Canadian Dictionary of Finance and Investment Terms

Jerry White
M.A., M.B.A., D. LIT.
Chairman, Independent Financial Publishers, Inc.
Financial Commentator, Canwest Global Television
C.F.R.B. and Sound Source Radio Network

John Downes
Editor, *Beating the Dow*
Former Vice President, AVCO Financial Services, Inc.
Office for Economic Development, City of New York

Jordan Elliot Goodman
Wall Street Correspondent
Money Magazine, Time-Warner Incorporated
Commentator
NBC News, Mutual Broadcasting System

BARRON'S

All inquiries should be addressed to:
Barron's Educational Series, Inc.
250 Wireless Boulevard
Hauppauge, NY 11788

Library of Congress Catalog Card No. 95-31641

International Standard Book No. 0-8120-9325-9

Library of Congress Cataloging-in-Publication Data
White, Jerry, 1946–
    Canadian dictionary of finance and investment terms / Jerry White,
John Downes, Jordan Elliot Goodman.
        p.   cm.
    ISBN 0-8120-9325-9
    1. Finance — Dictionaries. 2. Investments—Dictionaries.
3. Finance — Canada — Dictionaries. I. Downes, John, 1936– .
II. Goodman, Jordan Elliot. III. Title.
  HG151.W47   1995
  332'.03—dc20   95-31641
                                        CIP

PRINTED IN THE UNITED STATES OF AMERICA

5678   5500   98765432

CONTENTS

PREFACE

Canadians retiring in the early years of the 21st century face a finance and investment environment that underwent a revolution during their working years. Deregulation and the mass marketing of investments beginning in the 1970s, double digit inflation in the 1980s bracketed by two major recessions, and the return to frugality forced by corporate downsizing and huge Federal and provincial deficits in the 1990s, all occurred as the mega-trends of computerization and globalization gained momentum.

Deregulation in the financial marketplace made a vast range of innovative financial and investment products and services available to people at all economic levels. At the same time, investment decision-making has become more difficult as economic pressures have threatened ever higher taxes, trade policies have caused declines in the Canadian dollar, and ongoing separatist tensions have added to the volatility of the financial markets.

The North American Free Trade Agreement (NAFTA) has brought economic benefits along with painful economic adjustments, while the fall of the Iron Curtain has accelerated the trend toward globalization of the financial markets. These trends have also expanded investment choices while adding new dimensions of risk.

The computer and advanced communications systems have created both greater simplicity and greater complexity in the universe of finance and investment. By linking markets and processing massive information, these systems have given rise to investment vehicles, transactions, and methods of limiting risk not previously imaginable.

By the mid-1990s, real estate values had fallen to ten-year lows, net family disposable income had returned to 1980s levels, fixed income rates on guaranteed investment certificates and savings accounts had dropped to levels not seen in thirty years, and inflation was virtually non-existent. Downsizing by Canadian companies had eliminated a significant portion of the white collar labour force and growing numbers of Canadians were working out of their homes. The Federal government reported a $1 trillion-plus Canadian Pension Plan deficit, as budget-balancing forced greater austerity on a population living longer and retiring earlier.

Thus, as we prepare for a new millenium, Canadian investors have unprecedented opportunities to invest wisely, but the burden on individuals to take personal responsibility for their financial futures has become significantly greater. The key to successful investing is knowledge. Those who understand today's language of finance and investment will have an advantage over those who do not.

This first comprehensive guide to the language of Canadian finance and investment covers the 20th century's major developments in investments, taxation, economics, consumer and corporate finance, and related fields.

The authors were helped by many organizations and people, among them: The American Association of Individual Investors, American Bankers Association, American Council of Life Insurance, American Express Company, American Institute of Certified Public Accountants, American

iv

Society of CLU & ChFC (Chartered Life Underwriters), American Stock Exchange, Associated Credit Bureaus, Bankers Trust Company, The Bond Buyer, Boston Stock Exchange, Chase Manhattan Bank NA, Chicago Board Options Exchange, Coffee, Sugar & Cocoa Exchange, Commodity Futures Trading Commission, DD&W Limited, Dow Jones, Employee Benefit Research Institute, Fannie Mae, Federal Energy Regulatory Commission, Federal Reserve Bank of New York, Federal Trade Commission, FINEX, Frank Russell Company, Futures Industry Association, Goldman, Sachs & Company, Health Insurance Institute of America, Hulbert Financial Digest, IBC/Donoghue Incorporated, Insurance Information Institute, Intermarket Management Incorporated, Internal Revenue Service, International Petroleum Exchange, International Swaps and Derivatives Association, Investment Management Consultants Association, Investment Program Association, J.P. Morgan, Richard J. Kittrell, Esq./Kittrell & Kittrell P.C., Liquidity Financial Corporation, Mercer & Company, Merrill Lynch, Montreal Exchange, Morgan Stanley, Morningstar, Mortgage Bankers Association, Municipal Bond Investors Assurance Corporation, National Association of Investors Corporation, National Association of Real Estate Investment Trusts, National Association of Variable Annuities, National Credit Union Administration, New York Cotton Exchange, New York Life Insurance Company, New York Mercantile Exchange, New York Stock Exchange, Office of Thrift Supervision, Options Clearing Corporation, Options Institute, Pension Benefit Guaranty Corporation, Prudential Securities, Salomon Brothers Incorporated, Securities and Exchange Commission, Standard & Poor's, Toronto Stock Exchange, Trimedia Incorporated, U.S. Department of Commerce, U.S. Department of Labor, Value Line, Vancouver Stock Exchange, Visa International, The Weiser Walek Group, Wheat First Butcher Singer Incorporated, Wilshire Associates, Winnipeg Commodity Exchange, World Gold Council, Wrap Industry Association, and Zacks Investment Research.

Expert reviewing was provided by Paul Bates of Porthmeor Securities, Mark Borkowski of Mercantile Mergers and Acquisitions, Robert Walker, president of J. White & Associates, Inc.. Researchers Hartley, Meriam, Ian and Cayle White and we are in their debt. We also received material assistance from brokers, financial planners and professional advisors too numerous to mention.

Special thanks are due to Roberta Yafie, whose fact-checking and research went far beyond the call of duty, to Brian Cox of Barron's, who worked with us in championing the project, to Sheila Fletcher our Toronto-based developmental editor and, especially, to Mary Falcon, Barron's business editor, who handled an incredible amount of editorial work with skill and patience and really made it happen.

Jerry White
John Downes
Jordan Elliot Goodman

HOW TO USE THIS BOOK EFFECTIVELY

Alphabetization: All entries are alphabetized by letter rather than by word so that multiple-word terms are treated as single words. For example, **NET ASSET VALUE** follows **NET ASSETS** as though it were spelled **NETASSETVALUE**, without spacing. Similarly, **ACCOUNT EXECUTIVE** follows **ACCOUNTANT'S OPINION.** In unusual cases, abbreviations or acronyms appear as entries in the main text, in addition to appearing in the back of the book in the separate listing of Abbreviations and Acronyms. This is when the short form, rather than the formal name, predominates in common business usage. For example, NASDAQ is more commonly used in speaking of the National Association of Securities Dealers Automated Quotations system than the name itself, so the entry is at **NASDAQ.** Numbers in entry titles are alphabetized as if they were spelled out.

Abbreviations and Acronyms: A separate list of abbreviations and acronyms follows the Dictionary. It contains shortened versions of terms defined in the book, plus several hundred related business terms.

Cross references: In order to gain a fuller understanding of a term, it will sometimes help to refer to the definition of another term. In these cases the additional term is printed in SMALL CAPITALS. Such cross references appear in the body of the definition or at the end of the entry (or subentry). Cross references at the end of an entry (or subentry) may refer to related or contrasting concepts rather than give more information about the concept under discussion. As a rule, a term is printed in small capitals only the first time it appears in an entry. Where an entry is fully defined at another entry, a reference rather than a definition is provided; for example, **EITHER-OR ORDER** *see* ALTERNATIVE ORDER.

Italics: Italic type is generally used to indicate that another term has a meaning identical or very closely related to that of the entry. Occasionally, italic type is also used to highlight the fact that a word used is a business term and not just a descriptive phrase. Italics are also used for the titles of publications.

Parentheses: Parentheses are used in entry titles for two reasons. The first is to indicate that an entry's opposite is such an integral part of the concept that only one discussion is necessary; for example, **REALIZED PROFIT (OR LOSS).** The second and more common reason is to indicate that an abbreviation is used with about the same frequency as the term itself; for example, **OVER THE COUNTER (OTC).**

Examples, Illustrations, and Tables: The numerous examples in this Dictionary are designed to help readers gain understanding and to help them relate abstract concepts to the real world of finance and investment. Line drawings are provided in addition to text to clarify concepts best understood visually; for example, technical chart patterns used by securities analysts and graphic concepts used in financial analysis.

A

ABANDONMENT voluntarily giving up all rights, title, or claims to property that rightfully belongs to the owner. An example of abandoned property would be stocks, bonds, or mutual funds held in a brokerage account for which the firm is unable to locate the listed owner over a specified period of time, usually a few years. If ruled to be abandoned, the property may revert to the state under the laws of ESCHEAT. In addition to financial assets, other kinds of property that are subject to abandonment include patents, inventions, leases, trademarks, contracts, and copyrights.

ABC INVENTORY CONTROL SYSTEM system of dividing a firm's inventory system into three groups, A, B, and C, according to the contribution of each to the firm's overall investment in the inventory. The system facilitates the application of more effective and efficient inventory control techniques.

ABILITY TO PAY

Finance: borrower's ability to meet principal and interest payments on long-term obligations out of earnings. Also called *ability to service.* *See also* FIXED CHARGE COVERAGE.

Industrial relations: ability of an employer, especially a financial organization to meet a union's financial demands from operating income.

Municipal bonds: issuer's present and future ability to generate enough tax revenue to meet its contractual obligations, taking into account all factors concerned with municipal income and property values.

Taxation: the concept that tax rates should vary with levels of wealth or income; for example, the progressive income tax.

ABOVE PAR *see* PAR VALUE.

ABSORBED

Business: a cost that is treated as an expense rather than passed on to a customer.

Also, a firm merged into an acquiring company.

Cost accounting: indirect manufacturing costs (such as property taxes and insurance) are called absorbed costs. They are differentiated from variable costs (such as direct labour and materials). *See also* DIRECT OVERHEAD.

Finance: an account that has been combined with related accounts in preparing a financial statement and has lost its separate identity. Also called *absorption account* or *adjunct account.*

Securities: issue that an underwriter has completely sold to the public.

Also, in market trading, securities are absorbed as long as there are corresponding orders to buy and sell. The market has reached the *absorption point* when further assimilation is impossible without an adjustment in price. *See also* UNDIGESTED SECURITIES.

ACCELERATED COLLECTION *see* LOCK-BOX SERVICE.

ACCELERATED FUNDS TRANSFER a computer-based electronic funds transfer system for inter- and intra-account transfer, bill payment, accounts receivable collection, and overall management.

ACCELERATION CLAUSE provision, normally present in an INDENTURE agreement, mortgage, or other contract, that the unpaid balance is to become due and payable if specified events of default should occur. Such events include failure to meet interest, principal, or sinking fund payments; insolvency; and nonpayment of taxes on mortgaged property.

ACCEPTANCE

In general: agreement created when the drawee of a TIME DRAFT (bill of exchange) writes the word "accepted" above the signature and designates a date of payment. The drawee becomes the acceptor, responsible for payment at maturity.

Also, paper issued and sold by sales finance companies, such as General Motors Acceptance Corporation.

Banker's acceptance: time draft drawn on and accepted by a bank, the customary means of effecting payment for merchandise sold in import-export transactions and a source of financing used extensively in international trade. With the credit strength of a bank behind it, the banker's acceptance usually qualifies as a MONEY MARKET instrument. The liability assumed by the bank is called its acceptance liability. *See also* LETTER OF CREDIT.

Trade acceptance: time draft drawn by the seller of goods on the buyer, who becomes the acceptor, and which is therefore only as good as the buyer's credit.

ACCEPTANCE PAPER colloquial term for short-term promissory notes issued by sales finance companies to fund loans to consumers for cars, appliances, etc. *See also* FINANCE COMPANY PAPER.

ACCIDENT, DEATH AND DISMEMBERMENT INSURANCE insurance that provides benefits if the policyholder dies as a result of an accident or if he or she suffers the loss of a limb.

ACCIDENT INSURANCE mandatory auto insurance that provides coverage for medical payments over and above those paid by any provincial health plan.

ACCOUNT

In general: contractual relationship between a buyer and seller under which payment is made at a later time. The term *open account* or *charge account* is used, depending on whether the relationship is commercial or personal.

Also, the historical record of transactions under the contract, as periodically shown on the *statement of account*.

Banking: relationship under a particular name, usually evidenced by a deposit against which withdrawals can be made. Among them are demand, time, custodial, joint, trustee, corporate, special, and regular accounts. Administrative responsibility is handled by an *account officer.*

Bookkeeping: assets, liabilities, income, and expenses as represented by individual ledger pages to which debit and credit entries are chronologically posted to record changes in value. Examples are cash, accounts receivable, accrued interest, sales, and officers' salaries. The system of recording, verifying, and reporting such information is called accounting. Practitioners of accounting are called *accountants.*

Investment banking: financial and contractual relationship between parties to an underwriting syndicate, or the status of securities owned and sold.

Securities: relationship between a broker-dealer firm and its client wherein the firm, through its registered representatives, acts as agent in buying and selling securities and sees to related administrative matters. *See also* ACCOUNT STATEMENT.

ACCOUNTANT'S REVIEW report attached to financial statements that have been prepared without audit but reviewed by a firm of Chartered Accountants. The "Review Engagement Report" states that the review "consisted primarily of enquiry, analytical procedures and discussion" of the figures and "does not constitute an audit" or result in an audit opinion. Outsiders usually do not place full confidence in such figures. *See also* AUDITED FINANCIAL STATEMENTS.

ACCOUNT ANALYSIS informational report provided by a bank to its corporate customers with data detailing account service activity. Such reports are produced monthly as well as annually and usually detail: the average daily book balance, the average daily float, average available balances, itemized activity charges, earnings credit rate, the balanced required to compensate for services, and the balance available to support credit arrangement and other bank services.

ACCOUNT BALANCE net of debits and credits at the end of a reporting period. Term applies to a variety of account relationships, such as with banks, credit card companies, brokerage firms, and stores, and to classifications of transactions in a bookkeeping system. The same account may be an asset account balance or a liability account balance, depending on which side of the transaction you are on. For example, your bank balance is an asset account to you and a liability account to the bank. Your credit card (debit) balance is a liability account to you and an asset account (account receivable) to the credit card company.

ACCOUNTING PRINCIPLES BOARD (APB) board of the American Institute of Certified Public Accountants (AICPA) that issued (1959–73) a series of accountant's opinions constituting much of what is known as GENERALLY ACCEPTED ACCOUNTING PRINCIPLES. *See also* FINANCIAL ACCOUNTING STANDARDS BOARD (FASB).

ACCOUNT RECONCILIATION the process of adjusting the balance in your chequebook to match your bank statement. Your chequebook balance, plus outstanding cheques, less bank charges, plus interest (if any), should equal the balance shown on your bank statement.

ACCOUNTS PAYABLE amounts owing on open account to creditors for goods and services that are payable within one year or business cycle. Analysts look at the relationship of accounts payable to purchases for indications of sound day-to-day financial management. *See also* TRADE CREDIT.

ACCOUNTS RECEIVABLE money owed to a business for merchandise or services sold on open account, payable within one year or business cycle. Accounts receivable are a key factor in analyzing a company's LIQUIDITY—its ability to meet current obligations without additional revenues. *See also* ACCOUNTS RECEIVABLE TURNOVER; AGING SCHEDULE; COLLECTION RATIO.

ACCOUNTS RECEIVABLE FINANCING short-term financing whereby accounts receivable serve as collateral for working capital advances. *See also* FACTORING.

ACCOUNTS RECEIVABLE INSURANCE insurance that protects accounts receivable of a client owing money from physical loss because of fire, theft or any other named peril.

ACCOUNTS RECEIVABLE TURNOVER ratio obtained by dividing total credit sales by accounts receivable. The ratio indicates how many times the receivables portfolio has been collected during the accounting period. *See also* ACCOUNTS RECEIVABLE; AGING SCHEDULE; COLLECTION RATIO.

ACCOUNT STATEMENT
In general: any record of transactions and their effect on charge or open-account balances during a specified period.
Banking: summary of all cheques paid, deposits recorded, and resulting balances during a defined period. Also called a *bank statement.*
Securities: statement summarizing all transactions and showing the status of an account with a broker-dealer firm, including long and short positions. Such statements must be issued quarterly, but are generally provided monthly when accounts are active. Also, the OPTION AGREEMENT required when an option account is opened.

ACCRETION
1. asset growth through internal expansion, acquisition, or such causes as aging of whisky or growth of timber.
2. adjustment of the difference between the price of a bond bought at an original discount and the par value of the bond.

ACCRUAL BASIS accounting method whereby income and expense items are recognized as they are earned or incurred, even though they may not have been received or actually paid in cash. Accrual accounting provides an accurate picture of a company's performance buy cannot assist in monitoring cash flow. The alternative is CASH BASIS accounting.

ACCRUED BENEFITS pension benefits that an employee has earned based on his or her years of service at a company. *See also* VESTING.

ACCRUED INTEREST interest that has accumulated between the most recent payment and the sale of a bond or other fixed-income security. At the time of sale, the buyer pays the seller the bond's price plus accrued interest, calculated by multiplying the coupon rate by the number of days that have elapsed since the last payment.

ACCRUED MARKET DISCOUNT increase in market value of a DISCOUNT BOND that occurs because of its approaching MATURITY DATE (when it is redeemable at PAR) and not because of declining market interest rates.

ACCUMULATED DIVIDEND dividend due, usually to holders of cumulative preferred stock, but not paid. It is carried on the books as a liability until paid. *See also* CUMULATIVE PREFERRED.

ACCUMULATION
Corporate finance: profits that are not paid out as dividends but are instead added to the company's capital base. *See also* ACCUMULATED PROFITS TAX.
Investments: purchase of a large number of shares in a controlled way so as to avoid driving the price up. An institution's accumulation program, for instance, may take weeks or months to complete.
Mutual funds: investment of a fixed dollar amount regularly and reinvestment of dividends and capital gains.

ACCUMULATION AREA price range within which buyers accumulate shares of a stock. Technical analysts spot accumulation areas when a stock does not drop below a particular price. Technicians who use the ON-BALANCE VOLUME method of analysis advise buying stocks that have hit their accumulation area, because the stocks can be expected to attract more buying interest. *See* chart on next page. *See also* DISTRIBUTION AREA.

ACES acronym for *Advanced Computerized Execution System,* run by the NASDAQ stock market. ACES automates trades between order-entry and market-maker firms that have established trading relationships with each other, designating securities at specified quantities for automatic execution. Once trading parameters are set, ACES facilitates order entry, best-price order execution and limited-order maintenance, as well as a variety of inventory control capabilities. Trades are then automatically reported for public dissemination and sent for comparison and clearing.

ACCUMULATION AREA

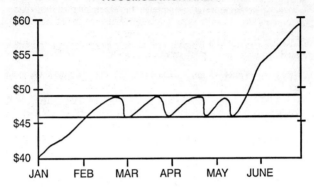

ACID TEST current cash and "near" cash assets (e.g., government bonds and current receivables, but excluding inventory) compared to the current debts (bank loans, payables). The acid test shows how much and how quickly cash can be found if a company gets into trouble.

ACID-TEST RATIO *See* QUICK RATIO.

ACKNOWLEDGMENT verification that a signature on a banking or brokerage document is legitimate and has been certified by an authorized person. Acknowledgment is needed when transferring an account from one broker to another, for instance. In banking, an acknowledgment verifies that an item has been received by the paying bank and is or is not available for immediate payment.

ACQUIRED SURPLUS uncapitalized portion of the net worth of a successor company in a POOLING OF INTERESTS combination. In other words, the part of the combined net worth not classified as CAPITAL STOCK.

    In a more general sense, the surplus acquired when a company is purchased.

ACQUISITION one company taking over controlling interest in another company. Investors are always looking out for companies that are likely to be acquired, because those who want to acquire such companies are often willing to pay more than the market price for the shares they need to complete the acquisition. *See also* MERGER; POOLING OF INTERESTS; TAKEOVER.

ACQUISITION COST
    Finance: price plus CLOSING COSTS to buy a company, real estate or other property.
    Investments: SALES CHARGE incurred to buy a LOAD FUND or the original price, plus brokerage commissions, of a security. *See also* TAX BASIS.

ACQUISITION FEE *see* LOAD.

ACROSS THE BOARD movement in the stock market that affects almost all stocks in the same direction. When the market moves up across the board, almost every stock gains in price.

An across-the-board pay increase in a company is a raise of a fixed percent or amount for all employees.

ACTIVE BOND CROWD members of the bond department of the New York Stock Exchange, the most important bond traders in North America, responsible for the heaviest volume of bond trading. The opposite of the active crowd is the CABINET CROWD, which deals in bonds that are infrequently traded. Investors who buy and sell bonds in the active crowd will tend to get better prices for their securities than in the inactive market, where spreads between bid and asked prices are wider.

ACTIVE BOX collateral available for securing brokers' loans or customers' margin positions in the place—or *box*—where securities are held in safekeeping for clients of a broker-dealer or for the broker-dealer itself. Securities used as collateral must be owned by the firm or hypothecated—that is, pledged or assigned—by the customer to the firm, then by the broker to the lending bank. For margin loans, securities must be hypothecated by the customer to the broker.

ACTIVE MARKET heavy volume of trading in a particular stock, bond, or commodity. The spread between bid and asked prices is usually narrower in an active market than when trading is quiet.

Also, a heavy volume of trading on the exchange as a whole. Institutional money managers prefer such a market because their trades of large blocks of stock tend to have less impact on the movement of prices when trading is generally active.

ACTUALS any physical commodity, such as gold, soybeans, or pork bellies. Trading in actuals ultimately results in delivery of the commodity to the buyer when the contract expires. This contrasts with trading in commodities of, for example, index options, where the contract is settled in cash, and no physical commodity is delivered upon expiration. However, even when trading is in actuals most futures and options contracts are closed out before the contract expires, and so these transactions do not end in delivery.

ACTUARY mathematician employed by an insurance company to calculate premiums, reserves, dividends, and insurance, pension, and annuity rates, using risk factors obtained from experience tables. These tables are based on both the company's history of insurance claims and other industry and general statistical data.

ADDITIONAL BONDS TEST test limiting the amount of new bonds that can be issued. Since bonds are secured by assets or revenues of a corporate or governmental entity, the underwriters of the bond must insure that the bond issuer can meet the debt service requirements of any additional bonds. The test usually sets specific financial benchmarks, such as what portion of an issuer's revenues or cash flow can be devoted to paying interest.

ADDITIONAL PAID-IN CAPITAL *see* PAID-IN CAPITAL.

ADEQUACY OF COVERAGE test of the extent to which the value of an asset, such as real property, securities, or a contract subject to currency exchange rates, is protected from potential loss either through INSURANCE or HEDGING.

ADJUSTABLE RATE *see* FLOATING RATE.

ADJUSTED BALANCE METHOD formula for calculating finance charges based on ACCOUNT BALANCE remaining after adjusting for payments and credits posted during the billing period. Interest charges under this method are lower than those under the AVERAGE DAILY, PREVIOUS BALANCE, and PAST DUE BALANCE METHODS.

ADJUSTED BASIS base price from which to judge capital gains or losses upon sale of an asset like a stock or bond. The cost of commissions in effect is deducted at the time of sale when net proceeds are used for tax purposes. The price must be adjusted to account for any stock splits that have occurred since the initial purchase before arriving at the adjusted basis.

ADMINISTRATOR court-appointed individual or bank charged with carrying out the court's decisions with respect to a decedent's estate until it is fully distributed to all claimants. Administrators are appointed when a person dies without having made a will or without having named an executor, or when the named executor cannot or will not serve. The term *administratrix* is sometimes used if the individual appointed is a woman, and the term *personal representative* is also used to describe the role.

   In a general sense, an administrator is a person who carries out an organization's policies.

AD VALOREM Latin term meaning "according to value" and referring to a way of assessing custom, duties, or taxes on property. As one example, ad valorem DUTY assessment is based on value of the imported item rather than on its weight or quantity.

ADVANCE
Employee benefits: cash given to an employee before it is needed or earned. A travel advance is supplied so that an employee has cash to use on an upcoming business trip. A salary advance is provided to help the employee cover emergency expenses.
Securities: increase in the price of stocks, bonds, commodities, or other assets. Often heard when referring to the movement of broad indexes, e.g., "The Toronto Stock Exchange 300 advanced 12 points today."

Trade: advance payment for goods or services that will be delivered in the near future. For example, home contractors require an advance from homeowners to pay for building materials.

ADVANCE-DECLINE (A-D) measurement of the number of stocks that have advanced and the number that have declined over a particular period. It is the ratio of one to the other and shows the general direction of the market. It is considered bullish if more stocks advance than decline on any trading day. It is bearish if declines outnumber advances. The steepness of the A-D line graphically shows whether a strong bull or bear market is underway.

ADVANCE-DECLINE LINE

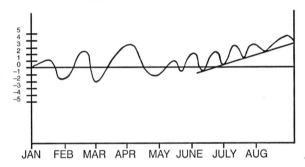

ADVERSE OPINION opinion expressed by a company's independent auditors that the firm's financial statements do not accurately reflect the company's current financial position or operating results. An adverse opinion is a far more serious finding than a QUALIFIED OPINION, in which only some issues are of concern to the auditor. Investors should be extremely cautious about investing in any company with an adverse opinion from its auditors.

ADVERSE SELECTION tendency of people with significant potential to file claims wanting to obtain insurance coverage. For example, those with severe health problems want to buy health insurance, and people going to a dangerous place such as a war zone want to buy more life insurance. Companies employing workers in dangerous occupations want to buy more worker's compensation coverage. In order to combat the problem of adverse selection, insurance companies try to reduce their exposure to large claims by either raising premiums or limiting the availability of coverage to such applicants.

ADVISORY LETTER newsletter aiming to offer financial advice to subscribers. The letter may offer a broad economic and market outlook, or it may focus on a particular sector of the stock, bond, or commodity markets. Some advisory letters specialize in recommending only mutual funds. Some letters also advise their subscribers of new recommendations through a toll-free hotline, which can be updated much more quickly than a printed letter.

AFFIDAVIT written statement made under oath before an authorized person, such as a notary public.

AFFILIATE
In general: two companies are affiliated when one owns less than a majority of the voting stock of the other, or when both are subsidiaries of a third company. A SUBSIDIARY is a company of which more than 50% of the voting shares are owned by another corporation, termed the PARENT COMPANY. A subsidiary is always, by definition, an affiliate, but subsidiary is the preferred term when majority control exists. In everyday use, affiliate is the correct word for intercompany relationships, however indirect, where the parent-subsidiary relationship does not apply.

AFFILIATED COMPANY company with less than 50% of its shares owned by another corporation or one whose stock is owned by the same controlling interests as that of another corporation.

AFFILIATED CORPORATION corporation that is an AFFILIATE.

AFFILIATED PERSON individual in a position to exert direct influence on the actions of a corporation. Among such persons are owners of 10% or more of the voting shares, directors, and senior elected officers and any persons in a position to exert influence through them— such as members of their immediate family and other close associates. Sometimes called a *control person.*

AFTER-HOURS DEALING OR TRADING trading of stocks and bonds after regular trading hours on organized exchanges. This may occur when there is a major announcement about positive or negative earnings or a takeover at a particular company. The stock price may therefore soar or plummet from the level at which it closed during regular trading hours. Some brokerage firms specialize in making over-the-counter markets around the clock to accommodate after-hours dealing. *See* MAKE A MARKET.

AFTERMARKET *see* SECONDARY MARKET.

AFTERTAX REAL RATE OF RETURN amount of money, adjusted for inflation, that an investor can keep, out of the income and capital gains earned from investments. Every dollar loses value to inflation, so investors have to keep an eye on the aftertax real rate of return whenever they commit their capital. By and large, investors seek a rate of return that will match if not exceed the rate of inflation.

AGAINST THE BOX SHORT SALE by the holder of a LONG POSITION in the same stock. *Box* refers to the physical location of securities held in safekeeping. When a stock is sold against the box, it is sold short, but only in effect. A short sale is usually defined as one where the seller does not own the shares. Here the seller *does* own the shares (holds a long position) but does not wish to disclose ownership; or perhaps the long shares are too inaccessible to deliver in the time required; or he may be holding his existing position to get the benefit of long-term capital gains tax treatment. In any event, when the sale is made against the box, the shares needed to cover are borrowed, probably from a broker.

AGED FAIL contract between two broker-dealers that is still not settled 30 days after the settlement date. At that point the open balance no longer counts as an asset, and the receiving firm must adjust its capital accordingly.

AGENCY

In general: relationship between two parties, one a principal and the other an AGENT who represents the principal in transactions with a third party.

Finance: certain types of accounts in trust institutions where individuals, usually trust officers, act on behalf of customers. Agency services to corporations are related to stock purchases and sales. Banks also act as agents for individuals.

Investment: act of buying or selling for the account and risk of a client. Generally, an agent, or broker, acts as intermediary between buyer and seller, taking no financial risk personally or as a firm, and charging a commission for the service.

AGENCY SECURITIES securities issued by U.S. government-sponsored entities (GSEs) and federally related institutions.

GSEs currently issuing securities comprise eight privately owned, publicly chartered entities created to reduce borrowing costs for certain sectors of the economy, such as farmers, homeowners, and students. They include the Federal Farm Credit Bank System, Farm Credit Financial Assistance Corporation, Federal Home Loan Bank, FEDERAL HOME LOAN MORTGAGE CORPORATION, FEDERAL NATIONAL MORTGAGE ASSOCIATION (FNMA), STUDENT LOAN MARKETING ASSOCIATION (SLMA), FINANCING CORPORATION (FICO), and RESOLUTION TRUST CORPORATION (RTC). GSEs issue discount notes (with maturities ranging from overnight to 360 days) and bonds. With the exception of the Farm Credit Financial Assistance Corporation, GSE securities are not backed by the full faith and credit of the U.S. government. Other GSEs that formerly issued directly now borrow from the FEDERAL FINANCING BANK.

Federally related institutions are arms of the U.S. government and generally have not issued securities directly into the marketplace since the Federal Financing Bank was established to meet their consolidated borrowing needs in 1973. They include the EXPORT-IMPORT BANK (EXIMBANK) of the United States, the Commodity Credit Corporation, the Farmers Housing Administration, the General

Services Administration, the GOVERNMENT NATIONAL MORTGAGE ASSO-CIATION (GNMA), the Maritime Administration, the Private Export Funding Corporation, the Rural Electrification Administration, the Rural Telephone Bank, the SMALL BUSINESS ADMINISTRATION (SBA), the Tennessee Valley Authority (TVA), and the Washington Metropolitan Area Transit Authority. Except for the Private Export Funding Corporation and the TVA, federally related institution obligations are backed by the full faith and credit of the U.S. government.

Agency securities are exempt from SEC registration and from state and local income taxes.

Agency securities can be purchased by pension funds and institutional investors, and the rates charged are important indicators of market trends.

AGENT individual authorized by another person, called the principal, to act in the latter's behalf in transactions involving a third party. Banks are frequently appointed by individuals to be their agents, and so authorize their employees to act on behalf of principals. Agents have three basic characteristics:

1. They act on behalf of and are subject to the control of the principal.

2. They do not have title to the principal's property.

3. They owe the duty of obedience to the principal's orders.

See also ACCOUNT EXECUTIVE; BROKER; TRANSFER AGENT.

AGENT FOR EXECUTOR a trust company hired by the named executor to provide advice and administration services for a fee.

AGGREGATE EXERCISE PRICE

1. in stock options trading, the number of shares in a put or call CONTRACT (normally 100) multiplied by the EXERCISE PRICE. The price of the option, called the PREMIUM, is a separate figure not included in the aggregate exercise price. A July call option on 100 XYZ at 70 would, for example, have an aggregate exercise price of 100 (number of shares) times $70 (price per share), or $7000, if exercised on or before the July expiration date.

2. in index options, the exercise price × $100.

AGGREGATE SUPPLY in MACROECONOMICS, the total amount of goods and services supplied to the market at alternative price levels in a given period of time; also called *total output*. The central concept in SUPPLY-SIDE ECONOMICS, it corresponds with aggregate demand, defined as the total amount of goods and services demanded in the economy at alternative income levels in a given period, including both consumer and producers' goods; aggregate demand is also called *total spending*. The aggregate supply curve describes the relationship between price levels and the quantity of output that firms are willing to provide.

AGGRESSIVE GROWTH MUTUAL FUND mutual fund holding stocks of rapidly growing companies. While these companies may be large or small, they all share histories of and prospects for above-average profit growth. Aggressive growth funds are designed solely for capital appreciation, since they produce little or no income from dividends. This type of mutual fund is typically more volatile than the overall stock market, meaning its shares will rise far more than the average stock during bull markets and will fall much farther than the typical stock in a bear market. Investors in aggressive growth funds must realize that the value of their shares will fluctuate sharply over time. Aggressive growth funds are also called *maximum capital gains funds* or *capital appreciation funds.*

AGING SCHEDULE classification of trade ACCOUNTS RECEIVABLE by date of sale. Usually prepared by a company's auditor, the *aging,* as the schedule is called, is a vital tool in analyzing the quality of a company's receivables investment. It is frequently required by grantors of credit.

The schedule is most often seen as: (1) a list of the amount of receivables by the month in which they were created; (2) a list of receivables by maturity, classified as current or as being in various stages of delinquency. The following is a typical aging schedule.

dollars (in thousands)

Current (under 30 days)	$14,065	61%
1–30 days past due	3,725	16
31–60 days past due	2,900	12
61–90 days past due	1,800	8
Over 90 days past due	750	3
	$23,240	100%

The aging schedule reveals patterns of delinquency and shows where collection efforts should be concentrated. It helps in evaluating the adequacy of the reserve for BAD DEBTS, because the longer accounts stretch out the more likely they are to become uncollectible. Using the schedule can help prevent the loss of future sales, since old customers who fall too far behind tend to seek out new sources of supply.

AGREEMENT AMONG UNDERWRITERS contract between participating members of an investment banking SYNDICATE; sometimes called *syndicate contract* or *purchase group agreement.* It is distinguished from the *underwriting agreement,* which is signed by the company issuing the securities and the SYNDICATE MANAGER, acting as agent for the underwriting group.

The agreement among underwriters, (1) appoints the originating investment banker as syndicate manager and agent; (2) appoints additional managers, if considered advisable; (3) defines the members' proportionate liability (usually limited to the amount of their participation) and agrees to pay each member's share on settlement date; (4) authorizes the manager to form and allocate units to a SELLING GROUP, and agrees to abide by the rules of the selling group agreement; (5)

states the life of the syndicate, usually running until 30 days after termination of the selling group, or ending earlier by mutual consent.

AIR POCKET STOCK stock that falls sharply, usually in the wake of such negative news as unexpected poor earnings. As shareholders rush to sell, and few buyers can be found, the price plunges dramatically, like an airplane hitting an air pocket.

ALBERTA STOCK EXCHANGE (ASE) exchange dating back to the incorporation of the Calgary Stock Exchange in 1913 by an act of the Alberta government. Trading commenced following the discovery of oil in the Turner Valley in 1914, and the Exchange's trading history has closely paralleled significant oil and gas discoveries in Western Canada. In 1974, the name was changed to the ASE.

In 1983, the ASE was the first exchange in Canada to accept corporate bonds for listing along with equities. Since 1988, the ASE has operated an Automated Trade Execution System (ATES), in which trading is fully automated.

Currently, approximately 30% of all trading is on ATES. The ASE is located at 300 Fifth Avenue S.W., Calgary, Alberta T2P 3C4.

ALLIGATOR SPREAD spread in the options market that "eats the investor alive" with high commission costs. The term is used when a broker arranges a combination of puts and calls that generates so much commission the client is unlikely to turn a profit even if the markets move as anticipated.

ALL IN underwriting shorthand for *all included,* referring to an issuer's interest rate after giving effect to commissions and miscellaneous related expenses.

ALL OR NONE (AON)
Investment banking: an offering giving the issuer the right to cancel the whole issue if the underwriting is not fully subscribed.
Securities: buy or sell order marked to signify that no partial transaction is to be executed. The order will not automatically be canceled, however, if a complete transaction is not executed; to accomplish that, the order entry must be marked FOK, meaning FILL OR KILL.

ALL ORDINARIES INDEX the major index of Australian stocks, representing 280 of the most active listed companies, or the majority of the equity capitalization (excluding foreign companies) listed on the AUSTRALIA STOCK EXCHANGE (ASX).The index is made up of 23 subindices representing various industry categories, and it summarizes market price movements by following changes in the aggregate market values of the companies listed.

ALLOTMENT amount of securities assigned to each of the participants in an investment banking SYNDICATE formed to underwrite and distribute a new issue, called *subscribers* or *allottees.* The financial responsibilities of the subscribers are set forth in an allotment notice, which is prepared by the SYNDICATE MANAGER.

ALLOWANCE deduction from the value of an invoice, permitted by a seller of goods to cover damages or shortages. *See also* RESERVE.

ALPHA

1. coefficient measuring the portion of an investment's RETURN arising from specific (nonmarket) risk. In other words, alpha is a mathematical estimate of the amount of return expected from an investment's inherent values, such as the rate of growth in earnings per share. It is distinct from the amount of return caused by VOLATILITY, which is measured by the BETA coefficient. For example, an alpha of 1.25 indicates that a stock is projected to rise 25% in price in a year when the return on the market and the stock's beta are both zero. An investment whose price is low relative to its alpha is undervalued and considered a good selection.

   In the case of a MUTUAL FUND, alpha measures the relationship between the fund's performance and its beta over a three-year period.

2. on the London Stock Exchange, now called the International Stock Exchange of the United Kingdom and Republic of Ireland (ISE), the designation *alpha stocks* applied to the largest and most actively traded companies in a classification system that was adopted after the BIG BANG in October 1986 and was replaced in January 1991 with the NORMAL MARKET SIZE (NMS) classification system.

ALPHABET STOCK categories of General Motors' common stock associated with particular acquisitions, such as "E" stock issued to acquire Electronic Data Systems and "H" stock issued to acquire Hughes Aircraft. The significance of the categories is that they have different voting rights and pay dividends tied to the operating performance of the particular divisions. Alphabet stock differs from CLASSIFIED STOCK, which is typically designated Class A and Class B, in that classified stock implies a hierarchy of powers and privileges whereas alphabet stock simply separates differences.

ALTERNATE APPOINTMENT alternate executor, appointed if the first named executor cannot or will not act.

ALTERNATIVE MINIMUM TAX (AMT) a federal tax ensuring taxpayers cannot use tax shelters or write-offs to reduce taxable income below $40,000.

ALTERNATIVE ORDER order giving a broker a choice between two courses of action; also called an *either-or order* or a *one cancels the other order.* Such orders are either to buy or to sell, never both. Execution of one course automatically makes the other course inoperative. An example is a combination buy limit/buy stop order, wherein the buy limit is below the current market and the buy stop is above.

AMENDMENT addition to, or change, in a legal document. When properly signed, it has the full legal effect of the original document.

AMERICAN DEPOSITARY RECEIPT (ADR) system devised by the American investment community whereby the original stock certificate of a foreign security is registered in the name of an American trust company or a U.S. bank and held in safekeeping by it. The trust company or bank then issues receipts against this stock, and these are traded as ADRs. The system developed because purchasers of foreign securities found that it could take several months to have foreign stock issues registered in their name.

AMERICAN DEPOSITARY SHARE (ADS) share issued under a deposit agreement representing the underlying ordinary share which trades in the issuer's home market. The terms ADS and ADR tend to be used interchangeably. Technically, the ADS is the instrument that actually is traded, while the ADR is the certificate that represents a number of ADSs.

AMERICAN STOCK EXCHANGE (AMEX) stock exchange with the second biggest volume of trading in the United States. Located at 86 Trinity Place in downtown Manhattan, the Amex was known until 1921 as the *Curb Exchange,* and it is still occasionally referred to as the *Curb* today. For the most part, the stocks and bonds traded on the Amex are those of small to medium-size companies, as contrasted with the huge companies whose shares are traded on the New York Stock Exchange. A large number of oil and gas companies, in particular, are traded on the Amex. The Amex also houses the trading of options on many New York Stock Exchange stocks and some OVER THE COUNTER stocks and has expanded its listings of DERIVATIVES in recent years. More foreign shares are traded on the Amex than on any other U.S. exchange. Hours: 9:30 A.M.–4:00 P.M., Monday through Friday.

AMERICAN STYLE OPTION option, common in North America, that can be exercised any time during its life up to and including the last trading day.

AMORTIZATION accounting procedure that gradually reduces the cost value of a limited life or intangible asset through periodic charges to income. For fixed assets the terms used is DEPRECIATION, and for wasting assets (natural resources) it is depletion, both terms meaning essentially the same thing as amortization. Most companies follow the conservative practice of writing off, through amortization, INTANGIBLE ASSETS such as goodwill. It is also common practice to amortize any premium over par value paid in the purchase of preferred stock or bond investments. The purpose of amortization is to reflect resale or redemption value.

Amortization also refers to the reduction of debt by regular payments of interest and principal sufficient to pay off a loan by maturity.

Discount and expense on funded debt are amortized by making applicable charges to income in accordance with a predetermined schedule. While this is normally done systematically, charges to profit and loss are permissible at any time in any amount of the remaining discount and expense. Such accounting is detailed in a company's annual report.

AMSTERDAM STOCK EXCHANGE the stock exchange in the Netherlands, founded in 1602, is the oldest in the world. Most of the stocks traded on the exchange are Dutch-based, and energy firms represent the largest sector. The Central Bureau of Statistics (CBS) All Share Index and the Total Return Index include all ordinary shares of Dutch companies listed on the exchange. Trading hours are 9:30 A.M. to 4:30 P.M., Monday through Friday. Settlement is almost exclusively without physical delivery.

ANALYSIS *see* FUNDAMENTAL ANALYSIS; TECHNICAL ANALYSIS.

ANALYST person in a brokerage house, bank trust department, or mutual fund group who studies a number of companies and makes buy or sell recommendations on the securities of particular companies and industry groups. Most analysts specialize in a particular industry, but some investigate any company that interests them, regardless of its line of business. Some analysts have considerable influence, and can therefore affect the price of a company's stock when they issue a buy or sell recommendation. *See also* CREDIT ANALYST.

AND INTEREST phrase used in quoting bond prices to indicate that, in addition to the price quoted, the buyer will receive ACCRUED INTEREST.

ANGEL INVESTMENT GRADE bond, as distinguished from FALLEN ANGEL.

ANKLE BITER stock issue having a MARKET CAPITALIZATION of less than $500 million. Generally, such small-capitalization stocks are more speculative than "high-cap" issues, but their greater growth potential gives them more RELATIVE STRENGTH in recessions. *See also* SMALL FIRM EFFECT.

ANNUAL BASIS statistical technique whereby figures covering a period of less than a year are extended to cover a 12-month period. The procedure, called *annualizing,* must take seasonal variations (if any) into account to be accurate.

ANNUAL CLEANUP provision normally included in a line-of-credit agreement requiring a borrower to "clean up" its loans (have a zero loan balance) for a specified time during one or more periods a year. The time will vary by the term of the firm's loan agreement. This requirement ensures that funds obtained by borrowing against a line of credit will be kept for short term only.

ANNUALIZE to convert to an annual basis. For example, if a mutual fund earns 1% in a month, it would earn 12% on an annualized basis, by multiplying the monthly return by 12. Many economists annualize a monthly number such as auto sales or housing starts to make it easier to compare to prior years.

ANNUAL MEETING once-a-year meeting when the managers of a company report to stockholders on the year's results, and the board of directors stands for election for the next year. The chief executive officer usually comments on the outlook for the coming year and, with other senior officers, answers questions from shareholders. Stockholders can also request that resolutions on corporate policy be voted on by all those owning stock in the company Stockholders unable to attend the annual meeting may vote for directors and pass on resolutions through the use of PROXY material, which must legally be mailed to all shareholders of record.

ANNUAL PERCENTAGE RATE (APR) cost of credit that consumers pay, expressed as a simple annual percentage.

ANNUAL RENEWABLE TERM INSURANCE *see* TERM INSURANCE.

ANNUAL REPORT formal yearly record of a corporation's financial condition that must be distributed to shareholders under SECURITIES AND EXCHANGE COMMISSION regulations. Included in the report is a description of the company's operations as well as its balance sheet and income statement. The long version of the annual report with more detailed financial information—called the 10-K—is available upon request from the corporate secretary.

ANNUAL RETURN TOTAL RETURN per year from an investment, including dividends or interest and capital gains or losses but excluding commissions and other transactions costs and taxes. A *compound annual return* represents the annual rate at which money would have to compound to reach the cumulative figure resulting from annual total returns. It is a discount rate and different from *average annual return*, which is simply an arithmetic mean of annual returns.

ANNUITANT person who will receive the income produced by a Registered Retirement Savings Plan (RRSP) when the assets of the fund are invested in an annuity or a Registered Retirement Income Fund (RRIF). If the RRSP is in your name, you are the annuitant. If it is a spousal plan, your spouse is the annuitant.

ANNUITIZE to begin a series of payments from the capital that has built up in an ANNUITY. The payments may be a fixed amount, or for a fixed period of time, or for the lifetimes of one or two *annuitants,* thus guaranteeing income payments that cannot be outlived. *See also* DEFERRED PAYMENT ANNUITY; FIXED ANNUITY; IMMEDIATE PAYMENT ANNUITY; VARIABLE ANNUITY.

ANNUITY form of contract sold by life insurance companies that guarantees a fixed or variable payment to the annuitant at some future time, usually retirement. In a FIXED ANNUITY the amount will ultimately be paid out in regular installments varying only with the payout method elected. In a VARIABLE ANNUITY, the payout is based on a guaranteed number of units; unit values and payments depend on the value of the underlying investments. All capital in the annuity grows TAX-DEFERRED. Key considerations when buying an annuity are the financial soundness of the insurance company *(see* BEST'S RATING), the returns it has paid in the past, and the level of fees and commissions paid to salesmen.

A common class of annuities are life annuities, which pay the agreed amount to the annuitant until his or her death. A life annuity is a kind of life insurance policy, in reverse in which the annuitant insures against outliving his or her money. The insurance company pools the money of a large number of such investors. The financial losers are those who die earlier than expected. Their losses provide the extra money to pay those who live longer than expected.

To meet the demand for different patterns of retirement income and risk management, financial service providers have developed many types of annuities that are generally available with monthly, quarterly, semi-annual and annual payment arrangement.

Types of annuities include systematic withdrawal with principal and interest, 20-year, and annuity to death with principal reverting to the surviving spouse or to the estate.

Three factors determine annuity payment amounts. The expected length of time it will be paid is calculated from the mortality tables, where the calculations can be quite complex for anything other than a straight life annuity. The initial amount contributed depends on the amount paid in available funds for the principal and the rate of interest based on what is current at the time the annuity is established.

ANNUITY CERTAIN annuity that pays a specified monthly level of income for a predetermined time period, frequently ten years. The annuitant is guaranteed by the insurance company to receive those payments for the agreed upon time period without exception or contingency. If the annuitant dies before the time period expires, the annuity payments are then made to the annuitant's designated beneficiaries. The level of payment in an annuity certain will be higher than for a LIFE ANNUITY because the insurance company knows exactly what its liability will be, whereas with a life annuity, payments depend on how long the annuitant lives.

ANOMALY used in mineral exploration, a statistical abnormality discovered by surveying and plotting geochemical or geophysical patterns over an area of ground. An anomaly suggests the possibility of a mineral deposit, but only one of thousands of anomalies ever leads to a worthwhile mineral discovery. Anomalies are often reported by mining stocks to attract investor interest in new promotions.

ANTICIPATION
In general: paying an obligation before it falls due.
Finance: repayment of debt obligations before maturity, usually to

save interest. If a formalized discount or rebate is involved, the term used is *anticipation rate*.

Mortgage instrument: when a provision allows prepayment without penalty, the mortgagee is said to have the *right of anticipation*.

Trade payments: bill that is paid before it is due, not discounted.

ANTITRUST LAWS U.S. federal legislation designed to prevent monopolies and restraint of trade. Landmark statutes include:
1. the Sherman Anti-Trust Act of 1890, which prohibited acts or contracts tending to create monopoly and initiated an era of trustbusting.
2. the Clayton Anti-Trust Act of 1914, which was passed as an amendment to the Sherman Act and dealt with local price discrimination as well as with the INTERLOCKING DIRECTORATES. It went further in the areas of the HOLDING COMPANY and restraint of trade.
3. the Federal Trade Commission Act of 1914, which created the Federal Trade Commission or FTC, with power to conduct investigations and issue orders preventing unfair practices in interstate commerce.

ANY-AND-ALL BID offer to pay an equal price for all shares tendered by a deadline; contrasts with TWO-TIER BID. *See also* TAKEOVER.

APPRAISAL FEE fee charged by an expert to estimate, but not determine, the market value of property. An appraisal is an opinion of value, and is usually required when real property is sold, financed, condemned, taxed, insured, or partitioned. The appraisal of a piece of real estate for insurance purposes may differ from an appraisal for determining property taxes. The appraisal fee is usually a set dollar amount, though in some cases may be calculated as a percentage of the value of the property appraised.

APPRECIATION increase in the value of an asset such as a stock, bond, commodity, or real estate.

APPROVED LIST list of investments that a mutual fund or other financial institution is authorized to make. The approved list may be statutory where a fiduciary responsibility exists. *See also* LEGAL LIST.

ARBITRAGE profiting from differences in price when the same security, currency, or commodity is traded on two or more markets. For example, an *arbitrageur* simultaneously buys one contract of gold in the Toronto market and sells one contract of gold in the New York market, locking in a profit because at that moment the price on the two markets is different, even after currency conversion is taken into account. (The arbitrageur's selling price is higher than the buying price.) *Index arbitrage* exploits price differences between STOCK INDEX FUTURES and underlying stocks. By taking advantage of momentary disparities in prices between markets, arbitrageurs perform the economic function of making those markets trade more efficiently. *See also* RISK ARBITRAGE.

ARBITRAGEUR person or firm engaged in ARBITRAGE. Arbitrageurs attempt to profit when the same security or commodity is trading at different prices in two or more markets. Those engaged in RISK ARBITRAGE attempt to profit from buying stocks of announced or potential TAKEOVER targets.

ARITHMETIC MEAN simple average obtained by dividing the sum of two or more items by the number of items.

ARM'S LENGTH TRANSACTION transaction that is conducted as though the parties were unrelated, thus avoiding any semblance of conflict of interest. For example, under current law parents may rent real estate to their children and still claim business deductions such as depreciation as long as the parents charge their children what they would charge if someone who is not a relative were to rent the same property.

ARREARAGE

In general: amount of any past-due obligation.

Investments: amount by which interest on bonds or dividends on CUMULATIVE PREFERRED stock is due and unpaid. In the case of cumulative preferred stock, common dividends cannot be paid by a company as long as preferred dividends are in arrears.

ARTIFICIAL CURRENCY *currency substitute,* such as SPECIAL DRAWING RIGHTS (SDRs) and EUROPEAN CURRENCY UNITS (ECUs).

ASCENDING TOPS chart pattern tracing a security's price over a period of time and showing that each peak in a security's price is higher than the preceding peak. This upward movement is considered bullish, meaning that the upward trend is likely to continue. *See also* DESCENDING TOPS.

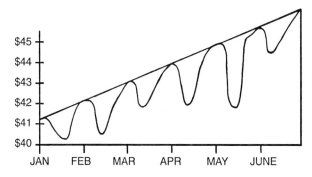

ASCENDING TOPS

ASE INDEX *see* STOCK INDEXES AND AVERAGES.

ASKED PRICE
  1. price at which a security or commodity is offered for sale on an exchange or in the over-the-counter market. Generally, it is the lowest round lot price at which a dealer will sell. Also called the *ask price, asking price, ask,* or OFFERING PRICE.
  2. per-share price at which mutual fund shares are offered to the public, usually the NET ASSET VALUE per share plus a sales charge, if any.

ASPIRIN acronym for *Australian Stock Price Riskless Indexed Notes.* Zero-coupon, four-year bonds guaranteed by the Treasury of New South Wales repayable at face value plus the percentage increase by which the Australian Stock Index of All Ordinaries (common stocks) rises above 1372 points during the period. *See also* ALL ORDINARIES INDEX.

ASSAY test of a metal's purity to verify that it meets the standards for trading on a commodities exchange. For instance, a 100 troy-ounce bar of refined gold must be assayed at a fineness of not less than 995 before the Comex will allow it to be used in settlement of a gold contract.

ASSESSED VALUATION dollar value assigned to property by a municipality for purposes of assessing taxes, which are based on the number of mills per dollar of assessed valuation. If a house is assessed at $100,000 and the tax rate is 50 mills, the tax is $5000.

ASSET anything having commercial or exchange value such as securities, deposits, or property owned by a business, institution, or individual. Assets held in RRSPs include cash, fixed income, and equities. *See also* CAPITAL ASSET; CURRENT ASSETS; DEFERRED CHARGE; FIXED ASSET; INTANGIBLE ASSET; NONCURRENT ASSET.

ASSET ALLOCATION apportioning of investment funds among categories of assets, such as CASH EQUIVALENTS, STOCK, FIXED-INCOME INVESTMENTS, and such tangible assets as real estate, precious metals, and collectibles. Also applies to subcategories such as government, municipal, and corporate bonds, and industry groupings of common stocks. Asset allocation affects both risk and return and is a central concept in personal financial planning and investment management.

ASSET ALLOCATION MUTUAL FUND mutual fund that switches between stocks, bonds, and money market securities to maximize shareholders' returns while minimizing risk. Such funds, which have become extremely popular in recent years, relieve individual shareholders of the responsibility of timing their entry or exit into different markets, since the fund manager is making those decisions. Theoretically, asset allocation funds provide a built-in buffer against declining stock and bond prices because the manager can move all the fund's assets into safe money market instruments. On the other hand, the manager has flexibility to invest aggressively in international and domestic stocks and bonds if he or she sees bull markets ahead for those securities

ASSET-BACKED SECURITIES bonds or notes backed by loan paper or accounts receivable originated by banks, credit card companies, or other providers of credit and often "enhanced" by a bank LETTER OF CREDIT or by insurance coverage provided by an institution other than the issuer. Typically, the originator of the loan or accounts receivable paper sells it to a specially created trust, which repackages it as securities with a minimum denomination of $1000 and a term of five years or less. The securities are then underwritten by brokerage firms who reoffer them to the public. Examples are CERTIFICATES FOR AUTOMOBILE RECEIVABLES (CARs) and so-called *plastic bonds,* backed by credit card receivables. Because the institution that originated the underlying loans or receivables is neither the obligor nor the guarantor, investors should evaluate the quality of the original paper, the worth of the guarantor or insurer, and the extent of the protection. *See also* PASS-THROUGH SECURITY.

ASSET COVERAGE extent to which a company's net assets cover a particular debt obligation, class of preferred stock, or equity position.

Asset coverage is calculated as follows: from assets at their total book value or liquidation value, subtract intangible assets, current liabilities, and all obligations prior in claim to the issue in question. Divide the result by the dollar amount of the subject issue (or loan) to arrive at the asset coverage ratio. The same information can be expressed as a percentage or, by using units as the divisor, as a dollar figure of coverage per unit. The variation to determine preferred stock coverage treats all liabilities as paid; the variation to arrive at common stock coverage considers both preferred stock and liabilities paid. The term most often used for the common stock calculation is *net book value per share of common stock.*

These calculations reveal *direct* asset coverage. *Overall* asset coverage is obtained by including the subject issue with the total of prior obligations and dividing the aggregate into total tangible assets at liquidating value.

Asset coverage is important as a cushion against losses in the event of liquidation.

ASSET FINANCING financing that seeks to convert particular assets into working cash in exchange for a security interest in those assets. The term is replacing *commercial financing* as major banks join commercial finance companies in addressing the financing needs of companies that do not fit the traditional seasonal borrower profile. Although the prevalent form of asset financing continues to be loans against accounts receivable, *inventory loans* are common and *second mortgage loans,* predicated as they usually are on market values containing a high inflation factor, seem to gain popularity by the day. *See also* ACCOUNTS RECEIVABLE FINANCING.

ASSET-LIABILITY MANAGEMENT matching an individual's level of debt and amount of assets. Someone who is planning to buy a new car, for instance, would have to decide whether to pay cash, thus lowering assets, or to take out a loan, thereby increasing debts (or liabilities). Such decisions should be based on interest rates, on earning power, and on the comfort level with debt. Financial institutions carry out asset-liability management when they match the maturity of their deposits with the length of their loan commitments to keep from being adversely affected by rapid changes in interest rates.

ASSET PLAY stock market term for a stock that is attractive because the current price does not reflect the value of the company's assets. For example, an analyst could recommend a hotel chain, not because its hotels are run well but because its real estate is worth far more than is recognized in the stock's current price. Asset play stocks are tempting targets for takeovers because they provide an inexpensive way to buy assets.

ASSET STRIPPER corporate raider who takes over a company planning to sell large assets in order to repay debt. The raider calculates that after selling the assets and paying off the debt, he or she will be left with valuable assets that are worth more than his or her purchase price.

ASSET STRUCTURE mix and type of assets on a firm's balance sheet. The mix of assets depends on the current fixed-asset breakdown; the type of assets depends on which current and fixed assets are best for a given firm. A retail business would have a large current asset basis and minimal fixed assets; a service business would be nearly all current assets, and a manufacturer would be more heavily weighted to fixed assets such as land, machinery, and equipment.

ASSET VALUE net market value of a company's assets on a per-share basis as opposed to the market value of the shares. A company is undervalued by the stock market when asset value exceeds share value.

ASSIGN sign a document transferring ownership from one party to another. Ownership can be in a number of forms, including tangible property, rights (usually arising out of contracts), or the right to transfer ownership at some later time. The party who assigns is called the *assignor* and the party who receives the transfer of title—the assignment—is the *assignee.*

Stocks and registered bonds can be assigned by completing and signing a form printed on the back of the certificate—or, as is sometimes preferred for safety reasons, by executing a separate form, called an *assignment separate from certificate* or *stock/bond power.*

When the OPTIONS CLEARING CORPORATION learns of the exercise of an option, it prepares an assignment form notifying a broker-dealer that an option written by one of its clients has been exercised. The firm in turn assigns the exercise in accordance with its internal procedures.

An assignment for the benefit of creditors, sometimes called simply an *assignment,* is an alternative to bankruptcy, whereby the assets of a company are assigned to the creditors and liquidated for their benefit by a trustee

ASSIMILATION absorption of a new issue of stock by the investing public after all shares have been sold by the issue's underwriters. *See also* ABSORBED.

ASSUMED INTEREST RATE rate of interest that an insurance company uses to determine the payout on an ANNUITY contract. The higher the assumed interest rate, the higher the monthly payout will be.

ASSUMPTION act of taking on responsibility for the liabilities of another party, usually documented by an *assumption agreement.* In the case of a MORTGAGE assumption, the seller remains secondarily liable unless released from the obligations by the lender.

ATP acronym for *arbitrage trading program,* better known as PROGRAM TRADING. Program traders simultaneously place orders for stock index futures and the underlying stocks in an attempt to exploit price variations. Their activity is often blamed for excessive VOLATILITY.

AT PAR at a price equal to the face, or nominal, value of a security. *See also* PAR VALUE.

AT RISK exposed to the danger of loss. Investors in a limited partnership can claim tax deductions only if they can prove that there's a chance of never realizing any profit and of losing their investment as well. Deductions will be disallowed if the limited partners are not exposed to economic risk—if, for example, the general partner guarantees to return all capital to limited partners even if the business venture should lose money.

ATHENS STOCK EXCHANGE principal stock exchange in Greece. There are no restrictions on foreign membership on the exchange. The ASE Composite Index is traded daily. The exchange uses an automated trading system, XTS, for all listed companies. Equities are traded on account or for cash. Settlement of nearly all transactions is within two days, along with the physical exchange of security certificates or depository receipt. Hours: 10:30 A.M.–1:30 P.M., Monday through Friday.

ATTAINED AGE age at which a person is eligible to receive certain benefits. For example, someone may be eligible to receive the proceeds from a trust when they reach age 21. Or someone who has attained the age of 65 may be eligible for certain pension or other retirement benefits. In some cases, the person may have to take some action when they reach the attained age, such as retire from a company.

AT THE CLOSE ORDER
Securities: market order that is to be executed in its entirety at the closing price on the exchange of the stock named in the order. If it is not so executed, the order is to be treated as canceled.
Futures/Options: in futures and options, a MARKET ON CLOSE ORDER, which is a contract to be executed on some exchanges during the closing period, during which there is a range of prices.

AT THE MARKET *see* MARKET ORDER.

AT THE MONEY at the current price, as an option with an exercise price equal to or near the current price of the stock or underlying futures contract. *See also* DEEP IN/OUT OF THE MONEY; IN THE MONEY; OUT OF THE MONEY.

AT THE OPENING ORDER
Securities: market or limited price order to be executed on the opening trade of the stock on the exchange. If the order, or any portion of it, is not executed in this manner, it is to be treated as canceled.
Futures/Options: in futures and options, a MARKET ON OPEN ORDER, during which there is a range of prices at the opening.

ATTRIBUTION RULES rules under the Income Tax Act that provide that, where property is transferred, directly or through a trust, for the benefit of a spouse or certain minor children, the income (and in some cases, capital gains) on that property may be deemed to be income or gains of the transferrer and not of the transferee. This guarantees that the tax burden for the property is retained by the transferrer rather than being passed to the transferee.

AUCTION MARKET system by which securities are bought and sold through brokers on the securities exchanges, as distinguished from the over-the-counter market, where trades are negotiated. Best exemplified by the NEW YORK STOCK EXCHANGE, it is a double auction system or TWO-SIDED MARKET. That is because, unlike the conventional auction with one auctioneer and many buyers, here we have many sellers and many buyers. As in any auction, a price is established by competitive bidding between brokers acting as agents for buyers and sellers. That the system functions in an orderly way is the result of several trading rules: (1) The first bid or offer at a given price has priority over any other bid or offer at the same price. (2) The high bid and low offer "have the floor." (3) A new auction begins whenever all the offers or bids at a given price are exhausted. (4) Secret transactions are prohibited. (5) Bids and offers must be made in an audible voice.

AUCTION-RATE PREFERRED STOCK *see* DUTCH AUCTION PREFERRED STOCK.

AUDIT professional examination and verification of a company's accounting documents and supporting data for the purpose of rendering an opinion as to their fairness, consistency, and conformity with GENERALLY ACCEPTED ACCOUNTING PRINCIPLES.

AUDITED FINANCIAL STATEMENT financial statement prepared in accordance with accounting and auditing standards laid down by the Canadian Institute of Chartered Accountants. Management of a company is responsible for preparing the financial statement. The auditors are responsible for testing the amounts and disclosures and assessing accounting principles used and significant estimates made by management. The auditors' report concludes whether, in their opinion, the financial statements present fairly, in all material respects, the balance sheet and the results for the year.

The standard audit report has only three paragraphs. If there is an additional paragraph, the reason for the variation must be fully understood. It will almost certainly be queried by any financial institution. The "Notes" to the statement must also be studied carefully, particularly any referred to in the audit report. Important issues, such as concerns of the viability of the corporation on a "going concern" basis, may only be referred to in the "Notes."

An audit report attached to financial statements gives much weight and credibility when dealing with outsiders such as bankers and investors or when a company is up for sale.

AUDIT TRAIL step-by-step record by which accounting data can be traced to their source. Questions as to the validity or accuracy of an accounting figure can be resolved by reviewing the sequence of events from which the figure resulted.

AUNT MILLIE derogatory term for an unsophisticated investor. Wall Street professionals may say that "This investment will interest Aunt Millie," meaning that it is simple to understand. It may also imply that such small investors will not be able to appreciate the amount of risk posed by the investment relative to the opportunity for profit. Brokers and financial advisors, using the KNOW YOUR CUSTOMER rule, should not recommend complex and risky investments to Aunt Millie investors.

AUSTRALIAN OPTIONS MARKET (AOM) established in 1976 to trade put and call options in the securities of 38 leading Australian companies. Trading is by open outcry and is quote driven, with liquidity provided by market makers. The Options Automated Trading System, known as OATS, was started in October 1989.

AUSTRALIA STOCK EXCHANGE (ASX) six trading floors, formerly independent entities in Adelaide, Brisbane, Hobart (Tasmania), Melbourne, Perth, and Sydney, are linked through the Stock Exchange Automated Trading System (SEATS). Administrative headquarters is in Sydney. The most important Australian stocks are tracked by the ALL ORDINARIES INDEX. Settlement is five business days after a transaction, with less actively traded shares taking longer. In October 1993, the ASX launched Flexible Auxiliary Security Transfer (FAST), a computerized system. SEATS trading hours are 10 A.M.–4 P.M. (EST) Monday through Friday; dealings are permitted outside these hours according to the exchange's after-hours trading rules.

AUTEX SYSTEM electronic system for alerting brokers that other brokers want to buy or sell large blocks of stock. Once a match is made, the actual transaction takes place over the counter or on the floor of an exchange.

AUTHENTICATION identification of a bond certificate as having been issued under a specific indenture, thus validating the bond. Also, legal verification of the genuineness of a document, as by the certification and seal of an authorized public official.

AUTHENTICITY genuineness, attested to by a reliable seller of precious metals, of the metal content of a bar of precious metal, e.g., gold or silver. The silver or gold content must not be less than .999.

AUTHORIZED CAPITAL total number of shares that a company can sell, a figure that is based on the amount of money required and the percent of dilution its owners are prepared to accept. Of these, the shares sold to the public are called issued capital.

AUTHORIZED SHARES maximum number of shares of any class a company may legally create under the terms of its ARTICLES OF INCORPORATION. Normally, a corporation provides for future increases in authorized stock by vote of the stockholders. The corporation is not required to issue all the shares authorized and may initially keep issued shares at a minimum to hold down taxes and expenses. Also called *authorized stock.*

AUTO INSURANCE insurance protection for the owner of a vehicle against damage or loss, also providing legal liability protection.

AUTOMATED BOND SYSTEM (ABS) New York Stock Exchange computerized system that records bids and offers for inactively traded bonds until they are cancelled or executed. Before the ABS, such limit orders were kept in steel cabinets, giving rise to the terms CABINET SECURITY and CABINET CROWD (traders in inactive bonds).

AUTOMATED CLEARING HOUSE (ACH) clearing house for settling accounts between member banks via electronic equipment or magnetic tape. The ACH obviates the need for paper in transferring account debit and other financial activity.

AUTOMATIC DISTRIBUTION SERVICE service by which a bank distributes data for customers. The customer submits data for payments or deposits, either on paper or magnetic tape, to any branch of his or her bank. The funds are then deposited into any account in any financial institution. Payments to different banks take somewhat longer. (Also known as *direct delivery service, payment distribution, direct deposit*).

AUTOMATIC FUNDS TRANSFER fast and accurate transfer of funds, often internationally, from one account or investment vehicle to another without direct management, using modern electronic and telecommunications technology. A broker's instant transfer of stock sale proceeds to a money market fund is one example.

AUTOMATIC INVESTMENT PROGRAM any program in which an investor can accumulate or withdraw funds automatically. Some of the most popular automatic investment programs include:

- mutual fund debit programs, in which a mutual fund will automatically debit a preset amount from a bank savings or chequing account to buy fund shares on a weekly, monthly, quarterly, or annual basis.
- mutual fund reinvestment programs, in which all dividends and capital gains are automatically reinvested in more shares of the fund.
- stock dividend reinvestment plans, in which companies offer their shareholders the opportunity to reinvest their dividends in more shares of the company, and in some cases, buy additional shares at a discount with little or no brokerage commissions.
- savings bond payroll savings plans, which allow employees to purchase savings bonds through payroll deduction.

In addition to allowing automatic purchases of shares, automatic investment programs also permit participants to withdraw a set amount of money on a regular basis. These are known as AUTOMATIC WITHDRAWAL plans. For example, a retiree may request that a mutual fund automatically sell a fixed dollar amount of shares every month and send him or her a cheque.

AUTOMATIC PREMIUM LOAN loan that keeps the policy and all of its provisions in force when a premium is not paid until the cash value is used up. These premium loans along with interest may be repaid at any time before the cash value is exhausted.

AUTOMATIC REINVESTMENT *see* CONSTANT DOLLAR PLAN; DIVIDEND REINVESTMENT PLAN.

AUTOMATIC TRANSFER *see* ACCELERATED FUND TRANSFER.

AUTOMATIC WITHDRAWAL mutual fund program that entitles shareholders to a fixed payment each month or each quarter. The payment comes from dividends, including realized capital gains and income on securities held by the fund.

AVAILABILITY number of days that elapse in converting book balance to available balance.

AVAILABLE BALANCE book balances less float. Available balances can be invested, disbursed or wired out.

AVERAGE appropriately weighted and adjusted ARITHMETIC MEAN of selected securities designed to represent market behaviour generally or important segments of the market. Among the most familiar averages are the Toronto Stock Exchange 300 Average.

Because the evaluation of individual securities involves measuring price trends of securities in general or within an industry group, the various averages are important analytical tools.

See also STOCK INDEXES AND AVERAGES.

AVERAGE AVAILABLE BALANCE sum of daily available balances in the account divided by the number of days in the period, usually calculated for a 30-day or monthly banking period.

AVERAGE COLLECTED BALANCE   sum of daily balances in an account, less the total of uncollected items, divided by the number of days in the period. This is usually calculated on a monthly basis on the financial report.

AVERAGE COST
   Investing: average cost of shares of stock or in a fund bought at different prices. *See also* AVERAGE DOWN; AVERAGE UP; CONSTANT DOLLAR PLAN.
   Manufacturing: total of fixed and variable costs divided by units of production. Companies with relatively low average costs are better able to withstand price-cutting pressures from competition. Term also describes INVENTORY valuation method whereby the cost of goods available for sale is divided by the number of units available for sale.

AVERAGE DAILY BALANCE method for computing interest or finance charges on bank deposit accounts, credit cards, and charge accounts. Deposit accounts use the daily closing balance divided by the number of days in the period and apply the interest rate to that. Credit and charge cards divide the balances owed each day by the number of days and apply the finance charge. The average daily balance method, widely used by department stores, is less favourable to the consumer than the ADJUSTED BALANCE METHOD used for interest earned on bank deposit accounts but more favourable than the PREVIOUS BALANCE METHOD used by most credit cards.

AVERAGE DOWN strategy to lower the average price paid for a company's shares. An investor who wants to buy 1000 shares, for example, could buy 400 at the current market price and three blocks of 200 each as the price fell. The average cost would then be lower than it would have been if all 1000 shares had been bought at once. Investors also average down in order to realize tax losses. Say someone buys shares at $20, then watches them fall to $10. Instead of doing nothing, the investor can buy at $10, then sell the $20 shares at a capital loss, which can be used at tax time to offset other gains. However, the WASH SALE rule says that in order to claim the capital loss, the investor must not sell the $20 stock until at least 30 days after buying the stock at $10. *See also* CONSTANT DOLLAR PLAN.

AVERAGE EQUITY average daily balance in a trading account. Brokerage firms calculate customer equity daily as part of their procedure for keeping track of gains and losses on uncompleted transactions, called MARK TO THE MARKET. When transactions are completed, profits and losses are booked to each customer's account together with brokerage commissions. Even though daily fluctuations in equity are routine, average equity is a useful guide in making trading decisions and ensuring sufficient equity to meet MARGIN REQUIREMENTS.

AVERAGE LIFE average length of time before the principal of a debt issue is scheduled to be repaid through AMORTIZATION or SINKING FUND payments. *See also* HALF-LIFE.

AVERAGE NUMBER OF SHARES OUTSTANDING   sum of the proportion of time in a period that shares were outstanding, times the number of outstanding shares. For example, if 1500 shares were outstanding for the first 6 months and 1800 were outstanding for the next 3 months, the average number of shares outstanding during the 9 month period would be 1600 shares. This calculation is done using only common shares that are outstanding or owned by shareholders.

AVERAGE UP buy on a rising market so as to lower the overall cost. Buying an equal number of shares at $50, $52, $54, and $58, for instance, will make the average cost $53.50. This is a mathematical reality, but it does not determine whether the stock is worth buying at any or all of these prices.

AVERAGE RATE OF RETURN means of evaluating proposed capital expenditures, calculated by dividing the average profits after taxes expected from a project by the average investment required by the project.

AVERAGES AND INDICES statistical tools that measure the state of the stock market or the economy, based on the performance of the stocks or other prime economic indicators. The Dow Jones Industrial Average, the TSE 300 Composite Index, and the Montreal Exchange Index indicate general trends in the stock markets while the Consumer Price Index reflects the rate of price increase of a fixed base of consumer goods.

AVERAGING *see* CONSTANT DOLLAR PLAN.

AWAY FROM THE MARKET expression used when the bid on a LIMIT ORDER is lower or the offer price is higher than the current market price for the security. Away from the market limit orders are held by the specialist for later execution unless FILL OR KILL (FOK) is stipulated on the order entry.

B

BACKDATING
In general: dating any statement, document, cheque or other instrument earlier than the date drawn.

BACK-END LOAD redemption charge an investor pays when withdrawing money from an investment. Most common in mutual funds and annuities, the back-end load is designed to discourage withdrawals. Back-end loads typically decline for each year that a shareholder remains in a fund. For example, if the shareholder sells shares in the first year, a 5% sales charge is levied. The charge is 4% in the second year, 3% in the third year, 2% in the fourth year, 1% in the fifth year, and no fee is charged if shares are sold after the fifth year. Also called *contingent deferred sales load, deferred sales charge, exit fee, redemption charge.*

BACK-IN conversion of a smaller, cost-free interest to a larger, working interest in a well, normally occurring when the original capital investment in the well has been returned.

BACKLOG value of unfilled orders placed with a manufacturing company. Whether the firm's backlog is rising or falling is a clue to its future sales and earnings.

BACK MONTHS in futures and options trading, the months with the expiration dates furthest out in time. *See also* FURTHEST MONTH.

BACK OFFICE bank or brokerage house departments not directly involved in selling or trading. The back office sees to accounting records, compliance with government regulations, and communication between branches. When stock-market trading is particularly heavy, order processing can be slowed by massive volume; this is called a back office crunch.

BACK TAXES taxes that have not been paid when due. Taxpayers may owe back taxes if they underreported income or overstated deductions, either accidentally, or by design.

BACK UP turn around; reverse a stock market trend. When prices are moving in one direction, traders would say of a sudden reversal that the market backed up. *See* chart on next page.

BACKUP LINE BANK LINE of credit in the name of an issuer of commercial paper, covering maturing notes in the event that new notes cannot be marketed to replace them. Ideally, the unused line should always equal the commercial paper outstanding. In practice, something less than total coverage is commonplace, particularly because the compensating balances normally required in support of the line are also available to meet maturing paper.

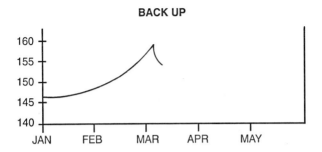

BACKWARDATION
1. pricing structure in commodities or foreign-exchange trading in which deliveries in the near future have a higher price than those made later on. Backwardation occurs when demand is greater in the near future. *See also* CONTANGO; INVERTED MARKET.
2. London Stock Exchange term for the fees and interest due on short sales of stock with delayed delivery.

BAD DEBT open account balance or loan receivable that has proven uncollectible and is written off. Traditionally, companies and financial institutions have maintained a RESERVE for uncollectible accounts, charging the reserve for actual bad debts and making annual, tax deductible charges to income to replenish or increase the reserve. The relationship of bad debt write-offs and recoveries to accounts receivable can reveal how liberal or conservative a firm's credit and charge-off policies are.

BAD DELIVERY opposite of GOOD DELIVERY.

BAD TITLE title to property that does not clearly confer ownership. Most frequently applied to real estate, a bad title may prevent a home-owner from selling the property. Title may be clouded by unpaid taxes or other unsatisfied liens, an incorrect survey, or uncorrected building violations, among other causes. Steps must be taken to rectify these problems before title to a property can be legally transferred. Also called *cloud on title.*

BAILING OUT selling a security or commodity quickly without regard to the price received. An investor bails out of a position if losses are mounting quickly and he or she is no longer able to sustain further losses. For example, someone who has sold a stock short may bail out by covering his or her position at a loss if the stock rises sharply.

BALANCE AND ACTIVITY REPORT *see* ACCOUNT ANALYSIS.

BALANCED BUDGET *see* BUDGET.

BALANCED FUND investment fund that the manager invests in bonds, debentures, or preferred shares in varying ratios with common stocks. This fund provides regular income, moderate growth, and safety of capital. It allocates its money among the three basic types of investments—cash equivalent investments, bonds, and common stocks. In some balanced funds, the portfolio mix remains fairly stable from one period to another and the fund's manager adopts a more or less "buy-and-hold" investment strategy. In other balanced funds, the manager changes the portfolio mix continuously, putting more weight on the investment type that is expected to outperform the other two for the coming period. This strategy of changing the portfolio mix continuously to increase the return on investment is called an asset allocation strategy; it is a kind of market-timing strategy.

BALANCED MUTUAL FUND fund that buys common stock, preferred stock, and bonds in an effort to obtain the highest return consistent with a low-risk strategy. A balanced fund typically offers a higher yield than a pure stock fund and performs better than such a fund when stocks are falling. In a rising market, however, a balanced mutual fund usually will not keep pace with all-equity funds.

BALANCE OF PAYMENTS system of recording all of a country's economic transactions with the rest of the world during a particular time period. Double-entry bookkeeping is used, and there can be no surplus or deficit on the overall balance of payments. The balance of payments is typically divided into three accounts—current, capital, and gold—and these can show a surplus or deficit. The current account covers imports and exports of goods and services; the capital account covers movements of investments; and the gold account covers gold movements. The balance of payments helps a country evaluate its competitive strengths and weaknesses and forecast the strength of its currency. From the standpoint of a national economy, a surplus on a part of the balance of payments is not necessarily good, nor is a deficit necessarily bad; the state of the national economy and the manner of financing the deficit are important considerations. *See also* BALANCE OF TRADE.

BALANCE OF SALE portion of the selling price taken back by the seller of a company in a note, debenture, or mortgage.

BALANCE OF TRADE net difference over a period of time between the value of a country's imports and exports of merchandise. Movable goods such as automobiles, foodstuffs, and apparel are included in the balance of trade; payments abroad for services and for tourism are not. When a country exports more than it imports, it is said to have a favourable balance of trade; when imports predominate the balance is called unfavourable. The balance of trade should be viewed in the context of the country's entire international economic position, however. For example, a country may consistently have an unfavourable balance of trade that is offset by considerable exports of services; this country would be judged to have a good international economic position. *See also* BALANCE OF PAYMENTS.

BALANCE SHEET financial report, also called *statement of condition* or *statement of financial position,* showing the status of a company's assets, liabilities, and owners' equity on a given date, usually the close of a month. The name comes from the fact that the asset and liability columns are "balanced," the net difference being the capital paid in, plus or minus retained earnings or losses, referred to as SHAREHOLDERS' EQUITY. One way of looking at a business enterprise is as a mass of capital (ASSETS) arrayed against the sources of that capital (LIABILITIES and EQUITY). Assets are equal to liabilities and equity, and the balance sheet is a listing of the items making up the two sides of the equation. Unlike a PROFIT AND LOSS STATEMENT, which shows the results of operations over a period of time, a balance sheet shows the state of affairs at one point in time. It is a snapshot, not a motion picture, and must be analyzed with reference to comparative prior balance sheets and other operating statements.

BALLOON final payment on a debt that is substantially larger than the preceding payments. Loans or mortgages are structured with balloon payments when some projected event is expected to provide extra cash flow or when refinancing is anticipated. Balloon loans are sometimes called *partially amortized loans.*

BALLOON INTEREST in serial bond issues, the higher COUPON rate on bonds with later maturities.

BALLOON MATURITY bond issue or long-term loan with larger dollar amounts of bonds or payments falling due in the later years of the obligation.

BAN *see* BOND ANTICIPATION NOTE.

BANKER'S ACCEPTANCE short-term promissory note issued by major corporations, backed by one of the banks, and repayable on a specified date. They are sold below the face or par value and then mature at the face value (discounted). A minimum of $25,000 is required for investment in a banker's acceptance. *See also* ACCEPTANCE.

BANKING GROUP group of investment firms, each of which individually assumes financial responsibility for part of an underwriting.

BANK LINE bank's moral commitment, as opposed to its contractual commitment, to make loans to a particular borrower up to a specified maximum during a specified period, usually one year. Interest is charged only on the amount withdrawn. Because a bank line—also called a *line of credit*—is not a legal commitment, it is not customary to charge a commitment fee, although a standby fee is charged. It is common, however, to require that compensating balances be kept on deposit—typically 10% of the line, with an additional 10% of any borrowings under the line. A line about which a customer is officially notified is called an *advised line* or *confirmed line*. A line that is an internal policy guide about which the customer is not informed is termed a *guidance line*.

BANKMAIL bank's agreement with a company involved in a TAKEOVER not to finance another acquirer's bid.

BANK OF CANADA RATE minimum rate charged by the Bank of Canada for advances to the chartered banks. It is usually 25 bonus points above the Treasury bill rate.

BANK QUALITY *see* INVESTMENT GRADE.

BANK RATE minimum rate at which the Bank of Canada makes short-term advances to the chartered banks, other members of the Canadian Payments Association, and investment dealers who are money market "jobbers." Since 1980, the bank rate has been set at 1.4 of 1% (25 basis points) above the weekly average tender rate of 91-day Government of Canada Treasury bills.

BANKRUPT legal status of an individual or company that is unable to pay its creditors and whose assets are therefore administered for its creditors by a Trustee in Bankruptcy.

BANK STATEMENT periodic statement of a customer's account detailing credits and debits posted to the account during the period and the book balance as of the statement cutoff date.

BANK WIRE private wire service for financial institutions for which a service or subscription fee is paid. It serves as a cooperative service for institutions across North America.

BARBELL PORTFOLIO portfolio of bonds distributed like the shape of a barbell, with most of the portfolio in short-term and long-term bonds, but few bonds in intermediate maturities. This portfolio can be adjusted to emphasize short- or long-term bonds, depending on whether the investor thinks interest rates are rising or falling. A portfolio with a higher concentration in medium-term bonds than short- or long-term bonds is called a *bell-shaped curve portfolio*.

BAREFOOT PILGRIM unsophisticated investor who has lost his or her shirt and shoes in securities trading.

BAROMETER selective compilation of economic and market data designed to represent larger trends. Consumer spending, housing starts, and interest rates are barometers used in economic forecasting. The Dow Jones Industrial Average, TSE 300 Index, and the Standard & Poor's 500 Stock Index are prominent stock market barometers.

A *barometer stock* has a price movement pattern that reflects the market as a whole, thus serving as a market indicator. Canadian bank stocks and major resource stocks such as Royal Bank, CIBC, Inco, and Stelco are considered barometers, along with such U.S. corporations as General Motors and IBM.

BARRON'S CONFIDENCE INDEX weekly index of corporate bond yields published by *Barron's*, a Dow Jones financial newspaper. The index shows the ratio of Barron's average yield on 10 top-grade bonds to the Dow Jones average yield on 40 bonds. People who are worried about the economic outlook tend to seek high quality, whereas investors who feel secure about the economy are more likely to buy lower-rated bonds. The spread between high- and low-grade bonds thus reflects investor opinion about the economy.

BARTER trade of goods or services without use of money. When money is involved, whether in such forms as wampum, checks, or bills or coins, a transaction is called a SALE. Although barter is usually associated with undeveloped economies, it occurs in modern complex societies. In conditions of extreme inflation, it can be a preferred mode of commerce. Where a population lacks confidence in its currency or banking system, barter becomes commonplace. In international trade, barter can provide a way of doing business with countries whose soft currencies would otherwise make them unattractive trading partners.

BASE MARKET VALUE average market price of a group of securities at a given time. It is used as a basis of comparison in plotting dollar or percentage changes for purposes of market INDEXING.

BASE METAL commercial metal such as copper, lead or zinc. The term was coined to describe a metal "inferior" to previous metals such as gold and silver.

BASE PERIOD particular time in the past used as a yardstick when measuring economic data. A base period is usually a year or an average of years; it can also be a month or other time period. The Canadian Consumer Price Index is based on the period 1981 for a fixed basket of consumer goods and services.

BASE RATE interest rate charged by banks to their best corporate customers in Great Britain. It is the British equivalent of the PRIME RATE in the United States and Canada. Many other consumer loan rates are pegged to the base rate in Britain.

BASIC LIFE INSURANCE insurance that usually guarantees death benefits regardless of the cause of death (other than by murder or suicide). It does not have a fixed term.

BASIS difference between the cash price and the futures price of a commodity.

BASIS POINT smallest measure used in quoting yields on bills, notes, and bonds. One basis point is .01%, or one one-hundredth of a percent of yield. Thus, 100 basis points equal 1%. A bond's yield that increased from 8.00% to 8.50% would be said to have risen 50 basis points.

BASIS PRICE

In general: price an investor uses to calculate capital gains when selling a stock or bond. *See also* BASIS.

Odd-lot trading: the price arbitrarily established by an exchange floor official at the end of a trading session for a buyer or seller of an odd lot when the market bid and asked prices are more than $2 apart, or if no round-lot transactions have occurred that day. The customer gets the basis price plus or minus the odd-lot differential, if any. This procedure for determining prices is rare, since most odd lots are transacted at the market bid (if a sale) or asked (if a buy) or at prices based on the next round-lot trade.

BASKET

1. unit of 15 or more stocks used in PROGRAM TRADING.
2. program trading vehicles offered by the New York Stock Exchange (called *Exchange Stock Portfolio* or *ESP*) and the Chicago Board Options Exchange (called *Market Basket*) to institutional investors and index arbitrageurs. Both baskets permit the purchase in one trade of all the stocks making up the STANDARD & POOR'S INDEX of 500 stocks. ESP's design requires a minimum trade of approximately $5 million, and Market Basket's, around $1.7 million. The baskets were introduced in late 1989 to solve problems revealed when institutions tried to negotiate large block trades on BLACK MONDAY and to head off an exodus of program trading business to overseas exchanges.
    See also SPIDERS.

BEAR investor who believes that stock prices will go down. A bear's strategies include buying options to sell stock in the future (buying puts), selling options to sell stock in the future that the investor does not own (selling naked calls), and selling stock that the investor does not own and repurchasing it later when the price declines (selling stock short).

BEARER BOND *see* COUPON BOND.

BEARER FORM security not registered on the books of the issuing corporation and thus payable to the one possessing it. A bearer bond has coupons attached, which the bondholder sends in or presents on the interest date for payment, hence the alternative name COUPON BONDS. Bearer stock certificates are negotiable without endorsement and are transferred by delivery. Dividends are payable by presentation of dividend coupons, which are dated or numbered. Most securities issued today, with the exception of foreign stocks, are in registered form, including municipal bonds issued since 1983.

BEARER SECURITY security (stock or bond) that does not have the owner's name recorded in the books of the issuing company or on the security itself and that is payable to the holder. *See also* REGISTERED SECURITY.

BEAR HUG TAKEOVER bid so attractive in terms of price and other features that TARGET COMPANY directors, who might be opposed for other reasons, must approve it or risk shareholder protest.

BEAR MARKET prolonged period of falling prices. A bear market in stocks is usually brought on by the anticipation of declining economic activity, and a bear market in bonds is caused by rising interest rates.

BEAR RAID attempt by investors to manipulate the price of a stock by selling large numbers of shares short. The manipulators pocket the difference between the initial price and the new, lower price after this maneuver.

BEAR SPREAD strategy in the options market designed to take advantage of a fall in the price of a security or commodity. Someone executing a bear spread could buy a combination of calls and puts on the same security at different *strike prices* in order to profit as the security's price fell. Or the investor could buy a put of short maturity and a put of long maturity in order to profit from the difference between the two puts as prices fell. *See also* BULL SPREAD.

BEAR TRAP situation confronting short sellers when a bear market reverses itself and turns bullish. Anticipating further declines, the bears continue to sell, and then are forced to buy at higher prices to cover. *See also* SELLING SHORT.

BELL signal that opens and closes trading on major exchanges—sometimes actually a bell but sometimes a buzzer sound.

BELLWETHER security seen as an indicator of a market's direction. In stocks, 3M Company (MMM) is considered both an economic and a market bellwether because it sells to a diverse range of other producers and because so much of its stock is owned by institutional investors who have much control over supply and demand on the stock market. Institutional trading actions tend to influence smaller investors and therefore the market generally.

BELOW PAR *see* PAR VALUE.

BENEFICIAL OWNER person who enjoys the benefits of ownership even though title is in another name. When shares of a mutual fund are held by a custodian bank or when securities are held by a broker in STREET NAME, the real owner is the beneficial owner, even though, for safety or convenience, the bank or broker holds title.

BENEFICIARY (INDIVIDUAL, COMPANY, OR ORGANIZATION)
1. party to whom an inheritance passes as the result of being named in a will.

2. recipient of the proceeds of a life insurance policy.
3. party in whose favour a LETTER OF CREDIT is issued.
4. one to whom the amount of an ANNUITY is payable.
5. party for whose benefit a TRUST exists.
6. heir to the assets of an RRSP. (When a spouse is named as the beneficiary to an RRSP, the money is transferred tax-free.)

BENEFIT-COST RATIO profitability index. B–C ratios are used to evaluate capital expenditure proposals. They are calculated by dividing the present value of net cash flows from a project by the initial investment in it. If the B–C ratio is greater or equal to one, a project is acceptable; otherwise, it should be rejected.

BEQUEST giving of assets, such as stocks, bonds, mutual funds, real estate, and personal property, to beneficiaries through the provisions of a will.

BEST EFFORT arrangement whereby investment bankers, acting as agents, agree to do their best to sell an issue to the public. Instead of buying the securities outright, these agents have an option to buy and an authority to sell the securities. Depending on the contract, the agents exercise their option and buy enough shares to cover their sales to clients, or they cancel the incompletely sold issue altogether and forgo the fee. Best efforts deals, which were common prior to 1900, entailed risks and delays from the issuer's standpoint. What is more, the broadening of the securities markets has made marketing new issues easier, and the practice of outright purchase by investment bankers, called FIRM COMMITMENT underwriting, has become commonplace. For the most part, the best efforts deals we occasionally see today are handled by firms specializing in the more speculative securities of new and unseasoned companies. *See also* BOUGHT DEAL.

BEST'S RATING rating of financial soundness given to insurance companies by Best's Rating Service. The top rating is A+. A Best's rating is important to buyers of insurance or annuities because it informs them whether a company is financially sound. Best's Ratings are also important to investors in insurance stocks.

BETA
1. coefficient measuring a stock's relative VOLATILITY. The beta is the covariance of a stock in relation to the rest of the stock market. Any stock with a higher beta is more volatile than the market, and any with a lower beta can be expected to rise and fall more slowly than the market. The lowest theoretical beta is 0, which indicates no movement, while a high beta (e.g., 2) indicates wild up and down swings for small movement in the market. A conservative investor whose main concern is preservation of capital should focus on stocks with low betas, whereas one willing to take high risks in an effort to earn high rewards should look for high-beta stocks. *See also* ALPHA.

2. on the London Stock Exchange, the designation *beta stocks* applies to the second tier in a four-level hierarchy introduced with BIG BANG in October 1986 and replaced in January, 1991 with the NORMAL MARKET SIZE (NMS) classification system. With ALPHA stocks representing the equivalent of North American BLUE CHIP issues, beta stocks represented smaller issues that were less actively traded. *See also* DELTA (2); GAMMA STOCKS.

BETWEEN-DEALER MARKET *see* OVER-THE-COUNTER.

BID
1. price a prospective buyer is ready to pay. Term is used by traders who MAKE A MARKET (maintain firm bid and OFFER prices) in a given security by standing ready to buy or sell round lots at publicly quoted prices and by the SPECIALIST in a stock, who performs a similar function on an exchange.
2. TENDER OFFER in a TAKEOVER attempt.
3. any offer to buy at a specified price.
   See also ANY-AND-ALL BID; COMPETITIVE BID; TREASURIES.

BID AND ASKED bid is the highest price a prospective buyer is prepared to pay at a particular time for a trading unit of a given security; asked is the lowest price acceptable to a prospective seller of the same security. Together, the two prices constitute a QUOTATION or a QUOTE; the difference between the two prices is the SPREAD. Although the bid and asked dynamic is common to all securities trading, "bid and asked" usually refers to UNLISTED SECURITIES traded OVER THE COUNTER.

BID-ASKED SPREAD difference between BID and offer prices. The term *asked* is usually used in OVER-THE COUNTER trading; *offered* is used in exchange trading. The bid and asked (or offered) prices together comprise a QUOTATION (or *quote*).

BIDDER party that is ready to buy at a specified price in a TWO-SIDED MARKET or DUTCH AUCTION.

BIDDING UP practice whereby the price bid for a security is successively moved higher lest an upswing in prices leaves orders unexecuted. An example would be an investor wanting to purchase a sizable quantity of shares in a rising market, using buy limit orders (orders to buy at a specified price or lower) to ensure the most favourable price. Since offer prices are moving up with the market, the investor must move his or her limit buy price upward to continue accumulating shares. To some extent the buyer is contributing to the upward price pressure on the stock, but most of the price rise is out of the buyer's control.

BID PRICE *see* BID.

BID WANTED (BW) announcement that a holder of securities wants to sell and will entertain bids. Because the final price is subject to negotiation, the bid submitted in response to a BW need not be specific. A BW is frequently seen on published market quotation sheets.

BIG BANG deregulation on October 27, 1986, of London-based securities markets, an event comparable to MAY DAY in the United States and marking a major step toward a single world financial market.

BIG BLUE popular name for International Business Machines Corporation (IBM), taken from the colour of its logotype.

BIG BOARD popular term for the NEW YORK STOCK EXCHANGE.

BIG PRODUCER broker who is very successful, and thereby produces a large volume of commission dollars for the brokerage firm he or she represents. Big producers typically will bring in $1 million or more per year in commissions for their firms. In order to retain big producers, many brokerage firms try to tie them to the firm with GOLDEN HANDCUFFS.

BIG SIX largest North American accounting firms as measured by revenue. They do the accounting and auditing for most major corporations, signing the auditor's report that appears in every annual report. They also offer various consulting services. Over time, there have been several mergers among the top accounting firms, which formerly were called the Big Eight. In alphabetical order they are: Arthur Andersen & Co.; Coopers & Lybrand; Deloitte & Touche; Ernst & Young; KPMG Peat Marwick; and Price Waterhouse & Co.

BIG THREE the three large automobile companies in America, which are, alphabetically, Chrysler, Ford, and General Motors. Since the automobile business has such a major influence on the direction of the economy, the Big Three's fortunes are closely followed by investors, analysts, and economists. Because auto company profits rise and fall with the economy, they are considered to be CYCLICAL STOCKS.

    In Switzerland, the term Big Three refers to the three most dominant banking institutions—Credit Suisse, Swiss Bank Corporation, and Union Bank of Switzerland.

BIG UGLIES stocks that are out of favour with the investing public. These usually are large industrial companies such as steel or chemical firms that are not in glamorous businesses. Because they are unpopular, Big Uglies typically sell at low price/earnings and price/book value ratios.

BILL
In general: (1) short for *bill of exchange,* an order by one person directing a second to pay a third. (2) document evidencing a debtor's obligation to a creditor, the kind of bill we are all familiar with. (3) paper currency, like the $5 bill. (4) *bill of sale,* a document used to transfer the title to certain goods from seller to buyer in the same way a deed to real property passes.
Investments: short for *due bill,* a statement of money owed. Commonly used to adjust a securities transaction when dividends,

interest, and other distributions are reflected in a price but have not yet been disbursed. For example, when a stock is sold ex-dividend, but the dividend has not yet been paid, the buyer would sign a due bill stating that the amount of the dividend is payable to the seller.

A due bill may accompany delivered securities to give title to the buyer's broker in exchange for shares or money.

BILLING CYCLE interval between periodic billings for goods sold or services rendered, normally one month, or a system whereby bills or statements are mailed at periodic intervals in the course of a month in order to distribute the clerical workload.

BILL OF EXCHANGE *see* DRAFT.

BINDER sum of money paid to evidence good faith until a transaction is finalized. In insurance, the binder is an agreement executed by an insurer (or sometimes an agent) that puts insurance coverage into force before the contract is signed and the premium paid. In real estate, the binder holds the sale until the closing and is refundable.

BLACK FRIDAY sharp drop in a financial market. The original Black Friday was September 24, 1869, when a group of financiers tried to corner the gold market and precipitated a business panic followed by a depression. The panic of 1873 also began on Friday, and Black Friday has come to apply to any debacle affecting the financial markets.

BLACK MONDAY October 19, 1987, when the Dow Jones Industrial Average plunged a record 508 points following sharp drops the previous week, reflecting investor anxiety about inflated stock price levels, federal budget and trade deficits, and foreign market activity. Many blamed PROGRAM TRADING for the extreme VOLATILITY.

BLACK-SCHOLES OPTION PRICING MODEL model developed by Fischer Black and Myron Scholes to gauge whether options contracts are fairly valued. The model incorporates such factors as the volatility of a security's return, the level of interest rates, the relationship of the underlying stock's price to the *strike price* of the option, and the time remaining until the option expires. Current valuations using this model are developed by the Options Monitor Service and are available from Standard & Poor's Trading Systems, 11 Broadway, New York, NY 10004.

BLANK CHEQUE cheque drawn on a bank account and signed by the maker, but with the amount of the cheque to be supplied by the drawee. Term is used as a metaphor for any situation where inordinate trust is placed in another person.

BLANK CHEQUE OFFERING INITIAL PUBLIC OFFERING (IPO) by a company whose business activities have yet to be determined and which is therefore speculative. Similar to the BLIND POOL concept of limited partnerships.

BLANKET RECOMMENDATION communication sent to all customers of a brokerage firm recommending that they buy or sell a particular stock or stocks in a particular industry regardless of investment objectives or portfolio size.

BLENDED RATE mortgage financing term used when a lender, to avoid assuming an old mortgage at an obsoletely low rate, offers the incentive to refinance at a rate somewhere between the old rate and the rate on a new loan.

BLIND POOL limited partnership that does not specify the properties the general partner plans to acquire. If, for example, a real estate partnership is offered in the form of a blind pool, investors can evaluate the project only by looking at the general partner's track record. In a *specified pool,* on the other hand, investors can look at the prices paid for property and the amount of rental income the buildings generate, then evaluate the partnership's potential. In general, blind pool partnerships do not perform better or worse than specified pool partnerships.

BLIND TRUST trust in which a fiduciary third party, such as a bank or money management firm, is given complete discretion to make investments on behalf of the trust beneficiaries. The trust is called blind because the beneficiary is not informed about the holdings of the trust. Blind trusts often are set up when there is a potential conflict of interest involving the beneficiary and the investments held in the trust. For example, a politician may be required to place assets in a blind trust so that his or her votes are not influenced by the trust's portfolio holdings.

BLITZKREIG TENDER OFFER TAKEOVER jargon for a tender offer that is completed quickly, usually because it was priced attractively. *Blitzkreig* translates from the German as "lightning-like war" and was used to describe World War II bombing raids.

BLOCK a large amount of stock sold as a single unit. The term is most often used to describe a unit of 1000 shares or more.

BLOCK TRADE *see* BLOCK.

BLOWOUT quick sale of all shares in a new offering of securities. Corporations like to sell securities in such environments, because they get a high price for their stock. Investors are likely to have a hard time getting the number of shares they want during a blowout. Also called *going away* or *hot issue.*

BLUE CHIP common stock of a nationally known company that has a long record of profit growth and dividend payment and a reputation for quality management, products, and services. Some examples of blue chip stocks: Bell Canada, General Motors Canada, Canadian Pacific,

Royal Bank of Canada; and in the U.S., International Business Machines, General Electric, and Du Pont. Blue chip stocks typically are relatively high priced and have moderate dividend yields.

BLUE-SKY LAW law of a kind passed by various provinces and U.S. states to protect investors against securities fraud. These laws require sellers of new stock issues or mutual funds to register their offerings and provide financial details on each issue so that investors can base their judgments on relevant data. The term is said to have originated with a judge who asserted that a particular stock offering had as much value as a patch of blue sky.

BOARD OF ARBITRATION group of three or fewer individuals selected to adjudicate cases between securities firms and claims brought by customers. Both parties in the dispute agree to one representative each and one independent.

BOARD LOT regular trading unit that has uniformly been decided upon by stock exchanges, usually 100 shares. *See also* ODD LOT.

BOARD OF DIRECTORS group of individuals elected, usually at an annual meeting, by the shareholders of a corporation and empowered to carry out certain tasks as spelled out in the corporation's charter. Among such powers are appointing senior management, naming members of executive and finance committees (if any), issuing additional shares, and declaring dividends. Boards normally include the top corporate executives, termed *inside directors,* as well as OUTSIDE DIRECTORS chosen from business and from the community at large to advise on matters of broad policy. Directors meet several times a year and are paid for their services.

BOARD ROOM
   Brokerage house: room where customers can watch an electronic board that displays stock prices and transactions.
   Corporation: room where the board of directors holds its meetings.

BO DEREK STOCK perfect stock with an exemplary record of earnings growth, product quality, and stock price appreciation. These stocks are named after the movie "10" in which Bo Derek was depicted as the perfect woman.

BOGEY target for purchasing or selling a security or achieving some other objective. An investor's bogey may be a 10% rate of return from a particular stock. Or it may be locking in an 8% yield on a bond. A money manager's bogey may be to beat the TSE 300 Index.

BOILERPLATE standard legal language, often in fine print, used in most contracts, wills, indentures, prospectuses, and other legal documents. Although what the boilerplate says is important, it rarely is subject to change by the parties to the agreement, since it is the product of years of legal experience.

BOILER ROOM place where high-pressure salespeople use banks of telephones to call lists of potential investors (known in the trade as sucker lists) in order to peddle speculative, even fraudulent, securities. They are called boiler rooms because of the high-pressure selling. The Ontario Securities Commission is fighting these operations, as is the Bank of Canada.

BOLSA Spanish term for *stock exchange.* There are Bolsas in Spain, Mexico, Chile, Argentina, and many other Spanish-speaking countries. In French, the term is BOURSE; in Italian, Borsa.

BOLSA DE VALORES DE SAO PAULO (BOVESPA) largest of Brazil's nine stock exchanges. Open outcry and computer assisted trading system (CATS) sessions are held simultaneously, in two sessions, from 9:30 A.M. to 1 P.M., and 3 P.M. to 4 P.M., Monday through Friday. Stock options of the 20 most actively traded companies are traded in the open outcry, while other stocks and options are traded only on the CATS system. Stock options and an option with a strike price quoted in points tied to the U.S. dollar are traded on the exchange as well. Physical settlement is on the first business day following the trade, and financial settlement is on the second business day.

BOMBAY STOCK EXCHANGE (BSE) largest of 22 stock exchanges in India. As such, it is the best indicator of economic and stock market activity in India. Settlement differs for "A" and "B" category stocks. The former, also known as the forward list, consists of the large capitalized companies, and involves a 14-day period, after which all transactions are settled on a net basis. The "B" group has a one-week settlement period. Trading Hours: 11:30 A.M.–2:30 P.M., Monday through Friday.

BOND any interest-bearing or discounted government or corporate security that obligates the issuer to pay the bondholder a specified sum of money, usually at specific intervals, and to repay the principal amount of the loan at maturity. Bondholders have an IOU from the issuer, but no corporate ownership privileges, as stockholders do.

An owner of *bearer bonds* presents the bond coupons and is paid interest, whereas the owner of *registered bonds* appears on the records of the bond issuer.

A SECURED BOND is backed by collateral which may be sold by the bondholder to satisfy a claim if the bond's issuer fails to pay interest and principal when they are due. An *unsecured bond* or DEBENTURE is backed by the full faith and credit of the issuer, but not by any specific collateral.

A CONVERTIBLE bond gives its owner the privilege of exchange for other securities of the issuing company at some future date and under prescribed conditions.

Also, a bond, in finance, is the obligation of one person to repay a debt taken on by someone else, should that other person default. A bond can also be money or securities deposited as a pledge of good faith.

A surety or PERFORMANCE BOND is an agreement whereby an insurance company becomes liable for the performance of work or services provided by a contractor by an agreed-upon date. If the contractor does not do what was promised, the surety company is financially responsible. *See also* INDENTURE; ZERO COUPON SECURITY.

BOND DISCOUNT amount by which the MARKET PRICE of a bond is lower than its FACE VALUE. Outstanding bonds with fixed COUPONS go to discounts when market interest rates rise. Discounts are also caused when supply exceeds demand and when a bond's CREDIT RATING IS reduced. When opposite conditions exist and market price is higher than face value, the difference is termed a *bond premium.* Premiums also occur when a bond issue with a CALL FEATURE is redeemed prior to maturity and the bondholder is compensated for lost interest. *See also* ORIGINAL ISSUE DISCOUNT.

BOND EQUIVALENT YIELD restatement of a DISCOUNT YIELD as its interest-bearing equivalent.

BONDHOLDER owner of a bond. Bondholders may be individuals or institutions such as corporations, banks, insurance companies, or mutual funds. Bondholders are entitled to regular interest payments as due and return of principal when the bond matures. Bondholders may own corporate, government, or municipal issues. For corporate bonds, bondholders' claims on the assets of the issuing corporation take precedence over claims of stockholders in the event of liquidation. Unlike stockholders, however, straight bondholders do not own an equity interest in the issuing company. Some bonds, such as convertible bonds, do have some claim on the equity of the issuing corporation.

BOND MUTUAL FUND mutual fund holding bonds. Such funds may specialize in a particular kind of bond, such as government, corporate, convertible, high-yield, mortgage-backed, municipal, foreign, or zero-coupon bonds. Other bond mutual funds will buy some or all of these kinds of bonds. Most bond mutual funds are designed to produce current income for shareholders. Bond funds also produce capital gains when interest rates fall and capital losses when interest rates rise. Unlike the bonds in these funds, the funds themselves never mature. There are two types of bond mutual funds: open- and closed-end. *Open-end funds* continually create new shares to accommodate new money as it flows into the funds and they always trade at NET ASSET VALUE. *Closed-end funds* issue a limited number of shares and trade on stock exchanges. Closed-end funds trade at either higher than their net asset value (a premium) or lower than their net asset value (a discount), depending on investor demand for the fund.

BOND OPTION contract giving the holder the right to buy or sell bonds at a fixed price during a specified time period. Bond options can be used to reduce the risk of interest rate fluctuations.

BOND PREMIUM *see* BOND DISCOUNT.

BOND POWER form used in the transfer of registered bonds from one owner to another. Sometimes called *assignment separate from certificate,* it accomplishes the same thing as the assignment form on the back of the bond certificate, but has a safety advantage in being separate. Technically, the bond power appoints an attorney-in-fact with the power to make a transfer of ownership on the corporation's books.

BOND RATING method of evaluating the possibility of default by a bond issuer. Standard & Poor's, Moody's Investors Service, and Dominion and Canada Bond Rating Services, analyze the financial strength of each bond's issuer, whether a corporation or a government body. Their ratings range from AAA (highly unlikely to default) to D (in default). Bonds rated BB or below are not INVESTMENT GRADE—in other words, institutions such as registered pension plans, insurance companies, and trust companies under federal legislation would not consider these acceptable securities. *See also* RATING.

BOND RATIO *leverage* ratio measuring the percentage of a company's capitalization represented by bonds. It is calculated by dividing the total bonds due after one year by the same figure plus all equity. A bond ratio over 33% indicates high leverage—except in utilities, where higher bond ratios are normal. *See also* DEBT-TO-EQUITY RATIO.

BOND SWAP simultaneous sale of one bond issue and purchase of another. The motives for bond swaps vary: *maturity swaps* aim to stretch out maturities but can also produce a profit because of the lower prices on longer bonds; *yield swaps* seek to improve return and *quality swaps* seek to upgrade safety; *tax swaps* create tax-deductible losses through the sale, while the purchase of a substitute bond effectively preserves the investment. *See also* SWAP, SWAP ORDER.

BOND YIELD complicated calculation involving annual interest payments and amortizing the difference between its current market price and par value over the life of the bond. This yield can be obtained from a bond yield table or from a computer.

BON VOYAGE BONUS *see* GREENMAIL.

BOOK
1. in an underwriting of securities, (1) preliminary indications of interest rate on the part of prospective buyers of the issue ("What is the book on XYZ Company?") or (2) record of activity in the syndicate account ("Who is managing the book on XYZ?").
2. record maintained by a specialist of buy and sell orders in a given security. The term derives from the notebook that specialists traditionally used for this purpose. Also, the aggregate of sell orders left with the specialist, as in BUY THE BOOK.
3. as a verb, to book is to give accounting recognition to something. ("They booked a profit on the transaction.")

4. collectively, books are the journals, ledgers, and other accounting records of a business.
   See also BOOK VALUE.

BOOK BALANCE ledger credit for funds on deposit prior to any reduction for float, uncollected funds, or reserve requirement.

BOOK PROFIT OR LOSS *see* UNREALIZED PROFIT OR LOSS.

BOOK VALUE

1. value at which an asset is carried on a balance sheet. For example, a piece of manufacturing equipment is put on the books at its cost when purchased. Its value is then reduced each year as depreciation is charged to income. Thus, its book value at any time is its cost minus accumulated depreciation. However, the primary purpose of accounting for depreciation is to enable a company to recover its cost, not replace the asset or reflect its declining usefulness. Book value may therefore vary significantly from other objectively determined values, most notably MARKET VALUE.

2. net asset value of a company's securities, calculated by using the following formula:
   Total assets *minus* intangible assets (goodwill, patents, etc.) *minus* current liabilities *minus* any long-term liabilities and equity issues that have a prior claim (subtracting them here has the effect of treating them as paid) *equals* total net assets available for payment of the issue under consideration.
   The total net asset figure, divided by the number of bonds, shares of preferred stock, or shares of common stock, gives the *net asset value*—or book value—per bond or per share of preferred or common stock.
   Book value can be a guide in selecting underpriced stocks and is an indication of the ultimate value of securities in liquidation. *See also* ASSET COVERAGE.

BOOT STRAP to help a company start from scratch. Entrepreneurs founding a company with little capital are said to be boot strapping it in order to become established.

BORROWING POWER OF SECURITIES amount of money that customers can invest in securities on MARGIN, as listed every month on their brokerage account statements. This margin limit usually equals 50% of the value of their stocks, 30% of the value of their bonds, and the full value of their CASH EQUIVALENT assets, such as MONEY MARKET account funds. The term also refers to securities pledged (hypothecated) to a bank or other lender as loan COLLATERAL. The loan value in this case depends on lender policy and type of security.

BOSTON STOCK EXCHANGE (BSE) established in 1834, the BSE is the first American exchange to open its membership to foreign brokers. It is the only U.S. exchange with a foreign linkage, with the

Montreal Stock Exchange, established in 1984. In 1994, the exchange introduced competing specialists in an auction market environment. The BSE uses a three-day settlement. Trading hours are Monday through Friday, 9:30 A.M.–4 P.M., with a limited crossing network at 5 P.M., matching the New York Stock Exchange's Session No. 1.

BOT
   1. stockbroker shorthand for bought, the opposite of SL for sold.
   2. in finance, abbreviation for balance of trade.
   3. in the mutual savings bank industry, abbreviation for board of trustees.

BOTTOM
In general: support level for market prices of any type. When prices fall below that level and appear to be continuing downward without check, we say that the *bottom dropped out.* When prices begin to trend upward again, we say they have *bottomed out.*
Economics: lowest point in an economic cycle.
Securities: lowest market price of a security or commodity during a day, a season, a year, a cycle. Also, lowest level of prices for the market as a whole, as measured by any of the several indexes.

BOTTOM FISHER investor who is on the lookout for stocks that have fallen to their bottom prices before turning up. In extreme cases, bottom fishers buy stocks and bonds of bankrupt or near-bankrupt firms.

BOTTOM LINE colloquial expression most frequently referring to the profit (earnings) of a company, that is the bottom line in the profit and loss statement. In smaller businesses, it frequently refers to Profit Before Tax, since lower small business tax rates distort the final figure.

BOTTOM-UP APPROACH TO INVESTING search for outstanding performance of individual stocks before considering the impact of economic trends. The companies may be identified from research reports, stock screens, or personal knowledge of the products and services. This approach assumes that individual companies can do well, even in an industry that is not performing well. *See also* TOP-DOWN APPROACH TO INVESTING.

BOUGHT DEAL in securities underwriting, a FIRM COMMITMENT to purchase an entire issue outright from the issuing company. Differs from a STAND-BY COMMITMENT, wherein, with conditions, a SYNDICATE of investment bankers agrees to purchase part of an issue if it is not fully subscribed. Also differs from a BEST EFFORTS commitment, wherein the syndicate agrees to use its best efforts to sell the issue. Most issues in recent years have been bought deals. Typically, the syndicate puts up a portion of its own capital and borrows the rest from commercial banks. Then, perhaps through a selling group, the syndicate resells the issue to the public at slightly more than the purchase price.

BOUNCE return of a cheque by a bank because it is not payable, usually due to insufficient funds. In securities, the rejection and subsequent RECLAMATION of a security because of *bad delivery.* Term also refers to stock price's sudden decline and recovery.

BOURSE French term for *stock exchange. See* PARIS BOURSE.

BOUTIQUE small, specialized brokerage firm that deals with a limited clientele and offers a limited product line. A highly regarded securities analyst may form a research boutique, which clients use as a resource for buying and selling certain stocks. A boutique is the opposite of a FINANCIAL SUPERMARKET, which offers a wide variety of services to a wide variety of clients.

BOX physical location of securities or other documents held in safe-keeping. The term derives from the large metal tin, or tray, in which brokerage firms and banks actually place such valuables. Depending on rules and regulations concerned with the safety and segregation of clients' securities, certificates held in safekeeping may qualify for stock loans or as bank loan collateral.

BRACKET CREEP edging into higher tax brackets as income rises to compensate for inflation.

BRANCH OFFICE MANAGER person in charge of a branch of a securities brokerage firm or bank. Branch office managers who oversee the activities of three or more brokers must pass tests administered by various stock exchanges. A customer who is not able to resolve a conflict with a REGISTERED REPRESENTATIVE should bring it to the attention of the branch office manager, who is responsible for resolving such differences.

BREADTH OF THE MARKET percentage of stocks participating in a particular market move. Analysts say there was good breadth if two thirds of the stocks listed on an exchange rose during a trading session. A market trend with good breadth is more significant and probably more long-lasting than one with limited breadth, since more investors are participating. Breadth-of-the-market indexes are alternatively called ADVANCE/DECLINE indexes.

BREAK
Finance: in a pricing structure providing purchasing discounts at different levels of volume, a point at which the price changes—for example, a 10% discount for ten cases.
Investments: (1) sudden, marked drop in the price of a security or in market prices generally; (2) discrepancy in the accounts of brokerage firms; (3) stroke of good luck.

BREAKEVEN ANALYSIS technique for evaluating the relationship between a firm's fixed costs, variable costs, profits, and sales. The breakeven point is the volume of sales at which the firm's revenues equal its total operating cost. It can be measured in either units or dollars.

BREAKEVEN CASH ANALYSIS approach for calculating a firm's breakeven point focusing on its position rather than on its accounting profit. It is calculated by subtracting non-cash charges from the firm's fixed costs in order to find the fixed cash costs prior to calculating the breakeven point. The purpose of this calculation is to determine how much cash a firm must earn to cover its fixed-cash outflow each month or quarter. It is a more stringent measure than the profit breakeven point, as failure to earn cash costs would result in insolvency.

BREAKEVEN POINT

Finance: the point at which sales equal costs. The point is located by breakeven analysis, which determines the volume of sales at which fixed and variable costs will be covered. All sales over the breakeven point produce profits; any drop in sales below that point will produce losses.

Because costs and sales are so complex, breakeven analysis has limitations as a planning tool and is being supplanted by computer based financial planning systems. *See also* LEVERAGE (operating).

Securities: dollar price at which a transaction produces neither a gain nor a loss.

In options strategy the term has the following definitions:

1. long calls and short uncovered calls: strike price plus premium.
2. long puts and short uncovered puts: strike price minus premium.
3. short covered call: purchase price minus premium.
4. short put covered by short stock: short sale price of underlying stock plus premium.

BREAKOUT rise in a security's price above a resistance level (commonly its previous high price) or drop below a level of support (commonly the former lowest price). A breakout is taken to signify a continuing move in the same direction.

BREAKOUT

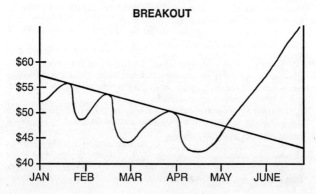

BREAKPOINT SALE in mutual funds, the dollar investment required to make the fundholder eligible for a lower sales charge. *See also* LETTER OF INTENT; RIGHT OF ACCUMULATION.

BREAKUP VALUE *see* PRIVATE MARKET VALUE.

BRETTON WOODS AGREEMENT OF 1944 *see* FIXED EXCHANGE RATE.

BRIDGE LOAN short-term loan, also called a *swing loan,* made in anticipation of intermediate-term or long-term financing. It may be taken out to cover the purchase or construction of an asset until permanent financing, frequently a previously arranged mortgage loan, can be drawn down against the completed asset.

BROADENED BASE EARNINGS computation of the earnings per share of a company that includes a pro rata share of the earnings of all unconsolidated subsidiaries and associated companies.

BROKER
Insurance: person who finds the best insurance deal for a client and then sells the policy to the client.
Real estate: person who represents the seller and gets a commission when the property is sold.
Securities: person who acts as an intermediary between a buyer and seller, usually charging a commission. A broker who specializes in stocks, bonds, commodities, or options acts as AGENT and must be registered with the exchange where the securities are traded. Hence the term *registered representative. See also* ACCOUNT EXECUTIVE; DEALER; DISCOUNT BROKER.

BROKER CALL LOAN RATE rate of loans made by brokers to customers that can be called or paid on request.

BROKER-DEALER *see* DEALER.

BROUGHT OVER THE WALL when somebody in the research department of an investment bank is pressed into the service of the underwriting department in reference to a particular corporate client, the individual has been "brought over the ("Chinese") wall" that legally divides the two functions and, being thus privy to INSIDE INFORMATION, is precluded from providing opinions about the company involved. *See also* CHINESE WALL.

BRUSSELS STOCK EXCHANGE (BSE) largest and most active of the three stock exchanges in Belgium; other exchanges are in Antwerp and Liege. A Computerized Automated Trading System, called CATS, replaced open outcry for the forward market in 1989; the cash market was computerized in 1993. Cash market trading hours are 12:30 P.M.–2:30 P.M.; forward market, 10 A.M.–4 P.M. Both trade Monday through Friday.

BUCKET SHOP illegal brokerage firm, of a kind now almost extinct, which accepts customer orders but does not execute them right away as Securities and Exchange Commission regulations require. Bucket-shop brokers confirm the price the customer asked for, but in fact make the trade at a time advantageous to the broker, whose profit is the difference between the two prices. Sometimes bucket shops neglect to fill the customer's order and just pocket the money. *See also* BOILER ROOM.

BUDGET estimate of revenue and expenditure for a specified period. Of the many kinds of budgets, a CASH BUDGET shows cash flow, an expense budget shows projected expenditures, and a CAPITAL BUDGET shows anticipated capital outlays. The term refers to a preliminary financial plan. In a *balanced budget* revenues cover expenditures.

BUDGET DEFICIT excess of spending over income for a government, corporation, or individual over a particular period of time. The budget deficit as of June 30, 1995, accumulated by the federal government, is $56 billion and, with the addition of provincial debt, it exceeds $800 billion. Individuals who consistently spend more than they earn will accumulate huge debts, which may ultimately force them to declare bankruptcy if the debt cannot be serviced.

BUDGETING financial planning for the future by individuals and companies to cover projected costs, finance planned investments, and to accumulate cash.

Companies prepare annual budgets of revenues, expenses, capital expenditures, and cash needed. This information is available to prospective lenders.

BUDGET SURPLUS excess of income over spending for a government, corporation, or individual over a particular period of time. A government with a budget surplus may choose to start new programs or cut taxes. A corporation with a surplus may expand the business through investment or acquisition, or may choose to buy back its own stock. An individual with a budget surplus may choose to pay down debt or increase spending or investment.

BULGE quick, temporary price rise that applies to an entire commodities or stock market, or to an individual commodity or stock.

BULGE BRACKET the group of firms in an underwriting syndicate that share the largest participation. TOMBSTONE ads list the participants alphabetically within groupings organized by size of participation and presented in tiers. The first and lead grouping is the "bulge bracket." *See also* MEZZANINE BRACKET.

BULL person who thinks prices will rise and who profits by buying options to buy stocks in the future (calls); selling options to sell stocks in the future (puts); and paying only part of the purchase price for stocks (buying on margin). One can be bullish on the prospects for an individual stock, bond, or commodity, an industry segment, or the market as a whole. In a more general sense, bullish means optimistic, so a person can be bullish on the economy as a whole.

BULLION bars and ingots of gold, silver, platinum, palladium, and other precious metals. Sizes range from one ounce to 400 ounces. These precious metals are used for smelting in industry; jewellery production, and also as security by investors and collectors against currency collapse.

BULLION COINS coins composed of metal such as gold, silver, platinum, or palladium. Bullion coins provide the purest play on the "up or down" price moves of the underlying metal, and are the most actively traded. These coins trade at a slight premium over their metal content, unlike NUMISMATIC COINS, which trade on their rarity and artistic value. Some of the most popular bullion coins minted by major governments around the world include Canadian Maple Leaf, the American Eagle, the South African Kruggerand, and the Australian Kangaroo. In addition to trading bullion in coin form, nearly pure precious metals also are available in bar form.

BULLION DEALERS dealers who trade in gold and who are members of the London Gold Market or any reputable affiliate or agent of such a member; to be distinguished from people listed in the "Yellow Pages" of the telephone book under "Gold Dealers." The latter tend to deal in smaller quantities and at a substantial markup over current daily market rates.

BULL MARKET prolonged rise in the prices of stocks, bonds, or commodities. Bull markets usually last at least a few months and are characterized by high trading volume.

BULL SPREAD option strategy, executed with puts or calls, that will be profitable if the underlying stock rises in value. The following are three varieties of bull spread:
Vertical spread: simultaneous purchase and sale of options of the same class at different strike prices, but with the same expiration date.
Calendar spread: simultaneous purchase and sale of options of the same class and the same price but at different expiration dates.
Diagonal spread: combination of vertical and calendar spreads wherein the investor buys and sells options of the same class at different strike prices and different expiration dates.

An investor who believes, for example, that XYZ stock will rise, perhaps only moderately, buys an XYZ 30 call for 1½ and sells an XYZ 35 call for ½; both options are OUT OF THE MONEY. The 30 and 35 are strike prices and the 1½ and ½ are premiums. The net cost of this spread, or the difference between the premiums, is $1. If the stock rises to 35 just prior to expiration, the 35 call becomes worthless and the 30 call is worth $5. Thus the spread provides a profit of $4 on an investment of $1. If on the other hand the price of the stock goes down, both options expire worthless and the investor loses the entire premium.

BUNCHING

1. combining many round-lot orders for execution at the same time on the floor of an exchange. This technique can also be used with odd lot orders, when combining many small orders can save the odd-lot differential for each customer.
2. pattern on the ticker tape when a series of trades in the same security appear consecutively.
3. aggregating income items or deductions in a single year to minimize taxes in that year.

BURN RATE in venture capital financing, the rate at which a start-up company spends capital to finance overhead before generating a positive cash flow from operations.

BUSINESS COMBINATION *see* MERGER.

BUSINESS CYCLE recurrence of periods of expansion (RECOVERY) and contraction (RECESSION) in economic activity with effects on inflation, growth, and employment. One cycle extends from a GNP base line through one rise and one decline and back to the base line, a period averaging about 5 years in Canada and about 2½ years in the United States. A business cycle affects profitability and CASH FLOW, making it a key consideration in corporate dividend policy, and is a factor in the rise and fall of the inflation rate, which in turn affects return on investments.

BUSINESS DAY

In general: hours when most businesses are in operation. Although individual working hours may differ, and particular firms may choose staggered schedules, the conventional business day is 9 A.M. to 5 P.M., Monday to Friday.

Finance and investments: day when financial marketplaces are open for trading. In figuring the settlement date on a *regular way* securities transaction—which is the fifth business day after the trade date—Saturday, Sunday, and a legal holiday would not be counted, for example.

BUSINESS INTERRUPTION INSURANCE insurance available to cover lost income in the event of the complete or partial shutdown of a business from specified causes, e.g., fire, evacuation, etc.

BUSINESS SEGMENT REPORTING reporting the results of the divisions, subsidiaries, or other segments of a business separately so that income, sales, and assets can be compared. When not a separate part of the business structure, a segment is generally defined as any grouping of products and services comprising a significant industry, which is one representing 10% or more of total revenues, assets, or income.

BUSTED CONVERTIBLES CONVERTIBLES that trade like fixed-income investments because the market price of the common stock they convert to has fallen so low as to render the conversion feature valueless.

BUST-UP TAKEOVER LEVERAGED BUYOUT in which TARGET COMPANY assets or activities are sold off to repay the debt that financed the TAKEOVER.

BUTTERFLY SPREAD complex option strategy that involves selling two calls and buying two calls on the same or different markets, with several maturity dates. One of the options has a higher exercise price and the other has a lower exercise price than the other two options. An investor in a butterfly spread will profit if the underlying security makes no dramatic movements because the premium income will be collected when the options are sold.

BUY acquire property in return for money. Buy can be used as a synonym for bargain.

BUY AND HOLD STRATEGY strategy that calls for accumulating shares in a company over the years. This allows the investor to pay favourable long-term capital gains tax on profits and requires far less attention than a more active trading strategy.

BUY AND WRITE STRATEGY conservative options strategy that entails buying stocks and then writing covered call options on them. Investors receive both the dividends from the stock and the premium income from the call options. However, the investor may have to sell the stock below the current market price if the call is exercised.

BUYBACK purchase of a long contract to cover a short position, usually arising out of the short sale of a commodity. Also, purchase of identical securities to cover a short sale. Synonym: *short covering. See also* STOCK BUYBACK.
Bond buyback: corporation's purchase of its own bonds at a discount in the open market. This is done in markets characterized by rapidly rising interest rates and commensurately declining bond prices.

BUY DOWN cash payment by a mortgage lender allowing the borrower to receive a lower rate of interest on a mortgage loan. For example, a home builder having trouble selling homes may offer a buy down with a local lender which will enable home buyers to qualify for mortgages that they would otherwise not qualify for. The buy down may lower the mortgage rate for the life of the loan, or sometimes just for the first few years of the loan.

BUYER'S MARKET market situation that is the opposite of a SELLER'S MARKET.

BUY HEDGE *see* LONG HEDGE.

BUY IN
Options trading: procedure whereby the responsibility to deliver or accept stock can be terminated. In a transaction called *buying-in* or CLOSING PURCHASE, the writer buys an identical option (only the

premium or price is different). The second of these options offsets the first, and the profit or loss is the difference in premiums.

Securities: transaction between brokers wherein securities are not delivered on time by the broker on the sell side, forcing the buy side broker to obtain shares from other sources.

BUYING CLIMAX rapid rise in the price of a stock or commodity, setting the stage for a quick fall. Such a surge attracts most of the potential buyers of the stock, leaving them with no one to sell their stock to at higher prices. This is what causes the ensuing fall. Technical chartists see a buying climax as a dramatic runup, accompanied by increased trading volume in the stock.

BUYING ON MARGIN buying securities with credit available through a relationship with a broker, called a MARGIN ACCOUNT.

BUYING POWER amount of money available to buy securities, determined by tabulating the cash held in brokerage accounts, and adding the amount that could be spent if securities were margined to the limit. The market cannot rise beyond the available buying power. *See also* PURCHASING POWER.

BUY MINUS order to buy a stock at a price lower than the current market price. Traders try to execute a buy minus order on a temporary dip in the stock's price.

BUY ON THE BAD NEWS strategy based on the belief that, soon after a company announces bad news, the price of its stock will plummet. Those who buy at this stage assume that the price is about as low as it can go, leaving plenty of room for a rise when the news improves. If the adverse development is indeed temporary, this technique can be quite profitable. *See also* BOTTOM FISHER.

BUY ORDER in securities trading, an order to a broker to purchase a specified quality of a security at the MARKET PRICE or at another stipulated price.

BUYOUT purchase of at least a controlling percentage of a company's stock to take over its assets and operations. A buyout can be accomplished through negotiation or through a tender offer. A LEVERAGED BUYOUT occurs when a small group borrows the money to finance the purchase of the shares. The loan is ultimately repaid out of cash generated from the acquired company's operations or from the sale of its assets. *See also* GOLDEN PARACHUTE.

BUY-SELL legal agreement between two or more shareholders setting out the conditions under which each may sell his or her shares. Such agreement may include "shotgun," "piggyback," right of "first refusal" or similar clauses. The need for such agreements is frequently overlooked by partners and shareholders in smaller businesses who are unwilling to consider the possibility of the company's dissolution or shareholder conflict. An "out" clause is crucial for every shareholder or partner situation.

BUY/SELL AGREEMENT INSURANCE   insurance that funds a buy/sell agreement between partners or practitioners should one partner die. The surviving partner can buy out the deceased's shares from the estate.

BUY STOP ORDER BUY ORDER marked to be held until the market price rises to the STOP PRICE, then to be entered as a MARKET ORDER to buy at the best available price. Sometimes called a *suspended market order,* because it remains suspended until a market transaction elects, activates, or triggers the stop. Such an order is not permitted in the over-the-counter market. *See also* STOP ORDER.

BUY THE BOOK order to a broker to buy all the shares available from the specialist in a security and from other brokers and dealers at the current offer price. The book is the notebook in which specialists kept track of buy and sell orders before computers. The most likely source of such an order is a professional trader or a large institutional buyer.

BYLAWS rules governing the internal management of an organization which, in the case of business corporations, are drawn up at the time of incorporation. The charter is concerned with such broad matters as the number of directors and the number of authorized shares; the bylaws, which can usually be amended by the directors themselves, cover such points as the election of directors, the appointment of executive and finance committees, the duties of officers, and how share transfers may be made. Bylaws, which are also prevalent in not-for-profit organizations, cannot countermand laws of the government.

C

CABINET CROWD members of a stock exchange who trade in infrequently traded bonds. Also called *inactive bond crowd* or *book crowd.* Buy and sell LIMIT ORDERS for these bonds are kept in steel racks, called cabinets, at the side of the bond trading floor; hence the name cabinet crowd.

CABINET SECURITY stock or bond listed on a major exchange but not actively traded. There are a considerable number of such bonds and a limited number of such stocks, mainly those trading in ten-share units. Cabinets are the metal storage racks that LIMIT ORDERS for such securities are filed in pending execution or cancellation. *See also* CABINET CROWD.

CAC 40 INDEX broad-based index of common stocks on the Paris Bourse, based on 40 of the 100 largest companies listed on the forward segment of the official list (reglement menseul); it has a base of 100. It is comparable to the Dow Jones Industrial Average. There are index futures and index options contracts based on the CAC 40 index.

CADILLAC PLAN *see* TOP-HAT PLAN.

CAFETERIA EMPLOYEE BENEFIT PLAN plan offering employees some mandatory benefits and numerous options among their employee benefits. Each employee is able to pick the benefits that are most valuable in his or her particular situation. For example, a young employee with children may want to receive more life and health insurance than a mid-career employee who is more concerned with building up retirement plan assets.

CAFETERIA PLAN *see* CAFETERIA EMPLOYEE BENEFIT PLAN.

CAGE section of a brokerage firm's back office where funds are received and disbursed.
     Also, the installation where a bank teller works.

CALENDAR list of securities about to be offered for sale. Separate calendars are kept for municipal bonds, corporate bonds, government bonds, and new stock offerings.

CALENDAR DAY any day of the year, as opposed to BUSINESS DAY. An event taking place in 7 calendar days will occur earlier than an event taking place in 7 business days since, in the latter case, the weekend will intervene.

CALENDAR SPREAD options strategy that entails buying two options on the same security with different maturities. If the EXERCISE PRICE is the same (a June 50 call and a September 50 call) it is a HORIZONTAL SPREAD. If the exercise prices are different (a June 50 call and a

September 45 call), it is a DIAGONAL SPREAD. Investors gain or lose as the difference in price narrows or widens.

CALL

Banking: demand to repay a secured loan usually made when the borrower has failed to meet such contractual obligations as timely payment of interest. When a banker calls a loan, the entire principal amount is due immediately.

Bonds: right to redeem outstanding bonds before their scheduled maturity. The first dates when an issuer may call bonds are specified in the prospectus of every issue that has a call provision in its indenture. *See also* CALLABLE; CALL PRICE.

Options: right to buy a specific number of shares at a specified price by a fixed date. Investors buy calls when they expect the price of a stock to rise. *See also* CALL OPTION.

CALLABLE redeemable by the issuer before the scheduled maturity. The issuer must pay the holders a premium price if such a security is retired early. Bonds are usually called when interest rates fall so significantly that the issuer can save money by floating new bonds at lower rates. *See also* CALL PRICE; DEMAND LOAN.

CALLABLE PREFERRED SHARE *see* REDEEMABLE.

CALL DATE date on which a bond may be redeemed before maturity. If called, the bond may be redeemed at PAR or at a slight premium to par. For example, a bond may be scheduled to mature in 20 years but may have a provision that it can be called in 10 years if it is advantageous for the issuer to refinance the issue. The date 10 years from the issue date is the call date. When buying a bond, it is important to know the bond's call date, because you cannot be assured that you will receive interest from that bond beyond the call date.

CALLED AWAY term for a bond redeemed before maturity, or a call or put option exercised against the stockholder, or a delivery required on a short sale.

CALL FEATURE part of the agreement a bond issuer makes with a buyer, called the indenture, describing the schedule and price of redemptions before maturity. Most corporate and municipal bonds have 10-year call features (termed CALL PROTECTION by holders); government securities usually have none. *See also* CALL PRICE.

CALL LOAN any loan repayable on demand, used to finance purchases of securities. In newspaper money rate tables it is used as a synonym for *broker loan* or *broker overnight loan*. *See* BROKER LOAN RATE.

CALL LOAN RATE *see* BROKER LOAN RATE.

CALL MONEY money lent by banks to stock exchange brokers for which payment can be demanded at any time. Also called *day-to-day money; demand money.*

CALL OPTION right to buy 100 shares of a particular stock or stock index at a predetermined price before a preset deadline, in exchange for a premium. For buyers who think a stock will go up dramatically, call options permit a profit from a smaller investment than it would take to buy the stock. These options can also produce extra income for the seller, who gives up ownership of the stock if the option is exercised.

CALL PREMIUM amount that the buyer of a call option has to pay to the seller for the right to purchase a stock or stock index at a specified price by a specified date.

    In bonds, preferreds, and convertibles, the amount over par that an issuer has to pay to an investor for redeeming the security early.

CALL PRICE price at which a bond or preferred stock with a *call provision* or CALL FEATURE can be redeemed by the issuer; also known as *redemption price.* To compensate the holder for loss of income and ownership, the call price is usually higher than the par value of the security, the difference being the CALL PREMIUM. *See also* CALL PROTECTION.

CALL PROTECTION length of time during which a security cannot be redeemed by the issuer.

CALL PROVISION clause in a bond's INDENTURE that allows the issuer to redeem the bond before maturity. The call provision will spell out the first CALL DATE and whether the bond will be called at PAR or at a slight premium to par. Some preferred stock issues also have call provisions spelling out the conditions of a redemption.

CALL RISK risk to a bondholder that a bond may be redeemed before scheduled maturity. Bondholders should read the CALL PROVISIONS in a bond's INDENTURE to understand the earliest potential CALL DATE for their bond. The main risk of having a bond called before maturity is that the investor will be unable to replace the bond's yield with another similar-quality bond paying the same yield. The reason the bond issuer will call the bond is that interest rates will have fallen from the time of issuance, and the bond can be refinanced at lower rates.

CANADA PENSION PLAN (CPP) mandatory contributory defined benefit indexed pension plan started in 1966 by the federal government for all Canadians. CPP provides monthly pensions to retirees, widowed spouses, orphans, the disabled, and children of disabled contributors. It also pays death benefits to the spouse and dependent children. Employees and employers make equal contributions. Self-employed persons must make contributions equal to the sum of the employee and employer contributions. The Canada Pension Plan (CPP) has been very successful for a large sector of the population that previously had insufficient retirement income because of a lack of employer plans. However, while the contribution rate has recently been raised substantially, it will have to be raised even more because the plan it still underfunded due to insufficient contributions in earlier years.

The current deduction rate is 2.6% of earnings, up to a limit of Maximum Pensionable Earnings, currently $34,000. Thus, employee and employer each contribute up to $806 p.a. A self-employed person would have a maximum contribution of $1612 p.a. This is expected to rise dramatically after 1997. CPP is an important part of the retirement income package. CPP indexation (deductions/contributions as a percent of income) is adjusted annually in January.

CANADIAN DEALING NETWORK, INC. (CDN) the organized over-the-counter stock market of Canada. The CDN became a subsidiary of the TORONTO STOCK EXCHANGE in 1991. Previously, CDN was known as the Canadian Over-the-counter Automated Trading System (COATS).

CANADIAN INVESTOR PROTECTION FUND established in 1969 as the National Contingency Fund, it became the Canadian Investor Protection Fund in 1990. The fund is financed entirely by members of the securities industry through the five Sponsoring Self-Regulatory Organizations (SSROs): The Toronto, Alberta and the Vancouver Stock Exchanges (TSE, ASE and VSE), the Montreal Exchange (ME) and the Investment Dealers Association of Canada (IDAC). From the moment an investor becomes a customer of a member of any one of the 5 SSROs, the accounts of that customer are covered by the Fund. The Fund covers customers' losses of securities and cash balances, within the limits described below, from the insolvency of a member firm of any one of the SSROs. The Fund does not cover customers' losses that result from changing market values.

The Fund is a trust established to protect customers in the event of the insolvency of a member of any of the SSROs. It is administered by a board of 9 governors, 5 of whom represent the SSROs, and 3 of whom represent the investing public. The president and chief executive officer of the Fund is also a governor.

The assets of the Fund are contributed by the securities industry through regular annual and periodic special assessments of member firms and the net income earned thereon. The Fund also has a line of credit provided by 2 Canadian chartered banks (different banks at different times). The aggregate of all assessments in a calendar year may not exceed 1% of the aggregate gross revenues of all member firms of the SSROs in that year. Subject to this 1% limitation, the Fund can levy assessments on member firms through the SSROs whenever required.

All customer accounts are covered either as part of the customer's general account or as a separate account (*see* INSURANCE AND INVESTOR PROTECTION ACCOUNT). The amount is currently $500,000 per account.

CANADIAN PAYMENTS ASSOCIATION association established in the 1980 revision of the Bank Act that operates a highly automated national clearing system for interbank payments. Members include chartered banks, trust and loan companies, and some credit unions and the Caisses Populaires.

CANCEL

In general: void a negotiable instrument by annulling or paying it; also, prematurely terminate a bond or other contract.

Securities trading: void an order to buy or sell. *See also* GOOD TILL CANCELED ORDER.

CAP

Bonds: highest level interest rate that can be paid on a floating-rate debt instrument. For example, a variable-rate note might have a cap of 8%, meaning that the yield cannot exceed 8% even if the general level of interest rates goes much higher than 8%.

Mortgages: highest interest rate level that an adjustable-rate mortgage (ARM) can rise to over a particular period of time. For example, an ARM contract may specify that the rate cannot jump more than two points in any year, or a total of six points during the life of the mortgage.

Stocks: short for CAPITALIZATION, or the total current value of a company's outstanding shares in dollars. A stock's capitalization is determined by multiplying the total number of shares outstanding by the stock's price. Analysts also refer to small-, medium- and large-cap stocks as a way of distinguishing the capitalizations of companies they are interested in. Many mutual funds restrict themselves to the small-, medium- or large-cap universes. *See also* COLLAR.

CAPACITY

Debt: ability to repay loans, as measured by credit grantors. Creditors judge an applicant's ability to repay a loan based on assets and income, and assign a certain capacity to service debt. If someone has many credit cards and credit lines outstanding, even if there are no outstanding balances, that is using up that person's debt capacity.

Economics: the amount of productive capacity in the economy is known as *industrial capacity.* If more than 85% of industrial capacity is in use, economists worry that production bottlenecks may form and create inflationary pressure. On the other hand, if less than 80% of capacity is in use, industrial production may be slack and inflationary pressures low.

CAPACITY UTILIZATION RATE percentage of production capacity in use by a particular company, an industry, or the entire economy. While in theory a business can operate at 100% of its productive capacity, in practice the maximum output is less than that, because machines need to be repaired, employees take vacations, etc. The operating rate is expressed as a percentage of the potential 100% production output. For example, a company may be producing at an 85% operating rate, meaning its output is 85% of the maximum that could be produced with its existing resources. *See also* CAPACITY.

CAPITAL
  Economics: machinery, factories, and inventory required to produce other products that can be sold.
  Investing: invested in securities, the investor's home, and other fixed assets, plus cash.

CAPITAL ASSET long-term asset that is not bought or sold in the normal course of business. Generally, the term includes FIXED ASSETS— land, buildings, equipment, furniture and fixtures, and so on. The Internal Revenue Service definition of capital assets includes security investments.

CAPITAL ASSET PRICING MODEL (CAPM) sophisticated model of the relationship between *expected risk* and *expected return.* The model is grounded in the theory that investors demand higher returns for higher risks. It says that the return on an asset or a security is equal to the risk-free return—such as the return on a short-term government security—plus a risk premium.

CAPITAL BUDGET program for financing long-term outlays such as plant expansion, research and development, and advertising. Among methods used in arriving at a capital budget are NET PRESENT VALUE (NPV), INTERNAL RATE OF RETURN (IRR), and PAYBACK PERIOD.

CAPITAL COST ALLOWANCE tax shield that allows a business to deduct the cost of depreciating capital assets from overall income. Under the Income Tax Act, this is regarded as a necessary expense for producing income. A capital cost allowance is calculated in such a way that it allows an investor to recover, over a period of time, the original amount invested without having to pay taxes on the portion of the income earned from the investment.

CAPITAL EXPENDITURE outlay of money to acquire or improve CAPITAL ASSETS such as buildings and machinery on which the returns are expected to extend for longer than one year. Such expenses are capitalized on the balance sheet as opposed to expenses that are written off on the income statement.

CAPITAL FLIGHT movement of large sums of money from one country to another to escape political or economic turmoil or to seek higher rates of return. For example, periods of high inflation or political revolution have brought about an exodus of capital from many Latin American countries to the United States, which is seen as a safe haven.

CAPITAL FORMATION creation or expansion, through savings, of capital or of *producer's goods*—buildings, machinery, equipment—that produce other goods and services, the result being economic expansion.

CAPITAL GAIN positive difference between proceeds of sale of an asset and the asset's original cost (or adjusted cost base if the asset was purchased after 1972). For individuals, only 75% of capital gains are taxable, while for a company, 100% of capital gains are taxable.

As of February 22, 1994, the $100,000 personal capital gains exemption was eliminated.

CAPITAL GAINS the profit realized when there is a difference between the market price paid for a security and the price at which it is sold.

CAPITAL GOODS goods used in the production of other goods—industrial buildings, machinery, equipment—as well as highways, office buildings, government installations. In the aggregate such goods form a country's productive capacity.

CAPITAL GROWTH increase in market value of the securities held in a mutual fund.

CAPITAL-INTENSIVE requiring large investments in CAPITAL ASSETS, Motor-vehicle and steel production are capital-intensive industries. To provide an acceptable return on investment, such industries must have a high margin of profit or a low cost of borrowing. Sometimes used to mean a high proportion of fixed assets to labor.

CAPITAL INTERNATIONAL INDEXES indexes maintained by Morgan Stanley's Capital International division which track most major stock markets throughout the world. The Capital International World Index tracks prices of major stocks in all the major markets worldwide. There are also many indexes for European, North American, and Asian markets. Most mutual funds and other institutional investors measure their performance against Capital International indexes.

CAPITAL INVESTMENT *see* CAPITAL EXPENDITURE.

CAPITALISM economic system in which (1) private ownership of property exists; (2) aggregates of property or capital provide income for the individuals or firms that accumulated it and own it; (3) individuals and firms are relatively free to compete with others for their own economic gain; (4) the profit motive is basic to economic life.

Among the synonyms for capitalism are LAISSEZ-FAIRE economy, private enterprise system, and free-price system. In this context *economy* is interchangeable with *system*.

CAPITALIZATION total amount, expressed in dollars or as a percentage, of all debt, preferred and common stock, contributed surplus and retained earnings of a company. *See also* CAPITALIZE; CAPITAL STRUCTURE; MARKET CAPITALIZATION.

CAPITALIZATION RATE rate of interest used to convert a series of future payments into a single PRESENT VALUE.

CAPITALIZATION RATIO analysis of a company's capital structure showing what percentage of the total is debt, preferred stock, common stock, and other equity. The ratio is useful in evaluating the relative RISK and leverage that holders of the respective levels of security have. *See also* BOND RATIO.

CAPITALIZE
1. convert a schedule of income into a principal amount, called *capitalized value,* by dividing by a rate of interest.
2. issue securities to finance *capital outlays* (rare).
3. record capital outlays as additions to asset accounts, not as expenses. *See also* CAPITAL EXPENDITURE.
4. convert a lease obligation to an asset/liability form of expression called a *capital lease,* that is, to record a leased asset as an owned asset and the lease obligation as borrowed funds.
5. record an expenditure initially as an asset on the balance sheet rather than as an earnings statement expense, and then write it off or amortize it (as an earnings statement expense) over a period of years. Examples include capitalized leases, interest, and research and development.
6. turn something to one's advantage economically—for example, sell umbrellas on a rainy day.

CAPITAL LOSS loss that occurs when the market price of a security falls below the price paid to buy it.

CAPITAL MARKETS markets where capital funds—debt and equity—are traded. Included are private placement sources of debt and equity as well as organized markets and exchanges. *See also* PRIMARY MARKET.

CAPITAL OUTFLOW exodus of capital from a country. A combination of political and economic factors may encourage domestic and foreign owners of assets to sell their holdings and move their money to other countries that offer more political stability and economic growth potential. If a capital outflow becomes large enough, some countries may try to restrict investors' ability to remove money from the country with currency controls or other measures.

CAPITAL OUTLAY *see* CAPITAL EXPENDITURE.

CAPITAL REQUIREMENTS
1. permanent financing needed for the normal operation of a business; that is, the long-term and working capital.
2. appraised investment in fixed assets and normal working capital. Whether patents, rights, and contracts should be included is moot.

CAPITAL SHARES one of the two classes of shares in a dual-purpose investment company. The capital shares entitle the owner to all appreciation (or depreciation) in value in the underlying portfolio in addition to all gains realized by trading in the portfolio. The other class of shares in a dual-purpose investment company are INCOME SHARES, which receive all income generated by the portfolio. If the fund guarantees a minimum level of income payable to the income shareholders, it may be necessary to sell some securities in the portfolio if the existing securities do not provide a high enough level of dividends and interest. In this case, the value of the capital shares will fall.

CAPITAL STOCK stock authorized by a company's charter and having PAR VALUE, STATED VALUE, or NO PAR VALUE. The number and value of issued shares are normally shown, together with the number of shares authorized, in the capital accounts section of the balance sheet.

Informally, a synonym for COMMON STOCK, though capital stock technically also encompasses PREFERRED STOCK.

CAPITAL STRUCTURE corporation's financial framework, including LONG-TERM DEBT, PREFERRED STOCK, and NET WORTH. It is distinguished from FINANCIAL STRUCTURE, which includes additional sources of capital such as short-term debt, accounts payable, and other liabilities. It is synonymous with *capitalization,* although there is some disagreement as to whether capitalization should include long-term loans and mortgages. Analysts look at capital structure in terms of its overall adequacy and its composition as well as in terms of the DEBT-TO-EQUITY RATIO, called *leverage. See also* CAPITALIZATION RATIO; PAR VALUE.

CAPITAL SURPLUS
1. EQUITY—or NET WORTH—not otherwise classifiable as CAPITAL STOCK or RETAINED EARNINGS. Here are five ways of creating surplus:
   a. from stock issued at a premium over par or stated value.
   b. from the proceeds of stock bought back and then sold again.
   c. from a reduction of par or stated value or a reclassification of capital stock.
   d. from donated stock.
   e. from the acquisition of companies that have capital surplus.
2. common umbrella term for more specific classifications such as ACQUIRED SURPLUS, ADDITIONAL PAID-IN CAPITAL, DONATED SURPLUS, and REEVALUATION SURPLUS (arising from appraisals). Most common synonyms: *paid-in surplus; surplus.*

CAPITAL TURNOVER annual sales divided by average stockholder equity (net worth). When compared over a period, it reveals the extent to which a company is able to grow without additional capital investment. Generally, companies with high profit margins have a low capital turnover and vice versa. Also called *equity turnover.*

CAPTIVE AGENT insurance agent working exclusively for one company. Such an agent will tend to have more in-depth knowledge of that company's policies than an INDEPENDENT AGENT, who can sell policies from many companies. Captive agents are usually paid on a combination of salary and commissions earned from selling policies, in the first few years they sell policies. Later, they are usually paid exclusively on a commission basis.

CAPTIVE FINANCE COMPANY company, usually a wholly owned subsidiary, that exists primarily to finance consumer purchases from the parent company. Prominent examples are General Motors Acceptance Corporation and Ford Motor Credit Company. Although these subsidiaries stand on their own financially, parent companies frequently make SUBORDINATED LOANS to add to their equity positions. This supports the high leverage on which the subsidiaries operate and assures their active participation in the COMMERCIAL PAPER and bond markets.

CARROT EQUITY British slang for an equity investment with a KICKER in the form of an opportunity to buy more equity if the company meets specified financial goals.

CARRYBACK, CARRYFORWARD *see* TAX LOSS CARRYBACK, CARRYFORWARD.

CARRYING CHARGE
Commodities: charge for carrying the actual commodity, including interest, storage, and insurance costs.
Margin accounts: fee that a broker charges for carrying securities on credit.
Real estate: carrying cost, primarily interest and taxes, of owning land prior to its development and resale.
Retailing: seller's charge for installment credit, which is either added to the purchase price or to unpaid installments.

CARRYOVER *see* TAX LOSS CARRYBACK, CARRYFORWARD.

CARS *see* CERTIFICATE FOR AUTOMOBILE RECEIVABLES.

CARTE BLANCHE full authority to take action. For example, an employee may be given carte blanche to enter into contracts with suppliers. The term also refers to the ability to fill in any amount on a blank cheque. For example, a father may sign a blank cheque and give it to his son to fill in when the son makes a major purchase. Carte Blanche is also the brand name of a widely used travel and entertainment card which requires that all balances be paid in full every month.

CARTEL group of businesses or nations that agree to influence prices by regulating production and marketing of a product. The most famous contemporary cartel is the Organization of Petroleum Exporting Countries (OPEC), which, notably in the 1970s, restricted oil production and sales and raised prices. A cartel has less control over an industry than a MONOPOLY. A number of nations, including Canada, have laws prohibiting cartels. TRUST is sometimes used as a synonym for cartel.

CASH asset account on a balance sheet representing paper currency and coins, negotiable money orders and checks, and bank balances. Also, transactions handled in cash. In the financial statements of annual reports, cash is usually grouped with CASH EQUIVALENTS, defined as all highly liquid securities with a known market value and a maturity, when acquired, of less than three months.

To cash is to convert a negotiable instrument, usually into paper currency and coins. *See also* CASH EQUIVALENTS.

CASH ADVANCE loan taken out against a line of credit or credit card. Normally, the bank begins to charge interest from the date of the loan. Many banks also levy a flat fee for each cash advance. The interest rate charged on the cash advance is usually different from the rate charged on purchases made with the same card. Frequently, the cash advance rate is higher. In many cases advance rates are variable, and are usually tied to a certain number of percentage points over the prime rate.

CASH AND CARRY purchase of gold bullion by investors who could simultaneously sell gold futures a year or more from the initial purchase date, knowing that the price of the futures would be sufficiently high that they could earn a risk-free return on this investment. (This is no longer risk-free since the price of gold has not risen as it did between 1963 and 1979.)

CASH ASSET RATIO balance sheet LIQUIDITY RATIO representing cash (and equivalents) and marketable securities divided by current liabilities. Stricter than the *quick ratio.*

CASH BASIS
Accounting: method that recognizes revenues when cash is received and recognizes expenses when cash is paid out. In contrast, the *accrual method* recognizes revenues when goods or services are sold and recognizes expenses when obligations are incurred. A third method, called *modified cash basis,* uses accrual accounting for long-term assets and is the basis usually referred to when the term cash basis is used.

CASHBOOK accounting book that combines cash receipts and disbursements. Its balance ties to the cash account in the general ledger on which the balance sheet is based.

CASH BUDGET estimated cash receipts and disbursements for a future period. A comprehensive cash budget schedules daily, weekly, or monthly expenditures together with the anticipated CASH FLOW from collections and other operating sources. Cash flow budgets are essential in establishing credit and purchasing policies, as well as in planning credit line usage and short-term investments in COMMERCIAL PAPER and other securities.

CASH COMMODITY commodity that is owned as the result of a completed contract and must be accepted upon delivery. Contrasts with futures contracts, which are not completed until a specified future date. The cash commodity contract specifications are set by the commodity exchanges.

CASH COMPENSATION cash payments in the form of salaries, bonuses, and commissions, paid to employees for their services.

CASH CONVERSION CYCLE *or* CASH CYCLE elapsed time, usually expressed in days, from the outlay of cash for raw materials to the receipt of cash after the finished goods have been sold. Because a profit is built into the sales, the term *earnings cycle* is also used. The shorter the cycle, the more WORKING CAPITAL a business generates and the less it has to borrow. This cycle is directly affected by production efficiency, credit policy, and other controllable factors.

CASH COW business that generates a continuing flow of cash. Such a business usually has well-established brand names whose familiarity stimulates repeated buying of the products. For example, a magazine company that has a high rate of subscription renewals would be considered a cash cow. Stocks that are cash cows have dependable dividends.

CASH DISCOUNT TRADE CREDIT feature providing for a deduction if payment is made early. For example: trade terms of "2% 10 days net 30 days" allow a 2% cash discount for payment in 10 days. Term also refers to the lower price some merchants charge customers who pay in cash rather than with credit cards, in which case the merchant is passing on all or part of the merchant fee it would otherwise pay to the credit card company.

CASH DIVIDEND cash payment to a corporation's shareholders, distributed from current earnings or accumulated profits and taxable as income. Cash dividends are distinguished from STOCK DIVIDENDS, which are payments in the form of stock. *See also* YIELD.

INVESTMENT COMPANY cash dividends are usually made up of dividends, interest income, and capital gains received on its investment portfolio.

CASH EARNINGS cash revenues less cash expenses—specifically excluding noncash expenses such as DEPRECIATION.

CASH EQUIVALENTS instruments or investments of such high liquidity and safety that they are virtually as good as cash. Examples are a MONEY MARKET FUND and a TREASURY BILL.

CASH FLOW
1. in a larger financial sense, an analysis of all the changes that affect the cash account during an accounting period. The STATEMENT OF CASH FLOWS included in annual reports analyzes all changes affecting cash in the categories of operations, investments, and financing. For example: net operating income is an increase; the purchase of a new building is a decrease; and the issuance of stock or bonds is an increase. When more cash comes in than goes out, we speak of a *positive cash flow;* the opposite is a *negative cash flow.* Companies with assets well in excess of liabilities may nevertheless go bankrupt because they cannot generate enough cash to meet current obligations.
2. in investments, NET INCOME plus DEPRECIATION and other noncash charges. In this sense, it is synonymous with CASH EARNINGS.

Investors focus on cash flow from operations because of their concern with a firm's ability to pay dividends. *See also* CASH BUDGET.

CASH FLOW PER SHARE measure to determine the underlying value of a share and the liquidity of the firm. It represents the ratio of the cash flow divided by the total number of shares outstanding. Companies with a high cash flow per share may be undervalued and good investments.

CASH FLOWS actual payment or receipt of dollars by a company. Cash flows do not necessarily occur when an obligation is incurred or an item is sold.

CASHIERING DEPARTMENT *see* CAGE.

CASH ITEM any item immediately convertible into cash, such as a cheque, depository transfer cheque, or preauthorized cheque.

CASH LETTER letter detailing transit routings, amounts, and totals that accompanies a batch of items sent directly to a bank or to a cheque processing centre, containing items drawn on that bank as well as on other banks within the region. The cash letter facilitates the processing of the items in the collection by the processing centres and ensures the cash or items are credited to the firm's accounts more quickly.

CASH MANAGEMENT
Corporate finance: efficient mobilization of cash into income-producing applications, using computers, telecommunications technology, innovative investment vehicles, and LOCK BOX arrangements.

CASH MARKET transactions in the cash or spot markets that are completed; that is, ownership of the commodity is transferred from seller to buyer and payment is given on delivery of the commodity. The cash market contrasts with the futures market, in which contracts are completed at a specified time in the future.

CASH-ON-CASH RETURN method of yield computation used for investments lacking an active secondary market, such as LIMITED PARTNERSHIPS. It simply divides the annual dollar income by the total dollars invested; a $10,000 investment that pays $1000 annually thus has a 10% cash-on-cash return. Investments having a market value and a predictable income stream to a designated maturity or call date, such as bonds, are better measured by CURRENT YIELD or YIELD-TO-MATURITY (or to call).

CASH ON DELIVERY (COD)
Commerce: transaction requiring that goods be paid for in full by cash or certified cheque or the equivalent at the point of delivery. The term *collect on delivery* has the same abbreviation and same meaning. If the customer refuses delivery, the seller has round-trip shipping costs to absorb or other, perhaps riskier, arrangements to make.

Securities: a requirement that delivery of securities to institutional investors be in exchange for assets of equal value—which, as a practical matter, means cash. Alternatively called *delivery against cost* (DAC) or *delivery versus payment* (DVP). On the other side of the trade, the term is *receive versus payment.*

CASH RATIO ratio of cash and marketable securities to current liabilities; a refinement of the QUICK RATIO. The cash ratio tells the extent to which liabilities could be liquidated immediately. Sometimes called *liquidity ratio.*

CASH SETTLEMENT means of settling some futures and options contracts. The seller pays the buyer the cash value of the underlying interest.

CASH SURRENDER VALUE in insurance, the amount the insurer will return to a policyholder on cancellation of the policy. Sometimes abbreviated *CSVLI* (cash surrender value of life insurance), it shows up as an asset on the balance sheet of a company that has life insurance on its principals, called *key man insurance.* Insurance companies make loans against the cash value of policies, often at a better-than-market rate.

CASH TURNOVER number of times each year a firm's cash cycle occurs, i.e., cash is turned over. It can be calculated by dividing the firm's cash cycle in days into the number of days in the year. The higher the cash turnover, the more efficiently cash is being moved, and vice versa. It reflects the company's efficiency in managing cash, its liquidity, and the effectiveness of credit, collection, payables, and the manufacturing process.

CASH VALUE amount of money available when a business owner stops paying premiums, thereby surrendering the insurance coverage. He or she then may take payment of the cash value in a lump sum or as an income over a specified period.

CASH VALUE INSURANCE life insurance that combines a death benefit with a potential tax-deferred buildup of money (called cash value) in the policy. The three main kinds of cash value insurance are WHOLE LIFE INSURANCE, VARIABLE LIFE INSURANCE, and UNIVERSAL LIFE INSURANCE. In whole life, cash value is accumulated based on the return on the company's investments in stocks, bonds, real estate, and other ventures. In variable life, the policyholder chooses how to allocate the money among stock, bond, and money market options. In universal life, a policyholder's cash value is invested in investments such as money market securities to build cash value. All cash values inside an insurance policy remain untaxed until they are withdrawn from the policy. Unlike cash value insurance, TERM LIFE INSURANCE offers only a death benefit, and no cash value buildup.

CASUALTY-INSURANCE insurance that protects a business or homeowner against property loss, damage, and related liability.

CATS AND DOGS speculative stocks that have short histories of sales, earnings, and dividend payments. In bull markets, analysts say disparagingly that even the cats and dogs are going up.

CAVEAT EMPTOR, CAVEAT SUBSCRIPTOR *buyer beware, seller beware.* A variation on the latter is *caveat venditor.*

CEILING highest level allowable in a financial transaction. For example, someone buying a stock may place a ceiling on the stock's price, meaning they are not willing to pay more than that amount for the shares. The issuer of a bond may place a ceiling on the interest rate it is willing to pay. If market interest rates rise beyond that ceiling, the underwriter must cancel the issue. *See also* CAP.

CENTRAL BANK country's bank that (1) issues currency; (2) administers monetary policy, including OPEN MARKET OPERATIONS; (3) holds deposits representing the reserves of other banks; and (4) engages in transactions designed to facilitate the conduct of business and protect the public interest. In Canada, central banking is a function of the Bank of Canada; in the U.S., of the Federal Reserve Board; in the U.K., of the Bank of England.

CENTRALIZED CONTROL OF CASH offers central control over company funds, either on paper or by "zero balancing" field accounts. This means that wherever the company's money is (as long as it is in the bank somewhere), it receives credit for the full net balance. By concentrating money in this way, a company can invest short-term surplus or pay down its operating loan. Money that is spread over numerous accounts in several locations receives a lower interest rate and incurs higher bank charges.

CENTRALIZED MONEY MANAGEMENT *see* CENTRALIZED CONTROL OF CASH.

CERTAIN TERM ANNUITY annuity paying equal amounts to a specified date, e.g., 20 years from its start date. This differs from a life annuity that pays a variable amount until the death of the annuitant.

CERTIFICATE formal declaration that can be used to document a fact, such as a birth certificate.
    The following are certificates with particular relevance to finance and investments.
1. auditor's certificate, sometimes called certificate of accounts, or ACCOUNTANT'S OPINION.
2. bond certificate, certificate of indebtedness issued by a corporation containing the terms of the issuer's promise to repay principal and pay interest, and describing collateral, if any. Traditionally, bond certificates had coupons attached, which were exchanged for payment of interest. Now that most bonds are issued in registered form, coupons are less common. The amount of a certificate is the par value of the bond.

3. CERTIFICATE OF DEPOSIT.
4. certificate of INCORPORATION.
5. certificate of indebtedness, government debt obligation having a maturity shorter than a bond and longer than a treasury bill.
6. PARTNERSHIP certificate, showing the interest of all participants in a business partnership.
7. PROPRIETORSHIP certificate, showing who is legally responsible in an individually owned business.
8. STOCK CERTIFICATE, evidence of ownership of a corporation showing number of shares, name of issuer, amount of par or stated value represented or a declaration of no-par value, and rights of the shareholder. Preferred stock certificates also list the issuer's responsibilities with respect to dividends and voting rights, if any.

CERTIFICATE OF DEPOSIT (CD) fixed-term deposits, such as guaranteed investment certificates and term deposits, issued by banks and trust companies. Capital is guaranteed by the Canada Deposit Insurance Corporation up to a specific maximum, usually $60,000. Certificates of Deposit can be purchased for terms ranging between 1 and 6 years.

CERTIFIED CHEQUE cheque for which a bank guarantees payment. It legally becomes an obligation of the bank, and the funds to cover it are immediately withdrawn from the depositor's account.

CERTIFIED FINANCIAL STATEMENTS financial statements accompanied by an ACCOUNTANT'S OPINION.

CERTIFIED PUBLIC ACCOUNTANT (CPA) accountant who has passed certain exams, achieved a certain amount of experience, reached a certain age, and met all other statutory and licensing requirements of the province where he or she works. In addition to accounting and auditing, CPAs prepare tax returns for corporations and individuals.

CHAIRMAN OF THE BOARD member of a corporation's board of directors who presides over its meetings and who is the highest ranking officer in the corporation. The chairman of the board may or may not have the most actual executive authority in a firm. The additional title of CHIEF EXECUTIVE OFFICER (CEO) is reserved for the principal executive, and depending on the particular firm, that title may be held by the chairman, the president, or even an executive vice president. In some corporations, the position of chairman is either a prestigious reward for a past president or an honorary position for a prominent person, a large stockholder, or a family member; it may carry little or no real power in terms of policy or operating decision making.

CHARGE OFF *see* BAD DEBT.

CHARGES in a futures contract, the investor pays a commission on the transactions, delivery, transportation and insurance charges. If the investor takes delivery of the precious metal and requests storage, there is a commission on the storage charges. Investors in gold bullion also pay a processing fee for the bars acquired. A larger processing fee is charged on the purchase of four 100 ounce bars, than on the purchase of one 400 ounce bar. Prospective buyers should check with a broker about all the charges involved in any transactions they contemplate.

CHARITABLE REMAINDER TRUST IRREVOCABLE TRUST that pays income to one or more individuals until the GRANTOR'S death, at which time the balance, which is tax free, passes to a designated charity. It is a popular tax-saving alternative for individuals who have no children or who are wealthy enough to benefit both children and charity.

The charitable remainder trust is the reverse of a *charitable lead trust,* whereby a charity receives income during the grantor's life and the remainder passes to designated family members upon the grantor's death. The latter trust reduces estate taxes while enabling the family to retain control of the assets.

CHARTER *see* ARTICLES OF INCORPORATION.

CHARTERED FINANCIAL PLANNER generalist in personal finance who has completed a comprehensive study program offered through the Canadian Institute of Financial Planning.

CHARTING *see* TECHNICAL ANALYSIS.

CHARTIST technical analyst who charts the patterns of stocks, bonds, and commodities to make buy and sell recommendations to clients. Chartists believe recurring patterns of trading can help them forecast future price movements. *See also* TECHNICAL ANALYSIS.

CHASING THE MARKET purchasing a security at a higher price than intended because prices have risen sharply, or selling it at a lower level when prices fall. For example, an investor may want to buy shares of a stock at $20 and place a limit order to do so. But when the shares rise above $25, and then $28, the customer decides to enter a market order and buy the stock before it goes even higher. Investors can also chase the market when selling a stock. For example, if an investor wants to sell a stock at $20 and it declines to $15 and then $12, that investor may decide to sell it at the market price before it declines even further.

CHASTITY BONDS bonds that become redeemable at par value in the event of a TAKEOVER.

CHATTEL MORTGAGE charge over movable goods or equipment as opposed to real estate.

CHEQUE bill of exchange, or draft on a bank drawn against deposited funds to pay a specified sum of money to a specified person on demand. A cheque is considered as cash and is NEGOTIABLE when endorsed.

CHECKING THE MARKET canvassing securities market-makers by telephone or other means in search of the best bid or offer price.

CHICAGO BOARD OF TRADE *see* SECURITIES AND COMMODITIES EXCHANGES.

CHICAGO BOARD OPTIONS EXCHANGE *see* SECURITIES AND COMMODITIES EXCHANGES.

CHICAGO MERCANTILE EXCHANGE *see* SECURITIES AND COMMODITIES EXCHANGES.

CHIEF EXECUTIVE OFFICER (CEO) officer of a firm principally responsible for the activities of a company. CEO is usually an additional title held by the CHAIRMAN OF THE BOARD, the president, or another senior officer such as a vice chairman or an executive vice president.

CHIEF FINANCIAL OFFICER (CFO) executive officer who is responsible for handling funds, signing checks, keeping financial records, and financial planning for a corporation. He or she typically has the title of vice president-finance or financial vice president in large corporations, that of treasurer or controller (also spelled comptroller) in smaller companies. Since many state laws require that a corporation have a treasurer, that title is often combined with one or more of the other financial titles.

The controllership function requires an experienced accountant to direct internal accounting programs, including cost accounting, systems and procedures, data processing, acquisitions analysis, and financial planning. The controller may also have internal audit responsibilities.

The treasury function is concerned with the receipt, custody, investment, and disbursement of corporate funds and for borrowings and the maintenance of a market for the company's securities.

CHIEF OPERATING OFFICER (COO) officer of a firm, usually the president or an executive vice president, responsible for day-to-day management. The chief operating officer reports to the CHIEF EXECUTIVE OFFICER and may or may not be on the board of directors (presidents typically serve as board members). *See also* CHAIRMAN OF THE BOARD.

CHINESE WALL imaginary barrier between the investment banking, corporate finance, and research departments of a brokerage house and the sales and trading departments. Since the investment banking side has sensitive knowledge of impending deals such as takeovers, new stock and bond issues, divestitures, spinoffs and the like, it would be unfair to the general investing public if the sales and trading side of the firm had advance knowledge of such transactions. The investment banking department uses code names and logs of the people who have access to key information in an attempt to keep the identities of the parties secret until the deal is publicly announced.

CHRISTMAS TREE assemblage of valves and fittings at the wellhead that control production in oil and gas wells. Also known as casing head, wellhead, or bradenhead.

CHUNNEL tunnel crossing the English Channel between Great Britain and France. The Chunnel project took years to build and cost billions of dollars, but was finally opened for passenger and freight traffic in 1994. The Chunnel was built and is operated by Euro-Tunnel PLC.

CHURNING excessive trading of a client's account. Churning increases the broker's commissions, but usually leaves the client worse off or no better off than before. Churning is illegal under SEC and exchange rules, but is difficult to prove.

CINCINNATI STOCK EXCHANGE (CSE) stock exchange established in 1887. The CSE became the first completely automated stock exchange, handling members' transactions without the benefit of a physical trading floor by using computers. The CSE has nominal jurisdiction over the National Securities Trading System (NSTS), known popularly as the "Cincinnati experiment." Participating brokerage firms enter orders into the NSTS computer, which then matches orders and clears the orders back to the brokers. The NSTS contains some of the features envisioned for a national exchange market system.

CIRCLE underwriter's way of designating potential purchasers and amounts of a securities issue during the REGISTRATION period, before selling is permitted. Registered representatives canvass prospective buyers and report any interest to the underwriters, who then circle the names on their list.

CIRCUIT BREAKERS measures instituted by the major stock and commodities exchanges to halt trading temporarily in stocks and stock index futures when the market has fallen by a specified amount in a specified period. Circuit breakers were instituted after BLACK MONDAY in 1987 and modified following another sharp market drop in October 1989. They are subject to change from time to time, but may include trading halts, curtailment of automated trading systems, and/or price movement limits on index futures. Their purpose is to prevent a market free-fall by permitting a rebalancing of buy and sell orders. *See also* PROGRAM TRADING.

CLAIM area of land or water "claimed" by a prospector or mining organization for the purpose of exploring the claim for a certain length of time and subject to certain conditions. Claims are first staked out and then recorded in a government claim recording office. A common size of a claim in Canada is about 40 acres (16.2 hectares) which is the industry and provincial standard of permissible mineral rights claims.

CLASS
  1. securities having similar features. Stocks and bonds are the two main classes; they are subdivided into various classes—for example, mortgage bonds and debentures, issues with different rates of interest, common and preferred stock, or Class A and Class B common. The different classes in a company's capitalization are itemized on its balance sheet.

2. options of the same type—put or call—with the same underlying security. A class of option having the same expiration date and EXERCISE PRICE is termed a SERIES.

CLASS A/CLASS B SHARES *see* CLASSIFIED STOCK.

CLASS ACTION legal complaint filed on behalf of a group of shareholders having an identical grievance. Shareholders in a class action are typically represented by one lawyer or group of attorneys, who like this kind of business because the awards tend to be proportionate to the number of parties in the class.

CLASSIFIED STOCK separation of equity into more than one CLASS of common, usually designated Class A and Class B. The distinguishing features, set forth in the corporation charter and bylaws, usually give an advantage to the Class A shares in terms of voting power, though dividend and liquidation privileges can also be involved. Classified stock is less prevalent today than in the 1920s, when it was used as a means of preserving minority control.

CLAYTON ANTI-TRUST ACT *see* ANTITRUST LAWS.

CLEAR
Banking: COLLECTION of funds on which a cheque is drawn, and payment of those funds to the holder of the cheque. *See also* CLEARING HOUSE FUNDS.
Finance: asset not securing a loan and not otherwise encumbered. As a verb, to clear means to make a profit: "After all expenses, we *cleared* $1 million."
Securities: COMPARISON of the details of a transaction between brokers prior to settlement; final exchange of securities for cash on delivery.

CLEAR DAY day following a Sunday or a holiday that is added to a stated period (allowed for tendering and closing) under Ontario takeover legislation.

CLEARING CORPORATION corporation through which transactions relating to stock options are cleared. The corporation becomes the buyer to every seller, and the seller to every buyer. It also helps to ensure the financial integrity of the market.

CLEARING HOUSE organization established by banks and trust companies in the same locality, through which cheques and other instruments are exchanged and net balances settled. There are regional facilities to expedite transfers and to cut down on float.

CLEAR TITLE title that is clear of all claims or disputed interests. It is necessary to have clear title to a piece of real estate before it can be sold by one party to another. In order to obtain a clear title, it is usually necessary to have a title search performed by a title company, which may find various clouds on the title such as an incomplete certificate of occupancy, outstanding building violations, claims by neighbors for pieces of the property, or an inaccurate survey. Once these objections have been resolved, the owner will have a clear and marketable title. *See also* BAD TITLE; CLOUD ON TITLE.

CLONE FUND in a FAMILY OF FUNDS, new fund set up to emulate a successful existing fund.

CLOSE
1. the price of the final trade of a security at the end of a trading day.
2. the last half hour of a trading session on the exchanges.
3. in commodities trading, the period just before the end of the session when trades marked for execution AT THE CLOSE are completed.
4. to consummate a sale or agreement. In a REAL ESTATE closing, for example, rights of ownership are transferred in exchange for monetary and other considerations. At a *loan* closing, notes are signed and cheques are exchanged. At the close of an *underwriting* deal, cheques and securities are exchanged.
5. in accounting, the transfer of revenue and expense accounts at the end of the period—called *closing the books*.

CLOSE A POSITION to eliminate an investment from one's portfolio. The simplest example is the outright sale of a security and its delivery to the purchaser in exchange for payment. In commodities futures and options trading, traders commonly close out positions through offsetting transactions. Closing a position terminates involvement with the investment; HEDGING, though similar, requires further actions.

CLOSED-END INVESTMENT COMPANY   investment company with a fixed number of shares that can be bought and sold on a stock exchange through brokers and dealers. *See also* OPEN-END INVESTMENT COMPANY.

CLOSE MARKET market in which there is a narrow spread between BID and OFFER prices. Such a market is characterized by active trading and multiple competing market makers. In general, it is easier for investors to buy and sell securities and get good prices in a close market than in a wide market characterized by wide differences between bid and offer prices.

CLOSED CORPORATION corporation owned by a few people, usually management or family members. Shares have no public market. Also known as *private corporation* or *privately held corporation*.

CLOSED-END FUND type of fund that has a fixed number of shares usually listed on a major stock exchange. Unlike open-end mutual funds, closed end funds do not stand ready to issue and redeem shares on a continuous basis. They tend to have specialized portfolios of stocks, bonds, CONVERTIBLES, or combinations thereof, and may be oriented toward income, capital gains, or a combination of these objectives. Because the managers of closed-end funds are perceived to be less responsive to profit opportunities than open-end fund managers, who must attract and retain shareholders, closed-end fund shares often sell at a discount from net asset value. A closed-end fund's equity base is relatively fixed and seldom changes materially. The shares can be traded among investors in an *aftermarket*; in fact, the shares or units of most of Canada's closed-end funds trade on the stock exchanges or in the OTC market. *See also* DUAL-PURPOSE FUND.

CLOSED-END MANAGEMENT COMPANY INVESTMENT COMPANY that operates a mutual fund with a limited number of shares outstanding. Unlike an OPEN-END MANAGEMENT COMPANY, which creates new shares to meet investor demand, a closed-end fund has a set number of shares. These are often listed on an exchange. *See also* CLOSED-END FUND.

CLOSED-END MORTGAGE mortgage-bond issue with an indenture that prohibits repayment before maturity and the repledging of the same collateral without the permission of the bondholders; also called closed mortgage. It is distinguished from an OPEN-END MORTGAGE, which is reduced by amortization and can be increased to its original amount and secured by the original mortgage.

CLOSED FUND MUTUAL FUND that has become too large and is no longer issuing shares.

CLOSED OUT liquidated the position of a client unable to meet a margin call or cover a short sale. *See also* CLOSE A POSITION.

CLOSELY HELD corporation most of whose voting stock is held by a few shareholders; differs from a CLOSED CORPORATION because enough stock is publicly held to provide a basis for trading. Also, the shares held by the controlling group and not considered likely to be available for purchase.

CLOSING COSTS expenses involved in transferring real estate from a seller to a buyer, among them lawyer's fees, survey charges, title searches and insurance, and fees to file deeds and mortgages.

CLOSING PRICE price of the last transaction completed during a day's trading session on an organized securities exchange. *See also* CLOSING RANGE.

CLOSING PURCHASE option seller's purchase of another option having the same features as an earlier one. The two options cancel each other out and thus liquidate the seller's position.

CLOSING QUOTE last bid and offer prices recorded by a specialist or market maker at the close of a trading day.

CLOSING RANGE range of prices (in commodities trading) within which an order to buy or sell a commodity can be executed during one trading day.

CLOSING SALE sale of an option having the same features (i.e., of the same series) as an option previously purchased. The two have the effect of canceling each other out. Such a transaction demonstrates the intention to liquidate the holder's position in the underlying securities upon exercise of the buy.

CLOSING TICK gauge of stock market strength that nets the number of stocks whose stock exchange closing prices were higher than their previous trades, called an UPTICK or plus tick, against the number that closed on a DOWNTICK or minus tick. When the closing tick is positive, that is, when more stocks advanced than declined in the last trade, traders say the market closed on an uptick or was "buying at the close," a bullish sign. "Selling at the close," resulting in a minus closing tick or downtick, is bearish. *See also* TRIN.

CLOSING TRANSACTION transaction in which an investor who has written or sold an option terminates his or her position by buying an option with the same terms.

CLOSING TRIN *see* TRIN.

CLOUD ON TITLE any document, claim, unreleased lien, or encumbrance that may superficially impair or injure the title to a property or make the title doubtful because of its apparent or possible validity. Clouds on title are usually uncovered in a TITLE SEARCH. These clouds range from a recorded mortgage paid in full, but with no satisfaction of mortgage recorded, to a property sold without a spouse's release of interest, to an heir of a prior owner with a questionable claim to the property. The property owner may initiate a quitclaim deed or a quiet title proceeding to remove the cloud on title from the record. Also called *bad title*.

CME Chicago Mercantile Exchange. *See* SECURITIES AND COMMODITIES EXCHANGES.

CMO *see* COLLATERALIZED MORTGAGE OBLIGATION (CMO).

CMO REIT specialized type of REAL ESTATE INVESTMENT TRUST (REIT) that invests in the residual cash flows of COLLATERALIZED MORTGAGE OBLIGATIONS (CMOs). CMO cash flows represent the spread (difference) between the rates paid by holders of the underlying mortgage loans and the lower, shorter term rates paid to investors in the CMOs. Spreads are subject to risks associated with interest rate levels and are considered risky investments. Also called *equity CMOs*.

COATTAIL INVESTING following on the coattails of other successful investors, usually institutions, by trading the same stocks when their actions are made public. This risky strategy assumes the research that guided the investor wearing the coat is still relevant by the time the coattail investor reads about it.

CODE OF ARBITRATION *see* BOARD OF ARBITRATION.

CODICIL legal document that amends a will.

C.O.D. TRANSACTION *see* DELIVERY VERSUS PAYMENT.

COFFEE, SUGAR AND COCOA EXCHANGE (CSCE) New York-based commodity exchange trading futures and options on SOFTS, as typical commodities are called. The CSCE trades futures and options on coffee "C," No. 11 sugar, cocoa, nonfat dry milk, and cheddar cheese. Only futures contracts are traded on No. 14 sugar and white sugar. The exchange shares the trading floor at the COMMODITIES EXCHANGE CENTER with the NEW YORK MERCANTILE EXCHANGE and NEW YORK COTTON EXCHANGE. Contracts trade Monday through Friday, with trading hours falling between 9 A.M. and 3:15 P.M.

COINSURANCE sharing of an insurance risk, common when claims could be of such size that it would not be prudent for one company to underwrite the whole risk. Typically, the underwriter is liable up to a stated limit, and the coinsurer's liability is for amounts above that limit.

Policies on hazards such as fire or water damage often require coverage of at least a specified coinsurance percentage of the replacement cost. Such clauses induce the owners of property to carry full coverage or close to it.

COLA acronym for *cost-of-living adjustment,* which is an annual addition to wages or benefits to compensate employees or beneficiaries for the loss of purchasing power due to inflation. Many union contracts contain a COLA providing for salary increases at or above the change in the previous year's CONSUMER PRICE INDEX (CPI).

COLD CALLING practice of making unsolicited calls to potential customers by brokers. Brokers hope to interest customers in stocks, bonds, mutual funds, financial planning, or other financial products and services in their cold calls. In parts of Canada and in some countries such as Great Britain, cold calling is severely restricted or even prohibited.

COLLAR in new issue underwriting, the lowest rate acceptable to a buyer of bonds or the lowest price acceptable to the issuer. Also used to mean the index level at which a CIRCUIT BREAKER is triggered.

COLLATERAL ASSET pledged to a lender until a loan is repaid. If the borrower defaults, the lender has the legal right to seize the collateral and sell it to pay off the loan.

COLLATERAL TRUST BOND bond secured by stocks or bonds of companies that are controlled by the issuing company, or other negotiable securities, acceptable to the lender and of equivalent value that are deposited with a trustee.

COLLATERALIZE *see* ASSIGN; COLLATERAL; HYPOTHECATION.

COLLATERAL TERM LIFE INSURANCE insurance that pays off a business's bank or other loans if the business is unable to do so because of the death of the sole owner or a partner.

COLLECTIBLE rare object collected by investors. Examples: stamps, coins, oriental rugs, antiques, baseball cards, photographs. Collectibles typically rise sharply in value during inflationary periods, when people are trying to move their assets from paper currency as an inflation hedge, then drop in value during low inflation. Collectible trading for profit can be quite difficult, because of the limited number of buyers and sellers.

COLLECTION
1. presentation of a negotiable instrument such as a draft or cheque to the place at which it is payable. The term refers not only to cheque clearing and payment, but to such special banking services as foreign collections, coupon collection, and collection of returned items (bad cheques).
2. referral of a past due account to specialists in collecting loans or accounts receivable, either an internal department or a private collection agency.
3. in a general financial sense, conversion of accounts receivable into cash.

COLLECTION PERIOD *see* COLLECTION RATIO.

COLLECTION RATIO ratio of a company's accounts receivable to its average daily sales. Average daily sales are obtained by dividing sales for an accounting period by the number of days in the accounting period—annual sales divided by 365, if the accounting period is a year. That result, divided into accounts receivable (an average of beginning and ending accounts receivable is more accurate), is the collection ratio—the average number of days it takes the company to convert receivables into cash. It is also called *average collection period. See* ACCOUNTS RECEIVABLE TURNOVER for a discussion of its significance.

COLLECTIVE BARGAINING process by which members of the labour force, operating through authorized union representatives, negotiate with their employers concerning wages, hours, working conditions, and benefits.

COMBINATION
1. arrangement of options involving two long or two short positions with different expiration dates or strike (exercise) prices. A trader could order a combination with a long call and a long put or a short call and a short put.
2. joining of competing companies in an industry to alter the competitive balance in their favour is called a combination in restraint of trade.
3. joining two or more separate businesses into a single accounting entity; also called *business combination. See also* MERGER.

COMBINATION ANNUITY *see* HYBRID ANNUITY.

COMBINATION ORDER *see* ALTERNATIVE ORDER.

COMBINED FINANCIAL STATEMENT financial statement that brings together the assets, liabilities, net worth, and operating figures of two or more affiliated companies. In its most comprehensive form, called a combining statement, it includes columns showing each affiliate on an "alone" basis; a column "eliminating" offsetting intercompany transactions; and the resultant combined financial statement. A combined statement is distinguished from a CONSOLIDATED FINANCIAL STATEMENT of a company and subsidiaries, which must reconcile investment and capital accounts. Combined financial statements do not necessarily represent combined credit responsibility or investment strength.

COMEX division of NEW YORK MERCANTILE EXCHANGE, following its merger with the NYMEX. Formerly known as the Commodity Exchange, it is the the leading U.S. market for metals futures and options trading. Futures and futures options are traded on copper, the Eurotop 100, gold, and silver. *See also* NEW YORK MERCANTILE EXCHANGE; SECURITIES AND COMMODITIES EXCHANGES.

COMFORT LETTER
1. independent auditor's letter, required in securities underwriting agreements, to assure that information in the registration statement and prospectus is correctly prepared and that no material changes have occurred since its preparation. It is sometimes called *cold comfort letter*—cold because the accountants do not state positively that the information is correct, only that nothing has come to their attention to indicate it is not correct. The letter is necessary because the report is not signed by the auditor until after the Securities Commission(s) has reviewed the prospectus and any required changes have been made.
2. letter from one to another of the parties to a legal agreement stating that certain actions not clearly covered in the agreement will—or will not—be taken. Such declarations of intent usually deal with matters that are of importance only to the two parties and do not concern other signers of the agreement.

COMMERCIAL HEDGERS companies that take positions in commodities markets in order to lock in prices at which they buy raw materials or sell their products. For instance, ALCAN might hedge its holdings of aluminum with contracts in aluminum futures, or Eastman Kodak, which must buy great quantities of silver for making film, might hedge its holdings in the silver futures market.

COMMERCIAL LOAN short-term (typically 90-day) renewable loan to finance the seasonal WORKING CAPITAL needs of a business, such as purchase of inventory or production and distribution of goods. Commercial loans—shown on the balance sheet as notes payable—rank second only to TRADE CREDIT in importance as a source of short-term financing. Interest is based on the prime rate. *See also* CLEAN.

COMMERCIAL PAPER short-term obligations with maturities ranging from 2 to 270 days issued by banks, corporations, and other borrowers to investors with temporarily idle cash. Such instruments are unsecured and usually discounted, although some are interest-bearing. They can be issued directly—*direct issuers* do it that way—or through brokers equipped to handle the enormous clerical volume involved. Issuers like commercial paper because the maturities are flexible and because the rates are usually marginally lower than bank rates. Investors—actually lenders, since commercial paper is a form of debt—like the flexibility and safety of an instrument that is issued only by top-rated concerns and is nearly always backed by bank lines of credit. Rating agencies that assign ratings to commercial paper are: Dominion and Canada Bond Rating Services, Dun & Bradstreet, Moody's, and Standard & Poor's.

COMMERCIAL PROPERTY real estate that includes income-producing property, such as office buildings, restaurants, shopping centres, hotels, industrial parks, warehouses, and factories. Commercial property usually must be zoned for business purposes. It is possible to invest in commercial property directly, or through REAL ESTATE INVESTMENT TRUSTS or REAL ESTATE LIMITED PARTNERSHIPS. Investors receive income from rents and capital appreciation if the property is sold at a profit. Investing in commercial property also entails large risks, such as nonpayment of rent by tenants or a decline in property values because of overbuilding or low demand.

COMMERCIAL WELLS oil and gas drilling sites that are productive enough to be commercially viable. A limited partnership usually syndicates a share in a commercial well.

COMMINGLING
Securities: mixing customer-owned securities with those owned by a firm in its proprietary accounts. REHYPOTHECATION—the use of customers' collateral to secure brokers' loans—is permissible with customer consent, but certain securities and collateral must by law be kept separate.
Trust banking: pooling the investment funds of individual accounts, with each customer owning a share of the total fund. Similar to a MUTUAL FUND.

COMMISSION
Real estate: percentage of the selling price of the property, paid by the seller.
Securities: fee paid to a broker for executing a trade based on the number of shares traded or the dollar amount of the trade. Fees vary from broker to broker.

COMMISSION BROKER broker, usually a floor broker, who executes trades of stocks, bonds, or commodities for a commission.

COMMITMENT FEE lender's charge for contracting to ho
available. Fee may be replaced by interest when money is borrc
both fees and interest may be charged, as with a REVOLVING CREDIT.

**COMMITTEE ON UNIFORM SECURITIES IDENTIFICATION
PROCEDURES (CUSIP)** committee that assigns identifying num-
bers and codes for all securities. These CUSIP numbers and symbols
are used when recording all buy or sell orders in North America. For
International Business Machines the CUSIP symbol is IBM and the
CUSIP number is 45920010.

COMMODITIES bulk goods such as grains, metals, and foods traded
on a commodities exchange or on the SPOT MARKET. *See also* SECURI-
TIES AND COMMODITIES EXCHANGES.

COMMODITIES EXCHANGE CENTER *see* SECURITIES AND COM-
MODITIES EXCHANGES.

COMMODITIES FUTURES EXCHANGE   an exchange in which
futures contracts for commodities are traded through an open option
system. Some of the commodity exchanges are: CBT (Chicago Board
of Trade), CME (Chicago Mercantile Exchange), KCBT (Kansas City
Board of Trade), ME (Montreal Exchange), NYCSCE (Coffee, Sugar,
and Cocoa Exchange [New York]), NYCX (Commodity Exchange in
New York), NYFE (New York Futures Exchange), NYM (New York
Mercantile Exchange), TFE (Toronto Futures Exchange), and Winn
(Winnipeg Commodity Exchange). *See* SECURITIES AND COMMODITIES
EXCHANGE.

COMMODITY-BACKED BOND bond tied to the price of an underlying commodity. An investor whose bond is tied to the price of silver or
gold receives interest pegged to the metal's current price, rather than a
fixed dollar amount. Such a bond is meant to be a hedge against inflation, which drives up the prices of most commodities.

COMMODITY FUTURES CONTRACT FUTURES CONTRACT tied to
the movement of a particular commodity. This enables contract buyers
to buy a specific amount of a commodity at a specified price on a particular date in the future. The price of the contract is determined using
the OPEN OUTCRY system on the floor of a commodity exchange such
as the Chicago Board of Trade or the Commodity Exchange in New
York. There are commodity futures contracts based on meats such as
cattle and pork bellies; grains such as corn, oats, soybeans and wheat;
metals such as gold, silver, and platinum; and energy products such as
heating oil, natural gas, and crude oil. For a complete listing of commodity futures contracts, *see* SECURITIES AND COMMODITIES
EXCHANGES.

COMMODITY FUTURES TRADING COMMISSION (CFTC)
independent agency created by Congress in 1974 responsible for regulating the U.S. commodity futures and options markets. The CFTC is

responsible for insuring market integrity and protecting market participants against manipulation, abusive trade practices, and fraud.

COMMODITY INDICES indices that measure either the price or performance of physical commodities, or the price of commodities as represented by the price of futures contracts that are listed on commodity exchanges. The Journal of Commerce Index, Reuters Index and The Economist Index are three that measure industrial performance and raw commodities. Due to the complexities of holding physical commodities, however, investors tend to focus on futures indices that are liquid baskets of commodities. Institutional investors prohibited from investing directly in the futures market can include commodities in their portfolios through these indices.

Among the commodity indices that measure futures price performance are:

Bankers Trust Commodity Index (BTCI) is a weighted, composite measure of the values of a basket of five commodities. Energy prices are based on NEW YORK MERCANTILE EXCHANGE contracts. Aluminum is based on the LONDON METAL EXCHANGE contract, while gold and silver are based on London spot fixings. The base prices used are the average prices of each component commodity over the first quarter of 1984. The components are: crude oil—45/$30.191; gold—18/$384.18; aluminum—17/$1,543.67; heating oil—10/$0.8340; silver—10/$9.0043. The value of the index on any given day is calculated by multiplying the current price by the base weight and dividing this figure by the base price.

Energy and Metals Index (ENMET) is a geometrically weighted index based on the prices of futures contracts and developed by Merrill Lynch. ENMET comprises six commodities: crude oil (40%), natural gas (15%), gold (20%), silver (5%), copper (15%), aluminum (5%). The index is weighted to show optimal historic correlation with the CONSUMER PRICE INDEX and the PRODUCER PRICE INDEX. The index is computed daily.

Goldman Sachs Commodity Index (GSCI) consists of 22 commodities. All but the industrials, which trade on the LONDON METAL EXCHANGE, trade on U.S. futures markets. There are five component groups: energy—crude oil (15.89%), natural gas (15.73%), heating oil (9.94%), unleaded gasoline (9.70%); agriculture—wheat (8.87%), corn (6.34%), soybeans (2.99%), cotton (2.96%), sugar (2.84%), coffee (1.09%), cocoa (0.29%); livestock—live cattle (9.35%), live hogs (4.24%); industrials—aluminum (2.86%), copper (2.07%), zinc (0.77%), nickel (0.48%), lead (0.29%), tin (0.12%); precious metals—gold (2.53%), platinum (0.40%), silver (0.26%). Each commodity is weighted by quantity of world production as a means of measuring the impact of commodity performance on the global economy. The index includes a rolling yield, achievable by continually rolling forward the futures positions, and it is investable. Price movement reflects spot price changes in the underlying commodities. Commodity yield reflects roll yield and Treasury bill yield. Because delivery of the underlying commodity never occurs, the investor can keep his or her money invested in Treasury bills. Additionally, there are six sub-indices, representing each of the commodity component groups, calculated daily on real-time prices. Futures and options on the index are traded on the Chicago Mercantile Exchange. Other investment products based on the GSCI and the GSCI sub-indices include structured notes, swaps, customized over-the-counter options and principal-guaranteed annuity contracts.

Investable Commodity Index (ICI) is a broad-based index of 16 commodities based on exchange-traded commodity futures and developed by Intermarket Management, Inc. The index measures the reinvested total returns of an equally weighted, fully collateralized basket: grains (19%)—wheat, corn, soybeans; metals (19%)—gold, silver, copper; energy (25%)—crude oil, heating oil, gasoline, natural gas; livestock (12%)—live cattle, live hogs; food and fibre (25%)— cocoa, coffee, sugar, cotton. The ICI is a rolling index, and represents the compounded daily percentage change in the geometric mean of the 16 commodities' prices plus 100% of the daily compounded 13-week U.S. Treasury bill returns.

J. P. Morgan Commodity Index (JPMCI) uses a dollar-weighted arithmetic average of total returns by investment in 11 metals and energy commodities. The index is composed of base metals (22%)— aluminum (9%), copper (8%), nickel (2%), zinc (3%); energy (55%)— West Texas Intermediate crude oil (33%), heating oil (10%), natural gas (7%), unleaded gasoline (5%); and precious metals (23%)—gold (15%), silver (5%), platinum (3%). As a total return index, returns are derived from changes in commodity futures prices, from rolling long futures positions through time along a sloping forward curve, and by full collateralization of the value of the index with Treasury bills. The index has a positive correlation with growth and inflation, and a negative correlation with bond and equity returns. The index is rebalanced monthly to maintain constant dollar weight.

Knight-Ridder Commodity Research Bureau Index (KR-CRB Index) is made up of 21 commodities whose futures trade on U.S. exchanges. The index is viewed widely as a broad measure of overall commodity price trends. There are six component groups: industrials (28.6%)—crude oil, heating oil, unleaded gasoline, copper, lumber, cotton; grains (23.8%)—corn, wheat, soybeans, soy meal, soy oil; metals (14.3%)—gold, silver, platinum; meats (14.3%)—cattle, hogs, pork bellies; imports (14.3%)—coffee, cocoa, sugar; miscellaneous (4.7%)—orange juice. Equal weighting is used for both arithmetic averaging of individual commodity months and for geometric averaging of the 21 commodity averages. As a result, no single month or commodity has undue impact on the index. Futures and options on the KR-CRB Index trade on the NEW YORK FUTURES EXCHANGE (NYFE). Futures are settled at contract maturity by cash payment. Values of the index are computed by Knight-Ridder Financial Publishing and disseminated by the NYFE every 15 seconds during the trading day.

COMMODITY PAPER inventory loans or advances secured by commodities. If the commodities are in transit, a bill of lading is executed by a common carrier. If they are in storage, a trust receipt acknowledges that they are held and that proceeds from their sale will be transmitted to the lender; a warehouse receipt lists the goods.

COMMON MARKET *see* EUROPEAN ECONOMIC COMMUNITY.

COMMON SHARES unit of equity ownership in a company. The holders of common shares participate in the risks and rewards of a company. They usually have one vote per share and theoretically have a say in the management of the company. They elect the directors, who in turn appoint the management.

COMMON STOCK units of ownership of a public corporation. Owners typically are entitled to vote on the selection of directors and other important matters as well as to receive dividends on their holdings. In the event that a corporation is liquidated, the claims of secured and unsecured creditors and owners of bonds and preferred stock take precedence over the claims of those who own common stock. For the most part, however, common stock has more potential for appreciation. *See also* CAPITAL STOCK.

COMMON STOCK EQUIVALENT preferred stock or bond convertible into common stock, or warrant to purchase common stock at a specified price or discount from market price. Common stock equivalents represent potential dilution of existing common shareholder's equity, and their conversion or exercise is assumed in calculating fully diluted earnings per share. *See also* FULLY DILUTED EARNINGS PER SHARE.

COMMON STOCK FUND MUTUAL FUND that invests only in common stocks.

COMMON STOCK RATIO percentage of total capitalization represented by common stock. From a creditor's standpoint a high ratio represents a margin of safety in the event of LIQUIDATION. From an investor's standpoint, however, a high ratio can mean a lack of *leverage*. What the ratio should be depends largely on the stability of earnings. Electric utilities can operate with low ratios because their earnings are stable. As a general rule, when an industrial company's stock ratio is below 30%, analysts check on earnings stability and fixed charge coverage in bad times as well as good.

COMPANY organization engaged in business as a proprietorship, partnership, corporation, or other form of enterprise. Originally, a firm made up of a group of people as distinguished from a sole proprietorship. However, since few proprietorships owe their existence exclusively to one person, the term now applies to proprietorships as well.

COMPANY DOCTOR executive, usually recruited from the outside, specialized in corporate turnarounds.

COMPANY NAME AND LOCATION name that is registered under the Corporations Act. Location refers to its head office. A company's name is not always the same as the one under which it conducts business but it may be the name of the parent or the holding company.

COMPANY SECRETARY officer of the company responsible for ensuring that the company carries out its legal obligations (e.g., informing shareholders of meetings, new developments, etc.); ensuring that the company's share register is kept up to date; and maintaining complete and accurate minutes of meetings of the company's Board of Directors.

COMPARATIVE STATEMENTS financial statements covering different dates but prepared consistently and therefore lending themselves to comparative analysis, as accounting convention requires. Comparative figures reveal trends in a company's financial development and permit insight into the dynamics behind static balance sheet figures.

COMPARISON
1. short for *comparison ticket*, a memorandum exchanged prior to settlement by two brokers in order to confirm the details of a transaction to which they were parties. Also called comparison sheet.
2. verification of collateral held against a loan, by exchange of information between two brokers or between a broker and a bank.

COMPENSATING BALANCE *or* **COMPENSATORY BALANCE** average balance required by a bank for holding credit available. The more or less standard requirement for a bank line of credit, for example, is 10% of the line plus an additional 10% of the borrowings. Compensating balances increase the effective rate of interest on borrowings.

COMPENSATION cash and non-cash payments to employees in return for employment services.

COMPETITIVE BID sealed bid, containing price and terms, submitted by a prospective underwriter to an issuer, who awards the contract to the bidder with the best price and terms. Many municipalities and virtually all railroads and public utilities use this bid system. Industrial corporations generally prefer NEGOTIATED UNDERWRITING on stock issues but do sometimes resort to competitive bidding in selecting underwriters for bond issues.

COMPETITIVE TRADER *see* REGISTERED COMPETITIVE TRADER.

COMPLETE AUDIT usually the same as an unqualified audit, because it is so thoroughly executed that the auditor's only reservations have to do with unobtainable facts. A complete audit examines the system of internal control and the details of the books of account, including subsidiary records and supporting documents. This is done with an eye to locality, mathematical accuracy, accountability, and the application of accepted accounting principles.

COMPLETION PROGRAM oil and gas limited partnership that takes over drilling when oil is known to exist in commercial quantities. A completion program is a conservative way to profit from oil and gas drilling, but without the capital gains potential of exploratory wildcat drilling programs.

COMPLIANCE DEPARTMENT department set up in all organized stock exchanges to oversee market activity and make sure that trading complies with exchange regulations. A company that does not adhere to the rules can be delisted, and a trader or brokerage firm that violates the rules can be barred from trading.

COMPOSITE TAPE *see* TAPE.

COMPOUND ANNUAL RETURN investment return, discounted retroactively from a cumulative figure, at which money, compounded annually, would reach the cumulative total. Also called INTERNAL RATE OF RETURN.

COMPOUNDED YIELD yield that occurs when the interest income from initial capital earns interest. A semiannual compounded yield is more attractive than an annual compound yield.

COMPOUND GROWTH RATE rate of growth of a number, compounded over several years. Securities analysts check a company's compound growth rate of profits for five years to see the long-term trend.

COMPOUND INTEREST interest earned on principal plus interest that was earned earlier. If $100 is deposited in a bank account at 10%, the depositor will be credited with $110 at the end of the first year and $121 at the end of the second year. That extra $1, which was earned on the $10 interest from the first year, is the compound interest. This example involves interest compounded annually: interest can also be compounded on a daily, quarterly, half-yearly, or other basis. *See also* COMPOUND ANNUAL RETURN.

COMPREHENSIVE GENERAL LIABILITY INSURANCE insurance that protects a law firm from suits for negligence not connected with the practice of law, e.g., someone being injured in the course of business.

COMPUTERIZED MARKET TIMING SYSTEM system of picking buy and sell signals that puts together voluminous trading data in search of patterns and trends. Often, changes in the direction of moving average lines form the basis for buy and sell recommendations. These systems, commonly used by commodity funds and by services that switch between mutual funds, tend to work well when markets are moving steadily up or down, but not in trendless markets.

CONCENTRATOR SERVICE *see* CENTRALIZED CASH CONTROL.

CONCERT PARTY person ACTING IN CONCERT.

CONCESSION
1. selling group's per-share or per-bond compensation in a corporate underwriting.
2. right, usually granted by a government entity, to use property for a specified purpose, such as a service station on a highway.

CONDITIONAL CALL OPTIONS form of CALL PROTECTION available to holders of some HIGH-YIELD BONDS. In the event the bond is called, the issuing corporation is obligated to substitute a non-callable bond having the same life and terms as the bond that is called.

CONDOMINIUM form of real estate ownership in which individual residents hold a deed and title to their houses or apartments and pay a maintenance fee to a management company for the upkeep of common property such as grounds, lobbies, and elevators as well as for other amenities. Condominium owners pay real estate taxes on their units and can sublet or sell as they wish.

CONDUIT THEORY theory regulating investment companies such as REAL ESTATE INVESTMENT TRUSTS and MUTUAL FUNDS holding that since such companies are pure conduits for all capital gains, dividends, and interest to be passed through to shareholders, the investment company should not be taxed at the corporate level. As long as the investment company adheres to certain regulations, shareholders are therefore taxed only once—at the individual level—on income and capital gains. In contrast, shareholders of corporations are taxed twice: once at the corporate level in the form of corporate income taxes and once at the individual level in the form of individual income taxes on all dividends paid by the corporation.

CONFIRMATION
1. formal memorandum from a broker to a client giving details of a securities transaction. When a broker acts as a dealer, the confirmation must disclose that fact to the customer. *See also* CONTRACT.
2. document sent by a company's auditor to its customers and suppliers requesting verification of the book amounts of receivables and payables. *Positive confirmations* request that every balance be confirmed, whereas *negative confirmations* request a reply only if an error exists.

CONFORMED COPY copy of an original document with the essential legal features, such as the signature and seal, being typed or indicated in writing.

CONGLOMERATE corporation composed of companies in a variety of businesses. Conglomerates were popular in the 1960s, when they were thought to provide better management and sounder financial backing, and therefore to generate more profit, than small independent companies. However, some conglomerates became so complex that they were difficult to manage. In the 1980s and 1990s, many conglomerates sold off divisions and concentrated on a few core businesses. Analysts generally consider stocks of conglomerates difficult to evaluate because they are involved in so many unrelated businesses.

CONSERVATOR individual appointed by a court to manage the property of a person who lacks the capacity to manage his or her own property. A conservator may be charged with liquidating the assets of a business in bankruptcy, or may have to take control of the personal finances of an incompetent individual who needs to be protected by the court.

CONSIDERATION something of value that one party gives to another in exchange for a promise or act. In law, a requirement of valid contracts. A consideration can be in the form of money, commodities, or personal services; in many industries the forms have become standardized.

CONSIGNMENT CHEQUES cheques signed and issued by a company and supplied with a prearranged cover deposit to the bank. The bank balances, reconciles, and stores the company's cheques, substantially reducing the company's bookkeeping workload and disbursement costs. Such arrangements include payroll, withholding taxes, and payments to government.

CONSOLIDATED FINANCIAL STATEMENT financial statement that brings together all assets, liabilities, and operating accounts of a parent company and its subsidiaries. *See also* COMBINED FINANCIAL STATEMENT.

CONSOLIDATED TAPE combined tapes of the New York Stock Exchange and the American Stock Exchange. It became operative in June 1975. Network A covers NYSE-listed securities and identifies the originating market. Network B does the same for Amex-listed securities and also reports on securities listed on regional exchanges.

CONSOLIDATION combining of the assets and liabilities of a parent company and its subsidiaries, or investments in which the company owns 50% or more into a total, eliminating any inter-company transfers and debts to avoid double counting.

CONSOLIDATION LOAN loan that combines and refinances other loans or debt. It is normally an installment loan designed to reduce the dollar amount of an individual's monthly payments.

CONSORTIUM group of companies formed to promote a common objective or engage in a project of benefit to all the members. The relationship normally entails cooperation and a sharing of resources, sometimes even common ownership.

CONSTANT DOLLAR PLAN method of accumulating assets by investing a fixed amount of dollars in securities at set intervals. The investor buys more shares when the price is low and fewer shares when the price is high; the overall cost is lower than it would be if a constant number of shares were bought at set intervals. Also called *dollar cost averaging.*

CONSTANT DOLLARS dollars of a base year, used as a gauge in adjusting the dollars of other years in order to ascertain actual purchasing power. Denoted as C$ by the FINANCIAL ACCOUNTING STANDARDS BOARD (FASB), which defines constant dollars as hypothetical units of general purchasing power.

CONSTANT RATIO PLAN type of FORMULA INVESTING whereby a predetermined ratio is maintained between stock and FIXED INCOME INVESTMENTS through periodic adjustments. For example, an investor with $200,000 and a 50-50 formula might start out with $100,000 in stock and $100,000 in bonds. If the stock increased in value to $150,000 and the bonds remained unchanged over a given adjustment period, the investor would restore the ratio at $125,000-$125,000 by selling $25,000 of stock and buying $25,000 of bonds.

CONSTRAINED SHARE COMPANIES banks, trusts, insurance, broadcasting and communication companies having constraints on the number of shares they are permitted to transfer to persons who are not Canadian citizens or Canadian residents.

CONSTRUCTION LOAN short-term real estate loan to finance building costs. The funds are disbursed as needed or in accordance with a prearranged plan, and the money is repaid on completion of the project, usually from the proceeds of a mortgage loan. The rate is normally higher than prime, and there is usually an origination fee. The effective yield on these loans tends to be high, and the lender has a security interest in the real property.

CONSUMER CREDIT debt assumed by consumers for purposes other than home mortgages. Consumers can borrow through credit cards, lines of credit, loans against insurance policies, and many other methods. The Interest Act, Usury Act, and the Bank Act all help to protect the Canadian consumer with respect to full and true disclosure of interest costs and terms.

CONSUMER DURABLES products bought by consumers that are expected to last three years or more. These include automobiles, appliances, boats, and furniture. Economists look at the trend in consumer expenditure on durables as an important indicator of the strength of the economy, since consumers need confidence to make such large and expensive purchases. Stock market analysts also classify companies that produce appliances, furniture, cars, and similar items as consumer durables manufacturers, contrasting them with consumer non-durables manufacturers, which make consumable items such as food or drugs.

CONSUMER FINANCE COMPANY *see* FINANCE COMPANY.

CONSUMER GOODS goods bought for personal or household use, as distinguished from CAPITAL GOODS or *producer's goods,* which are used to produce other goods. The general economic meaning of consumer goods encompasses consumer services. Thus the *market basket* on which the CONSUMER PRICE INDEX is based includes clothing, food, and other goods as well as utilities, entertainment, and other services.

CONSUMER PRICE INDEX monthly estimate of changes in the retail prices of goods and services bought by Canadians living in communities with a population of 30,000 people or more, in all parts of the country. The index is based on a shopping basket of 300 goods and services normally bought by families of 2 to 6 people with annual incomes of $4000 to $12,000 in 1967. It is a weighted index that assigns greater importance to changes in the price of food and housing than of entertainment. The current base year is 1971, i.e., 1971 is equal to 100. The CPI therefore shows inflation trends and is used in cost-of-living (COLA) clauses for wage increases and an indexation of the income tax and social benefits program.

CONSUMPTION TAX *see* VALUE-ADDED TAX (VAT).

CONTANGO
1. pricing situation in which futures prices get progressively higher as maturities get progressively longer, creating negative spreads as contracts go farther out. The increases reflect carrying costs, including storage, financing, and insurance. The reverse condition, an inverted market, is termed BACKWARDATION.
2. in finance, the costs that must be taken into account in analyses involving forecasts.

CONTINGENT BENEFICIARY person named in an insurance policy to receive the policy benefits if the primary beneficiary dies before the benefits become payable.

CONTINGENT DEFERRED SALES LOAD sales charge levied by a mutual fund if a customer sells fund shares within a specified number of years. Instead of charging a traditional FRONT END LOAD of 5%, for example, a brokerage firm may offer the same fund with a contingent deferred sales load. Customers who sell the fund within the first year pay a 5% load. In the second year, the charge would be 4%. Each year the charge declines by one percentage point until there is no fee for selling fund shares after the fifth year. Also called *back-end load.*

CONTINGENT LIABILITIES
Banking: potential obligation of a guarantor or accommodation endorser; or the position of a customer who opens a letter of credit and whose account will be charged if a draft is presented. The bank's own ultimate responsibility for letters of credit and other commitments, individually and collectively, is its contingent liability.

Corporate reports: pending lawsuits, judgments under appeal, disputed claims, and the like, representing potential financial liability.

CONTINUOUS DISCLOSURE press release that a reporting issuer must issue under the Ontario Securities Act as soon as a material change occurs in its affairs and, in any event, within 10 days. *See also* TIMELY DISCLOSURE.

CONTRA BROKER broker on the opposite side—the buy side of a sell order or the sell side of a buy order.

CONTRACT in general, agreement by which rights or acts are exchanged for lawful consideration. To be valid, it must be entered into by competent parties, must cover a legal and moral transaction, must possess mutuality, and must represent a meeting of minds. Countless transactions in finance and investments are covered by contracts.

CONTRACT HIGH AND LOW high and low transaction prices since the listing of a futures contract.

CONTRACT SIZE securities group of 100 shares that is known as a call contract. Also the number of single calls traded equal to 100 times the volume for the last business day and equal to 100 times the open interest for the total number traded for the specific contract expiration date.

In gold and silver, gold fixing contract size is 100 ounces.

CONTRACTUAL PLAN mutual fund savings plan that allows an investor to save over the long term, usually 10 years or more. Such plans have high fixed costs, usually at the beginning, and are justified only if the investor completes the term of the plan.

CONTRA ORDER *see* CROSS.

CONTRARIAN investor who does the opposite of what most investors are doing at any particular time. According to contrarian opinion, if everyone is certain that something is about to happen, it won't. This is because most people who say the market is going up are fully invested and have no additional purchasing power, which means the market is at its peak. When people predict decline they have already sold out, so the market can only go up. Some mutual funds follow a contrarian investment strategy, and some investment advisers suggest only out-of-favour securities, whose price/earnings ratio is lower than the rest of the market or industry.

CONTRIBUTED CAPITAL payments made in cash or property to a corporation by its stockholders either to buy capital stock, to pay an assessment on the capital stock, or as a gift. Also called *paid-in capital*. The contributed or paid-in capital of a corporation is made up of capital stock and capital (or contributed) surplus, which is contributed (or paid-in) capital in excess of PAR value or STATED VALUE. Donated capital and DONATED SURPLUS are freely given forms of contributed (paid-in) capital, but DONATED STOCK refers to fully paid (previously issued) capital stock that is given as a gift to the issuing corporation.

CONTRIBUTED SURPLUS component of shareholders' equity that originates from sources other than earnings, such as initial sale of stock above par value.

CONTRIBUTION accounting term meaning amount "contributed" in net cash flow toward overhead by a given product or manufacturing activity, after deduction of all direct costs associated with the production of that product.

CONTRIBUTORY PLAN *see* COST-SHARING.

CONTROLLED COMMODITY commodities regulated by the Commodity Exchange Authority. They are domestically produced agricultural products.

CONTROLLED WILDCAT DRILLING drilling for oil and gas in an area adjacent to but outside the limits of a proven field. Also known as a *field extension.* Limited partnerships drilling in this area take greater risks than those drilling in areas of proven energy reserves, but the rewards can be considerable if oil is found.

CONTROLLER *or* **COMPTROLLER** chief accountant of a company. In small companies the controller may also serve as treasurer.

CONTROLLING INTEREST ownership of more than 50% of a corporation's voting shares. A much smaller interest, owned individually or by a group in combination, can be controlling if the other shares are widely dispersed and not actively voted.

CONTROL PERSON *see* AFFILIATED PERSON.

CONTROL STOCK shares owned by holders who have a CONTROLLING INTEREST.

CONVENTIONAL MORTGAGE residential mortgage loan, usually from a bank, trust company, or a mortgage company, for a fixed term of 3, 5, 7, or 10 years with fixed monthly payments of a blend of interest, principal, and sometimes property taxes.

CONVENTIONAL OPTION put or call contract arranged off the trading floor of a listed exchange and not traded regularly. It was commonplace when options were banned on certain exchanges, but is now rare.

CONVERGENCE movement of the price of a futures contract toward the price of the underlying CASH COMMODITY. At the start of the contract price is higher because of the time value. But as the contract nears expiration the futures price and the cash price converge.

CONVERSION
1. exchange of a convertible security such as a bond into a fixed number of shares of the issuing corporation's common stock.
2. transfer of mutual-fund shares without charge from one fund to another fund in a single family; also known as fund switching.
3. exchange of currency of one country for that of another.
4. in insurance, switch from short-term to permanent life insurance.

CONVERSION FEATURE right to convert a particular holding to another form of holding, such as the SWITCHING within a mutual fund family, the right to convert certain preferred stock or bonds to common stock, or the right to switch from one type of insurance policy to another. *See also* CONVERTIBLES.

CONVERSION PARITY common-stock price at which a convertible security can become exchangeable for common shares of equal value.

CONVERSION PREMIUM amount by which the price of a convertible tops the market price of the underlying stock. If a stock is trading at $50 and the bond convertible at $45 is trading at $50, the premium is $5. If the premium is high the bond trades like any fixed income bond. If the premium is low the bond trades like a stock.

CONVERSION PRICE the dollar value at which convertible bonds, debentures, or preferred stock can be converted into common stock, as announced when the convertible is issued.

CONVERSION RATIO relationship that determines how many shares of common stock will be received in exchange for each convertible bond or preferred share when the conversion takes place. It is determined at the time of issue and is expressed either as a ratio or as a conversion price from which the ratio can be figured by dividing the par value of the convertible by the conversion price. The indentures of most convertible securities contain an antidilution clause whereby the conversion ratio may be raised (or the conversion price lowered) by the percentage amount of any stock dividend or split, to protect the convertible holder against dilution.

CONVERSION TRADE buying an option to sell (put), selling an option to buy (call), and then buying the underlying security. Thus, puts are transformed into calls and calls into puts, all without risk.

CONVERSION VALUE
In general: value created by changing from one form to another. For example, converting rental property to condominiums adds to the value of the property.
Convertibles: the price at which the exchange can be made for common stock.

CONVERTIBLE ADJUSTABLE PREFERRED STOCK *see* CAPS.

CONVERTIBLE DEBENTURE debenture that is convertible into common shares at the option of the owner.

CONVERTIBLE PREFERRED SHARE preferred share that may be converted into some other class of stock (usually common) at a predetermined price for a stated period of time.

CONVERTIBLES corporate securities (usually preferred shares or bonds) that are exchangeable for a set number of another form (usually common shares) at a prestated price. Convertibles are appropriate for investors who want higher income than is available from common stock, together with greater appreciation potential than regular bonds offer. From the issuer's standpoint, the convertible feature is usually designed as a sweetener, to enhance the marketability of the stock or preferred. A company can force conversion by calling in such shares for redemption if the redemption price is below the market price.

CONVEXITY mathematical concept that measures sensitivity of the market price of an interest-bearing bond to changes in interest rate levels. *See also* DURATION.

COOK THE BOOKS to falsify the financial statements of a company intentionally. A firm in financial trouble may want to cook the books to prevent investors from pushing down the company's stock price. Companies may also falsify their records to lower their tax liabilities. The practice is illegal because it violates federal competition and fraud regulations as well as provincial securities rules.

COOPERATIVE organization owned by its members.

In real estate, a property whose residents own shares in a cooperative giving them exclusive use of their apartments. Decisions about common areas—hallways, elevators, grounds—are made by a vote of members' shares. Members also approve sales of apartments.

Agriculture cooperatives help farmers sell their products more efficiently. Food cooperatives buy food for their members at wholesale prices, but usually require members to help run the organization.

COPENHAGEN STOCK EXCHANGE main securities market in Denmark. Both stocks and bonds are traded on the exchange using ELECTRA, the electronic trading system in which all Danish stock brokerage houses are connected. The market also offers futures and options based on Danish equities traded on the exchange and supervised by the Guarantee Fund for Danish Options and Futures. Stocks and bonds are settled three business days after the trading day. For stocks, the price is paid on delivery of share certificates. Bonds are settled through the Danish Securities Centre. Trading is conducted Monday through Friday, 9 A.M.–3:30 P.M.

CORE cylindrical piece of rock that is extracted from the earth and removed to the surface for examination and analysis. Core samples determine the mining stock evaluation. *See also* DRILL.

CORNERING THE MARKET purchasing a security or commodity in such volume that control over its price is achieved. A cornered market in a security would be unhappy news for a short seller, who would have to pay an inflated price to cover. Cornering has been illegal for some years.

CORPORATE BOND debt instrument issued by a private corporation, as distinct from one issued by a government agency or a municipality. Corporates typically have four distinguishing features: (1) they are taxable; (2) they have a par value of $1000; (3) they have a term maturity—which means they come due all at once—and are paid for out of a sinking fund accumulated for that purpose; (4) they are traded on major exchanges, with prices published in newspapers.

CORPORATE CHARTER *see* ARTICLES OF INCORPORATION.

CORPORATE EQUIVALENT YIELD comparison that dealers in government bonds include in their offering sheets to show the after-tax yield of government bonds selling at a discount and corporate bonds selling at par.

CORPORATE FINANCING COMMITTEE NATIONAL ASSOCIATION OF SECURITIES DEALERS standing committee that reviews documentation submitted by underwriters in compliance with Securities and Exchange Commission requirements to ensure that proposed markups are fair and in the public interest.

CORPORATE INSIDER *see* INSIDER.

CORPORATION legal entity, created under provincial or federal statute, separate and distinct from the persons who own it, giving rise to a jurist's remark that it has "neither a soul to damn nor a body to kick." Nonetheless, it is regarded by the courts as an artificial person; it may own property, incur debts, sue, or be sued. It has three chief distinguishing features:
1. limited liability; owners can lose only what they invest.
2. easy transfer of ownership through the sale of shares of stock.
3. continuity of existence.
    Other factors helping to explain the popularity of the corporate form of organization are its ability to obtain capital through expanded ownership, and the shareholders' ability to profit from the growth of the business. *See also* LIMITED LIABILITY.

CORPUS Latin for *body*.
1. in trust banking, the property in a trust—real estate, securities and other personal property, cash in bank accounts, and any other items included by the donor.
2. body of an investment or note, representing the principal or capital as distinct from the interest or income.

CORRECTION reverse movement, usually downward, in the price of an individual stock, bond, commodity, or index. If prices have been rising on the market as a whole, then fall dramatically, this is known as a *correction within an upward trend.* Technical analysts note that markets do not move straight up or down and that corrections are to be expected during any long-term move.

CORRECTION

Correction is Here

CORRELATION COEFFICIENT statistical measure of the degree to which the movements of two variables are related.

CORRESPONDENT, CORRESPONDENT BANK financial organization that regularly performs services for another in a market inaccessible to the other e.g., in a foreign country. In banking there is usually a depository relationship that compensates for expenses and facilitates transactions.

COST ACCOUNTING branch of accounting concerned with providing the information that enables the management of a firm to evaluate production costs.

COST BASIS original price of an asset, used in determining capital gains. It usually is the purchase price, but in the case of an inheritance it is the appraised value of the asset at the time of the donor's death.

COST-BENEFIT ANALYSIS method of measuring the benefits expected from a decision, calculating the cost of the decision, then determining whether the benefits outweigh the costs. Corporations use this method in deciding whether to buy a piece of equipment, and the government uses it in determining whether federal programs are achieving their goals.

COST OF CAPITAL rate of return that a business could earn if it chose another investment with equivalent risk—in other words, the OPPORTUNITY COST of the funds employed as the result of an investment decision. Cost of capital is also calculated using a weighted average of a firm's costs of debt and classes of equity. This is also called the *composite cost of capital.*

COST OF CARRY out-of-pocket costs incurred while an investor has an investment position, among them interest on long positions in margin accounts, dividends lost on short margin positions, and incidental expenses.

COST OF FUNDS interest cost paid by a financial institution for the use of money. Brokerage firms' cost of funds comprise the total interest expense to carry an inventory of stocks and bonds. In the banking industry, the cost of funds is the amount of interest the bank must pay on money market accounts, passbooks, GICs, and other liabilities.

COST OF GOODS SOLD figure representing the cost of buying raw materials and producing finished goods. Depreciation is considered a part of this cost but is usually listed separately. Included in the direct costs are clear-cut factors such as direct factory labour as well as others that are less clear-cut, such as overhead. *Cost of sales* may be used as a synonym or may mean selling expenses. See also DIRECT OVERHEAD; FIRST IN, FIRST OUT; LAST IN, FIRST OUT.

COST-OF-LIVING ADJUSTMENT (COLA) adjustment of wages designed to offset changes in the cost of living, usually as measured by the CONSUMER PRICE INDEX. COLAs are key bargaining issues in labour contracts and are politically sensitive elements of social security payments and federal pensions because they affect millions of people.

COST-OF-LIVING INDEX *see* CONSUMER PRICE INDEX.

COST OF SALES *see* COST OF GOODS SOLD.

COST-PLUS CONTRACT contract basing the selling price of a product on the total cost incurred in making it plus a stated percentage or a fixed fee—called a *cost-plus-fixed-fee contract.* Cost-plus contracts are common when there is no historical basis for estimating costs and the producer would run a risk of loss—defense contracts involving sophisticated technology, for example. The alternative is a FIXED PRICE contract.

COST-PUSH INFLATION inflation caused by rising prices, which follow on the heels of rising costs. This is the sequence: When the demand for raw materials exceeds the supply, prices go up. As manufacturers pay more for these raw materials they raise the prices they charge merchants for the finished products, and the merchants in turn raise the prices they charge consumers. *See also* DEMAND-PULL INFLATION; INFLATION.

COST RECORDS
   1. investor records of the prices at which securities were purchased, which provide the basis for computing capital gains.
   2. in finance, anything that can substantiate the costs incurred in producing goods, providing services, or supporting an activity designed to be productive. Ledgers, schedules, vouchers, and invoices are cost records.

COST SHARING principle by which both a company and its employees contribute to the financing of a benefits program.

COUNCIL OF ECONOMIC ADVISERS group of economists appointed by the President of the United States to provide counsel on economic policy. The council helps to prepare the President's budget message to Congress, and its chairman frequently speaks for the administration's economic policy.

COUNTERCYCLICAL STOCKS stocks that tend to rise in value when the economy is turning down or is in recession. Traditionally, companies in industries with stable demand, such as drugs, food, and tobacco, are considered countercyclical. Some firms actually do better when the economy or stock market is in turmoil. For example, firms offering money market mutual funds may enjoy an inflow of cash when stock prices fall. Temporary-help firms may benefit if companies are cutting costs by laying off full-time employees and replacing them with temps. Companies that can perform various functions for other companies more efficiently and at lower cost (called *outsourcing firms*) will tend to benefit during economic downturns. *See also* CYCLICAL STOCKS.

COUPON expressed rate of interest income paid by the issuer of a bond.
   Bank bonds actually have detachable coupons that can be cashed on maturity. It is usually attached to the bond. For example, a bond with a 12% coupon yields a fixed 12% interest income on invested capital, as long as the bond is purchased on its issue date, or at par value. The average coupon on a bond fund portfolio reflects the interest income the fund will generate, and will fluctuate as the portfolio manager trades the bonds in the portfolio.

COUPON BOND bond issued with detachable coupons that must be presented to a paying agent or the issuer for semiannual interest payment. These are bearer bonds, so whoever presents the coupon is entitled to the interest. Once universal, the coupon bond has been gradually giving way to the REGISTERED BOND, some of which pay interest through electronic transfers.

COUPON COLLECTION *see* COLLECTION.

COUPON-EQUIVALENT RATE same as EQUIVALENT BOND YIELD.

COUPON YIELD (OR RATE) *see* COUPON.

COVARIANCE statistical term for the correlation between two variables multiplied by the standard deviation for each of the variables.

COVENANT promise in a trust indenture or other formal debt agreement that certain acts will be performed and others refrained from. Designed to protect the lender's interest, covenants cover such matters as working capital, debt-equity ratios, and dividend payments. Also called *restrictive covenant* or *protective covenant.*

COVER
1. to buy back contracts previously sold; said of an investor who has sold stock or commodities short.
2. in corporate finance, to meet fixed annual charges on bonds, leases, and other obligations, out of earnings.
3. amount of net-asset value underlying a bond or equity security. Coverage is an important aspect of a bond's safety rating.

COVERAGE *see* FIXED-CHARGE COVERAGE.

COVERAGE RATIO ratios, such as times interest earned, total debt coverage, and overall coverage ratio, which measure the ability of a firm to meet its fixed financial obligations. The higher the ratios, the better.

COVERED OPTION option contract backed by the shares underlying the option. For instance, someone who owns 300 shares of XYZ and sells three XYZ call options is in a covered option position. If the XYZ stock price goes up and the option is exercised, the investor has the stock to deliver to the buyer. Selling a call brings a premium from the buyer. *See also* NAKED OPTION.

COVERED SELLER *see* COVERED WRITER.

COVERED WRITER seller of covered options—in other words, an owner of stock who sells options against it to collect premium income. For example, when writing a CALL OPTION, if a stock price stays stable or drops, the seller will be able to hold onto the stock. If the price rises sharply enough, it will have to be given up to the option buyer.

COVERED WRITING status of a call option seller who is considered to be covered if he or she owns 100 shares for each call option contract.

COVERING SHORT *see* COVER.

CPI *see* CONSUMER PRICE INDEX (CPI).

CRAM-DOWN DEAL merger or leveraged buyout slang for situation in which stockholders are forced, for lack of attractive alternatives, to accept undesirable terms, such as JUNK BONDS instead of cash or equity.

CRASH precipitate drop in stock prices and economic activity, as in the crash of 1929 or BLACK MONDAY in 1987. Crashes are usually brought on by a loss in investor confidence following periods of highly inflated stock prices.

CREDIT

In general: loans, bonds, charge-account obligations, and open-account balances with commercial firms. Also, available but unused bank letters of credit and other standby commitments as well as a variety of consumer credit facilities.

On another level, discipline in which lending officers and industrial credit people are professionals. At its loftiest it is defined in Dun & Bradstreet's motto: "Credit—Man's Confidence in Man."

Accounting: entry—or the act of making an entry—that increases liabilities, owners' equity, revenue, and gains, and decreases assets and expenses. *See also* CREDIT BALANCE.

Customer's statement of account: adjustment in the customer's favour, or increase in equity.

CREDIT ANALYST person who (1) analyzes the record and financial affairs of an individual or a corporation to ascertain creditworthiness or (2) determines the credit ratings of corporate and municipal bonds by studying the financial condition and trends of the issuers.

CREDIT BALANCE

In general: account balance in the customer's favour. See *also* CREDIT.

Securities: in cash accounts with brokers, money deposited and remaining after purchases have been paid for, plus the uninvested proceeds from securities sold. In margin accounts, (1) proceeds from short sales, held in escrow for the securities borrowed for these sales; (2) free credit balances, or net balances, which can be withdrawn at will. SPECIAL MISCELLANEOUS ACCOUNT balances are not counted as free credit balances.

CREDIT BUREAU agency that gathers information about the credit history of consumers and relays it to credit grantors for a fee. Credit bureaus maintain files on millions of consumers detailing which lines of credit they have applied for and received, and whether they pay their bills in a timely fashion. Bureaus receive this information from credit grantors such as credit card issuers, retail stores, gasoline companies, and others. Credit grantors look at this information, which is constantly being updated, in making their decision as to whether or not to grant credit to a particular consumer, and if so, how much credit is appropriate.

CREDIT CARD plastic card issued by a bank, trust company, retail store, oil company, or other credit grantor giving consumers the right to charge purchases and pay for them later. Most credit cards offer a grace period of about 25 days, during which interest charges do not accrue. After that, consumers pay nondeductible CONSUMER INTEREST on the remaining balance until it is paid off. Some credit cards start charging interest from the day the purchase is registered. Most credit cards also permit consumers to obtain cash on their card in the form of a CASH ADVANCE.

CREDIT INSURANCE protection against *abnormal* losses from unpaid accounts receivable, often a requirement of banks lending against accounts receivable.

In consumer credit, life or accident coverage protecting the creditor against loss in the event of death or disability, usually stated as a percentage of the loan balance.

CREDIT LIMIT credit card term, meaning the maximum balance allowed for a particular customer.

CREDITOR party that extends credit, such as a trade supplier, a bank lender, or a bondholder.

CREDITOR'S COMMITTEE group representing firms that have claims on a company in financial difficulty or bankruptcy; sometimes used as an alternative to legal bankruptcy, especially by smaller firms.

CREDIT RATING formal evaluation of an individual's or company's credit history and capability of repaying obligations. Any number of firms investigate, analyze, and maintain records on the credit responsibility of individuals and businesses—Crediteland Equifax (individuals) and Dun & Bradstreet (commercial firms), for example. The bond ratings assigned by Standard & Poor's, Canadian & Dominion Bond Rating Services, and Moody's are also a form of credit rating. Most large companies and lending institutions assign credit ratings to existing and potential customers.

CREDIT RISK financial and moral risk that an obligation will not be paid and a loss will result.

CREDIT SCORING objective methodology used by credit grantors to determine how much, if any, credit to grant to an applicant. Credit scoring is devised by three different methods: by a third-party firm, by the credit grantor, or by the credit bureau in cooperation with the credit grantor. Some of the most common factors in scoring are income, assets, length of employment, length of living in one place, and past record of using credit. Any negative events in the past, such as bankruptcies or tax delinquencies, will sharply reduce an applicant's credit score.

CREDIT SPREAD difference in the value of two options, when the value of the one sold exceeds the value of the one bought. The opposite of a DEBIT SPREAD.

CREDIT UNION not-for-profit financial institution typically formed by employees of a company, a labor union, or a religious group and operated as a cooperative. Credit unions may offer a full range of financial services and pay higher rates on deposits and charge lower rates on loans than banks or trust companies.

CREDIT WATCH used by bond RATING agencies to indicate that a company's credit is under review and its rating subject to change. The implication is that if the rating is changed, it will be lowered, usually because of some event that affects the income statement or balance sheet adversely.

CREDITWORTHINESS general eligibility of a person or company to borrow money. *See* CREDIT RATING; CREDIT SCORING.

CROSS securities transaction in which the same broker acts as agent in both sides of the trade. The practice—called crossing—is legal only if the broker first offers the securities publicly at a price higher than the bid. *See also* ORDER; PUT-THROUGH.

CROSS ON THE FLOOR *see* CROSS.

CROSSED TRADE manipulative practice prohibited on major exchanges whereby buy and sell orders are offset without recording the trade on the exchange, thus perhaps depriving the investor of the chance to trade at a more favourable price. Also called *crossed sale.*

CROWD group of exchange members with a defined area of function tending to congregate around a trading post pending execution of orders. These are specialists, floor traders, odd-lot dealers, and other brokers as well as smaller groups with specialized functions—the INACTIVE BOND CROWD, for example.

CROWDING OUT heavy federal borrowing at a time when businesses and consumers also want to borrow money. Because the government can pay any interest rate it has to and individuals and businesses can't, the latter are crowded out of credit markets by high interest rates. Crowding out can thus cause economic activity to slow.

CROWN JEWELS the most desirable entities within a diversified corporation as measured by asset value, earning power and business prospects. The crown jewels usually figure prominently in takeover attempts; they typically are the main objective of the acquirer and may be sold by a takeover target to make the rest of the company less attractive.

CUM DIVIDEND with dividend; said of a stock whose buyer is eligible to receive a declared dividend. Stocks are usually cum dividend for trades made on or before the fifth day preceding the RECORD DATE, when the register of eligible holders is closed for that dividend period. Trades after the fifth day go EX-DIVIDEND.

CUM RIGHTS with rights; said of stocks that entitle the purchaser to buy a specified amount of stock that is yet to be issued. The cut-off date when the stocks go from cum rights to EX-RIGHTS (without rights) is stipulated in the prospectus accompanying the rights distribution.

CUMULATIVE PREFERRED preferred stock whose dividends if omitted because of insufficient earnings or any other reason accumulate until paid out. They have precedence over common dividends, which cannot be paid as long as a cumulative preferred obligation exists. Most preferred stock issued today is cumulative.

CUMULATIVE PREFERRED SHARE preferred share, unpaid dividend of which accumulate in arrears. They must be paid to the preferred shareholder before any dividend can be paid to the common shareholder or before the preferred shares are redeemed.

CUMULATIVE VOTING voting method that improves minority shareholders' chances of naming representatives on the board of directors. In regular or statutory voting, stockholders must apportion their votes equally among candidates for director. Cumulative voting allows shareholders to cast all their votes for one candidate. Assuming one vote per share, 100 shares owned, and six directors to be elected, the regular method lets the shareholder cast 100 votes for each of six candidates for director, a total of 600 votes. The cumulative method lets the same 600 votes be cast for one candidate or split as the shareholder wishes. Cumulative voting is a popular cause among advocates of corporate democracy, but it remains the exception rather than the rule.

CURB *see* AMERICAN STOCK EXCHANGE.

CURRENCY notes and coins used as legal tender in the country in which they are minted.

CURRENCY FUTURES contracts in the futures markets that are for delivery in a major currency such as Canadian dollars, U.S. dollars, British pounds, French francs, German marks, Swiss francs, or Japanese yen. Corporations that sell products around the world can hedge their currency risk with these futures.

CURRENCY IN CIRCULATION paper money and coins circulating in the economy, counted as part of the total money in circulation, which includes DEMAND DEPOSITS in banks.

CURRENT ACCOUNT (1) an active TRADE CREDIT account; (2) an account with an extender of credit that is up to date; (3) *See* BALANCE OF PAYMENTS.

CURRENT AGGREGATE VALUE term used for index options. It is the level of the index at any time × $100.

CURRENT ASSETS cash, accounts receivable, inventory, and other assets that are likely to be converted into cash, sold, exchanged, or expensed in the normal course of business, usually within a year.

CURRENT INCOME money that is received on an ongoing basis from investments in the form of dividends, interest, rents, or other income sources.

CURRENT LIABILITY debt or other obligation coming due within a year.

CURRENT MARKET VALUE present worth of a client's portfolio at today's market price, as listed in a brokerage statement every month— or more often if stocks are bought on margin or sold short. For listed stocks and bonds the current market value is determined by closing prices; for over-the-counter securities the bid price is used.

CURRENT MATURITY interval between the present time and the maturity date of a bond issue, as distinguished from original maturity, which is the time difference between the issue date and the maturity date. For example, in 1997 a bond issued in 1995 to mature in 2015 would have an original maturity of 20 years and a current maturity of 18 years.

CURRENT RATIO current assets divided by current liabilities. The ratio shows a company's ability to pay its current obligations from current assets. For the most part, a company that has a small inventory and readily collectible accounts receivable can operate safely with a lower current ratio than a company whose cash flow is less dependable. *See also* QUICK RATIO; WORKING CAPITAL.

CURRENT RETURN annual income from an investment expressed as a percentage of the investment's current value: on stock, calculated by dividing yearly dividend by market price; on bonds, by dividing yearly interest by current price.

CURRENT YIELD
1. annual interest on a bond divided by the market price. It is the actual income rate of return as opposed to the coupon rate (the two would be equal if the bond were bought at par) or the yield to maturity. For example, a 10% (coupon rate) bond with a face (or par) value of $1000 is bought at a market price of $800. The annual income from the bond is $100. But since only $800 was paid for the bond, the current yield is $100 divided by $800, or 12½%.
2. in money market mutual funds, the current yield reflects the portfolio's average earnings in the most recent 7-day period converted to an annual percentage. Unlike a GIC's stated yield, current yield does not indicate anticipated earnings.

CUSHION
1. interval between the time a bond is issued and the time it can be called. Also termed CALL PROTECTION.
2. margin of safety for a corporation's financial ratios. For instance, if its DEBT-TO-EQUITY RATIO has a cushion of up to 40% debt, anything over that level might be cause for concern.
3. *see* LAST IN, FIRST OUT.

CUSHION BOND callable bond with a coupon above current market interest rates that is selling for a premium. Cushion bonds lose less of their value as rates rise and gain less in value as rates fall, making them suitable for conservative investors interested in high income.

CUSHION THEORY theory that a stock's price must rise if many investors are taking short positions in it, because those positions must be covered by purchases of the stock. Technical analysts consider it particularly bullish if the short positions in a stock are twice as high as the number of shares traded daily. This is because price rises force short sellers to cover their positions, making the stock rise even more.

CUSIP NUMBER number identifying all stocks and registered bonds, using the COMMITTEE ON UNIFORM SECURITIES IDENTIFICATION PROCEDURES (CUSIP). Brokers will use a security's CUSIP number to look it up on a computer terminal to get further information. The CUSIP number will also be listed on any trading confirmation tickets. The CUSIP system makes it easier to settle and clear trades. Foreign securities use a similar identification system called the CUSIP International Numbering System (CINS).

CUSTODIAN bank or other financial institution that keeps custody of stock certificates and other assets of a mutual fund, individual, or corporate client.

CUSTODY legal responsibility for someone else's assets or for a child. Term implies management as well as safekeeping. Currently, tax law states that all child support payments paid to a former spouse are taxable in their hands and deductible by the support payer. This is now under review.

CUSTOMER'S LOAN CONSENT agreement signed by a margin customer permitting a broker to borrow margined securities to the limit of the customer's debit balance for the purpose of covering other customers' short positions and certain failures to complete delivery.

CUSTOMER'S MAN traditionally a synonym for *registered representative, account executive,* or *account representative.* Now used rarely, as more women work in brokerages.

CUTOFF POINT in capital budgeting, the minimum rate of return acceptable on investments.

CYCLE *see* BUSINESS CYCLE.

CYCLICAL STOCK stock that tends to rise quickly when the economy turns up and to fall quickly when the economy turns down. Examples are housing, automobiles, and paper. Stocks of noncyclical industries—such as foods, insurance, drugs—are not as directly affected by economic changes.

D

DAILY TRADING LIMIT maximum that many commodities and options markets are allowed to rise or fall in one day. When a market reaches its limit early and stays there all day, it is said to be having an up-limit or down-limit day. Exchanges usually impose a daily trading limit on each contract. For example, the Chicago Board of Trade limit is two points ($2000 per contract) up or down on its treasury bond futures options contract.

DAISY CHAIN trading between market manipulators to create the appearance of active volume as a lure for legitimate investors. When these traders drive the price up, the manipulators unload their holdings, leaving the unwary investors without buyers to trade with in turn.

DATA BASE store of information that is sorted, indexed, and summarized and accessible to people with computers. Data bases containing market and stock histories are available from a number of commercial sources.

DATED DATE date from which accrued interest is calculated on new bonds and other debt instruments. The buyer pays the issuer an amount equal to the interest accrued from the dated date to the issue's settlement date. With the first interest payment on the bond, the buyer is reimbursed.

DATE OF ISSUE
Bonds: date on which a bond is issued and effective. Interest accrues to bondholders from this date.
Insurance: date on which a policy is issued. Normally, the policy is also declared effective on that date, though not in every case.
Stocks: date on which a new stock is publicly issued and begins trading.

DATE OF RECORD date on which a shareholder must officially own shares in order to be entitled to a dividend. For example, the board of directors of a corporation might declare a dividend on November 1 payable on December 1 to stockholders of record on November 15. After the date of record the stock is said to be EX-DIVIDEND. Also called *record date.*

DATING in commercial transactions, extension of credit beyond the supplier's customary terms—for example, 90 days instead of 30 days. In industries marked by high seasonality and long lead time, dating, combined with ACCOUNTS RECEIVABLE FINANCING, makes it possible for manufacturers with lean capital to continue producing goods. Also called *seasonal dating, special dating.*

DAWN RAID British term for a practice whereby a RAIDER instructs brokers to buy all the available shares of another company at the opening of the market, thus giving the acquirer a significant holding before the TARGET COMPANY gets wise to the undertaking. In London-based markets, the practice is restricted by the *City Code on Takeovers and Mergers. See also* SATURDAY NIGHT SPECIAL.

DAY LOAN loan from a bank to a broker for the purchase of securities pending delivery through the afternoon clearing. Once delivered the securities are pledged as collateral and the loan becomes a regular broker's call loan. Also called *morning loan.*

DAY OF DEPOSIT TO DAY OF WITHDRAWAL ACCOUNT bank account that pays interest based on the actual number of days that money is on deposit. Also called *actual balance method.*

DAY ORDER order to buy or sell securities that expires unless executed or canceled the day it is placed. All orders are day orders unless otherwise specified. The main exception is a GOOD-TILL-CANCELED ORDER, though even it can be executed the same day if conditions are right.

DAY-TO-DAY MONEY *see* CALL MONEY.

DAY TRADE purchase and sale of a position during the same day.

DEAD CAT BOUNCE sharp rise in stock prices after a severe decline. The saying refers to the fact that a dead cat dropped from a high place will bounce. Often, the bounce is the result of short-sellers covering their positions at a profit.

DEALER
1. individual or firm acting as a PRINCIPAL in a securities transaction. Principals trade for their own account and risk. When buying from a broker acting as a dealer, a customer receives securities from the firm's inventory; the confirmation must disclose this. When specialists trade for their own account, as they must as part of their responsibility for maintaining an orderly market, they act as dealers. Since most brokerage firms operate both as brokers and as principals, the term *broker-dealer* is commonly used.
2. one who purchases goods or services for resale to consumers. The element of inventory risk is what distinguishes a dealer from an agent or sales representative.

DEALER MARKET securities market in which transactions are between principals acting as DEALERS for their own accounts rather than between brokers acting as agents for buyers and sellers.

DEALER'S SPREAD *see* MARKDOWN; UNDERWRITING SPREAD.

DEAL FLOW rate of new deals being referred to the investment banking division of a brokerage firm. This might refer to proposals for new stock and bond issues, as well as mergers, acquisitions, and takeovers.

DEAL STOCK stock that may be rumoured to be a TAKEOVER target or the party to some other major transaction such as a merger or leveraged buyout. The stock may be subject to a rumour of a prospective deal, or a deal may have been announced that attracts additional bidders and the company is said to be *in play*. Arbitrageurs and other speculators will attempt to buy deal stocks before the deal is finalized or profit when the stock price rises. Of course, if there is no deal, these speculators may lose money if the stock falls back to its pre-rumour price.

DEAR MONEY British equivalent of TIGHT MONEY.

DEATH BENEFIT amount of money to be paid to beneficiaries when a policyholder dies. The death benefit is the face value of the policy less any unpaid policy loans or other insurance company claims against the policy. Beneficiaries are not taxed on the death benefit when they receive it.

DEATH PLAY stock bought on the expectation that a key executive will die and the shares will gain value as a result. For example, there might be reason to believe that upon the imminent death of a CEO, a company will be broken up and that the shares will be worth more at their PRIVATE MARKET VALUE.

DEATH VALLEY CURVE venture capital term that describes a start-up company's rapid use of capital. When a company begins operations, it uses a great deal of its equity capital to set up its offices, hire personnel, and do research and development. It may be several months or even years before the company has products or services to sell, creating a stream of revenues. The Death Valley Curve is the time period before revenues begin, when it is difficult for the company to raise more equity or issue debt to help it through its cash-flow difficulties.

DEBENTURE similar to a bond, a debenture is a formal written obligation of a company to repay a specified sum on a certain date(s). Debentures are normally registered and are frequently secured by one or more assets, but not usually in first position, i.e., the most senior.

A debenture usually contains negative covenants (what the borrower may not do, e.g., allow current ratio to fall below 1:1) and positive covenants (what the borrower must do, such as pay interest when due). Failure to meet a covenant gives the debenture holder the right to certain remedies, e.g., call the loan, put in a receiver, etc. *See also* FIXED CHARGE; FLOATING CHARGE.

DEBENTURE STOCK stock issued under a contract providing for fixed payments at scheduled intervals and more like preferred stock than a DEBENTURE, since their status in liquidation is equity and not debt.

Also, a type of bond issued by Canadian and British corporations, which refer to debt issues as stock.

DEBIT BALANCE
1. account balance representing money owed to the lender or seller.
2. money a margin customer owes a broker for loans to purchase securities.

DEBIT CARD card issued by a bank to allow customers access to their funds electronically. Debit cards could replace cheques as a method of payment for goods and services, and are more convenient because they are more widely accepted than cheques. Debit cards can also be used to withdraw cash from automated banking machines. Unlike credit cards, however, consumers do not have the advantage of the FLOAT on their money since funds are withdrawn immediately.

DEBIT SPREAD difference in the value of two options, when the value of the one bought exceeds the value of the one sold. The opposite of a CREDIT SPREAD.

DEBT
1. money, goods, or services that one party is obligated to pay to another in accordance with an expressed or implied agreement. Debt may or may not be secured.
2. general name for bonds, notes, mortgages, and other forms of paper evidencing amounts owed and payable on specified dates or on demand.

DEBT BOMB situation in which a major financial institution defaults on its obligations, causing major disruption to the financial system of the institution's home country. If a major multinational bank were to run into such trouble, it could have a major negative impact on the global financial system.

DEBT CEILING *see* DEBT LIMIT.

DEBT FINANCING loans used as a means of raising capital.

DEBT INSTRUMENT written promise to repay a debt; for instance, a BILL, NOTE, BOND, BANKER'S ACCEPTANCE, CERTIFICATE OF DEPOSIT, or COMMERCIAL PAPER.

DEBTOR any individual or company that owes money. If debt is in the form of a loan from a financial institution, you might use *borrower.* If indebtedness is in the form of securities, such as bonds, you would refer to the *issuer. See also* OBLIGOR.

DEBT LIMIT maximum amount of debt that a municipality can incur. If a municipality wants to issue bonds for an amount greater than its debt limit, it usually requires approval from the voters.

DEBT RETIREMENT repayment of debt. The most common method of retiring corporate debt is to set aside money each year in a SINKING FUND.

Most municipal bonds and some corporates are issued in serial form, meaning different portions of an issue—called series—are retired at different times, usually on an annual or semiannual schedule.

Sinking fund bonds and serial bonds are not classes of bonds, just methods of retiring them that are adaptable to debentures, convertibles, and so on. *See also* REFUNDING.

DEBT SECURITY security representing money borrowed that must be repaid and having a fixed amount, a specific maturity or maturities, and usually a specific rate of interest or an original purchase discount. For instance, a BILL, BOND, COMMERCIAL PAPER, or a NOTE.

DEBT SERVICE cash required in a given period, usually one year, for payments of interest and current maturities of principal on outstanding debt. In corporate bond issues, the annual interest plus annual sinking fund payments; in government bonds, the annual payments into the debt service fund. *See also* ABILITY TO PAY.

DEBT SERVICE COVERAGE

Corporate finance: amount, usually expressed as a ratio, of CASH FLOW available to meet annual interest and principal payments on debt, including SINKING FUND payments.

Government finance: export earnings required to cover annual principal and interest payments on a country's external debts.

Personal finance: ratio of monthly installment debt payments, excluding mortgage loans and rent, to monthly take-home pay.

See also FIXED-CHARGE COVERAGE.

DEBT SWAP exchange, between banks, of a loan, usually to a third-world country in local currency. *See also* SWAP.

DEBT-TO-EQUITY RATIO

1. total liabilities divided by total shareholders' equity. This shows to what extent owner's equity can cushion creditors' claims in the event of liquidation.
2. total long-term debt divided by total shareholders' equity. This is a measure of LEVERAGE—the use of borrowed money to enhance the return on owners' equity.
3. long-term debt and preferred stock divided by common stock equity. This relates securities with fixed charges to those without fixed charges.

DECLARATION DATE date on which a company announces the amount and date of its next dividend payment. There is normally an interim period of a few days between the declaration date and the EX-STOCK DIVIDEND date which allows people to buy shares and still qualify to receive the upcoming dividend.

DECLARE authorize the payment of a dividend on a specified date, an act of the board of directors of a corporation. Once declared, a dividend becomes an obligation of the issuing corporation.

DECREASING TERM LIFE INSURANCE form of life insurance coverage in which premiums remain constant for the life of the policy while the death benefit declines. Term insurance premiums usually increase every year as the policyholder ages, and the policy is renewed. If there is less need for coverage because, for example, children have become self-sufficient, it may be prudent to decrease the amount of outstanding coverage.

DEDUCTIBLE

Insurance: amount of money that the policyholders must pay out of their pockets before reimbursements from the insurance company begin. The deductible is usually set as a fixed dollar amount, though in some cases it can also be a percentage of the premium paid or some other formula. Some group health insurance plans set the deductible at a set percentage of the employee's salary, for example. In general, the higher a deductible a policyholder will accept, the lower insurance premiums will be. The insurance company is willing to lower its premiums because the company is no longer liable for small claims.

Taxes: *see* TAX DEDUCTIBLE.

DEDUCTION

1. expense allowed by the Department of National Revenue as a subtraction from adjusted gross income in arriving at a person's taxable income.
2. adjustment to an invoice allowed by a seller for a discrepancy, shortage, and so on.

DEED written instrument containing some transfer, bargain, or contract relating to property—most commonly, conveying the legal title to real estate from one party to another.

DEEMED DISPOSITION transfer of property that occurs under certain circumstances, according to taxation rules, even without a purchase or sale, e.g., there is a deemed disposition upon death, upon emigration from Canada, or upon the contribution of a security to one's self-directed RRSP.

DEEMED REALIZATION transfer of assets that is considered "a sale" by Revenue Canada though no cash or other consideration may be involved. For example, this could take the form of a transfer to a family trust or family member for a note or mortgage but no cash.

DEEP DISCOUNT BOND bond selling for a discount of more than about 20% from its face value. Unlike a CURRENT COUPON BOND, which has a higher interest rate, a deep discount bond will appreciate faster as interest rates fall and drop faster as rates rise. Unlike ORIGINAL ISSUE DISCOUNT bonds, deep discounts were issued at a par value of $1000.

DEEP IN/OUT OF THE MONEY CALL OPTION whose exercise price is well below the market price of the underlying stock (deep *in* the money) or well above the market price (deep *out of* the money). The situation would be exactly the opposite for a PUT OPTION. The premium for buying a deep-in-the-money option is high, since the holder has the right to purchase the stock at a striking price considerably below the current price of the stock. The premium for buying a deep-out-of-the-money option is very small, on the other hand, since the option may never be profitable.

DEFAULT failure of a debtor to make timely payments of interest and principal as they come due or to meet some other provision of a bond indenture. In the event of default, bondholders may make claims against the assets of the issuer in order to recoup their principal.

DEFAULT RISK risk that a debtholder will not receive interest and principal when due. One way to gauge default risk is the RATINGS issued by credit rating agencies such as Moody's, and Standard & Poor's. The higher the rating (AAA or Aaa is highest), the less risk of default. Some bonds such as Canada, Alberta, and B.C. government bonds are considered guaranteed against risk and default, while lower-rated provinces such as Newfoundland and Québec may be considered at greater risk.

DEFEASANCE
In general: provision found in some debt agreements whereby the contract is nullified if specified acts are performed.
Corporate finance: short for in-substance defeasance, a technique whereby a corporation discharges old, low-rate debt without repaying it prior to maturity. The corporation uses newly purchased securities with a lower face value but paying higher interest or having a higher market value. The objective is a cleaner (more debt free) balance sheet and increased earnings in the amount by which the face amount of the old debt exceeds the cost of the new securities.

In another type of defeasance, a company instructs a broker to buy, for a fee, the outstanding portion of an old bond issue of the company. The broker then exchanges the bond issue for a new issue of the company's stock with an equal market value. The broker subsequently sells the stock at a profit.

DEFENSIVE SECURITIES stocks and bonds that are more stable than average and provide a safe return on an investor's money. When the stock market is weak, defensive securities tend to decline less than the overall market.

DEFENSIVE STOCK *see* DEFENSIVE SECURITIES.

DEFERRAL OF TAXES postponement of tax payments from this year to a later year. For instance, an RRSP defers taxes until the money is withdrawn.

DEFERRED ACCOUNT account that postpones taxes until a later date. Some examples: RRSPS, ANNUITIES and DEFERRED PROFIT SHARING PLANS.

DEFERRED ANNUITY *see* DEFERRED PAYMENT ANNUITY.

DEFERRED CHARGE expenditure carried forward as an asset until it becomes relevant, such as an advance rent payment or insurance premium. The opposite is *deferred income,* such as advance rent received.

DEFERRED COMPENSATION currently earned compensation that, under the terms of a profit-sharing, pension, or stock option plan, is not actually paid until a later date and is therefore not taxable until that date.

DEFERRED INCOME TAX income tax that is deferred by the use of larger allowable deductions in calculating taxable income than those used in calculating net income in the financial statements. An acceptable practice, it is usually the result of timing differences and represents differences in accounting reporting guidelines and tax reporting guidelines.

DEFERRED INTEREST BOND bond that pays interest at a later date. A zero coupon bond and a stopped bond are examples of this.

DEFERRED LOAD FUND open-ended fund on which no sales charge or commission is applied when the fund is purchased but carrying a sales charge on redemption. Such loads are usually high if redeemed early, but decline over time to zero—usually 6 years. Also called a BACK-END or REAR-END LOAD.

DEFERRED PAYMENT ANNUITY ANNUITY whose contract provides that payments to the annuitant be postponed until a number of periods have elapsed—for example, when the annuitant attains a certain age. Also called a *deferred annuity.*

DEFERRED PROFIT SHARING PLAN plan that allows a business owner to set aside a portion of the firm's profits for employees.

DEFERRED SALES CHARGE *see* BACK-END LOAD.

DEFICIENCY LETTER written notice from a securities commission to a prospective issuer of securities that the preliminary prospectus needs revision or expansion. Deficiency letters require prompt action; otherwise, the registration period may be prolonged.

DEFICIT
1. excess of liabilities and debts over income and assets. Deficits usually are corrected by borrowing or by selling assets.
2. in finance, an excess of expenditures over budget.

DEFICIT FINANCING borrowing by a government agency to make up for a revenue shortfall. Deficit financing stimulates the economy for a time but eventually can become a drag on the economy by pushing up interest rates. *See also* CROWDING OUT; KEYNESIAN ECONOMICS.

DEFICIT NET WORTH excess of liabilities over assets and capital stock, perhaps as a result of operating losses. Also called *negative net worth.*

DEFICIT SPENDING excess of government expenditures over government revenue, creating a shortfall that must be financed through borrowing. *See also* DEFICIT FINANCING.

DEFINED BENEFIT PENSION PLAN plan that promises to pay a specified amount to each person who retires after a set number of years of service. Such plans pay no taxes on their investments. Employees contribute to them in some cases; in others, all contributions are made by the employer.

DEFLATION decline in the prices of goods and services. Deflation is the reverse of INFLATION; it should not be confused with DISINFLATION, which is a slowing down in the rate of price increases. Generally, the economic effects of deflation are the opposite of those produced by inflation, with two notable exceptions: (1) prices that increase with inflation do not necessarily decrease with deflation—union wage rates, for example; (2) while inflation may or may not stimulate output and employment, marked deflation has always affected both negatively.

DEFLATOR statistical factor used to convert current dollar activity into inflation-adjusted activity—in effect, a measure of prices. The change in the gross domestic product (GDP) deflator, for example, is a measure of economy-wide inflation.

DEGREE OF FINANCIAL LEVERAGE (DFL) measure of a firm's financial leverage; the higher the DFL, the greater the financial leverage and therefore the greater the financial risk.

DEGREE OF TOTAL LEVERAGE (DTL) measure of a firm's total leverage; the higher the DTL, the greater the total leverage and therefore the greater the total risk.

DELAYED DELIVERY delivery of securities later than the scheduled date, which is ordinarily three business days after the trade date. A contract calling for delayed delivery, known as SELLER'S OPTION, is usually agreed to by both parties to a trade. *See also* DELIVERY DATE.

DELAYED OPENING postponement of the start of trading in a stock until a gross imbalance in buy and sell orders is overcome. Such an imbalance is likely to follow on the heels of a significant event such as a takeover offer.

DELINQUENCY failure to make a payment on an obligation when due. In finance company parlance, the amount of past due balances, determined either on a contractual or recency-of-payment basis.

DELISTED STOCK shares of a company that are no longer traded on a stock exchange because of the repeated failure of the company to follow the stock exchange rules, bankruptcy of the company, or the redemption of the shares, i.e., the company buys back the shares from its shareholders. *See also* DELISTING.

DELISTING removal of a company's security from an exchange because the firm did not abide by some regulation or the stock does not meet certain financial ratios or sales levels.

DELIVERY *see* DELIVERY DATE; GOOD DELIVERY.

DELIVERY DATE
   1. first day of the month in which delivery is to be made under a futures contract. Since sales are on a SELLER'S OPTION basis, delivery can be on any day of the month, as long as proper notice is given.
   2. third business day following a REGULAR WAY transaction of stocks or bonds.

DELIVERY MONTH *see* SERIES MONTH.

DELIVERY NOTICE
   1. notification from the seller to the buyer of a futures contract indicating the date when the actual commodity is to be delivered.
   2. in general business transactions, a formal notice documenting that goods have been delivered or will be delivered on a certain date.

DELIVERY VERSUS PAYMENT securities industry procedure, common with institutional accounts, whereby delivery of securities sold is made to the buying customer's bank in exchange for payment, usually in the form of cash. (Institutions are required by law to require "assets of equal value" in exchange for delivery.) Also called CASH ON DELIVERY, delivery against payment, delivery against cash, or, from the sell side, RECEIVE VERSUS PAYMENT.

DELTA
   1. measure of the relationship between an option price and the underlying futures contract or stock price. For a call option, a delta of 0.50 means a half-point rise in premium for every dollar that the stock goes up. For a put option contract, the premium rises as stock prices fall. As options near expiration, IN-THE-MONEY contracts approach a delta of 1.
   2. on the London Stock Exchange, *delta stocks* were the smallest capitalization issues before the system was replaced with today's NORMAL MARKET SIZE.

DELTA HEDGING HEDGING method used in OPTION trading and based on the change in premium (option price) caused by a change in the price of the underlying instrument. The change in the premium for each one-point change in the underlying security is called DELTA and the relationship between the two price movements is called the *hedge ratio.* For example, if a call option has a hedge ratio of 40, the call should rise 40% of the change in the security move if the stock goes down. The delta of a put option, conversely, has a negative value. The value of the delta is usually good the first one-point move in the underlying security over a short time period. When an option has a high hedge ratio, it is usually more profitable to buy the option than to be a WRITER because the greater percentage movement vis a vis the underlying security's price and the relatively little time value erosion allow the purchaser greater leverage. The opposite is true for options with a low hedge ratio.

DEMAND DEPOSIT account balance which, without prior notice to the bank, can be drawn on by cheque, cash withdrawal from an automated banking machine, or by transfer to other accounts using the telephone or home computers.

DEMAND LOAN loan with no set maturity date that can be called for repayment when the lender chooses. Banks usually bill interest on these loans at fixed intervals.

DEMAND MONEY *see* CALL MONEY.

DEMAND-PULL INFLATION price increases occurring when supply is not adequate to meet demand. *See also* COST-PUSH INFLATION.

DEMONETIZATION withdrawal from circulation of a specified form of currency. For example, the Jamaica Agreement between major INTERNATIONAL MONETARY FUND countries officially demonetized gold starting in 1978, ending its role as the major medium of international settlement.

DENKS acronym for *dual-employed, no kids,* referring to a family unit in which both husband and wife work, and there are no children. Without the expense and responsibility for children, DENKS have a larger disposable income than couples with children, making them a prime target for marketers of luxury goods and services, particularly various types of investments.

DENOMINATION face value of currency units, coins, and securities. *See also* PAR VALUE.

DENTAL PLAN taxable, contributory plan on the part of the employer and employee that covers some or all expenses of an insured person's dental work. Coverage for spouse and children is usually included.

DEPLETION using up of wasting assets such as oil, gas, and minerals as a result of production. Minerals are a wasting asset or depleting resource because, once mined, they cannot be replaced. Revenue Canada allows certain deductions called depletion allowances to the extractive industries.

DEPOSIT
1. cash, cheques, or drafts placed with a financial institution for credit to a customer's account. Banks broadly differentiate between demand deposits (chequing accounts on which the customer may draw at any time) and time deposits, which usually pay interest and have a specified maturity or require notice before withdrawal.
2. securities placed with a bank or other institution or with a person for a particular purpose.
3. sums lodged with utilities, landlords, and service companies as security.
4. money put down as evidence of an intention to complete a contract and to protect the other party in the event that the contract is not completed.

DEPOSITARY RECEIPT *see* AMERICAN DEPOSITARY RECEIPT.

DEPOSIT CUTOFF specific point in the banking day by which cheques must be deposited at a bank in order to take advantage of the bank's direct send network and ensure greatest availability of the cash from the cheques to the business for its use. Enables banks to control volume of cheques and eliminates the need to make several mailings of transit items each day.

DEPOSIT INSURANCE *see* CANADIAN DEPOSIT INSURANCE CORPORATION.

DEPOSITORY TRANSFER CHEQUE (DTC) device for effecting the transfer of funds from one corporate bank account to another. DTCs are preprinted, nonnegotiable, usually unsigned demand deposit instruments, payable only to the bank of deposit for credit to a specific corporate account.

DEPRECIATED COST original cost of a fixed asset less accumulated DEPRECIATION; this is the *net book value* of the asset.

DEPRECIATION
Economics: consumption of capital during production—in other words, wearing out of plant and capital goods, such as machines and equipment.
Finance: amortization of fixed assets, such as plant and equipment, so as to allocate the cost over their depreciable life. Depreciation reduces taxable income but does not reduce cash. If an item is sold at a profit, tax must be paid on the profit.

   Among the most commonly used methods are STRAIGHT-LINE DEPRECIATION; ACCELERATED DEPRECIATION; the ACCELERATED COST RECOVERY SYSTEM, and the MODIFIED ACCELERATED COST RECOVERY SYSTEM. Others include the annuity, appraisal, compound interest, production, replacement, retirement, and sinking fund methods.
Foreign Exchange: decline in the price of one currency relative to another.

DEPRESSED MARKET market characterized by more supply than demand and therefore weak (depressed) prices. *See also* SYSTEMATIC RISK.

DEPRESSED PRICE price of a product, service, or security that is weak because of a DEPRESSED MARKET. Also refers to the market price of a stock that is low relative to comparable stocks or to its own ASSET VALUE because of perceived or actual risk. Such stocks are identified by high dividend yield, abnormally low PRICE/EARNINGS RATIOS and other such yardsticks. *See also* FUNDAMENTAL ANALYSIS.

DEPRESSION economic condition characterized by falling prices, reduced purchasing power, an excess of supply over demand, rising unemployment, accumulating inventories, deflation, plant contraction, public fear and caution, and a general decrease in business activity. The Great Depression of the 1930s, centered in the United States, Canada, and Europe, had worldwide repercussions.

DEREGULATION greatly reducing government regulation in order to allow freer markets to create a more efficient marketplace. Industries such as communications and transportation have also been deregulated, with similar results: increased competition, heightened innovation, and mergers among weaker competitors. Some government oversight usually remains after deregulation.

DERIVATIVE short for *derivative instrument,* a contract whose value is based on the performance of an underlying financial asset, index, or other investment. For example, an ordinary *option* is a derivative because its value changes in relation to the performance of an underlying stock. A more complex example would be an option on a FUTURES CONTRACT, where the option value varies with the value of the futures contract which, in turn, varies with the value of an underlying commodity or security. Derivatives are available based on the performance of assets, interest rates, currency exchange rates, and various domestic and foreign indexes. Derivatives afford leverage and, when used properly by knowledgeable investors, can enhance returns and be useful in HEDGING portfolios. They gained notoriety in the late '80s, however, because of problems involved in PROGRAM TRADING, and in the '90s, when a number of mutual funds, municipalities, corporations, and leading banks suffered large losses because unexpected movements in interest rates adversely affected the value of derivatives. *See also* BEARS, CERTIFICATES OF ACCRUAL ON TREASURY SECURITIES (CATS); COLLATERALIZED BOND OBLIGATION (CBO); COLLATERALIZED MORTGAGE OBLIGATION (CMO); CUBS; INDEX OPTIONS; OEX; SPIDERS; STRIP; SUBSCRIPTION RIGHT; SUBSCRIPTION WARRANT; SWAP; TIGER.

DERIVATIVE INSTRUMENT *see* DERIVATIVE.

DESCENDING TOPS chart pattern wherein each new high price for a security is lower than the preceding high. The trend is considered bearish. *See* chart on next page.

DESIGNATED ORDER TURNAROUND (DOT) electronic system used by the New York Stock Exchange to expedite execution of small MARKET ORDERS by routing them directly from the member firm to the SPECIALIST, thus bypassing the FLOOR BROKER. A related system called *Super DOT* routes LIMIT ORDERS.

DEUTSCHE BORSE AG operating company for the German cash and derivatives markets: the DEUTSCHE TERMINBORSE, the financial futures exchange, and the FRANKFURT STOCK EXCHANGE. Deutsche Borse provides the staff, facilities, premises, and financial resources for both operations. It also serves as the clearing house for DTB in a separate division.

DEUTSCHE TERMINBORSE (DTB) Germany's first fully computerized exchange, and the first German exchange for trading financial futures, opened in January 1990. In January 1994, DTB merged with

DESCENDING TOPS

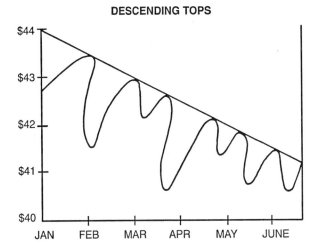

There is no open outcry system. Cooperative agreements have been undertaken for electronic linkages with the MATIF, the French derivatives exchange; MATIF members began trading DTB contracts in France in September 1994; DTB members also trade MATIF contracts via terminals in Germany. The exchange trades options on 16 German blue chip stocks, and three products linked to the DAX Index, the German stock index: DAX options, DAX futures, and options on DAX futures. The DTB trades four interest rate futures contracts with a full range of maturities: FIBOR futures (3 months), BOBL futures (3.3 to 5 years), BUND futures (8.5 to 10 years) and BUXL futures (15 to 30 years). Options are traded on BOBL and BUND futures.

DEVALUATION lowering of the value of a country's currency relative to gold and/or the currencies of other nations. Devaluation can also result from a rise in value of other currencies relative to the currency of a particular country.

DEVELOPMENTAL DRILLING PROGRAM drilling for oil and gas in an area with proven reserves to a depth known to have been productive in the past. Limited partners in such a program, which is considerably less risky than an EXPLORATORY DRILLING PROGRAM or WILDCAT DRILLING, have a good chance of steady income, but little chance of enormous profits.

DEWKS acronym for *dual-employed, with kids,* referring to a family unit in which both husband and wife work and there are children. Marketers selling products for children, including various investments, target DEWKS.

DIAGONAL SPREAD strategy based on a long and short position in the same class of option (two puts or two calls in the same stock) at different striking prices and different expiration dates. Example: a six-month call sold with a striking price of 40 and a three-month call sold with a striking price of 35. *See also* CALENDAR SPREAD; VERTICAL SPREAD.

DIALING AND SMILING expression for COLD CALLING by securities brokers and other salespeople. Brokers must not only make unsolicited telephone calls to potential customers, but also gain the customer's confidence with their upbeat tone of voice and sense of concern for the customer's financial well-being.

DIALING FOR DOLLARS expression for COLD CALLING in which brokers make unsolicited telephone calls to potential customers, hoping to find people with investable funds. The term has a derogatory implication, and is typically applied to salespeople working in BOILER ROOMS, selling speculative or fraudulent investments such as PENNY STOCKS.

DIFF short for *Euro-rate differential,* a futures contract traded on the Chicago Mercantile Exchange that is based on the interest rate spread between the U.S. dollar and the British pound, the German mark, or the Japanese yen.

DIFFERENTIAL small extra charge sometimes called the *odd-lot-differential*—usually ⅛ of a point—that dealers add to purchases and subtract from sales in quantities less than the standard trading unit or ROUND LOT. Also, the extent to which a dealer widens his or her round lot quote to compensate for lack of volume.

DIGITS DELETED designation on securities exchange tape meaning that because the tape has been delayed, some digits have been dropped. For example, 26½... 26⅝... 26⅛ becomes 6½... 6⅝... 6⅛.

DILUTION decrease in the proportional share of various owners in a firm, possibly resulting from new share issues. The dilution of ownership usually results in the dilution of earnings, although the long-term effect may be to increase per-share earnings.

DINKS acronym for *dual-income, no kids,* referring to a family unit in which there are two incomes and no children. The two incomes may result from both husband and wife working, or one spouse holding down two jobs. Since the couple do not have children, they typically have more disposable income than those with children, and therefore are the prime targets of marketers selling luxury products and services, including various investments. *See also* DENKS; DEWKS.

DIP slight drop in securities prices after a sustained uptrend. Analysts often advise investors to buy on dips, meaning buy when a price is momentarily weak.

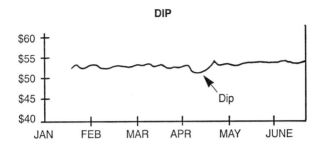

DIP

DIRECT DELIVERY SERVICE *see* AUTOMATIC DISTRIBUTION SERVICE.

DIRECT DEPOSIT SERVICE *see* AUTOMATIC DISTRIBUTION SERVICE; CENTRALIZED CASH CONTROL.

DIRECT HOLDING holding(s) of an individual or company in other companies, when the holding is direct as opposed to through another company. For example, if Company A owns 500,000 of Company B's 1,000,000 outstanding shares, Company A has a 50% direct interest in Company B. Company B, in turn owns 300,000 of Company C's outstanding 500,000 shares. Company B, then, has a 60% direct interest in Company C. Company A, by virtue of its 50% direct interest in Company B, has a 30% indirect interest in Company C.

DIRECT INVESTMENT (1) purchase of a controlling interest in a foreign (international) business or subsidiary. (2) in domestic finance, the purchase of a controlling interest or a minority interest of such size and influence that active control is a feasible objective.

DIRECT LOAN loan requiring a mortgage against equipment or other property that is being financed.

DIRECTOR person elected to direct company policy by common shareholders voting at the annual meeting. *See also* BOARD OF DIRECTORS.

DIRECT OVERHEAD portion of overhead costs—rent, lights, insurance—allocated to manufacturing, by the application of a standard factor termed a *burden rate.* This amount is absorbed as an INVENTORY cost and ultimately reflected as a COST OF GOODS SOLD.

DIRECT PARTICIPATION PROGRAM program letting investors participate directly in the cash flow and tax benefits of the underlying investments.

DIRECT PLACEMENT direct sale of securities to one or more professional or sophisticated investors. Such securities may or may not be registered. They may be bonds, private issues of stock, limited partnership interests, mortgage-backed securities, venture capital investments, or other sophisticated instruments. These investments typically require large minimum purchases. Direct placements offer higher potential returns than many publicly offered securities, but also present more risk. Buyers of direct placements are large, sophisticated financial institutions including insurance companies, banks, mutual funds, foundations, and pension funds that are able to evaluate such offerings. Also called *private placement.*

DIRECT PURCHASE purchasing shares in a no-load or low-load OPEN-END MUTUAL FUND directly from the fund company. Investors making direct purchases deal directly with the fund company over the phone, in person at investor centres, or by mail. This contrasts with the method of purchasing shares in a LOAD FUND through a financial intermediary such as a broker or financial planner, who collects a commission for offering advice on which fund is appropriate for the client. Many companies also now allow shareholders to purchase stock directly from the company, thereby avoiding brokers and sales commissions.

DIRTY FLOAT intervention in the foreign exchange market by the government, which insists that it is not intervening. This is done to give the impression that the currency is being allowed to float while preventing a major fluctuation or to keep the currency in a range despite negative economic or political news.

DIRTY STOCK stock that fails to meet the requirements for GOOD DELIVERY.

DISABILITY INCOME INSURANCE insurance policy that pays benefits to a policyholder when that person becomes incapable of performing one or more occupational duties, either temporarily or on a long-term basis, or totally. The policy is designed to replace a portion of the income lost because of the insured's disability. Payments begin after a specified period, called the *elimination period,* of several weeks or months.

　　Some policies remain in force until the person is able to return to work, or to return to a similar occupation, or is eligible to receive benefits from another program such as Canada Pension and Workers' Compensation. Disability insurance payments are normally tax-free to beneficiaries as long as they paid the policy premiums. Many employers offer disability income insurance to their employees, though people are able to buy coverage on an individual basis as well.

DISASTER OUT CLAUSE rarely applied clause in an underwriting agreement allowing the underwriter to rescind the agreement, should a law, event, or major financial occurrence transpire that adversely affects financial markets in general or the issuer in particular. These would include a material change in the financial condition of the business, such as bankruptcy; a change in law affecting the business; or an Act of God, such as a natural disaster or a fire that destroyed assets.

DISBURSEMENT paying out of money in the discharge of a debt or an expense, as distinguished from a distribution.

DISCHARGE OF BANKRUPTCY order terminating bankruptcy proceedings, ordinarily freeing the debtor of all legal responsibility for specified obligations.

DISCHARGE OF LIEN order removing a lien on property after the originating legal claim has been paid or otherwise satisfied.

DISCLAIMER CLAUSE disclaimer carried on the front page of a corporation's prospectus when securities are offered for sale. It is required by the Securities Commission to indicate that the Commission itself has in no way approved the merits of the securities being offered for sale.

DISCLAIMER OF OPINION auditor's statement, sometimes called an *adverse opinion,* that an ACCOUNTANT'S OPINION cannot be provided because of limitations on the examination or because some condition or situation exists, such as pending litigation, that could impair the financial strength or profitability of the client.

DISCLOSURE release by companies of all information, positive or negative, that might bear on an investment decision, as required by the Securities Commission and the stock exchanges. *See also* FINANCIAL PUBLIC RELATIONS; INSIDE INFORMATION; INSIDER.

DISCONTINUED OPERATIONS operations of a business that have been sold, abandoned, or otherwise disposed of. Accounting regulations require that continuing operations be reported separately in the income statement from discontinued operations, and that any gain or loss from the disposal of a segment (an entity whose activities represent a separate major line of business or class of customer) be reported along with the operating results of the discontinued segment.

DISCOUNT
1. difference between a bond's current market price and its face or redemption value.
2. manner of selling securities such as treasury bills, which are issued at less than face value and are redeemed at face value.
3. relationship between two currencies. The French franc may sell at a discount to the English pound, for example.
4. to apply all available news about a company in evaluating its current stock price. For instance, taking into account the introduction of an exciting new product.
5. method whereby interest on a bank loan or note is deducted in advance.
6. reduction in the selling price of merchandise or a percentage off the invoice price in exchange for quick payment.

DISCOUNT BOND bond selling below its redemption value. *See also* DEEP DISCOUNT BOND.

DISCOUNT BROKER brokerage house that executes orders to buy and sell securities at commission rates sharply lower than those charged by a FULL SERVICE BROKER.

DISCOUNT DIVIDEND REINVESTMENT PLAN *see* DIVIDEND REINVESTMENT PLAN.

DISCOUNTED CASH FLOW value of future expected cash receipts and expenditures at a common date, which is calculated using NET PRESENT VALUE or INTERNAL RATE OF RETURN and is a factor in analyses of both capital investments and securities investments. The net present value (NPV) method applies a rate of discount (interest rate) based on the marginal cost of capital to future cash flows to bring them back to the present. The internal rate of return (IRR) method finds the average return on investment earned through the life of the investment. It determines the discount rate that equates the present value of future cash flows to the cost of the investment. The benefit-cost ratio or profitability index is also used.

DISCOUNTING THE NEWS bidding a firm's stock price up or down in anticipation of good or bad news about the company's prospects.

DISCOUNT POINTS *see* POINT.

DISCOUNT RATE
1. in the United States, interest rate that the Federal Reserve charges member banks for loans, using government securities or ELIGIBLE PAPER as collateral. This provides a floor on interest rates, since banks set their loan rates a notch above the discount rate. The Bank of Canada rate is a trend-setting rate that mirrors the impact of the U.S. discount rate on banks.
2. interest rate used in determining the PRESENT VALUE of future CASH FLOWS. *See also* CAPITALIZATION RATE.

DISCOUNT YIELD yield on a security sold at a discount. To figure the annual yield, divide the discount ($250) by the face amount ($10,000) and multiply that number by the approximate number of days in the year (360) divided by the number of days to maturity (90). The calculation looks like this:

$$\frac{\$250}{\$10,000} \times \frac{360}{90} = .025 \times 4 = .10 = 10\%.$$

DISCRETIONARY ACCOUNT account empowering a broker or adviser to buy and sell without the client's prior knowledge or consent. Some clients set broad guidelines, such as limiting investments to blue chip stocks.

DISCRETIONARY INCOME amount of a consumer's income spent after essentials like food, housing, and utilities and prior commitments have been covered. The total amount of discretionary income can be a key economic indicator because spending this money can spur the economy.

DISCRETIONARY ORDER order to buy a particular stock, bond, or commodity that lets the broker decide when to execute the trade and at what price.

DISCRETIONARY TRUST

1. mutual fund or unit trust whose investments are not limited to a certain kind of security. The management decides on the best way to use the assets.

2. personal trust that lets the trustee decide how much income or principal to provide to the beneficiary. This can be used to prevent the beneficiary from dissipating funds.

DISHONOR to refuse to pay, as in the case of a cheque that is returned by a bank because of insufficient funds.

DISINFLATION slowing down of the rate at which prices increase—usually during a recession, when sales drop and retailers are not always able to pass on higher prices to consumers. Not to be confused with DEFLATION, when prices actually drop.

DISINTERMEDIATION movement of funds from low-yielding accounts at traditional banking institutions to higher-yielding investments in the general market—for example, withdrawal of funds from a passbook savings account paying 5½% to buy a T-bill paying 10%. As a counter move, banks may pay higher rates to depositors, then charge higher rates to borrowers, which leads to tight money and reduced economic activity. Since banking DEREGULATION, disintermediation is not the economic problem it once was.

DISINVESTMENT reduction in capital investment either by disposing of capital goods (such as plant and equipment) or by failing to maintain or replace capital assets that are being used up.

DISPOSABLE PERSONAL INCOME money remaining after payment of personal taxes, and statutory payments, such as Unemployment Insurance and Canada Pension. *See also* DISCRETIONARY INCOME.

DISTRESS SALE sale of property under distress conditions. For example, stock, bond, mutual fund or futures positions may have to be sold in a portfolio if there is a MARGIN CALL. Real estate may have to be sold because a bank is in the process of FORECLOSURE on the property. A brokerage firm may be forced to sell securities from its inventory if it has fallen below various capital requirements imposed by stock exchanges and regulators. Because distress sellers are being forced to sell, they usually do not receive as favourable a price as if they were able to wait for ideal selling conditions.

DISTRIBUTING SYNDICATE group of brokerage firms or investment bankers that join forces in order to facilitate the DISTRIBUTION of a large block of securities. A distribution is usually handled over a period of time to avoid upsetting the market price. The term distributing syndicate can refer to a primary distribution or a secondary distribution, but the former is more commonly called simply a syndicate or an underwriting syndicate.

DISTRIBUTION

Corporate finance: allocation of income and expenses to the appropriate subsidiary accounts.

Economics: (1) movement of goods from manufacturers; (2) way in which wealth is shared in any particular economic system.

Estate law: parceling out of assets to the beneficiaries named in a will, as carried out by the executor under the guidance of a court.

Mutual funds and closed-end investment companies: payout of realized capital gains on securities in the portfolio of the fund or closed-end investment company.

Securities: sale of a large block of stock in such manner that the price is not adversely affected. Technical analysts look on a pattern of distribution as a tipoff that the stock will soon fall in price. The opposite of distribution, known as ACCUMULATION, may signal a rise in price.

DISTRIBUTION AREA price range in which a stock trades for a long time. Sellers who want to avoid pushing the price down will be careful not to sell below this range. ACCUMULATION of shares in the same range helps to account for the stock's price stability. Technical analysts consider distribution areas in predicting when stocks may break up or down from that price range. *See also* ACCUMULATION AREA.

DISTRIBUTION COMPANY company that has the exclusive right to offer shares of one or more investment funds to the public, directly or through other investment fund dealers or brokers. When you buy shares in a fund, you will be dealing with the distribution company, and not the management company.

DISTRIBUTION PERIOD period of time, usually a few days, between the date a company's board of directors declares a stock dividend, known as the DECLARATION DATE, and the DATE OF RECORD, by which the shareholder must officially own shares to be entitled to the dividend.

DISTRIBUTION PLAN plan adopted by a mutual fund to charge certain distribution costs, such as advertising, promotion and sales incentives, to shareholders. The plan will specify a certain percentage, usually .75% or less, which will be deducted from fund assets annually. *See also* 12b-1 MUTUAL FUND.

DISTRIBUTION STOCK stock part of a block sold over a period of time in order to avoid upsetting the market price. May be part of a primary (underwriting) distribution or a secondary distribution following SHELF REGISTRATION.

DISTRIBUTOR wholesaler of goods to dealers that sell to consumers.

DIVERSIFICATION
1. spreading of risk by putting assets in several categories of investments—stocks, bonds, money market instruments, and precious metals, for instance, or several industries, or a mutual fund, with its broad range of stocks in one portfolio.
2. at the corporate level, entering into different business areas, as a CONGLOMERATE does.

DIVESTITURE disposition of an asset or investment by outright sale, employee purchase, liquidation, and so on.

Also, one corporation's orderly distribution of large blocks of another corporation's stock, which were held as an investment.

DIVIDEND distribution of earnings to shareholders, prorated by class of security and paid in the form of money, stock, scrip, or, rarely, company products or property. The amount is decided by the board of directors and is usually paid quarterly. Dividends must be declared as income in the year they are received.

Mutual fund dividends are paid out of income, usually on a quarterly basis from the fund's investments. Dividend income paid out by the fund is subject to the dividend tax credit if the fund is Canadian, offering a 25% advantage to investors. Income is taxed in full if the dividends are foreign. *See also* EQUALIZING DIVIDEND; EXTRA DIVIDEND.

DIVIDEND CAPTURE *See* DIVIDEND ROLLOVER PLAN.

DIVIDEND COVER British equivalent of the dividend PAYOUT RATIO.

DIVIDEND DISCOUNT MODEL mathematical model used to determine the price at which a stock should be selling based on the discounted value of projected future dividend payments. It is used to identify undervalued stocks representing capital gains potential.

DIVIDEND FUND a mutual fund that invests primarily in Canadian preferred and common stocks with high dividend yields. The preferential tax treatment of dividends over interest-bearing investments makes this type of fund highly attractive to some investors.

DIVIDEND IN ARREARS ACCUMULATED DIVIDEND on CUMULATIVE PREFERRED stock, which is payable to the current holder. Preferred stock in a TURNAROUND situation can be an attractive buy when it is selling at a discount and has dividends in arrears.

DIVIDEND INCOME dividends paid on preferred and some common shares owned by the mutual fund or held in a portfolio as the dividend income of the fund or portfolio.

DIVIDEND PAYOUT RATIO percentage of earnings paid to shareholders in cash. In general, the higher the payout ratio, the more mature the company. Electric and telephone utilities tend to have the highest payout ratios, whereas fast-growing companies usually reinvest all earnings and pay no dividends.

DIVIDEND RECORD publication of Standard & Poor's Corporation that provides information on corporate policies and payment histories.

DIVIDEND REINVESTMENT PLAN automatic reinvestment of shareholder dividends in more shares of the company's stock. Some companies absorb most or all of the applicable brokerage fees, and some also discount the stock price. Dividend reinvestment plans allow shareholders to accumulate capital over the long term using DOLLAR COST AVERAGING. For corporations, dividend reinvestment plans are a means of raising capital funds without the FLOTATION COSTS of a NEW ISSUE.

DIVIDEND REQUIREMENT amount of annual earnings necessary to pay contracted dividends on preferred stock.

DIVIDEND ROLLOVER PLAN method of buying and selling stocks around their EX-DIVIDEND dates so as to collect the dividend and make a small profit on the trade. This entails buying shares about two weeks before a stock goes ex-dividend. After the ex-dividend date the price will drop by the amount of the dividend, then work its way back up to the earlier price. By selling slightly above the purchase price, the investor can cover brokerage costs, collect the dividend, and realize a small capital gain in three or four weeks. Also called *dividend capture*. *See also* TRADING DIVIDENDS.

DIVIDENDS PAYABLE dollar amount of dividends that are to be paid, as reported in financial statements. These dividends become an obligation once declared by the board of directors and are listed as liabilities in annual and quarterly reports.

DIVIDENDS-RECEIVED DEDUCTION tax deduction allowed to a corporation owning shares in another corporation for the dividends it receives. In most cases, the deduction is 70%, but in some cases it may be as high as 100% depending on the level of ownership the dividend-receiving company has in the dividend-paying entity.

DIVIDEND YIELD annual percentage of return earned by an investor on a common or preferred stock. The yield is determined by dividing the amount of the dividends per share by the current market price per share of the stock. For example, a stock paying a $1 dividend per year that sells for $10 a share has a 10% dividend yield. The dividend yields of stocks are listed in the stock tables of most daily newspapers.

DOCUMENTARY DRAFT *see* DRAFT.

DOLLAR BEARS traders who think the dollar will fall in value against other foreign currencies. Dollar bears may implement a number of investment strategies to capitalize on a falling dollar, such as buying Japanese yen, Deutsche marks, British pounds or other foreign currencies directly, or buying futures or options contracts on those currencies.

DOLLAR COST AVERAGING *see* CONSTANT DOLLAR PLAN.

DOLLAR DRAIN amount by which a foreign country's imports from Canada exceed its exports to Canada. As the country spends more dollars to finance the imports than it receives in payment for the exports, its dollar reserves drain away.

DOLLAR PRICE bond price expressed as a percentage of face value (normally $1000) rather than as a yield. Thus a bond quoted at 97½ has a dollar price of $975, which is 97½% of $1000.

DOLLAR SWAPS conversion of local currency into another country's currency and investing it in a term deposit for a fixed rate over a specified period of time. A futures contract to reconvert the funds received from this transaction back into local currency is purchased at the same time. Both exchange rates as well as the term deposit rate are known at the time the transaction is set up, so the yield can be calculated based on these rates. A risk in this type of investment is that the foreign country in which funds have been invested might impose foreign currency regulations restricting outflow of funds from the country.

DOLLAR-WEIGHTED RETURN portfolio accounting method that measures changes in total dollar value, treating additions and withdrawals of capital as a part of the RETURN along with income and capital gains and losses. For example, a portfolio (or group of portfolios) worth $100 million at the beginning of a reporting period and $120 million at the end would show a return of 20%; this would be true even if the investments lost money, provided enough new money was infused. While dollar weighting enables investors to compare absolute dollars with financial goals, manager-to-manager comparisons are not possible unless performance is isolated from external cash flows; this is accomplished with the TIME-WEIGHTED RETURN method.

DOMICILE place where a person has established permanent residence. It is important to establish a domicile for the purpose of filing federal and provincial income taxes, and for filing estate taxes upon death. The domicile is created based on obtaining a driver's license, registering to vote, and having a permanent home to which one returns. Usually, one must be a resident in a province for at least 183 days of the year to establish a domicile.

DONATED STOCK fully paid capital stock of a corporation contributed without CONSIDERATION to the same issuing corporation. The gift is credited to the DONATED SURPLUS account at PAR VALUE.

DONATED SURPLUS shareholder's equity account that is credited when contributions of cash, property, or the firm's own stock are freely given to the company. Also termed *donated capital.* Not to be confused with contributed surplus or contributed capital, which is the balances in CAPITAL STOCK accounts plus capital contributed in excess of par or STATED VALUE accounts.

DO NOT INCREASE abbreviated *DNI*. Instruction on good-till-cancelled buy limit and sell stop orders that prevent the quantity from changing in the event of a stock SPLIT or stock dividend.

DO NOT REDUCE (DNR) instruction on a LIMIT ORDER to buy, or on a STOP ORDER to sell, or on a STOP-LIMIT ORDER to sell, not to reduce the order when the stock goes EX-DIVIDEND and its price is reduced by the amount of the dividend as usually happens. DNRs do not apply to rights or stock dividends.

DONOR individual who donates property to another through a TRUST. Also called a *grantor.* Donors also make tax-deductible charitable contributions of securities or physical property to nonprofit institutions such as schools, philanthropic groups, and religious organizations.

DON'T FIGHT THE TAPE don't trade against the market trend. If stocks are falling, as reported on the BROAD TAPE, some analysts say it would be foolish to buy aggressively. Similarly, it would be fighting the tape to sell short during a market rally.

DON'T KNOW Wall Street slang for a *questioned trade.* Brokers exchange comparison sheets to verify the details of transactions between them. Any discrepancy that turns up is called a don't know or a *QT.*

DOT (and SUPER-DOT) SYSTEM acronym for *Designated Order Turnaround,* New York Stock Exchange AUTOMATED ORDER ENTRY SYSTEMS for expediting small and moderate-sized orders. DOT handles market orders and Super DOT limited price orders. The systems bypass floor brokers and rout orders directly to the SPECIALIST, who executes through a CONTRA BROKER or against the SPECIALIST'S BOOK.

DOUBLE AUCTION SYSTEM *see* AUCTION MARKET.

DOUBLE BOTTOM technical chart pattern showing a drop in price, then a rebound, then another drop to the same level. The pattern is usually interpreted to mean the security has much support at that price and should not drop further. However, if the price does fall through that level, it is considered likely to reach a new low. *See also* DOUBLE TOP.

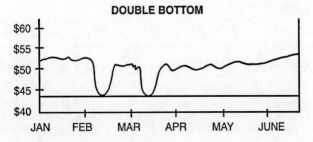

DOUBLE BOTTOM

DOUBLE INDEMNITY INSURANCE insurance that pays double the principal amount if loss occurs due to certain specified causes, e.g., accidental death.

DOUBLE TAXATION taxation of earnings at the corporate level, then again as stockholder dividends.

DOUBLE TOP technical chart pattern showing a rise to a high price, then a drop, then another rise to the same high price. This means the security is encountering resistance to a move higher. However, if the price does move through that level, the security is expected to go on to a new high. *See also* DOUBLE BOTTOM.

DOUBLE TOP

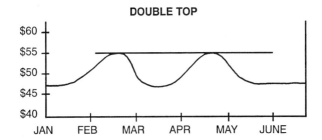

DOUBLE UP sophisticated stock buying (or selling short) strategy that reaffirms the original rationale by doubling the risk when the price goes (temporarily it is hoped) the wrong way. For example, an investor with confidence in XYZ buys 10,000 shares at $40. When the price drops to $35, the investor buys 10,000 additional shares, thus doubling up on a stock he or she feels will ultimately rise.

DOUBLE WITCHING DAY day when two related classes of options and futures expire. For example, index options and index futures on the same underlying index may expire on the same day, leading to various strategies by ARBITRAGEURS to close out positions. *See also* TRIPLE WITCHING HOUR.

DOW JONES AVERAGES *see* STOCK INDEXES AND AVERAGES.

DOW JONES INDUSTRIAL AVERAGE *see* STOCK INDEXES AND AVERAGES.

DOWNSIDE RISK estimate that a security will decline in value and the extent of the decline, taking into account the total range of factors affecting market price.

DOWNSIZING term for a corporate strategy popular in the 1990s whereby a company reduces its size and complexity, thereby presumably increasing its efficiency and profitability. Downsizing is typically accomplished through RESTRUCTURING, which means reducing the number of employees and, often, the SPIN-OFF of activities unrelated to the company's core business.

DOWNSTREAM flow of corporate activity from parent to subsidiary. Financially, it usually refers to loans, since dividends and interest generally flow upstream.

DOWNTICK sale of a security at a price below that of the preceding sale. If a stock has been trading at $15 a share, for instance, the next trade is a downtick if it is at 14⅞. Also known as MINUS TICK.

DOWNTURN shift of an economic or stock market cycle from rising to falling.

DOW THEORY theory that a major trend in the stock market must be confirmed by a similar movement in the Dow Jones Industrial Average and the Dow Jones Transportation Average. According to Dow Theory, a significant trend is not confirmed until both Dow Jones indexes reach the new highs or lows; if they don't, the market will fall back to its former trading range. Dow Theory proponents often disagree on when a true breakout has occurred and, in any case, miss a major portion of the up or down move while waiting for their signals.

DRAFT signed, written order by which one party (drawer) instructs another party (drawee) to pay a specified sum to a third party (payee). Payee and drawer are usually the same person. In transactions payable to companies outside of Canada, a draft is usually called a *bill of exchange*. When prepared without supporting papers, it is a *clean draft*. With papers or documents attached, it is a *documentary draft*. A *sight draft* is payable on demand. *A time draft* is payable either on a definite date or at a fixed time after sight or demand.

DRAFT PROSPECTUS prospectus prepared for internal use and discussion by the company issuing securities and the underwriters. It is not for outside distribution and shows only basic data on the company with little final detail about the terms of the planned underwriting. It is not a legal document and does not have to be drawn up strictly to securities commission standards. It is an earlier version of a preliminary prospectus and cannot be used in offering the security.

DRAWBACK rebate of taxes or duties paid on imported goods that have been re-exported. It is in effect a government subsidy designed to encourage domestic manufacturers to compete overseas.

DRAWEE BANK bank on which an item is drawn and to which it must be presented in order for cash to be collected.

DRAWER *see* DRAFT.

DRESSING UP A PORTFOLIO practice of money managers to make their portfolio look good at the end of a reporting period. For example, a mutual fund or pension fund manager may sell certain stocks that performed badly during the quarter shortly before the end of that quarter to avoid having to report that holding to shareholders. Or they may buy stocks that have risen during the quarter to show shareholders that they owned winning stocks. Because these portfolio changes are largely cosmetic, they have little effect on portfolio performance except they increase transaction costs. In the final few days of a quarter, market analysts frequently comment that certain stocks rose or fell because of end-of-quarter WINDOW DRESSING.

DRILLING PROGRAM *see* BALANCED DRILLING PROGRAM; COMPLETION PROGRAM; DEVELOPMENTAL DRILLING PROGRAM; EXPLORATORY DRILLING PROGRAM; OIL AND GAS LIMITED PARTNERSHIP.

DRIP *see* DIVIDEND REINVESTMENT PLAN.

DRIP FEED supplying capital to a new company as its growth requires it, rather than in a lump sum at the beginning. *See also* EVERGREEN FUNDING.

DROP-DEAD DAY day on which a deadline, such as the expiration of the national debt limit, becomes absolutely final.

DROP-DEAD FEE British term meaning a fee paid to a lender only if a deal requiring financing from that lender falls through.

DUAL LISTING listing of a security on more than one exchange, thus increasing the competition for bid and offer prices as well as the liquidity of the securities.

DUE BILL *see* BILL.

DUE DATE date on which a debt-related obligation is required to be paid.

DUE DILIGENCE MEETING meeting conducted by the underwriter of a new offering at which brokers can ask representatives of the issuer questions about the issuer's background and financial reliability and the intended use of the proceeds. Brokers who recommend investment in new offerings without very careful due diligence work may face lawsuits if the investment should go sour later. Although, in itself, the legally required due diligence meeting typically is a perfunctory affair, most companies, recognizing the importance of due diligence, hold informational meetings, often in different regions of the country, at which top management representatives are available to answer questions of securities analysts and institutional investors.

DUE-ON-SALE CLAUSE clause in a mortgage contract requiring the borrower to pay off the full remaining principal outstanding on a mortgage when the mortgaged property is sold, transferred, or in any way encumbered. Due-on-sale clauses prevent the buyer of the property from assuming the mortgage loan.

DUMPING

International finance: selling goods abroad below cost in order to eliminate a surplus or to gain an edge on foreign competition.

Securities: offering large amounts of stock with little or no concern for price or market effect.

DUN & BRADSTREET (D & B) company that combines credit information obtained directly from commercial firms with data solicited from their creditors, then makes this available to subscribers in reports and a ratings directory. D & B also offers an accounts receivable collection service and publishes financial composite ratios and other financial information. A subsidiary, MOODY'S INVESTOR'S SERVICE, rates bonds and commercial paper.

DUN'S NUMBER short for Dun's Market Identifier. It is published as part of a list of firms giving information such as an identification number, address code, number of employees, corporate affiliations, and trade styles. Full name: Data Universal Numbering System.

DURABLE GOODS items such as automobiles and appliances with a normal life expectancy of 3 years or more.

DURABLE POWER OF ATTORNEY legal document by which a person with assets (the principal) appoints another person (the agent) to act on the principal's behalf, even if the principal becomes incompetent. If the power of attorney is not "durable," the agent's authority to act ends if the principal becomes incompetent. The agent's power to act for the principal may be broadly stated, allowing the agent to buy and sell securities, or narrowly stated to limit activity to selling a car.

DURATION concept first developed by Frederick Macaulay in 1938 that measures bond price VOLATILITY by measuring the "length" of a bond. It is a weighted-average term-to-maturity of the bond's cash flows, the weights being the present value of each cash flow as a percentage of the bond's full price. A Salomon Brothers' study compared it to a series of tin cans equally spaced on a seesaw. The size of each can represents the cash flow due, the contents of each can represent the present values of those cash flows, and the intervals between them represent the payment periods. Duration is the distance to the fulcrum that would balance the seesaw. The duration of a zero-coupon security would thus equal its maturity because all the cash flows—all the weights—are at the other end of the seesaw. The greater the duration of a bond, the greater its percentage volatility. In general, duration rises with maturity, falls with the frequency of coupon payments, and falls as the yield rises (the higher yield reduces the present values of the cash flows.) Duration (the term *modified duration* is used in the strict sense because of modifications to Macaulay's formulation) as a measure of percentage of volatility is valid only for small changes in yield. For working purposes, duration can be defined as the approximate percentage change in price for a 100-basis-point change in yield.

A duration of 5, for example, means the price of the bond will change by approximately 5% for a 100-basis point change in yield.

For larger yield changes, volatility is measured by a concept called *convexity*. That term derives from the price-yield curve for a normal bond, which is convex. In other words, the price is always falling at a slower rate as the yield increases. The more convexity a bond has, the merrier, because it means the bond's price will fall more slowly and rise more quickly on a given movement in general interest rate levels. As with duration, convexity on straight bonds increases with lower coupon, lower yield, and longer maturity. Convexity measures the rate of change of duration, and for an option-free bond it is always positive because changes in yield do not affect cash flows. When a bond has a call option, however, cash flows are affected. In that case, duration gets smaller as yield decreases, resulting in *negative convexity.*

When the durations of the assets and the liabilities of a portfolio, say that of a pension fund, are the same, the portfolio is inherently protected against interest-rate changes and you have what is called *immunization*. The high volatility and interest rates in the early 1980s caused institutional investors to use duration and convexity as tools in immunizing their portfolios.

DUTCH AUCTION auction system in which the price of an item is gradually lowered until it meets a responsive bid and is sold. Contrasting is the two-sided or DOUBLE AUCTION SYSTEM exemplified by the major stock exchanges. *See also* BILL.

DUTY tax imposed on the importation, exportation, or consumption of goods. *See also* TARIFF.

E

EACH WAY commission made by a broker involved on both the purchase and the sale side of a trade. *See also* CROSSED TRADE.

EAFE acronym for the *Europe and Australasia, Far East Equity* index, calculated by the Morgan Stanley Capital International (MSCI) group. EAFE is composed of stocks screened for liquidity, cross-ownership, and industry representation. Stocks are selected by MSCI's analysts in Geneva. The index acts as a benchmark for managers of international stock portfolios. There are financial futures and options contracts based on EAFE.

EARLY WITHDRAWAL PENALTY charge assessed against holders of fixed-term investments if they withdraw their money before maturity. Such a penalty would be assessed, for instance, if someone who has a one-year GIC withdrew the money after four months.

EARNED INCOME income (especially wages and salaries) generated by providing goods or services. Also, pension or annuity income.

EARNED SURPLUS *see* RETAINED EARNINGS.

EARNEST MONEY good faith deposit given by a buyer to a seller prior to consummation of a transaction. Earnest money is usually forfeited in the event the buyer is unwilling or unable to complete the sale. In real estate, earnest money is the down payment, which is usually put in an escrow account until the closing.

EARNING ASSET income-producing asset. For example, a company's building would not be an earning asset normally, but a financial investment in other property would be if it provided rental income.

EARNING CREDIT RATE (ECR) rate used by a bank to determine the earnings allowance for a customer's demand deposit balances. Depending upon the bank, the rate may be arbitrarily set or tied to some market rate.

EARNINGS BEFORE TAXES corporate profits after interest has been paid to bondholders, but before taxes have been paid.

EARNINGS MOMENTUM pattern of increasing rate of growth in EARNINGS PER SHARE from one period to another, which usually causes a stock price to go up. For example, a company whose earnings per share are up 15% one year and 35% the next has earnings momentum and should see a gain in its stock price.

EARNINGS PER FULLY DILUTED SHARE earnings per common share calculated on the assumption that all convertible securities are converted into common shares and all outstanding rights, warrants, options, and contingents issued are exercised.

EARNINGS PER SHARE portion of a company's profit allocated to each outstanding share of common stock. For instance, a corporation that earned $10 million last year and has 10 million shares outstanding would report earnings of $1 per share. The figure is usually calculated after paying taxes and after paying preferred shareholders and bondholders. In smaller, private companies, it is usually calculated pre-tax. *See also* SHARE PROFIT.

EARNINGS-PRICE RATIO relationship of earnings per share to current stock price. Also known as *earnings yield,* it is used in comparing the relative attractiveness of stocks, bonds, and money market instruments. Inverse of PRICE-EARNINGS RATIO.

EARNINGS REPORT statement issued by a company to its shareholders and the public at large reporting its earnings for the latest period, which is either on a quarterly or annual basis. The report will show revenues, expenses, and net profit for the period. Earnings reports are released to the press and reported in newspapers and electronic media, and are also mailed to shareholders of record. Also called *profit and loss statement* (P&L) or *income statement.*

EARNINGS STATEMENT financial statement showing a company's revenues and expenditures and whether it has shown a profit or a loss during a financial period.

EARNINGS SURPRISE EARNINGS REPORT that reports a higher or lower profit than analysts have projected. If earnings are higher than expected, a company's stock price will usually rise sharply. If profits are below expectations, the company's stock will often plunge. Many analysts study earnings surprises very carefully on the theory that when a company reports a positive or negative surprise, it is typically followed by another surprise in the same direction.

EARNINGS YIELD *see* EARNINGS-PRICE RATIO.

EARN-OUT in mergers and acquisitions, supplementary payments, not part of the original ACQUISITION COST, based on future earnings of the acquired company above a predetermined level.

EASY MONEY *see* TIGHT MONEY.

EATING SOMEONE'S LUNCH expression that an aggressive competitor is beating their rivals. For example, an analyst might say that one retailer is "eating the lunch" of a competitive retailer in the same town if it is gaining market share through an aggressive pricing strategy. The implication of the expression is that the winning competitor is taking food away from the losing company or individual.

EATING STOCK a block positioner or underwriter who can't find buyers may find himself eating stock, that is, buying it for his own account.

ECONOMETRICS use of computer analysis and modeling techniques to describe in mathematical terms the relationship between key economic forces such as labour, capital, interest rates, and government policies, then test the effects of changes in economic scenarios. For instance, an econometric model might show the relationship of housing starts and interest rates.

ECONOMIC GROWTH RATE rate of change in the GROSS NATIONAL PRODUCT, as expressed in an annual percentage. If adjusted for inflation, it is called the *real economic growth rate.* Two consecutive quarterly drops in the growth rate mean recession, and two consecutive advances in the growth rate reflect an expanding economy.

ECONOMIC INDICATORS key statistics showing the direction of the economy. Among them are the unemployment rate, inflation rate, factory utilization rate, and balance of trade. *See also* LEADING INDICATORS.

ECONOMICS study of the economy. Classic economics concentrates on how the forces of supply and demand allocate scarce product and service resources. MACROECONOMICS studies a nation or the world's economy as a whole, using data about inflation, unemployment and industrial production to understand the past and predict the future. MICROECONOMICS studies the behavior of specific sectors of the economy, such as companies, industries, or households. Over the years, various schools of economic thought have gained prominence, including KEYNESIAN ECONOMICS, MONETARISM and SUPPLY-SIDE ECONOMICS.

ECONOMIES OF SCALE economic principle that as the volume of production increases, the cost of producing each unit decreases. Therefore, building a large factory will be more efficient than a small factory because the large factory will be able to produce more units at a lower cost per unit than the smaller factory. The introduction of mass production techniques in the early twentieth century, such as the assembly line production of Ford Motor Company's Model T, put the theory of economies of scale into action.

ECU *see* EUROPEAN CURRENCY UNIT (ECU).

EDUCATIONAL SAVINGS PLAN plan that provides funds for the postsecondary education of an insured person's children. Maximum contributions are $1500 per year, with a total per child of $31,500. For tax purposes, income must be declared by the child on withdrawal for tuition.

EEC *see* EUROPEAN ECONOMIC COMMUNITY.

EFFECTIVE DATE
In general: date on which an agreement takes effect.
Securities: date when an offering registered with the Securities Commission may commence.
Banking and insurance: time when an insurance policy goes into effect. From that day forward, the insured party is covered by the contract.

EFFECTIVE DEBT total debt owed by a firm, including the capitalized value of lease payments.

EFFECTIVE NET WORTH net worth plus subordinated debt, as viewed by senior creditors. In small business banking, loans payable to principals are commonly subordinated to bank loans. The loans for principals thus can be regarded as effective net worth as long as a bank loan is outstanding and the subordination agreement is in effect.

EFFECTIVE RATE yield on a debt instrument as calculated from the purchase price. The effective rate on a bond is determined by the price, the coupon rate, the time between interest payments, and the time until maturity. Every bond's effective rate thus depends on when it was bought. The effective rate is a more meaningful yield figure than the coupon rate. *See also* RATE OF RETURN.

EFFECTIVE TAX RATE tax rate paid by a taxpayer. It is determined by dividing the tax paid by the taxable income in a particular year. For example, if a taxpayer with a taxable income of $100,000 owes $30,000 in a year, he or she has an effective tax rate of 30%. The effective tax rate is useful in tax planning, because it gives a taxpayer a realistic understanding of the amount of taxes he or she is paying after allowing for all deductions, credits, and other factors affecting tax liability.

EFFECTIVE YIELD yield that results when the number quoted is the potential earning power of the fund on the date it was calculated. It can refer to interest and also to the total yield, including capital gain.

EFFICIENT MARKET theory that market prices reflect the knowledge and expectations of all investors. Those who adhere to this theory consider it futile to seek undervalued stocks or to forecast market movements. Any new development is reflected in a firm's stock price, they say, making it impossible to beat the market. This vociferously disputed hypothesis also holds that an investor who throws darts at a newspaper's stock listings has as good a chance to outperform the market as any professional investor.

EFFICIENT PORTFOLIO portfolio that has a maximum expected return for any level of risk or a minimum level of risk for any expected return. It is arrived at mathematically, taking into account the expected return and standard deviation of returns for each security, as well as the covariance of returns between different securities in the portfolio.

EITHER-OR ORDER *see* ALTERNATIVE ORDER.

ELASTICITY OF DEMAND AND SUPPLY
Elasticity of demand: responsiveness of buyers to changes in price. Demand for luxury items may slow dramatically if prices are raised, because these purchases are not essential, and can be postponed. On the other hand, demand for necessities such as food, telephone service, and emergency surgery is said to be inelastic. It remains about the same despite price changes because buyers cannot postpone their purchases without severe adverse consequences.

Elasticity of supply: responsiveness of output to changes in price. As prices move up, the supply normally increases. If it does not, it is said to be inelastic. Supply is said to be elastic if the rise in price means a rise in production.

ELECT
In general: choose a course of action. Someone who decides to incorporate a certain provision in a will elects to do so.
Securities trading: make a conditional order into a market order. If a customer has received a guaranteed buy or sell price from a specialist on the floor of an exchange, the transaction is considered elected when that price is reached. If the guarantee is that a stock will be sold when it reaches 20, and a stop order is put at that price, the sale will be elected at 20.

ELECTRONIC FUNDS TRANSFER SYSTEM system that uses electronic equipment to consolidate information currently recorded on paper, thus reducing the amount of paper handled by banks and the amount of time taken to handle transactions.

ELEPHANTS expression describing large institutional investors. The term implies that such investors, including mutual funds, pension funds, banks, and insurance companies, tend to move their billions of dollars in assets in a herd-like manner, driving stock and bond prices up and down in concert. CONTRARIAN investors specialize in doing the opposite of the elephants—buying when institutions are selling and selling when the elephants are buying. The opposite of elephants are SMALL INVESTORS, who buy and sell far smaller quantities of stocks and bonds.

ELIGIBILITY REQUIREMENTS
Insurance: requirements by an insurance company to qualify for coverage. For example, a life insurance company may require that because of a person's health condition, a potential policyholder would need to pay a higher premium to obtain coverage. In this circumstance, the policyholder's ability to pay becomes a primary issue.

For employer group health insurance coverage, an employer may require a person be a full-time employee for coverage of the employee and the employee's dependents.
Pensions: conditions an employee must satisfy to become a participant in a pension plan, such as completing one year of service and reaching the age of 21.

ELVES ten technical analysts who predict the direction of stock prices over the next six months on the "Wall Street Week" television show on the Public Broadcasting System. If five or more analysts are bullish or bearish at one time, the Wall Street Week Elves Index is giving a signal to buy or sell.

EMANCIPATION freedom to assume certain legal responsibilities normally associated only with adults, said of a minor who is granted this freedom by a court. If both parents die in an accident, for instance, the

18-year-old eldest son or daughter may be emancipated by a judge to act as guardian for his younger brothers and sisters.

EMBARGO government prohibition against the shipment of certain goods to another country. An embargo is most common during wartime, but is sometimes applied for economic reasons as well. For instance, the Organization of Petroleum Exporting Countries placed an embargo on the shipment of oil to the West in the early 1970s to protest Israeli policies and to raise the price of petroleum.

EMERGENCY FUND cash reserve that is available to meet financial emergencies, such as large medical bills or unexpected auto or home repairs. Most financial planners advocate maintaining an emergency reserve of two to three months' salary in a liquid interest-bearing account such as a money market mutual fund or bank money market deposit account.

EMERGING COMPANY MARKETPLACE (ECM) discontinued service of the AMERICAN STOCK EXCHANGE that focused on the needs of small, growth companies meeting special listing requirements. ECM provided matching of public orders, short sale protection, specialist oversight and support, and offered other services and programs designed to promote corporate visibility (through separate listings in newspaper stock tables, for example).

EMERGING MARKETS FREE (EMF) INDEX index developed by Morgan Stanley Capital International to follow stock markets in Mexico, Malaysia, Chile, Jordan, Thailand, the Philippines, and Argentina, countries selected because of their accessibility to foreign investors.

EMINENT DOMAIN right of a government entity to seize private property for the purpose of constructing a public facility. Federal, provincial, and municipal governments can seize people's homes under eminent domain laws as long as the homeowner is compensated at fair market value. Some public projects that may necessitate such CONDEMNATION include airports, highways, hospitals, schools, parks, or government office buildings.

EMPLOYEE RETIREMENT INCOME SECURITY ACT (ERISA) 1974 law governing the operation of most private pension and benefit plans, The law eased pension eligibility rules, set up the PENSION BENEFIT GUARANTY CORPORATION, and established guidelines for the management of pension funds.

EMPLOYEE STOCK OWNERSHIP PLAN (ESOP) program encouraging employees to purchase stock in their company. Employees may participate in the management of the company and even take control to rescue the company or a particular plant that would otherwise go out of business. Employees may offer wage and work rule concessions in return for ownership privileges in an attempt to keep a marginal facility operating.

EMPLOYMENT situation in which everyone who is willing and able to work has a job, whether full or part time, and including family workers contributing directly in the operation of a farm, business, or professional practice owned or operated by a related member of the same household.

ENCUMBERED owned by one party but subject to another party's valid claim. A homeowner owns his or her mortgaged property, for example, but the bank has a security interest in it as long as the mortgage loan is outstanding.

ENDORSE transfer ownership of an asset by signing the back of a negotiable instrument. One can endorse a cheque to receive payment or endorse a stock or bond certificate to transfer ownership.
See also QUALIFIED ENDORSEMENT.

ENDOWMENT permanent gift of money or property to a specified institution for a specified purpose. Endowments may finance physical assets or be invested to provide ongoing income to finance operations.

ENDOWMENT INSURANCE insurance that pays the face amount of the policy on a specified future date, called the maturity date. If the policyowner dies before the maturity date, the face amount is paid to the beneficiary. Premiums are equal and cash values accumulate.

ENERGY MUTUAL FUND mutual fund that invests solely in energy stocks such as oil, oil service, gas, solar energy, and coal companies and makers of energy-saving devices.

ENTERPRISE a business firm. The term often is applied to a newly formed venture.

ENTREPRENEUR person who takes on the risks of starting a new business. Many entrepreneurs have technical knowledge with which to produce a saleable product or to design a needed new service. Often, VENTURE CAPITAL is used to finance the startup in return for a piece of the equity. Once an entrepreneur's business is established, shares may be sold to the public as an INITIAL PUBLIC OFFERING, assuming favorable market conditions.

ENVIRONMENTAL FUND MUTUAL FUND specializing in stocks of companies having a role in the bettering of the environment. Not to be confused with a SOCIAL CONSCIOUSNESS MUTUAL FUND, which aims in part to satisfy social values, an environmental fund is designed to capitalize on financial opportunities related to the environmental movement.

EOM DATING arrangement—common in the wholesale drug industry, for example—whereby all purchases made through the 25th of one month are payable within 30 days of the end of the following month; EOM means *end of month*. Assuming no prompt payment discount, purchases through the 25th of April, for example, will be payable by the end of June. If a discount exists for payment in ten days, payment would have to be made by June 10th to take advantage of it. End of month dating with a 2% discount for prompt payment (10 days) would be expressed in the trade either as: *2%-10 days, EOM, 30,* or *2/10 prox. net 30,* where prox., or proximo, means "the next."

EPS *see* EARNINGS PER SHARE.

EQUALIZING DIVIDEND special dividend paid to compensate investors for income lost because a change was made in the quarterly dividend payment schedule.

EQUILIBRIUM PRICE
1. price when the supply of goods in a particular market matches demand.
2. for a manufacturer, the price that maximizes a product's profitability.

EQUILIBRIUM PRICE

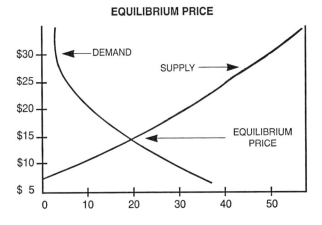

EQUIPMENT LEASING PARTNERSHIP limited partnership that buys equipment such as computers, railroad cars, and airplanes, then leases it to businesses. Limited partners receive income from the lease payments as well as tax benefits such as depreciation. Whether a partnership of this kind works out well depends on the GENERAL PARTNER'S expertise. In the past, there have been boat/yacht and aircraft leases in Canada. Most have been disallowed.

EQUIPMENT TRUST CERTIFICATE bond, more common in the United States than in Canada, usually issued by a transportation company such as a railroad or shipping line, used to pay for new equipment. The certificate gives the bondholder the first right to the equipment in the event that interest and principal are not paid when due. Title to the equipment is held in the name of the trustee, usually a bank, until the bond is paid off.

EQUITABLE OWNER beneficiary of property held in trust.

EQUITY

In general: fairness. Law courts, for example, try to be equitable in their judgments when splitting up estates or settling divorce cases.

Banking: difference between the amount a property could be sold for and the claims held against it.

Brokerage account: excess of securities over debit balance in a margin account. For instance, equity would be $28,000 in a margin account with stocks and bonds worth $50,000 and a debit balance of $22,000.

Investments: ownership interest possessed by shareholders in a corporation—stock as opposed to bonds. Investors in equity funds benefit from both capital gains and dividend income.

Personal finance: payment of principal of a debt, in order to build ownership value in the item. To arrive at the equity value, take the amount of principal and subtract any debts against the property.

EQUITY EARNINGS share owed to a company of an unconsolidated subsidiary's earnings. The equity accounting method is used when a company owns 20% to 50% of a subsidiary.

EQUITY FINANCING raising money by issuing shares of common or preferred stock. Usually done when prices are high and the most capital can be raised for the smallest number of shares.

EQUITY FUNDING type of investment combining a life insurance policy and a mutual fund. The fund shares are used as collateral for a loan to pay the insurance premiums, giving the investor the advantages of insurance protection and investment appreciation potential.

EQUITY KICKER offer of an ownership position in a deal that involves loans. For instance, a mortgage real estate limited partnership that lends to real estate developers might receive as an equity kicker a small ownership position in a building that can appreciate over time. When the building is sold, limited partners receive the appreciation payout. In return for that equity kicker, the lender is likely to charge a lower interest rate on the loan. Convertible features and warrants are offered as equity kickers to make securities attractive to investors.

EQUITY REIT REAL ESTATE INVESTMENT TRUST that takes an ownership position in the real estate it invests in. Stockholders in equity REITs earn dividends on rental income from the buildings and earn appreciation if properties are sold for a profit. .

EQUIVALENT BOND YIELD comparison of discount yields and yields on bonds with coupons. Also called *coupon-equivalent rate*.

ERM acronym for *exchange rate mechanism,* by which participating member countries agree to maintain the value of their own currencies through intervention.

ESCALATOR CLAUSE provision in a contract allowing cost increases to be passed on. In an employment contract, an escalator clause might call for wage increases to keep employee earnings in line with inflation. In a lease, an escalator clause could obligate the tenant to pay for increases in fuel or other costs.

ESCROW money, securities, or other property or instruments held by a third party until the conditions of a contract are met.

ESCROWED SHARES outstanding shares of a company that, while entitled to vote and receive dividends, may not be bought or sold unless special approval is obtained. This technique is commonly used by mining and oil companies when treasury shares are issued for new properties. Shares can be released from escrow (i.e., freed to be bought and sold) only with the permission of applicable authorities such as a stock exchange and/or securities commission.

ESTATE all the assets a person possesses at the time of death—such as securities, real estate, interests in business, physical possessions, and cash. The estate is distributed to heirs according to the dictates of the person's will or, if there is no will, a court ruling.

ESTATE PLANNING planning for the orderly handling, disposition, and administration of an estate when the owner dies. Estate planning includes drawing up a will, setting up trusts, and minimizing estate taxes, perhaps by passing property to heirs before death or by setting up an INTER VIVUS TRUST or a TESTAMENTARY TRUST.

ESTATE TAX the deemed disposition on death tax payable on capital gains on the estate at the deceased's capital gains rate. In the United States, it is a tax imposed by a state or the federal government on assets left to heirs in a will.

ETHICAL FUND funds whose investment decisions are guided by moral criteria that vary from fund to fund. One ethical fund may avoid investing in companies that profit from tobacco or armaments, whereas other funds may avoid companies that pollute the environment. *See also* SOCIAL CONSCIOUSNESS MUTUAL FUND.

EUROBOND bond denominated in Canadian dollars or other currencies and sold to investors outside the country whose currency is used. The bonds are usually issued by large underwriting groups composed of banks and issuing houses from many countries. An example of a Eurobond transaction might be a dollar-denominated debenture issued by Bell Canada through an underwriting group comprising the overseas affiliate of a New York investment banking house, a bank in Holland, and a consortium of British merchant banks; a portion of the issue is sold to French investors through Swiss investment accounts.

The Eurobond market is an important source of capital for multinational companies and foreign governments, including Third World governments.

EUROCURRENCY money deposited by corporations and national governments in banks away from their home countries, called *Eurobanks*. The terms Eurocurrency and Eurobanks do not necessarily mean the currencies or the banks are European, though more often than not, that is the case. For instance, dollars deposited in a British bank or Italian lire deposited in a Japanese bank are considered to be Eurocurrency. The Eurodollar is only one of the Eurocurrencies, though it is the most prevalent. Also known as *Euromoney*.

EURODOLLAR U.S. currency held in banks outside the United States, mainly in Europe, and commonly used for settling international transactions. Some securities are issued in Eurodollars—that is, with a promise to pay interest in dollars deposited in foreign bank accounts.

EURODOLLAR BOND bond that pays interest and principal in Eurodollars, U.S. dollars held in banks outside the United States, primarily in Europe. Such a bond is not registered with the Securities and Exchange Commission, and because there are fewer regulatory delays and costs in the Euromarket, Eurodollar bonds generally can be sold at lower than U.S. interest rates. *See also* EUROBOND.

EUROPEAN COMMUNITY (EC) with ratification of the Maastricht Treaty on European Union in November 1993, the former name of European Economic Community was dropped. The EC is part of the EUROPEAN UNION. The EC is an economic and, increasingly, political alliance formed in 1957 by Germany, France, Belgium, Luxembourg, the Netherlands and Italy to foster trade and cooperation among its members and "an ever closer union among the peoples of Europe." Membership was subsequently extended to the UK, Ireland and Denmark (1973); Greece (1981); and Spain and Portugal (1986). Austria, Finland, and Sweden became members in 1995. Norway rejected membership in November 1994. Tariff barriers between the member states have been abolished, and import duties vis-a-vis non-EC countries have been standardized. Many former European dependencies in African, Caribbean, and Pacific countries have preferential trade terms with the EC through the Rome Convention. EC headquarters is in Brussels, administered by the European Commission, the executive arm of the European Union. By December 1992, most remaining non-tariff trade barriers between the member states had been eliminated, and common standards in many industries had been adopted. Also known as the *European Union,* of which it is a part and, anachronistically, the *Common Market.*

EUROPEAN CURRENCY UNIT (ECU) one of two international currency substitutes ("artificial currencies"), the other being the SPECIAL DRAWING RIGHTS (SDRs) of the INTERNATIONAL MONETARY FUND (IMF).

Like the SDR, the ECU is a currency basket comprising a predetermined amount of a number of different currencies. Whereas SDRs represent five currencies, ECUs include all the EUROPEAN ECONOMIC COMMUNITY (EEC) currencies except the Spanish peseta and the Portuguese escudo. Currency substitutes are less volatile than the currencies making them up and are expected to be used increasingly for commercial purposes as the European Community develops.

EUROPEAN OPTIONS EXCHANGE (EOE) the Dutch derivatives exchange, trading equity, index, bond, currency, and metal options. Futures and options are traded on its EOE Index, as well as the Eurotop 100 Index, the Dutch Top 5 Index and the U.S. dollar. Futures are traded on the notional bond. Options are traded on the OMX Index, XMI LEAPS, MMI Index (listed on the AMERICAN STOCK EXCHANGE), Jumbo dollar, gold and Guilder bond.

EUROPEAN-STYLE EXERCISE system of exercising options contracts in which the option buyer can exercise the contract only on the last business day prior to expiration (normally Friday). This system is widely used with index options traded on various U.S. exchanges.

EUROPEAN UNION (EU) umbrella term referring to a "three-pillar" construction comprising the EUROPEAN COMMUNITY (EC) and two new pillars: Common Foreign and Security Policy (including defense) and Justice and Home Affairs (notably cooperation between police and other authorities on crime, terrorism, and immigration issues). The EU is governed by a five-part institutional system, including the European Commission, the EU Council of Ministers, the European Parliament and the European Court of Justice, and the Court of Auditors, which monitors EU budget spending. Under the Maastricht Treaty on European Union of Nov. 1, 1993, the directly elected Parliament gained co-decision powers with the Council and Commission.

EUROYEN BOND EUROCURRENCY deposits in Japanese yen.

EVALUATOR independent expert who appraises the value of property for which there is limited trading—antiques in an estate, perhaps, or rarely traded stocks or bonds. The fee for this service is sometimes a flat amount, sometimes a percentage of the appraised value.

EVENT RISK risk that a bond will suddenly decline in credit quality and warrant a lower RATING because of a TAKEOVER-related development, such as additional debt or a RECAPITALIZATION.

EVERGREEN FUNDING similar to DRIP FEED, British term for the gradual infusion of capital into a new or recapitalized enterprise. In Canada and the United States, the term *evergreen* is used to describe short-term loans that are continuously renewed rather than repaid.

EXACT INTEREST interest paid by a bank or other financial institution and calculated on a 365-days-per-year basis, as opposed to a

360-day basis, called ordinary interest. The difference—the ratio is 1.0139—can be material when calculating daily interest on large sums of money.

EX-ALL sale of a security without dividends, rights, warrants, or any other privileges associated with that security.

EXCESS MARGIN equity in a brokerage firm's customer account, expressed in dollars, above the legal minimum for a margin account or the maintenance requirement. For instance, with a margin requirement of $25,000, as set by REGULATION T and a maintenance requirement of $12,500 set by the stock exchange, the client whose equity is $100,000 would have excess margin of $75,000 and $87,500 in terms of the initial and maintenance requirements, respectively.

EXCHANGE
Barter: to trade goods and services with another individual or company for other goods and services of equal value.
Corporate finance: offer by a corporation to exchange one security for another. For example, a company may want holders of its convertible bonds to exchange their holdings for common stock. Or a company in financial distress may want its bondholders to exchange their bonds for stock in order to reduce or eliminate its debt load. *See also* SWAP.
Currency: trading of one currency for another. Also known as *foreign exchange.*
Mutual funds: process of switching from one mutual fund to another, either within one fund family or between fund families, if executed through a brokerage firm offering funds from several companies. In many cases, fund companies will not charge an additional LOAD if the assets are kept within the same family. If one fund is sold to buy another, a taxable event has occurred, meaning that capital gains or losses have been realized.
Trading: central location where securities or futures trading takes place.

EXCHANGEABLE DEBENTURE like CONVERTIBLES, with the exception that this type of debenture can be converted to the common stock of a SUBSIDIARY or AFFILIATE of the issuer.

EXCHANGE CONTROLS government regulation of foreign exchange (currency trading).

EXCHANGE DISTRIBUTION block trade carried out on the floor of an exchange between customers of a member firm. Someone who wants to sell a large block of stock in a single transaction can get a broker to solicit and bunch a large number of orders. The seller transmits the securities to the buyers all at once, and the trade is announced on the BROAD TAPE as an exchange distribution. The seller, not the buyers, pays a special commission to the broker who executes the trade.

EXCHANGE FUND ACCOUNT federal government account operated by the Bank of Canada to hold funds and conduct transactions in Canada's foreign exchange reserves on instructions from the Minister of Finance.

EXCHANGE MEMBERS *see* MEMBER FIRM; SEAT.

EXCHANGE PRIVILEGE right of a shareholder to switch from one mutual fund to another within one fund family—often, at no additional charge. This enables investors to put their money in an aggressive growth-stock fund when they expect the market to turn up strongly, then switch to a money-market fund when they anticipate a downturn. Some discount brokers allow shareholders to switch between fund families in pursuit of the best performance.

EXCHANGE RATE price at which one country's currency can be converted into another's. The exchange rate between the Canadian dollar and the British pound is different from the rate between the dollar and the West German mark, for example. A wide range of factors influences exchange rates, which generally change slightly each trading day. Some rates are fixed by agreement; *see* FIXED EXCHANGE RATE.

EXCHANGE TRADE OPTION trading of listed equity options that commenced on several recognized North American stock exchanges in the 1970s. In the ensuing period, exchange-traded options have grown in popularity, providing investors with greater liquidity.

EXCLUSION
Contracts: item not covered by a contract. For example, an insurance policy may list certain hazards, such as acts of war, that are excluded from coverage.
Taxes: on a tax return, items that must be reported, but not taxed. For example, corporations are allowed to exclude 70% of dividends received from other domestic corporations. Gift tax rules allow DONORS to exclude up to $10,000 worth of gifts to donees annually.

EXCLUSIVE LISTING written listing agreement giving an agent the right to sell a specific property for a period of time with a definite termination date, frequently three months. There are two types of exclusive listings. With the exclusive agency, the owner reserves the right to sell the property himself or herself without owing a commission; the exclusive agent is entitled to a commission if he or she personally sells the property, or if it is sold by anyone other than the seller. Under the exclusive right to sell, a broker is appointed as exclusive agent, entitled to a commission if the property is sold by the owner, the broker, or anyone else. "Right to sell" means the right to find a buyer. Sellers opt for exclusive listings because they think an agent will give their property more attention. An agent with an exclusive listing will not have to share the commission with any other agent as he or she would under a multiple-listing arrangement. If the property is not sold within the specified time, the seller may expand the selling group through an open, multiple listing.

EX-DIVIDEND interval between the announcement and the payment of the next dividend. An investor who buys shares during that interval is not entitled to the dividend. Typically, a stock's price moves up by the dollar amount of the dividend as the ex-dividend date approaches, then falls by the amount of the dividend after that date. A stock that has gone ex-dividend is marked with an *x* in newspaper listings.

EX-DIVIDEND DATE date on which a stock goes EX-DIVIDEND, typically the fourth business day before the dividend is paid to shareholders of record. Option contracts are usually adjusted for stock dividends but not for cash.

EXECUTION
Law: the signing, sealing, and delivering of a contract or agreement making it valid.
Securities: carrying out a trade. A broker who buys or sells shares is said to have executed an order.

EXECUTOR/EXECUTRIX administrator of the estate who gathers the estate assets; files the estate tax returns and final personal income tax returns, and administers the estate; pays the debts of and charges against the estate; and distributes the balance in accordance with the terms of the will. The executor's responsibility is relatively short term, one to three years, ending when estate administration is completed. An executor (executrix if a female) may be a bank trust officer, a lawyer, or a family member or trusted friend. Also commonly referred to as *personal representative*.

EXEMPTION DNR-allowed direct reductions from gross income. Personal and dependency exemptions are allowed for: individual taxpayers; elderly and disabled taxpayers; dependent children and other dependents and a taxpayer's spouse.

EXEMPT LIFE INSURANCE life insurance that passes a test in the Income Tax Act so that it is not subject to tax while the policy remains in force (Regulation 306). Such policies include those with deliberate premium overcharges and/or no payment until demise.

EXEMPT LIST large professional buyers of securities, mostly financial institutions, that are offered a portion of a new issue by one member of the banking group on behalf of the whole syndicate. They are exempt from normal market restrictions and disclosure such as those required when selling to the public.

EXEMPT MARKET unregulated market for sophisticated participants in government bonds, corporate issues, and commercial paper. A prospectus has not been required to raise money privately from private investors (largely institutions, but also wealthy individuals), and registration with a securities commission for those so dealing has not been needed.

EXEMPT PURCHASER category of institutional investors for whom it is not necessary for the issuer to file a prospectus with the applicable securities commission on the sale of a new issue of securities.

EXERCISE make use of a right available in a contract. In options trading a buyer of a call contract may exercise the right to buy underlying shares at a particular price by informing the option seller. A put buyer's right is exercised when the underlying shares are sold at the agreed-upon price.

EXERCISE LIMIT limit on the number of option contracts of any one class that can be exercised in a span of five business days. For options on stocks, the exercise limit is usually 2000 contracts.

EXERCISE NOTICE notification by a broker that a client wants to exercise a right to buy the underlying stock in an option contract.

EXERCISE PRICE price at which the stock or commodity underlying a call or put option can be purchased (call) or sold (put) over the specified period. For instance, a call contract may allow the buyer to purchase 100 shares of XYZ at any time in the next three months at an exercise or STRIKE PRICE of $63.

EXERCISING A CALL exercise of the right by the owner of a call contract to purchase stock at the lower strike price if its market price has risen above the strike price on the expiration date. If the stock is then sold on the market, it will realize a profit from the difference between the strike price and the market price paid for the calls.

EXERCISING AN OPTION making use of a right available in a contract with respect to an option. The exercise of an equity (stock or bond) option calls for delivery of the underlying security within 3 business days following the tender of an exercise notice, whereas the index options settlement is made in cash on the next business day.

EXERCISING A PUT exercise of the right of the put owner to sell the underlying security at the exercise price.

EXHAUST PRICE price at which broker must liquidate a client's holding in a stock that was bought on margin and has declined, but has not had additional funds put up to meet the MARGIN CALL.

EXIT FEE *see* BACK-END LOAD.

EXPECTED RETURN *see* MEAN RETURN.

EXPENSE RATIO amount, expressed as a percentage of total investment, that shareholders pay annually for mutual fund operating expenses and management fees. These expenses include shareholder service, salaries for money managers and administrative staff, and investor centres, among many others. The expense ratio, which may be as low as 0.2% or as high as 2% of shareholder assets, is taken out of the fund's current income and is disclosed in the prospectus to shareholders.

EXPERIENCE RATING insurance company technique to determine the correct price of a policy premium. The company analyzes past loss experience for others in the insured group to project future claims. The premium is then set at a rate high enough to cover those potential claims and still earn a profit for the insurance company. For example, life insurance companies charge higher premiums to smokers than to non-smokers because smokers' experience rating is higher, meaning their chance of dying is much higher.

EXPIRATION
Banking: date on which a contract or agreement ceases to be effective.
Options trading: last day on which an option can be exercised. If it is not, traders say that the option *expired worthless.*

EXPIRATION CYCLE cycle of expiration dates used in short-term options trading. For example, contracts may be written for one of three cycles: January, April, July, October; February, May, August, November; March, June, September, December. Since options are traded in three-, six-, and nine-month contracts, only three of the four months in the set are traded at once. In our example, when the January contract expires, trading begins on the October contract. Commodities futures expiration cycles follow other schedules.

EXPIRATION DATE in the bond market, the Saturday following the third Friday of each expiration month. The expiration date is the last day on which the option holder may exercise his or her option.

EXPIRATION MONTH month during which bond options expire. Such options are introduced with terms of 3, 6, and 9 months, expiring in the months of March, June, September, and December.

EX-PIT TRANSACTION purchase of commodities off the floor of the exchange where they are regularly traded and at specified terms.

EXPLORATORY DRILLING PROGRAM search for an undiscovered reservoir of oil or gas—a very risky undertaking. Exploratory wells are called *wildcat* (in an unproven area); *controlled wildcat* (in an area outside the proven limits of an existing field); or *deep test* (within a proven field but to unproven depths). Exploratory drilling programs are usually syndicated, and units are sold to limited partners.

EX-RIGHTS without the RIGHT to buy a company's stock at a discount from the prevailing market price, which was distributed until a particular date. Typically, after that date the rights trade separately from the stock itself. *See also* EX-WARRANTS; EX-DIVIDEND.

EX-RIGHTS DATE date after which the buyer of a common stock or convertible bond is not entitled to a previously declared rights offering.

EX-STOCK DIVIDENDS interval between the announcement and payment of a stock dividend. An investor who buys shares during that interval is not entitled to the announced stock dividend; instead, it goes to the seller of the shares, who was the owner on the last recorded date before the books were closed and the stock went EX-DIVIDEND. Stocks cease to be ex-dividend after the payment date.

EXTENDED COVERAGE insurance protection that is extended beyond the original term of the contract. For example, consumers can buy extended warranties when they purchase cars or appliances, which will cover repairs beyond the original warranty period.

EXTENDED HEALTH CARE INSURANCE insurance that covers medical expenses such as prescription drugs, ambulance services, and physiotherapy. Extended care is care beyond that offered by government plans and for a longer period.

EXTENDIBLE BOND bond or debenture with terms granting the holder the option to extend the maturity date by a specified number of years.

EXTENDIBLE DEBENTURE *see* EXTENDIBLE BOND.

EXTENSION OF TIME FOR FILING TAXES time period beyond the original tax filing date. A Canadian resident in the United States for 183 days or a retiree in the United States receiving CPP and OAS can apply for an extension of time to file.

EXTERNAL FUNDS funds brought in from outside the corporation, perhaps in the form of a bank loan, or the proceeds from a bond offering, or an infusion of cash from venture capitalists. External funds supplement internally generated CASH FLOW and are used for expansion, as well as for seasonal WORKING CAPITAL needs.

EXTRA *see* EXTRA DIVIDEND.

EXTRA DIVIDEND dividend paid to shareholders in addition to the regular dividend. Such a payment is made after a particularly profitable year in order to reward shareholders and engender loyalty.

EXTRAORDINARY CALL early redemption of a revenue bond by the issuer due to elimination of the source of revenue to pay the stipulated interest. For example, a mortgage revenue municipal bond may be subject to an extraordinary call if the issuer is unable to originate mortgages to homeowners because mortgage rates have dropped sharply, making the issuer's normally below-market mortgage interest rate suddenly higher than market rates. In this case, the bond issuer is required to return the money raised from the bond issue to bondholders because the issuer will not be able to realize the expected interest payments from mortgages. Extraordinary calls may also be necessary if another revenue-producing project such as a road or bridge is not able to be built for some reason. Calls are usually made at PAR. Also called a *special call*.

EXTRAORDINARY ITEM nonrecurring occurrence that must be explained to shareholders in an annual or quarterly report. Such occurrences are not typical of the normal business activities of the company; do not happen on a regular basis over a number of years; and are not regarded as a recurring factor in the ordinary operations of the company. Some examples: writeoff of a division, acquisition of another company, sale of a large amount of real estate, or uncovering of employee fraud that negatively affects the company's financial condition. Earnings are usually reported before and after taking into account the effects of extraordinary items.

EX-WARRANTS stock sold with the buyer no longer entitled to the WARRANT attached to the stock. Warrants allow the holder to buy stock at some future date at a specified price. Someone buying a stock on June 3 that had gone ex-warrants on June 1 would not receive those warrants. They would be the property of the stockholder of record on June 1.

F

FACE VALUE value of a bond, note, mortgage, or other security as given on the certificate or instrument. Corporate bonds are usually issued with $1000 face values, municipal bonds with $5000 face values, and federal government bonds with $10,000 face values. Although the bonds fluctuate in price from the time they are issued until redemption, they are redeemed at maturity at their face value, unless the issuer defaults. If the bonds are retired before maturity, bondholders normally receive a slight premium over face value. The face value is the amount on which interest payments are calculated; it is no indication of market value. Thus, a 10% bond with a face value of $1000 pays bondholders $100 per year. Face value is also referred to as PAR VALUE or *nominal value.*

FACILITY INSURANCE vehicle insurance that may be obtained by a driver with a bad driving record when no regular insurer is willing to carry the policy.

FACTORING type of financial service whereby a firm sells or transfers title to its accounts receivable to a factoring company, which then acts as principal, not as agent. The receivables are sold without recourse, meaning that the factor cannot turn to the seller in the event accounts prove uncollectible. Factoring can be done either on a *notification basis,* where the seller's customers remit directly to the factor, or on a *non-notification basis,* where the seller handles the collections and remits to the factor. There are two basic types of factoring:

1. **Discount factoring** arrangement whereby seller receives funds from the factor prior to the average maturity date, based on the invoice amount of the receivable, less cash discounts, less an allowance for estimated claims, returns, etc. Here the factor is compensated by an interest rate based on daily balances and typically 2% to 3% above the bank prime rate.

2. **Maturity factoring** arrangement whereby the factor, who performs the entire credit and collection function, remits to the seller for the receivables sold each month on the average due date of the factored receivables. The factor's commission on this kind of arrangement ranges from 0.75% to 2%, depending on the bad debt risk and the handling costs.

   Factors also accommodate clients with "overadvances," loans in anticipation of sales, which permit inventory building prior to peak selling periods. Factoring has traditionally been most closely associated with the garment industry, but is used by companies in other industries as well.

FAIL POSITION securities undelivered due to the failure of selling clients to deliver the securities to their brokers so the latter can deliver them to the buying brokers. Since brokers are constantly buying and selling, receiving and delivering, the term usually refers to a net delivery position—that is, a given broker owes more securities to other brokers on sell transactions than other brokers owe to it on buy transactions. *See also* FAIL TO DELIVER; FAIL TO RECEIVE.

FAIL TO DELIVER situation where the broker-dealer on the sell side of a contract has not delivered securities to the broker-dealer on the buy side. A fail to deliver is usually the result of a broker not receiving delivery from its selling customer. As long as a fail to deliver exists. the seller will not receive payment. *See also* FAIL TO RECEIVE.

FAIL TO RECEIVE situation where the broker-dealer on the buy side of a contract has not received delivery of securities from the broker-dealer on the sell side. As long as a fail to receive exists, the buyer will not make payment for the securities. *See also* FAIL TO DELIVER.

FAIR MARKET VALUE price at which an asset or service passes from a willing seller to a willing buyer. It is assumed that both buyer and seller are rational and have a reasonable knowledge of relevant facts. *See also* MARKET.

FAIRNESS OPINION professional judgment offered for a fee by an investment banker on the fairness of the price being offered in a merger, takeover, or leveraged buyout. For example, if management is trying to take over a company in a leveraged buyout, it will need a fairness opinion from an independent source to verify that the price being offered is adequate and in the best interests of shareholders. If shareholders sue on the grounds that the offer is not adequate, management will rely on the fairness opinion in court to prove its case. Fairness opinions are also obtained when a majority shareholder is trying to buy out the minority shareholders of a company.

FALLEN ANGELS bonds that were INVESTMENT GRADE at the time they were issued but have since declined in quality to below investment grade (BB or lower). Fallen angels are a type of JUNK BOND, but the latter term is usually reserved for bonds that are originally issued with ratings of BB or lower.

FALL OUT OF BED sharp drop in a stock's price, usually in response to negative corporate developments. For example, a stock may fall out of bed if a takeover deal falls apart or if profits in the latest period fall far short of expectations.

FAMILY OF FUNDS *see* FUND FAMILY.

FANNIE MAE (FEDERAL NATIONAL MORTGAGE ASSOCIATION) publicly owned, government-sponsored corporation established in 1938 to purchase both government-backed and conventional mortgages from lenders and securitize them. Its objective is to increase the affordability of home mortgage funds for low-, moderate- and middle-income home buyers. Fannie Mae is a congressionally chartered, shareholder-owned company, and the largest source of home mortgage funds in the United States. Fannie Mae is a large issuer of debt securities which are used to finance its activities. Equity shares of Fannie Mae are traded on the New York Stock Exchange.

FAR MONTH trading month that is farthest in the future in an options or futures contract. This may be a few months or up to a year or more. Under normal conditions, there is far less trading activity in the far month contracts than in the NEAREST MONTH or SPOT DELIVERY MONTH contracts. Also called *furthest month.*

FARMOUT AGREEMENT agreement whereby a party develops an oil or gas well on leases owned by others in return for earning an interest in those leases.

FARTHER OUT; FARTHER IN relative length of option-contract maturities with reference to the present. For example, an options investor in January would call an option expiring in October farther out than an option expiring in July. The July option is farther in than the October option. *See also* DIAGONAL SPREAD.

FASB *see* FINANCIAL ACCOUNTING STANDARDS BOARD.

FAST MARKET market in which activity in an option or its underlying interest is so fast that posted options quotations cannot be kept up to date.

FAT CAT wealthy person who has become lazy living off the dividends and interest from investments. Fat cats also tend to be offered special treatment by brokers and other financial professionals because they have so much money and their accounts can therefore generate large fees and commissions.

FAVOURABLE TRADE BALANCE situation that exists when the value of a nation's exports is in excess of the value of its imports. *See* BALANCE OF PAYMENTS; BALANCE OF TRADE.

FAVORITE FIFTY *See* NIFTY FIFTY.

FEDERAL DEFICIT federal shortfall that results when the government spends more in a fiscal year than it receives in revenue. To cover the shortfall, the government usually borrows from the public by floating long- and short-term debt. Some economists think that massive federal deficits can lead to high interest rates and inflation, since they compete with private borrowing by consumers and businesses.

FEDERAL DEPOSIT INSURANCE CORPORATION (FDIC) United States federal agency established in 1933 that guarantees (within limits) funds on deposit in member banks and thrift institutions and performs other functions such as making loans to or buying assets from member institutions to facilitate mergers or prevent failures. In 1989, the U.S. Congress passed savings and loan association bailout legislation that reorganized FDIC into two insurance units: the BANK INSURANCE FUND (BIF) continues the traditional FDIC functions with respect to banking institutions; the SAVINGS ASSOCIATION INSURANCE FUND (SAIF) insures thrift institution deposits, replacing the FEDERAL SAVINGS AND LOAN INSURANCE CORPORATION (FSLIC), which ceased to exist.

FEDERAL FUNDS

1. funds deposited by commercial banks at Federal Reserve Banks, including funds in excess of bank reserve requirements. Banks may lend federal funds to each other on an overnight basis at the federal funds rate. Member banks may also transfer funds among themselves or on behalf of customers on a same-day basis by debiting and crediting balances in the various reserve banks. *See* FED WIRE.
2. money used by the Federal Reserve to pay for its purchases of government securities.
3. funds used to settle transactions where there is no FLOAT.

FEDERAL INCOME TAXES *see* INCOME TAXES.

FEDERAL RESERVE BANK in the United States; one of the 12 banks that, with their branches, make up the FEDERAL RESERVE SYSTEM. These banks are located in Boston, New York, Philadelphia, Cleveland, Richmond, Atlanta, Chicago, St. Louis, Minneapolis, Kansas City, Dallas, and San Francisco. The role of each Federal Reserve Bank is to monitor the commercial and savings banks in its region to ensure that they follow Federal Reserve Board regulations and to provide those banks with access to emergency funds from the DISCOUNT WINDOW. The reserve banks act as depositories for member banks in their regions, providing money transfer and other services. Each of the banks is owned by the member banks in its district.

FEDERAL RESERVE BOARD (FRB) governing board of the FEDERAL RESERVE SYSTEM. Its seven members are appointed by the President of the United States, subject to Senate confirmation, and serve 14-year terms. The Board establishes Federal Reserve System policies on such key matters as reserve requirements and other bank regulations, sets the discount rate, tightens or loosens the availability of credit in the economy, and regulates the purchase of securities on margin.

FEDERAL RESERVE SYSTEM in the United States, system established by the Federal Reserve Act of 1913 to regulate the U.S. monetary and banking system. The Federal Reserve System (the Fed) comprises 12 regional Federal Reserve Banks, their 24 branches, and all national and state banks that are part of the system. National banks are stockholders of the FEDERAL RESERVE BANK in their region.

The Federal Reserve System's main functions are to regulate the national money supply, set reserve requirements for member banks, supervise the printing of currency at the mint, act as clearinghouse for the transfer of funds throughout the banking system, and examine member banks to make sure they meet various Federal Reserve regulations. Although the members of the system's governing board are appointed by the President of the United States and confirmed by the Senate, the Federal Reserve System is considered an independent entity, which is supposed to make its decisions free of political influence. Governors are appointed for terms of 14 years, which further assures their independence. *See also* FEDERAL OPEN MARKET COMMITTEE; FEDERAL RESERVE BOARD; OPEN MARKET OPERATIONS.

FEDERAL TRADE COMMISSION (FTC) in the United States, federal agency established in 1914 to foster free and fair business competition and prevent monopolies and activities in restraint of trade. It administers both antitrust and consumer protection legislation.

FED WIRE in the United States, high-speed, computerized communications network that connects all 12 Federal Reserve Banks, their 24 branches, the Federal Reserve Board office in Washington, D.C., U.S. Treasury offices in Washington, D.C., and Chicago, and the Washington, D.C. office of the Commodity Credit Corporation; also spelled FedWire and Fedwire. The Fed wire has been called the central nervous system of money transfer in the United States. It enables banks to transfer reserve balances from one to another for immediate available credit and to transfer balances for business customers. Using the Fed wire, Federal Reserve Banks can settle interdistrict transfers resulting from cheque collections, and the Treasury can shift balances from its accounts in different reserve banks quickly and without cost. It is also possible to transfer bearer short-term Government securities within an hour at no cost. This is done through a procedure called CPD (Commissioner of Public Debt of the Treasury) transfers, whereby one Federal Reserve Bank "retires" a seller's security, while another reserve bank makes delivery of a like amount of the same security from its unissued stock to the buyer.

FIDUCIARY person, company, or association holding assets in trust for a beneficiary. The fiduciary is charged with the responsibility of investing the money wisely for the beneficiary's benefit. Some examples of fiduciaries are executors of wills and estates, receivers in bankruptcy, trustees, and those who administer the assets of underage or incompetent beneficiaries.

FIFO *see* FIRST IN, FIRST OUT.

FILL execute a customer's order to buy or sell a stock, bond, or commodity. An order is filled when the amount of the security requested is supplied. When less than the full amount of the order is supplied, it is known as a *partial fill.*

FILL OR KILL (FOK) order to buy or sell a particular security which, if not executed immediately, is canceled. Often, fill or kill orders are placed when a client wants to buy a large quantity of shares of a particular stock at a particular price. If the order is not executed because it will significantly upset the market price for that stock, the order is withdrawn.

FINAL PROSPECTUS prospectus that supersedes the preliminary prospectus and is accepted for filing by applicable provincial securities commissions. The final prospectus shows all required information pertinent to the new issue and a copy must be given to each first-time buyer of the new issue.

FINANCE CHARGE cost of credit, including interest, paid by a customer for a consumer loan. Under the Bank Act, the finance charge must be disclosed in advance to the customer.

FINANCE COMPANY company engaged in making loans to individuals or businesses. Unlike a bank, it does not receive deposits but rather obtains its financing from banks, institutions, and other money market sources. Generally, finance companies fall into three categories: (1) consumer finance companies, also known as *small loan* or *direct loan companies,* lend money to individuals; (2) sales finance companies, also called *acceptance companies,* purchase retail and wholesale paper from automobile and other consumer and capital goods dealers; (3) commercial finance companies, also called *commercial credit companies,* make loans to manufacturers and wholesalers; these loans are secured by accounts receivable, inventories, and equipment. Finance companies typically enjoy high credit ratings and are thus able to borrow at the lowest market rates, enabling them to make loans at rates not much higher than banks. Even though their customers usually do not qualify for bank credit, these companies have experienced a low rate of default. Finance companies in general tend to be interest rate-sensitive—increases and decreases in market interest rates affect their profits directly.

FINANCIAL ACCOUNTING STANDARDS BOARD (FASB) independent board responsible for establishing and interpreting generally accepted accounting principles. It was formed in 1973 to succeed and continue the activities of the Accounting Principles Board (APB). *See* GENERALLY ACCEPTED ACCOUNTING PRINCIPLES.

FINANCIAL ADVISER professional adviser offering financial counsel. Some financial advisers charge a fee and earn commissions on the products they recommend to implement their advice. Other advisers only charge fees, and do not sell any products or accept commissions. Some financial advisers are generalists, while others specialize in specific areas such as investing, insurance, estate planning, taxes, or other areas.

FINANCIAL ANALYSIS analysis of the FINANCIAL STATEMENT of a company. *See also* FUNDAMENTAL ANALYSIS.

FINANCIAL ASSETS assets in the form of stocks, bonds, rights, certificates, bank balances, etc., as distinguished from tangible, physical assets. For example, real property is a physical asset, but shares in a REAL ESTATE INVESTMENT TRUST (REIT) or the stock or bonds of a company that held property as an investment would be financial assets.

FINANCIAL BREAKEVEN POINT level of earnings before interest and taxes (EBIT) necessary for a firm to be just able to meet its fixed financial obligations, i.e., the level of earnings before interest and taxes at which the earnings per share just equal zero. The higher the financial breakeven point, the more financially risky the firm is considered.

FINANCIAL FUTURE FUTURES CONTRACT based on a financial instrument. Such contracts usually move under the influence of interest rates. As rates rise, contracts fall in value; as rates fall, contracts gain in value. These include Treasury bills, certificates of deposit, foreign notes, and banker's acceptances. Traders use these futures to speculate on the direction of interest rates. Financial institutions (banks, trust companies, insurance companies, brokerage firms) use them to hedge financial portfolios against adverse fluctuations in interest rates.

FINANCIAL INSTITUTION institution that collects funds from the public to place in financial assets such as stocks, bonds, money market instruments, bank deposits, or loans. Depository institutions (banks, trusts, and credit unions) pay interest on deposits and invest the deposit money mostly in loans. Nondepository institutions (insurance companies, pension plans) collect money by selling insurance policies or receiving employer contributions and pay it out for legitimate claims or for retirement benefits.

FINANCIAL INTERMEDIARY commercial bank, trust company, credit union, or other "middleman" that smooths the flow of funds between "savings surplus units" and "savings deficit units." In an economy viewed as three sectors—households, businesses, and government—a *savings surplus unit* is one where income exceeds consumption; a *savings deficit unit* is one where current expenditures exceed current income and external sources must be called upon to make up the difference. As a whole, households are savings surplus units, whereas businesses and governments are savings deficit units. Financial intermediaries redistribute savings into productive uses and, in the process, serve two other important functions: By making savers infinitesimally small "shareholders" in huge pools of capital, which in turn are lent out to a wide number and variety of borrowers, the intermediaries provide both diversification of risk and liquidity to the individual saver.

FINANCIAL LEASE lease in which the service provided by the lessor to the lessee is limited to financing equipment. All other responsibilities related to the possession of equipment, such as maintenance, insurance, and taxes, are borne by the lessee. A financial lease is usually noncancellable and is fully paid out *(amortized)* over its term.

FINANCIAL MARKET market for the exchange of capital and credit in the economy. Money markets concentrate on short-term debt instruments; capital markets trade in long-term debt and equity instruments. Examples of financial markets: stock market, bond market, commodities market, and foreign exchange market.

FINANCIAL NEEDS APPROACH technique to assess the proper amount of life insurance for an individual. The person, either on his or her own or with the help of an insurance adviser, must estimate the financial needs of survivors in case the person dies unexpectedly. Projections for expenses, income, taxes, funeral costs, and other financial factors lead to an understanding of the amount of insurance proceeds that would be needed to allow the survivors to continue in their present lifestyle. Once the optimal amount of insurance protection is determined, various kinds of TERM and CASH VALUE INSURANCE programs can be designed to meet these needs.

FINANCIAL PLANNER professional who analyzes personal financial circumstances and prepares a program to meet financial needs and objectives. Financial planners, who may be accountants, bankers, lawyers, insurance agents, real estate or securities brokers, or independent practitioners, should have knowledge in the areas of wills and estate planning, retirement planning, taxes, insurance, family budgeting, debt management, and investments.

  Fee-only planners charge on the basis of service and time and have nothing to sell. *Commission-only planners* offer their services free but sell commission-producing products such as MUTUAL FUNDS, LIMITED PARTNERSHIPS, insurance products, stocks, and bonds. *Fee-plus-commission planners* charge an upfront fee for consultation and their written plan, then charge commissions on the financial products they sell. *Fee-offset planners* charge fees against which they apply credits when they sell commission-producing products.

FINANCIAL POSITION status of a firm's assets, liabilities, and equity accounts as of a certain time, as shown on its FINANCIAL STATEMENT. Also called *financial condition.*

FINANCIAL PUBLIC RELATIONS branch of public relations specializing in corporate disclosure responsibilities, stockholder relations, and relations with the professional investor community.

FINANCIAL PYRAMID
1. risk structure many investors aim for in spreading their investments between low-, medium-, and high-risk vehicles. In a financial pyramid, the largest part of the investor's assets is in safe, liquid investments that provide a decent return. Next, some money is invested in stocks and bonds that provide good income and the possibility for long-term growth of capital. Third, a smaller portion of one's capital is committed to speculative investments which may offer higher returns if they work out well. At the top of the financial pyramid, where only a small amount of money is committed, are high-risk ventures that have a slight chance of success, but which will provide substantial rewards if they succeed.
2. acquisition of holding company assets through financial leverage. *See* PYRAMIDING.

  Financial pyramid is not to be confused with fraudulent selling schemes, also sometimes called *pyramiding.*

FINANCIAL PYRAMID

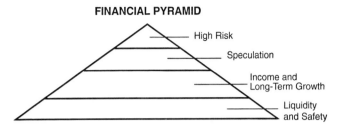

FINANCIAL STATEMENT written record of the financial status of an individual, association, or business organization. The financial statement includes a BALANCE SHEET and an INCOME STATEMENT (or operating statement or profit and loss statement) and may also include a STATEMENT OF CASH FLOWS, a statement of changes in retained earnings, and other analyses.

FINANCIAL STRUCTURE makeup of the right-hand side of a company's BALANCE SHEET, which includes all the ways its assets are financed, such as trade accounts payable and short-term borrowings as well as long-term debt and ownership equity. Financial structure is distinguished from CAPITAL STRUCTURE, which includes only long-term debt and equity. A company's financial structure is influenced by a number of factors, including the growth rate and stability of its sales, its competitive situation (i.e., the stability of its profits), its asset structure, and the attitudes of its management and its lenders. It is the basic frame of reference for analyses concerned with financial leveraging decisions.

FINANCIAL SUPERMARKET company that offers a wide range of financial services under one roof. For example, some large retail organizations offer mutual fund, insurance, and real estate brokerage, as well as banking services. For customers, having all their assets with one institution can make financial transactions and planning more convenient and efficient, since money does not constantly have to be shifted from one institution to another. For institutions, such all-inclusive relationships are more profitable than dealing with just one aspect of a customer's financial needs. Institutions often become financial supermarkets in order to capture all the business of their customers.

FINANCIAL TABLES tables found in newspapers listing prices, dividends, yields, price/earnings ratios, trading volume, and other important data on stocks, bonds, mutual funds, and futures contracts. While local newspapers may carry limited tables, more extensive listings are available in *Barron's, Investor's Business Daily,* the *Wall Street Journal, Financial Post,* and the *Report on Business* of the *Globe and Mail.*

FINDER'S FEE fee charged by a person or company acting as a finder (intermediary) in a transaction.

FINE OUNCE European terminology for an ounce of metal of 99.9% purity. Gold and silver are weighted according to the troy system of measurement (not the same as the avoirdupois system):

    1 troy pound = 12 ounces or 240 pennyweight
    1 troy ounce = 20 pennyweight, 480 grains, or 31.103 grams
    1 pennyweight = 24 grains, 0.05 ounces, or 1.555 grams
    1 grain = 0.042 pennyweight, or 0.002285 ounces

FIRE INSURANCE insurance that provides coverage for damage caused by fire and certain other perils.

FIRM

1. general term for a business, corporation, partnership, or proprietorship. Legally, a firm is not considered a corporation since it may not be incorporated and since the firm's principals are not recognized as separate from the identity of the firm itself. This might be true of a law or accounting firm, for instance.
2. solidity with which an agreement is made. For example, a firm order with a manufacturer or a firm bid for a stock at a particular price means that the order or bid is assured.

FIRM BID undertaking to buy (firm bid) a specified amount of securities at a specified price for a specified period of time, unless released from its obligation by the seller.

FIRM COMMITMENT

Lending: term used by lenders to refer to an agreement to make a loan to a specific borrower within a specific period of time and, if applicable, on a specific property. *See also* COMMITMENT FEE.

Securities underwriting: arrangement whereby investment bankers make outright purchases from the issuer of securities to be offered to the public; also called *firm commitment underwriting.* The underwriters, as the investment bankers are called in such an arrangement, make their profit on the difference between the purchase price—determined through either competitive bidding or negotiation—and the public offering price. Firm commitment underwriting is to be distinguished from conditional arrangements for distributing new securities, such as standby commitments and best efforts commitments. The word *underwriting* is frequently misused with respect to such conditional arrangements. It is used correctly only with respect to firm commitment underwritings or, as they are sometimes called, BOUGHT DEALS. *See also* BEST EFFORT; STANDBY COMMITMENT.

FIRM OFFER *see* FIRM BID.

FIRM ORDER

Commercial transaction: written or verbal order that has been confirmed and is not subject to cancellation.

Securities: (1) order to buy or sell for the proprietary account of the broker-dealer firm; (2) buy or sell order not conditional upon the customer's confirmation.

FIRM QUOTE securities industry term referring to any round lot bid or offer price of a security stated by a market maker and not identified as a nominal (or subject) quote. Under National Association of Securities Dealers' (NASD) rules and practice, quotes requiring further negotiation or review must be identified as nominal quotes. *See also* NOMINAL QUOTATION.

FIRST CALL DATE first date specified in the indenture of a corporate or municipal bond contract on which part or all of the bond may be redeemed at a set price. An XYZ bond due in 2030, for instance, may have a first call date of May 1, 2013. This means that, if XYZ wishes, bondholders may be paid off starting on that date in 2013. Bond brokers typically quote yields on such bonds with both yield to maturity (in this case, 2030) and yield to call (in this case, 2013). *See also* DURATION; YIELD TO CALL; YIELD TO MATURITY.

FIRST IN, FIRST OUT (FIFO) method of accounting for inventory whereby, quite literally, the inventory is assumed to be sold in the chronological order in which it was purchased. For example, the following formula is used in computing the cost of goods sold:

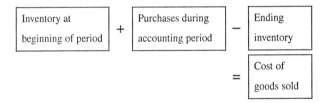

Under the FIFO method, inventory costs flow from the oldest purchases forward, with beginning inventory as the starting point and ending inventory representing the most recent purchases. The FIFO method contrasts with the LIFO or LAST IN, FIRST OUT method, which is FIFO in reverse. The significance of the difference becomes apparent when inflation or deflation affects inventory prices. In an inflationary period, the FIFO method produces a higher ending inventory, a lower cost of goods sold figure, and a higher gross profit. LIFO, on the other hand, produces a lower ending inventory, a higher cost of goods sold figure, and a lower reported profit.

FIRST MORTGAGE real estate loan that gives the mortgagee (lender) a primary lien against a specified piece of property. A primary lien has precedence over all other mortgages in case of default. *See also* JUNIOR MORTGAGE; SECOND MORTGAGE.

FIRST NOTICE DAY first day of the delivery period when notice of intent to deliver actual commodities from seller to buyer via the clearinghouse are sent out. The first notice day varies with each contract.

FIRST PREFERRED STOCK preferred stock that has preferential claim on dividends and assets over other preferred issues and common stock.

FIRST REFUSAL right of a second party to buy shares or property on the same terms and conditions as were offered to a first party. The right usually has a short time period of about 10 or 30 days attached to it.

FISCAL AGENT usually a bank or a trust company acting for a corporation under a corporate trust agreement. The fiscal agent handles such matters as disbursing funds for dividend payments, redeeming bonds and coupons, handling taxes related to the issue of bonds, and paying rents.

FISCAL POLICY federal taxation and spending policies designed to level out the business cycle and achieve full employment, price stability, and sustained growth in the economy. Fiscal policy basically follows the economic theory of the 20th-century English economist John Maynard Keynes that insufficient demand causes unemployment and excessive demand leads to inflation. It aims to stimulate demand and output in periods of business decline by increasing government purchases and cutting taxes, thereby releasing more disposable income into the spending stream, and to correct overexpansion by reversing the process. Working to balance these deliberate fiscal measures are the so-called built-in stabilizers, such as the progressive income tax and unemployment benefits, which automatically respond countercyclically. Fiscal policy is administered independently of MONETARY POLICY, by which the Bank of Canada attempts to regulate economic activity by controlling the money supply. The goals of fiscal and monetary policy are the same, but Keynesians and Monetarists disagree as to which of the two approaches works best. At the basis of their differences are questions dealing with the velocity (turnover) of money and the effect of changes in the money supply on the equilibrium rate of interest (the rate at which money demand equals money supply). *See also* KEYNESIAN ECONOMICS.

FISCAL YEAR (FY) accounting period covering 12 consecutive months, 52 consecutive weeks, 13 four-week periods, or 365 consecutive days, at the end of which the books are closed and profit or loss is determined. A company's fiscal year is often, but not necessarily, the same as the calendar year. A seasonal business will frequently select a fiscal rather than a calendar year, so that its year-end figures will show it in its most liquid condition, which also means having less inventory to verify physically. The FY of the Canadian Government ends March 31.

FIT a situation where the features of a particular investment perfectly match the portfolio requirements of an investor.

FITCH INVESTORS SERVICE, INC. New York- and Denver-based RATING firm, which rates corporate and municipal bonds, preferred stock, commercial paper, and obligations of health-care and not-for-profit institutions.

FITCH SHEETS sheets indicating the successive trade prices of securities listed on the major exchanges. They are published by Francis Emory Fitch, Inc. in New York City.

FIXATION setting of a present or future price of a commodity, such as the twice-daily London GOLD FIXING. In other commodities, prices are fixed further into the future for the benefit of both buyers and sellers of that commodity.

FIXED ANNUITY investment contract sold by an insurance company that guarantees fixed payments, either for life or for a specified period, to an annuitant. In fixed annuities, the insurer takes both the investment and the mortality risks. A fixed annuity contrasts with a VARIABLE ANNUITY, where payments depend on an uncertain outcome, such as prices in the securities markets. See *also* ANNUITY.

FIXED ASSET tangible property used in the operations of a business, but not expected to be consumed or converted into cash in the ordinary course of events. Plant, machinery and equipment, furniture and fixtures, and leasehold improvements comprise the fixed assets of most companies. They are normally represented on the balance sheet at their net depreciated value.

FIXED BENEFITS payments to a BENEFICIARY that are fixed rather than variable.

FIXED-CHARGE COVERAGE ratio of profits before payment of interest and income taxes to interest on bonds and other contractual long-term debt. It indicates how many times interest charges have been earned by the corporation on a pretax basis. Since failure to meet interest payments would be a default under the terms of indenture agreements, the coverage ratio measures a margin of safety. For example, if the annual blended payments on a term loan are $10,000 and the company's profit before tax and depreciation is $25,000, the company would have 2½ times coverage. The amount of safety desirable depends on the stability of a company's earnings. (Too much safety can be an indication of an undesirable lack of leverage.) In cyclical companies, the fixed-charge coverage in periods of recession is a telling ratio. Analysts also find it useful to calculate the number of times that a company's *cash flow*—i.e., *after*-tax earnings plus noncash expenses (for example, depreciation)—covers fixed charges. Also known as *times fixed charges.*

FIXED COST cost that remains constant regardless of sales volume. Fixed costs include salaries of executives, interest expense, rent, depreciation, and insurance expenses. They contrast with *variable costs* (direct labour, materials costs), which are distinguished from *semivariable costs.* Semivariable costs vary, but not necessarily in direct relation to sales. They may also remain fixed up to a level of sales, then increase when sales enter a higher range. For example, expenses associated with a delivery truck would be fixed up to the level of sales where a second truck was required. Obviously, no costs are purely fixed; the assumption, however, serves the purposes of cost accounting for limited planning periods. Cost accounting is also concerned with the allocation of portions of fixed costs to inventory costs, also called indirect costs, overhead, factory overhead, and supplemental overhead. *See also* DIRECT OVERHEAD; VARIABLE COST.

FIXED CURRENCY currency set at a fixed rate of exchange against a hard currency and not allowed to float on the open market according to supply and demand and market conditions. In 1962, Canada fixed its currency against the U.S. dollar at 92.5 cents U.S., after which it was allowed to float.

FIXED EXCHANGE RATE set rate of exchange between the currencies of countries. At the Bretton Woods international monetary conference in 1944, a system of fixed exchange rates was set up, which existed until the early 1970s, when a FLOATING EXCHANGE RATE system was adopted.

FIXED EXPENSES *see* FIXED COSTS.

FIXED/FLOATING CHARGE charge registered against a specific asset. Contrast with "floating" charge, which is registered against all assets (unspecified) and ranks in priority behind "fixed" charges. A "first fixed and floating charge" debenture would list a first charge against certain assets and a floating charge against all others.

FIXED-INCOME INVESTMENT security that pays a fixed rate of return. This usually refers to government bonds, which pay a fixed rate of interest until the bonds mature, and to preferred stock, paying a fixed dividend. Such investments are advantageous in a time of low inflation, but do not protect holders against erosion of buying power in a time of rising inflation, since the bondholder or preferred shareholder gets the same amount of interest or dividends, even though consumer goods cost more.

FIXED INCOME SECURITIES *see* FIXED-INCOME INVESTMENT.

FIXED PREMIUM equal installments payable to an insurance company for INSURANCE or an ANNUITY. *See also* SINGLE-PREMIUM DEFERRED ANNUITY (SPDA) and SINGLE-PREMIUM LIFE INSURANCE.

FIXED PRICE
Contracts: type of contract where the price is preset and invariable, regardless of the actual costs of production. *See also* COST-PLUS CONTRACT.
Investment: in a public offering of new securities, price at which investment bankers in the underwriting SYNDICATE agree to sell the issue to the public. The price remains fixed as long as the syndicate remains in effect. The proper term for this kind of system is *fixed price offering system.* In contrast, Eurobonds, which are also sold through underwriting syndicates, are offered on a basis that permits discrimination among customers; i.e., the underwriting spread may be adjusted to suit the particular buyer. *See also* EUROBOND.

FIXED RATE (LOAN) type of loan in which the interest rate does not fluctuate with general market conditions. There are fixed rate mortgage (also known as conventional mortgage) and consumer installment loans, as well as fixed rate business loans. Fixed rate loans tend to have higher original interest rates than flexible rate loans such as an ADJUSTABLE RATE MORTGAGE (ARM), because lenders are not protected against a rise in the cost of money when they make a fixed rate loan.

The term fixed rate may also refer to fixed currency exchange rates. *See* FIXED EXCHANGE RATE.

FIXTURE attachment to real property that is not intended to be moved and would create damage to the property if it were moved—for example, a plumbing fixture. Fixtures are classified as part of real estate when they share the same useful life. Otherwise, they are considered equipment.

FLAG technical chart pattern resembling a flag shaped like a parallelogram with masts on either side, showing a consolidation within a trend. It results from price fluctuations within a narrow range, both preceded and followed by sharp rises or declines. If the flag—the consolidation period—is preceded by a rise, it will usually be followed by a rise; a fall will follow a fall.

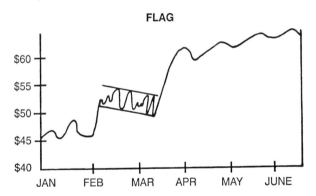

FLAG

FLASH tape display designation used when volume on an exchange is so heavy that the tape runs more than five minutes behind. The flash interrupts the display to report the current price—called the *flash price*—of a heavily traded security. Current prices of two groups of 50 stocks are flashed at five-minute intervals as long as the tape is seriously behind.

FLAT quoted market price of a bond or debenture and its total cost (as opposed to an accrued interest transaction, bond plus interest to date). Bonds and debentures in default of interest trade flat. Bonds are usually sold/bought inclusive of dealer markdown (markup).

FLAT MARKET market characterized by HORIZONTAL PRICE MOVEMENT. It is usually the result of low activity. However, STABILIZATION, consolidation, and DISTRIBUTION are situations marked by both horizontal price movement and active trading.

FLAT SCALE
Industry: labour term denoting a uniform rate of pay that makes no allowance for volume, frequency, or other factors.
Municipal bonds: bond trader's term describing a situation where shorter and longer term yields show little difference over the maturity range of a new serial bond issue.

FLAT TAX tax applied at the same rate to all levels of income. It is often discussed as an alternative to the PROGRESSIVE TAX. Proponents of a flat tax argue that people able to retain larger portions of higher income would have an added incentive to earn, thus stimulating the economy. Advocates also note its simplicity. Opponents argue it is a REGRESSIVE TAX in effect, comparing it to the sales tax, a uniform tax that puts a greater burden on households with lower incomes. If Canada moves to a flat tax, it will be between 17 and 20% of total income less certain deductions regardless of income. It is called a SINGLE TAX SYSTEM in Canada as it includes allowances for age, RRSPs, and children before application of the tax.

FLEXIBLE BUDGET statement of projected revenue and expenditure based on various levels of production. It shows how costs vary with different rates of output or at different levels of sales volume.

FLEXIBLE EXCHANGE RATE *see* FLOATING EXCHANGE RATE.

FLEXIBLE EXPENSES in personal finance, expenses that can be adjusted or eliminated, such as those for luxuries, as opposed to fixed expenses, such as rent or car payments.

FLEXIBLE MUTUAL FUND fund that can invest in stocks, bonds, and cash in whatever proportion the fund manager thinks will maximize returns to shareholders at the lowest level of risk. Flexible funds, also called ASSET ALLOCATION funds, can provide high returns if they are fully invested in stocks when stock prices soar, and they can also protect shareholders' assets by going largely to cash during a stock bear market. Flexible mutual funds are popular because the fund manager, not the shareholder, must make the difficult decisions on asset allocation and market timing. Some flexible funds allow managers to buy securities anywhere in the world in their quest to maximize shareholder returns.

FLIGHT OF CAPITAL *see* CAPITAL FLIGHT.

FLIGHT TO QUALITY moving capital to the safest possible investment to protect oneself from loss during an unsettling period in the market. For example, when a major bank fails, cautious money market investors may buy only government-backed money market securities instead of those issued by major banks. A flight to quality can be measured by the differing yields resulting from such a movement of capital. In the example just given, the yields on bank-issued money market paper will rise since there will be less demand for it, and the rates on government securities will fall, because there will be more demand for them.

FLIP-IN POISON PILL *see* POISON PILL.

FLIP-OVER POISON PILL *see* POISON PILL.

FLIPPING buying shares in an INITIAL PUBLIC OFFERING and selling them immediately for a profit. Brokerage firms underwriting new stock issues tend to discourage flipping, and will often try to allocate shares to investors who say they plan to hold on to the shares for some time. Still, the temptation to flip a new issue once it has risen in price sharply is too irresistible for many investors lucky enough to be allocated shares in a HOT ISSUE. An investor who flips stocks is called a *flipper.*

FLOAT
Banking: time between the deposit of a cheque in a bank and payment. Long floats are to the advantage of chequewriters, whose money may earn interest until a cheque clears. They are to the disadvantage of depositors, who must wait for a cheque to clear before they have access to the funds. As a rule, the further away the paying bank is from the deposit bank, the longer it will take for a cheque to clear.
Investments: number of shares of a corporation that are outstanding and available for trading by the public. A small float means the stock will be more volatile, since a large order to buy or sell shares can influence the stock's price dramatically. A larger float means the stock will be less volatile.

FLOATER
Bonds: debt instrument with a variable interest rate tied to another interest rate. A FLOATING RATE NOTE, for instance, provides a holder with additional interest if the applicable interest rate rises and less interest if the rate falls. It is generally best to buy floaters if it appears that interest rates will rise. If the outlook is for falling rates, investors typically favour fixed rate instruments. Floaters spread risk between issuers and debtholders.
Insurance: endorsement to a homeowner's or renter's insurance policy, a form of property insurance for items that are moved from location to location. Typically, a floater is bought to cover jewellery, furs, and other items whose full value is not covered in standard homeowner's or renter's policies. A standard homeowner's policy typically covers $1000 to $2000 for jewellery, furs, and watches. Also called a *rider.*

FLOAT FUNDS status of funds in the process of collection. Float is experienced from the time a sale is made until the seller's account receives collected funds on the customer's cheque. Because it has the dimension of both time and money, float is often computed as the product of the funds being collected and the time involved to collect them, expressed in Dollar-Days ($D).

FLOATING AN ISSUE *see* NEW ISSUE; UNDERWRITE.

FLOATING DEBT continuously renewed or refinanced short-term debt of companies or governments used to finance ongoing operating needs.

FLOATING CURRENCY currency that is allowed to float up and down according to a market exchange rate such as the U.S. dollar. The Canadian dollar was unfixed and allowed to float in the 1960s.

FLOATING EXCHANGE RATE movement of a foreign currency exchange rate in response to changes in the market forces of supply and demand; also known as *flexible exchange rate.* Currencies strengthen or weaken based on a nation's reserves of hard currency and gold, its international trade balance, its rate of inflation and interest rates, and the general strength of its economy. Nations generally do not want their currency to be too strong, because this makes the country's goods too expensive for foreigners to buy. A weak currency, on the other hand, may signify economic instability if it has been caused by high inflation or a weak economy. The opposite of the floating exchange rate is the FIXED EXCHANGE RATE system. *See also* PAR VALUE OF CURRENCY.

FLOATING RATE variable interest rate on preferred shares, causing dividend amounts to fluctuate with the current interest rates.

FLOATING RATE NOTE debt instrument with a variable interest rate. Interest adjustments are made periodically, often every six months, and are tied to a money-market index such as Treasury bill rates. Floating rate notes usually have a maturity of about five years. They provide holders with protection against rises in interest rates, but pay lower yields than fixed rate notes of the same maturity. Also known as a FLOATER.

FLOATING SECURITIES
1. securities bought for the purpose of making a quick profit on resale and held in a broker's name.
2. outstanding stock of a corporation that is traded on an exchange.
3. unsold units of a newly issued security.

FLOOR in general, the lower limit of something. In securities, the part of a stock exchange where active trading takes place or the price at which a STOP LOSS order is activated. *See also* FLOOR BROKER.

FLOOR BROKER member of an exchange who is an employee of a member firm and executes orders, as agent, on the floor of the exchange for clients. The floor broker receives an order via teletype machine from his or her firm's trading department, then proceeds to the appropriate trading post on the exchange floor. There he or she joins other brokers and the specialist in the security being bought or sold, and executes the trade at the best competitive price available. On completion of the transaction, the customer is notified through his registered representative back at the firm, and the trade is printed on the consolidated ticker tape, which is displayed electronically around the country. A floor broker should not be confused with a FLOOR TRADER, who trades as a principal for his or her own account, rather than as a broker.

FLOOR FINANCING financing of floor stock by car dealers and furniture and large appliance dealers. The lender maintains legal ownership of the floor items while the retailer displays them for sale. Ownership changes when the stock is paid for by the customer. *See also* INVENTORY FINANCING.

FLOOR TICKET summary of the information entered on the ORDER TICKET by the registered representative on receipt of a buy or sell order from a client. The floor ticket gives the floor broker the information needed to execute a securities transaction. The information required on floor tickets is specified by securities industry rules.

FLOOR TRADER member of a stock brokerage company who trades on the floor of that exchange on behalf of his or her company's clients. The term should not be confused with FLOOR BROKER. *See also* REGISTERED COMPETITIVE TRADER.

FLOTATION (FLOATATION) COST cost of issuing new stocks or bonds. It varies with the amount of underwriting risk and the job of physical distribution. It comprises two elements: (1) the compensation earned by the investment bankers (the underwriters) in the form of the spread between the price paid to the issuer (the corporation or government agency) and the offering price to the public, and (2) the expenses of the issuer (legal, accounting, printing, and other out-of-pocket expenses). Flotation costs are higher for stocks than for bonds, reflecting the generally wider distribution and greater volatility of common stock as opposed to bonds, which are usually sold in large blocks to relatively few investors. Flotation costs as a percentage of gross proceeds are greater for smaller issues than for larger ones. This occurs because the issuer's legal and other expenses tend to be relatively large and fixed; also, smaller issues tend to originate with less established issuers, requiring more information development and marketing expense. An issue involving a RIGHTS OFFERING can involve negligible underwriting risk and selling effort and therefore minimal flotation cost, especially if the underpricing is substantial.

    The UNDERWRITING SPREAD is the key variable in flotation cost, historically ranging from 23.7% of the size of a small issue of common stock to as low as 1.25% of the par value of high-grade bonds. Spreads are determined by both negotiation and competitive bidding.

FLOW OF FUNDS
Economics: in referring to the national economy, the way funds are transferred from savings surplus units to savings deficit units through financial intermediaries. *See also* FINANCIAL INTERMEDIARY.

FLOW-THROUGH SHARES   term meaning that tax deductions and credits, normally available only to a corporation, may flow through to owners of the corporation's flow-through shares. Canadian exploration and mining companies are able to issue such shares at a premium because investors are considered to be funding exploration and development costs and are therefore entitled to deduct these expenses from all other income.

FLUCTUATION
1. change in prices or interest rates, either up or down. Fluctuation may refer to either slight or dramatic changes in the prices of stocks, bonds, or commodities. *See also* FLUCTUATION LIMIT.
2. the ups and downs in the economy.

FLUCTUATION LIMIT limits placed on the daily ups and downs of futures prices by the commodity exchanges. The limit protects traders from losing too much on a particular contract in one day. If a commodity reaches its limit, it may not trade any further that day. *See also* LIMIT UP, LIMIT DOWN.

FLURRY sudden increase in trading activity in a particular security. For example, there will be a flurry of trading in the stock of a company that was just the target of a surprise takeover bid. There are often trading flurries right after a company releases its quarterly earnings.

FOB *see* FREE ON BOARD.

FOOTSIE popular name for the *Financial Times'* FT-SE 100 Index (Financial Times-Stock Exchange 100 stock index), a market-value (capitalization)-weighted index of 100 blue chip stocks traded on the London Stock Exchange.

FORBES 500 annual listing by *Forbes* magazine of the largest U.S. publicly-owned corporations ranked four ways: by sales, assets, profits, and market value. *See also* FORTUNE 500.

FORCED CONVERSION when a CONVERTIBLE security is called in by its issuer. Convertible owners may find it to their financial advantage either to sell or to convert their holdings into common shares of the underlying company or to accept the call price. Such a conversion usually takes place when the convertible is selling above its CALL PRICE because the market value of the shares of the underlying stock has risen sharply. *See also* CONVERTIBLE.

FORECASTING projecting current trends using existing data.
Stock market forecasters predict the direction of the stock market by relying on technical data of trading activity and fundamental statistics on the direction of the economy.
Economic forecasters foretell the strength of the economy, often by utilizing complex econometric models as a tool to make specific predictions of future levels of inflation, interest rates, and employment. *See also* ECONOMETRICS.

Forecasting can also refer to various PROJECTIONS used in business and financial planning.

FORECLOSURE process by which a homeowner who has not made timely payments of principal and interest on a mortgage loses title to the home. The holder of the mortgage, whether it be a bank, a trust company, or an individual, must go to court to seize the property, which may then be sold to satisfy the claims of the mortgage.

FOREIGN CURRENCY FUTURES AND OPTIONS futures and options contracts based on foreign currencies, such as the Japanese yen, Deutsche mark, British pound, and French franc. The buyer of a foreign currency futures contract acquires the right to buy a particular amount of that currency by a specific date at a fixed rate of exchange, and the seller agrees to sell that currency at the same fixed price. *Call options* give call buyers the right, but not the obligation, to buy the underlying currency at a particular price by a particular date. Call options on foreign currency futures give call buyers the right to a long underlying futures contracts. Those buying *put options* have the right to sell the underlying currencies at a specific price by a specific date. Most buyers and sellers of foreign currency futures and options do not exercise their rights to buy or sell, but trade out of their contracts at a profit or loss before they expire. SPECULATORS hope to profit by buying or selling a foreign currency futures or options contract before a currency rises or falls in value. HEDGERS buy or sell such contracts to protect their cash market position from fluctuations in currency values. These contracts are traded on SECURITIES AND COMMODITIES EXCHANGES throughout the world.

FOREIGN DIRECT INVESTMENT
1. investment in Canadian businesses by foreign citizens; usually involves majority stock ownership of the enterprise.
2. joint ventures between foreign and Canadian companies.

FOREIGN EXCHANGE instruments employed in making payments between countries—paper currency, notes, cheques, bills of exchange, and electronic notifications of international debits and credits.

FOREIGN EXCHANGE FORWARD CONTRACT *see* CONTRACT, FUTURES.

FOREIGN EXCHANGE RATE *see* EXCHANGE RATE. *See also* FOREIGN EXCHANGE.

FOREIGN INVESTMENT investment in Canada that originated outside of the country.

FOREIGN TRADE POLICY regulation of exports and imports by government. Generally, governments promote exports, and impose restrictions on imports to achieve a favourable balance of trade that will benefit the domestic economy.

FOREIGN FUND funds that invest in the shares of foreign corporations, e.g., Japan, various European countries, and Australia.

FORFEITURE loss of rights or assets due to failure to fulfill a legal obligation or condition and as compensation for resulting losses or damages.

FORM 4 in the United States, a document, filed with the Securities and Exchange Commission and the pertinent stock exchange, which is used to report changes in the holdings of (1) those who own at least 10% of a corporation's outstanding stock and (2) directors and officers, even if they own no stock. When there has been a major change in ownership, Form 4 must be filed within ten days of the end of the month in which the change took place. Form 4 filings must be constantly updated during a takeover attempt of a company when the acquirer buys more than 10% of the outstanding shares.

FORM 10-K in the United States, an annual report required by the Securities and Exchange Commission of every issuer of a registered security, every exchange-listed company, and any company with 500 or more shareholders or $1 million or more in gross assets. The form provides for disclosure of total sales, revenue, and pretax operating income, as well as sales by separate classes of products for each of a company's separate lines of business for each of the past five years. A source and application of funds statement presented on a comparative basis for the last two fiscal years is also required. Form 10-K becomes public information when filed with the SEC.

FORMULA INVESTING investment technique based on a predetermined timing or asset allocation model that eliminates emotional decisions. One type of formula investing, called dollar cost averaging, involves putting the same amount of money into a stock or mutual fund at regular intervals, so that more shares will be bought when the price is low and less when the price is high. Another formula investing method calls for shifting funds from stocks to bonds or vice versa as the stock market reaches particular price levels. If stocks rise to a particular point, a certain amount of the stock portfolio is sold and put in bonds. On the other hand, if stocks fall to a particular low price, money is brought out of bonds into stocks. *See also* CONSTANT DOLLAR PLAN; CONSTANT RATIO PLAN.

FORTUNE 500 listings of the top 500 U.S. industrial corporations, and one of four Fortune 500 listings compiled by *Fortune* magazine. The companies are ranked by 12 indices, among them sales, profits, assets, stockholders' equity, earnings per share growth over a 10-year span, total return to investors in the year, and the 10-year annual rate of total return to investors. In separate listings, companies also are ranked by performance, within 26 industries, and within states. Headquarters city, phone number and the name of the chief executive officer are included. The Global 500 covers 27 industrial categories, from aerospace to metals to tobacco. The Service 500 of U.S. companies is divided into 8 categories: 100 diversified service companies, 100 commercial banks, 50 diversified financial companies, 50 savings institutions, 50 life insurance companies and 50 utilities. Its international companion is the Global Service 500.

FORWARD CONTRACT purchase or sale of a specific quantity of a commodity, government security, foreign currency, or other financial instrument at the current or SPOT PRICE, with delivery and settlement at a specified future date. Because it is a completed contract—as opposed to an options contract, where the owner has the choice of completing or not completing—a forward contract can be a COVER for the sale of a FUTURES CONTRACT. Forward contracts are largely used by exporters and importers who wish to establish costs or prices on future goods. *See* HEDGE.

FORWARD EXCHANGE TRANSACTION purchase or sale of foreign currency at an exchange rate established now but with payment and delivery at a specified future time. Most forward exchange contracts have one-, three-, or six-month maturities, though contracts in major currencies can normally be arranged for delivery at any specified date up to a year, and sometimes up to three years.

FORWARD RATE rate at which foreign currency has been bought or sold for delivery at a specified future date. Payment is not made until the future specified delivery date.

FOR YOUR INFORMATION (FYI) prefix to a security price quote by a market maker that indicates the quote is "for your information" and is not a firm offer to trade at that price. FYI quotes are given as a courtesy for purposes of valuation. FVO (for valuation only) is sometimes used instead.

401(k) PLAN in the United States, a plan whereby employees may elect, as an alternative to receiving taxable cash in the form of compensation or a bonus, to contribute pretax dollars to a qualified tax-deferred retirement plan. Elective deferrals are limited to about $9000 a year (the amount is revised each year by the IRS based on inflation). Many companies, to encourage employee participation in the plan, match employee contributions anywhere from 10% to 100% annually. All employee contributions and employer matching funds can be invested in several options, usually including several stock mutual funds, bond mutual funds, a GUARANTEED INVESTMENT CONTRACT, a money market fund, and company stock. Employees control how the assets are allocated among the various choices, and can usually move the money at least once a year, and sometimes even daily. Withdrawals from 401(k) plans prior to age 59½ are subject to a 10% penalty tax except for death, disability, termination of employment, or qualifying hardship. Withdrawals after the age of 59½ are subject to taxation in the year the money is withdrawn. "Highly compensated" employees are subject to special limitations. 401(k) plans have become increasingly popular in recent years, in many cases supplanting traditional DEFINED BENEFIT PENSION PLANS. Employees favour them because they cut their tax bills in the year of contribution and their savings grow tax deferred until retirement. Companies favour these plans because they are less costly than traditional pension plans and also shift the responsibility for asset allocation to employees. Also called *cash or deferred arrangement* (CODA) or *salary reduction plan.*

403(b) PLAN type of INDIVIDUAL RETIREMENT ACCOUNT (IRA) covered in Section 403(b) of the Internal Revenue Code that permits employees of qualifying nonprofit organizations to set aside tax-deferred funds.

FOURTH MARKET in the United States, the direct trading of large blocks of securities between institutional investors to save brokerage commissions. The fourth market is aided by computers, notably by a computerized subscriber service called *INSTINET,* an acronym for Institutional Networks Corporation.

FRACTIONAL DISCRETION ORDER buy or sell order for securities that allows the broker discretion within a specified fraction of a point. For example, "Buy 1000 XYZ at 28, discretion ½ point" means that the broker may execute the trade at a maximum price of 28½.

FRACTIONAL SHARE unit of stock less than one full share. For instance, if a shareholder is in a dividend reinvestment program, and the dividends being reinvested are not adequate to buy a full share at the stock's current price, the shareholder will be credited with a fractional share until enough dividends accumulate to purchase a full share.

FRANCHISE
In general: (1) privilege given a dealer by a manufacturer or franchise service organization to sell the franchisor's products or services in a given area, with or without exclusivity. Such arrangements are sometimes formalized in *a franchise agreement,* which is a contract between the franchisor and franchisee wherein the former may offer consultation, promotional assistance, financing, and other benefits in exchange for a percentage of sales or profits. (2) The business owned by the franchisee, who usually must meet an initial cash investment requirement.
Government: legal right given to a company or individual by a government authority to perform some economic function. For example, an electrical utility might have the right, under the terms of a franchise, to use city property to provide electrical service to city residents.

FRANCHISED MONOPOLY monopoly granted by the government to a company. The firm will be protected from competition by government exclusive license, permit, patent, or other device.

FRANKFURT STOCK EXCHANGE the German securities exchange, supported financially and administratively by the DEUTSCHE BORSE AG. The stock exchange, however, is responsible for rules of admission and trading, and supervision. There are three membership classes: banks that trade securities for their own accounts or on behalf of third parties; Kursmaklers, who act as intermediaries for trades in securities in the

Official Market and at the same time determine their prices; and Free Maklers, who act as intermediaries in any securities. Branches of foreign brokerage firms, which under their national laws are not banks, are treated as banks. There are three markets, based on capitalization: the Official Market, Regular Market, Free Market. Trading is by open outcry and IBIS, a computer-assisted system launched in 1991.

FRAUD intentional misrepresentation, concealment, or omission of the truth for the purpose of deception or manipulation to the detriment of a person or an organization. Fraud is a legal concept and the application of the term in a specific instance should be determined by a legal expert.

FREDDIE MAC
1. nickname for FEDERAL HOME LOAN MORTGAGE CORPORATION (FHLMC).
2. mortgage-backed securities, issued in minimum denominations of $25,000, that are packaged, guaranteed, and sold by the FHLMC. Mortgage-backed securities are issues in which residential mortgages are packaged and sold to investors.

FREE AND OPEN MARKET market in which price is determined by the free, unregulated interchange of supply and demand. The opposite is a *controlled market,* where supply, demand, and price are artificially set, resulting in an *inefficient market.*

FREED UP securities industry jargon meaning that the members of an underwriting syndicate are no longer bound by the price agreed upon and fixed in the AGREEMENT AMONG UNDERWRITERS. They are thus free to trade in the security on a market basis.

FREE ON BOARD (FOB) transportation term meaning that the invoice price includes delivery at the seller's expense to a specified point and no further. For example, "FOB our Toronto warehouse" means that the buyer must pay all shipping and other charges associated with transporting the merchandise from the seller's warehouse in Toronto to the buyer's receiving point. Title normally passes from seller to buyer at the FOB point by way of a bill of lading.

FREE RIGHT OF EXCHANGE ability to transfer securities from one name to another without paying the charge associated with a sales transaction. The free right applies, for example, where stock in STREET NAME (that is, registered in the name of a broker-dealer) is transferred to the customer's name in order to be eligible for a dividend reinvestment plan. *See also* REGISTERED SECURITY.

FREE STOCK (1) stock that is fully paid for and is not assigned as collateral. (2) stock held by an issuer following a PRIVATE PLACEMENT but that can be traded free of the restrictions bearing on a LETTER SECURITY.

FREEZE OUT put pressure on minority shareholders after a takeover to sell their shares to the acquirer.

FRIENDLY TAKEOVER merger supported by the management and board of directors of the target company. The board will recommend to shareholders that they approve the takeover offer, because it represents fair value for the company's shares. In many cases, the acquiring company will retain many of the existing managers of the acquired company to continue to run the business. A friendly takeover is in contrast to a HOSTILE TAKEOVER, in which management actively resists the acquisition attempt by another company or RAIDER.

FRINGE BENEFITS compensation to employees in addition to salary. Some examples of fringe benefits are paid holidays, retirement plans, life and health insurance plans, subsidized cafeterias, company cars, stock options, and expense accounts. In many cases, fringe benefits can add significantly to an employee's total compensation, and are a key ingredient in attracting and retaining employees. In considering fringe benefits, the potential employee should keep in mind that almost all fringe benefits in Canada are taxable except certain medical/dental benefits.

FRONT-END LOAD sales charge applied to an investment at the time of initial purchase. There may be a front-end load on a mutual fund, for instance, which is sold by a broker. Annuities, life insurance policies, and limited partnerships can also have front-end loads. From the investor's point of view, the earnings from the investment should make up for this up-front fee within a relatively short period of time. *See also* INVESTMENT COMPANY.

FRONTIER AREAS areas of Canada that have potential and known reserves, but are beyond the economic reach of the market. These include the MacKenzie Delta Beaufort Sea area, the Arctic Islands, and the offshore areas of the Atlantic and Pacific oceans.

FRONT OFFICE sales personnel in a brokerage, insurance, or other financial services operation. Front office workers produce revenue, in contrast to BACK OFFICE workers, who perform administrative and other support functions for the front office.

FRONT RUNNING practice whereby a securities or commodities trader takes a POSITION to capitalize on advance knowledge of a large upcoming transaction expected to influence the market price. In the stock market, this might be done by buying an OPTION on stock expected to benefit from a large BLOCK transaction. In commodities, DUAL TRADING is common practice and provides opportunities to profit from front running.

FROZEN ACCOUNT
   Banking: bank account from which funds may not be withdrawn until a lien is satisfied and a court order is received freeing the balance.
   A bank account may also be frozen by court order in a dispute over the ownership of property.

FULL DISCLOSURE
In general: requirement to disclose all material facts relevant to a transaction.
Securities industry: public information requirements established by the Securities Commission, and the major stock exchanges.
See also DISCLOSURE.

FULL REPLACEMENT COVERAGE *see* GUARANTEED REPLACEMENT COST COVERAGE INSURANCE.

FULL-SERVICE BROKER broker who provides a wide range of services to clients. Unlike a DISCOUNT BROKER, who just executes trades, a full-service broker offers advice on which stocks, bonds, commodities, and mutual funds to buy or sell. A full-service broker may also offer an ASSET MANAGEMENT ACCOUNT; advice on financial planning, tax shelters, and LIMITED PARTNERSHIPS; and new issues of stock. A full-service broker's commissions will be higher than those of a discount broker. The term *brokerage* is gradually being replaced by variations of the term *financial services* as the range of services offered by brokers expands.

FULL TRADING AUTHORIZATION freedom, even from broad guidelines, allowed a broker or adviser under a DISCRETIONARY ACCOUNT.

FULLY DEPRECIATED said of a fixed asset to which all the DEPRECIATION the tax law allows has been charged. Asset is carried on the books at its RESIDUAL VALUE, although its LIQUIDATING VALUE may be higher or lower.

FULLY DILUTED EARNINGS PER (COMMON) SHARE figure showing earnings per common share after assuming the exercise of warrants and stock options, and the conversion of convertible bonds and preferred stock (all potentially *dilutive* securities). Actually, it is more analytically correct to define the term as the smallest earnings per common share figure that can be obtained by computing earnings per share (EPS) for all possible combinations of assumed exercise or conversion (because antidilutive securities—securities whose conversion would add to EPS—may not be assumed to be exercised or converted). Fully diluted EPS must be reported on the profit and loss statement when the figure is 97% or less of earnings available to common shareholders divided by the average number of common shares outstanding during the period. *See also* DILUTION; PRIMARY EARNINGS PER (COMMON) SHARE.

FULLY DISTRIBUTED term describing a new securities issue that has been completely resold to the investing public (that is, to institutions and individuals and other investors rather than to dealers).

FULLY INVESTED said of an investor or a portfolio when funds in cash or CASH EQUIVALENTS are minimal and assets are totally committed to other investments, usually stock. To be fully invested is to have an optimistic view of the market.

FULLY VALUED said of a stock that has reached a price at which analysts think the underlying company's fundamental earnings power has been recognized by the market. If the stock goes up from that price, it is called OVERVALUED. If the stock goes down, it is termed UNDERVALUED.

FUND *see* FUND FAMILY; FUNDING; MUTUAL FUND.

FUNDAMENTAL ANALYSIS
Economics: research of such factors as interest rates, gross national product, inflation, unemployment, and inventories as tools to predict the direction of the economy.
Investment: analysis of the balance sheet and income statements of companies in order to forecast their future stock price movements. Fundamental analysts consider past records of assets, earnings, sales, products, management, and markets in predicting future trends in these indicators of a company's success or failure. By appraising a firm's prospects, these analysts assess whether a particular stock or group of stocks is UNDERVALUED or OVERVALUED at the current market price. The other major school of stock market analysis is TECHNICAL ANALYSIS, which relies on price and volume movements of stocks and does not concern itself with financial statistics.

FUNDAMENTALIST analyst who believes that stock prices are determined by the future course of earnings and dividends. In order to assess potential earnings and dividends, the fundamentalist studies, among other things, economics, industry conditions, and corporate financial statements.

FUNDED DEBT
  1. debt that is due after one year and is formalized by the issuing of bonds or long-term notes.
  2. bond issue whose retirement is provided for by a SINKING FUND.
     See also FLOATING DEBT.

FUNDED PENSION PLAN pension plan in which all liabilities are fully funded. A pension plan's administrator knows the potential payments necessary to make to pensioners over the coming years. In order to be funded, the plan must have enough capital contributions from the plan sponsor, plus returns from investments, to pay those claims. Employees are notified annually of the financial strength of their pension plans, and whether or not the plans are fully funded. If the plans are not funded, the PENSION BENEFIT GUARANTY CORPORATION (PBGC), which guarantees pension plans, will act to try to get the plan sponsor to contribute more money to the plan. If a company fails with an underfunded pension plan, the PBGC will step in to make the promised payments to pensioners.

FUND FAMILY mutual fund company offering funds with many investment objectives. A fund family may offer several types of stock, bond, and money market funds and allow free switching among their funds. Large no-load fund families include Altamira and Royal Bank while independent load companies include Investors, Trimark, Mackenzie, Fidelity, AGF, and Templeton. Such firms distribute their funds with a sales charge through brokerage firms and financial planners. Many investors find it convenient to place most of their assets with one or two fund families because of the convenience offered by such switching privileges. In recent years, several discount brokerage firms have offered the ability to shift assets from one fund family to another, making it less important than it had been to consolidate assets in one fund family. *See also* INVESTMENT COMPANY.

FUNDING
1. refinancing a debt on or before its maturity; also called REFUNDING and, in certain instances, PREREFUNDING.
2. putting money into investments or another type of reserve fund, to provide for future pension or welfare plans.
3. in corporate finance, the word *funding* is preferred to *financing* when referring to bonds in contrast to stock. A company is said to be funding its operations if it floats bonds.
4. to provide funds to finance a project, such as a research study. *See also* SINKING FUND.

FUND MANAGER manager of a pool of money such as a mutual fund, pension fund, insurance fund, or bank-pooled fund. His or her job is to maximize the fund's returns at the least risk possible. Each fund manager tries his or her best to realize the fund's objectives, whether it be growth, income, or some combination of the two. Different fund managers use different styles to accomplish their objectives. For example, some stock fund managers use the value style of investing, while others concentrate on growth stocks. In picking a fund, it is important to know the fund manager's style, and how long he or she has been managing the fund. This information is generally available for publicly offered mutual funds from fund company literature or fund representatives.

FUND OF FUNDS mutual fund that invests in other mutual funds. The concept behind such funds is that they are able to move money between the best funds in the industry, and thereby increase shareholders' returns with more diversification than is offered by a single fund.

FUND RESERVE percentage of customer deposits set aside as an asset for the bank.

FUND SWITCHING moving money from one mutual fund to another, within the same FUND FAMILY. Purchases and sales of funds may be done to time the ups and downs of the stock and bond markets, or because investors' financial needs have changed. Several newsletters and fund managers specialize in advising clients on which funds to switch into and out of, based on market conditions. Switching among funds within a fund family is usually allowed without sales charges. Discount brokerages allow convenient switching of funds among fund families. Unless practiced inside a tax-deferred account such as an IRA or Keogh account, a fund switch creates a taxable event, since CAPITAL GAINS OR LOSSES are realized.

FUNGIBLES bearer instruments, securities, or goods that are equivalent, substitutable, and interchangeable. Commodities such as soybeans or wheat, common shares of the same company, and dollar bills are all familiar examples of fungibles.

Fungibility (interchangeability) of listed options, by virtue of their common expiration dates and strike prices, makes it possible for buyers and sellers to close out their positions by putting offsetting transactions through the OPTIONS CLEARING CORPORATION. *See also* OFFSET; STRIKE PRICE.

FUN MONEY money that is not necessary for everyday living expenses, and can therefore be risked in volatile, but potentially highly profitable, investments. If the investment pans out, the investor has had some fun speculating. If the investment turns sour, the investor's lifestyle has not been put at risk because he or she could afford to lose the money.

FUTURES CONTRACT agreement to buy or sell a specific amount of a commodity or financial instrument at a particular price on a stipulated future date. The price is established between buyer and seller on the floor of a commodity exchange, using the OPEN OUTCRY system. A futures contract obligates the buyer to purchase the underlying commodity and the seller to sell it, unless the contract is sold to another before settlement date, which may happen if a trader waits to take a profit or cut a loss. This contrasts with options trading, in which the option buyer may choose whether or not to exercise the option by the exercise date. *See also* FORWARD CONTRACT; FUTURES MARKET.

FUTURES MARKET commodity exchange where FUTURES CONTRACTS are traded. Different exchanges specialize in particular kinds of contracts. The major exchanges are Amex Commodity Exchange, the Commodity Exchange Inc. (Comex), the New York Coffee, Sugar and Cocoa Exchange, the New York Cotton Exchange, the New York Mercantile Exchange, and the New York Futures Exchange, all in New York; the Chicago Board of Trade, the International Monetary Market, the Chicago Mercantile Exchange, the Chicago Rice and Cotton Exchange, and the MidAmerica Commodity Exchange, all in Chicago; the Kansas City Board of Trade, in Kansas City, MO; the Minneapolis Grain Exchange, in Minneapolis; and Montreal Futures.

FUTURES OPTION OPTION on a FUTURES CONTRACT.

FUTURE VALUE reverse of PRESENT VALUE.

FVO (FOR VALUATION ONLY) *see* FOR YOUR INFORMATION.

G

GAAP *see* GENERALLY ACCEPTED ACCOUNTING PRINCIPLES (GAAP).

GAIJIN non-Japanese investor in Japan. The Japanese refer to foreign competitors, on both the individual and institutional levels, as gaijin. In particular, the large, prestigious American and European brokerage firms that compete with the major Japanese brokerage firms, such as Nomura and Nikko, are called gaijin.

GAIN profit on a securities transaction. A gain is realized when a stock, bond, mutual fund, futures contract, or other financial instrument is sold for more than its purchase price. If the instrument was held for more than a year, the gain is taxable at more favourable capital gains tax rates. If held for under a year, the gain is taxed at regular income tax rates.

GAMMA STOCKS obsolete classification of stocks traded on the London Stock Exchange. Ranking third behind ALPHA and BETA stocks in capitalization and activity, gamma stocks are less regulated, requiring just two market makers quoting indicative share prices. *See also* NORMAL MARKET SIZE (NMS).

GAP
Finance: amount of a financing need for which provision has yet to be made. For example, ABC company might need $1.5 million to purchase and equip a new plant facility. It arranges a mortgage loan of $700,000, secures equipment financing of $400,000, and obtains new equity of $150,000. That leaves a gap of $250,000 for which it seeks gap financing. Such financing may be available from provincial and municipal governments concerned with promoting economic development, although most municipalities provide assistance of a nonfinancial nature only.
Securities: securities industry term used to describe the price movement of a stock or commodity when one day's trading range for the stock or commodity does not overlap the next day's, causing a range, or gap, in which no trade has occurred. This usually takes place because of some extraordinary positive or negative news about the company or commodity. *See* chart on next page. *See also* PRICE GAP.

GAP OPENING opening price for a stock that is significantly higher or lower than the previous day's closing price. For example, if XYZ Company was the subject of a $50 takeover bid after the market closed with its shares trading at $30, its share price might open the next morning at $45 a share. There would therefore be a gap between the closing price of $30 and the opening price of $45. The same phenomenon can occur on the downside if a company reports disappointing earnings or a takeover bid falls through, for example.

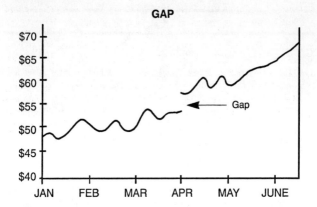

GAP

GARBATRAGE stock traders' term, combining garbage and ARBITRAGE, for activity in stocks swept upward by the psychology surrounding a major takeover. For example, when two leading entertainment stocks, Time, Inc., and Warner Communications, Inc., were IN PLAY in 1989, stocks with insignificant involvement in the entertainment sector became active. Garbatrage would not apply to activity in bona fide entertainment stocks moving on speculation that other mergers would follow in the wake of Time-Warner. *See also* RUMORTRAGE.

GARNISHMENT court order to an employer to withhold all or part of an employee's wages and send the money to the court or to a person who has won a lawsuit against the employee. An employee's wages will be *garnished* until the court-ordered debt is paid. Garnishing may be used in a divorce settlement or for repayment of creditors.

GATHER IN THE STOPS stock-trading tactic that involves selling a sufficient amount of stock to drive down the price to a point where stop orders (orders to buy or sell at a given price) are known to exist. The stop orders are then activated to become market orders (orders to buy or sell at the best available price), in turn creating movement which touches off other stop orders in a process called SNOWBALLING. Because this can cause sharp trading swings, floor officials on the exchanges have the authority to suspend stop orders in individual securities if that seems advisable. *See also* STOP ORDER.

GENERAL ACCOUNT account such as cash margin, short sale, options, futures and foreign currency belonging to a customer of a member firm of any one of the five sponsoring Self-Regulatory Organizations, e.g., Toronto Stock Exchange, Investment Dealers Association. Such accounts are combined and treated as one general account, entitling them to the maximum coverage offered by the Canadian Investor Protection Fund (CIPF). *See also* CANADIAN INVESTOR PROTECTION FUND.

GENERAL AGREEMENT ON TARIFFS AND TRADE (GATT)
United Nations-associated international treaty organization headquartered in Geneva that works to eliminate barriers to trade between nations. In December 1994, the United States Congress approved a pact that reduced tariffs, enhanced international copyright protections, and generally liberalized trade.

GENERAL AND ADMINISTRATIVE EXPENSE   costs of the accounting/financing division of a company and of administration and management, including any outside professionals, such as accountants or lawyers, who are not on staff as salaried employees. The overhead of the business.

GENERAL LEDGER formal ledger containing all the financial statement accounts of a business. It contains offsetting debit and credit accounts, the totals of which are proved by a trial balance. Certain accounts in the general ledger, termed *control accounts,* summarize the detail booked on separate subsidiary ledgers.

GENERAL LIEN LIEN against an individual that excludes real property. The lien carries the right to seize personal property to satisfy a debt. The property seized need not be the property that gave rise to the debt.

GENERAL LOAN AND COLLATERAL AGREEMENT continuous agreement under which a securities broker-dealer borrows from a bank against listed securities to buy or carry inventory, finance the underwriting of new issues, or carry the margin accounts of clients. Synonymous with *broker's loan. See also* BROKER LOAN RATE; MARGIN ACCOUNT; UNDERWRITE.

GENERALLY ACCEPTED ACCOUNTING PRINCIPLES (GAAP)
conventions, rules, and procedures that define accepted accounting practice, including broad guidelines as well as detailed procedures. The basic doctrine was set forth by the Accounting Principles Board of the American Institute of Certified Public Accountants, which was superseded in 1973 by the FINANCIAL ACCOUNTING STANDARDS BOARD (FASB), an independent self-regulatory organization.

GENERAL MORTGAGE BOND bond that is secured by a blanket mortgage on the company's property, but that is usually subordinated to one or more other specific mortgage bonds.

GENERAL PARTNER
1. one of two or more partners who are jointly and severally responsible for the debts of a partnership.
2. managing partner of a LIMITED PARTNERSHIP, who is responsible for the operations of the partnership and, ultimately, any debts taken on by the partnership. The general partner's liability is unlimited. In a real estate partnership, the general partner will pick the properties to be bought and will manage them. In an oil and gas partnership, the general partner will select drilling sites and oversee drilling activity.

In return for these services, the general partner collects certain fees and often retains a percentage of ownership in the partnership.

GHOSTING illegal manipulation of a company's stock price by two or more market makers. One firm will push a stock's price higher or lower, and the other firms will follow their lead in collusion to drive the stock's price up or down. The practice is called ghosting because the investing public is unaware of this coordinated activity among market makers who are supposed to be competing with each other.

GIC *see* GUARANTEED INVESTMENT CERTIFICATE.

GIFT INTER VIVOS gift of property from one living person to another, without consideration.

GILT-EDGED SECURITY stock or bond of a company that has demonstrated over a number of years that it is capable of earning sufficient profits to cover dividends on stocks and interest on bonds with great dependability. The term is used with corporate bonds more often than with stocks, where the term BLUE CHIP is more common.

GILTS bonds issued by the British government. Gilts are the equivalent in Canada of Treasury bills and Canada bonds and of Treasury securities in the United States in that they are perceived to have no risk of default. Income earned from investing in gilts is therefore guaranteed. Gilt yields act as the benchmark against which all other British bond yields are measured. Gilt futures are traded on the LONDON INTERNATIONAL FINANCIAL FUTURES EXCHANGE. The name gilt is derived from the original British government certificates, which had gilded edges.

GINNIE MAE nickname for the GOVERNMENT NATIONAL MORTGAGE ASSOCIATION and the securities guaranteed by that agency. *See also* GINNIE MAE PASS-THROUGH.

GINNIE MAE PASS-THROUGH in the United States, security, backed by a pool of mortgages and guaranteed by the GOVERNMENT NATIONAL MORTGAGE ASSOCIATION (Ginnie Mae), which passes through to investors the interest and principal payments of homeowners. Homeowners make their mortgage payments to the bank or savings and loan that originated their mortgage. After deducting a service charge (usually ½%), the bank forwards the mortgage payments to the pass-through buyers, who may be institutional investors or individuals. Ginnie Mae guarantees that investors will receive timely principal and interest payments even if homeowners do not make mortgage payments on time.

The introduction of Ginnie Mae pass-throughs has benefited the home mortgage market, since more capital has become available for lending. Investors, who are able to receive high, government-guaranteed interest payments, have also benefited. For investors, however, the rate of principal repayment on a Ginnie Mae pass-through is uncertain. If interest rates fall, principal will be repaid faster, since homeowners will refinance their mortgages. If rates rise, principal will be repaid more slowly, since homeowners will hold onto the underlying mortgages. *See also* HALF-LIFE.

GIVE UP

1. term used in a securities transaction involving three brokers, as illustrated by the following scenario: Broker A, a FLOOR BROKER, executes a buy order for Broker B, another member firm broker who has too much business at the time to execute the order. The broker with whom Broker A completes the transaction (the sell side broker) is Broker C. Broker A "gives up" the name of Broker B, so that the record shows a transaction between Broker B and Broker C even though the trade was actually executed between Broker A and Broker C.

2. another application of the term: A customer of brokerage firm ABC Co. travels out of town and, finding no branch office of ABC, places an order with DEF Co., saying he is an account of ABC. After confirming the account relationship, DEF completes a trade with GHI Co., advising GHI that DEF is acting for ABC ("giving up" ABC's name). ABC will then handle the clearing details of the transaction with GHI. Alternatively, DEF may simply send the customer's order directly to ABC for execution. Whichever method is used, the customer pays only one commission.

GLAMOUR STOCK stock with a wide public and institutional following. Glamour stocks achieve this following by producing steadily rising sales and earnings over a long period of time. In bull (rising) markets, glamour stocks tend to rise faster than market averages. Although a glamour stock is often in the category of a BLUE CHIP stock, the glamor is characterized by a higher earnings growth rate.

GLOBAL BOND FUND *see* GLOBAL MUTUAL FUND.

GLOBAL DEPOSITARY RECEIPT receipt for shares in a foreign-based corporation traded in capital markets around the world. AMERICAN DEPOSITARY RECEIPTS permit foreign corporations to offer shares to American citizens while Global Depositary Receipts (GDRs) allow companies in Canada, Europe, Asia, the United States and Latin America to offer shares in many markets around the world. The advantage to the issuing company is that they can raise capital in many markets, as opposed to just their home market. The advantage of GDRs to local investors is that they do not have to buy shares through the issuing company's home exchange, which may be difficult and expensive. In addition, the share price and all dividends are converted into the shareholder's home currency. Many GDRs are issued by companies in emerging markets such as China, India, Brazil, and South Korea and are traded on major stock exchanges, particularly the London SEAQ International Trading system. Because the companies issuing GDRs are not as well established and do not use the same accounting systems as traditional Western corporations, their stocks tend to be more volatile and less liquid.

GLOBAL MUTUAL FUND mutual fund that can invest in stocks and bonds throughout the world. Such funds typically have a portion of their assets in American markets as well as Europe, Asia, and developing countries. Global funds differ from INTERNATIONAL MUTUAL FUNDS, which invest only in non-Canadian securities. The advantage of global funds is that the fund managers can buy stocks or bonds anywhere they think has the best opportunities for high returns. Thus if one market is underperforming, they can shift assets to markets with better potential. Though some global funds invest in both stocks and bonds, most funds specialize in either stocks or bonds.

GNOMES OF ZÜRICH term coined by Labour ministers of Great Britain, during the sterling crisis of 1964, to describe the financiers and bankers in Zürich, Switzerland, who were engaged in foreign exchange speculation.

GNP *see* GROSS NATIONAL PRODUCT.

GOAL financial objective set by an individual or institution. For example, an individual investor might set a goal to accumulate enough capital to finance a child's college education. A pension fund's goal is to build up enough money to pay pensioners their promised benefits. Investors may also set specific price objectives when buying a security. For example, an investor buying a stock at $30 may set a price goal of $50, at which point he or she will sell shares, or at least reevaluate whether or not to continue holding the stock. Also called *target price.*

GODFATHER OFFER takeover offer that is so generous that management of the target company is unable to refuse it out of fear of shareholder lawsuits.

GOING AHEAD unethical securities brokerage act whereby the broker trades first for his or her own account before filling his customers' orders.

GOING-CONCERN VALUE value of a company as an operating business to another company or individual. The excess of going-concern value over asset value, or LIQUIDATING VALUE, is the value of the operating organization as distinct from the value of its assets. In acquisition accounting, going-concern value in excess of asset value is treated as an intangible asset, termed *goodwill.* Goodwill is generally understood to represent the value of a well-respected business name, good customer relations, high employee morale, and other such factors expected to translate into greater than normal earning power. However, because this intangible asset has no independent market or liquidation value, accepted accounting principles require that goodwill be written off over a period of time.

GOING LONG purchasing a stock, bond, or commodity for investment or speculation. Such a security purchase is known as a LONG POSITION.

The opposite of going long is GOING SHORT, when an investor sells a security he or she does not own and thereby creates a SHORT POSITION.

GOING PRIVATE movement from public ownership to private ownership of a company's shares either by the company's repurchase of shares or through purchases by an outside private investor. A company usually goes private when the market price of its shares is substantially below their BOOK VALUE and the opportunity thus exists to buy the assets cheaply. Another motive for going private is to ensure the tenure of existing management by removing the company as a takeover prospect.

GOING PUBLIC securities industry phrase used when a private company first offers its shares to the public. The firm's ownership thus shifts from the hands of a few private stockowners to a base that includes public shareholders. At the moment of going public, the stock is called an INITIAL PUBLIC OFFERING. From that point on, or until the company goes private again, its shares have a MARKET VALUE. *See also* NEW ISSUE; GOING PRIVATE.

GOING SHORT selling a stock or commodity that the seller does not have. An investor who goes short borrows stock from his or her broker, hoping to purchase other shares of it at a lower price. The investor will then replace the borrowed stock with the lower priced stock and keep the difference as profit. *See also* SELLING SHORT; GOING LONG.

GOLD precious metal used at one time in place of paper money as currency, i.e., traded in exchange for goods and services.

GOLD BARS bars made out of 99.5% to 99.99% pure gold which can be traded for investment purposes or held by central banks. Gold bars range in size from 400 troy ounces to as little as 1 ounce of gold; an individual can either hold on to these bars or store them in a safe deposit box. Central banks store gold bars weighing 400 troy ounces in vaults.

GOLD BOND bond backed by gold. Such debt obligations are issued by gold-mining companies, who peg interest payments to the level of gold prices. Investors who buy these bonds therefore anticipate a rising gold price. Silver mining firms similarly issue silver-backed bonds.

GOLDBUG analyst enamoured of gold as an investment. Goldbugs usually are worried about possible disasters in the world economy, such as a depression or hyperinflation, and recommend gold as a HEDGE.

GOLD BULLION gold in its purest form. The metal may be smelted into GOLD COINS or GOLD BARS of different sizes of 1 kg and up and refined to between .995 and .999 fineness or 99.5% and 99.9% purity. The standard bar traded is the 400-oz. bar. The price of gold bullion is set by market forces of supply and demand. Twice a day, the latest gold price is fixed at the London GOLD FIXING. Gold bullion is traded in physical form, and also through futures and options contracts. Certain gold-oriented mutual funds also hold small amounts of gold bullion.

GOLD CERTIFICATE paper certificate providing evidence of ownership of gold bullion. An investor not wanting to hold the actual gold in his or her home because of lack of security, for example, may prefer to hold gold in certificate form; the physical gold backing the certificate is held in a secure bank vault. Certificate owners pay a small custodial charge each year to the custodian bank.

GOLD COIN coin minted in gold. Bullion coins are minted by governments and are traded mostly on the value of their gold content. Major gold bullion coins include the Canadian Maple Leaf, the American Eagle, the Mexican Peso, the Australian Kangaroo, and the South African Kruggerand. Other gold coins, called NUMISMATIC COINS, are minted in limited quantity and trade more on the basis of their aesthetic value and rarity, rather than on their gold content. Numismatic coins are sold at a hefty markup to their gold content, and are therefore not as pure a play on gold prices as bullion coins.

GOLD FUTURES contract between a buyer and a seller in which the buyer or seller puts down a small deposit (margin) with a broker for the eventual purchase or sale in full of the gold. Prior to the delivery month, both the buyer and seller can offset their obligations by selling and buying similar contracts respectively. The buyer or seller who has not offset his or her position is obligated to take delivery.

GOLDEN BOOT inducement, using maximum incentives and financial benefits, for an older worker to take "voluntary" early retirement, thus circumventing age discrimination laws.

GOLDEN HANDCUFFS contract that ties a broker to a brokerage firm. If the broker stays at the firm, he or she will earn lucrative commissions, bonuses, and other compensation. But if the broker leaves and tries to lure clients to another firm, the broker must promise to give back to the firm much of the compensation received while working there. Golden handcuffs are a response by the brokerage industry to the frequent movement of brokers from one firm to another.

GOLDEN HANDSHAKE generous payment by a company to a director, senior executive, or consultant who is let go before his or her contract expires because of a takeover or other development. *See also* GOLDEN PARACHUTE.

GOLDEN HELLO bonus paid by a securities firm, usually in England, to get a key employee away from a competing firm.

GOLDEN PARACHUTE lucrative contract given to a top executive to provide lavish benefits in case the company is taken over by another firm, resulting in the loss of the job. A golden parachute might include generous severance pay, stock options, or a bonus.

GOLD FIXING daily determination of the price of gold by selected gold specialists and bank officials in London, Paris, and Zürich. The price is fixed at 10:30 A.M. and 3:30 P.M. London time every business day, according to the prevailing market forces of supply and demand.

GOLD MUTUAL FUND mutual fund investing in gold mining shares. Some funds limit themselves to shares in North American mining companies, while others can buy shares anywhere in the world, including predominantly South Africa and Australia. Such mutual funds offer investors diversification among many gold mining companies, somewhat reducing risks. Still, such funds tend to be volatile, since the prices of gold mining shares tend to move up or down far more than the price of gold itself. Gold funds also tend to pay dividends, since many gold mining companies pay dividends based on gold sales.

GOLD PRICE price of gold agreed to at one of the two daily London gold fixings.

GOLD STANDARD monetary system under which units of currency are convertible into fixed amounts of gold. Such a system is said to be anti-inflationary.

GOODBYE KISS *see* GREENMAIL.

GOOD DELIVERY securities industry designation meaning that a certificate has the necessary endorsements and meets all other requirements (signature guarantee, proper denomination, and other qualifications), so that title can be transferred by delivery to the buying broker, who is then obligated to accept it. Exceptions constitute *bad delivery. See also* DELIVERY DATE.

GOOD FAITH DEPOSIT
In general: token amount of money advanced to indicate intent to pursue a contract to completion.
Commodities: initial margin deposit required when buying or selling a futures contract. Such deposits generally range from 2% to 10% of the contract value.
Securities:
1. deposit, usually 25% of a transaction, required by securities firms of individuals who are not known to them but wish to enter orders with them.
2. deposit left with a municipal bond issuer by a firm competing for the underwriting business. The deposit typically equals 1% to 5% of the principal amount of the issue and is refundable to the unsuccessful bidders.

GOOD THROUGH order to buy or sell securities or commodities at a stated price for a stated period of time, unless canceled, executed, or changed. It is a type of LIMIT ORDER and may be specified GTW (good this week), GTM (GOOD-THIS-MONTH ORDER), or for shorter or longer periods.

GOOD-TILL-CANCELED ORDER (GTC) brokerage customer's order to buy or sell a security, usually at a particular price, that remains in effect until executed or canceled. If the GTC order remains unfilled after a long period of time, a broker will usually periodically (e.g., every 30 days) confirm that the customer still wants the transaction to occur if the stock reaches the target price. *See also* DAY ORDER; GOOD-THIS-MONTH ORDER; OPEN ORDER; TARGET PRICE.

GOODWILL *see* GOING-CONCERN VALUE.

GOVERNMENT BOND evidence of government debt to the purchaser or bondholder. It is of fixed duration, earning a fixed amount of interest, and has varying market values generally, corresponding to changes in the level of interest rates.

GOVERNMENT NATIONAL MORTGAGE ASSOCIATION (GNMA) in the United States, a government-owned corporation, nicknamed Ginnie Mae, which is an agency of the U.S. Department of Housing and Urban Development. GNMA guarantees, with the full faith and credit of the U.S. Government, full and timely payment of all monthly principal and interest payments on the mortgage-backed PASS-THROUGH SECURITIES of registered holders. The securities, which are issued by private firms, such as MORTGAGE BANKERS and savings institutions, and typically marketed through security broker-dealers, represent pools of residential mortgages insured or guaranteed by the Federal Housing Administration (FHA), the Farmer's Home Administration (FmHA), or the Veterans Administration (VA). *See also* GINNIE MAE PASS-THROUGH.

GOVERNMENT OBLIGATIONS government debt instruments (federal and provincial savings bonds, federal Treasury bills, and federal agency bonds such as CMHC) the government has pledged to repay.

GRACE PERIOD period of time provided in most loan contracts and insurance policies during which default or cancellation will not occur even though payment is due.
Credit cards: number of days between when a credit card bill is sent and when the payment is due without incurring interest charges. Most banks offer credit card holders a 25-day grace period, though some offer more and others fewer days.
Insurance: number of days, typically 30, during which insurance coverage is in force and premiums have not been paid.
Loans: provision in some long-term loans, particularly EUROCURRENCY syndication loans to foreign governments and multinational firms by groups of banks, whereby repayment of principal does not begin until some point well into the lifetime of the loan. The grace period, which can be as long as five years for international transactions for corporations, is an important point of negotiation between a borrower and a lender; borrowers sometimes will accept a higher interest rate to obtain a longer grace period.

GRADUATED CALL WRITING strategy of writing (selling) covered CALL OPTIONS at gradually higher EXERCISE PRICES so that as the price of the underlying stock rises and the options are exercised, the seller winds up with a higher average price than the original exercise price. The premiums naturally rise as the underlying stock rises, representing income to the seller that helps offset the loss if the stock should decline.

GRADUATED LEASE longer-term lease in which payments, instead of being fixed, are adjusted periodically based on appraisals or a benchmark rate, such as increases in the CONSUMER PRICE INDEX.

GRADUATED-PAYMENT MORTGAGE (GPM) mortgage featuring lower monthly payments at first, which steadily rise until they level off after a few years. GPMs, also known as "jeeps," are designed for young couples whose income is expected to grow as their careers advance. A graduated-payment mortgage allows such a family to buy a house that would be unaffordable if mortgage payments started out at a high level. Persons planning to take on such a mortgage must be confident that their income will be able to keep pace with the rising payments.

GRAHAM AND DODD METHOD OF INVESTING investment approach outlined in Benjamin Graham and David Dodd's landmark book *Security Analysis,* published in the 1930s. Graham and Dodd founded the modern discipline of security analysis with their work. They believed that investors should buy stocks with undervalued assets and that eventually those assets would appreciate to their true value in the marketplace. Graham and Dodd advocated buying stocks in companies where current assets exceed current liabilities and all long-term debt, and where the stock is selling at a low PRICE/EARNINGS RATIO. They suggested that the stocks be sold after a profit objective of between 50% and 100% was reached, which they assumed would be three years or less from the time of purchase. Analysts today who call themselves Graham and Dodd investors hunt for stocks selling below their LIQUIDATING VALUE and do not necessarily concern themselves with the potential for earnings growth.

GRANDFATHER CLAUSE provision included in a new rule that exempts from the rule a person or business already engaged in the activity coming under regulation.

GRANT OF PROBATE CERTIFICATE certificate issued to an executor by the court confirming the executor's authority as set out in a will to administer a particular estate. Also called Grant of Letter Probate and Letters Probate.

GRANTOR
Investments: options trader who sells a CALL OPTION or a PUT OPTION and collects PREMIUM INCOME for doing so. The grantor sells the right to buy a security at a certain price in the case of a call, and the right to sell at a certain price in the case of a put.
Law: one who executes a deed conveying title to property or who creates a trust. Also called a *settlor.*

GRAVEYARD MARKET bear market wherein investors who sell are faced with substantial losses, while potential investors prefer to stay liquid, that is, to keep their money in cash or cash equivalents until market conditions improve. Like a graveyard, those who are in can't get out and those who are out have no desire to get in.

GRAY KNIGHT acquiring company that, acting to advance its own interests, outbids a WHITE KNIGHT but that, not being unfriendly, is preferable to a hostile bidder.

GREY MARKET
Consumer goods: sale of products by unauthorized dealers, frequently at discounted prices. Consumers who buy grey market goods may find that the manufacturer refuses to honour the product warranty. In some cases, grey market goods may be sold in a country they were not intended for, so, for example, instructions may be in another language than the home market language.
Securities: sale of securities that have not officially been issued yet by a firm that is not a member of the underwriting syndicate. Such trading in the when-issued, or grey, market can provide a good indication of the amount of demand for an upcoming new stock or bond issue.

GREATER FOOL THEORY theory that even though a stock or the market as a whole is FULLY VALUED, speculation is justified because there are enough fools to push prices further upward.

GREENMAIL payment of a premium to a raider trying to take over a company through a proxy contest or other means. Also known as BON VOYAGE BONUS, it is designed to thwart the takeover. By accepting the payment, the raider agrees not to buy any more shares or pursue the takeover any further for a specified number of years. *See also* GOODBYE KISS.

GREEN SHOE clause in an underwriting agreement saying that, in the event of exceptional public demand, the issuer will authorize additional shares for distribution by the syndicate.

GRESHAM'S LAW theory in economics that bad money drives out good money. Specifically, people faced with a choice of two currencies of the same nominal value, one of which is preferable to the other because of metal content or because it resists mutilation, will hoard the good money and spend the bad money, thereby driving the good money out of circulation. The observation is named for Sir Thomas Gresham, master of the mint in the reign of Queen Elizabeth I.

GROSS EARNINGS personal taxable income before adjustments made to arrive at ADJUSTED GROSS INCOME.

GROSS INCOME total personal income before exclusions and deductions.

GROSS LEASE property lease under which the lessor (landlord) agrees to pay all the expenses normally associated with ownership (insurance, taxes, utilities, repairs). An exception might be that the lessee (tenant) would be required to pay real estate taxes above a stipulated amount or to pay for certain special operating expenses (snow removal, grounds care in the case of a shopping centre, or institutional advertising, for example). Gross leases are the most common type of lease contract and are typical arrangements for short-term tenancy. They normally contain no provision for periodic rent adjustments, nor are there preestablished renewal arrangements. *See also* NET LEASE.

GROSS NATIONAL EXPENDITURE total level of demand in the economy for goods and services. It shows how the GNP is used up through consumer spending, investment, and government spending.

GROSS NATIONAL PRODUCT (GNP) total output by the country of goods and services. The change in the GNP from one period to the next shows the growth rate (or its lack) for the period and is a strong indicator of the direction of the country's economy. *See also* GROSS DOMESTIC PRODUCT.

GROSS PER BROKER gross amount of commission revenues attributable to a particular REGISTERED REPRESENTATIVE during a given period. Brokers, who typically keep one third of the commissions they generate, are often expected by their firms to meet productivity quotas based on their gross.

GROSS PROFIT profit after deduction of all costs of material, labour, and factory overhead, but before selling and administrative costs. Gross margin is gross profit expressed as a percentage of sales. Also called *gross margin*. *See also* NET PROFIT.

GROSS SALES total sales at invoice values, not reduced by customer discounts, returns or allowances, or other adjustments. *See also* NET SALES.

GROSS SPREAD difference (spread) between the public offering price of a security and the price paid by an underwriter to the issuer. The spread breaks down into the manager's fee, the dealer's (or underwriter's) discount, and the selling concession (i.e., the discount offered to a selling group). *See also* CONCESSION; FLOTATION (FLOATATION) COST.

GROSS-UP AND CREDIT SYSTEM procedure intended to encourage Canadians to invest in preferred and common shares of taxable, dividend-paying Canadian corporations; not available on interest from bonds. The taxpayer pays tax based on grossing up (i.e., adding 25% to the amount of dividends actually received) and obtains a credit against federal and provincial tax based on the grossed-up amount.

GROUND LEASE lease on the land. Typically, the land will be under a building, which will have its own leases with tenants.

GROUP INSURANCE insurance coverage bought for and provided to a group instead of an individual. For example, an employer may buy disability, health, and term life insurance for its employees at a far better rate than the employees could obtain on their own. Credit unions, trade associations, and other groups may also offer their members preferential group insurance rates. Group insurance is not only advantageous to employees or group members because it is cheaper than they could obtain on their own, but some people may be able to get coverage under the group umbrella when they would be denied coverage individually because of pre-existing conditions or other factors.

GROUP OF TEN ten major industrialized countries that try to coordinate monetary and fiscal policies to create a more stable world economic system. The ten are Belgium, Canada, France, Germany, Italy, Japan, the Netherlands, Sweden, the United Kingdom, and the United States. Also known as the *Paris Club*.

GROUP ROTATION tendency of stocks in one industry to outperform and then underperform other industries. This may be due to the economic cycle or what industry is popular or unpopular with investors at any particular time. For example, CYCLICAL stocks in the auto, paper, or steel industry may be group leaders when the economy is showing robust growth, while stocks of stable-demand firms such as drug or food companies may be market leaders in a recession. Alternatively, investor demand for stocks in certain industries, such as biotechnology, computer software, or real estate investment trusts may rise and fall because of enthusiasm or disappointment with the group, creating rotation into or out of such stocks. Market analysts watch which industry group is coming into and going out of vogue in recommending stocks that might lead or lag in coming months.

GROUP SALES term used in securities underwriting that refers to block sales made to institutional investors. The securities come out of a syndicate "pot" with credit for the sale prorated among the syndicate members in proportion to their original allotments.

GROWTH AND INCOME FUND MUTUAL FUND that seeks earnings growth as well as income. These funds invest mainly in the common stock of companies with a history of capital gains but that also have a record of consistent dividend payments. They also invest in securities that are convertible into common stocks, such as warrants and options.

GROWTH FUND mutual fund that invests in growth stocks. The goal is to provide capital appreciation for the fund's shareholders over the long term. Growth funds are more volatile than more conservative income or money market funds. They tend to rise faster than conservative funds in bull (advancing) markets and to drop more sharply in bear (falling) markets. *See also* GROWTH STOCK.

GROWTH RATE percentage rate at which the economy, stocks, or earnings are growing. The economic growth rate is normally determined by the growth of the GROSS DOMESTIC PRODUCT. Individual companies try to establish a rate at which their earnings grow over time. Firms with long-term earnings growth rates of more than 15% are considered fast-growing companies. Analysts also apply the term *growth rate* to specific financial aspects of a company's operations, such as dividends, sales, assets, and market share. Analysts use growth rates to compare one company to another within the same industry.

GROWTH STOCK stock of a corporation that has exhibited faster-than-average gains in earnings over the last few years and is expected to continue to show high levels of profit growth. Over the long run, growth stocks tend to outperform slower-growing or stagnant stocks. Growth stocks are riskier investments than average stocks, however, since they usually sport higher price/earnings ratios and make little or no dividend payments to shareholders. *See also* PRICE/EARNINGS RATIO.

G-7 FINANCE MINISTERS the finance ministers of the seven largest industrial countries: Canada, France, Germany, Great Britain, Italy, Japan, and the United States. In recent years, the Russian finance minister has also been invited to participate in G-7 meetings. Such meetings take place at least once a year and are important in coordinating economic policy among the major industrial countries. The political leaders of the G-7 countries also meet once a year, usually in June, at the Economic Summit, which is held in one of the seven countries.

GUARANTEE to take responsibility for payment of a debt or performance of some obligation if the person primarily liable fails to perform. A guarantee is a CONTINGENT LIABILITY of the guarantor—that is, it is a potential liability not recognized in accounts until the outcome becomes probable in the opinion of the company's accountant.

GUARANTEED INCOME SUPPLEMENT (GIS)   income-tested monthly pension supplement for OAS pensioners who have little other income. The annual amount received is adjusted every year for changes in the pensioner's financial circumstances and marital status, and the pensioner must reapply every year. GIS is distinguished from OAS because only recipients who are resident in Canada are eligible, while OAS can be paid to nonresidents. GIS is not included in taxable income. GIS indexation is adjusted quarterly.

GUARANTEED INSURABILITY feature offered as an option in life and health insurance policies that enables the insured to add coverage at specified future times and at standard rates without evidence of insurability.

GUARANTEED INVESTMENT CERTIFICATE (GIC) deposit instrument most commonly available from trust companies, requiring a minimum investment (usually $1000) at a predetermined rate of interest for a stated term. Rates vary with market conditions and the bank rate. Generally nonredeemable prior to maturity but there can be exceptions.

GICs are most attractive to older investors as the investment is insured to $60,000 and there is little perceived risk. However, mortgage-backed securities and government bonds (other than savings bonds) offer better interest rates.

GUARANTEED REPLACEMENT COST COVERAGE INSURANCE policy that pays for the full cost of replacing damaged property without a deduction for depreciation and without a dollar limit. This policy is different from an actual cash value policy, which takes into account depreciation for lost and damaged items, if the damage resulted from an insured peril.

GUARANTEE LETTER letter by a commercial bank that guarantees payment of the EXERCISE PRICE of a client's PUT OPTION (the right to sell a given security at a particular price within a specified period) if or when a notice indicating its exercise, called an assignment notice, is presented to the option seller (writer).

GUARANTEE OF SIGNATURE certificate issued by a bank or brokerage firm vouching for the authenticity of a person's signature. Such a document may be necessary when stocks, bonds, or other registered securities are transferred from a seller to a buyer. Banks also require guarantees of signature before they will process certain transactions.

GUARDIAN individual who has the legal right to care for another person as a parent or to act as an administrator of the assets of a person declared incompetent for mental or physical reasons. Guardians can be *testamentary*, meaning appointed in a parent's will; *general*, meaning having the general responsibility to care for another person and that person's estate; or *special*, meaning the guardian has limited authority, such as half the responsibility of a general guardian but not the other.

GUN JUMPING
1. trading securities on information before it becomes publicly disclosed.
2. illegally soliciting buy orders in an underwriting, before REGISTRATION is complete.

GUNSLINGER aggressive portfolio manager who buys speculative stocks, often on margin. In the great bull market of the 1960s, several hot fund managers gained reputations and had huge followings as gunslingers by producing enormous returns while taking great risks. However, the bear market of the early 1970s caused many of these gunslingers to lose huge amounts of money, and in most cases, their followings. The term is still used when referring to popular managers who take big risks in search of high returns.

H

HAIRCUT securities industry term referring to the formulas used in the valuation of securities for the purpose of calculating a broker-dealer's net capital. The haircut varies according to the class of a security, its market risk, and the time to maturity. For example, cash equivalent GOVERNMENTS could have a 0% haircut, equities could have an average 30% haircut, and fail positions (securities with past due delivery) with little prospect of settlement could have a 100% haircut. *See also* CASH EQUIVALENTS; FAIL POSITION.

HALF-STOCK common or preferred stock with a $50 par value instead of the more conventional $100 par value.

HAMMERING THE MARKET intense selling of stocks by those who think prices are inflated. Speculators who think the market is about to drop, and therefore sell short, are said to be hammering the market. *See also* SELLING SHORT.

HANDS-OFF INVESTOR investor willing to take a passive role in the management of a corporation. An individual or corporation with a large stake in another company may decide to adopt a "hands-off" policy if it is satisfied with the current performance of management. However, if management falters, it may become more actively involved in corporate strategy.

HANDS-ON INVESTOR investor who takes an active role in the management of the company whose stock he or she has bought.

HANDY AND HARMAN SILVER QUOTATION dealer in precious metals with a very large requirement for silver. Their quotation is the average price for which they can purchase silver in order to meet their need for that day. Photographic film manufacturers are heavy users of silver, as are jewelers and silversmiths.

HANG SENG INDEX the major indicator of stock market performance in Hong Kong. The index comprises 33 companies, divided into four sub-indices: financial (4), property (9), utilities (6), commerce and industry (14). It is computed on an arithmetic basis, weighted by market capitalization, and strongly influenced by large capitalization stocks such as Hongkong Bank, Hang Seng Bank, Hongkong Land and Cheung Kong.

HARD CURRENCY currency that is sought after as a stable standard of exchange and security. The major hard currencies are the U.S. dollar, Swiss franc, Deutschemark, and Japanese yen.

HARD DOLLARS actual payments made by a customer for services, including research, provided by a brokerage firm. For instance, if a broker puts together a financial plan for a client, the fee might be $1000 in hard dollars. This contrasts with SOFT DOLLARS, which refers to compensation by way of the commissions a broker would receive if he were to carry out any trades called for in that financial plan. Brokerage house research is sold for either hard or soft dollars.

HARD MONEY (HARD CURRENCY)

1. currency in which there is widespread confidence. It is the currency of an economically and politically stable country, such as the U.S. or Switzerland. Countries that have taken out loans in hard money generally must repay them in hard money.

2. gold or coins, as contrasted with paper currency, which is considered *soft money*. Some hard-money enthusiasts advocate a return to the GOLD STANDARD as a method of reducing inflation and promoting economic growth.

HEAD AND SHOULDERS patterns resembling the head and shoulders outline of a person, which is used to chart stock price trends. The pattern signals the reversal of a trend. As prices move down to the right shoulder, a head and shoulders top is formed, meaning that prices should be falling. A reverse head and shoulders pattern has the head at the bottom of the chart, meaning that prices should be rising.

HEAD AND SHOULDERS

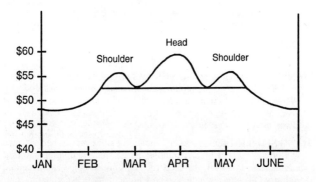

HEALTH INSURANCE in popular usage, any insurance plan that covers medical expenses or health care services over and above that supplied by provincial hospital and medical plans. In insurance, protection against loss by sickness or bodily injury, in which sense it is synonymous with accident and health, accident and sickness, accident, or disability income insurance.

HEAVY MARKET stock, bond, or commodity market with falling prices resulting from a larger supply of offers to sell than bids to buy.

HEDGE/HEDGING strategy used to offset investment risk. A perfect
hedge is one eliminating the possibility of future gain or loss.

A stockholder worried about declining stock prices, for instance,
can hedge his or her holdings by buying a PUT OPTION on the stock or
selling a CALL OPTION. Someone owning 100 shares of XYZ stock,
selling at $70 per share, can hedge his or her position by buying a put
option giving him or her the right to sell 100 shares at $70 at any time
over the next few months. This investor must pay a certain amount of
money, called a PREMIUM, for these rights. If XYZ stock falls during
that time, the investor can exercise his or her option—that is, sell the
stock at $70—thereby preserving the $70 value of the XYZ holdings.
The same XYZ stockholder can also hedge his or her position by selling a call option. In such a transaction, he or she sells the right to buy
XYZ stock at $70 per share for the next few months. In return, the
stockholder receives a premium. If XYZ stock falls in price, that premium income will offset to some extent the drop in value of the stock.

SELLING SHORT is another widely used hedging technique.

Investors often try to hedge against inflation by purchasing assets
that will rise in value faster than inflation, such as gold, real estate, or
other tangible assets.

Large commercial firms that want to be assured of the price they
will receive or pay for a commodity will hedge their position by buying and selling simultaneously in the FUTURES MARKET. For example,
Redpath Sugar, will hedge its supplies of sugar in the futures market
to limit the risk of a rise in sugar prices.

Managers of large pools of money such as pension and mutual
funds frequently hedge their exposure to currency or interest rate risk
by buying or selling futures or options contracts. For example, a
GLOBAL MUTUAL FUND manager with a large position in Japanese
stocks who thinks the Japanese yen is about to fall in value against the
U.S. dollar may buy futures or options on the Japanese yen to offset
the projected loss on the currency.

HEDGE CLAUSE disclaimer seen in market letters, security research
reports, or other printed matter having to do with evaluating
investments, which purports to absolve the writer from responsibility
for the accuracy of information obtained from usually reliable sources.
Despite such clauses, which may mitigate liability, writers may still be
charged with negligence in their use of information. Typical language
of a hedge clause: "The information furnished herein has been
obtained from sources believed to be reliable, but its accuracy is not
guaranteed."

HEDGED TENDER SELLING SHORT a portion of the shares being tendered to protect against a price drop in the event all shares tendered are
not accepted. For example, ABC Company or another company wishing to acquire ABC Company announces a TENDER OFFER at $52 a share
when ABC shares are selling at a market price of $40. The market price

of ABC will now rise to near the tender price of $52. An investor wishing to sell all his or her 2000 shares at $52 will tender 2000 shares, but cannot be assured all shares will be accepted. To lock in the $52 price on the tendered shares the investor thinks might not be accepted—say half of them or 1000 shares—he or she will sell short that many shares. Assuming the investor has guessed correctly and only 1000 shares are accepted, when the tender offer expires and the market price of ABC begins to drop, the investor will still have sold all 2000 shares for $52 or close to it—half to the tenderer and the other half when the short sale is consummated.

HEDGE FUND private investment partnership (for U.S. investors) or an off-shore investment corporation (for non-U.S. or tax-exempt investors) in which the general partner has made a substantial personal investment, and whose offering memorandum allows for the fund to take both long and short positions, use leverage and derivatives, and invest in many markets. Hedge funds often take large risks on speculative strategies, including PROGRAM TRADING, SELLING SHORT, SWAPS, and ARBITRAGE. A fund need not employ all of these tools all of the time; it must merely have them at its disposal. Since hedge funds are not limited to buying securities, they can potentially profit in any market environment, including one with sharply declining prices. Because they move billions of dollars in and out of markets quickly, hedge funds can have a significant impact on the day-to-day trading developments in the stock, bond, and futures markets.

Hedge funds entitle the general partner to an additional incentive management fee based upon positive returns—the higher the returns, the higher their fee. Hedge funds require that 65% of all investors be of the *accredited* type, defined as an individual or couple who have a net worth of at least $1 million, or an individual who had income in the previous year of at least $200,000, or a couple with at least $300,000 of income in the previous year. In reality, though, an investor needs much more than that.

The funds also require substantial minimum investments that can make it hard even for accredited investors to ante up. Minimums typically range from about $250,000 to $10 million. An investor gives up liquidity in hedge funds. They typically have a one-year lock-up for first-time investors.

HEDGER investor, possibly a farmer, manufacturer, portfolio manager, banker, etc., who uses the futures market to minimize the risk in his or her business.

HEDGE WRAPPER options strategy where the holder of a long position in an underlying stock buys an OUT OF THE MONEY put and sells an out of the money call. It defines a range where the stock will be sold at expiration of the option, whatever way the stock moves. The maximum profit is made if the call is exercised at expiration, since the holder gets the strike price plus any dividends. The maximum loss occurs if the put option is exercised, and represents the cost of the hedge wrapper less the strike price plus dividends received. The cost of the hedge wrapper less dividends received is the breakeven point. The strategy produces a loss whenever the breakeven price is higher than the strike price of the call.

HEIR one who inherits some or all of the estate of a deceased person by virtue of being in the direct line (*heir of the body*), or being designated in a will or by a legal authority (*heir at law*).

HELSINKI STOCK EXCHANGE smallest of the Nordic exchanges. Electronic trading began in 1992 with the switch to computer registered book entries. The Helsinki Stock Exchange Automated Trading System permits all 19 members to receive a feed from terminals in their own offices. The HEX Index includes all shares quoted on the Helsinki Stock Exchange (HSE), and share price indices also are computed for industry groups. The rapidly expanding derivatives market is traded on two options exchanges, open to international investors. The Finnish Options Market (FOM) trades equity and currency derivatives, offering standardized options and forward contracts on the Finnish Options Index (FOX). Trading is conducted Monday through Friday, 8:30 A.M.–5:05 P.M.

HEMLINE THEORY whimsical idea that stock prices move in the same general direction as the hemlines of women's dresses. Short skirts in the 1920s and 1960s were considered bullish signs that stock prices would rise, whereas longer dresses in the 1930s and 1940s were considered bearish (falling) indicators. Despite its sometimes uncanny way of being prophetic, the hemline theory has remained more in the area of wishful thinking than serious market analysis.

HIBOR acronym for *Hong Kong Interbank Offer Rate,* the annualized offer rate paid by banks for Hong Kong dollar-denominated three-month deposits. It acts as a benchmark for many interest rates throughout the Far East.

HIDDEN VALUES assets owned by a company but not yet reflected in its stock price. For example, a manufacturing firm may own valuable real estate that could be sold at a much higher price than it appears on the company's books, which is usually the price at which the real estate was purchased. Other undervalued assets that could have significant value include patents, trademarks, or exclusive contracts. Value-oriented money managers search for stocks with hidden values on their balance sheet in the hope that some day, those values will be realized through a higher stock price either by actions of the current management or by a takeover.

HIGH AND LOW high and low transaction prices that occur each trading day.

HIGH CREDIT
   Banking: maximum amount of loans outstanding recorded for a particular customer.
   Finance: the highest amount of TRADE CREDIT a particular company has received from a supplier at one time.

HIGH FLYER high-priced and highly speculative stock that moves up and down sharply over a short period. The stock of unproven high-technology companies might be high flyers, for instance.

HIGH-GRADE BOND bond rated triple-A or double-A by Dominion Bond Rating or Standard & Poor's or Moody's rating services. *See also* RATING.

HIGHJACKING Japanese term for a TAKEOVER.

HIGHLY CONFIDENT LETTER letter from an investment banking firm that it is "highly confident" that it will be able to arrange financing for a securities deal. This letter might be used to finance a leveraged buyout or multibillion-dollar takeover offer, for example. The board of directors of the target firm might request a highly confident letter in evaluating whether a proposed takeover can be financed. After the letter has been issued and the deal approved, the investment bankers will attempt to line up financing from banks, private investors, stock and bond offerings, and other sources. Though the investment banker professes to be highly confident he can arrange financing, the letter is not an ironclad guarantee of his ability to do so.

HIGHLY LEVERAGED TRANSACTION (HLT) loan, usually by a bank, to an already highly LEVERAGED COMPANY.

HIGH, LOW AND CLOSE highest and lowest price at which a security trades during a business day, and the closing price or last trade price of the day.

HIGHS stocks that have hit new high prices in daily trading for the current 52-week period. (They are listed as "highs" in daily newspapers.) Technical analysts consider the ratio between new highs and new LOWS in the stock market to be significant for pointing out stock market trends.

HIGH-TECH STOCK stock of companies involved in high-technology fields (computers, semiconductors, biotechnology, robotics, electronics). Successful high-tech stocks have above-average earnings growth and therefore typically very volatile stock prices.

HIGH-TICKET ITEMS items with a significant amount of value, such as jewellery and furs. Most standard homeowner's/renter's policies have limits on specific types of high-ticket items. Most policies have a limit of $1000–$2000 for all jewellery and furs. To provide appropriate coverage for these items, they should be scheduled separately in the form of a FLOATER or endorsement. Also called *valuables*.

HIGH-YIELD BOND bond that has RATING of BB or lower and that pays a higher yield to compensate for its greater risk. *See also* JUNK BOND.

HISTORICAL COST accounting principle requiring that all financial statement items be based on original cost or acquisition cost. The dollar is assumed to be stable for the period involved.

HISTORICAL TRADING RANGE price range within which a stock, bond, or commodity has traded since going public. A VOLATILE stock will have a wider trading range than a more conservative stock. Technical analysts see the top of a historical range as the RESISTANCE LEVEL and the bottom as the SUPPORT LEVEL. They consider it highly significant if a security breaks above the resistance level or below the support level. Usually such a move is interpreted to mean that the security will go onto new highs or new lows, thus expanding its historical trading range.

HISTORICAL YIELD yield provided by a mutual fund, typically a money market fund, over a particular period of time. For instance, a money market fund may advertise that its historical yield averaged 10% over the last year.

HIT informally, a significant securities loss or a development having a major impact on corporate profits, such as a large WRITE-OFF. Term is also used in the opposite sense to describe an investing success, similar to a "hit" in show business.

HIT THE BID to accept the highest price offered for a stock. For instance, if a stock's ask price is $50¼ and the current bid price is $50, a seller will hit the bid if he or she accepts $50 a share.

HOLD
Banking: retaining an asset in an account until the item has been collected. For example, a hold can be put on a certain amount of funds in a checking account if a certified check has been issued for that amount.
Securities: maintaining ownership of a stock, bond, mutual fund, or other security for a long period of time. Proponents of the BUY AND HOLD STRATEGY try to buy high-quality securities which they hope will grow in value over many years. By holding for a long time, the investor can delay capital gains taxes until the position is sold many years in the future.

Securities analysts also issue a HOLD recommendation if they are not enthusiastic enough about a security to recommend purchasing it, yet are not pessimistic enough to recommend selling it. However, many analysts who downgrade a stock from a buy to a hold rating are in fact saying that investors should sell the stock, since there are better opportunities to invest elsewhere.

HOLDER buyer of an option contract.

HOLDER OF RECORD owner of a company's securities as recorded on the books of the issuing company or its TRANSFER AGENT as of a particular date. Dividend declarations, for example, always specify payability to holders of record as of a specific date.

HOLDING COMPANY corporation that owns enough voting stock in another corporation to influence its board of directors and therefore to control its policies and management. A holding company need not own a majority of the shares of its subsidiaries or be engaged in similar activities. However, to gain the benefits of tax consolidation, which include tax-free dividends to the parent and the ability to share operating losses, the holding company must own 80% or more of the subsidiary's voting stock.

Among the advantages of a holding company over a MERGER as an approach to expansion are the ability to control sizeable operations with fractional ownership and commensurately small investment; the somewhat theoretical ability to take risks through subsidiaries with liability limited to the subsidiary corporation; and the ability to expand through unobtrusive purchases of stock, in contrast to having to obtain the approval of another company's shareholders.

Among the disadvantages of a holding company are partial multiple taxation when less than 80% of a subsidiary is owned, plus other special state and local taxes; the risk of forced DIVESTITURE (it is easier to force dissolution of a holding company than to separate merged operations); and the risks of negative leverage effects in excessive PYRAMIDING.

The following types of holding companies are defined in special ways and subject to particular legislation: public utility holding company (*see* PUBLIC UTILITY HOLDING COMPANY ACT), BANK HOLDING COMPANY, railroad holding company, and air transport holding company.

HOLDING PERIOD length of time an asset is held by its owner. Effective in 1994, capital assets held for 12 months or more qualify for special CAPITAL GAINS TAX treatment. *See also* ANTICIPATED HOLDING PERIOD; INVESTMENT LETTER.

HOLDING THE MARKET entering the market with sufficient buy orders to create price support for a security or commodity, for the purpose of stabilizing a downward trend.

HOME BANKING service offered by banks allowing consumers and small businesses to perform many banking functions at home through computers, telephones, and cable television links to the bank, thereby providing them with a number of convenience services. Bank customers are able to shift money between accounts, apply for loans and make loan payments, pay bills, check balances, and buy and sell securities, among other services. As home banking becomes easier and more convenient to use, more and more consumers sign up for it. It offers the advantages of privacy, speed, accuracy and the ability to perform transactions at any time. Most banks charge an extra fee for access to home banking services. Home banking does not currently offer the ability to obtain cash, for which customers must still visit a bank teller or automated banking machine.

HOMEOWNER'S EQUITY ACCOUNT credit line offered by banks, trust companies, brokerage firms, and other mortgage lenders allowing a homeowner to tap the built-up equity in his or her home. Such an account is, in effect, a REVOLVING CREDIT second mortgage, which can be accessed with the convenience of a cheque. Most lenders will provide a line of credit up to 70% or 80% of the appraised value of a home, minus any outstanding first mortgage debt. When a homeowner receives the loan, a LIEN is automatically placed against the house; the lien is removed when the loan is repaid. A homeowner's equity account often carries a lower interest rate than a second mortgage; typically, the rate is tied to the PRIME RATE. Many banks charge one or two percentage points higher than the prime rate.

HOMEOWNER'S INSURANCE POLICY policy protecting a homeowner against property and casualty perils. It will cover damage to the home from natural causes such as fire, lightning, windstorms, hail, rain, volcanic eruption, damage caused by falling objects, the weight of ice, snow or sleet, freezing of plumbing, heating or air conditioning systems, electrical discharges, or the rupture of water heating or protective sprinkler systems. In addition, man-made disasters such as riots, vandalism, damage from cars or airplanes, explosions, and theft will also be reimbursed. Flood, earthquake, war, and nuclear accident are not covered; flood and earthquake insurance can be purchased separately. In general, homeowners should try to purchase coverage that will pay for the replacement of damaged or stolen items at current market prices, not at the prices for which those items may have been acquired years ago. There are dollar limits for high-ticket items such as jewellery. A FLOATER or an endorsement, purchased separately, can provide the additional coverage needed.

The average homeowner's or renter's policy provides approximately $500,000 of liability protection. A special policy is required for homeowner's business risk coverage. Home business owners need both property and liability insurance, since the homeowner's policy provides only limited coverage for business equipment, in most cases up to $2,500 for business equipment in the home and $250 away from the home.

Most mortgage lenders require homeowners to obtain adequate insurance coverage before they agree to provide a mortgage.

HOME RUN large gain by an investor in a short period of time. Someone who aims to hit an investment home run may be looking for a potential TAKEOVER target, for example, since takeover bids result in sudden price spurts. Such investing is inherently more risky than the strategy of holding for the long term.

HORIZON ANALYSIS method of measuring the discounted cash flow (timeadjusted return) from an investment, using time periods or series *(horizons)* that differ from the investment's contractual maturity. The horizon date might be the end of a BUSINESS CYCLE or some other date determined in the perspective of the investor's overall portfolio requirements. Horizon analysis calculations, which include reinvestment assumptions, permit comparison with alternative investments that is more realistic in terms of individual portfolio requirements than traditional YIELD-TO-MATURITY calculations.

HORIZONTAL MERGER *see* MERGER.

HORIZONTAL PRICE MOVEMENT movement within a narrow price range over an extended period of time. A stock would have a horizontal price movement if it traded between $47 and $51 for over six months, for instance. Also known as *sideways price movement. See also* FLAT MARKET.

HORIZONTAL PRICE MOVEMENT

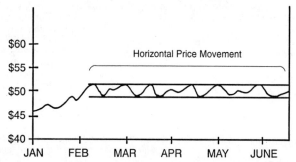

HORIZONTAL SPREAD options strategy that involves buying and selling the same number of options contracts with the same exercise price, but with different maturity dates; also called a CALENDAR SPREAD. For instance, an investor might buy ten XYZ call options with a striking price of $70 and a maturity date of October. At the same time, he or she would sell ten XYZ call options with the same striking price of $70 but a maturity date of July. The investor hopes to profit by moves in XYZ stock by this means.

HOSTILE TAKEOVER takeover of a company against the wishes of current management and the board of directors. This takeover may be attempted by another company or by a well-financed RAIDER. If the price offered is high enough, shareholders may vote to accept the offer even if management resists and claims that the company is actually worth even more. If the acquirer raises the price high enough, management may change its attitude, converting the hostile takeover into a friendly one. Management has many weapons at its disposal to fend off a hostile takeover, such as GREENMAIL, POISON PILLS, the SCORCHED EARTH POLICY, and SUICIDE PILLS, among others. Also called *unfriendly takeover. See also* TAKEOVER.

HOT ISSUE newly issued stock that is in great public demand. Hot issue stocks usually shoot up in price at their initial offering, since there is more demand than there are shares available.

HOT MONEY investment funds capriciously seeking high, short-term yields. Borrowers attracting hot money, such as banks issuing high-yielding CERTIFICATES OF DEPOSIT, should be prepared to lose it as soon as another borrower offers a higher rate.

HOT STOCK
   1. stock that has been stolen.
   2. newly issued stock that rises quickly in price. *See* HOT ISSUE.

HOUSE
   1. firm or individual engaged in business as a broker-dealer in securities and/or investment banking and related services.
   2. nickname for the London Stock Exchange.

HOUSE ACCOUNT account handled at the main office of a brokerage firm or managed by an executive of the firm; in other words, an account distinguished from one that is normally handled by a salesperson in the territory. Ordinarily, a salesperson does not receive a commission on a house account, even though the account may actually be in his or her territory.

HOUSE CALL brokerage house notification that the customer's EQUITY in a MARGIN ACCOUNT is below the maintenance level. If the equity declines below that point, a broker must call the client, asking for more cash or securities. If the client fails to deliver the required margin, his or her position will be liquidated.

HOUSE MAINTENANCE REQUIREMENT internally set and enforced rules of individual broker-dealers in securities with respect to a customer's MARGIN ACCOUNT. House maintenance requirements set levels of EQUITY that must be maintained to avoid putting up additional equity or having collateral sold out.

HOUSE OF ISSUE investment banking firm that underwrites a stock or bond issue and offers the securities to the public. *See also* UNDER-WRITE.

HOUSE POOR short of cash because the bulk of your money is tied up in your house. Implication is that without the real estate investment and associated mortgage, you would be financially comfortable.

HOUSE RULES securities industry term for internal rules and policies of individual broker-dealer firms concerning the opening and handling of customers' accounts and the activities of the customers in such accounts. House rules are designed to assure that firms are in comfortable compliance with the requirements of outside regulatory authorities and in most cases are more stringent than the outside regulations. *See also* HOUSE CALL; HOUSE MAINTENANCE REQUIREMENT.

HOUSING AFFORDABILITY INDEX *see* AFFORDABILITY INDEX.

HOUSING STARTS number of new residential housing units on which construction has started. Construction has started when the excavation of footings has begun. Housing starts is one of the measures used to assess the performance of the economy.

HULBERT RATING rating by *Hulbert Financial Digest* of Alexandria, Virginia, of how well the recommendations of various investment advisory newsletters have performed. The ratings cover performance as far back as 1980, if data are available. The *Digest* ranks over 150 investment advisory newsletters covering stocks, bonds, mutual funds, futures, and options by tabulating the profits and losses subscribers would have received had they followed the newsletter's advice exactly.

HUMAN CAPITAL skills acquired by a worker through formal education and experience that improve the worker's productivity and increase his or her income.

HUNG UP term used to describe the position of an investor whose stocks or bonds have dropped in value below their purchase price, presenting the problem of a substantial loss if the securities were sold.

HUNKERING DOWN trader's term for working to sell off a big position in a stock.

HURDLE RATE term used in the budgeting of capital expenditures, meaning the REQUIRED RATE OF RETURN in a DISCOUNTED CASH FLOW analysis. If the EXPECTED RATE OF RETURN on an investment is below the hurdle rate, the project is not undertaken. The hurdle rate should be equal to the INCREMENTAL COST OF CAPITAL.

HYBRID ANNUITY contract offered by an insurance company that allows an investor to mix the benefits of both fixed and variable annuities. Also called *combination annuity.* For instance, a portion of an annuity buyer's assets may be put in a FIXED ANNUITY, which promises a certain rate of return, and the remainder in a stock or bond fund VARIABLE ANNUITY, which offers a chance for higher return but takes more risk.

HYBRID INVESTMENT OR SECURITY investment vehicle that combines two different kinds of underlying investments. For example, a structured note, which is a form of a bond, may have the interest rate it pays tied to the rise and fall of a commodity's price. Hybrid investments are also called *derivatives.*

HYPERINFLATION *see* INFLATION.

HYPOTHECATION

Banking: pledging property to secure a loan. Hypothecation does not transfer title, but it does transfer the right to sell the hypothecated property in the event of default.

Securities: pledging of securities to brokers as collateral for loans made to purchase securities or to cover short sales, called margin loans. When the same collateral is pledged by the broker to a bank to collateralize a broker's loan, the process is called *rehypothecation.*

I

IBC/DONOGHUE'S MONEY FUND REPORT AVERAGE average for all major money market mutual fund yields, published weekly for 7- and 30-day simple and compound (assumes reinvested dividends) yields. IBC/Donoghue also tracks the average maturity of securities in money fund portfolios. A short maturity of about 30 days reflects the conviction of fund managers that interest rates are going to rise, and a long maturity of 60 days or more reflects a sentiment that rates are going to fall. The IBC/Donoghue's Money Fund Report Average is published in major newspapers, including the *Wall Street Journal, The New York Times* and *Barron's*.

In Canada, Fiscal Agents Bell Charts and Southam provide daily or monthly rates.

I/B/E/S INTERNATIONAL INC. provides the I/B/E/S data base, which comprises analysts' estimates of future earnings for thousands of publicly traded companies. These estimates are tabulated, and companies whose estimates have increased or decreased significantly are pinpointed. Reports also detail how many estimates are available on each company and the high, low, and average estimates for each. *See also* ZACK'S ESTIMATE SYSTEM.

IDLE FUNDS funds in an account in excess of the compensating balance requirement that have not been invested or put to use. The compensating balance requirement is specified by the loan agreement to compensate for services, cheques, etc.

IF, AS AND WHEN clause in a contract drawn up when new issues are sold before the security certificates are printed. This clause protects the dealer against delay in receiving the certificates.

ILLIQUID
Finance: firm that lacks sufficient CASH FLOW to meet current and maturing obligations.
Investments: not readily convertible into cash, such as a stock, bond, or commodity that is not traded actively and would be difficult to sell at once without taking a large loss. Other assets for which there is not a ready market, and which therefore may take some time to sell, include real estate and collectibles such as rare stamps, coins, or antique furniture.

IMBALANCE OF ORDERS too many orders of one kind—to buy or to sell—without matching orders of the opposite kind. An imbalance usually follows a dramatic event such as a takeover, the death of a key executive, or a government ruling that will significantly affect the company's business. If it occurs before the stock exchange opens, trading in the stock is delayed. If it occurs during the trading day, the specialist suspends trading until enough matching orders can be found to make for an orderly market.

IMF *see* INTERNATIONAL MONETARY FUND.

IMMEDIATE FAMILY parents, brothers, sisters, children, relatives supported financially, father-in-law, mother-in-law, sister-in-law, and brother-in-law.

IMMEDIATE OR CANCEL ORDER order requiring that all or part of the order be executed as soon as the broker enters a bid or offer; the portion not executed is automatically canceled. Such stipulations usually accompany large orders.

IMMEDIATE PAYMENT ANNUITY annuity contract bought with a single payment and with a specified payout plan that starts right away. Payments may be for a specified period or for the life of the annuitant and are usually on a monthly basis. *See also* ANNUITIZE.

IMMUNIZATION *see* DURATION.

IMM International Monetary Market of the CME.

IMPAIRED CAPITAL total capital that is less than the stated or par value of the company's CAPITAL STOCK. *See also* DEFICIT NET WORTH.

IMPAIRED CREDIT deterioration in the credit rating of a borrower, which may result in a reduction in the amount of credit made available by lenders. For example, a company may launch a product line that is a failure, and the resulting losses will seriously weaken the company's finances. Concerned lenders may reduce the firm's credit lines as a result. The same process can apply to an individual who has been late paying bills, or in an extreme case, has filed for bankruptcy protection. Also called *adverse credit.*

IMPORT DUTY *see* TARIFF.

IMPREST ACCOUNT technique for maintaining tight control over disbursing by branch office, subsidiary, or local affiliate. The local unit must provide proof of legitimate disbursements before corporate headquarters will refund its account. Balances in these accounts are maintained at a negotiated level.

IMPROVEMENTS INSURANCE insurance a tenant may acquire to protect improvements made to rented business premises.

IMPUTED INTEREST interest considered to have been paid in effect even though no interest was actually paid.

IMPUTED VALUE logical or implicit value that is not recorded in any accounts. Examples: in projecting annual figures, values are imputed for months about which actual figures are not yet available; cash invested unproductively has an imputed value consisting of what it would have earned in a productive investment (OPPORTUNITY COST).

INACTIVE ASSET asset not continually used in a productive way, such as an auxiliary generator.

INACTIVE BOND CROWD *see* CABINET CROWD.

INACTIVE POST trading post on the New York Stock Exchange at which inactive stocks are traded in 10-share units rather than the regular 100-share lots. Known to traders as *Post 30. See also* ROUND LOT.

INACTIVE STOCK/BOND security traded relatively infrequently, either on an exchange or over the counter. The low volume makes the security ILLIQUID, and small investors tend to shy away from it.

IN-AND-OUT purchase and sale of the same security within a short period—a day, week, even a month. An in-and-out trader is more interested in profiting from day-to-day price fluctuations than in dividends or long-term growth.

IN-AND-OUT TRADER one who buys and sells the same security in one day, aiming to profit from sharp price moves. *See also* DAY TRADE.

INCESTUOUS SHARE DEALING buying and selling of shares in each other's companies to create a tax or other financial advantage.

INCOME ASSET any investment asset that produces a regular income monthly, quarterly, or annually, such as interest and dividend income. This may include Guaranteed Investment Certificates, preferred shares, and a mutual fund income fund of dividend-bearing shares.

INCOME AVAILABLE FOR FIXED CHARGES *see* FIXED-CHARGE COVERAGE.

INCOME AVERAGING method of computing personal income tax whereby tax is figured on the average of the total of current year's income and that of the preceding years. Revenue Canada automatically uses an income averaging program to adjust taxes in a year when a taxpayer reports a large interest bonus or severance.

INCOME BOND obligation on which the payment of interest is contingent on sufficient earnings from year to year. Generally, an income bond that promises to repay principal but to pay interest only when earned. In some cases, unpaid interest on an income bond may accumulate as a claim against the company when the bond matures.

INCOME DIVIDEND payout to shareholders of interest, dividends, or other income received by a mutual fund. By law, all such income must be distributed to shareholders, who may choose to take the money in cash or reinvest it in more shares of the fund. All income dividends are taxable to shareholders in the year they are received.

INCOME MUTUAL FUND mutual fund designed to produce current income for shareholders. Some examples of income funds are government, mortgage-backed security, municipal, international, and junk bond funds. Several kinds of equity-oriented funds also can have income as their primary investment objective, such as utilities income funds and equity income funds. *See also* BOND FUND.

INCOME PROPERTY   real estate bought for the income it produces.

INCOME-SPLITTING   tax planning device frequently available to business owners to minimize total tax paid by the company and the shareholders. "Splitting" can refer to splitting between salaries and dividends, spousal salaries, etc.

INCOME STATEMENT *see* PROFIT AND LOSS STATEMENT; EARNINGS STATEMENT.

INCOME STOCK stock paying high and regular dividends to shareholders. Some industries known for income stocks include gas, electric, and telephone utilities; banks; and insurance companies. High-quality income stocks have established a long history of paying dividends, and in many cases have a track record of regularly increasing dividends. All dividends paid to shareholders of income stocks are taxable in the year received unless the stock is held in an RRSP.

INCOME TAX annual tax on income levied by the federal government and the provinces. There are two basic types: the personal income tax, levied on incomes of households and unincorporated businesses, and the corporate (or corporation) income tax, levied on net earnings of corporations.

The income tax was established in 1917 as a temporary measure to finance the war. It has risen to become a 1500-page Act that has been under constant amendment and reform. Major tax reform began as early as 1971 and again in 1981, with special commissions undertaking multi-year studies to attempt to simplify the Act and ensure greater fairness. The tax brackets were reduced to 3 brackets in 1991. Provincial governments now levy their own income tax as a percent of federal taxes paid (except Québec). There is a new taxpayer's Bill of Rights that was introduced in 1994 by the Department of National Revenue to give more equity and less arbitrary action.

The income tax system is a progressive, graduated income tax that permits personal deductions (credits) for the taxpayer, spouse, children (under 18), the aged (over 65), and the disabled. There are numerous schedules for special reporting of investment income, capital gains and losses, transfer of deductions, etc. The return can be filed electronically.

Most working Canadians pay withholding tax at the source or by quarterly installments.

INCONTESTABILITY CLAUSE provision in a life insurance contract stating that the insurer cannot revoke the policy after it has been in force for one or two years if the policyholder concealed important facts from the company during the application process. For example, a policyholder who stated that he or she had never had a heart attack, but in fact had experienced one, would still be covered by the policy if the insurance company had not discovered this discrepancy within one or two years. However, if a policyholder lies about his or her age on the application, the policy's death benefit can be adjusted higher retroactively to account for the insured's true age.

INCORPORATION process by which a company receives a provincial or federal charter allowing it to operate as a corporation. The fact of incorporation must be acknowledged in the company's legal name, using the word Limited, or Ltd. or Inc. or other acceptable variations. *See also* ARTICLES OF INCORPORATION.

INCREMENTAL CASH FLOW net of cash outflows and inflows attributable to a corporate investment project.

INCREMENTAL COST OF CAPITAL weighted cost of the additional capital raised in a given period. Weighted cost of capital, also called *composite cost of capital,* is the weighted average of costs applicable to the issues of debt and classes of equity that compose the firm's capital structure. Also called *marginal cost of capital.*

INDEMNIFY agree to compensate for damage or loss. The word is used in insurance policies promising that, in the event of a loss, the insured will be restored to the financial position that existed prior to the loss.

INDENTURE formal agreement, also called a deed of trust, between an issuer of bonds and the bondholder covering such considerations as: (1) form of the bond; (2) amount of the issue; (3) property pledged (if not a debenture issue); (4) protective COVENANTS including any provision for a sinking fund; (5) WORKING CAPITAL and CURRENT RATIO; and (6) redemption rights or call privileges.

INDEPENDENT AGENT agent representing several insurance companies. The agent is independent from all the companies he or she sells for, and can therefore in theory evaluate different insurance policies objectively. Independent agents pay all their own expenses and keep their own records and earn their income from commissions on the policies they sell. The opposite of an independent agent is a CAPTIVE AGENT, who works exclusively for one company.

INDEPENDENT AUDITOR chartered accountant (CA) (CGA in British Columbia) who provides the accountant's opinion.

INDEPENDENT LIFE INSURANCE insurance that provides death benefits in the event of the death of the spouse or child of a policyholder.

INDEX securities index specified by an exchange that is determined by inclusion and relative representation of the current market value of a group of securities. *See also* AVERAGES.

INDEX ARBITRAGE *see* ARBITRAGE.

INDEXATION *see* INDEXING, at meaning (2).

INDEX BOND bond whose cash flow is linked to the purchasing power of the dollar or a foreign currency. For example, a bond indexed to the CONSUMER PRICE INDEX (CPI) would ensure that the bondholder receives real value by making an upward adjustment in the interest rate to reflect higher prices.

INDEXED ANNUITY annuity that is referred to as inflation-indexed because it increases the payment each year by an agreed value, up to 4%. The word "indexed" may be misleading, because the annuity is not indexed to any inflation measure; it simply increases every year by a fixed percentage. The earlier payments are lower than a straight life annuity and the later payments (if the annuitant lives long enough) are higher. In periods of positive inflation, such an annuity does provide a reasonable hedge. An indexed annuity provides some tax relief since the higher tax on the higher nominal amount is deferred, relative to taxes on the straight life annuity.

INDEX FUND mutual fund that has a portfolio matching that of a broad-based portfolio. This may include the TSE 300, indexes of mid- and small-capitalization stocks, foreign stock indexes, and bond indexes, to name a few. Many institutional and individual investors, especially believers in the EFFICIENT MARKET theory, put money in index funds on the assumption that trying to beat the market averages over the long run is futile, and their investments in these funds will at least keep pace with the index being tracked. In addition, since the cost of managing an index fund is far cheaper than the cost of running an actively managed portfolio, index funds have a built-in cost advantage.

INDEXING
1. weighting one's portfolio to match a broad-based index such as TSE 300 so as to match its performance—or buying shares in an INDEX FUND.
2. tying wages, taxes, or other rates to an index. For example, a labour contract may call for indexing wages to the consumer price index to protect against loss of purchasing power in a time of rising inflation.

INDEX OF LEADING INDICATORS *see* LEADING INDICATORS.

INDEX OPTIONS calls and puts on indexes of stocks designed to reflect market conditions and fluctuate with the market. These options are traded on the TSE, New York, American, and Chicago Board Options Exchanges, among others. Broad-based indexes cover a wide range of companies and industries, whereas narrow-based indexes consist of stocks in one industry or sector of the economy. Index options allow investors to trade in a particular market or industry group without having to buy all the stocks individually. For instance, someone who thought oil stocks were about to fall could buy a put on the oil index instead of selling short shares in half a dozen oil companies.

INDEX PARTICIPATION *see* BASKET.

INDICATED YIELD coupon or dividend rate as a percentage of the current market price. For fixed rate bonds it is the same as CURRENT YIELD. For common stocks, it is the market price divided into the annual dividend. For preferred stocks, it is the market price divided into the contractual dividend.

INDICATION approximation of what a security's TRADING RANGE (bid and offer prices) will be when trading resumes after a delayed opening or after being halted because of an IMBALANCE OF ORDERS or another reason. Also called *indicated market.*

INDICATION OF INTEREST securities underwriting term meaning a dealer's or investor's interest in purchasing securities that are still *in registration* (awaiting clearance by) a securities commission. A broker who receives an indication of interest should send the client a preliminary prospectus on the securities. An indication of interest is not a commitment to buy, an important point because selling a security while it is in registration is illegal. *See also* CIRCLE.

INDICATOR technical measurement securities market analysts use to forecast the market's direction, such as investment advisory sentiment, volume of stock trading, direction of interest rates, and buying or selling by corporate insiders.

INDICES AND AVERAGES *see* AVERAGES AND INDICES.

INDIRECT COST AND EXPENSE *see* DIRECT OVERHEAD; FIXED COST.

INDIRECT HOLDING *see* DIRECT HOLDING.

INDIRECT LABOUR COSTS wages and related costs of factory employees, such as inspectors and maintenance crews, whose time is not charged to specific finished products.

INDIVIDUAL INSURANCE *see* PERSONAL INSURANCE.

INDUSTRIAL in stock market vernacular, general, catch-all category including firms producing or distributing goods and services that are not classified as utility, transportation, or financial companies. *See also* STOCK INDEXES AND AVERAGES; FORTUNE 500.

INEFFICIENCY IN THE MARKET failure of investors to recognize that a particular stock or bond has good prospects or may be headed for trouble. According to the EFFICIENT MARKET theory, current prices reflect all knowledge about securities. But some say that those who find out about securities first can profit by exploiting that information; stocks of small, little-known firms with a large growth potential most clearly reflect the market's inefficiency, they say.

INELASTIC DEMAND OR SUPPLY *see* ELASTICITY OF DEMAND OR SUPPLY.

IN ESCROW *see* ESCROW.

INFANT INDUSTRY ARGUMENT case made by developing sectors of the economy that their industries need protection against international competition while they establish themselves. In response to such pleas, the government may enact a TARIFF or import duty to stifle foreign competition. The infant industry argument is frequently made in developing nations that are trying to lessen their dependence on the industrialized world. In Brazil, for example, such infant industries as automobile production argue that they need protection until their technological capability and marketing prowess are sufficient to enable competition with well-established foreigners.

INFLATION rise in the prices of goods and services, as happens when spending increases relative to the supply of goods on the market—in other words, too much money chasing too few goods. Moderate inflation is a common result of economic growth. Hyperinflation, with prices rising at 100% a year or more, causes people to lose confidence in the currency and put their assets in hard assets like real estate or gold, which usually retain their value in inflationary times. *See also* COST-PUSH INFLATION; DEMAND-PULL INFLATION.

INFLATION HEDGE investment designed to protect against the loss of purchasing power from inflation. Traditionally, gold and real estate have a reputation as good inflation hedges, though growth in stocks also can offset inflation in the long run. Money market funds, which pay higher yields as interest rates rise during inflationary times, can also be a good inflation hedge. In the case of hyperinflation, hard assets such as precious metals and real estate are normally viewed as inflation hedges, while the value of paper-based assets such as stocks, bonds, and currency erodes rapidly.

INFLATION RATE rate of change in prices.

INFLATION RISK *see* RISK.

INFLEXIBLE EXPENSES *see* FLEXIBLE EXPENSES.

INFORMATION CIRCULAR document sent to shareholders with a proxy, providing details of matters to come before a shareholders' meeting.

INFRASTRUCTURE a nation's basic system of transportation, communication, and other aspects of its physical plant. Building and maintaining road, bridge, sewage, and electrical systems provides millions of jobs nationwide. For developing countries, building an infrastructure is a first step in economic development.

INGOT standard silver bar weighing about 1000 troy ounces.

INHERITANCE part of an estate acquired by an HEIR.

INITIAL INVESTMENT cash outflow that should be considered in evaluating capital expenditure. It is found by netting all inflows and outflows occurring at time zero for a proposed project.

INITIAL MARGIN amount of cash or eligible securities required to be deposited with a broker before engaging in margin transactions. A margin transaction is one in which the broker extends credit to the customer in a margin account, usually about 50% of the purchase price of the stocks.

INITIAL PUBLIC OFFERING (IPO) corporation's first offering of stock to the public. IPO's are almost invariably an opportunity for the existing investors and participating venture capitalists to make big profits, since for the first time their shares will be given a market value reflecting expectations for the company's future growth. *See also* HOT ISSUE.

INJUNCTION court order instructing a defendant to refrain from doing something that would be injurious to the plaintiff, or face a penalty. The usual procedure is to issue a temporary restraining order, then hold hearings to determine whether a permanent injunction is warranted.

IN PLAY stock affected by TAKEOVER rumors or activities.

INSIDE INFORMATION corporate affairs that have not yet been made public. The officers of a firm would know in advance, for instance, if the company was about to be taken over, or if the latest earnings report was going to differ significantly from information released earlier. Under Securities and Exchange Commission rules, an INSIDER is not allowed to trade on the basis of such information.

INSIDE MARKET bid or asked quotes between dealers trading for their own inventories. Distinguished from the retail market, where quotes reflect the prices that customers pay to dealers. Also known as *interdealer market; wholesale market.*

INSIDER person with access to key information before it is announced to the public. Usually the term refers to directors, officers, and key employees, but the definition has been extended legally to include relatives and others in a position to capitalize on INSIDE INFORMATION such as anyone owning more than 10% of the voting shares in a corporation. Insiders are prohibited from trading on their knowledge.

INSIDER REPORT report of all transactions in the shares of a company by those considered to be insiders of the company and submitted each month to securities commissions.

INSIDER TRADING practice of buying and selling shares in a company's stock by that company's management or board of directors, or by a holder of more than 10% of the company's shares. Managers may trade their company's stock as long as they disclose their activity within ten days of the close of the month within the time the transactions took place. However, it is illegal for insiders to trade based on their knowledge of material corporate developments that have not been announced publicly. Developments that would be considered *material* include news of an impending takeover, introduction of a new product line, a divestiture, a key executive appointment, or other news that could affect the company's stock positively or negatively. Insider trading laws have been extended to other people who have knowledge of these developments but who are not members of management, including investment bankers, lawyers, printers of financial disclosure documents, or relatives of managers and executives who learn of these material developments.

INSOLVENCY inability to pay debts when due. *See also* BANKRUPTCY; CASH FLOW; SOLVENCY.

INSTALLMENT DEBENTURE *see* SERIAL BOND.

INSTALLMENT RECEIPTS new issue of stock sold with the obligation that buyers will pay the issue price in a series of specified installments instead of in one lump sum payment. Also known as PARTIALLY PAID SHARES.

INSTALLMENT SALE
In general: sale made with the agreement that the purchased goods or services will be paid for in fractional amounts over a specified period of time.
Securities: transaction with a set contract price, paid in installments over a period of time. Gains or losses are generally taxable on a pro-rated basis.

INSTINET *see* FOURTH MARKET.

INSTITUTIONAL BROKER broker who buys and sells securities for banks, mutual funds, insurance companies, pension funds, or other institutional clients. Institutional brokers deal in large volumes of securities and generally charge their customers lower per-unit commission rates than individuals pay.

INSTITUTIONAL INVESTOR organization that trades large volumes of securities and has a steady flow of money to invest. Such organizations have become the major buyers and sellers on stock exchanges and, although they can influence prices on the stock exchanges, they tend not to exert any direct influence on the companies whose shares they buy. Some examples are mutual funds, banks, insurance companies, pension funds, labour union funds, corporate profit-sharing plans, and college endowment funds.

INSTRUMENT legal document in which some contractual relationship is given formal expression or by which some right is granted—for example, notes, contracts, agreements. *See also* NEGOTIABLE INSTRUMENT.

INSURABILITY conditions under which an insurance company is willing to insure a risk. Each insurance company applies its own standards based on its own underwriting criteria. For example, some life insurance companies do not insure people with high-risk occupations such as stuntmen or firefighters, while other companies consider these people insurable, though the premiums they must pay are higher than for those in low-risk professions.

INSURABLE INTEREST relationship between an insured person or property and the potential beneficiary of the policy. For example, a spouse or marital partner has an insurable interest in the other spouse's life, because he or she would be financially harmed if the spouse were to die. Therefore, he or she could receive the proceeds of the insurance policy if the spouse were to die while the policy was in force. If there is no insurable interest, an insurance company will not issue a policy.

INSURANCE system whereby individuals and companies that are concerned about potential hazards pay premiums to an insurance company, which reimburses them in the event of loss. The insurer profits by investing the premiums it receives. Some common forms of insurance cover business risks, automobiles, homes, boats, worker's compensation, and health. Life insurance guarantees payment to the beneficiaries when the insured person dies. In a broad economic sense, insurance transfers risk from individuals to a larger group, which is better able to pay for losses.

INSURANCE AGENT representative of an insurance company who sells the firm's policies. CAPTIVE AGENTS sell the policies of only one company, while INDEPENDENT AGENTS sell the policies of many companies. Agents must be licensed to sell insurance in the states where they solicit customers.

INSURANCE BROKER independent broker who searches for the best insurance coverage at the lowest cost for the client. Insurance brokers do not work for insurance companies, but for the buyers of insurance products. They constantly are comparing the merits of competing insurance companies to find the best deal for their customers.

INSURANCE CLAIM request for payment from the insurance company by the insured. For example, a homeowner files a claim if he or she suffered damage because of a fire, theft, or other loss. In life insurance, survivors submit a claim when the insured dies. The insurance company investigates the claim and pays the appropriate amount if the claim is found to be legitimate, or denies the claim if it determines the loss was fraudulent or not covered by the policy.

INSURANCE DIVIDEND money paid to cash value life insurance policyholders with participating policies, usually once a year. Dividend rates are based on the insurance company's mortality experience, administrative expenses, and investment returns. Lower mortality experience (the number of policyholders dying) and expenses, combined with high investment returns, will increase dividends. Technically, dividends are considered a return of the policyholder's premiums, and are thus not considered taxable income by the IRS. Policyholders may choose to take these dividends in cash or may purchase additional life insurance.

INSURANCE POLICY insurance contract specifying what risks are insured and what premiums must be paid to keep the policy in force. Policies also spell out DEDUCTIBLES and other terms. Policies for life insurance specify whose life is insured and which beneficiaries will receive the insurance proceeds. HOMEOWNER'S INSURANCE POLICIES specify which property and casualty perils are covered. *Health insurance policies* detail which medical procedures, drugs, and devices are reimbursed. *Auto insurance policies* describe the conditions under which car owners will be covered in case of accidents, theft, or other damage to their cars. *Disability policies* specify the qualifying conditions of disability and how long payments will continue. *Business insurance policies* describe which liabilities are reimbursable. The policy is the written document that both insured and insurance company refer to when determining whether or not a claim is covered.

INSURANCE PREMIUM payment made by the insured in return for insurance protection. Premiums are set based on the probability of risk of loss and competitive pressures with other insurers. An insurance company's actuary will figure out the expected loss ratio on a particular class of customers, and then individual applicants will be evaluated based on whether they present higher or lower risks than the class as a whole. If a policyholder does not pay the premium, the insurance or policy may lapse. If the policy is a cash value policy, the policyowner can choose to take a paid-up insurance policy with a lower face value amount or an extended term policy.

INSURANCE SETTLEMENT payment of proceeds from an insurance policy to the insured under the terms of an insurance contract. Insurance settlements may be either in the form of one lump-sum payment or a series of payments.

INSURED individual, group, or property that is covered by an INSURANCE POLICY. The policy specifies exactly which perils the insured is indemnified against. The insured may be a particular individual, such as someone covered by a life insurance policy. It may be a group of people, such as those covered by a group life insurance policy purchased by a company on behalf of its employees. The insured may also refer to property, such as a house and its possessions which are covered by a HOMEOWNER'S INSURANCE POLICY.

INTANGIBLE ASSET right or nonphysical resource that is presumed to represent an advantage to the firm's position in the marketplace. Such assets include copyrights, patents, TRADEMARKS, goodwill, computer programs, capitalized advertising costs, organization costs, licenses, LEASES, FRANCHISES, exploration permits, and import and export permits.

INTANGIBLE COST tax-deductible cost. Such costs are incurred in drilling, testing, completing, and reworking oil and gas wells—labour, core analysis, fracturing, drill stem testing, engineering, fuel, geologists' expenses; also abandonment losses, management fees, delay rentals, and similar expenses.

INTERBANK RATE *see* LONDON INTERBANK OFFERED RATE (LIBOR).

INTERCOMMODITY SPREAD spread consisting of a long position and a short position in different but related commodities—for example, a long position in gold futures and a short position in silver futures. The investor hopes to profit from the changing price relationship between the commodities.

INTERDELIVERY SPREAD futures or options trading technique that entails buying one month of a contract and selling another month in the same contract—for instance, buying a June wheat contract and simultaneously selling a September wheat contract. The investor hopes to profit as the price difference between the two contracts widens or narrows.

INTEREST
  1. cost of using money, expressed as a rate per period of time, usually one year, in which case it is called an annual rate of interest.
  2. share, right, or title in property.

INTEREST COVERAGE *see* FIXED-CHARGE COVERAGE.

INTEREST DEDUCTION DEDUCTION allowable for certain types of interest expense, such as for interest on a home mortgage or interest on a MARGIN ACCOUNT.

INTEREST-ONLY LOAN form of loan where the only current obligation is interest and where repayment of principal is deferred.

INTEREST OPTION insurance policyholder's choice to reinvest dividends with the insurer to earn a guaranteed rate of interest. A beneficiary may also reinvest proceeds to earn interest.

INTEREST RATE rate of interest charged for the use of money, usually expressed at an annual rate. The rate is derived by dividing the amount of interest by the amount of principal borrowed. For example, if a bank charged $10 per year in interest to borrow $100, it would be charging a 10% interest rate. The interest rate is proportionate to investment risk: the higher the risk, the higher the rate. Interest rates are quoted on bills, notes, bonds, credit cards, and many kinds of consumer and business loans.

INTEREST RATE FUTURES financial futures, excluding currency futures, which call for future delivery of interest rate instruments, e.g., bonds, Treasury bills, and term deposits.

INTEREST-RATE OPTIONS CONTRACT options contract based on an underlying debt security. Options, unlike futures, give their buyers the right, but not the obligation, to buy the underlying bond at a fixed price before a specific date in the future. Option sellers promise to sell the bonds at a set price anytime until the contract expires. In return for granting this right, the option buyer pays a premium to the option seller. Yield-based calls become more valuable as yields rise, and puts become more valuable as yields decline.

INTEREST-RATE RISK RISK that changes in interest rates will adversely affect the value of an investor's securities portfolio. For example, an investor with large holdings in long-term bonds and utilities has assumed a significant interest-rate risk, because the value of those bonds and utility stocks will fall if interest rates rise. Investors can take various precautionary measures to HEDGE their interest-rate risk, such as buying INTEREST-RATE FUTURES or INTEREST-RATE OPTIONS CONTRACTS.

INTEREST-SENSITIVE STOCK stock of a firm whose earnings change when interest rates change, such as a bank, and which therefore tends to go up or down on news of rate movements.

INTERIM CERTIFICATE temporary certificate sometimes delivered to purchasers of a new bond issue. Interim certificates are later exchanged for permanent or definitive certificates when these become available.

INTERIM DIVIDEND DIVIDEND declared and paid before annual earnings have been determined, generally quarterly. Most companies strive for consistency and plan quarterly dividends they are sure they can afford, reserving changes until fiscal year results are known.

INTERIM FINANCING temporary, short-term loan made conditional on a TAKEOUT by intermediate or long-term financing. Also called *bridge loan* financing.

INTERIM LOAN *see* CONSTRUCTION LOAN.

INTERIM STATEMENT financial report covering only a portion (e.g., 3 months) of a fiscal year. Public corporations supplement the annual report with quarterly statements informing shareholders of changes in the balance sheet and income statement, as well as other newsworthy developments.

INTERLOCKING DIRECTORATE membership on more than one company's board of directors. This is legal so long as the companies are not competitors.

INTERMEDIARY person or institution empowered to make investment decisions for others. Some examples are banks, trust companies, insurance companies, brokerage firms, mutual funds, and credit unions. These specialists are knowledgeable about investment alternatives and can achieve a higher return than the average investor can. Furthermore, they deal in large dollar volumes, have lower transaction costs, and can diversify their assets easily. Also called *financial intermediary*.

INTERMEDIATE TERM period between the short and long term, the length of time depending on the context. Stock analysts, for instance, mean 6 to 12 months, whereas bond analysts most often mean 3 to 10 years.

INTERMEDIATION placement of money with a financial INTERMEDIARY like a broker or bank, which invests it in bonds, stocks, mortgages, or other loans, money-market securities, or government obligations so as to achieve a targeted return. More formally called *financial intermediation*. The opposite is DISINTERMEDIATION, the withdrawal of money from an intermediary.

INTERNAL AUDITOR employee of a company who examines records and procedures to ensure against fraud and to make certain board directives and management policies are being properly executed.

INTERNAL CONTROL method, procedure, or system designed to promote efficiency, assure the implementation of policy, and safeguard assets.

INTERNAL EXPANSION asset growth financed out of internally generated cash—usually termed INTERNAL FINANCING—or through ACCRETION or APPRECIATION. *See also* CASH EARNINGS.

INTERNAL FINANCING funds produced by the normal operations of a firm, as distinguished from external financing, which includes borrowings and new equity. *See also* INTERNAL EXPANSION.

INTERNAL RATE OF RETURN (IRR) discount rate at which the present value of the future cash flows of an investment equal the cost of the investment. It is found by a process of trial and error; when the net present values of cash outflows (the cost of the investment) and cash inflows (returns on the investment) equal zero, the rate of discount being used is the IRR. When IRR is greater than the required return—called the hurdle rate in capital budgeting—the investment is acceptable

INTERNAL REVENUE SERVICE (IRS) in the United States, the agency charged with collecting nearly all federal taxes, including personal and corporate income taxes, social security taxes, and excise and gift taxes. Major exceptions include taxes having to do with alcohol, tobacco, firearms, and explosives, and customs duties and tariffs. The IRS administers the rules and regulations that are the responsibility of the U.S. Department of the Treasury and investigates and prosecutes (through the U.S. Tax Court) tax illegalities.

INTERNATIONAL BANK FOR RECONSTRUCTION AND DEVELOPMENT (IBRD) organization set up by the Bretton Woods Agreement of 1944 to help finance the reconstruction of Europe and Asia after World War II. That task accomplished, the *World Bank*, as

IBRD is known, turned to financing commercial and infrastructure projects, mostly in developing nations. It does not compete with commercial banks, but it may participate in a loan set up by a commercial bank. World Bank loans must be backed by the government in the borrowing country.

INTERNATIONAL FUND fund invested primarily in securities of countries other than Canada. Some international funds focus on one single country. In Canada, the most popular single-country funds are those that invest in U.S. securities.

INTERNATIONAL MARKET INDEX market-value weighted proprietary index of the American Stock Exchange which tracks the performance of 50 American Depositary Receipts traded on the American Stock Exchange, New York Stock Exchange and NASDAQ Market. Options are no longer traded on the index.

INTERNATIONAL MONETARY FUND (IMF) organization set up by the Bretton Woods Agreement in 1944. Unlike the World Bank, whose focus is on foreign exchange reserves and the balance of trade, the IMF focus is on lowering trade barriers and stabilizing currencies. While helping developing nations pay their debts, the IMF usually imposes tough guidelines aimed at lowering inflation, cutting imports, and raising exports. IMF funds come mostly from the treasuries of industrialized nations. *See also* INTERNATIONAL BANK FOR RECONSTRUCTION AND DEVELOPMENT.

INTERNATIONAL MONETARY MARKET (IMM) division of the Chicago Mercantile Exchange that trades futures in U.S. Treasury bills, foreign currency, certificates of deposit, and Eurodollar deposits.

INTERNATIONAL MUTUAL FUND mutual fund that invests in securities markets throughout the world so that if one market is in a slump, profits can still be earned in others. Fund managers must be alert to trends in foreign currencies as well as in world stock and bond markets. Otherwise, seemingly profitable investments in a rising market could lose money if the national currency is falling against the dollar.

INTERNATIONAL PETROLEUM EXCHANGE (IPE) London-based energy futures and options exchange, trading Brent crude oil futures and options, gas oil futures and options, and unleaded gasoline futures. Brent crude futures are cash settled. There are three classes of IPE membership: floor members who are voting members, hold seats on the exchange and own a share of the exchange; trade associates, which are companies with direct interests in producing, refining, or trading oil and oil products; and local floor members, individuals who can trade on the exchange floor. Trading is carried out on the IPE floor through floor members; anyone can trade through them. Locals can trade for their own accounts or for floor members and other locals, but not for clients. The IPE trades Monday through Friday, from 9:15 A.M. to 8:15 P.M.

INTERNATIONAL STOCK EXCHANGE OF THE U.K. AND THE REPUBLIC OF IRELAND (ISE) organization formed after BIG BANG to replace the London Stock Exchange following its merger with the International Securities Regulatory Organization (ISRO). ISRO is a professional trade association of brokers and dealers in the United Kingdom that functions as a self-regulatory organization. The term *London Stock Exchange* persists in investment parlance despite the name change.

INTERPOLATION estimation of an unknown number intermediate between known numbers. Interpolation is a way of approximating price or yield using bond tables that do not give the net yield on every amount invested at every rate of interest and for every maturity. Interpolation is based on the assumption that a certain percentage change in yield will result in the same percentage change in price. The assumption is not altogether correct, but the variance is small enough to ignore.

INTER VIVOS TRUST trust established between living persons—for instance, between father and child. In contrast, a TESTAMENTARY TRUST goes into effect when the person who establishes the trust dies. Also called *living trust.*

INTESTACY; INTESTATE a person who dies without a valid will is said to die *intestate* or *in intestacy.* A partial intestacy exists when a valid will does not dispose of the whole of the estate.

INTESTATE DISTRIBUTION distribution of assets to beneficiaries from the estate of a person who dies without a written will of instructions. This distribution is overseen by a PROBATE court and the appointed EXECUTOR of the estate. Each province has specific laws outlining how intestate distributions are to be made.

IN THE MONEY option contract on a stock whose current market price is above the striking price of a call option or below the striking price of a put option. A call option on XYZ at a striking price of 100 would be in the money if XYZ were selling for 102, for instance, and a put option with the same striking price would be in the money if XYZ were selling for 98. *See also* AT THE MONEY; OUT OF THE MONEY.

IN THE TANK slang expression meaning market prices are dropping rapidly. Stock market observers may say, "The market is in the tank" after a day in which stock prices fell.

INTRACOMMODITY SPREAD futures position in which a trader buys and sells contracts in the same commodity on the same exchange, but for different months. For instance, a trader would place an intracommodity spread if he or she bought a pork bellies contract expiring in December and at the same time sold a pork bellies contract expiring in April. The profit or loss would be determined by the price difference between the December and April contracts.

INTRADAY within the day; often used in connection with high and low prices of a stock, bond, or commodity. For instance, "The stock hit a new intraday high today" means that the stock reached an all-time high price during the day but fell back to a lower price by the end of the day. The listing of the high and low prices at which a stock is traded during a day is called the *intraday price range.*

INTRINSIC VALUE

Financial analysis: valuation determined by applying data inputs to a valuation theory or model. The resulting value is comparable to the prevailing market price.

Options trading: difference between the EXERCISE PRICE or strike price of an option and the market value of the underlying security. For example, if the strike price is $53 on a call option to purchase a stock with a market price of $55, the option has an intrinsic value of $2. Or, in the case of a put option, if the strike price was $55 and the market price of the underlying stock was $53, the intrinsic value of the option would also be $2. Options AT THE MONEY or OUT OF THE MONEY have no intrinsic value.

INVENTORY

Corporate finance: value of a firm's raw materials, work in process, supplies used in operations, and finished goods. Since inventory value changes with price fluctuations, it is important to know the method of valuation. There are a number of inventory valuation methods; the most widely used are FIRST IN, FIRST OUT (FIFO) and LAST IN, FIRST OUT (LIFO). Financial statements normally indicate the basis of inventory valuation, generally the lower figure of either cost price or current market price, which precludes potentially overstated earnings and assets as the result of sharp increases in the price of raw materials.

Personal finance: list of all assets owned by an individual and the value of each, based on cost, market value, or both. Such inventories are usually required for property insurance purposes and are sometimes required with applications for credit.

Securities: net long or short position of a dealer or specialist. Also, securities bought and held by a dealer for later resale.

INVENTORY FINANCING

Factoring: sometimes used as a synonym for overadvances in FAC-TORING, where loans in excess of accounts receivable are made against inventory in anticipation of future sales.

Finance companies: financing by a bank or sales finance company of the inventory of a dealer in consumer or capital goods. Such loans, also called wholesale financing or *floorplanning*, are secured by the inventory and are usually made as part of a relationship in which retail installment paper generated by sales to the public is also financed by the lender. *See also* FINANCE COMPANY.

INVENTORY TURNOVER ratio of annual sales to inventory, which shows how many times the inventory of a firm is sold and replaced during an accounting period; sometimes called *inventory utilization ratio*. Compared with industry averages, a low turnover might indicate a company is carrying excess stocks of inventory, an unhealthy sign because excess inventory represents an investment with a low or zero rate of return and because it makes the company more vulnerable to falling prices. A steady drop in inventory turnover, in comparison with prior periods, can reveal lack of a sufficiently aggressive sales policy or ineffective buying.

Two points about the way inventory turnover may be calculated: (1) Because sales are recorded at market value and inventories are normally carried at cost, it is more realistic to obtain the turnover ratio by dividing inventory into cost of goods sold rather than into sales. However, it is conventional to use sales as the numerator because that is the practice of Dun & Bradstreet and other compilers of published financial ratios, and comparability is of overriding importance. (2) To minimize the seasonal factor affecting inventory levels, it is better to use an average inventory figure, obtained by adding yearly beginning and ending inventory figures and dividing by 2.

INVERTED MARKET futures market where the nearby contracts sell at higher prices than the contracts for later delivery because of a short-term demand for the cash commodity. *See also* BACKWARDATION MARKET; CONTANGO MARKET.

INVERTED YIELD CURVE unusual situation where short-term interest rates are higher than long-term rates. Normally, lenders receive a higher yield when committing their money for a longer period of time; this situation is called a POSITIVE YIELD CURVE. An inverted YIELD CURVE occurs when a surge in demand for short-term credit drives up short-term rates on instruments like Treasury bills and money-market funds, while long-term rates move up more slowly, since borrowers are not willing to commit themselves to paying high interest rates for many years. This situation happened in the early 1980s, when short-term interest rates were around 22%, while long-term rates went up to only 18% or 19%. The existence of an inverted yield curve can be a sign of an unhealthy economy, marked by high inflation and low levels of confidence. Also called *negative yield curve. See* chart on next page.

INVESTMENT use of capital to create more money, either through income-producing vehicles or through more risk-oriented ventures designed to result in capital gains. *Investment* can refer to a financial investment (where an investor puts money into a vehicle) or to an investment of effort and time on the part of an individual who wants to reap profits from the success of his or her labour. Investment connotes the idea that safety of principal is important. SPECULATION, on the other hand, is far riskier.

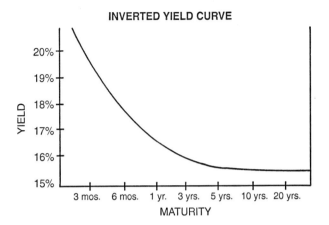

INVESTMENT ADVISOR professional who offers expertise to the public for a fee. An investment advisor is usually someone with special qualifications including professional expertise in stocks, mutual funds, insurance, or some other related activity.

INVESTMENT BANKER firm, acting as underwriter or agent, that serves as intermediary between an issuer of securities and the investing public. In what is termed FIRM COMMITMENT underwriting, the investment banker, either as manager or participating member of an investment banking syndicate, makes outright purchases of new securities from the issuer and distributes them to dealers and investors, profiting on the spread between the purchase price and the selling (public offering) price. Under a conditional arrangement called BEST EFFORT, the investment banker markets a new issue without underwriting it, acting as agent rather than principal and taking a commission for whatever amount of securities the banker succeeds in marketing. Under another conditional arrangement, called STANDBY COMMITMENT, the investment banker serves clients issuing new securities by agreeing to purchase for resale any securities not taken by existing holders of RIGHTS.

    Where a client relationship exists, the investment banker's role begins with preunderwriting counseling and continues after the distribution of securities is completed, in the form of ongoing expert advice and guidance, often including a seat on the board of directors. The direct underwriting responsibilities include preparing the Securities Commission registration statement; consulting on pricing of the securities; forming and managing the syndicate; establishing a selling group if desired; and PEGGING (stabilizing) the price of the issue during the offering and distribution period.

In addition to new securities offerings, investment bankers handle the distribution of blocks of previously issued securities, either through secondary offerings or through negotiations; maintain markets for securities already distributed; and act as finders in the private placement of securities.

Along with their investment banking functions, the majority of investment bankers also maintain broker-dealer operations, serving both wholesale and retail clients in brokerage and advisory capacities and offering a growing number of related financial services. *See also* FLOTATION COST; SECONDARY DISTRIBUTION; UNDERWRITE.

INVESTMENT CLIMATE economic, monetary, and other conditions affecting the performance of investments.

INVESTMENT CLUB group of people who pool their assets in order to make joint investment decisions. Each member of the club contributes a certain amount of capital, with additional money to be invested every month or quarter. Decisions on which stocks or bonds to buy are made by a vote of members. Besides helping each member become more knowledgeable about investing, these clubs allow people with small amounts of money to participate in larger investments, own part of a more diversified portfolio, and pay lower commission rates than would be possible for individual members on their own.

INVESTMENT COMPANY company that uses its capital to invest in other companies. There are two principal types: closed-end and open-end or mutual fund. Shares in closed-end investment companies are readily transferable in the open market and are bought and sold like other shares. Capitalization is fixed. Open-end funds sell their own new shares to investors, buy back their old shares, and are not listed. Open-end funds are so called because their capitalization is not fixed; they normally issue more shares as people want them.

INVESTMENT COUNSEL, INVESTMENT COUNSELOR professional with the responsibility for providing investment advice to clients and executing investment decisions. *See also* PORTFOLIO MANAGER.

INVESTMENT DEALER securities firm or an individual associated with one. When underwriting new securities or in most bond trading, the dealer acts as a principal, owning the securities bought or sold.

INVESTMENT FUND *see* INVESTMENT COMPANY.

INVESTMENT GRADE bond with a RATING of AAA to BBB. *See also* JUNK BOND.

INVESTMENT HISTORY body of prior experience establishing "normal investment practice" with respect to the account relationship between a member firm and its customer.

INVESTMENT INCOME income from securities and other nonbusiness investments; such as DIVIDENDS, INTEREST, and capital gains.

INVESTMENT INSTRUMENT each of the forms of investing in the money market, such as Treasury bills, commercial paper, banker's acceptances, dollar swaps, and certificates of deposit.

INVESTMENT MANAGEMENT in general, the activities of a portfolio manager. More specifically, it distinguishes between managed and unmanaged portfolios.

INVESTMENT OBJECTIVE financial objective that an investor uses to determine which kind of investment is appropriate. For example, if the investor's objective is growth of capital, he or she may opt for growth-oriented mutual funds or individual stocks. If the investor is more interested in income, he or she might purchase income-oriented mutual funds or individual bonds instead. Consideration of investment objectives, combined with the risk tolerance of investors, helps an investor narrow the search to an investment vehicle designed for his or her needs at a particular time.

INVESTMENT OPPORTUNITIES SCHEDULE schedule or graph that lists the best (i.e., highest) internal rate of return (IRR) to the worst (i.e., lowest IRR) investment opportunities available at a given time.

INVESTMENT PHILOSOPHY style of investment practised by an individual investor or money manager. For example, some investors follow the growth philosophy, concentrating on stocks with steadily rising earnings. Others are value investors, searching for stocks that have fallen out of favour, and are therefore cheap relative to the true value of their assets. Some managers favour small-capitalization stocks, while others stick with large blue-chip companies. Some managers have a philosophy of remaining fully invested at all times, while others believe in market timing, so that their portfolios can accumulate cash if the managers think stock or bond prices are about to fall.

INVESTMENT SERVICE counseling service operated by banks. Apart from arranging the bank's standard term deposit, guaranteed investment certificates, etc., the bank's investment department can counsel customers on foreign currency investments and some outside vehicles. Treasury accounts can also be arranged and daily interests negotiated on surplus current account balances.

INVESTMENT SOFTWARE software designed to aid investors' decision-making. Some software packages allow investors to perform TECHNICAL ANALYSIS, charting stock prices, volume, and other indicators. Other programs allow FUNDAMENTAL ANALYSIS, permitting investors to SCREEN STOCKS based on financial criteria such as earnings, price/earnings ratios, book value, and dividend yields. Some software offers recordkeeping, so that investors can keep track of the value of their portfolios, and the prices at which they bought or sold securities. Many software packages allow investors to tap into databases to update securities prices, scan news items, and execute trades. Specialty programs allow investors to value options, calculate yield analysis on bonds, and screen mutual funds.

INVESTMENT STRATEGY plan to allocate assets among such choices as stocks, bonds, CASH EQUIVALENTS, commodities, and real estate. An investment strategy should be formulated based on an investor's outlook on interest rates, inflation, and economic growth, among other factors, and also taking into account the investor's age, tolerance for risk, amount of capital available to invest, and future needs for capital, such as for financing children's college educations or buying a house. An investment adviser will help to devise such a strategy. *See also* INVESTMENT ADVISORY SERVICE.

INVESTMENT STRATEGY COMMITTEE committee in the research department of a brokerage firm that sets the overall investment strategy the firm recommends to clients. The director of research, the chief economist, and several top analysts typically sit on this committee. The group advises clients on the amount of money that should be placed into stocks, bonds, or CASH EQUIVALENTS, as well as the industry groups or individual stocks or bonds that look particularly attractive.

INVESTOR individual (or institution) who puts money at risk but whose principal concern is the minimization of risk, in contrast to the speculator, who is prepared to accept calculated risk in the hope of making better-than-average profits, or the gambler, who is prepared to take even greater risks.

INVESTOR RELATIONS DEPARTMENT in major listed companies, a staff position responsible for investor relations, reporting either to the chief financial officer or to the director of public relations. The actual duties will vary, depending on whether the company retains an outside financial public relations firm, but the general responsibilities are as follows:

- to see that the company is understood, in terms of its activities and objectives, and is favourably regarded in the financial and capital markets and the investment community; this means having input into the annual report and other published materials, coordinating senior management speeches and public statements with the FINANCIAL PUBLIC RELATIONS effort, and generally fostering a consistent and positive corporate image.
- to ensure full and timely public DISCLOSURE of material information, and to work with the legal staff in complying with the rules of the Securities Commission, the securities exchanges, and other regulatory authorities.
- to respond to requests for reports and information from shareholders, professional investors, brokers, and the financial media.
- to maintain productive relations with the firm's investment bankers, the specialists in its stock, major broker-dealers, and institutional

investors who follow the company or hold sizeable positions in its securities.

- to take direct measures, where necessary, to see that the company's shares are properly valued. This involves identifying the firm's particular investment audience and the professionals controlling its stock float, arranging analysts' meetings and other presentations, and generating appropriate publicity.

The most successful investor relations professionals have been those who follow a policy of full and open dissemination of relevant information, favorable and unfavorable, on a consistent basis. The least successful, over the long run, have been the "touts"—those who emphasize promotion at the expense of credibility.

INVOICE bill prepared by a seller of goods or services and submitted to the purchaser. The invoice lists all the items bought, together with amounts.

IOCC clearing organization called the International Options Clearing Corporation, whose members are the Amsterdam, Montreal, Vancouver, and Sydney Stock Exchanges.

IRREDEEMABLE BOND
1. bond without a CALL FEATURE (issuer's right to redeem the bond before maturity) or a REDEMPTION privilege (holder's right to sell the bond back to the issuer before maturity).
2. PERPETUAL BOND.

IRREVOCABLE something done that cannot legally be undone, such as an IRREVOCABLE TRUST.

IRREVOCABLE LIVING TRUST trust usually created to achieve some tax benefit, or to provide a vehicle for managing assets of a person the creator believes cannot or should not be managing his or her own property. This trust cannot be changed or reversed by the creator of the trust.

IRREVOCABLE TRUST trust that cannot be changed or terminated by the one who created it without the agreement of the BENEFICIARY.

IRS *see* INTERNAL REVENUE SERVICE.

IRS PRIVATE LETTER RULING *see* PRIVATE LETTER RULING.

ISIS *see* INTERMARKET SURVEILLANCE INFORMATION SYSTEM (ISIS).

INTERNATIONAL SECURITIES REGULATORY ORGANIZATION (ISRO) *see* INTERNATIONAL STOCK EXCHANGE OF THE UNITED KINGDOM AND THE REPUBLIC OF IRELAND (ISE).

ISSUE
1. stock or bonds sold by a corporation or a government entity at a particular time.

2. selling new securities by a corporation or government entity, either through an underwriter or by a private placement.
3. descendants, such as children and grandchildren. For instance, "This woman's estate will be passed, at her death, to her issue."

ISSUED AND OUTSTANDING shares of a corporation, authorized in the corporate charter, which have been issued and are outstanding. These shares represent capital invested by the firm's shareholders and owners, and may be all or only a portion of the number of shares authorized. Shares that have been issued and subsequently repurchased by the company are called *treasury stock,* because they are held in the corporate treasury pending reissue or retirement. Treasury shares are legally issued but are not considered outstanding for purposes of voting, dividends, or earnings per share calculations. Shares authorized but not yet issued are called *unissued shares.* Most companies show the amount of authorized, issued and outstanding, and treasury shares in the capital section of their annual reports. *See also* TREASURY STOCK.

ISSUED CAPITAL proportion of authorized capital that has been sold to the public in the form of common and preferred shares.

ISSUER legal entity that has the power to issue and distribute a security. Issuers include corporations, municipalities, foreign and domestic governments and their agencies, and investment trusts. Issuers of stock are responsible for reporting on corporate developments to shareholders and paying dividends once declared. Issuers of bonds are committed to making timely payments of interest and principal to bondholders.

ISSUER BID offer by an issuer to security holders to buy back any of its shares or other securities convertible into its shares. Such an offer is made when management wishes to increase control or to reduce debt.

J

JANUARY BAROMETER in the United States, a market forecasting tool popularized by *The Stock Traders Almanac*, whose statistics show that with 88% consistency since 1950, the market has risen in years when the STANDARD & POOR'S INDEX of 500 stocks was up in January and dropped when the index for that month was down.

JANUARY EFFECT in the United States, a phenomenon that stocks (especially small stocks) have historically tended to rise markedly during the period starting on the last day of December and ending on the fourth trading day of January. The January Effect is owed to year-end selling to create tax losses, recognize capital gains, effect portfolio WINDOW DRESSING, or raise holiday cash; since such selling depresses the stocks but has nothing to do with their fundamental worth, bargain hunters quickly buy in, causing the January rally.

JEEP *see* GRADUATED PAYMENT MORTGAGE.

JITNEY execution and clearing of orders by one member of a stock exchange for the account of another member. Example: Broker A is a small firm whose volume of business is not sufficient to maintain a trader on the floor of the exchange. Instead it gives its orders to Broker B for execution and clearing and pays a reduced percentage of the normal commission.

JOBBER
1. wholesaler, especially one who buys in small lots from manufacturers, importers, and/or other wholesalers and sells to retailers.
2. London Stock Exchange term for MARKET MAKER.

JOB LOT unit of trading that is smaller than a full contract; allowed by some exchanges. The Chicago Board of Trade and the Winnipeg Grain Exchange both allow job lots of 1000 bushels as compared with the normal 5000.

JOHANNESBURG STOCK EXCHANGE (JSE) only stock exchange in South Africa, established in 1886. Gold and mining shares dominate the shares listed, though there are also many other industrial and service stocks trading on the exchange. The mining-related sector accounts for nearly 41% of market capitalization of all quoted companies. Futures contracts are traded on the All Share, All Gold, and Industrial indices; options are traded on All Share and All Gold. Share options are traded on some of the top mining stocks, including DeBeers Consolidated Mines Ltd., Driefontein Consolidated Ltd., Rustenburg Platinum Holdings Ltd., Barlow Rand Ltd., and Gencor Ltd. Trading is by open outcry. The exchange uses a weekly computerized clearing system for settlement between brokers. Trades executed in one week are settled the following week. Hours: 9:30 A.M.–4 P.M., Monday through Friday.

JOINT ACCOUNT bank or brokerage account owned jointly by two or more people. Joint accounts may be set up in two ways: (1) either all parties to the account must sign cheques and approve all withdrawals or brokerage transactions or (2) any one party can take such actions on his or her own. *See also* JOINT TENANTS WITH RIGHT OF SURVIVORSHIP.

JOINT ACCOUNT AGREEMENT form needed to open a JOINT ACCOUNT at a bank or brokerage. It must be signed by all parties to the account regardless of the provisions it may contain concerning signatures required to authorize transactions.

JOINT AND SURVIVOR ANNUITY annuity that makes payments for the lifetime of two or more beneficiaries, often a husband and wife. When one of the annuitants dies, payments continue to the survivor annuitant in the same amount or in a reduced amount as specified in the contract.

JOINT LIABILITY mutual legal responsibility by two or more parties for claims on the assets of a company or individual. *See also* LIABILITY.

JOINT LIFE ANNUITY annuity that names an annuitant and a second person, usually the annuitant's spouse. If the annuitant dies, the second person continues to receive payments for life. The annuitant can specify equal payments throughout, reduced payments for life, or guaranteed term. Joint life annuities provide lower payments than straight life to each annuity beneficiary.

JOINTLY AND SEVERALLY
In general: legal phrase used in definitions of liability meaning that an obligation may be enforced against all obligators jointly or against any one of them separately.
Securities: term used to refer to municipal bond underwritings where the account is undivided and syndicate members are responsible for unsold bonds in proportion to their participations. In other words, a participant with 5% of the account would still be responsible for 5% of the unsold bonds, even though that member might already have sold 10%. *See also* SEVERALLY BUT NOT JOINTLY.

JOINT OWNERSHIP equal ownership by two or more people, who have right of survivorship.

JOINT TENANCY *see* TENANCY IN COMMON. *See also* JOINT TENANTS WITH RIGHT OF SURVIVORSHIP.

JOINT TENANTS form of joint ownership in which the death of one joint owner results in the immediate transfer of ownership to the surviving joint owner or owners.

JOINT TENANTS WITH RIGHT OF SURVIVORSHIP when two or more people maintain a JOINT ACCOUNT with a brokerage firm or a bank, it is normally agreed that, upon the death of one account holder, ownership of the account assets passes to the remaining account holders. This transfer of assets escapes probate, but estate taxes may be due, depending on the amount of assets transferred.

JOINT VENTURE agreement by two or more parties to work on a project together. Frequently, a joint venture will be formed when companies with complementary technology wish to create a product or service that takes advantage of the strengths of the participants. A joint venture, which is usually limited to one project, differs from a partnership, which forms the basis for cooperation on many projects.

JOINT WILL single document setting forth the testamentary instructions of a husband and wife. The use of joint wills is not common in the United States, and it may create tax and other problems.

JONESTOWN DEFENSE tactics taken by management to ward off a hostile TAKEOVER that are so extreme that they appear suicidal for the company. For example, the company may try to sell its CROWN JEWELS or take on a huge amount of debt to make the company undesirable to the potential acquirer. The term refers to the mass suicide led by Jim Jones in Jonestown, Guyana, in the early 1980s. *See also* SCORCHED EARTH POLICY.

JUDGMENT decision by a court of law ordering someone to pay a certain amount of money. For instance, a court may order someone who illegally profited by trading on INSIDE INFORMATION to pay a judgment amounting to all the profits from the trade, plus damages. The term also refers to condemnation awards by government entities in payment for private property taken for public use.

JUNIOR BOND ISSUE *see* JUNIOR ISSUE.

JUNIOR DEBT *see* JUNIOR ISSUE.

JUNIOR ISSUE issue of debt or equity that is subordinate in claim to another issue in terms of dividends, interest, principal, or security in the event of liquidation. *See also* JUNIOR SECURITY; PREFERRED STOCK; PRIORITY; PRIOR LIEN BOND: PRIOR PREFERRED STOCK.

JUNIOR MORTGAGE mortgage that is subordinate to other mortgages—for example, a second or a third mortgage. If a debtor defaults, the first mortgage will have to be satisfied before the junior mortgage.

JUNIOR SECURITY security with lower priority claim on assets and income than a SENIOR SECURITY. For example, a PREFERRED STOCK is junior to a DEBENTURE, but a debenture, being an unsecured bond, is junior to a MORTGAGE BOND. COMMON STOCK is junior to all corporate securities.

JUNK BOND bond with a credit rating of BB or lower by RATING agencies. Although commonly used, the term has a pejorative connotation, and issuers and holders prefer the securities be called *high-yield* *bonds.* Junk bonds are issued by companies without long track records of sales and earnings, or by those with questionable credit strength. They are a popular means of financing TAKEOVERS. Since they are more volatile and pay higher yields than INVESTMENT GRADE bonds, many risk-oriented investors specialize in trading them.

JURY OF EXECUTIVE OPINION forecasting method whereby a panel of experts—perhaps senior corporate financial executives—prepare individual forecasts based on information made available to all of them. Each expert then reviews the others' work and modifies his or her own forecasts accordingly. The resulting composite forecast is supposed to be more realistic than any individual effort could be. Also known as *Delphi forecast.*

JUSTIFIED PRICE fair market price an informed buyer will pay for an asset, whether it be a stock, a bond, a commodity, or real estate. *See also* FAIR MARKET VALUE.

JUST TITLE title to property that is supportable against all legal claims. Also called *clear title, good title, proper title.*

K

KAFFIRS term used in Great Britain that refers to South African gold mining shares. These shares are traded over the counter in the U.S. in the form of American Depositary Receipts, which are claims to share certificates deposited in a foreign bank. Under South African law, Kaffirs must pay out almost all their earnings to shareholders as dividends. These shares thus not only provide stockholders with a gold investment to hedge against inflation, but also afford substantial income in the form of high dividend payments. However, investors in Kaffirs must also consider the political risks of investing in South Africa, as well as the risk of fluctuations in the price of gold. *See also* AMERICAN DEPOSITARY RECEIPT.

KANGAROOS nickname for Australian stocks. The term normally refers to stocks in the ALL ORDINARIES INDEX, and refers to the animal most closely associated with Australia.

KANSAS CITY BOARD OF TRADE (KCBT) futures exchange trading No. 2 red wheat futures and options; Value Line Index futures; and Mini Value Line futures and options. Hours: 8:30 A.M.–3:15 P.M., Monday through Friday.

KARAT unit of fineness for gold jewellery; 24 karat is equal to 100% pure gold; 18 karat is therefore 18/24 or 75% gold content. Some of the popular gold jewellery alloys and their gold content are:

> 24K = 100% gold of .999 fineness,
> 22K = 91% gold of .999 fineness,
> 14K = 58% gold of .999 fineness,
> 10K = 41% gold of .999 fineness.

KEY INDUSTRY industry of primary importance to a nation's economy. For instance, the mining industry is called a key industry since it is crucial to maintaining a country's exports. The automobile industry is also considered key since so many jobs are directly or indirectly dependent on it.

KEYNESIAN ECONOMICS body of economic thought originated by the British economist and government adviser, John Maynard Keynes (1883–1946), whose landmark work, *The General Theory of Employment, Interest and Money,* was published in 1935. Writing during the Great Depression, Keynes took issue with the classical economists, like Adam Smith, who believed that the economy worked best when left alone. Keynes believed that active government intervention in the marketplace was the only method of ensuring economic growth and stability. He held essentially that insufficient demand causes unemployment and that excessive demand results in inflation; government should therefore manipulate the level of aggregate demand by

of Malaysia. Trading must be carried out through one of the exchange's member firms at a fixed commission rate. Open outcry was phased out in November 1989 and SCORE, the System on Computerized Order Routing and Execution, was introduced. Settlement is through the Central Depository System (CDS), by book entry, with CDS accounts of buyers credited on the fifth day but held in lien until payment by the seventh market day, while sellers are debited on the fifth market day. The Kuala Lampur Composite Index is the benchmark index, with 11 other indices traded. Hours: 9:30 A.M.–12:30 P.M., and 2:30 P.M.–5 P.M., Monday through Friday.

L

LABOUR-INTENSIVE requiring large pools of workers. Said of an industry in which labour costs are more important than capital costs. Deep-shaft coal mining, for instance, is labour-intensive.

LADY MACBETH STRATEGY TAKEOVER tactic whereby a third party poses as a white knight then turns coat and joins an unfriendly bidder.

LAFFER CURVE curve named for U.S. economics professor Arthur Laffer, postulating that economic output will grow if marginal tax rates are cut. The curve is used in explaining SUPPLY-SIDE ECONOMICS, a theory that noninflationary growth is spurred when tax policies encourage productivity and investment.

LAGGING INDICATORS economic indicators that lag behind the overall pace of economic activity. The six most frequently used components of the lagging indicators are the unemployment rate, business spending, unit labour costs, bank loans outstanding, bank interest rates, and the book value of manufacturing and trade inventories.

LAISSEZ-FAIRE doctrine that interference of government in business and economic affairs should be minimal. Adam Smith's *The Wealth Of Nations* (1776) described laissez-faire economics in terms of an "invisible hand" that would provide for the maximum good for all, if businessmen were free to pursue profitable opportunities as they saw them. The growth of industry in England in the early 19th century and American industrial growth in the late 19th century both occurred in a laissez-faire capitalist environment. The laissez-faire period ended by the beginning of the 20th century, when large monopolies were broken up and government regulation of business became the norm. The Great Depression of the 1930s saw the birth of KEYNESIAN ECONOMICS, an influential approach advocating government intervention in economic affairs.

LANDLORD owner of property who rents it to a TENANT.

LAPSE expiration of a right or privilege because one party did not live up to its obligations during the time allowed. For example, a life insurance policy will lapse if the policyholder does not make the required premium payments on time. This means that the policyholder is no longer protected by the policy.

LAPSED OPTION OPTION that reached its expiration date without being exercised and is thus without value.

LAST IN FIRST OUT (LIFO) method of accounting for INVENTORY that ties the cost of goods sold to the cost of the most recent purchases. The formula for cost of goods sold is:

beginning inventory + purchases − ending inventory = cost of goods sold

In contrast to the FIRST IN, FIRST OUT (FIFO) method, in a period of rising prices LIFO produces a higher cost of goods sold and a lower gross profit and taxable income. The artificially low balance sheet inventories resulting from the use of LIFO in periods of inflation give rise to the term *LIFO cushion.*

LAST PRICE PAID OPTION CONTRACT cash amount, also known as the premium, paid by the buyer to the seller (writer) for the privilege of owning the option.

LAST SALE most recent trade in a particular security. Not to be confused with the final transaction in a trading session, called the CLOSING SALE. The last sale is the point of reference for two Securities and Exchange Commission rules: (1) On a national exchange, no SHORT SALE may be made below the price of the last regular sale. (2) No short sale may be made at the same price as the last sale unless the last sale was at a price higher than the preceding different price. PLUS TICK, MINUS TICK, ZERO MINUS TICK, and ZERO PLUS TICK, used in this connection, refer to the last sale.

LAST TRADING DAY final day during which a futures contract may be settled. If the contract is not OFFSET, either an agreement between the buying and selling parties must be arranged or the physical commodity must be delivered from the seller to the buyer.

LATE CHARGE fee charged by a grantor of credit when the borrower fails to make timely payment.

LATE TAPE delay in displaying price changes because trading on a stock exchange is particularly heavy. If the tape is more than five minutes late, the first digit of a price is deleted. For instance, a trade at $62\frac{3}{4}$ is reported as $2\frac{3}{4}$. *See also* DIGITS DELETED.

LAUNDER to make illegally acquired cash look as if it were acquired legally. The usual practice is to transfer the money through foreign banks, thereby concealing its purpose. SEC Rule 17a-8 prohibits using broker-dealers for this purpose.

LAW OF LARGE NUMBERS statistical concept holding that the greater the number of units in a projection, the less important each unit becomes. Group insurance, which gets cheaper as the group gets larger, is an example of the principle in application; actuarial abnormalities have less influence on total claims.

LAY OFF
Investment banking: reduce the risk in a standby commitment, under which the bankers agree to purchase and resell to the public any portion of a stock issue not subscribed to by shareowners who hold rights. The risk is that the market value will fall during the two to four weeks when shareholders are deciding whether to exercise or sell their rights. To minimize the risk, investment bankers (1) buy up the rights as they

are offered and, at the same time, sell the shares represented by these rights; and (2) sell short an amount of shares proportionate to the rights that can be expected to go unexercised—to ½% of the issue, typically. Also called *laying off.*

Labour: temporarily or permanently remove an employee from a payroll because of an economic slowdown or a production cutback, not because of poor performance or an infraction of company rules.

LEADER

1. stock or group of stocks at the forefront of an upsurge or a downturn in a market. Typically, leaders are heavily bought and sold by institutions that want to demonstrate their own market leadership.
2. product that has a large market share.

LEADING INDICATORS selection of statistical data that, on average, indicates highs and lows in the business cycle ahead of the economy as a whole. These relate to employment, capital investment, business starts and failures, profits, stock prices, inventory adjustment, housing starts, and certain commodity prices.

LEAPS acronym for Long-Term Equity AnticiPation Securities, LEAPS are long-term equity options traded on exchanges and over the counter. Instead of expiring in two near-term and two farther out months as most equity OPTIONS do, LEAPS expire in two or three years, giving the buyer a longer time for his or her strategy to come to fruition. LEAPS are traded on many individual stocks listed on the Toronto Stock Exchange, the New York Stock Exchange, the American Stock Exchange, and NASDAQ.

LEARNING CURVE predictable improvements following the early part of the life of a production contract, when costly mistakes are made.

LEASE contract granting use of real estate, equipment, or other fixed assets for a specified time in exchange for payment, usually in the form of rent. The owner of the leased property is called the lessor, the user the lessee. *See also* CAPITAL LEASE; FINANCIAL LEASE; OPERATING LEASE; SALE AND LEASEBACK.

LEASEBACK transaction in which one party sells property to another and agrees to lease the property back from the buyer for a fixed period of time. For example, a building owner wanting to get cash out of the building may decide to sell the building to a real estate or leasing company and sign a long-term lease to occupy the space. The original owner is thereby able to receive cash for the value of the property, which can be reinvested in the business as well as remain in the property. The new owner is assured of the stability of a long-term tenant and a steady income. Leaseback deals (also called sale and leaseback deals) also are executed for business equipment such as computers, cars, trucks, and airplanes.

LEASEHOLD asset representing the right to use property under a LEASE.

LEASEHOLD IMPROVEMENT modification of leased property. The cost is added to fixed assets and then amortized.

LEASE-PURCHASE AGREEMENT agreement providing that portions of LEASE payments may be applied toward the purchase of the property under lease.

LEASING use of specific assets without actual title. The lessee receives the services of the assets leased by the owner (lessor). A periodic tax-deductible payment is required. An operating lease is generally a short-term arrangement that can be cancelled, while a financial or capital lease is a long-term agreement that cannot be cancelled. Leases can be held on offices, equipment, furniture, cars, trucks, land, and computer software and hardware.

LEG
1. sustained trend in stock market prices. A prolonged bull or bear market may have first, second, and third legs.
2. one side of a spread transaction. For instance, a trader might buy a CALL OPTION that has a particular STRIKE PRICE and expiration date, then combine it with a PUT OPTION that has the same striking price and a different expiration date. The two options are called legs of the spread.
   Selling one of the options is termed LIFTING A LEG.

LEGACY gift under a WILL of cash or some other specific item of personal property, such as a stock certificate, a car, or a piece of jewellery. The legacy usually is conditioned, meaning the legatee is required to be employed by the TESTATOR—the person who makes the will—or related to the testator by marriage. In other cases, a legacy to a legatee who has not attained a certain age at the testator's death will be held in trust for the legatee, instead of being distributed outright.

LEGAL computerized data base maintained by the New York Stock Exchange to track enforcement actions against member firms, audits of member firms, and customer complaints. LEGAL is not an acronym, but is written in all capitals.

LEGAL AGE age at which a person can enter into binding contracts or agree to other legal acts without the consent of another adult. The legal age, also called the *age of majority,* is 18, 19, or 21, depending on the province.

LEGAL ENTITY person or organization that has the legal standing to enter into a contract and may be sued for failure to perform as agreed in the contract. A child under legal age is not a legal entity; a corporation is a legal entity since it is a person in the eyes of the law.

LEGAL LIABILITY (1) monies owed, shown on a balance sheet. (2) individual's or company's obligation to act responsibly or face compensatory penalties. *See also* LIABILITY.

LEGAL MONOPOLY exclusive right to offer a particular service within a particular territory. In exchange, the company agrees to have its policies and rates regulated. Hydro utilities are legal monopolies.

LEGAL OPINION
1. statement as to legality, written by an authorized official such as a city attorney or an attorney general.
2. statement as to the legality of a MUNICIPAL BOND issue, usually written by a law firm specializing in public borrowings. It is part of the *official statement,* the municipal equivalent of a PROSPECTUS. Unless the legality of an issue is established, an investor's contract is invalid at the time of issue and he cannot sue under it. The legal opinion is therefore required by a SYNDICATE MANAGER and customarily accompanies the transfer of municipal securities as long as they are outstanding.

LEGAL TRANSFER transaction that requires documentation other than the standard stock or bond power to validate the transfer of a stock certificate from a seller to a buyer—for example, securities registered to a corporation or to a deceased person. It is the selling broker's responsibility to supply proper documentation to the buying broker in a legal transfer.

LEGISLATIVE RISK risk that a change in legislation could have a major positive or negative effect on an investment. For instance, a company that is a large exporter may be a beneficiary of a trade agreement that lowers tariff barriers, and therefore may see its stock price rise. On the other hand, a company that is a major polluter may be harmed by laws that stiffen fines for polluting the air or water, thereby making its share price fall.

LEMON product or investment producing poor performance. A car that continually needs repairs is a lemon, and, in several states of the United States, consumers are guaranteed a full refund under so-called lemon laws. A promising stock that fails to live up to expectations is also called a lemon.

LENDER individual or firm that extends money to a borrower with the expectation of being repaid, usually with interest. Lenders create debt in the form of loans, and in the event of LIQUIDATION they are paid off before stockholders receive distributions. But the investor deals in both debt (bonds) and equity (stocks). It is useful to remember that investors in commercial paper, bonds, and other debt instruments are in fact lenders with the same rights and powers enjoyed by banks.

LENDING AGREEMENT contract between a lender and a borrower. *See also* INDENTURE; REVOLVING CREDIT; TERM LOAN.

LENDING AT A PREMIUM term used when one broker lends securities to another broker to cover customer's short position and imposes a charge for the loan. Such charges, which are passed on to the customer, are the exception rather than the rule, since securities are normally LOANED FLAT between brokers, that is, without interest. Lending at a premium might occur when the securities needed are in very heavy demand and are therefore difficult to borrow. The premium is in addition to any payments the customer might have to make to the lending broker to MARK TO THE MARKET or to cover dividends or interest payable on the borrowed securities.

LENDING AT A RATE paying interest to a customer on the credit balance created from the proceeds of a SHORT SALE. Such proceeds are held in ESCROW to secure the loan of securities, usually made by another broker, to cover the customer's short position. Lending at a rate is the exception rather than the rule.

LENDING SECURITIES securities borrowed from a broker's inventory, other MARGIN ACCOUNTS, or from other brokers, when a customer makes a SHORT SALE and the securities must be delivered to the buying customer's broker. As collateral, the borrowing broker deposits with the lending broker an amount of money equal to the market value of the securities. No interest or premium is ordinarily involved in the transaction.

LESS DEVELOPED COUNTRIES (LDC) countries that are not fully industrialized or do not have sophisticated financial or legal systems. These countries, also called members of the *Third World,* typically have low levels of per-capita income, high inflation and debt, and large trade deficits. The World Bank may be helping them by providing loan assistance. Loans to such countries are commonly called *LDC debt.*

LESSEE *see* LEASE.

LESSOR *see* LEASE.

LETTER OF CREDIT (L/C) instrument or document issued by a bank guaranteeing the payment of a customer's drafts up to a stated amount for a specified period. It substitutes the bank's credit for the buyer's and eliminates the seller's risk. It is used extensively in international trade. A *commercial letter of credit* is normally drawn in favour of a third party, called the beneficiary. A *confirmed letter of credit* is provided by a correspondent bank and guaranteed by the issuing bank. A *revolving letter of credit* is issued for a specified amount and automatically renewed for the same amount for a specified period, permitting any number of drafts to be drawn so long as they do not exceed its overall limit. A *traveler's letter of credit* is issued for the convenience of a traveling customer and typically lists correspondent banks at which drafts will be honoured. A *performance letter of credit* is issued to guarantee performance under a contract.

LETTER OF INTENT

1. any letter expressing an intention to take (or not take) an action, sometimes subject to other action being taken. For example, a bank might issue a letter of intent stating it will make a loan to a customer, subject to another lender's agreement to participate. The letter of intent, in this case, makes it possible for the customer to negotiate the participation loan.
2. preliminary agreement between two companies that intend to merge. Such a letter is issued after negotiations have been satisfactorily completed.

LEVEL DEBT SERVICE provision in a municipal charter stipulating that payments on municipal debt be approximately equal every year. This makes it easier to project the amount of tax revenue needed to meet obligations.

LEVERAGE

Operating leverage: extent to which a company's costs of operating are fixed (rent, insurance, executive salaries) as opposed to variable (materials, direct labour). In a totally automated company, whose costs are virtually all fixed, every dollar of increase in sales is a dollar of increase in operating income once the BREAKEVEN POINT has been reached, because costs remain the same at every level of production. In contrast, a company whose costs are largely variable would show relatively little increase in operating income when production and sales increased because costs and production would rise together. The leverage comes in because a small change in sales has a magnified percentage effect on operating income and losses. The *degree of operating leverage*—the ratio of the percentage change in operating income to the percentage change in sales or units sold—measures the sensitivity of a firm's profits to changes in sales volume. A firm using a high degree of operating leverage has a breakeven point at a relatively high sales level.

Financial leverage: debt in relation to equity in a firm's capital structure—its LONG-TERM DEBT (usually bonds), PREFERRED STOCK, and SHAREHOLDERS' EQUITY—measured by the DEBT-TO-EQUITY RATIO. The more long-term debt there is, the greater the financial leverage. Shareholders benefit from financial leverage to the extent that return on the borrowed money exceeds the interest costs and the market value of their shares rises. For this reason, financial leverage is popularly called *trading on the equity*. Because leverage also means required interest and principal payments and thus ultimately the risk of default, how much leverage is desirable is largely a question of stability of earnings. As a rule of thumb, an industrial company with a debt to equity ratio of more than 30% is highly leveraged, exceptions being firms with dependable earnings and cash flow, such as electric utilities.

Since long-term debt interest is a fixed cost, financial leverage tends to take over where operating leverage leaves off, further magnifying the effects on earnings per share of changes in sales levels. In general, high operating leverage should accompany low financial leverage, and vice versa.

Investments: means of enhancing return or value without increasing investment. Buying securities on margin is an example of leverage with borrowed money, and extra leverage may be possible if the leveraged security is convertible into common stock. RIGHTS, WARRANTS, and OPTION contracts provide leverage, not involving borrowings but offering the prospect of high return for little or no investment.

LEVERAGED BUYOUT takeover of a company, using borrowed funds. Most often, the target company's assets serve as security for the loans taken out by the acquiring firm, which repays the loan out of cash flow of the acquired company. Management may use this technique to retain control by converting a company from public to private. A group of investors may also borrow funds from banks, using their own assets as collateral, to take over another firm. In almost all leveraged buyouts, public shareholders receive a premium over the current market value for their shares. When a company that has gone private in a leveraged buyout offers shares to the public again, it is called a REVERSE LEVERAGED BUYOUT.

LEVEL LOAD sales charge that does not change over time. In some mutual funds, level load shares are called *C class shares,* compared to *A class* for upfront loads and *B class* for back-end loads. A level load will typically be 1% to 2% of assets each year, which is lower than an upfront load of 4% to 5% or the back-end load, which starts at 5% and declines each year until it disappears if the fund shares are held for five years. Though the level load may be lower than an upfront or back-end load, a higher commission is charged if the investor holds the fund for many years.

LEVEL PLAYING FIELD condition in which competitors operate under the same rules. For example, the insurance industry complains about the banks entering into the direct sale of life insurance by phone while the insurance companies have far stricter licensing and investing rules. Companies wanting to export to a particular country may complain that domestic companies are protected by various trade barriers, creating an uneven playing field. Various sections of the tax act may favour some companies more than others, prompting cries from the disadvantaged firms to "level the playing field."

LEVEL TERM INSURANCE life insurance policy with a fixed face value and rising insurance premiums.

LEVERAGED COMPANY company with debt in addition to equity in its capital structure. In its popular connotation, the term is applied to companies that are highly leveraged. Although the judgment is relative, industrial companies with more than one third of their capitalization in the form of debt are considered highly leveraged. *See also* LEVERAGE.

LEVERAGED RECAPITALIZATION corporate strategy to fend off potential acquirers by taking on a large amount of debt and making a large cash distribution to shareholders. For example, XYZ Company, selling at $50 a share, may borrow $3 billion to make a one-time distribution of $20 a share to stockholders. After the distribution, the stock price will drop to $30. By replacing equity with $3 billion in debt, XYZ is a far less attractive takeover target for a raider or other company than it was before. Also called *leveraged recap* for short.

LEVERAGED STOCK stock financed with credit, as in a MARGIN ACCOUNT. Although not, strictly speaking, leveraged stock, securities that are convertible into common stock provide an extra degree of leverage when bought on margin. Assuming the purchase price is reasonably close to the INVESTMENT VALUE and CONVERSION VALUE, the downside risk is no greater than it would be with the same company's common stock, whereas the appreciation value is much greater.

LIABILITY claim on the assets of a company or individual—excluding ownership EQUITY. Characteristics: (1) It represents a transfer of assets or services at a specified or determinable date. (2) The firm or individual has little or no discretion to avoid the transfer. (3) The event causing the obligation has already occurred. *See also* BALANCE SHEET.

LIABILITY INSURANCE insurance for money the policyholder is legally obligated to pay because of bodily injury or property damage caused to another person and covered in the policy. Liabilities may result from property damage, bodily injury, libel, or any other damages caused by the insured. The insurance company agrees to pay for such damages if they are awarded by a court, up to the limitations specified in the insurance contract. The insurer may also cover legal expenses incurred in defending the suit.

LIBOR *see* LONDON INTERBANK OFFERED RATE.

LICENCE legal document issued by a regulatory agency permitting an individual to conduct a certain activity, usually because the person has passed a training course qualifying him or her. For example, a securities licence is required for a broker to sell stocks, bonds, and mutual funds. An insurance licence is required before someone can sell insurance products. Before a driver's licence is granted, a driver must pass an examination proving that he or she knows how to drive safely. If the licenced individual violates the regulations, the licence can be revoked.

LIEN creditor's claim against property. For example, a mortgage is a lien against a house; if the mortgage is not paid on time, the house can be seized to satisfy the lien. Similarly, a bond is a lien against a company's assets; if interest and principal are not paid when due, the assets may be seized to pay the bondholders. As soon as a debt is paid, the lien is removed. Liens may be granted by courts to satisfy judgments. They must be registered under provincial law in order to be protected and enforceable. *See also* MECHANIC'S LIEN.

LIFE ANNUITY ANNUITY that makes a guaranteed fixed payment for the rest of the life of the annuitant. After the annuitant dies, beneficiaries receive no further payments.

LIFE CYCLE most common usage refers to an individual's progression from cradle to grave and the assumption that the choice of appropriate investments changes. Term also applies to the life of a product or of a business, consisting of inception, development, growth, expansion, maturity, and decline (or change). Recently, the term has entered into the vocabulary of the family-owned business, referring to generations of management. The post-World War II baby boom produced entrepreneurs who built businesses that now approach a juncture where a second generation either takes over management or sells out.

LIFE CYCLE PLANNING planning contemplated by the concept of LIFE CYCLE.

LIFE EXPECTANCY age to which an average person can be expected to live, as calculated by an ACTUARY. Insurance companies base their projections of benefit payouts on actuarial studies of such factors as sex, heredity, and health habits and base their rates on actuarial analysis. Life expectancy can be calculated at birth or at some other age and generally varies according to age. Thus, all persons at birth might have an average life expectancy of 70 years and all persons aged 40 years might have an average life expectancy of 75 years.

LIFE INCOME FUND *see* LOCKED-IN PENSION FUND.

LIFE INCOME RETIREMENT FUND *see* LOCKED-IN PENSION FUND.

LIFE INSURANCE insurance policy that pays a death benefit to beneficiaries if the insured dies. In return for this protection, the insured pays a premium, usually on an annual basis. *Term insurance* pays off upon the insured's death but provides no buildup of cash value in the policy. Term premiums are cheaper than premiums for *cash value policies* such as whole life, variable life, and universal life, which pay death benefits and also provide for the buildup of cash values in the policy. The cash builds up tax-deferred in the policy and is invested in stocks, bonds, real estate, and other investments. Policyholders can take out loans against their policies, which reduce the death benefit if they are not repaid. Some life insurance provides benefits to policyholders while they are still living, including income payments.

LIFE INSURANCE IN FORCE amount of life insurance that a company has issued, including the face amount of all outstanding policies together with all dividends that have been paid to policyholders. Thus a life insurance policy for $500,000 on which dividends of $10,000 have been paid would count as life insurance in force of $510,000.

LIFE INSURANCE POLICY contract between an insurance company and the insured setting out the provisions of the life insurance coverage. These provisions include premiums, loan procedures, face amounts, and the designation of beneficiaries, among many other clauses. Policies may be for term or permanent cash value types of coverage.

LIFETIME REVERSE MORTGAGE type of reverse mortgage agreement whereby a homeowner borrows against the value of the home, retains title, and makes no payments while living in the home. When the home ceases to be the primary residence of the borrower, as when the borrower dies, the lender sells the property, repays the loan, and remits any surplus to the borrower's estate. Such arrangements may be appropriate for older people who need cash and are HOUSE POOR. *See also* REVERSE ANNUITY MORTGAGE (RAM).

LIFE WITH GUARANTEED TERM ANNUITY annuity that guarantees annuitant an agreed-upon series of payments until death. If the annuitant dies before the end of the guaranteed term, the balance goes to the beneficiary. If the spouse is the stated beneficiary, the arrangement may allow the spouse to receive the rest of the payments as scheduled, or to receive the commuted value, that is, the present value of the future payment at the interest rate set in the policy. The guaranteed period, set by agreement, is usually 5 to 10 years and extends only until the annuitant or the annuitant's spouse (the younger of the two) reaches the age of 90. Payments are lower than a straight life policy, and decline as the guaranteed term increases.

LIFFE *see* LONDON INTERNATIONAL FINANCIAL FUTURES AND OPTIONS EXCHANGE.

LIFO *see* LAST IN, FIRST OUT.

LIFT rise in securities prices as measured by the Dow Jones Industrial Average or other market averages, usually caused by good business or economic news.

LIFTING A LEG closing one side of a HEDGE, leaving the other side as a long or short position. A leg, in Bay Street parlance, is one side of a hedged transaction. A trader might have a STRADDLE—that is, a call and a put on the same stock, at the same price, with the same expiration date. Making a closing sale of the put, thereby lifting a leg—or *taking off a leg,* as it is sometimes called—would leave the trader with the call, or the LONG LEG.

LIGHTEN UP to sell a portion of a stock or bond position in a portfolio. A money manager with a large profit in a stock may decide to realize some of the gains because he or she is unsure that the stock will continue to rise, or because of concern that too much of the fund's assets are tied up in the stock. As a result, the money manager will be "lightening up" his or her position in the stock. However, some of the stock remains in the portfolio.

LIMIT *see* LIMIT ORDER; LIMIT UP, LIMIT DOWN.

LIMITED COMPANY form of business most common in Britain and Canada, where registration under the Companies Act is comparable to incorporation under provincial law in Canada. It is abbreviated Ltd. or PLC.

LIMITED DISCRETION agreement between broker and client allowing the broker to make certain trades without consulting the client—for instance, sell an option position that is near expiration or sell a stock on which there has just been adverse news.

LIMITED LIABILITY underlying principle of the LIMITED COMPANY in Canada and the United Kingdom and the CORPORATION and the LIMITED PARTNERSHIP in the United States. LIABILITY is limited to an investor's original investment. In contrast, a general partner or the owner of a PROPRIETORSHIP has unlimited liability.

LIMITED PARTNERSHIP organization made up of a GENERAL PARTNER, who manages a project, and limited partners, who invest money but have limited liability, are not involved in day-to-day management, and usually cannot lose more than their capital contribution. Usually limited partners receive income, capital gains, and tax benefits; the general partner collects fees and a percentage of capital gains and income. Typical limited partnerships are in real estate, oil and gas, film and software, but they also finance research and development, and other projects. Typically, public limited partnerships are sold through brokerage firms, for minimum investments of $2500, whereas private limited partnerships are put together with fewer than 25 limited partners who invest more than $150,000 each.

LIMITED PARTNERSHIP MUTUAL FUND limited partnership offering a 3-year tax write-off and a share in the funds management and redemption fees. It is used to finance marketing and sales costs.

LIMITED PAY LIFE INSURANCE insurance for which premiums are payable for a limited period, e.g., 20 years. It is not usually convertible to a whole life policy and is not usually renewable.

LIMITED RISK risk in buying an options contract. For example, someone who pays a PREMIUM to buy a CALL OPTION on a stock will lose nothing more than the premium if the underlying stock does not rise during the life of the option. In contrast, a FUTURES CONTRACT entails *unlimited risk,* since the buyer may have to put up more money in the event of an adverse move. Thus options trading offers limited risk unavailable in futures trading.

Also, stock analysts may say of a stock that has recently fallen in price, that it now has limited risk, reasoning that the stock is unlikely to fall much further.

LIMITED TRADING AUTHORIZATION *see* LIMITED DISCRETION.

LIMITED WARRANTY warranty that imposes certain limitations, and is therefore not a full warranty. For example, an automaker may issue a warranty that covers parts, but not labour, for a particular period of time.

LIMIT ON CLOSE ORDER order to buy or sell a stated amount of a stock at the closing price, to be executed only if the closing price is a specified price or better, e.g., an order to sell XYZ at the close, if the closing price is $30 or higher.

LIMIT ORDER order to buy or sell a security or commodity at a specific price or better. The broker will execute the trade only within the price restriction. For example, a customer puts in a limit order to buy XYZ Corp. at 30 when the stock is selling for 32. Even if the stock reached 30⅛ the broker will not execute the trade. Similarly, if the client put in a limit order to sell XYZ Corp. at 33 when the price is 31, the trade will not be executed until the stock price hits 33.

LIMIT ORDER INFORMATION SYSTEM electronic system that informs subscribers about securities traded on participating exchanges, showing the specialist, the exchange, the order quantities, and the bid and offer prices. This allows subscribers to shop for the most favorable prices.

LIMIT PRICE price set in a LIMIT ORDER. For example, a customer might put in a limit order to sell shares at 45 or to buy at 40. The broker executes the order at the limit price or better.

LIMIT UP, LIMIT DOWN maximum price movement allowed for a commodity FUTURES CONTRACT during one trading day. In the face of a particularly dramatic development, a future's price may move limit up or limit down for several consecutive days.

LINE category of insurance, such as the *liability line,* or the amount of insurance on a given property, such as a $500,000 line on the buildings of the XYZ Company. Term is also used generally, to refer to a product line. *See also* BANK LINE.

LINE OF CREDIT *see* BANK LINE.

LIPPER MUTUAL FUND INDUSTRY AVERAGE average performance level of all mutual funds, as reported by Lipper Analytical Services of New York. The performance of all mutual funds is ranked quarterly and annually, by type of fund—such as aggressive growth fund or income fund. Mutual fund managers try to beat the industry average as well as the other funds in their category. *See also* MUTUAL FUND.

LIQUID ASSET cash or easily convertible into cash. Some examples: money-market fund shares, U.S. Treasury bills, bank deposits. An investor in an ILLIQUID investment such as a real estate or oil and gas LIMITED PARTNERSHIP is required to have substantial liquid assets, which would serve as a cushion if the illiquid deal did not work out favorably.

In a corporation's financial statements, liquid assets are cash, marketable securities, and accounts receivable.

LIQUIDATING DIVIDEND distribution of assets in the form of a DIV-
IDEND from a corporation that is going out of business. Such a payment
may come when a firm goes bankrupt or when management decides to
sell off a company's assets and pass the proceeds on to shareholders.

LIQUIDATING VALUE projected price for an asset of a company that
is going out of business—for instance, a real estate holding or office
equipment. Liquidating value, also called *auction value,* assumes that
assets are sold separately from the rest of the organization; it is distinguished from GOING CONCERN VALUE, which may be higher because of
what accountants term *organization value* or *goodwill.*

LIQUIDATION
1. dismantling of a business, paying off debts in order of priority, and
   distributing the remaining assets in cash to the owners.
2. process of converting securities or other property into cash.

LIQUIDITY ability to buy or sell an asset quickly and in large volume
without substantially affecting the asset's price. Shares in large blue-
chip stocks like General Motors or General Electric are liquid, because
they are actively traded and therefore the stock price will not be dramatically moved by a few buy or sell orders. However, shares in small
companies with few shares outstanding, or commodity markets with
limited activity, generally are not considered liquid, because one or
two big orders can move the price up or down sharply. A high level of
liquidity is a key characteristic of a good market for a security or a
commodity.
    Liquidity also refers to the ability to convert to cash quickly. For
example, a money market mutual fund provides instant liquidity since
shareholders can sell their shares at current market value back to the
fund, without having to wait for another buyer. Other examples of liquid accounts include chequing accounts, bank money market deposit
accounts, passbook accounts, and Treasury bills. The liquidity of a
company is directly related to the level of cash, marketable securities,
and other current assets it holds.

LIQUIDITY CRISIS period of "technical insolvency" in which a firm
is unable to meet due bills.

LIQUIDITY DIVERSIFICATION purchase of bonds whose maturities range from short to medium to long term, thus helping to protect
against sharp fluctuations in interest rates.

LIQUIDITY RATIO measure of a firm's ability to meet maturing short-
term obligations. *See also* CASH ASSET RATIO; CURRENT RATIO; NET
QUICK ASSETS; QUICK RATIO.

LIQUID STOCK stock is said to be liquid if it trades frequently, if there
is a small price difference between the bid and ask prices, and if there
are small price changes from sale to sale.

LISBON STOCK EXCHANGE largest of two exchanges in Portugal. Trading on the exchange takes place Monday through Friday from 9 A.M. to 3 P.M. for continuous trading and 9:30 A.M. to 4 P.M. for daily calls. TRADIS, a computerized trading system, links the Lisbon and Oporto (OSE) exchanges. Settlement takes place on the fourth business day following the trade. The OSE also trades several futures and options contracts.

LISTED OPTION put or call OPTION that an exchange has authorized for trading, properly called an *exchange-traded option.*

LISTED SECURITY stock or bond that has been accepted for trading by one of the organized and registered securities exchanges in Canada or the United States. Generally, the advantages of being listed are that the exchanges provide (1) an orderly marketplace; (2) liquidity; (3) fair price determination; (4) accurate and continuous reporting on sales and quotations; (5) information on listed companies; and (6) strict regulations for the protection of security holders. Each exchange has its own listing requirements. Listed securities include stocks, bonds, convertible bonds, preferred stocks, warrants, rights, and options, although not all forms of securities are accepted on all exchanges. Unlisted securities are traded in the OVER-THE-COUNTER market. *See also* LISTING REQUIREMENTS; STOCK EXCHANGE.

LISTED SHARE share that meets the listing requirements of a stock exchange and is traded on the exchange.

LISTED STOCK *see* LISTED SECURITY.

LISTING written employment agreement between a property owner and a real estate broker authorizing the broker to find a buyer or tenant for certain property. Oral listings, while not specifically illegal, are unenforceable under many state fraud statutes, and generally are not recommended. The most common form of listing is the exclusive-right-to-sell listing. Others include open listings and exclusive-agency listings. The listing usually states the amount of commission the seller will pay the broker and the time limit. In a buyer's listing, the buyer hires the broker to locate a property.

LISTING BROKER licensed real estate broker (agent) who secures a listing of a property for sale. A *listing* involves a contract authorizing the broker to perform services for the selling property owner. The listing broker may sell the property, but it may also be sold by the *selling broker,* a different agent, with the two sharing commissions, usually equally.

LISTING REQUIREMENTS rules that must be met before a stock is listed for trading on an exchange. The Toronto Stock Exchange requires five years of audit statements with a profit position and $5 million in worth. Among the requirements of the New York Stock Exchange: a corporation must have a minimum of one million publicly held shares with a minimum aggregate market value of $16 million as well as an annual net income topping $2.5 million before federal income tax.

LISTING STATEMENT stock exchange document published when a company's shares are accepted for listing. It provides basic information on the company, its business, management, assets, capitalization, and financial status.

LIST PRICE suggested retail price for a product according to the manufacturer. The list price is designed to guide retailers, though they remain free to sell products above or below list price.

LITTLE DRAGONS nickname for developing Asian nations such as Singapore, Hong Kong, South Korea, and Taiwan that pose a threat to Japan (the Big Dragon) because of their lower labour costs, high productivity, and pro-business attitudes. Also known as the *tigers*.

LIVING BENEFITS life insurance benefits upon which the insured can draw cash while still alive. Some policies allow benefits to be paid to the insured in cases of terminal illness or illness involving certain long-term care costs. Beneficiaries receive any balance upon the insured's death. Also known as *accelerated benefits*.

LIVING DEAD *see* ZOMBIES.

LIVING TRUST *see* INTER VIVOS TRUST.

LLOYD'S OF LONDON London-based corporation of underwriters (Lloyd's Underwriters) and insurance brokers (Lloyd's Brokers) most famous for the wide variety of risks it insures. Lloyd's is not itself an underwriter. Its business is underwritten by some 350 syndicates of Lloyd's Underwriters representing some 30,000 underwriters, who become members of the corporation by depositing a substantial sum of money and accepting unlimited liability. The insurance is marketed through some 260 Lloyd's brokers.

LOAD sales charge paid by an investor who buys shares in a load MUTUAL FUND or ANNUITY. Loads are usually charged when shares or units are purchased; a charge for withdrawing is called a BACK-END LOAD (or *rear-end load*). A fund that does not charge this fee is called a NO-LOAD FUND. *See also* INVESTMENT COMPANY.

LOAD FUND MUTUAL FUND that is sold for a sales charge by a brokerage firm or other sales representative. Such funds may be stock, bond, or commodity funds, with conservative or aggressive objectives. The stated advantage of a load fund is that the salesperson will explain the fund to the customer, and advise him or her when it is appropriate to sell the fund, as well as when to buy more shares. A NO-LOAD FUND, which is sold without a sales charge directly to investors by a fund company, does not give advice on when to buy or sell. Increasingly, traditional no-load funds are becoming *low-load funds,* imposing up-front charges of 3% or less with no change in services. *See also* INVESTMENT COMPANY.

LOAD SPREAD OPTION method of allocating the annual sales charge on some contractual mutual funds. In a CONTRACTUAL PLAN, the investor accumulates shares in the fund through periodic fixed payments. During the first four years of the contract, up to 20% of any single year's contributions to the fund may be credited against the sales charge, provided that the total charges for these four years do not exceed 64% of one year's contributions. The sales charge is limited to 9% of the entire contract.

LOAN transaction wherein an owner of property, called the LENDER, allows another party, the *borrower,* to use the property. The borrower customarily promises to return the property after a specified period with payment for its use, called INTEREST. The documentation of the promise is called a PROMISSORY NOTE when the property is cash.

LOAN AGREEMENT contract between the bank and the borrower in which the terms and conditions of a credit commitment are recorded.

LOAN AMORTIZATION reduction of debt by scheduled, regular payments of principal and interest sufficient to repay the loan at maturity.

LOAN COMMITMENT lender's agreement to make money available to a borrower in a specified amount, at a specified rate, and within a specified time. *See also* COMMITMENT FEE.

LOAN CROWD stock exchange members who lend or borrow securities required to cover the positions of brokerage customers who sell short—called a crowd because they congregate at a designated place on the floor of the exchange. *See also* LENDING SECURITIES.

LOANED FLAT loaned without interest, said of the arrangement whereby brokers lend securities to one another to cover customer SHORT SALE positions. *See also* LENDING AT A PREMIUM; LENDING AT A RATE; LENDING SECURITIES.

LOAN ORIGINATION FEE *see* POINT.

LOAN STOCK *see* LENDING SECURITIES.

LOAN-TO-VALUE RATIO (LTV) ratio of money borrowed to fair market value, usually in reference to real property. Residential mortgage loans conventionally have a maximum LTV of 80% (an $80,000 loan on a $100,0000 house).

LOAN VALUE
1. amount a lender is willing to lend against collateral. For example, at 50% of appraised value, a piece of property worth $800,000 has a loan value of $400,000.

LOCAL member of a futures exchange who trades for his or her own account. The traders in a futures pit are composed of locals and employees of various brokerage firms. Locals initiate their own transactions on the floor of the exchange. Some, termed *dual traders,* also execute orders on behalf of customers.

LOCAL TAXES taxes paid by an individual to his or her locality. This includes city income, property, sewer, water, school, and other taxes. These taxes are usually not deductible unless the taxpayer runs a home business.

LOCK BOX

1. cash management system whereby a company's customers mail payments to a post office box near the company's bank. The bank collects cheques from the lock box—sometimes several times a day—deposits them to the account of the firm, and informs the company's cash manager by telephone of the deposit. The bank also forwards any other enclosures to the company. This reduces processing FLOAT and puts cash to work more quickly. The bank's fee for its services must be weighed against the savings from reduced float to determine whether this arrangement is cost-effective.

2. bank service that entails holding a customer's securities and, as agent, receiving and depositing income such as dividends on stock and interest on bonds.

3. box rented in a post office where mail is stored until collected.

LOCK BOX SERVICE *see* LOCK BOX.

LOCKED IN

1. unable to take advantage of preferential tax treatment on the sale of an asset because the required HOLDING PERIOD has not elapsed. *See also* CAPITAL GAIN.

2. commodities position in which the market has an up or down limit day, and investors cannot get in or out of the market.

3. said of a rate of return that has been assured for a length of time through an investment such as a certificate of deposit or a fixed rate bond; also said of profits or yields on securities or commodities that have been protected through HEDGING techniques.

4. unable to sell because of either the absence of a market or some legal restriction on the sale of the security. Also refers to an investor holding a security that has declined below the purchase price who cannot sell without incurring a loss.

LOCKED-IN PENSION FUND   RRSP or retirement account that allows for pension portability for people who change jobs. The employer deposits the value of the accumulated contributions of both employer and employee into a locked-in RRSP or a locked-in retirement account (LIRA). (For a defined contribution plan, the calculation is easy; for a defined benefit plan, there can be complications.) A person may use these vehicles only to buy a life annuity that is essentially what the pension fund would have done: no cash withdrawals are permitted. The locked-in fund need not be transferred at once to an annuity and is ordinarily held until retirement, accumulating income, tax-free.

Recent changes in provincial pension legislation have created new types of funds for conversion of locked-in pensions. These funds are essentially types of RRIFs. A Life Income Fund (LIF) operates like an RRIF from inception. The minimum and maximum payments are set by the pension legislation of each province. The funds left in the LIF at the end of the year in which the purchaser turns 80 must be used to purchase an immediate life annuity. Pension legislation in all provinces except Newfoundland and PEI permits LIFs.

Alberta and Saskatchewan have created a Life Retirement Income Fund (LRIF) that does not require annuitization at age 80. The minimum withdrawal is the same as in an RRIF. The maximum is the greatest of: the accumulated income; the preceding year's income; and, in the first two years of the plan, 6% of the plan value. If the minimum exceeds the maximum, the withdrawal is the minimum.

LOCKED-IN RETIREMENT ACCOUNT *see* LOCKED-IN PENSION FUND.

LOCKED-IN RRSP *see* LOCKED-IN PENSION FUND.

LOCKED MARKET highly competitive market environment with identical bid and ask prices for a stock. The appearance of more buyers and sellers unlocks the market.

LOCK-UP OPTION privilege offered a WHITE KNIGHT (friendly acquirer) by a TARGET COMPANY of buying CROWN JEWELS or additional equity. The aim is to discourage a hostile TAKEOVER.

LONDON COMMODITY EXCHANGE (LCE) formerly the London Futures and Options Exchange (FOX), the LCE trades futures and options on robusta coffee, No. 7 cocoa, No. 5 white sugar, Baltic freight (Biffex), EEC wheat, EEC barley and potatoes; and futures on No. 7 premium raw sugar. The sugar contracts trade on the LCE's proprietary FAST electronic trading system. Hours: 9:30 A.M.–5 P.M. (floor), with FAST trading until 7:01 P.M. for the sugar contracts, Monday through Friday.

LONDON INTERNATIONAL FINANCIAL FUTURES AND OPTIONS EXCHANGE (LIFFE) three largest futures markets in the United Kingdom. Futures and options contracts on long- and short-term interest rates, denominated in world currencies: three-month sterling (short sterling), three-month Eurodollar, three-month Eurodeutschmark (Euromark), and three-month Euroswiss franc (Euroswiss); three-month Eurolira interest rate and three-month ECU futures; and long gilt futures and options. Bond trading includes German government bond (bund) futures and options, Italian government bond (BTP) futures and options, Japanese government bond (JGB) futures and medium-term German government bond (Bobl). LIFFE trades two indices, the FT-SE 100 Index future and option, and the FT-SE 250 Index future and option, and 71 equity options that include British Petroleum, RTZ, Hanson, and Unilever. Hours: 7:30 A.M.–4:15 P.M., Monday through Friday. Short sterling, Euromarks, Euroswiss, Long Gilt, bund, BTP, and Bobl futures contracts are traded "after hours" on the exchange's Automated Pit Trading (APT) system, between 4:20 P.M. and 8 P.M.; the JGB trades from 7 A.M. to 4 P.M. Trading on LIFFE's bond futures and options contracts is linked to trading on the CHICAGO BOARD OF TRADE. LIFFE traders can trade the CBOT's U.S. Treasury Bond, 10-year note and 5-year note futures and options during the London Morning prior to the opening of Chicago trading. The CBOT can trade LIFFE's Bund, BTP and long gilt futures and options during Chicago's day session and all of its evening session.

LONDON INTERBANK OFFERED RATE (LIBOR) rate that the most creditworthy international banks dealing in EURODOLLARS charge each other for large loans. The LIBOR rate is usually the base for other large Eurodollar loans to less creditworthy corporate and government borrowers. For instance, a Third World country may have to pay one point over LIBOR when it borrows money.

LONDON METAL EXCHANGE (LME) principal-to-principal market for base metals trading. The LME trades cash and three-month contracts on aluminum, copper, nickel, lead, zinc, tin, and aluminum alloy. Trading is conducted in two open-outcry rings, each followed by a kerb session (a private session on the side). Traded options contracts are available on the underlying futures contracts. Clearing is through the London Clearing House Ltd.

LONG term signifying ownership of a security. "I am long 100 on ABC" means that the speaker owns 100 shares of ABC corporation's stock. To be long on something is to own it.

LONG BOND in general, bond that matures in more than 10 years. Since these bonds commit investors' money for a long time, they normally pay investors a higher yield. In Wall Street parlance, the long bond is the 30-year Treasury.

LONG COUPON
1. bond issue's first interest payment covering a longer period than the remaining payments, or the bond issue itself. Conventional schedules call for interest payments at six-month intervals. A long COUPON results when a bond is issued more than six months before the date of the first scheduled payment. *See also* SHORT COUPON.
2. interest-bearing bond maturing in more than 10 years.

LONG HEDGE
1. FUTURES CONTRACT bought to protect against a rise in the cost of honouring a future commitment. Also called a *buy hedge*. The hedger benefits from a narrowing of the BASIS (difference between cash price and future price) if the future is bought below the cash price, and from a widening of the basis if the future is bought above the cash price.

    2. FUTURES CONTRACT or CALL OPTION bought in anticipation of a drop in interest rates, so as to lock in the present yield on a fixed-income security.

LONG LEG part of an OPTION SPREAD representing a commitment to buy the underlying security. For instance, if a spread consists of a long CALL OPTION and a short PUT OPTION, the long call is the long LEG.

LONG POSITION
    1. ownership of a security, giving the investor the right to transfer ownership to someone else by sale or by gift; the right to receive any income paid by the security; and the right to any profits or losses as the security's value changes.
    2. investor's ownership of securities held by a brokerage firm.

LONG TERM
    1. investment approach to the stock market in which an investor seeks appreciation by holding a stock for a year or more.
    2. bond or debenture with a maturity of 10 years or longer.
        See also LONG BOND; LONG-TERM DEBT; LONG-TERM FINANCING; LONG-TERM GAIN; LONG-TERM LOSS.

LONG-TERM BOND bond or debenture maturing in more than 10 years.

LONG-TERM DEBT liability due in a year or more. Normally, interest is paid periodically over the term of the loan, and the principal amount is payable as notes or bonds mature. Also, a LONG BOND with a maturity of 10 years or more.

LONG-TERM DEBT RATIO *see* DEBT-TO-EQUITY RATIO (2). *See also* RATIO ANALYSIS.

LONG-TERM FINANCING liabilities not repayable in one year and all equity. *See also* LONG-TERM DEBT.

LONG-TERM GAIN gain on the sale of a CAPITAL ASSET where the HOLDING PERIOD was 12 months or more and the profit was subject to the long-term CAPITAL GAINS TAX.

LONG-TERM GOALS financial goals that an individual sets for five years or longer. Some examples of long-term goals include assembling a retirement fund, saving for a down payment on a house or for college tuition, buying a second home, or starting a business.

LONG-TERM INVESTOR someone who invests in stocks, bonds, mutual funds or other investment vehicles for a long time, typically at least five years, in order to fund LONG-TERM GOALS. A long-term investor looks for solid investments with a good long-term track record, such as a BLUE CHIP STOCK or a mutual fund with exemplary performance.

LONG-TERM LIABILITIES any monies owed that are not payable on demand or within one year. The *current portion of long-term debt* is a current liability, as distinguished from a long-term liability.

LONG-TERM LOSS negative counterpart to LONG-TERM GAIN as defined by the same legislation. A CAPITAL LOSS can be used to offset a CAPITAL GAIN plus $3000 of ORDINARY INCOME except that short-term losses exceeding short-term gains must first be applied to long-term gains, if any.

LONG-TERM PLANNING financial planning to accomplish LONG-TERM GOALS. A long-term plan will project how much money will be needed to fund retirement, pay college tuition, or buy a house in five years or more by designing an investment strategy to meet that goal.

LONG TRADING trading that involves buying futures contracts in the hope that the price will go up, and hanging onto the contract. Such an investor is said to be long in the market.

LOOPHOLE technicality making it possible to circumvent a law's intent without violating its letter. For instance, a TAX SHELTER may exploit a loophole in the tax law.

LOOSE CREDIT policy by the Bank of Canada to make loans less expensive and thus widely available in the economy. To do so, it uses moral suasion, buying and selling the Canadian dollar, reduc ing the bank rate. Also called EASY MONEY. The opposite policy is called TIGHT MONEY, in which the Bank of Canada sells securities and makes it more difficult and expensive to borrow, and thereby hopes to slow down economic activity. Tight money policy is used to dampen inflation in an overheated economy.

LOSS
1. opposite of PROFIT.
2. a return of less than the original amount of invested capital.

LOSS-CONTROL ACTIVITIES actions initiated by a company or individual at the urging of its insurance company to prevent accidents, losses or other insurance claims. For example, a home insurer may require smoke alarms. A commercial insurer may require certain safety procedures in a manufacturing plant.

LOSS LEADER concept, primarily in retailing, where an item is priced at a loss and widely advertised in order to draw trade into the store. The loss is considered a cost of promotion and is offset by the profits on other items sold. Concept is sometimes used by DISCOUNT BROKERS, who will advertise a particular transaction at a loss price to attract customers, who will enter into other transactions at a profit to the broker.

LOSS-OF-INCOME INSURANCE insurance coverage replacing income lost by a policyholder. For example, *business interruption insurance* will pay employee wages if a business is temporarily out of operation because of a fire, flood, or other disaster. *Disability insurance* will replace a portion of an insured disabled person's income while he or she is disabled due to injury or illness. *Worker's compensation insurance* will reimburse a worker who was injured on the job for lost wages during the disability period. *See also* DISABILITY INSURANCE.

LOSS PREVENTION programs instituted by individuals or companies to prevent losses. Businesses implement safety programs to prevent workplace injuries. Individuals install fire detectors, burglar alarms, and other protective devices to prevent losses caused by fire and theft. Car owners install special locks to prevent auto theft. Insurance companies usually offer discounts to businesses or individuals taking loss prevention measures.

LOSS RATIO ratio of losses paid or accrued by an insurer to premiums earned, usually for a one-year period. *See also* BAD DEBT.

LOSS RESERVE *see* BAD DEBT.

LOT in a general business sense, a lot is any group of goods or services making up a transaction. *See also* ODD LOT; ROUND LOT.

LOW bottom price paid for a security over the past year or since trading in the security began; in the latter sense also called *historic low.*

LOW BALANCE METHOD interest computation method on savings accounts where interest is based on the lowest balance during the period.

LOW GRADE bond RATING of B or lower.

LUMP SUM large payment of money received at one time instead of in periodic payments. People retiring from or leaving a company may receive a lump-sum distribution of the value of their pension, salary reduction or profit-sharing plan. When taking early retirement or severance, an employee can roll over $2000 a year tax-free into an RRSP for each year of service up to December 31, 1995 and $1500 for each year prior to 1989 if he or she was not a member of a registered pension plan. Lump sum withdrawals of no more than $5000 at a time are subject to a withholding tax of 10% (higher if more is withdrawn). Beneficiaries of life insurance policies may receive a death benefit in a lump sum. A consumer making a large purchase such as a car or boat may decide to pay in one lump sum instead of financing the purchase over time.

M

M1 currency in circulation outside of the chartered banks, together with the monies in Canadian dollar savings and chequing accounts held within financial institutions. It is one of the money supply indicators. The U.S. definition of M1 is different from the Canadian one because the U.S. includes chequable savings deposits that can also be withdrawn at any time, although they formally can require advance notice of withdrawal.

M2 M1 plus personal non-chequing term and savings deposits, some chequable and non-chequable notice deposits. The Canadian M2 is the same as the U.S. M2.

M3 M2 plus all non-personal term deposits, including certificates of deposits held by business corporations.

MACARONI DEFENSE defensive tactic used by a corporation trying to defeat a TAKEOVER attempt by a RAIDER or unfriendly bidder. The target corporation will issue a massive amount of bonds that must be redeemed at a mandatory higher redemption value if the company is taken over. The redemption value of these bonds therefore expands when the company is threatened—like macaroni when it is cooked—making the takeover prohibitively expensive to complete.

MACROECONOMICS analysis of a nation's economy as a whole, using such aggregate data as price levels, unemployment, inflation, and industrial production. *See also* MICROECONOMICS.

MADRID STOCK EXCHANGE the Bolsa de Madrid is the largest and most international of Spain's four stock exchanges. The Madrid Stock Exchange General Index is dominated by banks, utilities, and communications firms, and is based on trading frequency and liquidity. Trading is through an electronic trading system based on the CATS system developed by the Toronto Stock Exchange. Trading on the continuous market owned by the four exchanges is from 11 A.M. to 5 P.M., with pre-opening trading from 10 A.M. to 11 A.M. Trading on the exchanges is from 10 A.M. to 12:15 P.M. All trading is Monday through Friday. Settlement is five business days after the trade date.

MACRS *see* MODIFIED ACCELERATED COST RECOVERY SYSTEM (MACRS).

MAGNETIC INK CHARACTER RECOGNITION (MICR) magnetic characters encoded at the bottom of a cheque to facilitate use of automated equipment in the bank clearing process. A fully encoded MICR line may contain serial number of cheque, payer bank transit/routing symbol, account number, and dollar amount of cheque.

MAINTENANCE BOND a bond that guarantees against defects in workmanship or materials for a specified period following completion of a contract.

MAINTENANCE CALL call for additional money or securities when a brokerage customer's margin account equity falls below the requirements. *See also* MAINTENANCE REQUIREMENT; MINIMUM MAINTENANCE; SELL OUT.

MAINTENANCE FEE annual charge to maintain certain types of brokerage accounts.

MAINTENANCE REQUIREMENT *see* MINIMUM MAINTENANCE.

MAJORITY SHAREHOLDER one of the shareholders who together control more than half the outstanding shares of a corporation. If the ownership is widely scattered and there are no majority shareholders, effective control may be gained with far less than 51% of the outstanding shares. *See also* WORKING CONTROL.

MAJOR MEDICAL INSURANCE *see* EXTENDED HEALTH CARE INSURANCE.

MAJOR TREND underlying price trend prevailing in a market despite temporary declines or rallies.

MAKE A MARKET maintain firm bid and offer prices in a given security by standing ready to buy or sell ROUND LOTS at publicly quoted prices. The dealer is called a *market maker* in the over-the-counter market and a SPECIALIST on the exchanges. A dealer who makes a market over a long period is said to *maintain* a market. See *also* REGISTERED COMPETITIVE MARKET MAKER.

MAKE A PRICE *see* MAKE A MARKET.

MANAGED ACCOUNT investment account consisting of money that one or more clients entrust to a manager, who is usually licensed to be a portfolio manager and who then decides when and where to invest the money. Such an account may be handled by a bank trust department or by an investment advisory firm. Clients are charged a MANAGEMENT FEE And share in proportion to their participation in any losses and gains.

MANAGEMENT combined fields of policy and administration and the people who provide the decisions and supervision necessary to implement the owners' business objectives and achieve stability and growth. The formulation of policy requires analysis of all factors having an effect on short- and long-term profits. The administration of policies is carried out by the CHIEF EXECUTIVE OFFICER, his or her immediate staff, and everybody else who possesses authority delegated by people with supervisory responsibility. Thus the size of management can range from one person in a small organization to multilayered management hierarchies in large, complex organizations. The top members of management, called senior management, report to the owners of a firm; in large corporations, the CHAIRMAN OF THE BOARD, the PRESIDENT, and sometimes other key senior officers report to the BOARD OF DIRECTORS, comprising elected representatives of the owning stockholders. The application of scientific principles to decision-making is called management science. *See also* ORGANIZATION CHART.

MANAGEMENT BUYIN purchase of a large, and often controlling, interest in a company by an outside investor group that chooses to retain existing management. In many cases, the outside investors are venture capitalists who believe the company's products, services, and management have bright prospects. The investor group will usually place its representatives on the company's board of directors to monitor the progress of the company.

MANAGEMENT BUYOUT purchase of all of a company's publicly held shares by the existing management, which takes the company private. Usually, management will have to pay a premium over the current market price to entice public shareholders to go along with the deal. If management has to borrow heavily to finance the transaction, it is called a LEVERAGED BUYOUT (LBO). Managers may want to buy their company for several reasons: They want to avoid being taken over by a raider who would bring in new management; they no longer want the scrutiny that comes with running a public company; or they believe they can make more money for themselves in the long run by owning a larger share of the company, and eventually reap substantial profits by going public again with a REVERSE LEVERAGED BUYOUT.

MANAGEMENT COMPANY business entity that sets up, promotes, and manages a fund or funds. In order to buy shares in a fund, an investor must go to a distribution company, not to the management company. Same as INVESTMENT COMPANY.

MANAGEMENT FEE regular annual fee to a mutual fund, levied quarterly, in the amount of anywhere from 0.15% to 3.0%.

MANAGING UNDERWRITER leading—and originating—investment banking firm of an UNDERWRITING GROUP organized for the purchase and distribution of a new issue of securities. The AGREEMENT AMONG UNDERWRITERS authorizes the managing underwriter, or syndicate manager, to act as agent for the group in purchasing, carrying, and distributing the issue as well as complying with all federal and state requirements; to form the selling group; to determine the allocation of securities to each member; to make sales to the selling group at a specified discount—or CONCESSION—from the public offering price; to engage in open market transactions during the underwriting period to stabilize the market price of the security; and to borrow for the syndicate account to cover costs. *See also* FLOTATION COST; INVESTMENT BANKER; UNDERWRITE.

MANIPULATION buying or selling a security to create a false appearance of active trading and thus influence other investors to buy or sell shares. This may be done by one person or by a group acting in concert. Those found guilty of manipulation are subject to criminal and civil penalties. *See also* MINI-MANIPULATION.

MAPLE LEAF bullion coin minted by the government of Canada in gold (99.99% pure), silver (99.99% pure) and platinum (99.95% pure). The gold and platinum coins are available in one ounce, one-half ounce, one-quarter ounce, one-tenth ounce, one-fifteenth ounce and one-twentieth ounce sizes. The silver coin is available only in the one-ounce size. The Maple Leaf is actively traded throughout the world along with the American Eagle, South African Kruggerand, and other coins. The Maple Leaf usually sells at a slight premium to the bullion value of the coin. *See also* GOLD COIN.

MARGIN
In general: amount a customer deposits with a broker when borrowing from the broker to buy securities. Security industry procedures require 50% on most margin stock trades but this can vary to as low as 50% on speculative futures contracts.
Corporate finance: difference between the price received by a company for its products and services and the cost of producing them. Also known as *gross profit margin.*
Futures trading: good-faith deposit an investor must put up when buying or selling a contract. If the futures price moves adversely, the investor must put up more money to meet margin requirements.

MARGINABLE SECURITIES see MARGIN SECURITY.

MARGIN ACCOUNT brokerage account allowing customers to buy securities with money borrowed from the broker. The margin is the amount the investor pays toward the total cost of the security and is usually 50% or more of its cost, although it can range as low as 30% and as low as 5% for certain bonds. Margin requirements can be met with cash or with eligible securities. In the case of securities sold short, an equal amount of the same securities is normally borrowed without interest from another broker to cover the sale, while the proceeds are kept in trust as collateral for the lending broker.

MARGIN AGREEMENT document that spells out the rules governing a MARGIN ACCOUNT, including the HYPOTHECATION of securities, how much equity the customer must keep in the account, and the interest rate on margin loans. Also known as a *hypothecation agreement.*

MARGIN CALL demand, should the share or futures contract prices fall, that the lender (dealer) increase his or her security in anticipation of investor losses. The lender (dealer) may contact the investor who is required to post more collateral or cash to offset the loss of the investment value. Failure to do so would result in a default, sale of the investment, and demand for payment in full.

MARGINAL ANALYSIS principle that an investment (or action) should be undertaken when its marginal benefits exceed its marginal costs.

MARGINAL COST increase or decrease in the total costs of a business firm as the result of one more or one less unit of output. Also called *incremental cost* or *differential cost*. Determining marginal cost is important in deciding whether or not to vary a rate of production. In most manufacturing firms, marginal costs decrease as the volume of output increases due to economies of scale, which include factors such as bulk discounts on raw materials, specialization of labour, and more efficient use of machinery. At some point, however, diseconomies of scale enter in and marginal costs begin to rise; diseconomies include factors like more intense managerial supervision to control a larger work force, higher raw materials costs because local supplies have been exhausted, and generally less efficient input. The marginal cost curve is typically U-shaped on a graph.

MARGINAL COST

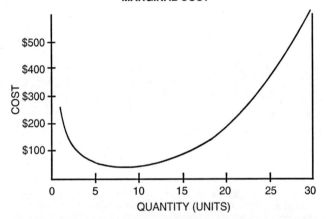

A firm is operating at optimum output when marginal cost coincides with average total unit cost. Thus, at less than optimum output, an increase in the rate of production will result in a marginal unit cost lower than average total unit cost; production in excess of the optimum point will result in marginal cost higher than average total unit cost. In other words, a sale at a price higher than marginal unit cost will increase the net profit of the manufacturer even though the sales price does not cover average total unit cost; marginal cost is thus the lowest amount at which a sale can be made without adding to the producer's loss or subtracting from his profits.

MARGINAL EFFICIENCY OF CAPITAL annual percentage yield earned by the last additional unit of capital. It is also known as *marginal productivity of capital, natural interest rate, net capital productivity,* and *rate of return over cost.* The significance of the concept to a business firm is that it represents the market rate of interest at which it begins to pay to undertake a capital investment. If the market rate is 10%, for example, it would not pay to undertake a project that has a return of 9½%, but any return over 10% would be acceptable. In a larger economic sense, marginal efficiency of capital influences long-term interest rates. This occurs because of the law of diminishing returns as it applies to the yield on capital. As the highest yielding projects are exhausted, available capital moves into lower yielding projects and interest rates decline. As market rates fall, investors are able to justify projects that were previously uneconomical. This process is called *diminishing marginal productivity* or *declining marginal efficiency of capital.*

MARGINAL REVENUE change in total revenue caused by one additional unit of output. It is calculated by determining the difference between the total revenues produced before and after a one-unit increase in the rate of production. As long as the price of a product is constant, price and marginal revenue are the same; for example, if baseball bats are being sold at a constant price of $10 apiece, a one-unit increase in sales (one baseball bat) translates into an increase in total revenue of $10. But it is often the case that additional output can be sold only if the price is reduced, and that leads to a consideration of MARGINAL COST—the added cost of producing one more unit. Further production is not advisable when marginal cost exceeds marginal revenue since to do so would result in a loss. Conversely, whenever marginal revenue exceeds marginal cost, it is advisable to produce an additional unit. Profits are maximized at the rate of output where marginal revenue equals marginal cost.

MARGINAL TAX RATE amount of tax imposed on an additional dollar of income. In the Canadian progressive income tax system, the marginal tax rate increases as income rises. Economists believing in SUPPLY-SIDE ECONOMICS hold that this reduces the incentive to be productive and discourages business investment. In urging that marginal tax rates be cut for individuals and businesses, they argue that the resulting increased work effort and business investment would reduce STAGFLATION. *See also* FLAT TAX.

MARGINAL UTILITY in economics, the addition to total satisfaction from goods or services (called *utility*) that is derived from consuming one more unit of that good or service.

MARGIN CALL demand that a customer deposit enough money or securities to bring a margin account up to the INITIAL MARGIN or MINIMUM MAINTENANCE requirements. If a customer fails to respond, securities in the account may be liquidated. *See also* FIVE HUNDRED DOLLAR RULE; SELL OUT.

MARGIN DEPARTMENT section within a brokerage firm that monitors customer compliance with margin regulations, keeping track of debits and credits, short sales, and purchases of stock on margin, and all other extensions of credit by the broker. Also known as the *credit department. See also* MARK TO THE MARKET.

MARGIN OF PROFIT relationship of gross profits to net sales. Returns and allowances are subtracted from gross sales to arrive at net sales. Cost of goods sold (sometimes including depreciation) is subtracted from net sales to arrive at gross profit. Gross profit is divided by net sales to get the profit margin, which is sometimes called the *gross margin.* The result is a ratio, and the term is also written as *margin of profit ratio.*

The term profit margin is less frequently used to mean the *net margin,* obtained by deducting operating expenses in addition to cost of goods sold and dividing the result by net sales. Operating expenses are usually shown on profit and loss statements as "selling, general and administrative (SG&A) expenses."

Both gross and net profit margins, when compared with prior periods and with industry statistics, can be revealing in terms of a firm's operating efficiency and pricing policies and its ability to compete successfully with other companies in its field.

MARGIN REQUIREMENT minimum amount that a client must deposit in the form of cash or eligible securities in a margin account (e.g., 50% in Canada). *See also* MARGIN; MARGIN SECURITY; MINIMUM MAINTENANCE; SELLING SHORT.

MARKDOWN
1. amount subtracted from the selling price, when a customer sells securities to a dealer in the OVER THE COUNTER market. Had the securities been purchased from the dealer, the customer would have paid a *markup,* or an amount added to the purchase price.
2. downward adjustment of the value of securities by banks and investment firms, based on a decline in market quotations.
3. reduction in the original retail selling price, which was determined by adding a percentage factor, called a markon, to the cost of the merchandise. Anything added to the markon is called a markup, and the term markdown does not apply unless the price is dropped below the original selling price.

MARKET
1. public place where products or services are bought and sold, directly or through intermediaries. Also called *marketplace.*
2. aggregate of people with the present or potential ability and desire to purchase a product or service; equivalent to demand.
3. securities markets in the aggregate, or the TSE or VSE in particular.
4. short for *market value,* the value of an asset based on the price it would command on the open market, usually as determined by the MARKET PRICE at which similar assets have recently been bought and sold.
5. as a verb, to sell. *See also* MARKETING.

MARKETABLE something that is easily bought or sold because it is in demand.

MARKETABILITY speed and ease with which a particular security may be bought and sold. A stock that has a large amount of shares outstanding and is actively traded is highly marketable and also liquid. In common use, marketability is interchangeable with LIQUIDITY, but liquidity implies the preservation of value when a security is bought or sold. *See also* LIQUIDITY.

MARKETABLE SECURITIES securities that are easily sold. On a corporation's balance sheet, they are assets that can be readily converted into cash—for example, government securities, banker's acceptances, and commercial paper. In keeping with conservative accounting practice, these are carried at cost or market value, whichever is lower.

MARKET ANALYSIS
1. research aimed at predicting or anticipating the direction of stock, bond, or commodity markets, based on technical data about the movement of market prices or on fundamental data such as corporate earnings prospects or supply and demand.
2. study designed to define a company's markets, forecast their directions, and decide how to expand the company's share and exploit any new trends.

MARKET BASKET *see* BASKET.

MARKET BREAK any sudden drop (BREAK) in the stock market as measured by STOCK INDEXES AND AVERAGES. In TSE parlance, BLACK MONDAY, when the TSE 300 Index dropped 22% in value.

MARKET BREADTH *see* BREADTH OF THE MARKET.

MARKET CAPITALIZATION value of a corporation as determined by the market price of its issued and outstanding common stock. It is calculated by multiplying the number of outstanding shares by the current market price of a share. Institutional investors often use market capitalization as one investment criterion, requiring, for example, that a company have a market capitalization of $100 million or more to qualify as an investment. Analysts look at market capitalization in relation to book, or accounting, value for an indication of how investors value a company's future prospects.

MARKET CORRECTION price reversal that often occurs when a given commodity has been overbought or oversold.

MARKET EYE financial information service that emanates from the British Broadcasting Company under the sponsorship of the INTERNATIONAL STOCK EXCHANGE OF THE UK AND THE REPUBLIC OF IRELAND (ISE). Market Eye supplies current market information plus statistical information on particular equity and debt issues and is a supplement to the Stock Exchange Automated Quotations System (SEAQ), which records trades.

MARKET IF TOUCHED ORDER (MIT) order to buy or sell a security or commodity as soon as a preset market price is reached, at which point it becomes a MARKET ORDER. When corn is selling for $4.75 a bushel, someone might enter a market if touched order to buy at $4.50. As soon as the price is dropped to $4.50, the contract would be bought on the customer's behalf at whatever market price prevails when the order is executed.

MARKET INDEX numbers representing weighted values of the components that make up the index. A stock market index, for example, is weighted according to the prices and number of outstanding shares of the various stocks. The Toronto Stock Exchange 300 Index and Standard & Poor's 500 Stock Index are two of the most widely followed, but myriad other indexes track stocks in various industry groups.

MARKETING moving goods and services from the provider to consumer. This involves product origination and design, development, distribution, advertising, promotion, and publicity as well as market analysis to define the appropriate market.

MARKET JITTERS state of widespread fear among investors, which may cause them to sell stocks and bonds, pushing prices downward. Investors may fear lower corporate earnings, negative economic news, tightening of credit by the Bank of Canada, foreign currency fluctations, or many other factors. In some cases, news may be good, but is interpreted as bad because investors are so fearful.

MARKET LETTER newsletter provided to brokerage firm customers or written by an independent market analyst, registered as an investment adviser, who sells the letter to subscribers. These letters assess the trends in interest rates, the economy, and the market in general. Brokerage letters typically reiterate the recommendations of their own research departments. Independent letters take on the personality of their writers—concentrating on growth stocks, for example, or basing their recommendations on technical analysis. A HULBERT RATING is an evaluation of such a letter's performance.

MARKET MAKER trader employed by a securities firm who is authorized and required by applicable self-regulatory organizations (SROs) to maintain reasonable liquidity in securities markets by making firm bids or offers for one or more designated securities. *See also* MAKE A MARKET.

MARKET OPENING the start of formal trading on an exchange, usually referring to the Toronto Exchange (TSE) and the New York Stock Exchange (NYSE) and marked by an opening bell. All stocks do not necessarily open trading at the bell, since there may be order imbalances causing a DELAYED OPENING. *See also* OPD; OPENING.

MARKET-ON-CLOSE (MOC) ORDER order to buy or sell stocks or futures and options contracts as near as possible to when the market closes for the day. Such an order may be a LIMIT ORDER which had not yet been executed during the trading day.

MARKET ORDER order to buy or sell a security at the best available price. Most orders executed on the exchanges, and any for which the buyer did not specify the price are market orders.

MARKET OUT CLAUSE escape clause sometimes written into FIRM COMMITMENT underwriting agreements which essentially allows the underwriters to be released from their purchase commitment if material adverse developments affect the securities markets generally. It is not common practice for the larger investment banking houses to write "outs" into their agreements, because the value of their commitment is a matter of paramount concern. *See also* UNDERWRITE.

MARKETPLACE *see* MARKET.

MARKET PRICE last reported price at which a security was sold on an exchange. For stocks or bonds sold OVER THE COUNTER, the combined bid and offer prices available at any particular time from those making a market in the stock. For an inactively traded security, evaluators or other analysts may determine a market price if needed—to settle an estate, for example. Also the midpoint between the bid and ask prices. The closer to maturity a bond gets, the closer to par value the price or quote.

In the general business world, market price refers to the price agreed upon by buyers and sellers of a product or service, as determined by supply and demand.

MARKET RESEARCH exploration of the size, characteristics, and potential of a market to find out, before developing any new product or service, what people want and need. Market research is an early step in marketing—which stretches from the original conception of a product to its ultimate delivery to the consumer.

In the stock market, market research refers to TECHNICAL ANALYSIS of factors such as volume, price advances and declines, and market breadth, which analysts use to predict the direction of prices.

MARKET RISK *see* SYSTEMATIC RISK.

MARKET SHARE percentage of industry sales of a particular company or product.

MARKET SWEEP second offer to institutional investors, made following a public TENDER OFFER, aimed at increasing the buyer's position from a significant interest to a controlling interest. The second offering is usually at a slightly higher price than the original tender offer.

MARKET TIMING decisions on when to buy or sell securities, in light of economic factors such as the strength of the economy and the direction of interest rates, or technical indications such as the direction of stock prices and the volume of trading. Investors in mutual funds may implement their market timing decisions by switching from a stock fund to a bond fund to a money market fund and back again, as the market outlook changes.

MARKET TONE general health and vigour of a securities market. The market tone is good when dealers and market makers are trading actively on narrow bid and offer spreads; it is bad when trading is inactive and bid and offer spreads are wide.

MARKET VALUE

In general: market price—the price at which buyers and sellers trade similar items in an open marketplace. In the absence of a market price, it is the estimated highest price a buyer would be warranted in paying and a seller justified in accepting, provided both parties were fully informed and acted intelligently and voluntarily.

Investments: current market price of a security—as indicated by the latest trade recorded.

Accounting: technical definition used in valuing inventory or marketable securities in accordance with the conservative accounting principle of "lower of cost or market." While cost is simply acquisition cost, market value is estimated net selling price less estimated costs of carrying, selling, and delivery, and, in the case of an unfinished product, the costs to complete production. The market value arrived at this way cannot, however, be lower than the cost at which a normal profit can be made.

MARKET VALUE-WEIGHTED INDEX index whose components are weighted according to the total market value of their outstanding shares. Also called *capitalization-weighted index*. The impact of a component's price change is proportional to the issue's overall market value, which is the share price times the number of shares outstanding. The weighting of each stock constantly shifts with changes in the stock's price and the number of shares outstanding. The index fluctuates in line with the price moves of the stocks.

MARKING UP OR DOWN increasing or decreasing the price of a security based on supply and demand forces. A securities dealer may mark up the price of a stock or bond if prices are rising, and may be forced to mark it down if demand is declining. The markup is the difference, or spread, between the price the dealer paid for the security and the price at which it is sold to the retail customer. *See also* MARKDOWN.

MARK TO THE MARKET

1. adjust the valuation of a security or portfolio to reflect current market values. For example, MARGIN ACCOUNTS are marked to the market to ensure compliance with maintenance requirements. OPTION and FUTURES CONTACTS are marked to the market at year end with PAPER PROFIT OR LOSS recognized for tax purposes.
2. in a MUTUAL FUND, the daily net asset value reported to shareholders is the result of marking the fund's current portfolio to current market prices.

MARKUP *see* MARKDOWN.

MARRIED PUT option to sell a certain number of securities at a particular price by a specified time, bought simultaneously with securities of the underlying company so as to hedge the price paid for the securities. *See also* OPTION; PUT OPTION.

MATCHED AND LOST report of the results of flipping a coin by two securities brokers locked in competition to execute equal trades.

MATCHED BOOK term used for the accounts of securities dealers when their borrowing costs are equal to the interest earned on loans to customers and other brokers.

MATCHED ORDERS
1. illegal manipulative technique of offsetting buy and sell orders to create the impression of activity in a security, thereby causing upward price movement that benefits the participants in the scheme.
2. action by a SPECIALIST to create an opening price reasonably close to the previous close. When an accumulation of one kind of order—either buy or sell—causes a delay in the opening of trading on an exchange, the specialist tries to find counterbalancing orders or trades long or short from his own inventory in order to narrow the spread.

MATERIAL CHANGE change in the affairs of a company that is expected to have significant effect on the market value of its securities.

MATERIALITY characteristic of an event or information that is sufficiently important (or *material*) to have a large impact on a company's stock price. For example, if a company was about to report its earnings, or make a takeover bid for another company, that would be considered material information. Material information is information the reasonable investor needs to make an informed decision about an investment.

MATIF SA France's futures exchange, formally known as Marche a Terme International de France. The MATIF uses a combination of open outcry (9 A.M. to 4:30 P.M.) and electronic trading on the Globex system (4:30 P.M. to 9 A.M.) for its notion bond futures and options, and ECU bond futures and options; for three-month PIBOR futures and options (8:30 A.M. to 4 P.M., 4 P.M. to 8:30 A.M.); and CAC 40 INDEX futures and options contracts (10 A.M. to 5 P.M., 5 P.M. to 10 A.M.). U.S. dollar/ Deutschmark and U.S. dollar/French franc options are traded by open outcry (9:15 A.M. to 5 P.M.) and on Globex and the THS after-hours telephone system (5 P.M. to 9:15 A.M.). The exchange also trades three commodities through open outcry: white sugar futures (10:45 A.M. to 1 P.M., 3 P.M. to 7 P.M.); potato futures (10:30 A.M. to 12:45 P.M., 2 P.M. to 4 P.M.); and rapeseed futures (11 A.M. to 1 P.M., 3:30 P.M. to 6:30 P.M.).

MATRIX TRADING bond swapping whereby traders seek to take advantage of temporary aberrations in YIELD SPREAD differentials between bonds of the same class but with different ratings or between bonds of different classes.

MATURE ECONOMY economy of a nation whose population has stabilized or is declining, and whose economic growth is no longer robust. Such an economy is characterized by a decrease in spending on roads or factories and a relative increase in consumer spending. Many of Western Europe's economies are considerably more mature than that of Canada and in marked contrast to the faster-growing economies of the Far East.

MATURITY
1. reaching the date at which a debt instrument is due and payable. A bond due to mature on January 1, 2010, will return the bondholder's principal and final interest payment when it reaches maturity on that date. Bond yields are frequently calculated on a YIELD-TO-MATURITY basis.
2. when referring to a company or economy, *maturity* means that it is well-established, and has little room for dynamic growth. For example, economists will say that an aging industrial economy has reached maturity. Or stock analysts will refer to a company's market as mature, meaning that demand for the company's products is stagnant.

MATURITY DATE
1. date on which the principal amount of a note, draft, acceptance bond, or other debt instrument becomes due and payable. Also termination or due date on which an installment loan must be paid in full.
2. in FACTORING, average due date of factored receivables, when the factor remits to the seller for receivables sold each month.

MATURITY MATCHING *see* DURATION (*immunization*).

MBSs mortgage-backed securities first sold in Canada in the late 1980s. MBSs represent ownership in a pool of residential mortgages, all CHMC-insured. There is very low risk, because principal and interest payments are fully guaranteed by the federal government. Since the monthly income from an MBS, unlike a mortgage fund, includes some repayment of principal as well as interest, the investor does not receive the full face amount at maturity.

These securities can be purchased through stockbrokers with a minimum investment of $5000. A closed fund, whose mortgages don't allow borrowers to repay, means a steady stream of interest payment to the investor. MBS yields are usually slightly higher than Government of Canada bonds with the same term.

ME Montreal Exchange.

MEALS AND ENTERTAINMENT EXPENSE expense for meals and entertainment that qualifies for a tax deduction. Under current tax law, employers may deduct 50% of meals and entertainment expenses that have a bona fide business purpose. For example, a business meal must include a discussion producing a direct business benefit.

MEAN RETURN in security analysis, expected value, or mean, of all the likely returns of investments comprising a portfolio; in capital budgeting, mean value of the probability distribution of possible returns. The portfolio approach to the analysis of investments aims at quantifying the relationship between risk and return. It assumes that while investors have different risk-value preferences, rational investors will always seek the maximum rate of return for every level of acceptable risk. It is the mean, or expected, return that an investor attempts to maximize at each level of risk. Also called *expected return*. *See also* CAPITAL ASSET PRICING MODEL, EFFICIENT PORTFOLIO, PORTFOLIO THEORY.

MECHANIC'S LIEN LIEN against buildings or other structures, allowed by some states to contractors, laborers, and suppliers of materials used in their construction or repair. The lien remains in effect until these people have been paid in full and may, in the event of a liquidation before they have been paid, give them priority over other creditors.

MEDIAN midway value between two points. There are an equal number of points above and below the median. For example, the number 5 is the median between the numbers 1 and 9, since there are 4 numbers above and below 5 in this sequence. Several important economic numbers use medians, including median household income and median home price.

MEDIUM TERM any investment period of 3 to 7 years.

MEDIUM-TERM BOND bond with a maturity of 2 to 10 years. *See also* INTERMEDIATE TERM; LONG TERM; SHORT TERM.

MEFF RENTA FIJA Spain's derivatives exchange, in Barcelona, responsible for interest rate and foreign exchange derivatives. The exchange trades futures on interest rates and options on futures, the 90-day Madrid Interbank Offered Rate (MIBOR) and one-year MIBOR; and 3-year and 10-year government bond futures and options contracts. The exchange is a subsidiary of MEFF Holding Corp. of Financial Derivatives.

MEFF RENTA VARIABLE Spain's stock index and equity derivatives market, located in Madrid, trading futures and options on the Iberian Exchange (IBEX)-35 index and options on individual stocks. The IBEX-35 is the official index of the continuous market of the Spanish Sociedad de Bolsas, owned by the four exchanges. It is comprised of the 35 largest and most liquid stocks traded on the CATS electronic trading system. The exchange is a subsidiary of MEFF Holding Corp. of Financial Derivatives.

ME INDEX indices published by the Montreal Exchange, charting its common stock prices since 1926. In 1984, the Canadian Market

Portfolio Index (XXM), was introduced with a base value of 1000 calculated on January 3, 1983. The XXM comprises 25 widely held, highly capitalized, interlisted Canadian stocks representing a variety of economic sectors. A non-weighted price index, it gives a reliable depiction of the evolution of stock prices across the country. It is calculated every 3 minutes during trading hours on the basis of the most recent stock transaction, regardless of the exchange upon which these sales occurred.

In 1984, the ME also included 6 Canadian Market sectorial indices covering banking, forest products, oil and gas, utilities, mining and minerals, and industrial products. The indices, as well as the XXM, are revised on an annual basis to ensure the proper representation of Canadian companies in each of the economic sectors they measure.

To be included in one of the ME's indices, a stock must be listed on the ME as well as one other Canadian exchange; be issued by a company incorporated in Canada or be held by a majority of Canadian investors; be a common as opposed to a preferred share; be listed for at least 2 years; have a market capitalization of at least $10 million; have an annual trading volume of at least 100,000 shares and an annual trading value of at least $4 million; have a minimum of 3.6 million shares outstanding and have traded at a price of at least $5 during the previous twelve months.

The Canadian Market Portfolio Index is composed of 25 high-quality, widely held common stocks. It is designed to provide an accurate average price against which investors can compare the performance of their own portfolios.

MEMBER FIRM brokerage firm that has at least one membership on a stock exchange or in the Investment Dealers Association of Canada, even though, by exchange rules, the membership is in the name of an employee and not of the firm itself. Such a firm enjoys the rights and privileges of membership, such as voting on exchange policy, together with the obligations of membership, such as the commitment to settle disputes with customers through exchange arbitration procedures.

MERC nickname for the Chicago Mercantile Exchange. The exchange trades many types of futures, futures options, and foreign currency futures contracts. *See also* SECURITIES AND COMMODITIES EXCHANGES.

MERCANTILE AGENCY organization that supplies businesses with credit ratings and reports on other firms that are or might become customers. Such agencies may also collect past due accounts or trade collection statistics, and they tend to industry and geographical specialization. The largest of the agencies, DUN & BRADSTREET, was founded in 1841 under the name Mercantile Agency. It provides credit information on companies of all descriptions along with a wide range of other credit and financial reporting services.

MERCATO ITALIANO FUTURES (MIF) the Italian futures market, based in Rome. The MIF is a screen-based market, trading 10-year and

5-year Italian Treasury bond (BTP) futures. The market uses the same computer network that handles the underlying secondary market in Italian government securities.

MERCHANDISE EXPORTS products or commodities produced in one country and sold and shipped to other countries.

MERCHANDISE IMPORTS goods and services consumed in one country but produced in other countries.

MERCHANT BANK
1. European financial institution that engages in investment banking, counseling, and negotiating in mergers and acquisitions, and a variety of other services including securities portfolio management for customers, insurance, the acceptance of foreign bills of exchange, dealing in bullion, and participating in commercial ventures. Deposits in merchant banks are negligible, and the prominence of such names as Rothschild, Baring, Lazard, and Hambro attests to their role as counselors and negotiators in large-scale acquisitions, mergers, and the like.

MERGER combination of two or more companies, either through a POOLING OF INTERESTS, where the accounts are combined; a purchase, where the amount paid over and above the acquired company's book value is carried on the books of the purchaser as goodwill; or a consolidation, where a new company is formed to acquire the net assets of the combining companies. Strictly speaking, only combinations in which one of the companies survives as a legal entity are called mergers or, more formally, statutory mergers; thus consolidations, or statutory consolidations, are technically not mergers, though the term merger is commonly applied to them. Mergers meeting the legal criteria for pooling of interests, where common stock is exchanged for common stock, are nontaxable and are called tax-free mergers. Where an acquisition takes place by the purchase of assets or stock using cash or a debt instrument for payment, the merger is a taxable capital gain to the selling company or its stockholders. There is a potential benefit to such taxable purchase acquisitions, however, in that the acquiring company can write up the acquired company's assets by the amount by which the market value exceeds the book value; that difference can then be charged off to depreciation with resultant tax savings.

Mergers can also be classified in terms of their economic function. Thus a *horizontal merger* is one combining direct competitors in the same product lines and markets; a *vertical merger* combines customer and company or supplier and company; a *market extension merger* combines companies selling the same products in different markets; a *product extension merger* combines companies selling different but related products in the same market; a *conglomerate merger* combines companies with none of the above relationships or similarities. *See also* ACQUISITION.

MEXICAN STOCK EXCHANGE the only stock exchange in Mexico, formally known as the Bolsa Mexicana de Valores, and owned by the 26 casas de bolsa, or stock brokerage companies. The Indice de Precios y Cotizaciones, or IPC, consists of the 40 most representative stocks, chosen every two months. The INMEX index is an underlying index for derivative products, reviewed every six months so a single issuer cannot account for more than 10% of the index. The trading floor is automated, and trading is conducted from 8:30 A.M. to 2 P.M., Monday through Friday. Trades are settled two days after the trade date. All trades are executed in Mexican pesos.

MEZZANINE BRACKET members of a securities underwriting group whose participations are of such a size as to place them in the tier second to the largest participants. In the newspaper TOMBSTONE advertisements that announce new securities offerings, the underwriters are listed in alphabetical groups, first the lead underwriters, then the mezzanine bracket, then the remaining participants.

MEZZANINE LEVEL stage of a company's development just prior to its going public, in VENTURE CAPITAL language. Venture capitalists entering at that point have a lower risk of loss than at previous stages and can look forward to early capital appreciation as a result of the MARKET VALUE gained by an INITIAL PUBLIC OFFERING.

MICROECONOMICS study of the behavior of basic economic units such as companies, industries, or households. Research on the companies in the airline industry would be a microeconomic concern, for instance. *See also* MACROECONOMICS.

MILAN STOCK EXCHANGE largest of regional stock exchanges in Italy, accounting for more than 90% of trading volume. The MIB indices, based on the prices of all listed shares, and the COMIT Index, calculated by the Banca Commerciale Italiana, are the most widely used. Extensive reforms and reorganization in Italy created the Consiglio di Borsa, the Italian Stock Exchange Council, which instituted computerized trading and a block market. The regional exchanges are located in Rome, Turin, Genoa, Bologna, Florence, Naples, Palermo, Trieste, and Venice. Electronic trading is conducted Monday through Friday from 8:45 A.M. to 10 A.M. (order entry, automatic fixing of opening price), and from 10 A.M. to 4 P.M. (continuous trading with automatic matching of buy and sell orders). An open outcry system is used in the second market, from 9 A.M. to 10 A.M. Milan's second market, Mercato Ristretto, is the largest in the country. Trades are settled on a monthly basis, between 15 and 45 days after the trade date.

MILL one-tenth of a cent, the unit most often used in expressing property tax rates. For example, if a town's tax rate is 5 mills per dollar of assessed valuation, and the assessed valuation of a piece of property is $100,000, the tax is $500, or 0.005 times $100,000.

MINI-MANIPULATION trading in a security underlying an option contract so as to manipulate the stock's price, thus causing an increase in the value of the options. In this way the manipulator's profit can be multiplied many times, since a large position in options can be purchased with a relatively small amount of money.

MINIMUM FLUCTUATION smallest possible price movement of a security or options or futures contract. For example, most stocks on the Toronto Stock Exchange trade with a minimum fluctuation of one-eighth of a point. Minimum fluctuations are set by the securities, futures, or options exchanges regulating each security or contract. Also called MINIMUM TICK.

MINIMUM OPERATING CASH estimated by dividing a firm's annual cash outlay by its cash turnover. The resulting value represents the minimum amount of cash or liquidity the firm is estimated to need during the year, assuming that there is a small degree of seasonal fluctuation in the expected income of the business.

MINIMUM PAYMENT minimum amount that a consumer is required to pay on a revolving charge account in order to keep the account in good standing. If the minimum payment is not made, late payment penalties are due. If the minimum is still not paid within a few months, credit privileges may be revoked. If a consumer pays just the minimum due, interest charges continue to accrue on all outstanding balances. In some cases, a credit card issuer will waive the minimum payment for a month or two, as long as the cardholder has demonstrated a good payment history. If the cardholder does not make any minimum payment in such a case, interest charges accrue on the entire outstanding balance.

MINIMUM TICK *see* MINIMUM FLUCTUATION.

MINORITY INTEREST interest of shareholders who, in the aggregate, own less than half the shares in a corporation. On the consolidated balance sheets of companies whose subsidiaries are not wholly owned, the minority interest is shown as a separate equity account or as a liability of indefinite term. On the income statement, the minority's share of income is subtracted to arrive at consolidated net income.

MINUS symbol (−) preceding a fraction or number in the change column at the far right of newspaper stock tables designating a closing sale lower than that of the previous day.

MINUS TICK *see* DOWNTICK.

MISERY INDEX index that combines the unemployment and inflation rates. The index was devised in the United States in the 1970s when both inflation and unemployment rose sharply. The misery index is often credited with political significance, since it may be difficult for a president to be re-elected if there is a high misery index. The misery index is also linked to consumer confidence—the lower the index, in general, the more confident consumers tend to be.

MISSING THE MARKET failing to execute a transaction on terms favourable to a customer and thus being negligent as a broker. If the order is subsequently executed at a price demonstrably less favourable, the broker, as the customer's agent, may have to make up the loss.

MIXED ACCOUNT brokerage account in which some securities are owned (in long positions) and some borrowed (in short positions).

MOCK TRADING simulated trading of stocks, bonds, commodities and mutual funds. Real money is not used. Students learning about investing in schools or brokerage training classes may go through exercises in mock trading, in which securities prices are tracked on a daily basis and fictional trades are made. With commodity futures and options, this may take the form of going through a simulated trading session on the trading floor or using computer programs to illustrate the futures and options strategies.

MODELING designing and manipulating a mathematical representation of an economic system or corporate financial application so that the effect of changes can be studied and forecast. For example, in ECONOMETRICS, a complex economic model can be drawn up, entered into a computer, and used to predict the effect of a rise in inflation or a cut in taxes on economic output.

MODERN PORTFOLIO THEORY *see* PORTFOLIO THEORY.

MODIFIED OR GRADED PREMIUM LIFE INSURANCE type of insurance for which lower premiums are paid in the earlier years than in the later years of the policy. Such insurance makes policyowning more accessible to those who are just starting their careers.

MOMENTUM rate of acceleration of an economic, price, or volume movement. An economy with strong growth that is likely to continue is said to have a lot of momentum. In the stock market, technical analysts study stock momentum by charting price and volume trends. *See also* EARNINGS MOMENTUM.

MONEP (Marche des Options Negociables de Paris) subsidiary of the PARIS BOURSE, continuously trading stock and index options. The CAC 40 INDEX was developed as an underlying index for derivative products traded on the MONEP and MATIF. Trading hours are 10 A.M. to 5 P.M., Monday through Friday, either electronically or by open outcry. The MONEP trades CAC 40 INDEX short-term (American style) and long-term (European style) options, and equity options.

MONETARIST economist who believes that the MONEY SUPPLY is the key to the ups and downs in the economy. Monetarists such as Milton Friedman think that the money supply has far more impact on the economy's future course than, say, the level of federal spending—a factor on which KEYNESIAN ECONOMICS puts great stress. Monetarists advocate slow but steady growth in the money supply.

MONETARY INDICATORS economic gauges of the effects of MONE-TARY POLICY, such as various measures of credit market conditions, Treasury BILL rates, and the Toronto Stock Exchange 300 Average (of common stocks).

MONETARY POLICY The Bank of Canada can loosen or tighten the money supply by affecting interest rates through its weekly auction, depending on whether it wishes to expand or contract the economy. Other instruments of monetary policy range from selective credit controls to simple but often highly effective MORAL SUASION. Monetary policy differs from FISCAL POLICY, which is carried out through government spending and taxation. Both seek to control the level of economic activity as measured by such factors as industrial production, employment, and prices.

MONETIZE THE DEBT to finance the national debt by printing new money, causing inflation.

MONEY legal tender as defined by a government and consisting of currency and coin. In a more general sense, money is synonymous with CASH, which includes negotiable instruments, such as checks, based on bank balances.

MONEY MANAGEMENT financial planner's responsibility for the general management of monetary matters, including banking, credit management, budgeting, taxation, and borrowing. Term is also a synonym for PORTFOLIO MANAGEMENT.

MONEY MANAGER *see* PORTFOLIO MANAGER.

MONEY MARKET market for SHORT-TERM DEBT INSTRUMENTS—negotiable certificates of deposit, Eurodollar certificates of deposit, commercial paper, banker's acceptances, Treasury bills. What these instruments have in common are safety and LIQUIDITY. The money market operates through dealers. New York City is the leading money market, followed by London and Tokyo. The dealers in the important money markets are in constant communication with each other and with major borrowers and investors to take advantage of ARBITRAGE opportunities, a practice which helps keep prices uniform worldwide. *See also* MONEY MARKET FUND.

MONEY MARKET FUND open-ended MUTUAL FUND that invests in commercial paper, banker's acceptances, repurchase agreements, Government of Canada Treasury bills, certificates of deposit, and other highly liquid and safe securities, and pays money market rates of interest with a minimum purchase as low as $100. Launched in the 1980s, these funds were especially popular in the early 1990s when interest rates soared. Management's fee is less than 1% of an investor's assets, and the unit price is often fixed at $10.

MONEY ORDER financial instrument that can be easily converted into cash by the payee named on the money order. The money order lists both the payee and the person who bought the instrument, known as the payor. Money orders are issued by financial institutions, post offices, and traveler's cheque issuers to people presenting cash or other forms of acceptable payment. Money orders often are used by people who do not have chequing accounts. They can be used to pay bills or any outstanding debts.

MONEY PURCHASE PLAN program for buying a pension annuity that provides for specified, regular payments, usually based on salary.

MONEY SPREAD *see* VERTICAL SPREAD.

MONEY SUPPLY total stock of money in the economy, consisting primarily of (1) currency in circulation and (2) deposits in savings and chequing accounts. Too much money in relation to the output of goods tends to push interest rates down and push prices and inflation up; too little money tends to push interest rates up, lower prices and output, and cause unemployment and idle plant capacity. *See also* M1; M2; M3.

MONOPOLY control of the production and distribution of a product or service by one firm or a group of firms acting in concert. In its pure form, monopoly, which is characterized by an absence of competition, leads to high prices and a general lack of responsiveness to the needs and desires of consumers. Monopolies persist in some degree as the result of such factors as patents, scarce essential materials, and high startup and production costs that discourage competition in certain industries. *Public monopolies*—those operated by the government, such as the post office or utilities—ensure the delivery of essential products and services at acceptable prices and generally avoid the disadvantages produced by private monopolies. MONOPSONY, the dominance of a market by one buyer or group of buyers acting together, is less prevalent than monopoly. *See also* CARTEL; OLIGOPOLY; PERFECT COMPETITION.

MONOPSONY situation in which one buyer dominates, forcing sellers to agree to the buyer's terms. For example, a tobacco grower may have no choice but to sell his tobacco to one cigarette company that is the only buyer for his product. The cigarette company therefore virtually controls the price at which it buys tobacco. The opposite of a monopsony is a MONOPOLY.

MONTHLY COMPOUNDING OF INTEREST *see* COMPOUND INTEREST.

MONTHLY INVESTMENT PLAN plan whereby an investor puts a fixed dollar amount into a particular investment every month, thus building a position at advantageous prices by means of *dollar cost averaging (see* CONSTANT DOLLAR PLAN).

MONTREAL EXCHANGE/BOURSE DE MONTREAL (ME)

Canada's oldest stock exchange and second-largest in dollar value of trading. The first record of trading securities in Montreal was in 1817. No formal stock exchange existed although a "board of brokers" operated with certain rules and membership criteria from 1863 until 1874, when the Montreal Stock Exchange (MSE) was incorporated under Québec charter. The Montreal Curb Market was organized in 1926 to provide trading facilities for securities not listed on the MSE. In 1953, the Montreal Curb Market formally incorporated as the Canadian Stock Exchange, and the Montreal and Canadian Stock Exchanges shared the same permanent executive staff and trading facilities. In 1974, the two exchanges merged into the MSE, and in 1982, the name was changed to ME. Stocks, bonds, futures and options are traded through a specialist system combined with automated systems, including the Electronic Order Book and electronic order routing, execution and trading system—the MORRE System. A system-to-system link between the Montreal Exchange (ME) and the Boston Stock Exchange (BSE) enables ME member firms to electronically route retail orders for U.S. securities directly to the BSE for automatic execution and confirmation at the best prevailing price in the Intermarket Trading System. The Canadian Market Portfolio Index (XXM) tracks the market performance of 25 highly capitalized Canadian corporations, while six sector indices track banking, forest products, industrial products, mining and minerals, oil and gas, and utilities. In the derivatives market, the exchange trades 10-year Government of Canada bond futures and options on the futures; 3-month Canadian bankers' acceptance (BAX) futures and options on the futures; 1-month Canadian bankers' acceptance futures (BAR); stock options; Canadian bond options; and LEAPS. Since 1965, the ME has been located at the Stock Exchange Tower, P.O. Box 61, 800 Victoria Square, Montreal, Québec H4Z 1A9. Trading hours are 9:30 A.M. to 4 P.M., Monday through Friday. Government bond futures are traded from 8:20 A.M. to 3 P.M. Settlement for securities is the third business day following the trade date; for futures and options, it is the day after a transaction by direct payment to the clearing corporation.

MOODY'S INVESTORS SERVICE

headquartered with its parent company, Dun & Bradstreet, in downtown Manhattan, Moody's is one of the two best known bond rating agencies in the United States, the other being Standard & Poor's. Moody's also rates commercial paper, preferred and common stocks, and municipal short-term issues. The six bound manuals it publishes annually, supplemented weekly or semiweekly, provide great detail on issuers and securities. The company also publishes the quarterly *Moody's Handbook of Common Stocks,* which charts more than 500 companies, showing industry group trends and company stock price performance. Also included are essential statistics for the past decade, an analysis of the company's financial background, recent financial developments, and the outlook.

Moody's rates most of the publicly held corporate and municipal bonds and many Treasury and government agency issues, but does not usually rate privately placed bonds.

MORAL SUASION persuasion through influence rather than coercion.

MORGAN STANLEY CAPITAL INTERNATIONAL INDICES indices maintained and calculated by Morgan Stanley's Capital International group (MSCI) which track more than 45 equity markets throughout the world. The MSCI indices are market capitalization weighted and cover both developed and emerging markets. In addition to the country indices, MSCI also calculates aggregate indices for the world, Europe, North America, Asia, and Latin America. Most international mutual funds and other international institutional investors measure their performance against MSCI indices.

MORNINGSTAR RATING SYSTEM system for rating open- and closed-end mutual funds and annuities by Morningstar Inc. of Chicago. The system rates funds from one to five stars, using a risk-adjusted performance rating in which performance equals total return of the fund. The system rates funds assessing down-side risk, which is linked to the three-month U.S. Treasury bill. If a fund underperforms the Treasury bill, it will lower the fund's rating. The score is plotted on a bell curve, and is applied to four distinct categories: all equities, fixed income, hybrids, municipals. The top 10% receive five stars; the top 22.5%, four stars; the top 35%, three stars; the bottom 22.5%, two stars; and the bottom 10%, one star. Morningstar is a subscription-based company, offering its ratings in binders, software, and CD-ROM form. It sells its data to America Online and Realities Telescan Analyzer and other databases, as well as metropolitan newspapers. Morningstar also sells information on U.S. equities and American Depository Receipts (ADRs), but star ratings are not calculated for them.

MORTALITY amount charged in an insurance policy for the risk of an individual dying.

MORTGAGE debt instrument by which the borrower (mortgagor) gives the lender (mortgagee) a lien on property as security for the repayment of a loan. The borrower has use of the property, and the lien is removed when the obligation is fully paid. A mortgage normally involves real estate. For personal property, such as machines, equipment, or tools, the lien is called a *chattel mortgage. See also* ADLUSTABLE RATE MORTGAGE; CLOSED-END MORTGAGE; CONSOLIDATED MORTGAGE BOND; MORTGAGE BOND; OPEN-END MORTGAGE; VARIABLE RATE MORTGAGE.

MORTGAGE-BACKED SECURITIES similar to bonds, the current $5000 units with 5-year terms are backed by a share in a pool of home mortgages insured under the National Housing Act. Units pay interest and a part of principal each month and, if homeowners prepay their mortgages, may pay out additional amounts of principal before normal maturity. Mortgage-backed securities trade in the bond market at prices reflecting current interest rates. *See* MORTGAGE-BACKED CERTIFICATE.

MORTGAGE BROKER one who places mortgage loans with lenders for a fee, but does not originate or service loans.

MORTGAGE FUND pool of residential first mortgages, some of which are insured by the federal government through Canada Mortgage and Housing Corporation. Interest payments flow through the fund to the unitholders regularly, normally once a month, while principal payments are reinvested in other mortgages. The minimum investment is $100.

As with bond funds, mortgage funds go down in price when interest rates go up.

MORTGAGE LIFE INSURANCE policy that pays off the balance of a mortgage on the death of the insured.

MORTGAGE SERVICING administration of a mortgage loan, including collecting monthly payments and penalties on late payments, keeping track of the amount of principal and interest that has been paid at any particular time, acting as escrow agent for funds to cover taxes and insurance, and, if necessary, curing defaults and foreclosing when a homeowner is seriously delinquent. For mortgage loans that are sold in the secondary market and packaged into a MORTGAGE-BACKED CERTIFICATE the local bank or savings and loan that originated the mortgage typically continues servicing the mortgages for a fee.

MOST ACTIVE LIST stocks with the most shares traded on a given day. Unusual VOLUME can be caused by TAKEOVER activity, earnings releases, institutional trading in a widely-held issue, and other factors.

MOVING AVERAGE average of security or commodity prices constructed on a period as short as a few days or as long as several years and showing trends for the latest interval. For example, a thirty-day moving average includes yesterday's figures; tomorrow the same average will include today's figures and will no longer show those for the earliest date included in yesterday's average. Thus every day it picks up figures for the latest day and drops those for the earliest day. *See* chart on next page.

MULTINATIONAL CORPORATION corporation that has production facilities or other fixed assets in at least one foreign country and makes its major management decisions in a global context. In marketing, production, research and development, and labor relations, its decisions must be made in terms of host-country customs and traditions. In finance, many of its problems have no domestic counterpart—the payment of dividends in another currency, for example, or the need to shelter working capital from the risk of devaluation, or the choices between owning and licensing. Economic and legal questions must be dealt with in drastically different ways. In addition to foreign exchange risks and the special business risks of operating in unfamiliar environments, there is the spectre of political risk—the risk that sovereign governments may interfere with operations or terminate them altogether.

MOVING AVERAGE

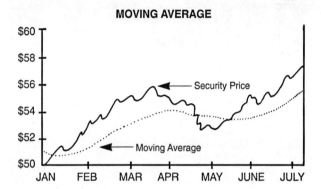

MULTIPLE *see* PRICE-EARNINGS RATIO.

MULTIPLE LISTING listing agreement used by a broker who is a member of a multiple-listing organization that is an exclusive right to sell with an additional authority and obligation on the part of the listing broker to distribute the listing to other brokers in the organization. These listings then are distributed in a multiple-listing service publication. Generally, the listing broker and the selling broker will split the commission, but terms for division can vary. A multiple-listing agreement benefits the seller by exposing property to a wider group of potential buyers than would be available from one exclusive broker, which should allow the sale to be completed more quickly, and for a higher price.

MULTIPLIER the multiplier has two major applications in finance and investments.
  1. *investment multiplier* or *Keynesian multiplier:* multiplies the effects of investment spending in terms of total income. An investment in a small plant facility, for example, increases the incomes of the workers who built it, the merchants who provide supplies, the distributors who supply the merchants, the manufacturers who supply the distributors, and so on. Each recipient spends a portion of the income and saves the rest. By making an assumption as to the percentage each recipient saves, it is possible to calculate the total income produced by the investment.

2. *deposit multiplier* or *credit multiplier:* magnifies small changes in bank deposits into changes in the amount of outstanding credit and the money supply. For example, a bank receives a deposit of $100,000, and the RESERVE REQUIREMENT is 20%. The bank is thus required to keep $20,000 in the form of reserves. The remaining $80,000 becomes a loan, which is deposited in the borrower's bank. When the borrower's bank sets aside the $16,000 required reserve out of the $80,000, $64,000 is available for another loan and another deposit, and so on. Carried out to its theoretical limit, the original deposit of $100,000 could expand into a total of $500,000 in deposits and $400,000 in credit.

MUTILATED SECURITY certificate that cannot be read for the name of the issue or the issuer, or for the detail necessary for identification and transfer, or for the exercise of the holder's rights. It is then the seller's obligation to take corrective action, which usually means having the transfer agent guarantee the rights of ownership to the buyer.

MUTUAL COMPANY corporation whose ownership and profits are distributed among members in proportion to the amount of business they do with the company. The most familiar examples are mutual insurance companies, whose members are policy holders entitled to name the directors or trustees and to receive dividends or rebates on future premiums.

MUTUAL FUND fund operated by an INVESTMENT COMPANY that raises money from shareholders and invests it in stocks, bonds, options, futures, currencies, or money market securities. These funds offer investors the advantages of diversification and professional management. A management fee is charged for these services, typically between 0.5% and 3% of assets per year. Funds that are sold through brokers or planners are called LOAD FUNDS, and those sold to investors directly from the fund companies are called NO-LOAD FUNDS. Mutual fund shares are redeemable on demand at NET ASSET VALUE by shareholders. All shareholders share equally in the gains and losses generated by the fund.

    Mutual funds come in many varieties. Some invest aggressively for capital appreciation, while others are conservative and are designed to generate income for shareholders. Investors need to assess their tolerance for risk before they decide which fund would be appropriate for them. In addition, the timing of buying or selling depends on the outlook for the economy, the state of the stock and bond markets, interest rates, and other factors.

MUTUAL FUND CASH-TO-ASSETS RATIO amount of mutual fund assets held in cash instruments. A fund manager may choose to keep a large cash position if he or she is bearish on the stock or bond market, or if he or she cannot find securities he or she thinks are attractive to buy. A large cash position (10% or more of the fund's assets in liquid instruments) may also accumulate if many investors buy fund shares and the fund manager cannot put all the money to work at once. On the other hand, a low cash-to-assets ratio is an indication that the fund manager is bullish, because he or she is fully invested and expects stock or bond prices to rise. Some analysts consider this ratio to be an important indicator of bullish or bearish sentiment among sophisticated investment managers. If many fund managers are increasing their cash positions, the fund managers are becoming more bearish—though some analysts consider it bullish for the market because the managers will have more cash to buy securities.

N

NAKED OPTION OPTION for which the buyer or seller has no underlying security position. A writer of a naked CALL OPTION, therefore, does not own a LONG POSITION in the stock on which the call has been written. Similarly, the writer of a naked PUT OPTION does not have a SHORT POSITION in the stock on which the put has been written. Naked options are very risky—although potentially very rewarding. If the underlying stock or stock index moves in the direction sought by the investor, profits can be enormous, because the investor would only have had to put down a small amount of money to reap a large return. On the other hand, if the stock moved in the opposite direction, the writer of the naked option could be subject to huge losses.

For instance, if someone wrote a naked call option at $60 a share on XYZ stock without owning the shares, and if the stock rose to $70 a share, the writer of the option would have to deliver XYZ shares to the call buyer at $60 a share. In order to acquire those shares, he or she would have to go into the market and buy them for $70 a share, sustaining a $10-a-share loss on his or her position. If, on the other hand, the option writer already owned XYZ shares when writing the option, he or she could just turn those shares over to the option buyer. This latter strategy is known as writing a COVERED CALL.

NAKED POSITION securities position that is not hedged from market risk—for example, the position of someone who writes a CALL or PUT option without having the corresponding LONG POSITION or SHORT POSITION on the underlying security. The potential risk or reward of naked positions is greater than that of covered positions. *See* COVERED CALL; HEDGE; NAKED OPTION.

NAKED WARRANT warrant owned by the investor rather than the stock to which the warrant pertains.

NAKED WRITER *see* UNCOVERED WRITER.

NAMED PERILS INSURANCE property insurance that covers risks specified in the policy. Contrasts with *all-risks insurance,* which specifies exclusions.

NARROWING THE SPREAD closing the SPREAD between the bid and asked prices of a security as a result of bidding and offering by market makers and specialists in a security. For example, a stock's bid price—the most anyone is willing to pay—may be $10 a share, and the asked price—the lowest price at which anyone will sell—may be $10¼. If a broker or market maker offers to buy shares at $10¼, while the asked price remains at $10¾, the spread has effectively been narrowed.

NARROW MARKET securities or commodities market characterized by light trading and greater fluctuations in prices relative to volume than would be the case if trading were active. The market in a particular stock is said to be narrow if the price falls more than a point between ROUND LOT trades without any apparent explanation, suggesting lack of interest and too few orders. The terms THIN MARKET and *inactive market* are used as synonyms for narrow market.

NASDAQ National Association of Securities Dealers Automated Quotations system, which is owned and operated by the NATIONAL ASSOCIATION OF SECURITIES DEALERS in the United States. NASDAQ is a computerized system that provides brokers and dealers with price quotations for securities traded OVER THE COUNTER as well as for many New York Stock Exchange listed securities. NASDAQ quotes are published in the financial pages of most newspapers. *See also* NATIONAL MARKET SYSTEM.

NASDAQ SMALL CAPITALIZATION COMPANIES separately listed group of some 2000 companies that have smaller capitalizations and are less actively traded than NASDAQ NATIONAL MARKET SYSTEM stocks, but that meet NASDAQ price and market value listing criteria and have at least two MARKET MAKERS.

NATIONAL ASSOCIATION OF SECURITIES DEALERS (NASD) in the United States, nonprofit organization formed under the joint sponsorship of the Investment Bankers' Conference and the Securities and Exchange Commission to comply with the MALONEY ACT. NASD members include virtually all investment banking houses and firms dealing in the OVER THE COUNTER market. Operating under the supervision of the SEC, the NASD's basic purposes are to (1) standardize practices in the field, (2) establish high moral and ethical standards in securities trading, (3) provide a representative body to consult with the government and investors on matters of common interest, (4) establish and enforce fair and equitable rules of securities trading, and (5) establish a disciplinary body capable of enforcing the above provisions. The NASD also requires members to maintain quick assets in excess of current liabilities at all times. Periodic examinations and audits are conducted to ensure a high level of solvency and financial integrity among members. A special Investment Companies Department is concerned with the problems of investment companies and has the responsibility of reviewing companies' sales literature in that segment of the securities industry. *See also* NASDAQ.

NATIONAL BANK commercial bank in the United States whose charter is approved by the U.S. Comptroller of the Currency rather than by a state banking department. National banks are required to be members of the FEDERAL RESERVE SYSTEM and to purchase stock in the FEDERAL RESERVE BANK in their district *(see* MEMBER BANK*)*. They must also belong to the FEDERAL DEPOSIT INSURANCE CORPORATION.

NATIONAL CONTINGENCY FUND established in 1969, it became the Canadian Investor Protection Fund in 1990. *See* CANADIAN INVESTOR PROTECTION FUND.

NATIONAL DEBT debt owed by the federal government. The national debt consists of all the debt and obligations of the Government of Canada including Goverment of Canada bonds, Treasury bills, and Canada savings bonds. There is no ceiling on the amount that the government can borrow, nor is there a balanced budget requirement. The national debt has increased from $200 billion in 1984 to $560 billion today.

NATIONALIZATION takeover of a private company's assets or operations by a government. The company may or may not be compensated for the loss of assets. In developing nations, an operation is typically nationalized if the government feels the company is exploiting the host country and exporting too high a proportion of the profits. By nationalizing the firm, the government hopes to keep profits at home. In developed countries, industries are often nationalized when they need government subsidies to survive. For instance, the French government nationalized steel and chemical companies in the mid-1980s in order to preserve jobs that would have disappeared if free market forces had prevailed. In some developed countries, however, nationalization is carried out as a form of national policy, often by Socialist governments, and is not designed to rescue ailing industries.

NATIONAL MARKET SYSTEM
1. in the United States, system of trading OVER THE COUNTER stocks under the sponsorship of the NATIONAL ASSOCIATION OF SECURITIES DEALERS (NASD) and NASDAQ. Stocks trading in the National Market System must meet certain criteria for size, profitability, and trading activity. More comprehensive information is available for National Market System stocks than for other stocks traded over the counter. For most over-the-counter stocks, newspapers list the stock name, dividend, trading volume, bid and ask prices, and the change in those prices during a trading day. For National Market System stocks, the listing includes the stock name, dividend, high and low price for the past 52 weeks, trading volume, high and low price during the trading day, closing price on that day, and price change for that day.
2. in the United States, national system of trading whereby the prices for stocks and bonds are listed simultaneously on the New York Stock Exchange and all regional exchanges. Buyers and sellers therefore are able to get the best prices by executing their trades on the exchange with the most favourable price at the time. This system is not to be confused with the national exchange market system (NEMS) being studied by the Securities and Exchange Commission and other planning groups. *See also* NATIONAL MARKET ADVISORY BOARD.

NATIONAL SECURITIES CLEARING CORPORATION (NSCC) in the United States, a securities clearing organization formed in 1977 by merging subsidiaries of the New York and American Stock Exchanges with the National Clearing Corporation. It functions essentially as a medium through which brokerage firms, exchanges, and other clearing corporations reconcile accounts with each other. *See also* CONTINUOUS NET SETTLEMENT.

NEARBYS months of futures or options contracts that are nearest to delivery (for futures) or expiration (for options). For example, in January, futures and options contracts settling in February and March would be considered nearbys. In general, nearby contracts are far more actively traded than contracts for more distant months. *See also* FURTHEST MONTH, NEAREST MONTH.

NEAREST MONTH in commodity futures or OPTION trading, the expiration dates, expressed as months, closest to the present. For a commodity or an option that had delivery or expiration dates available in September, December, March, and June, for instance, the nearest month would be September if a trade were being made in August. Nearest month contracts are always more heavily traded than FURTHEST MONTH contracts.

NEAR MONEY CASH EQUIVALENTS and other assets that are easily convertible into cash. Some examples are government securities, bank TIME DEPOSITS, and MONEY MARKET FUND shares. Bonds close to REDEMPTION date are also called near money.

NEGATIVE CARRY situation in which the cost of money borrowed to finance securities or financial futures positions is higher than the return on those positions. For example, if an investor borrowed at 10% to finance, or "carry," a bond yielding 8%, the bond position would have a negative carry. Negative carry does not necessarily mean a loss to the investor, however, and a positive yield can result on an aftertax basis. In this case, the yield from the 8% bond may be tax-exempt, whereas interest on the 10% loan is tax-deductible. In commodities, this would occur in any month in a BACKWARDATION where the price is higher than the spot month. With the negative carry, if the investor holds the physical position in copper, for example, it will continue to lose value.

NEGATIVE CASH FLOW situation in which a business spends more cash than it receives through earnings or other transactions in an accounting period. *See also* CASH FLOW.

NEGATIVE PLEDGE CLAUSE negative covenant or promise in an INDENTURE agreement that states the corporation will not pledge any of its assets if doing so would result in less security to the debtholders covered under the indenture agreement. Also called *covenant of equal coverage.*

NEGATIVE PLEDGE COVENANT like a negative pledge clause, an undertaking not to do certain things. It is frequently argued that negative pledge covenants are preferable to positive covenants because it is easier to establish if something that was not to have been done has in fact been done. For example in a debenture, a negative pledge covenant usually constitutes a default, which in turn gives rise to certain specific remedies that can be taken by the debenture or other security holder.

NEGATIVE WORKING CAPITAL situation in which the current liabilities of a firm exceed its current assets. For example, if the total of cash, MARKETABLE SECURITIES, ACCOUNTS RECEIVABLE and notes receivable, inventory, and other current assets is less than the total of ACCOUNTS PAYABLE, short-term notes payable, long-term debt due in one year, and other current liabilities, the firm has a negative working capital. Unless the condition is corrected, the firm will not be able to pay debts when due, threatening its ability to keep operating and possibly resulting in bankruptcy.

To remedy a negative working capital position, a firm has these alternatives: (1) it can convert a long-term asset into a current asset—for example, by selling a piece of equipment or a building, by liquidating a long-term investment, or by renegotiating a long-term loan receivable; (2) it can convert short-term liabilities into long-term liabilities—for example, by negotiating the substitution of a current account payable with a long-term note payable; (3) it can borrow long term; (4) it can obtain additional equity through a stock issue or other sources of paid-in capital; (5) it can retain or "plough back" profits. *See also* WORKING CAPITAL.

NEGATIVE YIELD CURVE situation in which yields on short-term securities are higher than those on long-term securities of the same quality. Normally, short-term rates are lower than long-term rates because those who commit their money for longer periods are taking more risk. But if interest rates climb high enough, borrowers become unwilling to lock themselves into high rates for long periods and borrow short-term instead. Therefore, yields rise on short-term funds and fall or remain stable on long-term funds. Also called an INVERTED YIELD CURVE. *See also* YIELD CURVE.

NEGOTIABLE
In general:
1. something that can be sold or transferred to another party in exchange for money or as settlement of an obligation.
2. matter of mutual concern to one or more parties that involves conditions to be worked out to the satisfaction of the parties. As examples: In a lender-borrower arrangement, the interest rate may be negotiable; in securities sales, brokerage commissions are now negotiable, having historically been fixed; and in divorce cases involving children, the terms of visiting rights are usually negotiable.

Investments: type of security the title to which is transferable by delivery. A stock certificate with the stock power properly signed is negotiable, for example.

NEGOTIABLE INSTRUMENT unconditional order or promise to pay an amount of money, easily transferable from one person to another. Examples: cheque, promissory note, draft (bill of exchange). The

Uniform Commercial Code requires that for an instrument to be negotiable it must be signed by the maker or drawer, must contain an unconditional promise or order to pay a specific amount of money, must be payable on demand or at a specified future time, and must be payable to order or to the bearer.

NEGOTIATED COMMISSION brokerage COMMISSION that is determined through negotiation.

NEGOTIATED UNDERWRITING underwriting of new securities issue in which the SPREAD between the purchase price paid to the issuer and the public offering price is determined through negotiation rather than multiple competitive bidding. The spread, which represents the compensation to the investment bankers participating in the underwriting (collectively called the *syndicate),* is negotiated between the issuing company and the MANAGING UNDERWRITER, with the consent of the group. Most corporate stock and bond issues and municipal revenue bond issues are priced through negotiation, whereas municipal general obligation bonds and new issues of public utilities are generally priced through competitive bidding. Competitive bidding is mandatory for new issues of public utilities holding companies. *See also* COMPETITIVE BID.

NEO abbreviation for *nonequity options.* This refers to options contracts on foreign currencies, bonds and other debt issues, commodities, metals, and stock indexes. In contrast, equity options have individual stocks as underlying values.

NEST EGG assets put aside for a person's retirement. Such assets are usually invested conservatively to provide the retiree with a secure standard of living for the rest of his or her life. Investment in an INDIVIDUAL RETIREMENT ACCOUNT would be considered part of a nest egg.

NET

In general: figure remaining after all relevant deductions have been made from the gross amount. For example: net sales are equal to gross sales minus discounts, returns, and allowances; net profit is gross profit less operating (sales, general, and administrative) expenses; net worth is assets (worth) less liabilities.

Investments: dollar difference between the proceeds from the sale of a security and the seller's adjusted cost of acquisition—that is, the gain or loss.

As a verb:

1. to arrive at the difference between additions and subtractions or plus amounts and minus amounts. For example, in filing tax returns, capital losses are netted against capital gains.

2. to realize a net profit, as in "last year we netted a million dollars after taxes."

NET AFTERTAX GAIN capital gain after income taxes.

NET ASSETS difference between a company's total assets and liabilities; another way of saying *owner's equity* or NET WORTH. *See* ASSET COVERAGE for a discussion of net asset value per unit of bonds, preferred stock, or common stock.

NET ASSET VALUE (NAV)
1. in mutual funds, the market value of a fund share, synonymous with *bid price.* In the case of no-load funds, the NAV, market price, and offering price are all the same figure, which the public pays to buy shares; load fund market or offer prices are quoted after adding the sales charge to the net asset value. NAV is calculated by most funds after the close of the exchanges each day by taking the closing market value of all securities owned plus all other assets such as cash, subtracting all liabilities, then dividing the result (total net assets) by the total number of shares outstanding. The number of shares outstanding can vary each day depending on the number of purchases and redemptions.
2. book value of a company's different classes of securities, usually stated as net asset value per bond, net asset value per share of preferred stock, and net book value per common share of common stock. The formula for computing net asset value is total assets less any INTANGIBLE ASSET less all liabilities and securities having a prior claim, divided by the number of units outstanding (i.e., bonds, preferred shares, or common shares). *See* BOOK VALUE for a discussion of how these values are calculated and what they mean.

NET CHANGE difference between the last trading price on a stock, bond, commodity, or mutual fund from one day to the next. The net change in individual stock prices is listed in newspaper financial pages. In the case of a stock that is entitled to a dividend one day, but not the next, the dividend is not considered in computing the change. Similarly, with stock splits, a stock selling at $100 the day before a two-for-one split and trading the next day at $50 would be considered unchanged. The designation +2½, for example, means that a stock's final price on that day was $2.50 higher than the final price on the previous trading day. The net change in prices of OVER THE COUNTER stocks is usually the difference between bid prices from one day to the next.

NET CURRENT ASSETS difference between current assets and current liabilities; another name for WORKING CAPITAL. Some security analysts divide this figure (after subtracting preferred stock, if any) by the number of common shares outstanding to arrive at working capital per share. Believing working capital per share to be a conservative measure of LIQUIDATING VALUE (on the theory that fixed and other noncurrent assets would more than compensate for any shrinkage in current assets if assets were to be sold), they compare it with the MARKET VALUE of the company's shares. If the net current assets per share figure, or "minimum liquidating value," is higher than the market price, these analysts view the common shares as a bargain (assuming, of course, that the company is not losing money and that its assets are conservatively valued). Other analysts believe this theory ignores the efficiency of capital markets generally and, specifically, obligations such as pension plans, which are not reported as balance sheet liabilities under present accounting rules.

NET EARNINGS *see* NET INCOME.

NET ESTATE *see* GROSS ESTATE.

NET INCOME
In general: sum remaining after all expenses have been met or deducted; synonymous with *net earnings* and with *net profit* or *net loss* (depending on whether the figure is positive or negative).
For a business: difference between total sales and total costs and expenses. Total costs comprise cost of goods sold including depreciation; total expenses comprise selling, general, and administrative expenses, plus INCOME DEDUCTIONS. Net income is usually specified as to whether it is before income taxes or after income taxes. Net income after taxes is the *bottom line* referred to in popular vernacular. It is out of this figure that dividends are normally paid. See *also* OPERATING PROFIT (OR LOSS).
For an individual: regular monthly gross income less source deductions such as taxes, CPP, UI, pension deductions, union dues, charitable donations, etc.; and less expenses incurred to produce gross income. Those expenses are mostly deductible for tax purposes.

NET INCOME PER SHARE OF COMMON STOCK amount of profit or earnings allocated to each share of common stock after all costs, taxes, allowances for depreciation, and possible losses have been deducted. Net income per share is stated in dollars and cents and is usually compared with the corresponding period a year earlier. For example, XYZ might report that second-quarter net income per share was $1.20, up from 90 cents in the previous year's second quarter. Also known as *earnings per common share* (EPS).

NET INCOME TO NET WORTH RATIO *see* RETURN ON EQUITY.

NET INVESTMENT INCOME PER SHARE income received by an investment company from dividends and interest on securities investments during an accounting period, less management fees and administrative expenses and divided by the number of outstanding shares. Short-term trading profits (net profits from securities held for less than six months) are considered dividend income. The dividend and interest income is received by the investment company, which in turn pays shareholders the net investment income in the form of dividends prorated according to each holder's share in the total PORTFOLIO.

NET LEASE financial lease stipulating that the user (rather than the owner) of the leased property shall pay all maintenance costs, taxes, insurance, and other expenses. Many real estate and oil and gas limited partnerships are structured as net leases with ESCALATOR CLAUSES, to provide limited partners with both depreciation tax benefits and appreciation of investment, minus cash expenses. *See also* GROSS LEASE.

NET PRESENT VALUE (NPV) method used in evaluating investments whereby the net present value of all cash outflows (such as the cost of the investment) and cash inflows (returns) is calculated using a given discount rate, usually a REQUIRED RATE OF RETURN. An investment is acceptable if the NPV is positive. In capital budgeting, the discount rate used is called the HURDLE RATE and is usually equal to the INCREMENTAL COST OF CAPITAL.

NET PROCEEDS amount (usually cash) received from the sale or disposition of property, from a loan, or from the sale or issuance of securities after deduction of all costs incurred in the transaction. In computing the gain or loss on a securities transaction for tax purposes, the amount of the sale is the amount of the net proceeds.

NET PROFIT *see* NET INCOME.

NET PROFIT MARGIN NET INCOME as a percentage of NET SALES. A measure of operating efficiency and pricing strategy, the ratio is usually computed using net profit before extraordinary items and taxes—that is, net sales less COST OF GOODS SOLD and SELLING, GENERAL, AND ADMINISTRATIVE (SG&A) EXPENSES.

NET QUICK ASSETS cash, MARKETABLE SECURITIES, and ACCOUNTS RECEIVABLE, minus current liabilities. *See also* QUICK RATIO.

NET REALIZED CAPITAL GAINS PER SHARE amount of CAPITAL GAINS that an investment company realized on the sale of securities, NET OF CAPITAL LOSSES and divided by the number of outstanding shares. Such net gains are distributed annually to shareholders in proportion to their shares in the total portfolio. Such distributions are eligible for favourable capital gains tax rates if the positions were held for at least a year. If held for less than a year, they would be subject to regular income taxes at the shareholder's tax bracket. *See also* REGULATED INVESTMENT COMPANY.

NET SALES gross sales less returns and allowances, freight out, and cash discounts allowed. Cash discounts allowed is seen less frequently than in past years, since it has become conventional to report as net sales the amount finally received from the customer. Returns are merchandise returned for credit; allowances are deductions allowed by the seller for merchandise not received or received in damaged condition; freight out is shipping expense passed on to the customer.

NET TANGIBLE ASSETS PER SHARE total assets of a company, less any INTANGIBLE ASSET such as goodwill, patents, and trademarks, less all liabilities and the par value of preferred stock, divided by the number of common shares outstanding. *See* BOOK VALUE for a discussion of what this calculation means and how it can be varied to apply to bonds or preferred stock shares. *See also* NET ASSET VALUE.

NET TRANSACTION securities transaction in which the buyer and seller do not pay fees or commissions. For instance, when an investor buys a new issue, no commission is due. If the stock is initially offered at $15 a share, the buyer's total cost is $15 per share.

NETWORK A *see* CONSOLIDATED TAPE.

NETWORK B *see* CONSOLIDATED TAPE.

NET WORKING CAPITAL CURRENT ASSETS minus CURRENT LIABILITIES. Usually simply called WORKING CAPITAL.

NET WORTH amount by which assets exceed liabilities. For a corporation, net worth is also known as *stockholders' equity* or NET ASSETS. For an individual, net worth is the total value of all possessions, such as a house, stocks, bonds, and other securities, minus all outstanding debts, such as mortgage and revolving-credit loans. In order to qualify for certain high-risk investments, brokerage houses require that an individual's net worth must be at or above a certain dollar level. *See also* BOOK VALUE.

NET YIELD RATE OF RETURN on a security net of out-of-pocket costs associated with its purchase, such as commissions or markups. *See also* MARKDOWN.

NEW ACCOUNT REPORT document filled out by a broker that details vital facts about a new client's financial circumstances and investment objectives. The report may be updated if there are material changes in a client's financial position. Based on the report, a client may or may not be deemed eligible for certain types of risky investments, such as commodity trading or highly leveraged LIMITED PARTNERSHIP deals. *See also* KNOW YOUR CUSTOMER.

NEW HIGH/NEW LOW stock prices that have hit the highest or lowest prices in the last year. Next to each stock's listing in a newspaper will be an indication of a new high with a letter "u" or a new low with the letter "d." Newspapers publish the total number of new highs and new lows each day on the Toronto, New York, and American Stock Exchanges and on the NASDAQ Stock Market. Technical analysts pay great attention to the trend of new highs and new lows. If the number of new highs is expanding, that is considered a bullish indicator. If the number of new lows is rising, that is considered bearish. Many analysts also track the ratio of new highs to new lows as a reflection of the general direction of the stock market.

NEW ISSUE stock or bond being offered to the public for the first time, the distribution of which is covered by a securities commission. New issues may be initial public offerings by previously private companies or additional stock or bond issues by companies already public and often listed on the exchanges. Proceeds may be used to retire outstanding securities of the company, to purchase fixed assets or for additional working capital. New debt issues are also offered by government bodies. *See also* HOT ISSUE; UNDERWRITE.

NEW LISTING security that has just begun to trade on a stock or bond exchange. A new listing on the Toronto Stock Exchange must meet all LISTING REQUIREMENTS, and may either be an INITIAL PUBLIC OFFERING or a company whose shares have previously traded on another exchange.

NEW MONEY amount of additional long-term financing provided by a new issue or issues in excess of the amount of a maturing issue or by issues that are being refunded.

NEW-MONEY POLICIES cash values, amount of insurance, and premiums that are guaranteed by the insuring company for a specified period of time only and using current interest rates.

NEW ORDERS FOR DURABLE GOODS signal of a recession or of growth. A drop in the growth of new orders and a buildup of inventory is a good indicator of a coming recession. Conversely, an increase in new orders and a reduction of inventories could be a sign of economic recovery.

NEW YORK COFFEE, SUGAR AND COCOA EXCHANGE *see* SECURITIES AND COMMODITIES EXCHANGES.

NEW YORK COTTON EXCHANGE (NYCE) oldest commodity exchange in New York, founded in 1870 by a group of cotton brokers and merchants. FINEX (Financial Exchange), the exchange's financial futures and options division, began operations in 1985. In December 1993, the NYCE acquired the NEW YORK FUTURES EXCHANGE (NYFE) from the New York Stock Exchange; it is a wholly owned subsidiary. The NYCE trades cotton futures and options (10:30 A.M.–2:40 P.M.). Through Citrus Associates of the New York Cotton Exchange Inc., it trades frozen concentrated orange juice futures and options (10:15 A.M.– 2:15 P.M.). In June 1994, FINEX Europe was opened in Dublin, creating a 24-hour market in most FINEX contracts. FINEX/FINEX Europe trades U.S. dollar index (USDX) futures and options, and U.S. dollar-based currency futures (7 P.M.–10 P.M., 3 A.M.–8 A.M., 8:05 A.M.–3 P.M.); and cross-rate currency futures (7 P.M.–10 P.M., 3 A.M.– 9 A.M., 9:05 A.M.–3 P.M.). The exchange also trades options on cross-rate futures. Futures and options on Treasury auction five-year U.S. Treasury note futures and Treasury auction two-year U.S. Treasury note futures (8:20 A.M.–3 P.M.) are traded only in New York.

NEW YORK CURB EXCHANGE *see* AMERICAN STOCK EXCHANGE.

NEW YORK FUTURES EXCHANGE (NYFE) wholly owned subsidiary of the NEW YORK COTTON EXCHANGE, acquired from the New York Stock Exchange in December 1993. The NYFE trades NYSE

Composite Index futures and options based on the NYSE Composite Index of approximately 2,000 common stocks traded on the New York Stock Exchange (9:30 A.M.–4:15 P.M.); and KR-CRB (Knight-Ridder—Commodity Research Bureau) Index futures and options based on the KR-CRB Index of 21 commodity components (9:40 A.M.–2:45 P.M.).

NEW YORK MERCANTILE EXCHANGE world's largest physical commodity futures exchange, following merger in 1994 with the COMMODITY EXCHANGE (COMEX). The exchange operates as two divisions since the merger. The NYMEX division trades light, sweet crude oil, heating oil, New York Harbor unleaded gasoline, natural gas and platinum futures and options; sour crude, propane and palladium futures; and crack spread options (intercommodity spreads) for heating oil-crude oil and unleaded gasoline-crude oil. The COMEX division trades futures and options in copper, gold, and silver, and the Eurotop 100 Index futures and options. Five-day copper, five-day gold, and five-day silver options also are traded. NYMEX division trading hours are Monday through Friday, from 8:10 A.M. to 3:20 P.M. COMEX division hours are Monday through Friday, from 8:10 A.M. to 3 P.M. The exchange operates the ACCESS after hours electronic trading system, Monday through Thursday from 5 P.M. to 8 A.M., and a Sunday evening session beginning at 7 P.M., trading crude oil, heating oil, and gasoline futures and options, and platinum, copper, gold and silver futures. The exchange has an electronic linkage with the Sydney Futures Exchange (SFE) to allow SFE members to trade NYMEX energy products directly, at non-member rates through the SFE's SYCOM electronic trading system.

NEW YORK STOCK EXCHANGE (NYSE) oldest (1792) and largest stock exchange in the United States, located at 11 Wall Street in New York City; also known as the *Big Board* and *The Exchange*. The NYSE is an unincorporated association governed by a board of directors headed by a full-time paid chairman and comprising 20 individuals representing the public and the exchange membership in about equal proportion. Operating divisions of the NYSE are market operations, member firm regulation and surveillance, finance and office services, product development and planning, and market services and customer relations. Staff groups handle other specialized functions, such as legal problems, government relations, and economic research; certain operational functions are handled by affiliated corporations, such as DEPOSITORY TRUST COMPANY, NATIONAL SECURITIES CLEARING CORPORATION (NSCC), and SECURITIES INDUSTRY AUTOMATION CORPORATION (SIAC). Total voting membership is currently fixed at 1366 "seats," which are owned by individuals, usually partners or officers of securities firms. The number of firms represented is about 550, 150 of which are specialists responsible for the maintenance of an orderly market in the securities they handle. Most members execute orders for the public, although a small number—about 30, who are called FLOOR TRADERS—deal exclusively for their own accounts. More than 1600 companies are listed on the NYSE, representing large firms meeting the exchange's uniquely stringent LISTING REQUIREMENTS. STOCKS, BONDS, WARRANTS, OPTIONS, and RIGHTS are traded at 22 horseshoe-shaped installations, called TRADING POSTS, on the FLOOR of the exchange. In the mid-1990s NYSE-listed shares made up more than half of the total shares traded on organized national exchanges in the United States. Hours: 9:30 A.M.–4:00 P.M., Monday through Friday.

NEW YORK STOCK EXCHANGE INDEX *see* STOCK INDEXES AND AVERAGES.

NEW ZEALAND FUTURES AND OPTIONS EXCHANGE electronic screen-trading exchange, purchased in 1992 by the SYDNEY FUTURES EXCHANGE, whose traders use the SFE's ATS 2000 trading system as a means of direct access to its markets. The Forty Index Futures (FIF) contract is based on the NZSE 40 Capital Index; options are traded on the futures. Futures are traded on the U.S. dollar, New Zealand dollar, and New Zealand wool; equity options are also traded. Futures and options are traded on 90-day bank bills, New Zealand 3-year and 10-year government stock.

NEW ZEALAND STOCK EXCHANGE automated, screen-based national trading system, based in Wellington. The principal index is the NZSE 40 Index of the 40 largest and most liquid stocks. Trading hours are 9:30 A.M. to 3:30 P.M., Monday through Friday. Clearing is through an automated broker-to-broker accounting system. Settlement is for cash on demand, unless otherwise stipulated. Maximum delivery time for a contract is five business days from the trade date.

NICHE particular specialty in which a firm has garnered a large market share. Often, the market will be small enough so that the firm will not attract very much competition. For example, a company that makes a line of specialty chemicals for use by only the petroleum industry is said to have a niche in the chemical industry. Stock analysts frequently favour such companies, since their profit margins can often be wider than those of firms facing more competition.

NICS acronym for *newly industrialized countries,* which are countries that have rapidly developing industrial economies. Some examples of NICS are Hong Kong, Singapore, Malaysia, South Korea, Mexico, Argentina, and Chile. NICS typically have instituted free-market policies which encourage exports to traditional Western industrialized countries and seek investment from Western corporations. Most NICS have increasingly been reducing trade barriers to imports from Western firms.

NIFTY FIFTY 50 stocks most favoured by institutions. The membership of this group is constantly changing, although companies that continue to produce consistent earnings growth over a long time tend to remain institutional favourites. Nifty Fifty stocks also tend to have higher than market average price/earnings ratios, since their growth prospects are well recognized by institutional investors. The Nifty Fifty stocks were particularly famous in the bull markets of the 1960s and early 1970s, when many of the price/earnings ratios soared to 50 or more. *See also* PRICE/EARNINGS RATIO.

NIKKEI INDEX *See* NIKKEI STOCK AVERAGE.

NIKKEI STOCK AVERAGE index of 225 leading stocks traded on the Tokyo Stock Exchange. Called the Nikkei Dow Jones Stock Average until it was renamed in May 1985, it is similar to the Dow Jones Industrial Average because it is composed of representative BLUE CHIP companies (termed *first-section* companies in Japan) and is a PRICE-WEIGHTED INDEX. That means that the movement of each stock, in yen or dollars respectively, is weighed equally regardless of its market capitalization. The Nikkei Stock Average, informally called the Nikkei Index and often still referred to as the Nikkei Dow, is published by the *Nihon Keizai Shimbun (Japan Economic Journal)* and is the most widely quoted Japanese stock index.

Also widely quoted is the Tokyo Stock Price Index (Topix) of all issues listed in the First Section.

NO-BRAINER term used to describe a market the direction of which has become obvious, and therefore requires little or no analysis. This means that most of the stocks will go up in a strong bull market and fall in a bear market, so that it does not matter very much which stock investors buy or sell.

NO-FAULT concept used in divorce law and automobile insurance in Alberta and Ontario whereby the parties involved are not required to prove blame in an action. The concept recognizes irreconcilable differences as a basis for divorce. In automobile insurance, the accident victim collects directly from his or her own insurance company for medical and hospital expenses, regardless of who was at fault. No-fault automobile insurance typically contains provisions aimed at discouraging frivolous lawsuits.

NOISE stock-market activity caused by PROGRAM TRADES and other phenomena not reflective of general sentiment.

NO-LOAD FUND MUTUAL FUND offered by an open-end investment company that imposes no sales charge (load) on its shareholders. Investors buy shares in no-load funds directly from the fund companies, rather than through a BROKER, as is done in load funds. Many no-load fund families *(see* FAMILY OF FUNDS) allow switching of assets between stock, bond, and money market funds. The net asset value, market price, and offer prices of this type of fund are exactly the same, since there is no sales charge. *See also* LOAD FUND.

NOMINAL DOLLARS dollars unadjusted for inflation. For example, economists will refer to a product that cost 100 nominal dollars several years ago, and now costs $150. However, adjusted for inflation, the product's current price may be much higher or lower. Most financial statements are reported in nominal dollars.

NOMINAL INTEREST RATE *see* NOMINAL YIELD.

NOMINAL QUOTATION bid and offer prices given by a market maker for the purpose of valuation, not as an invitation to trade. Securities industry rules require that nominal quotations be specifically identified as such; usually this is done by prefixing the quote with the letters FYI (FOR YOUR INFORMATION) or FVO (for valuation only).

NOMINAL RATE OF INTEREST rate of interest unadjusted for inflation. The actual interest rate charged by a bank on a loan is in nominal dollars. This is in contrast to interest rates that have been adjusted for either past or projected inflation, called REAL INTEREST RATES.

NOMINAL YIELD annual dollar amount of income received from a fixed-income security divided by the PAR VALUE of the security and stated as a percentage. Thus a bond that pays $90 a year and has a par value of $1000 has a nominal yield of 9%, called its *coupon rate.* Similarly, a preferred stock that pays a $9 annual dividend and has a par value of $100 has a nominal yield of 9%. Only when a stock or bond is bought exactly at par value is the nominal yield equal to the actual yield. Since market prices of fixed-income securities go down when market interest rates go up and vice versa, the actual yield, which is determined by the market price and coupon rate (nominal yield), will be higher when the purchase price is below par value and lower when the purchase price is above par value. *See also* RATE OF RETURN.

NOMINEE person or firm, such as a bank official or brokerage house, into whose name securities or other properties are transferred by agreement. Securities held in STREET NAME, for example, are registered in the name of a BROKER (nominee) to facilitate transactions, although the customer remains the true owner.

NONCALLABLE preferred stock or bond that cannot be redeemed at the option of the issuer. A bond may offer CALL PROTECTION for a particular length of time, such as ten years. After that, the issuer may redeem the bond if it chooses and can justify doing so. Bond yields are often quoted to the first date at which the bonds could be called. *See also* YIELD TO CALL.

NONCASH CHARGE items deducted for tax purposes on a firm's income statement, but that require no actual cash outlay. Depreciation, amortization, and depletion charges are the most common noncash charges.

NONCLEARING MEMBER member firm of an exchange that does not have the operational facilities for clearing transactions and thus pays a fee to have the services performed by another member firm, called a *clearing member.* The clearing process involves comparison and verification of information between the buying and selling brokers and then the physical delivery of certificates in exchange for payment, called the *settlement.*

NONCONTESTABILITY CLAUSE in the United States, provision found in insurance contracts stipulating that policyholders cannot be denied coverage after a specific period of time, usually two years, even if the policyholder provided inaccurate or even fraudulent information in his or her insurance application. In order to contest the policy, the insurer must find out about the incorrect information before the clause goes into effect. *See* INCONTESTABILITY CLAUSE.

NONCONTRIBUTORY PENSION PLAN pension plan that is totally funded by the employer, and to which employees are not expected to contribute. Most DEFINED BENEFIT PENSION PLANS are noncontributory.

NONCUMULATIVE term describing a preferred stock issue in which unpaid dividends do not accrue. Such issues contrast with CUMULATIVE PREFERRED issues, where unpaid dividends accumulate and must be paid before dividends on common shares. Most preferred issues are cumulative. On a noncumulative preferred, omitted dividends will, as a rule, never be paid. Some older railroad preferred stocks are of this type.

NONCUMULATIVE PREFERRED SHARE preferred share that does not receive a dividend that has passed and not been paid.

NONCURRENT ASSET asset not expected to be converted into cash, sold, or exchanged within the normal operating cycle of the firm, usually one year. Examples of noncurrent assets include FIXED ASSETS, such as real estate, machinery, and other equipment; LEASEHOLD IMPROVEMENTS; INTANGIBLE ASSETS, such as goodwill, patents, and trademarks; notes receivable after one year; other investments; miscellaneous assets not meeting the definition of a CURRENT ASSET. Prepaid expenses (also called DEFERRED CHARGES or *deferred expenses),* which include such items as rent paid in advance, prepaid insurance premiums, and subscriptions, are usually considered current assets by accountants. Credit analysts, however, prefer to classify these expenses as noncurrent assets, since prepayments do not represent asset strength and protection in the way that other current assets do, with their convertibility into cash during the normal operating cycle and their liquidation value should operations be terminated.

NONCURRENT LIABILITY LIABILITY due after one year.

NONDISCRETIONARY TRUST TRUST where the trustee has no power to determine the amount of distributions to the beneficiary. Contrast with DISCRETIONARY TRUST.

NONEXEMPT LIFE INSURANCE *see* EXEMPT LIFE INSURANCE.

NONFINANCIAL ASSETS assets that are physical, such as REAL ESTATE and PERSONAL PROPERTY.

NON-INTEREST-BEARING NOTE note that makes no periodic interest payments. Instead, the note is sold at a discount and matures at face value. Also called a ZERO-COUPON BOND.

NONMEMBER FIRM brokerage firm that is not a member of an organized exchange. Such firms execute their trades either through member firms, on regional exchanges, or in the THIRD MARKET. *See* MEMBER FIRM; REGIONAL STOCK EXCHANGES.

NONPARTICIPATING LIFE INSURANCE POLICY life insurance policy that does not pay dividends. Policyholders thus do not participate in the interest, dividends, and capital gains earned by the insurer on premiums paid. In contrast, PARTICIPATING INSURANCE POLICIES pay dividends to policyholders from earnings on investments.

NON-PARTICIPATING PREFERRED SHARE preferred share that is limited to a stipulated dividend.

NONPARTICIPATING PREFERRED STOCK *see* PARTICIPATING PREFERRED STOCK.

NONPERFORMING ASSET ASSET not effectual in the production of income. In banking, commercial loans 90 days past due and consumer loans 180 days past due are classified as nonperforming.

NONPRODUCTIVE LOAN type of commercial bank loan that increases the amount of spending power in the economy but does not lead directly to increased output; for example, a loan to finance a LEVERAGED BUYOUT. In the United States, the Federal Reserve has on occasion acted to curtail such lending as one of its early steps in implementing monetary restraint.

NONPUBLIC INFORMATION information about a company, either positive or negative, that will have a material effect on the stock price when it is released to the public. Insiders, such as corporate officers and members of the board of directors, are not allowed to trade on material nonpublic information until it has been released to the public, since they would have an unfair advantage over unsuspecting investors. Some examples of important nonpublic information are an imminent takeover announcement, a soon-to-be-released earnings report that is more favourable than most analysts expect, or the sudden resignation of a key corporate official. *See also* DISCLOSURE; INSIDER.

NONRATED bonds that have not been rated by one or more of the major rating agencies such as Standard & Poor's or Moody's Investor Services. Issues are usually nonrated because they are too small to justify the expense of getting a rating. Nonrated bonds are not necessarily better or worse than rated bonds, though many institutions cannot buy them because they need to hold bonds with an investment-grade rating.

NONRECOURSE LOAN type of financial arrangement used by limited partners, whereby the limited partners finance a portion of their participation with a loan secured by their ownership in the underlying venture. They benefit from the LEVERAGE provided by the loan. In case of default, the lender has no recourse to the assets of the partnership beyond those held by the limited partners who borrowed the money.

NONRECURRING CHARGE one-time expense or WRITE-OFF appearing in a company's financial statement; also called *extraordinary charge.* Nonrecurring charges would include, for example, a major fire or theft, the write-off of a division, and the effect of a change in accounting procedure.

NONREFUNDABLE provision in a bond INDENTURE that either prohibits or sets limits on the issuer's retiring the bonds with the proceeds of a subsequent issue, called REFUNDING. Such a provision often does not rule out refunding altogether but protects bondholders from REDEMPTION until a specified date. Other such provisions may preclude refunding unless new bonds can be issued at a specified lower rate. *See also* CALL PROTECTION.

NONREGISTERED FUND fund that, because it is not registered with Revenue Canada cannot be deducted from income tax, i.e., it is not eligible as an RRSP. Such funds are usually used for investments of disposable personal income and may be considered by individuals who have already placed in their RRSPs the limit allowed them by Revenue Canada for that particular year.

NONREVOLVING LINE OF CREDIT contractual agreement between a bank and its customer, usually a company, established for a one-time specific purpose with the related advance carried on a strictly reducing basis. The credit line, while being paid off, can be run back up as cash is needed.

NONVOTING STOCK corporate securities that do not empower a holder to vote on corporate resolutions or the election of directors. Such stock is sometimes issued in connection with a takeover attempt, when management creates nonvoting shares to dilute the target firm's equity and thereby discourage the merger attempt. Preferred stock is normally nonvoting stock. *See also* VOTING STOCK.

NOON RATE rate that shows the number of local dollars paid to buy another country's currency at the last transaction before noon on the date indicated.

NO-PAR ITEM cheque collected at its face value less drawee bank charges.

NO-PAR-VALUE STOCK stock with no set (par) value specified in the corporate charter or on the stock certificate; also called *no-par stock.* Companies issuing no-par value shares may carry whatever they receive for them either as part of the CAPITAL STOCK account or as part of the CAPITAL SURPLUS (paid-in capital) account, or both. Whatever amount is carried as capital stock has an implicit value, represented by the number of outstanding shares divided into the dollar amount of capital stock.

NORMALIZED EARNINGS earnings, either in the past or the future, that are adjusted for cyclical ups and downs in the economy. Earnings are normalized by analysts by generating a moving average over several years including up and down cycles. Analysts refer to normalized earnings when explaining whether a company's current profits are above or below its long-term trend.

NORMAL MARKET SIZE (NMS) share classification system that in 1991 replaced the alpha, beta, gamma, delta, system brought in with BIG BANG on the INTERNATIONAL STOCK EXCHANGE OF THE U.K. AND THE REPUBLIC OF IRELAND (ISE). The earlier system had unintentionally become a measure of corporate status, strength, and viability. The new system has 12 categories based on the size of the transactions that are normal for each security. The system fixes the size of transactions in which market makers are obligated to deal.

NORMAL RETIREMENT point at which a pension plan participant can retire and immediately receive unreduced benefits. Pension plans can specify age and length-of-service requirements that employees must meet to be eligible for retirement.

NORMAL TRADING UNIT standard minimum size of a trading unit for a particular security; also called a ROUND LOT. For instance, stocks have a normal trading unit of 100 shares, although inactive stocks trade in 10-share round lots. Any securities trade for less than a round lot is called an ODD LOT trade.

NOTE unsecured written promise to pay a specified amount to a certain entity on demand or on a specified date. *See also* PROMISSORY NOTE.

NOT-FOR-PROFIT type of incorporated organization in which no stockholder or trustee shares in profits or losses and which usually exists to accomplish some charitable, humanitarian, or educational purpose; also called *nonprofit.* Such groups are exempt from corporate income taxes but are subject to other taxes on income-producing property or enterprises. Donations to these groups are usually tax deductible for the donor. Some examples are hospitals, colleges and universities, foundations, and familiar groups such as the Red Cross.

NOTICE DAY any day during the delivery month when notices of intent to deliver the underlying commodities may be tendered.

NOTICE OF SALE advertisement placed by an issuer of municipal securities announcing its intentions to sell a new issue and inviting underwriters to submit COMPETITIVE BIDS.

NOT RATED indication used by securities rating services (such as Standard & Poor's or Moody's) and mercantile agencies (such as Dun & Bradstreet) to show that a security or a company has not been rated. It has neither negative nor positive implications. The abbreviation NR is used.

NOT-SUFFICIENT-FUNDS CHEQUE a bank cheque written against an inadequate balance. Also called *insufficient-funds cheque* and, informally, a *bounced cheque.*

NOVATION
1. agreement to replace one party to a contract with a new party. The novation transfers both rights and duties and requires the consent of both the original and the new party.
2. replacement of an older debt or obligation with a newer one.

NOW ACCOUNT *see* NEGOTIABLE ORDER OF WITHDRAWAL.

NUMISMATIC COIN coin that is valued based on its rarity, age, quantity originally produced, and condition. These coins are bought and sold as individual items within the coin collecting community. Most numismatic coins are legal tender coins that were produced in limited quantities to give them scarcity value. They are historic coins which also can be rare. The current price of gold is a minor factor when dealing with numismatic coins. Premiums are traditionally far higher than those of BULLION COINS, and values fluctuate to a much wider extent. For example, a $5 gold piece may contain $60 worth of gold and may sell for as much as $700. The minimum amount recovered from numismatic coin investments is always either its face value or its metal content. Most coins, however, sell substantially above these amounts. Since the markup over bullion value can vary widely from one dealer to another, investors need to shop around diligently to avoid paying exhorbitant markups.

O

OBLIGATION legal responsibility, as for a DEBT.

OBLIGOR one who has an obligation, such as an issuer of bonds, a borrower of money from a bank or another source, or a credit customer of a business supplier or retailer. The obligor *(obligator, debtor)* is legally bound to pay a debt, including interest, when due.

ODD LOT securities trade made for less than the NORMAL TRADING UNIT (termed a ROUND LOT). In stock trading, any purchase or sale of less than 100 shares is considered an odd lot, although inactive stocks generally trade in round lots of 10 shares. An investor buying or selling an odd lot pays a higher commission rate than someone making a round-lot trade. This odd-lot differential varies among brokers but for stocks is often ⅛ of a point (12½¢) per share. For instance, someone buying 100 shares of XYZ at $70 would pay $70 a share plus commission. At the same time, someone buying only 50 shares of XYZ would pay $70⅛ a share plus commission. *See also* ODD-LOT DEALER; ODD-LOT SHORT-SALE RATIO; ODD-LOT THEORY.

ODD-LOT DEALER originally a dealer who bought round lots of stock and resold it in odd lots to retail brokers who, in turn, accommodated their smaller customers at the regular commission rate plus an extra charge, called the odd-lot differential.

ODD-LOT THEORY historical theory that the ODD LOT investor—the small personal investor who trades in less than 100-share quantities—is usually guilty of bad timing and that profits can be made by acting contrary to odd-lot trading patterns. Heavy odd-lot buying in a rising market is interpreted by proponents of this theory as a sign of technical weakness and the signal of a market reversal. Conversely, an increase of odd-lot selling in a declining market is seen as a sign of technical strength and a signal to buy. In fact, analyses of odd-lot trading over the years fail to bear out the theory with any real degree of consistency, and it has fallen into disfavour in recent years. It is also a fact that odd-lot customers generally, who tend to buy market leaders, have fared rather well in the upward market that has prevailed over the last fifty years or so. *See also* ODD-LOT SHORT-SALE RATIO.

OEX pronounced as three letters, Wall Street shorthand for the Standard & Poor's 100 stock index, which comprises stocks for which options are traded on the Chicago Board Options Exchange. OEX index options are traded on the Chicago Board of Trade, and futures are traded on the Chicago Mercantile Exchange. *See also* STOCK INDEXES AND AVERAGES.

OFF-BALANCE-SHEET FINANCING financing that does not add debt on a balance sheet and thus does not affect borrowing capacity as it would be determined by financial ratios. The most common example would be a lease structured as an OPERATING LEASE rather than a CAPITAL LEASE and where management's intent is, in fact, to acquire an asset and corresponding liability without reflecting either on its balance sheet. Other examples include the sale of receivables with recourse, and bank financial instruments such as guarantees, letters of credit, and loan commitments. GENERALLY ACCEPTED ACCOUNTING PRINCIPLES (GAAP) require that information be provided in financial statements about off-balance-sheet financing involving credit, market, and liquidity risk.

OFF-BOARD off the exchange (the New York Stock Exchange is known in the United States as the Big Board, hence the term). The term is used either for a trade that is executed OVER THE COUNTER or for a transaction entailing listed securities that is not completed on a national exchange. Over-the-counter trading is handled by telephone, with competitive bidding carried on constantly by market makers in a particular stock. The other kind of off-board trade occurs when a block of stock is exchanged between customers of a brokerage firm, or between a customer and the firm itself if the brokerage house wants to buy or sell securities from its own inventory. *See also* THIRD MARKET.

OFFER price at which someone who owns a security offers to sell it; also known as the ASKED PRICE. This price is listed in newspapers for stocks traded OVER THE COUNTER. The bid price—the price at which someone is prepared to buy—is also shown. The bid price is always lower than the offer price. *See also* OFFERING PRICE.

OFFERING *see* PUBLIC OFFERING.

OFFERING CIRCULAR *see* PROSPECTUS.

OFFERING DATE date on which a distribution of stocks or bonds will first be available for sale to the public. *See also* DATED DATE; PUBLIC OFFERING.

OFFERING PRICE price per share at which a new or secondary distribution of securities is offered for sale to the public; also called PUBLIC OFFERING PRICE. For instance, if a new issue of XYZ stock is priced at $40 a share, the offering price is $40.

When mutual fund shares are made available to the public, they are sold at NET ASSET VALUE, also called the *offering price* or the ASKED PRICE, plus a sales charge, if any. In a NO-LOAD FUND, the offering price is the same as the net asset value. In a LOAD FUND, the sales charge is added to the net asset value, to arrive at the offering price. *See also* OFFER.

OFFER WANTED (OW) notice by a potential buyer of a security that he or she is looking for an offer by a potential seller of the security. The abbreviation OW is frequently seen in the PINK SHEETS (listing of stocks) and YELLOW SHEETS (listing of corporate bonds) published by the NATIONAL QUOTATION BUREAU for securities traded by OVER THE COUNTER dealers. *See also* BID WANTED.

OFF-FLOOR ORDER order to buy or sell a security that originates off the floor of an exchange. These are customer orders originating with brokers, as distinguished from orders of floor members trading for their own accounts (ON-FLOOR ORDERS). Exchange rules require that off-floor orders be executed before orders initiated on the floor.

OFFICIAL STATEMENT *see* LEGAL OPINION.

OFFSET

Accounting: (1) amount equaling or counterbalancing another amount on the opposite side of the same ledger or the ledger of another account. *See also* ABSORBED. (2) amount that cancels or reduces a claim.

Banking: (1) bank's legal right to seize deposit funds to cover a loan in default—called *right of offset.* (2) number stored on a bank card that, when related to the code number remembered by the cardholder, represents the depositor's identification number, called *PAN-PIN pair.*

Securities, commodities, options: (1) closing transaction involving the purchase or sale of an OPTION having the same features as one already held. (2) HEDGE, such as the SHORT SALE of a stock to protect a capital gain or the purchase of a future to protect a commodity price, or a STRADDLE representing the purchase of offsetting put and call options on a security.

OFFSHORE term used for any financial organization with a headquarters outside the country. A MUTUAL FUND with a legal domicile in the Bahamas or the Cayman Islands, for instance, is called an *offshore fund.*

OF RECORD on a company's books of record. If for example, a company announces that it will pay a dividend to shareholders of record January 15, every shareholder whose name appears on the company's books on that day will be sent a dividend cheque.

OIL AND GAS LIMITED PARTNERSHIP partnership consisting of one or more limited partners and one or more general partners that is structured to find, extract, and market commercial quantities of oil and natural gas. The limited partners, who assume no liability beyond the funds they contribute, buy units in the partnership, typically for at least $2500 a unit, from a broker registered to sell that partnership. All the limited partners' money then goes to the GENERAL PARTNER, the partner with unlimited liability, who either searches for oil and gas (an exploratory or wildcat well), drills for oil and gas in a proven oil field (a DEVELOPMENTAL DRILLING PROGRAM), or pumps petroleum and gas from an existing well (a COMPLETION PROGRAM). The riskier the chance of finding oil and gas, the higher the potential reward or loss to the limited partner. Conservative investors who mainly want to collect income from the sale of proven oil and gas reserves are safest with a developmental or completion program.

Limited partners also receive tax breaks, such as depreciation deductions for equipment used for drilling and oil depletion allowances for the value of oil extracted from the fields.

OIL PATCH provinces that produce and refine oil and gas. This includes Alberta and Saskatchewan. Economists refer to oil patch provinces when assessing the strength or weakness of a region of the country tied to movements in oil prices.

OLD AGE SECURITY PENSION (OAS)   pension available to Canadian citizens and legal residents of Canada aged 65 and over, who have lived in Canada for at least 10 years since turning 18. Those who no longer reside in Canada must have resided here for at least 20 years after turning 18. Residence in countries with which Canada has a social security pension agreement may also count towards the 20-year qualifying period. OAS is not dependent upon previous employment. OAS indexation is adjusted quarterly, and it is included in taxable income. After July 1, 1996, OAS will be subject to withholding tax if income exceeds $53,215.

OLIGOPOLY market situation in which a small number of selling firms control the market supply of a particular good or service and are therefore able to control the market price. An oligopoly can be *perfect*—where all firms produce an identical good or service (cement)—or *imperfect*—where each firm's product has a different identity but is essentially similar to the others (cigarettes). Because each firm in an oligopoly knows its share of the total market for the product or service it produces, and because any change in price or change in market share by one firm is reflected in the sales of the others, there tends to be a high degree of interdependence among firms; each firm must make its price and output decisions with regard to the responses of the other firms in the oligopoly, so that oligopoly prices, once established, are rigid. This encourages nonprice competition, through advertising, packaging, and service—a generally nonproductive form of resource allocation. Two examples of oligopoly in the United States are airlines serving the same routes and tobacco companies. *See also* OLIGOPSONY.

OLIGOPSONY market situation in which a few large buyers control the purchasing power and therefore the output and market price of a good or service; the buy-side counterpart of OLIGOPOLY. Oligopsony prices tend to be lower than the prices in a freely competitive market, just as oligopoly prices tend to be higher. For example, the large tobacco companies purchase all the output of a large number of small tobacco growers and therefore are able to control tobacco prices.

OMITTED DIVIDEND dividend that was scheduled to be declared by a corporation, but instead was not voted for the time being by the board of directors. Dividends are sometimes omitted when a company has run into financial difficulty and its board decides it is more important to conserve cash than to pay a dividend to shareholders. The announcement of an omitted dividend will typically cause the company's stock price to drop, particularly if the announcement is a surprise.

ON ACCOUNT
In general: in partial payment of an obligation.
Finance: on credit terms. The term applies to a relationship between a seller and a buyer wherein payment is expected sometime after delivery and the obligation is not documented by a NOTE. Synonymous with *open account.*

ON-BALANCE VOLUME TECHNICAL ANALYSIS method that attempts to pinpoint when a stock, bond, or commodity is being accumulated by many buyers or is being distributed by many sellers. The on-balance volume line is superimposed on the stock price line on a chart, and it is considered significant when the two lines cross. The chart indicates a buy signal when accumulation is detected and a sell signal when distribution is spotted. The on-balance method can be used to diagnose an entire market or an individual stock, bond, or commodity.

ONE DECISION STOCK stock with sufficient quality and growth potential to be suitable for a BUY AND HOLD STRATEGY.

ONE-SHARE-ONE VOTE RULE the principle that public companies should not reduce shareholder voting rights.

ON-FLOOR ORDER security order originating with a member on the floor of an exchange when dealing for his or her own account. The designation separates such orders from those for customers' accounts (OFF-FLOOR ORDERS), which are generally given precedence by exchange rules.

ON MARGIN *see* MARGIN.

ON THE CLOSE ORDER order to buy or sell a specified number of shares in a particular stock as close as possible to the closing price of the day. Brokers accepting on the close orders do not guarantee that the trade will be executed at the final closing price, or even that the trade can be completed at all. On an order ticket, on the close orders are abbreviated as "OTC" orders. *See also* AT THE CLOSE ORDER; MARKET-ON-CLOSE ORDER.

ON THE OPENING ORDER order to buy or sell a specified number of shares in a particular stock at the price of the first trade of the day. If the trader cannot buy or sell shares at that price, the order is immediately cancelled.

ON THE SIDELINES investors who refrain from investing because of market uncertainty are said to be on the sidelines. The analogy is to a football game, in which spectators on the sidelines do not actively participate in the game. Investors on the sidelines normally keep their money in short-term instruments such as money market mutual funds, which can be tapped instantly if the investor sees a good opportunity to reenter the stock or bond markets. Market commentators frequently say that trading activity was light "because investors stayed on the sidelines."

OPD ticker tape symbol designating (1) the first transaction of the day in a security after a DELAYED OPENING or (2) the opening transaction in a security whose price has changed significantly from the previous day's close—usually 2 or more points on stocks selling at $20 or higher, 1 or more points on stocks selling at less than $20.

OPEN
Securities:
1. status of an order to buy or sell securities that has still not been executed. A GOOD-TILL-CANCELED ORDER that remains pending is an example of an open order.
2. to establish an account with a broker.

Banking: to establish an account or a LETTER OF CREDIT.

Finance: unpaid balance.

See also OPEN-END LEASE; OPEN-END MANAGEMENT COMPANY; OPEN-END MORTGAGE; OPEN INTEREST; OPEN ORDER; OPEN REPO.

OPEN-END INVESTMENT COMPANY investment company that constantly issues and redeems shares without affecting the net asset value of the fund (see CLOSED-END INVESTMENT COMPANY). It uses its capital to invest in other companies. Its shareholders can participate directly because the open-end investment company will sell or rebuy its own shares at book value. See also MUTUAL FUND.

OPEN-END LEASE lease agreement providing for an additional payment after the property is returned to the lessor, to adjust for any change in the value of the property.

OPEN-END MANAGEMENT COMPANY INVESTMENT COMPANY that sells MUTUAL FUNDS to the public. The term arises from the fact that the firm continually creates new shares on demand. Mutual fund shareholders buy the shares at NET ASSET VALUE and can redeem them at any time at the prevailing market price, which may be higher or lower than the price at which the investor bought. The shareholder's funds are invested in stocks, bonds, or money market instruments, depending on the type of mutual fund company. The opposite of an open-end management company is a CLOSED-END MANAGEMENT COMPANY, which issues a limited number of shares, which are then traded on a stock exchange.

OPEN-END (MUTUAL) FUND see OPEN-END MANAGEMENT COMPANY.

OPENING
1. price at which a security or commodity starts a trading day. Investors who want to buy or sell as soon as the market opens will put in an order at the opening price.
2. short time frame of market opportunity. For instance, if interest rates have been rising for months, and for a few days or weeks they

fall, a corporation that has wanted to FLOAT bonds at lower interest rates might seize the moment to issue the bonds. This short time frame would be called an *opening in the market* or a *window of opportunity. See also* WINDOW.

OPENING TRANSACTION *see* PURCHASE TRANSACTION; SALE TRANSACTION.

OPEN INTEREST total number of contracts in a commodity or options market that are still open; that is, they have not been exercised, closed out, or allowed to expire. The term also applies to a particular commodity or, in the case of options, to the number of contracts outstanding on a particular underlying security. The level of open interest is reported daily in newspaper commodity and options pages. In trading of gold futures, the open interest is the number of contracts that remain to be settled or delivered for a particular delivery month. This open interest goes up by one every time a contract and a buyer is agreed to. In gold and silver options, it is the total number of contracts which are outstanding. It does not affect the price of the option or contract, but does affect liquidity.

OPEN ON THE PRINT BLOCK POSITIONER'S term for a BLOCK trade that has been completed with an institutional client and "printed" on the consolidated tape, but that leaves the block positioner open—that is, with a risk position to be covered. This usually happens when the block positioner is on the sell side of the transaction and sells SHORT what he lacks in inventory to complete the order.

OPEN ORDER buy or sell order for securities that has not yet been executed or canceled; a GOOD-TILL-CANCELED ORDER.

OPEN OUTCRY method of trading on a commodity exchange. The term derives from the fact that traders must shout out their buy or sell offers. When a trader shouts that she wants to sell at a particular price and another trader shouts that he wants to buy at that price, the two traders have made a contract that will be recorded.

OPERATING BUDGET estimate of operating revenues and expenses for a given period.

OPERATING EXPENSES costs of doing business, i.e., selling and general administrative costs, deducted from gross profit to arrive at a net income before taxes.

OPERATING INCOME *see* OPERATING PROFIT (OR LOSS).

OPERATING IN THE RED operating at a loss. *See* OPERATING PROFIT (OR LOSS).

OPERATING LEASE type of LEASE, normally involving equipment, whereby the contract is written for considerably less than the life of the equipment and the lessor handles all maintenance and servicing;

also called *service lease*. Operating leases are the opposite of capital leases, where the lessee acquires essentially all the economic benefits and risks of ownership. Common examples of equipment financed with operating leases are office copiers, computers, automobiles, and trucks. Most operating leases are cancelable, meaning the lessee can return the equipment if it becomes obsolete or is no longer needed.

OPERATING LEVERAGE *see* LEVERAGE.

OPERATING LOANS funds required to look after the day-to-day operating requirements of a business. This type of loan may be secured by receivables, inventory, or fixed and other assets, or other collateral.

OPERATING PROFIT MARGIN *see* NET PROFIT MARGIN.

OPERATING PROFIT (OR LOSS) the difference between the revenues of a business and the related costs and expenses, excluding income derived from sources other than its regular activities and before income deductions; synonymous with *net operating profit (or loss), operating income (or loss),* and *net operating income (or loss).* Income deductions are a class of items comprising the final section of a company's income statement, which, although necessarily incurred in the course of business and customarily charged before arriving at net income, are more in the nature of costs imposed from without than costs subject to the control of everyday operations. They include interest; amortized discount and expense on bonds; income taxes; losses from sales of plants, divisions, major items of property; prior-year adjustments; charges to contingency reserves; bonuses and other periodic profit distributions to officers and employees: write-offs of intangibles: adjustments arising from major changes in accounting methods, such as inventory valuation and other material and nonrecurrent items.

OPERATING RATE percentage of production capacity in use by a particular company, an industry, or the entire economy. While in theory a business can operate at 100% of its productive capacity, in practice the maximum output is less than that because machines need to be repaired, employees take vacations, etc. The operating rate is expressed as a percentage of the ideal 100% production output. For example, a company may be producing at an 85% operating rate, meaning its output is 85% of the maximum that could be produced with its existing resources. If a company has a low operating rate of under 50%, it usually is suffering meager profits or losses, though it has large potential for profit growth. A company operating at 80% of capacity or more is usually highly profitable, though it has less opportunity for improvement.

OPERATING RATIO any of a group of ratios that measure a firm's operating efficiency and effectiveness by relating various income and expense figures from the profit and loss statement to each other and to balance sheet figures. Among the ratios used are sales to cost of goods sold, operating expenses to operating income, net profits to gross income, net income to net worth. Such ratios are most revealing when compared with those of prior periods and with industry averages.

OPERATING RISK risk of being unable to cover operating costs measured by the variability of a firm's EBIT (Earnings Before Interest and Taxes). Increased operating leverage (i.e., use of borrowed money) increases a firm's operating risk.

OPERATIONS DEPARTMENT BACK OFFICE of a brokerage firm where all clerical functions having to do with clearance, settlement, and execution of trades are handled. This department keeps customer records and handles the day-to-day monitoring of margin positions.

OPINION *see* ACCOUNTANT'S OPINION.

OPINION SHOPPING dubious practice of changing outside auditors until one is found that will give an unqualified ACCOUNTANT'S OPINION.

OPM
1. other people's money; slang for the use of borrowed funds by individuals or companies to increase the return on invested capital. *See also* FINANCIAL LEVERAGE.
2. options pricing model. *See* BLACK-SCHOLES OPTION PRICING MODEL.

OPPORTUNITY COST
In general: highest price or rate of return an alternative course of action would provide.
Corporate finance: concept widely used in business planning; for example, in evaluating a CAPITAL INVESTMENT project, a company must measure the projected return against the return it would earn on the highest yielding alternative investment involving similar risk. *See also* COST OF CAPITAL.
Securities investments: cost of forgoing a safe return on an investment in hopes of making a larger profit. For instance, an investor might buy a stock that shows great promise but yields only 2%, even though a higher safe return is available in a money market fund yielding 5%. The 3% yield difference is called the opportunity cost.

OPTICAL SCANNING process whereby characters imprinted on documents can be read by machine and transferred directly to magnetic tape. Often used by banks as a service in conjunction with lock box to permit rapid credit file updating by corporations. Use of bank (or in-house) optical scanning services permits corporations to update computer accounts receivable files directly, thus reducing their cost for clerical intervention.

OPTIMUM CAPACITY level of output of manufacturing operations that produces the lowest cost per unit. For example, a tire factory may produce tires at $30 apiece if it turns out 10,000 tires a month, but the tires can be made for $20 apiece if the plant operates at its optimum capacity of 100,000 tires a month. *See also* MARGINAL COST.

OPTION

In general: right to buy or sell property that is granted in exchange for an agreed upon sum. If the right is not exercised after a specified period, the option expires and the option buyer forfeits the money. *See also* EXERCISE.

Securities: securities transaction agreement tied to stocks, commodities, or stock indexes. Options are traded on many exchanges.

1. a CALL OPTION gives its buyer the right to buy 100 shares of the underlying security at a fixed price before a specified date in the future—usually three, six, or nine months. For this right, the call option buyer pays the call option seller, called the writer, a fee called a PREMIUM, which is forfeited if the buyer does not exercise the option before the agreed-upon date. A call buyer therefore speculates that the price of the underlying shares will rise within the specified time period. For example, a call option on 100 shares of XYZ stock may grant its buyer the right to buy those shares at $100 apiece anytime in the next three months. To buy that option, the buyer may have to pay a premium of $2 a share, or $200. If at the time of the option contract XYZ is selling for $95 a share, the option buyer will profit if XYZ's stock price rises. If XYZ shoots up to $120 a share in two months, for example, the option buyer can EXERCISE his or her option to buy 100 shares of the stock at $100 and then sell the shares for $120 each, keeping the difference as profit (minus the $2 premium per share). On the other hand, if XYZ drops below $95 and stays there for three months, at the end of that time the call option will expire and the call buyer will receive no return on the $2 a share investment premium of $200.

2. the opposite of a call option is a PUT OPTION, which gives its buyer the right to sell a specified number of shares of a stock at a particular price within a specified time period. Put buyers expect the price of the underlying stock to fall. Someone who thinks XYZ's stock price will fall might buy a three-month XYZ put for 100 shares at $100 apiece and pay a premium of $2. If XYZ falls to $80 a share, the put buyer can then exercise his or her right to sell 100 XYZ shares at $100. The buyer will first purchase 100 shares at $80 each and then sell them to the put option seller (writer) at $100 each, thereby making a profit of $18 a share (the $20 a share profit minus the $2 a share cost of the option premium).

   In practice, most call and put options are rarely exercised. Instead, investors buy and sell options before expiration, trading on the rise and fall of premium prices. Because an option buyer must put up only a small amount of money (the premium) to control a large amount of stock, options trading provides a great deal of LEVERAGE and can prove immensely profitable. Options traders can write either covered options, in which they own the underlying security, or far riskier naked options, for which they do not own the underlying security. Often, options traders lose many premiums on unsuccessful trades before they make a very profitable trade. More sophisticated traders combine various call and put options in SPREAD and STRADDLE positions. Their profits or losses result from the narrowing or widening of spreads between option prices.

An *incentive stock option* is granted to corporate executives if the company achieves certain financial goals, such as a level of sales or profits. The executive is granted the option of buying company stock at a below-market price and selling the stock in the market for a profit. *See also* CALL; COVERED OPTION; DEEP IN (OUT OF) THE MONEY; IN THE MONEY; LEAPS; NAKED OPTION; OPTION WRITER; OUT OF THE MONEY.

OPTION ACCOUNT account at a brokerage firm that is approved to contain option positions or trades. Since certain option strategies require margin, an option account may be a margin account or a cash account. There are several prerequisites. The client must be given a copy of "Characteristics and Risks of Standardized Options Contracts," known as the Options Disclosure Documents, before the account can be approved. The client must complete an OPTION AGREEMENT in order to open the account. The client must show that he or she is suitable for options transactions, both in financial resources and investing experience, before the brokerage firm will approve the account for options trading.

OPTION AGREEMENT form filled out by a brokerage firm's customer when opening an option account. It details financial information about the customer, who agrees to follow the rules and regulations of options trading. This agreement, also called the *option information form*, assures the broker that the customer's financial resources are adequate to withstand any losses that may occur from options trading. The customer must receive a prospectus from the OPTIONS CLEARING CORPORATION before he or she can begin trading.

OPTION CLASS options that all have the same underlying instrument, e.g., a stock or bond futures contract.

OPTIONAL LIFE INSURANCE insurance that provides additional life insurance coverage for the policyholder.

OPTION CYCLE cycle of months in which options contracts expire. These cycles are used for options on stocks and indices, as well as options on commodities, currencies, and debt instruments. The three most common cycles are: January, April, July, October (JAJO); February, May, August, November (FMAN); and March, June, September, December (MJSD). In addition to these expiration months, options on individual stocks and indices generally also expire in the current month and subsequent month. As an example, an option in the February cycle trading during May would have May, June and August expiration months listed at a minimum. Because of option cycles, there are four days a year—in March, June, September, and December, when TRIPLE WITCHING DAY takes place, as several options contracts expire on the same day.

OPTIONAL DIVIDEND dividend that can be paid either in cash or in stock. The shareholder entitled to the dividend makes the choice.

OPTION-ELIGIBLE SECURITIES securities that meet the eligibility criteria as underlying securities for either Canadian (TransCanada Options, or TCO) or U.S. (Options Clearing Corporation, or OCC) exchange-traded put and call options. In Canada, option-eligible securities and preferred eligible securities require a minimum client margin (for purchase on margin) of 30% of their purchase price.

OPTION EXPIRY MONTH time limit on an option.

OPTION HOLDER someone who has bought a call or put OPTION but has not yet exercised or sold it. A call option holder wants the price of the underlying security to rise; a put option holder wants the price of the underlying security to fall.

OPTION MARGIN MARGIN REQUIREMENT applicable to OPTIONS, as set forth in REGULATION T and in the internal policies of individual brokers. Requirements vary with the type of option and the extent to which it is IN-THE-MONEY, but are strictest in the case of NAKED OPTIONS and narrow-based INDEX OPTIONS.

OPTION PREMIUM amount per share paid by an OPTION buyer to an option seller for the right to buy (call) or sell (put) the underlying security at a particular price within a specified period. Option premium prices are quoted in increments of eighths or sixteenths of 1% and are printed in the options tables of daily newspapers. A PREMIUM of $5 per share means an option buyer would pay $500 for an option on 100 shares. *See also* CALL OPTION; PUT OPTION.

OPTION PRICE market price at which an option contract is trading at any particular time. The price of an option on a stock reflects the fact that it covers 100 shares of a stock. So, for example, an option that is quoted at $7 would cost $700, because it would be an option for 100 shares of stock at a $7 cost per share covered. The option price is determined by many factors, including its INTRINSIC VALUE, time to expiration, volatility of the underlying stock, interest rates, dividends, and marketplace adjustments for supply and demand. Options on indices, debt instruments, currencies, and commodities also have prices determined by many of the same forces. Options prices are published daily in the business pages of many newspapers.

OPTIONS CLEARING CORPORATION (OCC) in the United States, a corporation that handles options transactions on the stock exchanges and is owned by the exchanges. It issues all options contracts and guarantees that the obligations of both parties to a trade are fulfilled. The OCC also processes the exchange of money on all options trades and maintains records of those trades. Its prospectus is given to all investors to read before they can trade in options. This prospectus outlines the rules and risks of trading and sets the standards for ethical conduct on the part of options traders. *See also* OPTION.

OPTION SERIES options of the same class (puts or calls with the same underlying security) that also have the same EXERCISE PRICE and maturity month. For instance, all XYZ October 80 calls are a series, as are all ABC July 100 puts. *See also* OPTION.

OPTION SPREAD buying and selling of options within the same CLASS at the same time. The investor who uses the OPTION spread strategy hopes to profit from the widening or narrowing of the SPREAD between the various options. Option spreads can be designed to be profitable in either up or down markets.

Some examples:

(1) entering into two options at the same EXERCISE PRICE, but with different maturity dates. For instance, an investor could buy an XYZ April 60 call and sell an XYZ July 60 call.

(2) entering into two options at different STRIKE PRICES with the same expiration month. For example, an investor could buy an XYZ April 60 call and sell an XYZ April 70 call.

(3) entering into two options at different strike prices with different expiration months. For instance, an investor could buy an XYZ April 60 call and sell an XYZ July 70 call.

OPTION WRITER person or financial institution that sells put and call options. A writer of a PUT OPTION contracts to buy 100 shares of stock from the put option buyer by a certain date for a fixed price. For example, an option writer who sells XYZ April 50 put agrees to buy XYZ stock from the put buyer at $50 a share any time until the contract expires in April.

A writer of a CALL OPTION, on the other hand, guarantees to sell the call option buyer the underlying stock at a particular price before a certain date. For instance, a writer of an XYZ April 50 call agrees to sell stock at $50 a share to the call buyer any time before April.

In exchange for granting this right, the option writer receives a payment called an OPTION PREMIUM. For holders of large portfolios of the premiums from stocks, option writing therefore is a source of additional income.

ORAL CONTRACT contract between two parties that has been spoken, but not agreed to in writing or signed by both parties. Oral contracts are usually legally enforceable, though not in the case of real estate.

OR BETTER indication, abbreviated OB on the ORDER TICKET of a LIMIT ORDER to buy or sell securities, that the broker should transact the order at a price better than the specified LIMIT PRICE if a better price can be obtained.

ORDER
Investments: instruction to a broker or dealer to buy or sell securities or commodities. Securities orders fall into four basic categories: MARKET ORDER, LIMIT ORDER, time order, and STOP ORDER.
Law: direction from a court of jurisdiction, or a regulation.

Negotiable instruments: payee's request to the maker, as on a cheque stating, "Pay to the order of (when presented by) John Doe."

Trade: request to buy, sell, deliver, or receive goods or services which commits the issuer of the order to the terms specified.

ORDER IMBALANCE large number of buy or sell orders for a stock, causing an unusually wide spread between bid and offer prices. Stock exchanges frequently halt trading of a stock with a significant order imbalance until more buyers or sellers appear and an orderly market can be reestablished. A significant order imbalance on the buying side can occur when there is an announcement of an impending takeover of the company, better-than-expected earnings, or other unexpected positive news. A significant order imbalance on the selling side can occur when a takeover offer has fallen through, a key executive has left the company, earnings came in far worse than expected, or there is other unexpected negative news.

ORDER ROOM department in a brokerage firm that receives all orders to buy or sell securities. ORDER TICKETS are processed through the order room.

ORDER SPLITTING practice prohibited by most stock exchanges in Canada and by rules of the National Association of Securities Dealers (NASD) whereby brokers might split orders in order to qualify them as small orders for purposes of automatic execution by the SMALL ORDER EXECUTION SYSTEM (SOES).

ORDER TICKET form completed by a registered representative (ACCOUNT EXECUTIVE) of a brokerage firm, upon receiving order instructions from a customer. It shows whether the order is to buy or to sell, the number of units, the name of the security, the kind of order (ORDER MARKET, LIMIT ORDER or STOP ORDER) and the customer's name or code number. After execution of the order on the exchange floor or in the firm's trading department (if over the counter), the price is written and circled on the order ticket, and the completing broker is indicated by number. The order ticket must be retained for a certain period in compliance with federal law.

ORDINARY INTEREST simple interest based on a 360-day year rather than on a 365-day year (the latter is called *exact interest*). The difference between the two bases when calculating daily interest on large sums of money can be substantial. The ratio of ordinary interest to exact interest is 1.0139.

ORGANIZATION CHART chart showing the interrelationships of positions within an organization in terms of authority and responsibility. There are basically three patterns of organization: *line organization,* in which a single manager has final authority over a group of foremen or middle management supervisors; *functional organization,* in which a general manager supervises a number of managers identified by function; and *line and staff organization,* which is a combination of line and functional organization, with specialists in particular functions holding staff positions where they advise line officers concerned with actual production.

ORGANIZED SECURITIES EXCHANGE STOCK EXCHANGE as distinguished from an OVER-THE-COUNTER MARKET. *See also* SECURITIES AND COMMODITIES EXCHANGES.

ORIGINAL COST
1. in accounting, all costs associated with the acquisition of an asset.
2. in public utilities accounting, the acquisition cost incurred by the entity that first devotes a property to public use; normally, the utility company's cost for the property. It is used to establish the rate to be charged customers in order to provide the utility company with a FAIR RATE OF RETURN on capital.

ORIGINAL MATURITY interval between the issue date and the maturity date of a bond, as distinguished from CURRENT MATURITY, which is the time difference between the present time and the maturity date. For example, in 1997 a bond issued in 1995 to mature in 2010 would have an original maturity of 15 years and a current maturity of 13 years.

ORIGINATOR
1. bank, savings and loan, or mortgage banker that initially made the mortgage loan comprising part of a pool of mortgages.
2. investment banking firm that worked with the issuer of a new securities offering from the early planning stages and that usually is appointed manager of the underwriting SYNDICATE; more formally called the *originating investment banker.*
3. in banking terminology, the initiator of money transfer instructions.

ORPHAN STOCK stock that has been neglected by research analysts. Since the company's story is rarely followed and the stock infrequently recommended, it is considered an orphan by investors. Orphan stocks may not attract much attention because they are too small, or because they have disappointed investors in the past. Because they are followed by so few investors, orphan stocks tend to trade at low price/earnings ratios. However, if the company assembles a solid record of rising profitability, it can be discovered again by research analysts, boosting the stock price and price/earnings ratio significantly. Investors who buy the stock when it is still a neglected orphan can thereby earn high returns. Also called a *wallflower.*

OSLO STOCK EXCHANGE smallest of the Scandinavian exchanges. Founded in 1819 as a foreign exchange market, it later was a commodity exchange; securities were launched in 1881. The stock exchanges in Bergen and Trondheim, Norway, are branches of the OSE. The OSE trades stocks, bonds, and stock options, and is considered the options market of Norway. Energy-related companies dominate the listings. The Oslo Stock Exchange General Price Index is made up of nearly 50 stocks. All trading is conducted electronically, and trades are settled a maximum of seven days from the transaction date. Trading hours are 8:30 A.M. to 4:30 P.M., Monday through Friday.

OTC *see* OVER THE COUNTER.

OTC BULLETIN BOARD electronic listing of bid and asked quotations of over-the-counter stocks not meeting the minimum-net worth and other requirements of the NASDAQ stock-listing system. The new system, which was developed by the National Association of Securities Dealers (NASD) and approved by the Securities and Exchange Commission in 1990, provides continuously updated data on domestic stocks and twice-daily updates on foreign stocks. It was designed to facilitate trading and provide greater surveillance of stocks traditionally reported on once daily in the PINK SHEETS published by NATIONAL QUOTATION BUREAU.

OTHER INCOME heading on a profit and loss statement for income from activities not in the normal course of business: sometimes called *other revenue.* Examples: interest on customers' notes, dividends and interest from investments, profit from the disposal of assets other than inventory, gain on foreign exchange, miscellaneous rent income. *See also* EXTRAORDINARY ITEM.

OTHER PEOPLE'S MONEY *see* OPM.

OTHER TSE INDEX approximately 15 stock indices, also calculated by the TSE, based on narrow industry groupings such as the Oil and Gas Index, the Gold and Silver Index, the Merchandising Index, and the High Technology Index.

OUT-OF-FAVOUR INDUSTRY OR STOCK industry or stock that is currently unpopular with investors. For example, the investing public may be disenchanted with an industry's poor earnings outlook. If interest rates were rising, interest-sensitive stocks such as banks and savings and loans would be out of favour because rising rates might harm these firms' profits. CONTRARIAN investors—those who consciously do the opposite of most other investors—tend to buy out-of-favour stocks because they can be bought cheaply. When the earnings of these stocks pick up, contrarians typically sell the stocks. Out-of-favour stocks tend to have a low PRICE/EARNINGS RATIO.

OUT OF LINE term describing a stock that is too high or too low in price in comparison with similar-quality stocks. A comparison of this sort is usually based on the PRICE/EARNINGS RATIO (PE), which measures how much investors are willing to pay for a firm's earnings prospects. If most computer industry stocks had PEs of 15, for instance, and XYZ Computers had a PE of only 10, analysts would say that XYZ's price is out of line with the rest of the industry.

OUT OF THE MONEY term used to describe an OPTION whose STRIKE PRICE for a stock is either higher than the current market value, in the case of a CALL, or lower, in the case of a PUT. For example, an XYZ December 60 CALL option would be out of the money when XYZ stock was selling for $55 a share. Similarly, an XYZ December 60 PUT OPTION would be out of the money when XYZ stock was selling for $65 a share.

Someone buying an out-of-the-money option hopes that the option will move IN THE MONEY, or at least in that direction. The buyer of the above XYZ call would want the stock to climb above $60 a share, whereas the put buyer would like the stock to drop below $60 a share.

OUTSIDE DIRECTOR member of a company's BOARD OF DIRECTORS who is not an employee of the company. Such directors are considered important because they are presumed to bring unbiased opinions to major corporate decisions and also can contribute diverse experience to the decision-making process. A retailing company may have outside directors with experience in finance and manufacturing, for instance. To avoid conflict of interest, outside directors never serve on the boards of two directly competing corporations. Directors receive fees from the company in return for their service, usually a set amount for each board meeting they attend.

OUTSTANDING
1. unpaid; used of ACCOUNTS RECEIVABLE and debt obligations of all types.
2. not yet presented for payment, as a cheque or draft.
3. stock held by shareholders, shown on corporate balance sheets under the heading of CAPITAL STOCK issued and outstanding.

OUT THE WINDOW term describing the rapid way a very successful NEW ISSUE of securities is marketed to investors. An issue that goes out the window is also called a BLOWOUT. *See also* HOT ISSUE.

OVERALL MARKET PRICE COVERAGE total assets less intangibles divided by the total of (1) the MARKET VALUE of the security issue in question and (2) the BOOK VALUE of liabilities and issues having a prior claim. The answer indicates the extent to which the market value of a particular CLASS of securities is covered in the event of a company's liquidation.

OVERBOOKED *see* OVERSUBSCRIBED.

OVERBOUGHT description of a security or a market that has recently experienced an unexpectedly sharp price rise and is therefore vulnerable to a price drop (called a CORRECTION by technical analysts). When a stock has been overbought, there are fewer buyers left to drive the price up further. *See also* OVERSOLD.

OVERDRAFT extension of credit by a lending institution. An overdraft cheque for which there are not sufficient funds (NSF) available may be rejected (bounced) by the bank. A bounced-cheque charge will be assessed on the cheque-writer's account. Alternatively, the bank customer may set up an overdraft loan account, which will cover NSF cheques. While the customer's cheque will clear, the account will be charged overdraft cheque fees or interest on the outstanding balance of the loan starting immediately.

OVERHANG sizable block of securities or commodities contracts that, if released on the market, would put downward pressure on prices. Examples of overhang include shares held in a dealer's inventory, a large institutional holding, a secondary distribution still in registration, and a large commodity position about to be liquidated. Overhang inhibits buying activity that would otherwise translate into upward price movement.

OVERHEAD
1. costs of a business that are not directly associated with the production or sale of goods or services. Also called INDIRECT COSTS AND EXPENSES, *burden* and, in Great Britain, *on costs*.
2. sometimes used in a more limited sense, as in manufacturing or factory overhead.
   See also DIRECT OVERHEAD.

OVERHEATING term describing an economy that is expanding so rapidly that economists fear a rise in INFLATION. In an overheated economy, too much money is chasing too few goods, leading to price rises, and the productive capacity of a nation is usually nearing its limit. *See also* MONETARY POLICY; OPTIMUM CAPACITY.

OVERISSUE shares of CAPITAL STOCK issued in excess of those authorized. Preventing overissue is the function of a corporation's REGISTRAR (usually a bank acting as agent), which works closely with the TRANSFER AGENT in canceling and reissuing certificates presented for transfer and in issuing new shares.

OVERNIGHT POSITION broker-dealer's LONG POSITION or SHORT POSITION in a security at the end of a trading day.

OVERNIGHT REPO in the United States, overnight REPURCHASE AGREEMENT; an arrangement whereby securities dealers and banks finance their inventories of Treasury bills, notes, and bonds. The dealer or bank sells securities to an investor with a temporary surplus of cash, agreeing to buy them back the next day. Such transactions are settled immediately available FEDERAL FUNDS, usually at a rate below the federal funds rate (the rate charged by banks lending funds to each other).

OVERSHOOT to exceed a target figure, such as an economic goal or an earnings projection.

OVERSOLD description of a stock or market that has experienced an unexpectedly sharp price decline and is therefore due, according to some proponents of TECHNICAL ANALYSIS, for an imminent price rise. If all those who wanted to sell a stock have done so, there are no sellers left, and so the price will rise. *See also* OVERBOUGHT.

OVERSUBSCRIBED underwriting term describing a new stock issue for which there are more buyers than available shares. An oversubscribed, or *overbooked,* issue often will jump in price as soon as its shares go on the market, since the buyers who could not get shares will want to buy once the stock starts trading. In some cases, an issuer will increase the number of shares available if the issue is oversubscribed. *See also* GREEN SHOE; HOT ISSUE.

OVER THE COUNTER (OTC)
1. security that is not listed and traded on an organized exchange.
2. market in which securities transactions are conducted through a telephone and computer network connecting dealers in stocks and bonds, rather than on the floor of an exchange.

Over-the-counter stocks are traditionally those of smaller companies that do not meet the LISTING REQUIREMENTS of the Toronto or New York Stock Exchange or the American Stock Exchange. In recent years, however, many companies that qualify for listing have chosen to remain with over-the-counter trading, because they feel that the system of multiple trading by many dealers is preferable to the centralized trading approach of the Toronto or New York Stock Exchange, where all trading in a stock has to go through the exchange SPECIALIST in that stock. The rules of over-the-counter stock trading are written and enforced largely by the NATIONAL ASSOCIATION OF SECURITIES DEALERS (NASD), a self-regulatory group. Prices of over-the-counter stocks are published in daily newspapers, with the NATIONAL MARKET SYSTEM stocks listed separately from the rest of the over-the-counter market. Other over-the-counter markets include those for government and municipal bonds. *See also* NASDAQ.

OVERVALUED description of a stock whose current price is not justified by the earnings outlook or the PRICE/EARNINGS RATIO. It is therefore expected that the stock will drop in price. Overvaluation may result from an emotional buying spurt, which inflates the market price of the stock, or from a deterioration of the company's financial strength. The opposite of overvalued is UNDERVALUED. *See also* FULLY VALUED.

OVERWRITING speculative practice by an OPTION WRITER who believes a security to be overpriced or underpriced and sells CALL OPTIONS or PUT OPTIONS on the security in quantity, assuming they will not be exercised. *See also* OPTION.

OWNER'S EQUITY PAID-IN CAPITAL, donated capital, and RETAINED EARNINGS less the LIABILITIES of a corporation. In a proprietorship or partnership, equity is each owner's original investment, plus any earnings and minus any withdrawals. In a corporation, equity is the sum of contributors, plus earnings retained after paying dividends.

P

PACIFIC STOCK EXCHANGE *see* REGIONAL STOCK EXCHANGES.

PAC-MAN STRATEGY technique used by a corporation that is the target of a takeover bid to defeat the acquirer's wishes. The TARGET COMPANY defends itself by threatening to take over the acquirer and begins buying its common shares. For instance, if company A moves to take over company B against the wishes of the management of company B, company B will begin buying shares in company A in order to thwart A's takeover attempt. The Pac-Man strategy is named after a popular video game of the early 1980s, in which each character that does not swallow its opponents is itself consumed. *See also* TAKEOVER; TENDER OFFER.

PAID-IN CAPITAL capital received from investors in exchange for stock, as distinguished from capital generated from earnings or donated. The paid-in capital account includes CAPITAL STOCK and contributions of stockholders credited to accounts other than capital stock, such as an excess over PAR value received from the sale or exchange of capital stock. It would also include surplus resulting from RECAPITALIZATION. Paid-in capital is sometimes classified more specifically as *additional paid-in capital, paid-in surplus,* or *capital surplus.* Such accounts are distinguished from RETAINED EARNINGS or its older variation, EARNED SURPLUS. *See also* DONATED STOCK.

PAID-IN SURPLUS *see* PAID-IN CAPITAL.

PAID UP a situation in which all payments due have been made. For example, if all premiums on a life insurance policy have been paid, it is known as a PAID-UP POLICY.

PAID-UP POLICY life insurance policy in which all premiums have been paid. Some policies require premium payments for a limited number of years, and if all premium payments have been made over those years, the policy is considered paid in full and requires no more premium payments. Such a policy remains in force until the insured person dies or cancels the policy.

PAINTING THE TAPE
1. illegal practice by manipulators who buy and sell a particular security among themselves to create artificial trading activity, causing a succession of trades to be reported on the CONSOLIDATED TAPE and luring unwary investors to the "action." After causing movement in the market price of the security, the manipulators hope to sell at a profit.
2. consecutive or frequent trading in a particular security, resulting in its repeated appearances on the ticker tape. Such activity is usually attributable to special investor interest in the security.

PAIRED SHARES common stocks of two companies under the same management that are sold as a unit, usually appearing as a single certificate printed front and back. Also called *Siamese shares* or *stapled stock.*

P & I abbreviations for *principal* and *interest* on bonds or mortgage-backed securities. A traditional debt instrument such as a bond makes periodic interest payments and returns bondholders' principal when the bond matures. But in many cases, the principal payment and each of the interest payments are separated from each other by brokerage firms and sold in pieces. When accomplished with government bonds, each of the individual interest payments and the final principal payment is sold as a "stripped" zero-coupon bond known as a STRIP. In the case of a mortgage-backed security, each of the interest payments and principal repayments from mortgagees is packaged into a COLLATERALIZED MORTGAGE OBLIGATION. A security composed of only interest payments is known as an *interest-only* or *IO* security. A security composed of just principal repayments is known as a *principal-only* or PO security. Both IOs and POs are forms of DERIVATIVE SECURITIES.

P & L *see* PROFIT AND LOSS STATEMENT.

PANIC BUYING OR SELLING flurry of buying or selling accompanied by high volume done in anticipation of sharply rising or falling prices. A sudden news event will trigger panic buying or selling, leaving investors little time to evaluate the fundamentals of individual stocks or bonds. Panic buying may be caused by an unexpected cut in interest rates or outcome of a political election. Short sellers may also be forced into panic buying if stock prices start to rise quickly, and they have to cover their short positions to prevent further losses. Panic selling may be set off by an international crisis such as a war or currency devaluation, the assassination of a head of state, or other unforeseen event. If stock prices start to fall sharply, investors may start to panic sell because they fear prices will fall much farther.

PAPER shorthand for *short-term commercial paper,* which is an unsecured note issued by a corporation. The term is also more loosely used to refer to all debt issued by a company, as in "ABC has $100 million in short and long-term paper outstanding."

PAPER DEALER brokerage firm that buys COMMERCIAL PAPER at one rate of interest, usually discounted, and resells it at a lower rate to banks and other investors, making a profit on the difference.

PAPER GAIN situation where, if, before the execution of the contract, the market price of the underlying commodity rises above the contract price, you have a paper gain of the difference in prices. *See also* PAPER PROFIT OR LOSS.

PAPER PROFIT OR LOSS unrealized CAPITAL GAIN or CAPITAL LOSS in an investment or PORTFOLIO. Paper profits and losses are calculated by comparing the current market prices of all stocks, bonds, mutual funds, and commodities in a portfolio to the prices at which those assets were originally bought. These profits or losses become realized only when the securities are sold.

PAPER TRADING *see* MOCK TRADING.

PAR equal to the nominal or FACE VALUE of a security. A bond selling at par, for instance, is worth the same dollar amount it was issued for or at which it will be redeemed at maturity—typically, $1000 per bond.

With COMMON STOCK, par value is set by the company issuing the stock At one time, par value represented the original investment behind each share of stock in goods, cash, and services, but today this is rarely the case. Instead, it is an assigned amount (such as $1 a share) used to compute the dollar accounting value of the common shares on a company's balance sheet. Par value has no relation to MARKET VALUE, which is determined by such considerations as NET ASSET VALUE, YIELD, and investors' expectations of future earnings. Some companies issue NO-PAR VALUE STOCK. *See also* STATED VALUE.

Par value has more importance for bonds and PREFERRED STOCK. The interest paid on bonds is based on a percentage of a bond's par value—a 10% bond pays 10% of the bond's par value annually. Preferred dividends are normally stated as a percentage of the par value of the preferred stock issue.

PAR BOND bond that is selling at PAR, the amount equal to its nominal value or FACE VALUE. A corporate bond redeemable at maturity for $1000 is a par bond when it trades on the market for $1000.

PARENT COMPANY company that owns or controls subsidiaries through the ownership of voting stock. A parent company is usually an operating company in its own right; where it has no business of its own, the term HOLDING COMPANY is often preferred.

PARETO'S LAW theory that the pattern of income distribution is constant, historically and geographically, regardless of taxation or welfare policies; also called *law of the trivial many and the critical few* or *80-20 law.* Thus, if 80% of a nation's income will benefit only 20% of the population, the only way to improve the economic lot of the poor is to increase overall output and income levels.

Other applications of the law include the idea that in most business activities a small percentage of the work force produces the major portion of output or that 20% of the customers account for 80% of the dollar volume of sales. The law is attributed to Vilfredo Pareto, an Italian-Swiss engineer and economist (1848–1923).

Pareto is also credited with the concept called *Paretian optimum* (or *optimality*) that resources are optimally distributed when an individual cannot move into a better position without putting someone else into a worse position.

PARI PASSU term indicating side-by-side at an equal rate or in equal installments or, in terms of security, ranking equally.

PARIS BOURSE national stock market of France, formed in 1991 when the computerized trading system in Paris was extended to the regional exchanges. The electronic system, modeled on the CATS (Computer Assisted Trading System) system at the TORONTO STOCK EXCHANGE, operates from 10 A.M. to 5 P.M., Monday through Friday. SOCIETES DE BOURSE are the brokerage firms that trade on the exchange. The CAC 40 INDEX is the underlying index for derivative products which are traded on the MONEP, a subsidiary of the Paris Bourse. The SBF 120 Index is made up of the top 120 stocks based on liquidity and capitalization. The SBF 250 Index is the indicator of the wider French economy. Settlement is three business days after the trade.

PARITY *see* CONVERSION PARITY.

PARITY PRICE price for a commodity or service that is pegged to another price or to a composite average of prices based on a selected prior period. As the two sets of prices vary, they are reflected in an index number on a scale of 100. Parity price is no longer commonly used in Canada.

The concept of parity is also widely applied in industrial wage contracts as a means of preserving the real value of wages.

PARKING placing assets in a safe investment while other investment alternatives are under consideration. For instance, an investor will park the proceeds of a stock or bond sale in an interest-bearing money market fund while considering what other stocks or bonds to purchase. Term also refers to an illegal practice whereby ownership of stock is concealed, and DISCLOSURE requirements circumvented, by holding stock in the name of a conspiring party.

PARTIAL DELIVERY term used when a broker does not deliver the full amount of a security or commodity called for by a contract. If 10,000 shares were to be delivered, for example, and only 7000 shares are transferred, it is called a partial delivery.

PARTICIPATING DIVIDEND dividend paid from PARTICIPATING PREFERRED STOCK.

PARTICIPATING FEATURE PREFERRED SHARE preferred share that, in addition to its fixed rate of prior dividend, share with the common shares in further dividend distributions and in capital distributions above its par value in liquidation.

PARTICIPATING LIFE INSURANCE POLICIES life insurance that pays dividends to policyholders. The policyholders participate in the success or failure of the company's underwriting and investment performance by having their dividends rise or fall. The fewer claims the company experiences and the better its investment performance, the higher the dividends. Policyholders have many choices in what they can do with the dividends. They can have them paid in cash, in which case the income is taxable in the year received; they can use them to reduce policy premiums; they can buy more paid-up insurance, either cash value or term; or they can put them in an account with the insurance company that earns interest. The opposite of a participating policy is a NONPARTICIPATING LIFE INSURANCE POLICY.

PARTICIPATING PREFERRED SHARE preferred share that has certain rights to share in the profit of the company over the above specified dividend rate.

PARTICIPATING PREFERRED STOCK PREFERRED STOCK that, in addition to paying a stipulated dividend, gives the holder the right to participate with the common stockholder in additional distributions of earnings under specified conditions. One example would be an arrangement whereby preferred shareholders are paid $5 per share, then common shareholders are paid $5 per share, and then preferred and common shareholders share equally in further dividends up to $1 per share in any one year.

Participating preferred issues are rare. They are used when special measures are necessary to attract investors. Most preferred stock is *nonparticipating preferred stock,* paying only the stipulated dividends.

PARTICIPATION LOAN
Commercial lending: loan made by more than one lender and serviced (administered) by one of the participants, called the *lead bank* or *lead lender.* Participation loans make it possible for large borrowers to obtain bank financing when the amount involved exceeds the lending limit or exposure desired by a bank.
Real estate: mortgage loan, made by a lead lender, in which other lenders own an interest.

PARTNERSHIP contract between two or more people in a joint business who agree to pool their funds and talent and share in the profits and losses of the enterprise. Those who are responsible for the day-to-day management of the partnership's activities, whose individual acts are binding on the other partners, and who are personally liable for the partnership's total liabilities are called *general partners.* Those who contribute only money and are not involved in management decisions are called *limited partners;* their liability is limited to their investment.

Partnerships are a common form of organization for service professions such as accounting and law. Each accountant or lawyer made a partner earns a percentage of the firm's profits.

Limited partnerships are also sold to investors by brokerage firms, financial planners, and other registered representatives. Limited partnerships invest in real estate, oil and gas, research and development, and filming. Some of these partnerships are oriented towards offering tax advantages and capital gains to limited partners.

See also GENERAL PARTNER; LIMITED PARTNERSHIP; OIL AND GAS LIMITED PARTNERSHIP.

PARTNERSHIP AGREEMENT written agreement among partners specifying the conduct of the partnership, including the division of earnings, procedures for dividing up assets if the partnership is dissolved, and steps to be followed when a partner becomes disabled or dies. Investors in LIMITED PARTNERSHIPS also receive partnership agreements, detailing their rights and responsibilities.

PAR VALUE *see* PAR.

PAR VALUE OF CURRENCY ratio of one nation's currency unit to that of another country, as defined by the official exchange rates between the two countries; also called *par of exchange* or *par exchange rate.* Since 1971, exchange rates have been allowed to float; that is, instead of official rates of exchange, currency values are being determined by the forces of supply and demand in combination with the buying and selling by countries of their own currencies in order to stabilize the market value, a form of PEGGING.

PASSBOOK book issued by a bank to record deposits, withdrawals, and interest earned in a savings account, usually known as a passbook savings account. The passbook lists the depositor's name and account number as well as all transactions. Passbook savings accounts, though usually offering low yields, are safe because deposits in them are insured up to $60,000 by Canadian Deposit Insurance Corporation. There are many alternatives to passbooks today, including ABMs, telephone banking services, and debit cards.

PASSED DIVIDEND *see* OMITTED DIVIDEND; CUMULATIVE PREFERRED.

PASSIVE income or loss from activities in which an individual does not materially participate, such as LIMITED PARTNERSHIPS, as distinguished from (1) income from wages and active trade or business or (2) *investment (or portfolio) income,* such as dividends and interest.

PASSIVE INVESTING investing in a MUTUAL FUND that replicates a market index, such as the STANDARD & POOR'S INDEX, thus assuring investment performance no worse (or better) than the market as a whole. An INDEX FUND charges a much lower MANAGEMENT FEE than an ordinary mutual fund.

PASS THE BOOK system to transfer responsibility for a brokerage firm's trading account from one office to another around the world as trading ends in one place and begins in another. For example, a firm may start the day with the "book" of the firm's securities inventory controlled in London. As the London market closes, the book will be passed to New York, then Los Angeles, then Tokyo, then Singapore, and back to London. Passing the book is necessary because markets are now traded 24 hours a day. Customers wanting to trade at any time will often be referred to the office handling the book at that time.

PASS-THROUGH SECURITY security, representing pooled debt obligations repackaged as shares, that passes income from debtors through the intermediary to investors. The most common type of pass-through is a MORTGAGE-BACKED SECURITY, usually Central Mortgage Housing Corporation guaranteed, where homeowners' principal and interest payments pass to investors, net of service charges.

PATENT exclusive right to a use a process or produce or sell a particular product for a designated period of time. Patents are normally for 17 years in Canada.

PATTERN technical chart formation made by price movements of stocks, bonds, commodities, or mutual funds. Analysts use patterns to predict future price movements. Some examples of patterns include ASCENDING TOPS; DOUBLE BOTTOM; FLAG; HEAD AND SHOULDERS; RISING BOTTOMS; SAUCER; and TRIANGLE. *See also* TECHNICAL ANALYSIS.

PAWNBROKER individual or employee of a pawn shop who lends money at a high rate of interest to a borrower leaving COLLATERAL such as jewellery, furs, appliances, or other valuable items. If the loan is repaid, the borrower gets the collateral back. If the loan is not repaid, the pawnbroker keeps the collateral, and in many cases, sells it to the public. Borrowers who turn to pawnbrokers and pawn shops typically do not have access to credit from banks or other financial institutions because they are in poor financial condition.

PAYABLES trade or liabilities evidenced by an invoice or other form of documentation.

PAYABLE-THROUGH DRAFT legal, cheque-like instruments drawn on and paid by the issuer rather than the bank. The bank serves only as agent in the clearing process with the drafts flowing through it to the issuer for examination and final payment authorization.

PAYBACK PERIOD in capital budgeting; the length of time needed to recoup the cost of a CAPITAL INVESTMENT. The payback period is the ratio of the initial investment (cash outlay) to the annual cash inflows for the recovery period. The major shortcoming of the payback period method is that it does not take into account cash flows after the payback period and is therefore not a measure of the profitability of an investment project. For this reason, analysts generally prefer the DISCOUNTED CASH FLOW methods of capital budgeting—namely, the INTERNAL RATE OF RETURN and the NET PRESENT VALUE methods.

PAYDOWN
Bonds: refunding by a company of an outstanding bond issue through a smaller new bond issue, usually to cut interest costs. For instance, a company that issued $100 million of 12% bonds a few years ago will pay down (refund) that debt with a new $80 million issue with an 8% yield. The amount of the net deduction is called the paydown.
Lending: repayment of principal short of full payment. *See also* ON ACCOUNT.

PAYEE person receiving payment through a cheque, bill, money order, promissory note, credit card, cash, or other payment method.

PAYER person making a payment to a PAYEE through a cheque, bill, money order, promissory note, cash, credit card, or other form of payment.

PAYING AGENT agent, usually a bank, that receives funds from an issuer of bonds or stock and in turn pays principal and interest to bondholders and dividends to stockholders, usually charging a fee for the service. Sometimes called *disbursing agent.*

PAYMENT DATE date on which a declared stock dividend or a bond interest payment is scheduled to be paid.

PAYMENT IN KIND payment for goods and services made in the form of other goods and services, not cash or other forms of money. Usually, payment in kind is made when the payee returns with the same kind of good or service. For example, if someone's tire blows out, the payee will buy another tire to replace the first one. In the securities world, PAYMENT-IN-KIND SECURITIES pay bondholders in more bonds instead of cash interest. Payment in kind is different from BARTER because the payor gets the same goods and services in return, not other goods or services of equivalent value, as is the case in barter.

PAYMENT-IN-KIND SECURITIES *see* PIK (PAYMENT-IN-KIND) SECURITIES.

PAYOUT RATIO percentage of a firm's profits that is paid out to shareholders in the form of dividends. Young, fast-growing companies reinvest most of their earnings in their business and usually do not pay dividends. Regulated electric, gas, and telephone utility companies have historically paid out larger proportions of their highly dependable earnings in dividends than have other industrial corporations. Since these utilities are limited to a specified return on assets and are thus not able to generate from internal operations the cash flow needed for expansion, they pay large dividends to keep their stock attractive to investors desiring yield and are able to finance growth through new securities offerings. *See also* RETENTION RATE.

PAYROLL WITHHOLDING *see* WITHHOLDING (tax at source).

PAY UP
1. situation when an investor who wants to buy a stock at a particular price hesitates and the stock begins to rise. Instead of letting the stock go, he "pays up" to buy the shares at the higher prevailing price.
2. when an investor buys shares in a high quality company at what is felt to be a high price. Such an investor will say "I realize that I am paying up for this stock, but it is worth it because it is such a fine company."

PBR abbreviation for price to BOOK VALUE ratio, which is the market value of a company's stock divided by its TANGIBLE NET WORTH. This ratio is especially significant to securities analysts where real estate not used in operations is a significant portion of assets, such as in the case of a typical Japanese company.

PC commonly used abbreviation for PARTICIPATION CERTIFICATE and, in brokerage parlance, for *plus commissions* (which are added to purchases and subtracted from sales).

PEACE DIVIDEND term used to describe the reallocation of spending from military purposes to peacetime priorities. After the end of World War II and at the end of the Cold War, government officials spoke of the peace dividend which could be spent on housing, education, social initiatives, deficit reduction, and other programs instead of on maintaining the military establishment.

PEGGING stabilizing the price of a security, commodity, or currency by intervening in a market. For example, until 1971 governments pegged the price of gold at certain levels to stabilize their currencies and would therefore buy it when the price dropped and sell when the price rose. Since 1971, a FLOATING EXCHANGE RATE system has prevailed, in which countries use pegging—the buying or selling of their own currencies—simply to offset fluctuations in the exchange rate.

In floating new stock issues, the managing underwriter is authorized to try to peg the market price and stabilize the market in the issuer's stock by buying shares in the open market.

PENALTY CLAUSE clause found in contracts, borrowing agreements, and savings instruments providing for penalties in the event a contract is not kept, a loan payment is late, or a withdrawal is made prematurely. *See also* PREPAYMENT PENALTY.

PENNANT technical chart pattern resembling a pointed flag, with the point facing to the right. Unlike a FLAG pattern, in which rallies and

PENNANT

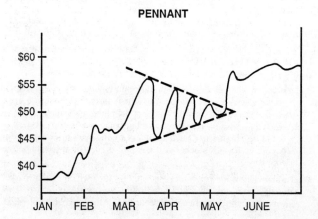

peaks occur in a uniform range, it is formed as the rallies and peaks that give it its shape become less pronounced. A pennant is also characterized by diminishing trade volume. With these differences, this pattern has essentially the same significance as a flag; that is, prices will rise or fall sharply once the pattern is complete.

PENNY STOCK stock that typically sells for less than $1 a share, although it may rise to as much as $10 a share after the initial PUBLIC OFFERING, usually because of heavy promotion. Penny stocks are issued by companies with a short or erratic history of revenues and earnings, and therefore such stocks are more VOLATILE than those of large, well-established firms traded on the Toronto, New York or London stock exchanges. Many brokerage houses therefore have special precautionary rules about trading in these stocks, and the term *penny stocks* is often used as a term of disparagement, although some have developed into investment calibre issues.

All penny stocks are traded OVER-THE-COUNTER, many of them in the local markets of Vancouver, Denver, or Salt Lake City. These markets have had a history of boom and bust, with a speculative fervour for oil, gas, and gold-mining stocks in the Denver penny stock market in the late 1970s turning to bust by the early 1980s.

PENSION FUND fund set up by a corporation, labour union, governmental entity, or other organization to pay the pension benefits of retired workers. Pension funds invest billions of dollars annually in the stock and bond markets, and are therefore a major factor in the supply-demand balance of the markets. Fund managers make actuarial assumptions about how much they will be required to pay out to pensioners and then try to ensure that the RATE OF RETURN on their portfolios equals or exceeds that anticipated payout need.

PENSION PARACHUTE pension agreement that specifies that in the event of a hostile takeover attempt, any excess assets in a company pension plan can be used for the benefit of pension plan participants, such as increasing pension payments. This prevents the raiding firm or individual from using the pension assets to finance the takeover, and therefore acts as an additional deterrent to help the firm ward off the acquisition. A pension parachute is a form of POISON PILL.

PENSION PLAN provides replacement for salary when a person is no longer working. In the case of Canada Pension Plan, employer and employee contribute, the the employer's contribution is deducted at source. In the case of a DEFINED BENEFIT PENSION PLAN, the employer or union contributes to the plan, which pays a predetermined benefit for the rest of the employee's life based on length of service and salary. Payments may be made either directly or through an annuity. Pension payments are taxable income to recipients in the year received. The employer or union has fiduciary responsibility to invest the pension funds in stocks, bonds, real estate, and other assets; earn a satisfactory rate of return; and make payments to retired workers.

In the case of a DEFINED CONTRIBUTION PENSION PLAN, employees choose whether or not to contribute to the plan offered by the employer, who may or may not match employee contributions. Pension benefits are determined by the amount of assets built up by the employee during his or her years of contributions. Self-employed individuals can also set up pension plans such as the Registered Retirement Savings Plan. *See also* VESTING.

PEOPLE PILL defensive tactic to ward off a hostile TAKEOVER. Management threatens that, in the event of a successful takeover, the entire management team will resign at once, leaving the company without experienced leadership. This is a version of the POISON PILL defense.

PER CAPITA in Latin translation, *per head*. In other words, *per person*.

PER CAPITA DEBT total bonded debt of a municipality, divided by its population. A more refined version, called *net per capita debt*, divides the total bonded debt less applicable sinking funds by the total population. The result of either ratio, compared with ratios of prior periods, reveals trends in a municipality's debt burden, which bond analysts evaluate, bearing in mind that, historically, defaults in times of recession have generally followed overexpansion of debts in prior booms.

PERCENTAGE-OF-COMPLETION CAPITALIZED COST METHOD *see* COMPLETED CONTRACT METHOD.

PERCENTAGE ORDER order to a securities broker to buy or sell a specified number of shares of a stock after a fixed number of these shares have been traded. It can be a LIMIT ORDER or a MARKET ORDER and usually applies to one trading day.

PERCS acronym for *preferred equity—redemption cumulative stock*. A form of preferred stock that allows common shareholders to exchange common stock for preferred shares, thereby retaining a high dividend rate. PERCS usually have little appreciation potential, however.

PERFECT COMPETITION market condition wherein no buyer or seller has the power to alter the market price of a good or service. Characteristics of a perfectly competitive market are a large number of buyers and sellers, a homogeneous (similar) good or service, an equal awareness of prices and volume, an absence of discrimination in buying and selling, total mobility of productive resources, and complete freedom of entry. Perfect competition exists only as a theoretical ideal. Also called *pure competition*.

PERFECT HEDGE *see* HEDGE/HEDGING.

PERFORMANCE BOND surety bond given by one party to another, protecting the second party against loss in the event the terms of a contract are not fulfilled. The surety company is primarily liable with the principal (the contractor) for nonperformance. For example, a homeowner having a new kitchen put in may request a performance bond from the home improvement contractor so that the homeowner would receive cash compensation if the kitchen was not done satisfactorily within the agreed upon time.

PERFORMANCE FEE *see* INCENTIVE FEE.

PERFORMANCE FUND MUTUAL FUND designed for growth of capital. A performance fund invests in high-growth companies that do not pay dividends or that pay small dividends. Investors in such funds are willing to take higher-than-average risks in order to earn higher-than-average returns on their invested capital. *See also* GROWTH STOCK; PERFORMANCE STOCK.

PERFORMANCE STOCK high-growth stock that an investor feels will significantly rise in value. Also known as GROWTH STOCK, such a security tends to pay either a small dividend or no dividend at all. Companies whose stocks are in this category tend to retain earnings rather than pay dividends in order to finance their rapid growth. *See also* PERFORMANCE FUND.

PERIODIC PAYMENT PLAN plan to accumulate capital in a mutual fund by making regular investments on a monthly or quarterly basis. The plan has a set pay-in period, which may be 10 or 20 years, and a mechanism to withdraw funds from the plan after that time. Participants in periodic payment plans enjoy the advantages of DOLLAR COST AVERAGING and the diversification among stocks or bonds that is available through a mutual fund. Some plans also include completion insurance, which assures that all scheduled contributions to the plan will continue so that full benefits can be passed on to beneficiaries in the event the participant dies or is incapacitated.

PERIODIC PURCHASE DEFERRED CONTRACT ANNUITY contract for which fixed-amount payments, called *premiums,* are paid either monthly or quarterly and that does not begin paying out until a time elected by the holder (the *annuitant).* In some cases, premium payments may continue after payments from the annuity have begun. A periodic purchase deferred contract can be either fixed or variable. *See also* FIXED ANNUITY; VARIABLE ANNUITY.

PERIOD-CERTAIN ANNUITY annuity that guarantees payments to an ANNUITANT for a particular period of time. For example, a 10-year period-certain annuity will make annuity payments for 10 years and no more. If the annuitant dies before the 10 years have expired, the payments will continue to the policy's beneficiaries for the remaining term. The monthly payment rate for a period-certain annuity is generally higher than the rate for a LIFE ANNUITY because the insurance company knows its maximum liability in advance.

PERIOD OF DIGESTION time period after the release of a NEW ISSUE of stocks or bonds during which the trading price of the security is established in the marketplace. Particularly when an INITIAL PUBLIC

OFFERING is released, the period of digestion may entail considerable VOLATILITY, as investors try to ascertain an appropriate price level for it.

PERMANENT FINANCING
Corporate finance: long-term financing by means of either debt (bonds or long-term notes) or equity (common or preferred stock).

PERMANENT OR WHOLE LIFE INSURANCE any type of life insurance, other than term, that has the following characteristics: a cash value that can be borrowed, used as collateral, or withdrawn by surrendering the policy; and a lump sum benefit payable at death.

PERPENDICULAR SPREAD option strategy using options with similar expiration dates and different strike prices (the prices at which the options can be exercised). A perpendicular spread can be designed for either a bullish or a bearish outlook.

PERPETUAL BOND bond that has no maturity date, is not redeemable and pays a steady stream of interest indefinitely; also called *annuity bond.* The only notable perpetual bonds in existence are the consols first issued by the British Treasury to pay off smaller issues used to finance the Napoleonic Wars (1814).

PERPETUAL INVENTORY inventory accounting system whereby book inventory is kept in continuous agreement with stock on hand; also called *continuous inventory.* A daily record is maintained of both the dollar amount and the physical quantity of inventory, and this is reconciled to actual physical counts at short intervals. Perpetual inventory contrasts with *periodic inventory.*

PERPETUAL WARRANT investment certificate giving the holder the right to buy a specified number of common shares of stock at a stipulated price with no expiration date. *See also* SUBSCRIPTION WARRANT.

PERQUISITE commonly known as a *perk.* A fringe benefit offered to an employee in addition to salary. Some examples of perquisites are reimbursement for educational expenses, legal services, vacation time, pension plans, life insurance coverage, company cars and aircraft, personal financial counseling, and employee assistance hotlines. In general, the higher an employee's position and the more valued he or she in a company, the more perks he or she receives.

PERSONAL ARTICLE FLOATER policy or an addition to a policy, used to cover personal valuables, such as jewellery and furs.

PERSONAL INCOME income received by persons from all sources: from participation in production, from both government and business TRANSFER PAYMENTS and from government interest (which is treated like a transfer payment). "Persons" refers to individuals, nonprofit institutions that primarily serve individuals, private noninsured welfare funds, and private trust funds. Personal income is calculated as the sum of wages and salary disbursements, other labour income, proprietors' income with inventory valuation and personal dividend income, personal interest income, and transfer payments to persons.

PERSONAL INSURANCE insurance that ensures an income stream or a lump-sum benefit to the beneficiary on the death or disability of the insured person.

PERSONAL INFLATION RATE rate of price increases as it affects a specific individual or couple. For example, a young couple with children who are buying and furnishing a home probably will have a much higher personal inflation rate than an elderly couple with their home paid off and self-supporting children, because the young couple need to buy many more things that are likely to rise in price than the elderly couple.

PERSONAL PROPERTY tangible and intangible assets other than real estate.

PERSONAL TAX RETURN tax return filed by an individual instead of a corporation.

PER STIRPES formula for distributing the assets of a person who dies intestate (without a will) according to the "family tree." Under such a distribution, the estate is allocated according to the number of children the deceased had, and distributed accordingly to those surviving the decedent. If any children predeceased the decedent, the share allocated to them would be equally divided among their children and so on.

PETRODOLLARS dollars paid to oil-producing countries and deposited in Western banks. When the price of oil skyrocketed in the 1970s, Middle Eastern oil producers built up huge surpluses of petrodollars that the banks lent to oil-importing countries around the world. By the mid-1980s and 1990s, these surpluses had shrunk because consumption increased while oil exporters spent a good deal of the money on development projects. The flow of petrodollars, therefore, is very important in understanding the current world economic situation. Also called *petrocurrency* or *oil money.*

PHANTOM STOCK PLAN executive incentive concept whereby an executive receives a bonus based on the market appreciation of the company's stock over a fixed period of time. The hypothetical (hence phantom) amount of shares involved in the case of a particular executive is proportionate to his or her salary level. The plan works on the same principle as a CALL OPTION (a right to purchase a fixed amount of stock at a set price by a particular date). Unlike a call option, however, the executive pays nothing for the option and therefore has nothing to lose.

PHILADELPHIA STOCK EXCHANGE *see* REGIONAL STOCK EXCHANGES.

PHILIPPINE STOCK EXCHANGE operates two trading floors, Manila and Makati; Manila is the larger. Trading hours are from

9:30 A.M. to 12 noon, Monday through Friday, with a 15-minute extension at closing prices, and a 10-minute break at 10:50 A.M. Settlement takes place on the fourth business day after a trade.

PHYSICAL COMMODITY actual commodity that is delivered to the contract buyer at the completion of a commodity contract in either the SPOT MARKET or the FUTURES MARKET. Some examples of physical commodities are corn, cotton, gold, oil, soybeans, and wheat. The quality specifications and quantity of the commodity to be delivered are specified by the exchange on which it is traded.

PHYSICAL INVENTORY *see* PHYSICAL VERIFICATION.

PHYSICAL VERIFICATION procedure by which an auditor actually inspects the assets of a firm, particularly inventory, to confirm their existence and value, rather than relying on written records. The auditor may use statistical sampling in the verification process.

PICKUP value gained in a bond swap. For example, bonds with identical coupon rates and maturities may have different market values, mainly because of a difference in quality, and thus in yields. The higher yield of the lower-quality bond received in such a swap compared with the yield of the higher-quality bond that was exchanged for it results in a net gain for the trader, called his or her pickup on the transaction.

PICKUP BOND bond that has a relatively high coupon (interest) rate and is close to the date at which it is callable—that is, can be paid off prior to maturity—by the issuer. If interest rates fall, the investor can look forward to picking up a redemption PREMIUM, since the bond will in all likelihood be called.

PICTURE investment jargon used to request bid and asked prices and quantity information from a specialist or from a dealer regarding a particular security. For example, the question "What's the picture on XYZ?" might be answered, "58⅜ [best bid] to ¾ [best offer is 58¾], 1000 either way [there are both a buyer and a seller for 1000 shares]."

PIGGYBACK clause in shareholders' agreement that allows a party the same rights as another if certain actions are taken by the other. A piggyback buy-sell would mean that if A sold shares, B would have the right either to force sales of his own shares at the same price (piggyback) or buy A's shares at the same price (RIGHT OF FIRST REFUSAL), as well as the alternative of doing nothing.

PIGGYBACKING illegal practice by a broker who buys or sells stocks or bonds in his or her personal account after a customer buys or sells the same security. The broker assumes that the customer is making the trade because of access to material, nonpublic information that will make the stock or bond rise or fall sharply. Trading following customer orders is a conflict of interest, and may be disciplined by the broker's firm or regulatory authorities if discovered.

PIGGYBACK WARRANT second series of warrants acquired upon exercise of primary warrants sold as part of a unit.

PINK SHEETS daily publication in the United States of the NATIONAL QUOTATION BUREAU that details the BID AND ASKED prices of OVER THE COUNTER (OTC) stocks not carried in daily OTC newspaper listings of NASDAQ. Brokerage firms subscribe to the pink sheets—named for their colour—because the sheets not only give current prices but list market makers who trade each stock. Debt securities are listed separately on YELLOW SHEETS. *See also* OTC BULLETIN BOARD.

PIN NUMBER acronym for *personal identification number.* Customers use PIN numbers to identify themselves, such as when performing transactions with a debit card at an automated banking machine.

PIPELINE term referring to the underwriting process that involves securities being proposed for public distribution. The phrase used is "in the pipeline." Underwriters attempt to have several securities issues waiting in the pipeline so that the issues can be sold as soon as market conditions become favorable.

PIT location at a futures or options exchange in which trading takes place. Pits are usually shaped like rings, often with several levels of steps, so that a large number of traders can see and be seen by each other as they conduct business.

PITI acronym for *principal, interest, taxes and insurance,* the primary components of monthly mortgage payments. Many mortgage lenders, to ensure that property taxes and homeowner's insurance premiums are paid on schedule, require that borrowers include these amounts in their monthly payments. The funds are then placed in trust until needed. When calculating how much a house will cost a borrower on a monthly basis, the payment is expressed for PITI.

PLACE to market new securities. The term applies to both public and private sales but is more often used with reference to direct sales to institutional investors, as in PRIVATE PLACEMENT. The terms FLOAT and *distribute* are preferred in the case of a PUBLIC OFFERING.

PLACER sand gravel deposit containing small particles of a valuable mineral such as gold, platinum, tin, or diamonds.

PLANT assets comprising land, buildings, machinery, natural resources, furniture and fixtures, and all other equipment permanently employed. Synonymous with FIXED ASSET.

    In a limited sense, the term is used to mean only buildings or only land and buildings: "property, plant, and equipment" and "plant and equipment."

PLAYING THE MARKET unprofessional buying and selling of stocks, as distinguished from SPECULATION. Both players and speculators are seeking capital gains, but while playing the market is more akin to gambling, speculating is done by professionals taking calculated risks.

PLAZA ACCORD agreement in August of 1985 in which the finance ministers of the Group of 5—the United States, Great Britain, France, Germany, and Japan—met at the Plaza Hotel in New York City to mount a concerted effort to reduce the value of the U.S. dollar against other major currencies. Though the dollar had already begun its decline months earlier, the Plaza Accord accelerated the move. The action was necessary because the dollar had become so strong that it was difficult for U.S. exporters to sell their products abroad, weakening the American economy.

PLC *see* PUBLIC LIABILITY COMPANY.

PLEDGING transferring property, such as securities or the CASH SURRENDER VALUE of life insurance, to a lender or creditor as COLLATERAL for an obligation. *Pledge* and *hypothecate* are synonymous, as they do not involve transfer of title. ASSIGN, although commonly used interchangeably with *pledge* and *hypothecate,* implies transfer of ownership or of the right to transfer ownership at a later date. *See also* HYPOTHECATION.

PLOUGH BACK to reinvest a company's earnings in the business rather than pay out those profits as dividends. Smaller, fast-growing companies usually plough back most or all earnings in their businesses, whereas more established firms pay out more of their profits as dividends.

PLUS
1. plus sign (+) that follows a price quotation on a bond, indicating that the price (normally quoted as a percentage of PAR value refined to 32ds) is refined to 64ths. Thus 95.16 + (95^{16}⁄$_{32}$+ or 95^{32}⁄$_{64}$+) means 95^{33}⁄$_{64}$.
2. plus sign after a transaction price in a listed security (for example, 39½+), indicating that the trade was at a higher price than the previous REGULAR WAY transaction. *See also* PLUS TICK.
3. plus sign before the figure in the column labeled "Change" in the newspaper stock tables, meaning that the closing price of the stock was higher than the previous day's close by the amount stated in the "Change" column.

POINT
Bonds: percentage change of the face value of a bond expressed as a point. For example, a change of 1% is a move of one point. For a bond with a $1000 face value, each point is worth $10, and for a bond with a $5000 face value, each point is $50.

Bond yields are quoted in basis points: 100 basis points make up 1% of yield. *See* BASIS POINT.

Futures/options: measure of price change equal to one one-hundredth of one cent in most futures traded in decimal units. In grains, it is one

quarter of one cent; in Treasury bonds, it is 1% of par. *See also* TICK.
Stocks: change of $1 in the market price of a stock. If a stock has risen
5 points, it has risen by $5 a share.

The movements of stock market averages, such as the Toronto
Stock Exchange 300 Index, are also quoted in points. However, those
points refer not to dollar amounts but to units of movement in the average, which is a composite of weighted dollar values. For example, a
20-point move in the TSE 300 from 4000 to 4020 does *not* mean the
TSE now stands at $4020.

POINT AND FIGURE CHART graphic technique used in TECHNICAL
ANALYSIS to follow the up or down momentum in the price moves of a
security. Point and figure charting disregards the element of time and
is solely used to record changes in price. Every time a price move is
upward, an X is put on the graph above the previous point. Every time
the price moves down, an O is placed one square down. When direction changes, the next column is used. The resulting lines of Xs and Os
will indicate whether the security being charted has been maintaining
an up or a down momentum over a particular time period.

POINT AND FIGURE CHART

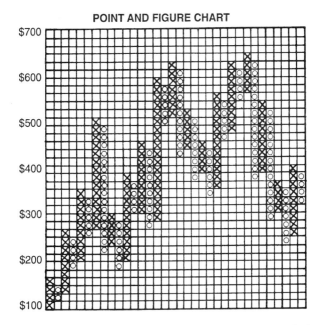

POISON PILL strategic move by a takeover-target company to make its
stock less attractive to an acquirer. For instance, a firm may issue a

new series of PREFERRED STOCK that gives shareholders the right to redeem it at a premium price after a TAKEOVER. Two variations: a *flip-in poison pill* allows all existing holders of target company shares except the acquirer to buy additional shares at a bargain price; a *flip-over poison pill* allows holders of common stock to buy (or holders of preferred stock to convert into) the acquirer's shares at a bargain price in the event of an unwelcome merger. Such measures raise the cost of an ACQUISITION, and cause DILUTION, hopefully deterring a takeover bid. A third type of poison pill, known as a PEOPLE PILL, is the threat that in the event of a successful takeover, the entire management team will resign at once, leaving the company without experienced leadership. Poison pills are relatively new in corporate Canada and there is some controversy over whom they are designed to protect. *See also* PENSION PARACHUTE; SUICIDE PILL.

POLICYHOLDER owner of an INSURANCE contract (policy). Term is commonly used synonymously with *insured,* although the two can be different parties and *insured* is the preferred designation for the person indemnified by the insurance company.

POLICY LIMIT limit of coverage provided by an insurance policy, known as a *maximum lifetime benefit.* For coverage of individuals, roughly two-thirds of existing policies have a limit of $1 million or more.

POLICY LOAN loan from an insurance company secured by the CASH SURRENDER VALUE of a life insurance policy. The amount available for such a loan depends on the number of years the policy has been in effect, the insured's age when the policy was issued, and the size of the death benefit. Such loans are often made at below-market interest rates to policyholders, although more recent policies usually only allow borrowing at rates that fluctuate in line with money market rates. If the loan is not repaid by the insured, the death benefit of the life insurance policy will be reduced by the amount of the loan plus accrued interest.

POOL
Capital budgeting: as used in the phrase "pool of financing," the concept that investment projects are financed out of a pool of funds rather than out of bonds, preferred stock, and common stock individually. A weighted average cost of capital is thus used in analyses evaluating the return on investment projects. *See also* COST OF CAPITAL.
Industry: joining of companies to improve profits by reducing competition.
Investments:
1. combination of resources for a common purpose or benefit. For example, an INVESTMENT CLUB pools the funds of its members, giving them the opportunity to share in a PORTFOLIO offering greater diversification and the hope of a better return on their money than they could get individually. A *commodities pool* entrusts the funds

of many investors to a trading professional and distributes profits and losses among participants in proportion to their interests.

2. group of investors joined together to use their combined power to manipulate security or commodity prices or to obtain control of a corporation.

POOLED SHARE *see* ESCROWED SHARE.

POOLING OF INTEREST interest that occurs when a company issues Treasury shares for the assets of another company so that the latter becomes a division or subsidiary of the acquiring company.

PORCUPINE PROVISIONS *see* SHARK REPELLENTS.

PORTABILITY ability of employees to retain benefits from one employer to the next when switching jobs. The term is most frequently used in connection with pension and insurance coverage.

PORTFOLIO combined holding of more than one stock, bond, commodity, real estate investment, CASH EQUIVALENT, or other asset by an individual or institutional investor. The purpose of a portfolio is to reduce risk by diversification. *See also* PORTFOLIO BETA SCORE; PORTFOLIO THEORY.

PORTFOLIO BETA SCORE relative VOLATILITY of an individual securities portfolio, taken as a whole, as measured by the BETA coefficients of the securities making it up. Beta measures the volatility of a stock relative to the market as a whole, as represented by an index such as Standard & Poor's 500 Stock Index. A beta of 1 means the stock has about the same volatility as the market.

PORTFOLIO INCOME *see* INVESTMENT INCOME.

PORTFOLIO INVESTMENT purchase of shares and bonds made with the objective of realizing income and capital gains, rather than for the purpose of gaining control of a company.

PORTFOLIO MANAGER professional responsible for the securities PORTFOLIO of an individual or INSTITUTIONAL INVESTOR. Also called a *money manager* or, especially when personalized service is involved, an INVESTMENT COUNSEL. A portfolio manager may work for a mutual fund, pension fund, profit-sharing plan, bank trust department, or insurance company. In return for a fee, the manager has the fiduciary responsibility to manage the assets prudently and choose whether stocks, bonds, CASH EQUIVALENTS, real estate, or some other assets present the best opportunities for profit at any particular time. *See also* PORTFOLIO THEORY; PRUDENT-MAN RULE.

PORTFOLIO THEORY sophisticated investment decision approach that permits an investor to classify, estimate, and control both the kind and the amount of expected risk and return; also called *portfolio management theory* or *modern portfolio theory.* Essential to portfolio theory are its quantification of the relationship between risk and return and the assumption that investors must be compensated for assuming risk. Portfolio theory departs from traditional security analysis in shifting emphasis from analyzing the characteristics of individual investments to determining the statistical relationships among the individual securities that comprise the overall portfolio. The portfolio theory approach has four basic steps: *security valuation*—describing a universe of assets in terms of expected return and expected risk; *asset allocation decision*—determining how assets are to be distributed among classes of investment, such as stocks or bonds; *portfolio optimization*—reconciling risk and return in selecting the securities to be included, such as determining which portfolio of stocks offers the best return for a given level of expected risk; and *performance measurement*—dividing each stock's performance (risk) into market-related (systematic) and industry/security-related (residual) classifications.

PORTFOLIO TURNOVER   frequency with which securities are bought and sold. A fund that shows a high portfolio turnover ratio and good performance is better managed than one that shows a high turnover ratio and poor performance.

POSITION
   Banking: bank's net balance in a foreign currency.
   Finance: firm's financial condition.
   Investments:
   1. investor's stake in a particular security or market. A LONG POSITION equals the number of shares *owned;* a SHORT POSITION equals the number of shares *owed* by a dealer or an individual. The dealer's long positions are called his *inventory of securities.*
   2. Used as a verb, to take on a long or a short position in a stock.

POSITION BUILDING   process of buying shares to accumulate a LONG POSITION or of selling shares to accumulate a SHORT POSITION. Large institutional investors who want to build a large position in a particular security do so over time to avoid pushing up the price of the security.

POSITION LIMIT
   Commodities trading: number of contracts that can be acquired in a specific commodity before a speculator is classified as a "large trader."
   Options trading: maximum number of exchange-listed OPTION contracts that can be owned or controlled by an individual holder, or by a group of holders acting jointly, in the same underlying security.

POSITION TRADER   commodities trader who takes a long-term approach—six months to a year or more—to the market. Usually possessing more than average experience, information, and capital, these traders ride through the ups and downs of price fluctuations until close to the delivery date, unless drastic adverse developments threaten. More like insurance underwriters than gamblers, they hope to achieve long-term profits from calculated risks as distinguished from pure speculation.

POSITIVE CARRY situation in which the cost of money borrowed to finance securities is lower than the yield on the securities. For example, if a fixed-income bond yielding 10% is purchased with a loan bearing 8% interest, the bond has positive carry. The opposite situation is called NEGATIVE CARRY.

POSITIVE YIELD CURVE situation in which interest rates are higher on long-term debt securities than on short-term debt securities of the same quality. For example, a positive yield curve exists when 10-year bonds yield 10% and 3-month Treasury bills yield 6%. Such a situation is common, since an investor who ties up his money for a longer time is taking more risk and is usually compensated by a higher yield. When short-term interest rates rise above long-term rates, there is a NEGATIVE YIELD CURVE, also called an INVERTED YIELD CURVE.

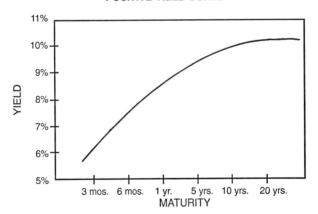

POSITIVE YIELD CURVE

POST
> **Accounting:** to transfer from a journal of original entry detailed financial data, in the chronological order in which it was generated, into a ledger book. Banks post checking account deposits and withdrawals in a ledger, then summarize these transactions on the monthly bank statement.
> **Investments:** horseshoe-shaped structure on the floor of the New York Stock Exchange where specialists trade specific securities. Video

screens surround the post, displaying the bid and offer prices available for stocks traded at that location. Also called *trading post.*

POSTDATED CHEQUE cheque dated in the future. It is not negotiable until the date becomes current.

POSTING in bookkeeping terminology, the transfer of data from a journal to a ledger.

POSTPONING INCOME technique to delay receipt of income into a later year to reduce current tax liability.

POT securities underwriting term meaning the portion of a stock or bond issue returned to the MANAGING UNDERWRITER by the participating investment bankers to facilitate sales to INSTITUTIONAL INVESTORS. Institutions buying from the pot designate the firms to be credited with pot sales. *See also* RETENTION.

POT IS CLEAN MANAGING UNDERWRITER'S announcement to members of the underwriting group that the POT—the portion of the stock or bond issue withheld to facilitate institutional sales—has been sold.

POWER OF ATTORNEY
In general: written document that authorizes a particular person to perform certain acts on behalf of the one signing the document. The document, which must be witnessed by a notary public or some other public officer, may bestow either *full power of attorney* or *limited power of attorney.* It becomes void upon the death of the signer.
Investments: *full power of attorney* might, for instance, allow assets to be moved from one brokerage or bank account to another. A *limited power of attorney,* on the other hand, would only permit transactions within an existing account. A broker given a limited power of attorney, for instance, may buy and sell securities in an account but may not remove them. Such an account is called a DISCRETIONARY ACCOUNT.
See also DISCRETIONARY ORDER; PROXY; STOCK POWER.

PRACTICE INSURANCE general and liability insurance to protect the physical property and finances of a legal, medical, or dental practice.

PREARRANGED TRADING questionable and probably fraudulent practice whereby commodities dealers arrange risk-free trades at predetermined prices, usually to gain tax advantages.

PREAUTHORIZED CHEQUE (PAC) preprinted, normally unsigned, instrument used to transfer funds from an individual to a corporation on a regular basis, with the individual's authorization. The individual sends a cheque marked "void," and the corporation then automatically receives the funds on a preset date.

PREAUTHORIZED CHEQUE PLAN *see* PREAUTHORIZED PAYMENT.

PREAUTHORIZED PAYMENT prearranged deductions from a bank account for the payment of a third party.

PRECEDENCE priority of one order over another on the floor of the exchanges, according to rules designed to protect the DOUBLE-AUCTION SYSTEM. The rules basically are that the highest bid and lowest offer have precedence over other bids and offers, that the first bid or first offer at a price has priority over other bids or offers at that price, and that the size of the order determines precedence thereafter, large orders having priority over smaller orders. Where two orders of equal size must compete for the same limited quantity after the first bid is filled, the impasse is resolved by a flip of the coin. *See also* MATCHED AND LOST. Exchange rules also require that public orders have precedence over trades for floor members' own accounts. *See also* OFF-FLOOR ORDER; ON-FLOOR ORDER.

PRECIOUS METALS gold, silver, platinum, and palladium. These metals are valued for their intrinsic value, backing world currencies, as well as their industrial applications. Fundamental issues of supply and demand are important factors in their prices, along with political and economic considerations, especially when producing countries are involved. Inflation fears will stimulate gold accumulation and higher prices, as will war and natural disaster, especially in major producing or consuming countries or regions. Precious metals are held by central banks and are considered a storehouse of value. While gold is often singled out, cultural factors assign different levels of significance to the metals. In the Far East, especially Japan, platinum traditionally is held in higher regard than gold, both in terms of physical metal and investment holdings, and for personal accumulation (e.g., jewellery and coins). Gold is favoured in the West. In India and the Middle East, silver is highly prized, and the dowries of Indian women are replete with silver jewelry and coins. Investors can buy physical metal in bars, BULLION and NUMISMATIC COINS, and jewellery. There are numerous investment vehicles that do not involve physical delivery: futures and options contracts, mining company stocks, bonds, mutual funds, commodity indices, and commodity funds. The values of these investment vehicles are influenced by metal price volatility, with commodity funds and indices, and futures and options, more sensitive to daily price swings. Many metals analysts and advisors recommend that 5% to 15% of investor portfolios be held in some form of precious metals as a long-term hedge against inflation and political turmoil.

PRECOMPUTE in installment lending, methods of charging interest whereby the total amount of annual interest either is deducted from the face amount of the loan at the time the loan proceeds are disbursed or is added to the total amount to be repaid in equal installments. In both cases, the EFFECTIVE RATE to the borrower is higher than the stated annual rate used in the computation. "Truth in lending" laws require that the effective annual rate be expressed in SIMPLE INTEREST terms.

PREEMPTIVE RIGHT right giving existing stockholders the opportunity to purchase shares of a NEW ISSUE before it is offered to others. Its purpose is to protect shareholders from dilution of value and control when new shares are issued.

PREFERRED DIVIDEND COVERAGE net income after interest and taxes (but before common stock dividends) divided by the dollar amount of preferred stock dividends. The result tells how many times over the preferred dividend requirement is covered by current earnings.

PREFERRED PRIOR STOCK preferred stock that, in liquidation of the issuing company, would rank ahead of other classes of preferred shares as to asset and dividend entitlement.

PREFERRED SHARE share that has some of the features of both debt and common stock. Preferred shares rank ahead of common shares in the event of liquidation but behind other creditors. Usually, preferred stock has a par value and shareholder's claim is limited to that account. Preferred shares state a dividend but payment is discretionary. The return is usually limited to the specified dividend.

PREFERRED STOCK class of CAPITAL STOCK that pays dividends at a specified rate and that has preference over common stock in the payment of dividends and the liquidation of assets. Preferred stock does not ordinarily carry voting rights, but it pays a higher level of investment income and retains a higher level of market stability than common stock.

Most preferred stock is *cumulative;* if dividends are passed (not paid for any reason), they accumulate and must be paid before common dividends. A PASSED DIVIDEND on *noncumulative preferred* stock is generally gone forever. PARTICIPATING PREFERRED STOCK entitles its holders to share in profits above and beyond the declared dividend, along with common shareholders, as distinguished from *nonparticipating preferred,* which is limited to the stipulated dividend. *Adjustable-rate preferred* stock pays a dividend that is adjustable, usually quarterly, based on changes in the Treasury bill rate or other money market rates. *Convertible preferred stock* is exchangeable for a given number of common shares and thus tends to be more VOLATILE than *nonconvertible preferred,* which behaves more like a fixed-income bond. *See also* CONVERTIBLE; CUMULATIVE PREFERRED; PARTICIPATING PREFERRED.

PREFERRED STOCK RATIO PREFERRED STOCK at PAR value divided by total CAPITALIZATION; the result is the percentage of capitalization—bonds and net worth—represented by preferred stock.

PRELIMINARY PROSPECTUS first document released by an underwriter of a NEW ISSUE to prospective investors. The document offers financial details about the issue but does not contain all the information that will appear in the final or statutory prospectus, and parts of the document may be changed before the final prospectus is issued.

Because portions of the cover page of the preliminary prospectus are printed in red ink, it is popularly called the *red herring.*

PREMIUM

In general: extra payment usually made as an incentive.

Bonds:

1. amount by which a bond sells above its face (PAR) value. For instance, a bond with a face value of $1000 would sell for a $100 premium when it cost $1100. The same meaning also applies to preferred stock. *See also* PREMIUM BOND; PREMIUM OVER BOND VALUE; PREMIUM OVER CONVERSION VALUE.

2. amount by which the REDEMPTION PRICE to the issuer exceeds the face value when a bond is called. *See also* CALL PREMIUM.

Insurance: fee paid to an insurance company for insurance protection. Also, the single or multiple payments made to build an ANNUITY fund.

Options: price a put or call buyer must pay to a put or call seller (writer) for an option contract. The premium is determined by market supply and demand forces. *See also* OPTION; PREMIUM INCOME.

Stocks:

1. charge occasionally paid by a short seller when stock is borrowed to make delivery on a SHORT SALE.

2. amount by which a stock's price exceeds that of other stocks to which it is comparable. For instance, securities analysts might say that XYZ Foods is selling at a 15% premium to other food company stocks—an indication that the stock is more highly valued by investors than its industry peers. It does not necessarily mean that the stock is overpriced, however. Indeed, it may indicate that the investment public has only begun to recognize the stock's market potential and that the price will continue to rise. Similarly, analysts might say that the food industry is selling for a 20% premium to Standard & Poor's 500 index, indicating the relative price strength of the industry group to the stock market as a whole.

3. in new issues, amount by which the trading price of the shares exceeds the OFFERING PRICE.

4. amount over market value paid in a *tender offer. See also* PREMIUM RAID.

PREMIUM BOND bond with a selling price above face or redemption value. A bond with a face value of $1000, for instance, would be called a premium bond if it sold for $1050. This price does not include any ACCRUED INTEREST due when the bond is bought. When a premium bond is called before scheduled maturity, bondholders are usually paid more than face value, though the amount may be less than the bond is selling for at the time of the CALL.

PREMIUM INCOME income received by an investor who sells a PUT OPTION or a CALL OPTION. An investor collects premium income by writing a COVERED OPTION, if he or she owns the underlying stock, or a NAKED OPTION, if he or she does not own the stock. An investor who sells options to collect premium income hopes that the underlying stock will not rise very much (in the case of a call) or fall very much (in the case of a put).

PREMIUM OVER BOND VALUE upward difference between the market value of a CONVERTIBLE bond and the price at which a straight bond of the same company would sell in the same open market. A convertible bond, eventually convertible to common stock, will normally sell at a PREMIUM over its bond value because investors place a value on the conversion feature. The higher the market price of the issuer's stock is relative to the price at which the bond is convertible, the greater the premium will be, reflecting the investor's tendency to view it more as a stock than as a bond. When the stock price falls near or below the conversion price, investors then tend to view the convertible as a bond and the premium narrows or even disappears. Other factors affecting the prices of convertible bonds generally include lower transaction costs on the convertibles than would be incurred in buying the stock outright, an attraction that exerts some upward pressure on the premium; the demand from life insurance companies and other institutional investors that are limited by law as to the common stock investments they can have and that gain their equity participation through convertibles; the duration period of the option to convert—the longer it is, the more valuable the future and the higher the premium; high dividends on the issuer's common stock, a factor increasing demand for the common versus the convertible, and therefore a downward pressure. *See also* PREMIUM OVER CONVERSION VALUE.

PREMIUM OVER CONVERSION VALUE amount by which the MARKET PRICE of a CONVERTIBLE preferred stock or convertible bond exceeds the price at which it is convertible. Convertibles (CVs) usually sell at a PREMIUM for two basic reasons: (1) if the convertible is a bond, the bond value—defined as the price at which a straight bond of the same company would sell in the same open market—is the lowest value the CV will reach; it thus represents DOWNSIDE RISK protection, which is given a value in the marketplace, generally varying with the VOLATILITY of the common stock; (2) the conversion privilege is given a value by investors because they might find it profitable eventually to convert the securities.

At relatively high common-stock price levels, a convertible tends to sell for its common stock equivalent and the conversion value becomes negligible. This occurs because investors are viewing the security as a common stock, not as a bond, and because conversion would be preferable to redemption if the bond were called. On the other hand, when the market value of the convertible is close to its bond value, the conversion feature has little value and the security is valued more as a bond. It is here that the CONVERSION PREMIUM is highest. The conversion premium is also influenced to some extent by transaction costs, insurance company investment restrictions, the duration of the conversion OPTION, and the size of common dividends. *See also* PRE-MIUM OVER BOND VALUE.

PREMIUM RAID surprise attempt to acquire a position in a company's stock by offering holders an amount—or premium—over the market value of their shares. The term *raid* assumes that the motive is control and not simply investment. Attempts to acquire control are regulated by federal laws that require disclosure of the intentions of those seeking shares. *See also* TENDER OFFER; WILLIAMS ACT.

PRENUPTIAL CONTRACT agreement between a future husband and wife that details how the couple's financial affairs are to be handled both during the marriage and in the event of divorce. The agreement may cover insurance protection, ownership of housing and securities, and inheritance rights. Such contracts may not be accepted in a court of law.

PREPAID EXPENSE expense that has been paid in advance of use of the good or service it has purchased. Insurance, fuel, oil, and telephone service may all be classed as prepaid expenses.

PREPAID INTEREST asset account representing interest paid in advance. The interest is expensed, that is, charged to the borrower's profit and loss statement (P & L), as it is earned by the lender. Synonymous with UNEARNED INTEREST, which is the preferred term when DISCOUNT is involved.

PREPAYMENT
In general: paying a debt obligation before it comes due.
Accounting: expenditure for a future benefit, which is recorded in a BALANCE SHEET asset account called a DEFERRED CHARGE, then written off in the period when the benefit is enjoyed. For example, prepaid rent is first recorded as an asset, then charged to expense as the rent becomes due on a monthly basis.
Banking: paying a loan before maturity. Some loans (particularly mortgages) have a prepayment clause that allows prepayment at any time without penalty, while others charge a fee if a loan is paid off before due.
Installment credit: making payments before they are due. *See also* RULE OF THE 78s.
Securities: paying a seller for a security before the settlement date.

PREPAYMENT PENALTY fee paid by a borrower to a bank when a loan or mortgage that does not have a prepayment clause is repaid before its scheduled maturity.

PRESENTMENT actual delivery of a negotiable instrument by a holder to the drawee for payment or acceptance, or to the maker for payment.

PRESENT VALUE value today of a future payment, or stream of payments, discounted at some appropriate compound interest—or discount—rate. For example, the present value of $100 to be received 10 years from now is about $38.55, using a discount rate equal to 10% interest compounded annually.

The present value method, also called the DISCOUNTED CASH FLOW method, is widely used in corporate finance to measure the return on a CAPITAL INVESTMENT project. In security investments, the method is used to determine how much money should be invested today to result in a certain sum at a future time. Present value calculations are facilitated by present value tables, which are compound interest tables in reverse. Also called *time value of money*.

PRESIDENT highest-ranking officer in a corporation after the CHAIRMAN OF THE BOARD, unless the title CHIEF EXECUTIVE OFFICER (CEO) is used, in which case the president can outrank the chairman. The president is appointed by the BOARD OF DIRECTORS and usually reports directly to the board. In smaller companies the president is usually the CEO, having authority over all other officers in matters of day-to-day management and policy decision-making. In large corporations the CEO title is frequently held by the chairman of the board, leaving the president as CHIEF OPERATING OFFICER, responsible for personnel and administration on a daily basis.

PRESIDENTIAL ELECTION CYCLE THEORY hypothesis of investment advisers that major stock market moves can be predicted based on the 4-year presidential election cycle in the United States. According to this theory, stocks decline soon after a president is elected, as the chief executive takes the harsh and unpopular steps necessary to bring inflation, government spending, and deficits under control. During the next two years or so, taxes may be raised and the economy may slip into a recession. About midway into the four-year cycle, stocks should start to rise in anticipation of the economic recovery that the incumbent president wants to be roaring at full steam by election day. The cycle then repeats itself with the election of a new president or the reelection of an incumbent. This theory worked remarkably well from the late 1960s to the mid-1980s.

PRETAX EARNINGS OR PROFITS NET INCOME (earnings or profits) before federal income taxes.

PRETAX RATE OF RETURN yield or capital gain on a particular security before taking into account an individual's tax situation. *See also* RATE OF RETURN.

PREVIOUS BALANCE METHOD method of charging credit card interest that uses the outstanding balance at the end of the previous month as the basis for the current month's interest computation. *See also* ADJUSTED BALANCE METHOD.

PRICE CHANGE net rise or fall of the price of a security at the close of a trading session, compared to the previous session's CLOSING PRICE. A stock that rose $2 in a day would have a + 2 after its final price in the newspaper stock listings. A stock that fell $2 would have a –2.

PRICE/EARNINGS RATIO (P/E) price of a stock divided by its earnings per share. The P/E ratio may either use the reported earnings from the latest year (called a *trailing P/E*) or employ an analyst's forecast of next year's earnings (called a *forward P/E*). The trailing P/E is listed along with a stock's price and trading activity in the daily newspapers. For instance, a stock selling for $20 a share that earned $1 last year has a trailing P/E of 20. If the same stock has projected earnings of $2 next year, it will have a forward P/E of 10.

The price/earnings ratio, also known as the *multiple,* gives investors an idea of how much they are paying for a company's earning power. The higher the P/E, the more investors are paying, and therefore the more earnings growth they are expecting. High P/E stocks—those with multiples over 20—are typically young, fast-growing companies. They are far riskier to trade than low P/E stocks, since it is easier to miss high-growth expectations than low-growth predictions. Low P/E stocks tend to be in low-growth or mature industries, in stock groups that have fallen out of favour, or in old, established, BLUE-CHIP companies with long records of earnings stability and regular dividends. In general, low P/E stocks have higher yields than high P/E stocks, which often pay no dividends at all.

PRICE GAP term used when a stock's price either jumps or plummets from its last trading range without overlapping that trading range. For instance, a stock might shoot up from a closing price of $20 a share, marking the high point of an $18–$20 trading range for that day, and begin trading in a $22–$24 range the next day on the news of a takeover bid. Or a company that reports lower than expected earnings might drop from the $18–$20 range to the $13–$15 range without ever trading at intervening prices. Price gaps are considered significant movements by technical analysts, who note them on charts, because such gaps are often indications of an OVERBOUGHT or OVERSOLD position.

PRICE INDEXES indices that track levels of prices and rates of inflation. The most common price index published by the government is the CONSUMER PRICE INDEX (CPI).

PRICE LEADERSHIP establishment of a price by a leading producer of a product that becomes the price adopted by other producers.

PRICE LIMIT *see* LIMIT PRICE.

PRICE RANGE high/low range in which a stock has traded over a particular period of time. In the daily newspaper, a stock's 52-week price range is given. In most companies' annual reports, a stock's price range is shown for the FISCAL YEAR.

PRICE SPREAD OPTIONS strategy in which an investor simultaneously buys and sells two options covering the same security, with the same expiration months, but with different exercise prices. For example, an investor might buy an XYZ May 100 call and sell an XYZ May 90 call.

PRICE SUPPORT government-set price floor designed to aid farmers or other producers of goods. For instance, the government sets a minimum price for sugar that it guarantees to sugar growers. If the market price drops below that level, the government makes up the difference. *See also* PARITY PRICE.

PRICE TICK minimum price fluctuation on the stock market.

PRICE-WEIGHTED INDEX index in which component stocks are weighted by their price. Higher-priced stocks therefore have a greater percentage impact on the index than lower-priced stocks. In recent years, the trend of using price-weighted indexes has given way to the use of MARKET-VALUE WEIGHTED INDEXES.

PRICEY term used of an unrealistically low bid price or unrealistically high offer price. If a stock is trading at $15, a pricey bid might be $10 a share, and a pricey offer $20 a share.

PRIMARY DISTRIBUTION sale of a new issue of stocks or bonds, as distinguished from a SECONDARY DISTRIBUTION, which involves previously issued stock. All issuances of bonds are primary distributions. Also called *primary offering,* but not to be confused with *initial public offering,* which refers to a corporation's *first* distribution of stock to the public.

PRIMARY EARNINGS PER (COMMON) SHARE earnings available to common stock (which is usually net earnings after taxes and preferred dividends) divided by the number of common shares outstanding. This figure contrasts with earnings per share after DILUTION, which assumes warrants, rights, and options have been exercised and convertibles have been converted. *See also* CONVERTIBLE; FULLY DILUTED EARNINGS PER (COMMON) SHARE; SUBSCRIPTION WARRANT.

PRIMARY MARKET market for new issues of securities, as distinguished from the SECONDARY MARKET, where previously issued securities are bought and sold. A market is primary if the proceeds of sales go to the issuer of the securities sold. The term also applies to government securities auctions and to opening option and futures contract sales.

PRIMARY OFFERING OF A NEW ISSUE *see* PRIMARY DISTRIBUTION.

PRIME
Banking: PRIME RATE.

PRIME PAPER highest quality COMMERCIAL PAPER, as rated by Moody's Investor's Service and other rating agencies. Prime paper is considered INVESTMENT GRADE, and therefore institutions with FIDUCIARY responsibility can invest in it. Moody's has three ratings of prime paper:

P-1: Highest quality
P-2: Higher quality
P-3: High quality
Commercial paper below P-3 is not considered prime paper.

PRIME RATE base rate that banks use in pricing commercial loans to their best and most creditworthy customers. The rate is determined by the Bank of Canada's decision to raise or lower prevailing interest rates for short-term borrowing. Though some banks charge their best customers more and some less than the prime rate, the rate tends to become standard across the banking industry when a major bank moves its prime up or down. The rate is a key interest rate, since loans to less-creditworthy customers are often tied to the prime rate. Many consumer loans, such as home equity, automobile, mortgage, and credit card loans, are tied to the prime rate.

PRINCIPAL
In General:
1. major party to a transaction, acting as either a buyer or a seller. A principal buys and sells for his or her own account and risk.
2. owner of a privately held business.
Banking and Finance:
1. face amount of a debt instrument or deposit on which interest is either owed or earned.
2. balance of a debt, separate from interest. *See also* PRINCIPAL AMOUNT.
Investments: basic amount invested, exclusive of earnings.

PRINCIPAL AMOUNT FACE VALUE of an obligation (such as a bond or a loan) that must be repaid at maturity, as separate from the INTEREST.

PRINCIPAL STOCKHOLDER stockholder who owns a significant number of shares in a corporation, usually a principal stockholder owns 10% or more of the voting stock of a REGISTERED COMPANY. These stockholders are often on the board of directors and are considered insiders, so that they must report buying and selling transactions in the company's stock. *See also* AFFILIATED PERSON; CONTROL STOCK; INSIDER.

PRINCIPAL SUM
Finance: also used as a synonym for PRINCIPAL, in the sense of the obligation due under a debt instrument exclusive of interest. Synonymous with CORPUS. *See also* TRUST.
Insurance: amount specified as payable to the beneficiary under a policy, such as the death benefit.

PRIORITY system used in an AUCTION MARKET, in which the first bid or offer price is executed before other bid and offer prices, even if subsequent orders are larger. Orders originating off the floor *(see* OFF-FLOOR ORDER*)* of an exchange also have priority over ON-FLOOR ORDERS. *See also* MATCHED AND LOST; PRECEDENCE.

PRIOR-PREFERRED STOCK PREFERRED STOCK that has a higher claim than other issues of preferred stock on dividends and assets in LIQUIDATION; also known as *preference shares*.

PRIVATE MARKET VALUE (PMV) aggregate market value of a company if each of its parts operated independently and had its own stock price. Also called *breakup value* or *takeover value*. Analysts look for high PMV in relation to market value to identify bargains and potential TARGET COMPANIES. PMV differs from LIQUIDATING VALUE, which excludes GOING CONCERN VALUE, and BOOK VALUE, which is an accounting concept.

PRIVATE PLACEMENT sale of blocks of securities to a small group of sophisticated investors, such as life insurance companies, trust companies, pension funds, and venture capital companies. It rarely involves amounts of less than $500,000.

PRIVATIZATION process of converting a publicly operated enterprise into a privately owned and operated entity. Many countries around the world have privatized formerly state-run enterprises such as banks, airlines, steel companies, utilities, phone systems, and large manufacturers. A wave of privatization swept through Russia and Eastern Europe after the fall of Communism in the early 1990s, and through some Latin American countries such as Peru, as new, democratic governments were established. When a company is privatized, shares formerly owned by the government, as well as management control, are sold to the public. The theory behind privatization is that these enterprises run far more efficiently and offer better service to customers when owned by stockholders instead of the government.

PROBATE judicial process whereby the will of a deceased person is presented to a court and an EXECUTOR or ADMINISTRATOR is appointed to carry out the will's instructions. Every province except Québec requires probate of a will and each has different probate fees. *See also* LETTERS PROBATE.

PROCEEDS
1. funds given to a borrower after all costs and fees are deducted.
2. money received by the seller of an asset after commissions are deducted—for example, the amount a stockholder receives from the sale of shares, less broker's commission. *See also* PROCEEDS SALE.

PROCEEDS SALE OVER THE COUNTER securities sale where the PROCEEDS are used to purchase another security.

PRODUCER PRICE INDEX (PPI) in the United States, a measure of change in wholesale prices (formerly called the *wholesale price index),* as released monthly by the U.S. Bureau of Labor Statistics. The index is broken down into components by commodity, industry sector, and stage of processing. The PPI tracks prices of foods, metals, lumber, oil and gas, and many other commodities, but does not measure the price of services. Economists look at trends in the PPI as an accurate precursor to changes in the CPI, since upward or downward pressure on wholesale prices is usually passed through to consumer prices over time. The PPI, published by the Bureau of Labor Statistics in the Department of Labor, is based at 100 in 1982 and is released monthly. Economists also look at the PPI excluding the volatile food and energy components, which they call the "core" PPI. The consumer equivalent of this index is the CONSUMER PRICE INDEX.

PRODUCTIVITY in labour and other areas of economics, the amount of output per unit of input, for example, the quantity of a product produced per hour of labour.

PROFESSIONAL LIABILITY money paid to an insurance company in exchange for benefits. Such insurance affords protection against claims arising from practising a profession, e.g., claims of negligence.

PROFIT
Finance: positive difference that results from selling products and services for more than the cost of producing these goods. *See also* NET PROFIT.
Investments: difference between the selling price and the purchase price of commodities or securities when the selling price is higher.

PROFITABILITY-RISK TRADE-OFF relationship between profitability and risk, involving management of working capital. The lower a firm's liquidity, the greater the risk of technical insolvency, and the higher the expected profits, and vice versa.

PROFIT AND LOSS STATEMENT (P & L) summary of the revenues, costs, and expenses of a company during an accounting period; also called INCOME STATEMENT, *operating statement, statement of profit and loss, income and expense statement.* Together with the BALANCE SHEET as of the end of the accounting period, it constitutes a company's financial statement. Revenue less costs of goods is the gross profit. From this are deducted itemized selling and administrative costs, to give a profit before taxes. What is left after deduction of taxes is "net" profit. *See also* COST OF GOODS SOLD; NET INCOME; NET SALES.

PROFIT CENTRE segment of a business organization that is responsible for producing profits on its own. A conglomerate with interests in hotels, food processing, and paper may consider each of these three businesses separate profit centres, for instance.

PROFIT FORECAST prediction of future levels of profitability by analysts following a company, as well as company officials. Investors base their buy and sell decisions on such earnings projections. Stock prices typically reflect analysts' profit expectations—companies expected to produce rapidly growing profits often have high price/earnings ratios. Conversely, projections of meager earnings result in lower P/E ratios. The company will often guide analysts so that their profit forecasts are not too high or too low, preventing unwelcome surprises. Analyst profit forecasts are tracked by the INSTITUTIONAL BROKERS ESTIMATE SYSTEM (I/B/E/S) and ZACKS ESTIMATE SYSTEM.

PROFIT MARGIN *see* MARGIN OF PROFIT.

PROFIT-SHARING PLAN agreement between a corporation and its employees that allows the employees to share in company profits. Annual contributions are made by the company, when it has profits, to a profit-sharing account for each employee, either in cash or in a deferred plan, which may be invested in stocks, bonds, or cash equivalents. The funds in a profit-sharing account generally accumulate tax deferred until the employee retires or leaves the company. Many plans allow employees to borrow against profit-sharing accounts for major expenditures such as purchasing a home or financing children's education. Because corporate profit-sharing plans have custody over billions of dollars, they are major institutional investors in the stock and bond markets.

PROFIT TAKING action by short-term securities or commodities traders to cash in on gains earned on a sharp market rise. Profit taking pushes down prices, but only temporarily; the term implies an upward market trend.

PRO FORMA Latin for "as a matter of form"; refers to a presentation of data, such as a BALANCE SHEET or INCOME STATEMENT, where certain amounts are hypothetical. For example, a pro forma balance sheet might show a debt issue that has been proposed but has not yet been consummated.

PROGRAM TRADING computer-driven buying (*buy program*) or selling (*sell program*) of baskets of 15 or more stocks by *index* ARBITRAGE specialists or institutional traders. "Program" refers to computer programs that constantly monitor stock, futures, and options markets, giving buy and sell signals when opportunities for arbitrage profits occur or when market conditions warrant portfolio accumulation or liquidation transactions. Also refers to switching or trading blocks of securities in order to change the asset mix of a portfolio. Program trading has been blamed for excessive volatility in the markets, especially on Black Monday in 1987, when PORTFOLIO INSURANCE—the since discredited use of index options and futures to hedge stock portfolios— was an important contributing factor.

PROGRESSIVE TAX income tax system in which those with higher incomes pay taxes at higher rates than those with lower incomes; also called *graduated tax*. The Canadian income tax system is based on the concept of progressivity. There are several tax brackets, based on the taxpayer's income, which determine the tax rate that applies to each taxpayer. *See also* FLAT TAX; REGRESSIVE TAX.

PROGRESS PAYMENTS
  1. periodic payments to a supplier, contractor, or subcontractor for work satisfactorily performed to date. Such schedules are provided in contracts and can significantly reduce the amount of WORKING CAPITAL required by the performing party.
  2. disbursements by lenders to contractors under construction loan arrangements. As construction progresses, bills and LIEN waivers are presented to the bank or savings and loan, which advances additional funds.

PROJECTION estimate of future performance made by economists, corporate planners, and credit and securities analysts. Economists use econometric models to project GROSS DOMESTIC PRODUCT (GDP), inflation, unemployment, and many other economic factors. Corporate financial planners project a company's operating results and CASH FLOW, using historical trends and making assumptions where necessary, in order to make budget decisions and to plan financing. Credit analysts use projections to forecast DEBT SERVICE ability. Securities analysts tend to focus their projections on earnings trends and cash flow per share in order to predict market values and dividend coverage. *See also* ECONOMETRICS.

PROJECT LINK econometric model linking all the economies in the world and forecasting the effects of changes in different economies on other economies. The project is identified with 1980 Nobel Memorial Prize in Economics winner Lawrence R. Klein. *See also* ECONOMETRICS.

PROMISSORY NOTE written promise committing the maker to pay the payee a specified sum of money either on demand or at a fixed or determinable future date, with or without interest. Instruments meeting these criteria are NEGOTIABLE. Often called, simply, a NOTE.

PROPERTY AND EQUIPMENT *see* FIXED ASSET.

PROPERTY INVENTORY personal finance term meaning a list of PERSONAL PROPERTY with cost and market values. A property inventory, which should be accompanied by photographs, is used to substantiate insurance claims and tax losses.

PROPERTY TAX tax assessed on property such as real estate. The tax is determined by several factors, including the use of the land (residential, commercial, or industrial), the assessed valuation of the property, and the tax rate, expressed in MILLS. Property taxes are usually assessed by county and local governments, school districts, and other special authorities such as for water and sewer service. Property taxes are usually deductible on federal income tax returns. If a mortgage lender requires that it pay all property taxes, borrowers must remit their property taxes as part of their monthly mortgage payments and the lender keeps the money in trust until property taxes are due. *See also* AD VALOREM, PITI.

PROPORTIONAL REPRESENTATION method of stockholder voting, giving individual shareholders more power over the election of directors than they have under STATUTORY VOTING, which, by allowing one vote per share per director, makes it possible for a majority shareholder to elect all the directors. The most familiar example of proportional representation is CUMULATIVE VOTING, under which a shareholder has as many votes as he or she has shares of stock, multiplied by the number of vacancies on the board, all of which can be cast for one director. This makes it possible for a minority shareholder or a group of small shareholders to gain at least some representation on the board. Another variety provides for the holders of specified classes of stock to elect a number of directors in certain circumstances. For example, if the corporation failed to pay preferred dividends, the preferred holders might then be given the power to elect a certain proportion of the board. Despite the advocacy of stockholders' rights activists, proportional representation has made little headway in Canadian corporations.

PROPRIETORSHIP unincorporated business owned by a single person. The individual proprietor has the right to all the profits from the business and also has responsibility for all the firm's liabilities.

PRO RATA Latin for "according to the rate"; a method of proportionate allocation. For example, a pro rata property tax rebate might be divided proportionately (prorated) among taxpayers based on their original assessments, so that each gets the same percentage.

PROSPECTUS formal written offer to sell securities that sets forth the plan for a proposed business enterprise or the facts concerning an existing one that an investor needs to make an informed decision. Prospectuses are also issued by MUTUAL FUNDS, describing the history, background of managers, fund objectives, a financial statement, and other essential data. A prospectus for a PUBLIC OFFERING must be filed with a securities commission and given to prospective buyers of the offering. The prospectus contains financial information and a description of a company's business history, officers, operations, pending litigation (if any), and plans (including the use of the proceeds from the issue).

Before investors receive the final copy of the prospectus, they may receive a PRELIMINARY PROSPECTUS, commonly called a *red herring*. This document is not complete in all details, though most of the major facts of the offering are usually included. The final prospectus is also called the *offering circular.*

Offerings of limited partnerships are also accompanied by prospectuses. Real estate, oil and gas, and other types of limited partnerships are described in detail, and pertinent financial information, the background of the general partners, and supporting legal opinions are also given.

PROTECTIONISM practice of protecting domestic goods and service industries from foreign competition with tariff and non-tariff barriers.

Protectionism causes higher prices for consumers because domestic producers are not exposed to foreign competition, and can therefore keep prices high. But domestic exporters also may suffer, because foreign countries tend to retaliate against protectionism with tariffs and barriers of their own. Many economists say that the Depression of the 1930s was precipitated by the protectionist trade barriers erected by the United States under the Smoot-Hawley Act, which led to retaliation by many countries throughout the world. In more recent years, many protectionist trade barriers have fallen through the passage of GATT, the General Agreement on Tariffs and Trade, which went into effect in 1995.

PROTECTIVE COVENANT *see* COVENANT.

PROVISION *see* ALLOWANCE.

PROVISION FOR INCOME TAXES item on a company's profit and loss statement (P & L) representing its estimated income tax liability for the year. Although taxes are actually paid according to a timetable determined by Revenue Canada and a certain portion of the liability may be accrued, the provision gives an indication of the company's effective tax rate, which analysts compare to other companies as one measure of effective management and profitability. EARNINGS BEFORE TAXES is the net earnings figure before provision for income taxes.

PROXY
In general: person authorized to act or speak for another.
Business:
1. written POWER OF ATTORNEY given by shareholders of a corporation, authorizing a specific vote on their behalf at corporate meetings. Such proxies normally pertain to election of the BOARD OF DIRECTORS or to various resolutions submitted for shareholders' approval.
2. person authorized to vote on behalf of a stockholder of a corporation.

PROXY FIGHT technique used by an acquiring company to attempt to gain control of a TAKEOVER target. The acquirer tries to persuade the shareholders of the TARGET COMPANY that the present management of the firm should be ousted in favour of a slate of directors favourable to the acquirer. If the shareholders, through their PROXY votes, agree, the acquiring company can gain control of the company without paying a PREMIUM price for the firm.

PRUDENT MAN RULE investment standard for those with responsibility for investing the money of others. In some provinces, the law requires that a fiduciary, such as a trustee, may invest funds only in a list of securities designated by the province of the federal government. In other provinces, the trustee may invest in a security if it is one that an ordinary prudent man or woman would buy if investing for the benefit of other people for whom he or she felt morally bound to provide. Most provinces apply the two standards.

PUBLIC, THE term for individual investors, as opposed to professional investors. Wall Street analysts like to deride the public for constantly buying at the top of a bull market and selling at the bottom of a bear market. The public participates in stock and bond markets both by buying individual securities and through intermediaries such as mutual funds and insurance companies. The term *public* is also used to describe a security that is available to be bought and sold by individual investors (as opposed to just large institutions or wealthy people, in which case the offering is a private one). Stocks that offer shares to the public are known as *publicly held*, in contrast to *privately held* concerns in which shares are owned by founders, employees, and a few large investors.

PUBLIC COMPANY company that offers stock for sale to the general public.

PUBLIC DEBT borrowings by governments to finance expenditures not covered by current tax revenues. *See also* AGENCY SECURITIES; MUNICIPAL BOND; TREASURIES.

PUBLIC HOLIDAYS *see* STATUTORY HOLIDAYS.

PUBLIC LIABILITY *see* LIABILITY INSURANCE.

PUBLICLY HELD company with shares outstanding that are held by public investors. A company converts from a privately held firm to a publicly held one through an INITIAL PUBLIC OFFERING (IPO) of stock.

PUBLIC OFFERING
1. offering to the investment public, after registration requirements of a securities commission have been complied with, of new securities, usually by an investment banker or a syndicate made up of several investment bankers, at a public offering price agreed upon between the issuer and the investment bankers.

    Public offering is distinguished from PRIVATE PLACEMENT of new securities, which is subject to different regulations. *See also* UNDERWRITE.
2. SECONDARY DISTRIBUTION of previously issued stock. *See also* SECONDARY OFFERING.

PUBLIC OFFERING PRICE price at which a NEW ISSUE of securities is offered to the public by underwriters. *See also* OFFERING PRICE; UNDERWRITE.

PUBLIC OUTCRY method used to sell and buy futures contracts in the gold and silver pits on the exchange floor—a refined term for screaming. The price of the contract is agreed upon verbally.

PUBLIC OWNERSHIP
Government: government ownership and operation of a productive facility for the purpose of providing some good or service to citizens. The government supplies the capital, controls management, sets prices, and generally absorbs all risks and reaps all profits—similar to

a private enterprise. When public ownership displaces private owner-ship in a particular instance, it is called NATIONALIZATION.

Investments: publicly traded portion of a corporation's stock.

PULLING IN THEIR HORNS move to defensive strategies on the part of investors. If the stock or bond market has experienced a sharp rise, investors may want to lock in profits by selling part of their positions or instituting hedging techniques to guard against a downturn. If stock prices fall after a steep runup, commentators will frequently say that "investors are pulling in their horns" to describe the reason for the downturn.

PURCHASE ACQUISITION accounting method used in a business MERGER whereby the purchasing company treats the acquired company as an investment and adds the acquired company's assets to its own at their fair market value. Any premium paid over and above the FAIR MARKET VALUE of the acquired assets is reflected as GOODWILL on the buyer's BALANCE SHEET and must be written off against future earnings. Until 1993, goodwill amortization was not deductible for tax purposes, so the reduction of reported future earnings was a disadvantage of this method of merger accounting as compared with the alternative POOLING OF INTERESTS method. The purchase acquisition method is mandatory unless all the criteria for a pooling of interests combination are met.

PURCHASE AND RESALE AGREEMENT method by which banks lend temporarily idle funds to money market dealers. The bank buys short-term securities from the money market dealer who agrees to repurchase the securities from the bank at a higher price at a specified future date.

PURCHASE FUND provision in some PREFERRED STOCK contracts and BOND indentures requiring the issuer to use its best efforts to purchase a specified number of shares or bonds annually at a price not to exceed par value. Unlike SINKING FUND provisions, which require that a cer-tain number of bonds be retired annually, purchase funds require only that a tender offer be made; if no securities are tendered, none are retired. Purchase fund issues benefit the investor in a period of rising rates when the redemption price is higher than the market price and the proceeds can be put to work at a higher return.

PURCHASE GROUP group of investment bankers that, operating under the AGREEMENT AMONG UNDERWRITERS, agrees to purchase a NEW ISSUE of securities from the issuer for resale to the investment public; also called the UNDERWRITING GROUP or *syndicate.* The purchase group is distinguished from the SELLING GROUP, which is organized by the purchase group and includes the members of the purchase group along with other investment bankers. The selling group's function is DISTRIBUTION.

The agreement among underwriters, also called the *purchase group agreement,* is distinguished from the underwriting or purchase agreement, which is between the underwriting group and the issuer. *See also* UNDERWRITE.

PURCHASE GROUP AGREEMENT *see* PURCHASE GROUP.

PURCHASE LOAN in consumer credit, a loan made at a rate of interest to finance a purchase.

PURCHASE ORDER written authorization to a vendor to deliver specified goods or services at a stipulated price. Once accepted by the supplier, the purchase order becomes a legally binding purchase CONTRACT.

PURCHASE TRANSACTION transaction in which an investor becomes the buyer of an option. He or she is initiating or increasing a long position.

PURCHASING POWER
Economics: value of money as measured by the goods and services it can buy. For example, the PURCHASING POWER OF THE DOLLAR can be determined by comparing an index of consumer prices for a given base year to the present.
Investment: amount of credit available to a client in a brokerage account for the purchase of additional securities. Purchasing power is determined by the dollar amount of securities that can be margined.

PURCHASING POWER OF THE DOLLAR measure of the amount of goods and services that a dollar can buy in a particular market, as compared with prior periods, assuming always an INFLATION or a DEFLATION factor and using an index of consumer prices. It might be reported, for instance, that one dollar in 1982 has 58 cents of purchasing power in the mid-90s because of the erosion caused by inflation. Deflation would increase the dollar's purchasing power.

PURE PLAY stock market jargon for a company that is virtually all devoted to one line of business. An investor who wants to invest in that line of business looks for such a pure play. For instance, Hudson's Bay Company may be considered a pure play in the retail business. Macmillan Bloedel is a pure play in the forest products business. The opposite of a pure play is a widely diversified company, such as a CONGLOMERATE.

PURE MONOPOLY situation in which one firm controls the entire market for a product. This may occur because the firm has a patent on a product or a license from the government to be a monopoly.

PUT right to sell a share of a certain stock at a stated price within a given period of time. A put is sold when the price of the stock is expected to fall.

PUT BOND bond that allows its holder to redeem the issue at specified intervals before maturity and receive full FACE VALUE. The bondholders may be allowed to put bonds back to the issuer either only once during the lifetime of the issue or far more frequently. In return for this privilege, a bond buyer sacrifices some yield when choosing a put bond over a fixed-rate bond, which cannot be redeemed before maturity.

PUT-CALL RATIO ratio of trading volume in put options to the trading volume in call options. The ratio provides a quantitative measure of the bullishness or bearishness of investors. A high volume of puts relative to calls indicates investors are bearish, whereas a high ratio of calls to puts shows bullishness. Many market technicians find the put-call ratio to be a good contrary indicator, meaning that when the ratio is high, a market bottom is near and when the ratio is low, a market top is imminent. This reading assumes that the majority of options investors are making the wrong move.

PUT OPTION

Bonds: bondholder's right to redeem a bond before maturity. *See also* PUT BOND.

Options: contract that grants the right to sell at a specified price a specific number of shares by a certain date. The put option buyer gains this right in return for payment of an OPTION PREMIUM. The put option seller grants this right in return for receiving this premium. For instance, a buyer of an XYZ May 70 put has the right to sell 100 shares of XYZ at $70 to the put seller at any time until the contract expires in May. A put option buyer hopes the stock will drop in price, while the put option seller (called a *writer)* hopes the stock will remain stable, rise, or drop by an amount less than his or her profit on the premium.

PUT-THROUGH *see* CROSS ON THE BOARD.

PUT TO SELLER phrase used when a PUT OPTION is exercised. The OPTION WRITER is obligated to buy the underlying shares at the agreed upon price. If an XYZ June 40 put were "put to seller," for instance, the writer would have to buy 100 shares of XYZ at $40 a share from the put holder even though the current market price of XYZ may be far less than $40 a share.

PYRAMIDING

In general: form of business expansion that makes extensive use of financial LEVERAGE to build complex corporate structures.

Fraud: scheme that builds on nonexistent values, often in geometric progression, such as a chain letter, now outlawed by mail fraud legislation. A famous example was the Ponzi scheme, perpetrated by Charles Ponzi in the late 1920s. Investors were paid "earnings" out of money received from new investors until the scheme collapsed.

Investments: using unrealized profits from one securities or commodities POSITION as COLLATERAL to buy further positions with funds borrowed from a broker. This use of leverage creates increased profits in a BULL MARKET, and causes MARGIN CALLS and large losses in a BEAR MARKET.

Marketing: legal marketing strategy whereby additional distributorships are sold side-by-side with consumer products in order to multiply market reach and maximize profits to the sales organization.

Q

QUALIFICATION PERIOD period of time during which an insurance company will not reimburse a policyholder for a claim. The qualification period, which may be several weeks or months, gives the insurance company time to uncover fraud or deception in the policyholder's application for coverage. Such periods, which are stated in the insurance contract, are commonplace in health insurance plans.

QUALIFIED ENDORSEMENT endorsement (signature on the back of a cheque or other NEGOTIABLE INSTRUMENT transferring the amount to someone other than the one to whom it is payable) that contains wording designed to limit the endorser's liability. "Without recourse," the most frequently seen example, means that if the instrument is not honoured, the endorser is not responsible. Where qualified endorsements are restrictive (such as "for deposit only") the term *restricted endorsement* is preferable.

QUALIFIED OPINION auditor's opinion accompanying financial statements that calls attention to limitations of the audit or exceptions the auditor takes to the statements. Typical reasons for qualified opinions: a pending lawsuit that, if lost, would materially affect the financial condition of the company; an indeterminable tax liability relating to an unusual transaction; inability to confirm a portion of the inventory because of inaccessible location. *See also* ACCOUNTANT'S OPINION.

QUALIFYING SHARE share of COMMON STOCK owned in order to qualify as a director of the issuing corporation.

QUALITATIVE ANALYSIS
In general: analysis that evaluates important factors that cannot be precisely measured.
Securities and credit analysis: analysis that is concerned with such questions as the experience, character, and general calibre of management; employee morale; and the status of labour relations rather than with the actual financial data about a company. *See also* QUANTITATIVE ANALYSIS.

QUALITY CONTROL process of assuring that products are made to consistently high standards of quality. Inspection of goods at various points in their manufacture by either a person or a machine is usually an important part of the quality control process.

QUALITY OF EARNINGS phrase describing a corporation's earnings that are attributable to increased sales and cost controls, as distinguished from artificial profits created by inflationary values in inventories or other assets. In a period of high inflation, the quality of earnings tends to suffer, since a large portion of a firm's profits is generated by the rising value of inventories. In a lower inflation period, a company that achieves higher sales and maintains lower costs produces a higher quality of earnings—a factor often appreciated by investors, who are frequently willing to pay more for a higher quality of earnings.

QUANT person with mathematical and computer skills who provides numerical and analytical support services in the securities industry.

QUANTISE to denominate an asset or liability in a currency other than the one in which it usually trades.

QUANTITATIVE ANALYSIS analysis dealing with measurable factors as distinguished from such qualitative considerations as the character of management or the state of employee morale. In credit and securities analysis, examples of quantitative considerations are the value of assets; the cost of capital; the historical and projected patterns of sales, costs, and profitability and a wide range of considerations in the areas of economics; the money market; and the securities markets. Although quantitative and qualitative factors are distinguishable, they must be combined to arrive at sound business and financial judgments. *See also* QUALITATIVE ANALYSIS.

QUANTO OPTION option in one currency or interest rate that pays out in another. A quanto option can be used when an investor favours a foreign index, but is bearish on the outlook for that country's currency.

QUARTERLY
In general: every three months (one quarter of a year).
Securities: basis on which earnings reports to shareholders are made; also, usual time frame of dividend payments.

QUARTER STOCK stock with a par value of $25 per share.

QUICK ASSETS cash, marketable securities, and accounts receivable. *See also* QUICK RATIO.

QUICKIE order that must either be filled as soon as it reaches the trading floor at the price specified or be canceled.

QUICK RATIO cash, MARKETABLE SECURITIES, and ACCOUNTS RECEIVABLE divided by current liabilities. By excluding inventory, this key LIQUIDITY ratio focuses on the firm's more LIQUID ASSETS, and helps answer the question "If sales stopped, could this firm meet its current obligations with the readily convertible assets on hand?" Assuming there is nothing happening to slow or prevent collections, a quick ratio of 1 to 1 or better is usually satisfactory. Also called *acid-test ratio, quick asset ratio.*

QUID PRO QUO
In general: from the Latin, meaning "something for something." By mutual agreement, one party provides a good or service for which he or she gets another good or service in return.

Securities industry: arrangement by a firm using institutional research that it will execute all trades based on that research with the firm providing it, instead of directly paying for the research. This is known as paying in SOFT DOLLARS.

QUORUM minimum number of people who must be present at a meeting in order to make certain decisions go into effect. A quorum may be required at a board of directors, committee, shareholder, legislative, or other meeting for any decisions to have legal standing. A quorum may be achieved by providing a PROXY as well as appearance in person.

QUOTATION
Business: price estimate on a commercial project or transaction.
Investments: highest bid and lowest offer (asked) price currently available on a security or a commodity. An investor who asks for a quotation ("quote") on XYZ might be told "60 to 60½," meaning that the best bid price (the highest price any buyer wants to pay) is currently $60 a share and that the best offer (the lowest price any seller is willing to accept) is $60½ at that time. Such quotes assume ROUND-LOT transactions—for example, 100 shares for stocks.

QUOTATION BOARD electronically controlled board at a brokerage firm that displays current price quotations and other financial data such as dividends, price ranges of stocks, and current volume of trading.

QUOTE *see* QUOTATION.

QUOTED PRICE price at which the last sale and purchase of a particular security or commodity took place.

R

RADAR ALERT close monitoring of trading patterns in a company's stock by senior managers to uncover unusual buying activity that might signal a TAKEOVER attempt. *See also* SHARK WATCHER.

RAIDER individual or corporate investor who intends to take control of a company by buying a controlling interest in its stock and installing new management.

RAINMAKER individual who brings significant amounts of new business to a brokerage firm. The rainmaker may bring in wealthy brokerage customers who generate a large dollar volume of commissions. Or he or she may be an investment banker who attracts corporate or municipal finance underwritings or merger and acquisition business. Because they are so important to the firm, rainmakers are usually given special PERQUISITES and bonus compensation.

RALLY marked rise in the price of a security, commodity future, or market after a period of decline or sideways movement.

R & D *see* RESEARCH AND DEVELOPMENT.

RANDOM WALK theory about the movement of stock and commodity futures prices hypothesizing that past prices are of no use in forecasting future price movements and that a portfolio of stocks chosen at random will perform as well as a portfolio of carefully selected securities. According to the theory, stock prices reflect reactions to information coming to the market in random fashion, so they are no more predictable than the walking pattern of a drunken person. The random walk theory was first espoused in 1900 by the French mathematician Louis Bachelier and revived in the 1960s. It is hotly disputed by advocates of TECHNICAL ANALYSIS, who say that charts of past price movements enable them to predict future price movements.

RANGE high and low end of a security, commodity future, or market's price fluctuations over a period of time. Daily newspapers publish the 52-week high and low price range of stocks traded on the Toronto, Montreal, and Vancouver Stock Exchange, and over-the-counter markets. Advocates of TECHNICAL ANALYSIS attach great importance to trading ranges because they consider it of great significance if a security breaks out of its trading range by going higher or lower. *See also* BREAKOUT.

RATE CAP *see* CAP.

RATE OF EXCHANGE *see* EXCHANGE RATE; PAR VALUE OF CURRENCY.

RATE OF INFLATION *see* CONSUMER PRICE INDEX; INFLATION RATE; PRODUCER PRICE INDEX.

RATE OF RETURN
  Fixed-income securities (bonds and preferred stock): CURRENT YIELD,

that is, the coupon or contractual dividend rate divided by the purchase price. *See also* YIELD TO AVERAGE LIFE; YIELD TO CALL; YIELD TO MATURITY.

Common stock: (1) dividend yield, which is the annual dividend divided by the purchase price. (2) TOTAL RETURN rate, which is the dividend plus capital appreciation.

Corporate finance: RETURN ON EQUITY or RETURN ON INVESTED CAPITAL.

Capital budgeting: INTERNAL RATE OF RETURN.

See also FAIR RATE OF RETURN; HORIZON ANALYSIS; MEAN RETURN; REAL INTEREST RATE; REQUIRED RATE OF RETURN; TOTAL RETURN; YIELD.

RATING

Credit and investments: evaluation of securities investment and credit risk by rating services such as Canada Bond Rating Service, Dominion Bond Rating Service, Duff & Phelps/MCM, Fitch Investors Service Inc., MOODY'S INVESTORS SERVICE, STANDARD & POOR'S CORPORATION, and VALUE LINE INVESTMENT SURVEY. *See also* CREDIT RATING; EVENT RISK; NOT RATED.

Insurance: using statistics, mortality tables, probability theory, experience, judgment, and mathematical analysis to establish the rates on which insurance premiums are based. There are three basic rating systems: *class rate,* applying to a homogeneous grouping of clients; *schedule system,* relating positive and negative factors in the case of a particular insured (for example, a smoker or nonsmoker in the case of a life policy) to a base figure; and *experience rating,* reflecting the historical loss experience of the particular insured. Also called *rate-making.*

Insurance companies are also rated. *See* BEST'S RATING.

LEADING BOND RATING SERVICES	RATING SERVICE			
Explanation of corporate/ municipal bond ratings	Duff & Phelps/MCM	Fitch	Moody's	Standard & Poor's
Highest quality, "gilt edged" High quality Upper medium grade	AAA AA A	AAA AA A	Aaa Aa A	AAA AA A
Medium grade Predominantly speculative Speculative, low grade	BBB BB B	BBB BB B	Baa Ba B	BBB BB B
Poor to default Highest speculation Lowest quality, no interest	CCC	CCC CC C	Caa Ca C	CCC CC C
In default, in arrears, questionable value		{ DDD DD D		DDD DD D

Fitch and Standard & Poor's may use + or – to modify some ratings. Moody's uses the numerical modifiers 1 (highest), 2, and 3 in the range from Aa1 through Ca3.

RATIO ANALYSIS method of analysis, used in making credit and investment judgments, which utilizes the relationship of figures found in financial statements to determine values and evaluate risks and compares such ratios to those of prior periods and other companies to reveal trends and identify eccentricities. Such analyses are commonly grouped into liquidity and activity ratios, debt ratios, and profitability ratios. Ratio analysis is only one tool among many used by analysts. *See also* ACCOUNTS RECEIVABLE TURNOVER; ACID TEST RATIO; BOND RATIO; CAPITALIZATION RATIO; CAPITAL TURNOVER; CASH RATIO; COLLECTION PERIOD; COMMON STOCK RATIO; CURRENT RATIO; DEBT-TO-EQUITY RATIO; DIVIDEND PAYOUT RATIO; EARNINGS-PRICE RATIO; FIXED CHARGE COVERAGE; LEVERAGE; NET TANGIBLE ASSETS PER SHARE; OPERATING RATIO; PREFERRED STOCK RATIO; PRICE-EARNINGS RATIO; PROFIT MARGIN; QUICK RATIO; RETURN ON EQUITY; RETURN ON INVESTED CAPITAL; RETURN ON SALES.

RATIO WRITER OPTIONS writer who sells more CALL contracts than he or she has underlying shares. For example, an investor who writes (sells) 10 calls, 5 of them covered by 500 owned shares and the other 5 of them uncovered (or "naked"), has a 2 for 1 ratio write.

RAW LAND property in its natural state, prior to grading, construction, and subdividing. The property has no sewers, electricity, streets, buildings, water service, telephone service, or other amenities. Investors in raw land hope that the land's value will rise in the future if it is developed. While they wait, however, they must pay property taxes on the land's value.

RAW MATERIAL unfinished goods used in the manufacture of a product. For example, a steelmaker uses iron ore and other metals in producing steel. A publishing company uses paper and ink to create books, newspapers, and magazines. Raw materials are carried on a company's balance sheet as inventory in the current assets section.

REACTION drop in securities prices after a sustained period of advancing prices, perhaps as the result of PROFIT TAKING or adverse developments. *See also* CORRECTION.

READING THE TAPE judging the performance of stocks by monitoring changes in price as they are displayed on the TICKER tape. An analyst reads the tape to determine whether a stock is acting strongly or weakly, and therefore is likely to go up or down. An investor reads the tape to determine whether a stock trade is going with or against the flow of market action. *See also* DON'T FIGHT THE TAPE.

REAGANOMICS economic program followed by the administration of U.S. President Ronald Reagan beginning in 1980. Reaganomics stressed lower taxes, higher defence spending, and curtailed spending for social services. After a reduction of growth in the money supply by the Federal Reserve Board combined with Reaganomics to produce a severe recession in 1981–82, the Reagan years were characterized by huge budget deficits, low interest and inflation rates, and continuous economic growth.

REAL ESTATE piece of land and all physical property related to it, including houses, fences, landscaping, and all rights to the air above and earth below the property. Assets not directly associated with the land are considered *personal property*.

REAL ESTATE AGENT licensed salesperson working for a licensed broker. The agent may hold an individual REAL ESTATE BROKER'S licence.

REAL ESTATE APPRAISAL estimate of the value of property, usually required when a property is sold, financed, condemned, taxed, insured, or partitioned. An appraisal is not a determination of value. Three approaches are used. To produce an accurate resale price for a residence, appraisers compare the price of the property to the prices of similar nearby properties that have sold recently. For new construction and service properties such as churches and post offices, appraisers look at the reproduction or replacement cost of the improvements, less depreciation, plus the value of the land. For investment properties such as apartment buildings and shopping centres, an estimated value is based on the capitalization of net operating income from a property at an acceptable market rate.

REAL ESTATE BROKER person who arranges the purchase or sale of property for a buyer or seller in return for a commission. Brokers must be licensed provincially to buy or sell real estate.

REAL ESTATE FUND mutual fund that invests primarily in income-producing real estate (such as rental apartment buildings, office buildings, shopping malls, industrial buildings) in order to achieve long-term growth through capital appreciation and reinvestment of income.

REAL ESTATE INVESTMENT TRUST (REIT) company, usually traded publicly, that manages a portfolio of real estate to earn profits for shareholders. REITs make investments in a diverse array of real estate such as shopping centres, medical facilities, nursing homes, office buildings, apartment complexes, industrial warehouses, and hotels. Some REITs, called EQUITY REITS, take equity positions in real estate; shareholders receive income from the rents received and from the properties and receive capital gains as buildings are sold at a profit.

REAL ESTATE LIMITED PARTNERSHIP LIMITED PARTNERSHIP that invests in real estate. The partnership buys properties such as apartment or office buildings, shopping centres, industrial warehouses, and hotels and passes rental income through to limited partners. If the properties appreciate in value over time, they can be sold and the profit passed through to limited partners. A GENERAL PARTNER manages the partnership, deciding which properties to buy and sell and handling administrative duties, such as distributions to limited partners.

REAL ESTATE RATE nominal rate of interest minus the percentage change in the Consumer Price Index (i.e., the rate of inflation). It is tied to the rate of mortgages.

REAL GAIN OR LOSS gain or loss adjusted for INFLATION. *See also* INFLATION ACCOUNTING.

REAL INCOME income of an individual, group, or country adjusted for changes in PURCHASING POWER caused by inflation. A price index is used to determine the difference between the purchasing power of a dollar in a base year and the purchasing power now. The resulting percentage factor, applied to total income, yields the value of that income in constant dollars, termed real income. For instance, if the cost of a market basket increases from $100 to $120 in ten years, reflecting a 20% decline in purchasing power, salaries must rise by 20% if real income is to be maintained.

REAL INTEREST RATE current interest rate minus inflation rate. The real interest rate may be calculated by comparing interest rates with present or, more frequently, with predicted inflation rates The real interest rate gives investors in bonds and other fixed-rate instruments a way to see whether their interest will allow them to keep up with or beat the erosion in dollar values caused by inflation. With a bond yielding 10% and inflation of 3%, for instance, the real interest rate of 7% would bring a return high enough to beat inflation. If inflation were at 15%, however, the investor would fall behind as prices rise.

REALIZED PROFIT (OR LOSS) profit or loss resulting from the sale or other disposal of a security. Capital gains taxes may be due when profits are realized: realized losses can be used to offset realized gains for tax purposes. Such profits and losses differ from a PAPER PROFIT OR LOSS, which (except for OPTION AND FUTURES CONTRACTS) has no tax consequences.

REAL PROPERTY land and all property attached to the land, such as houses, trees, fences, and all improvements.

REAL RATE OF RETURN RETURN on an investment adjusted for inflation.

REAL RETURN *see* REAL RATE OF RETURN.

REBATE
1. in lending, unearned interest refunded to a borrower if the loan is paid off before maturity.
2. in consumer marketing, payment made to a consumer after a purchase is completed, to induce purchase of a product. For instance, a customer who buys a television set for $500 may be entitled to a rebate of $50, which is received after sending a proof of purchase and a rebate form to the manufacturer. *See also* RULE OF THE 78s.

RECAPITALIZATION alteration of a corporation's CAPITAL STRUCTURE, such as an exchange of bonds for stock. BANKRUPTCY is a common reason for recapitalization; debentures might be exchanged for REORGANIZATION BONDS that pay interest only when earned. *See also* DEFEASANCE.

RECAPTURE

1. contract clause allowing one party to recover some degree of possession of an asset. In leases calling for a percentage of revenues, such as those for shopping centres, the recapture clause provides that the developer get a percentage of profits in addition to a fixed rent.
2. in the tax code, the reclamation by the government of tax benefits previously taken. For example, where a portion of the profit on the sale of a depreciable asset has been sheltered by capital cost allowance.

RECEIVABLES *see* ACCOUNTS RECEIVABLE.

RECEIVER court-appointed person who takes possession of, but not title to, the assets and affairs of a business or estate that is in a form of BANKRUPTCY called *receivership* or is enmeshed in a legal dispute. The receiver collects rents and other income and generally manages the affairs of the entity for the benefit of its owners and creditors until a disposition is made by the court.

RECESSION downturn in economic activity, defined by many economists as at least two consecutive quarters of decline in a country's GROSS DOMESTIC PRODUCT.

RECLAMATION

Banking: restoration or correction of a NEGOTIABLE INSTRUMENT—or the amount thereof—that has been incorrectly recorded by the *clearing house.*

Finance: restoration of an unproductive asset to productivity, such as by using landfill to make a swamp developable.

Securities: right of either party to a securities transaction to recover losses caused by *bad delivery* or other irregularities in the settlement process.

RECONCILIATION SERVICE mainly of use to companies with huge volume, a service provided by the bank that batches, sorts, and lists customers' cheques and provides detailed account reconciliation reports to their specification.

RECORD DATE *see* DATE OF RECORD; EX-DIVIDEND DATE; PAYMENT DATE.

RECOURSE legal ability the purchaser of a financial asset may have to fall back on the original creditor if the current debtor defaults. For example, an account receivable sold with recourse enables the buyer of the receivable to make claim on the seller if the account doesn't pay.

RECOURSE LOAN

1. loan for which an endorser or guarantor is liable for payment in the event the borrower defaults.

2. loan made to a LIMITED PARTNERSHIP whereby the lender, in addition to being secured by specific assets, has recourse against the general assets of the partnership. *See also* NONRECOURSE LOAN.

RECOVERY
Economics: period in a business cycle when economic activity picks up and the GROSS NATIONAL PRODUCT grows, leading into the expansion phase of the cycle.

Finance: (1) absorption of cost through the allocation of DEPRECIATION; (2) collection of an ACCOUNT RECEIVABLE that had been written off as a bad debt; (3) residual cost, or salvage value, of a fixed asset after all allowable depreciation.

Investment: period of rising prices in a securities or commodities market after a period of falling prices.

RECOVERY PERIOD
Economics: period of time in which the economy is emerging from a recession or depression. The recovery period is marked by rising sales and production, improved consumer confidence, and in many cases, rising interest rates.

Stocks: period of time in which a stock that has fallen sharply in price begins to rise again, thereby recovering some of its value.

REDEEMABLE BOND *see* CALLABLE.

REDEEMABLE PREFERRED SHARE preferred share for which the company reserves the right to redeem or pay out cash, usually for a small profit to the preferred shareholder. The shares are then cancelled by the company.

REDEMPTION repayment of a debt security or preferred stock issue, at or before maturity, at PAR or at a premium price.

Mutual fund shares are redeemed at NET ASSET VALUE when a shareholder's holdings are liquidated.

REDEMPTION DATE date on which a bond is scheduled to mature or be redeemed. If a bond is CALLED AWAY before scheduled maturity, the redemption date is the day that the bond will be taken back.

REDEMPTION FEES fees charged by a mutual fund on shareholders who sell fund shares within a short period of time. The time limit and size of the fee vary among funds, but the redemption fee usually is a relatively small percentage (1% or 2% of the amount withdrawn). Some mutual funds charge a small flat redemption fee of $5 or $10 to cover administrative charges. The intent of the redemption fee is to discourage rapid-fire shifts from one fund to another in an attempt to "time" swings in the stock or bond market. This fee often is confused with the contingent deferred sales charge, or BACK END SALES CHARGE, typically a feature of the bank sold fund.

REDEMPTION PRICE *see* CALL PRICE.

RED HERRING preliminary prospectus so called because certain information is printed in red ink around the border of the front page. It does not contain all the information found in the final prospectus. Its purpose is to ascertain the extent of public interest in an issue while it is being reviewed by a securities commission. *See also* PRELIMINARY PROSPECTUS.

REDLINING discrimination in the pattern of granting loans, insurance coverage, or other financial benefits practised in urban areas of the United States. Lenders or insurers who practise redlining "draw a red line" around a troubled area of a city and vow not to lend or insure property in that neighbourhood because of poor economic conditions and high default rates. Insurance companies withdraw from an area because of high claims experience and widespread fraud. With mortgage and business loans and insurance hard to obtain, redlining therefore tends to accelerate the decline of such neighbourhoods. Redlining is illegal because it discriminates against residents of an area on the basis of where they live. The U.S. Congress has enacted legislation such as the Community Reinvestment Act, which forces banks to lend to underprivileged areas, to combat redlining.

REFCORP *see* RESOLUTION FUNDING CORPORATION (REFCORP).

REFINANCING
Banking: extending the maturity date, or increasing the amount of existing debt, or both.
Bonds: REFUNDING; retiring existing bonded debt by issuing new securities to reduce the interest rate, or to extend the maturity date, or both.
Personal finance: revising a payment schedule, usually to reduce the monthly payments and often to modify interest charges.

REFLATION reversal of DEFLATION by deliberate government monetary action.

REFUND
Bonds: retirement of an existing bond issue through the sale of a new bond issue. When interest rates have fallen, issuers may want to exercise the CALL FEATURE of a bond and replace it with another debt instrument paying a lower interest rate. *See also* PREREFUNDING.
Commerce: return of merchandise for money. For example, a consumer who is not happy with a product has the right to return it for a refund of his money.
Taxes: *see* TAX REFUND.

REFUNDING
1. replacing an old debt with a new one, usually in order to lower the interest cost of the issuer. For instance, a corporation or municipality that has issued 10% bonds may want to refund them by issuing 7% bonds if interest rates have dropped. *See also* PREREFUNDING; REFINANCING.

    2. in merchandising, returning money to the purchaser, e.g., to a consumer who has paid for an appliance and is not happy with it.

REGIONAL STOCK EXCHANGES in the United States, organized national securities exchanges located outside of New York City and registered with the Securities and Exchange Commission. They include: the Boston, Cincinnati, Intermountain (Salt Lake City), Midwest (Chicago), Pacific (Los Angeles and San Francisco), Philadelphia (Philadelphia and Miami), and Spokane stock exchanges. These exchanges list not only regional issues, but many of the securities that are listed on the New York exchanges. Companies listed on the NEW YORK STOCK EXCHANGE and the AMERICAN STOCK EXCHANGE will often be listed on regional exchanges as well to broaden the market for their securities. Using the INTERMARKET TRADING SYSTEM (ITS), a SPECIALIST on the floor of one of the New York or regional exchanges can see competing prices for the securities he trades on video screens. Regional exchanges handle only a small percentage of the total volume of the New York exchanges, though most of the trading done on regional exchanges involves stocks listed on the New York exchanges. *See also* DUAL LISTING; GRADUATED SECURITY; SECURITIES AND COMMODITIES EXCHANGES.

REGISTERED ANNUITY annuity arranged so that the interest portion is level each year. If an annuity is purchased with money upon which tax has already been paid, only the interest portion of the payments is taxable in the future, but it is the interest portion of any blended payment that is usually higher in the early years. If the annuitant is close to the threshold for one of the tax brackets, a registered annuity may help to avoid high tax burdens by keeping the investor in the lower tax bracket.

REGISTERED BOND bond that is recorded in the name of the holder on the books of the issuer or the issuer's REGISTRAR and can be transferred to another owner only when ENDORSED by the registered owner. A bond registered for principal only, and not for interest, is called a *registered coupon bond.* One that is not registered is called a *bearer bond;* one issued with detachable coupons for presentation to the issuer or a paying agent when interest or principal payments are due is termed a COUPON BOND. Bearer bonds are NEGOTIABLE INSTRUMENTS payable to the holder and therefore do not legally require endorsement. Bearer bonds that may be changed to registered bonds are called *interchangeable bonds.*

REGISTERED COMPANY company that has filed a REGISTRATION STATEMENT with the Ontario, Alberta, Québec, or B.C. securities commissions in connection with a PUBLIC OFFERING of securities and must therefore comply with the commission's DISCLOSURE requirements. In the United States, such a company files registration with the U.S. Securities and Exchange Commission.

REGISTERED COMPETITIVE MARKET MAKER

1. U.S. securities dealer registered with the NATIONAL ASSOCIATION OF SECURITIES DEALERS (NASD) as a market maker in a particular OVER-THE-COUNTER stock—that is, one who maintains firm bid and offer prices in the stock by standing ready to buy or sell round lots. Such dealers must announce their quotes through NASDAQ, which requires that there be at least two market makers in each stock listed in the system; the bid and asked quotes are compared to ensure that the quote is a *representative spread. See also* MAKE A MARKET.

2. REGISTERED COMPETITIVE TRADER on the New York Stock Exchange. Such traders are sometimes called market makers because, in addition to trading for their own accounts, they are expected to help correct an IMBALANCE OF ORDERS. *See also* REGISTERED EQUITY MARKET MAKER.

REGISTERED EDUCATION SAVINGS PLAN plan allowing the accumulation of tax-sheltered contributions for education. Withdrawals are taxable. Contributions are not tax-deductible. Income is sheltered in the plan for up to 21 years as long as it is not withdrawn. *See also* EDUCATIONAL SAVINGS PLAN.

REGISTERED FINANCIAL PLANNER (RFP) *see* FINANCIAL PLANNER.

REGISTERED FUND fund normally registered with and regulated by Revenue Canada, i.e., eligible for an RRSP.

REGISTERED REPRESENTATIVE salesperson employed by a stock exchange member broker/dealer. As such, the registered representative gives advice on which securities to buy and sell, and collects as compensation a percentage of any commission income generated. To qualify as a registered representative, a person must acquire a background in the securities business, pass a series of tests, and be registered by the securities commission in the province in which he or she works.

REGISTERED RETIREMENT INCOME FUND (RRIF) continuation and mirror image of an RRSP. The RRSP funds can be partly or wholly transferred to an RRIF, and all RRSPs must be wound up by December 31st of the year in which the beneficiary turns 71. The funds accumulated are withdrawn in future years to provide retirement income. Income on the balance in the RRIF accumulates tax-free, but all payouts are fully taxable. A trustee holds the RRIF, and the person whose RRSP created it can either manage the money in a self-administered RRIF or use a guaranteed rate RRIF provided by the trustee. The investment restrictions on the RRIF are essentially the same as those on an RRSP.

The beneficiary may withdraw as much from the RRIF as desired, but there is a minimum withdrawal required, based on the market value of the plan's assets at the start of the year. The rules changed in 1993 to require lower minimum withdrawals after age 78. In addition, the old rule had required that all the funds be paid out by the time the beneficiary or the beneficiary's spouse reached age 90. The new rules allow the RRIF to continue to any age. Retirees who set up an RRIF prior to 1993 will continue to use the old rules until their 79th year, when they switch to the new ones. Of course, since there is no maximum limit on withdrawals, they can still withdraw all the funds by age 90.

A person may have more than one RRIF. The income from an RRIF is pension income. The funds in an RRIF in excess of the minimum withdrawal for the year can be used to buy life annuity. However, such annuity cannot have a guaranteed term extending beyond age 90 of the annuitant or spouse.

REGISTERED RETIREMENT SAVINGS PLAN (RRSP) plan to which tax deductible contributions are made to accumulate a retirement fund.

REGISTERED TAX DEFERRAL SAVINGS PLAN government-approved savings plans (such as registered pension plans, registered retirement savings plans, and registered retirement income funds) in which funds contributed by individuals are tax-deductible within certain limits, and investment earnings accumulate in the plans tax-free until deregistration or maturity of the plans.

REGISTERED SECURITY

1. security whose owner's name is recorded on the books of the issuer or the issuer's agent, called a *registrar*—for example, a REGISTERED BOND as opposed to a *bearer bond,* the former being transferable only by endorsement, the latter payable to the holder. Registered debt securities may be registered as to principal only or fully registered. In the latter case, interest is paid by cheque rather than by coupons attached to the certificate.

2. securities issue registered with a securities commission as a new issue or as a SECONDARY OFFERING. *See also* REGISTERED SECONDARY OFFERING; REGISTRATION.

REGISTRAR agency, usually a trust company, responsible for keeping track of the owners of bonds and the issuance of stock. The registrar, working with the TRANSFER AGENT, keeps current files of the owners of a bond issue and the stockholders in a corporation. The registrar also makes sure that no more than the authorized amount of stock is in circulation, receiving both the old cancelled certificate and the new certificate and recording and signing the new one. For bonds, the registrar certifies that a bond is a corporation's genuine debt obligation. The registrar is, in effect, an auditor checking on the accuracy of the work of the transfer agent, although in most cases the registrar and transfer agent are the same trust company.

REGISTRATION registration of new securities under the Securities Act of each province in which they will be offered for sale. This usually involves filing a prospectus, and must be done before a public offering may be made of the new securities or of outstanding securities by controlling stockholders.

REGISTRATION STATEMENT document detailing the purpose of a proposed public offering of securities. The statement outlines financial details, a history of the company's operations and management, and other facts of importance to potential buyers. *See also* REGISTRATION.

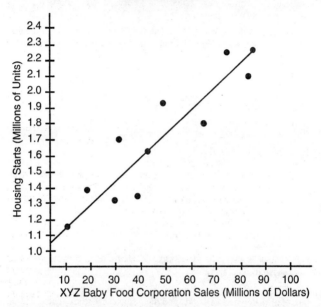

**REGRESSION ANALYSIS
SCATTER GRAPH**

REGRESSION ANALYSIS statistical technique used to establish the relationship of a dependent variable, such as the sales of a company, and one or more independent variables, such as family formations, GROSS NATIONAL PRODUCT, per capita income, and other ECONOMIC INDICATORS. By measuring exactly how large and significant each independent variable has historically been in its relation to the dependent variable, the future value of the dependent variable can be predicted. Essentially, regression analysis attempts to measure the degree of correlation between the dependent and independent variables, thereby establishing the latter's predictive value. For example, a manufacturer of baby food might want to determine the relationship between sales and housing starts as part of a sales forecast. Using a technique called a scatter graph, it might plot on the X and Y axes the historical sales for ten years and the historical annual housing starts for the same period. A line connecting the average dots, called the regression line, would reveal the degree of correlation between the two factors by showing the amount of unexplained variation—represented by the dots falling outside the line. Thus, if the regression line connected all the dots, it would demonstrate a direct relationship between baby food sales and housing starts, meaning that one could be predicted on the basis of the other. The proportion of dots scattered outside the regression line would indicate, on the other hand, the degree to which the relationship was less direct, a high enough degree of unexplained variation meaning there was no meaningful relationship and that housing starts have no predictive value in terms of baby food sales. This proportion of unexplained variations is termed the *coefficient of determination,* and its square root the CORRELATION COEFFICIENT. The correlation coefficient is the ultimate yardstick of regression analysis: a correlation coefficient of 1 means the relationship is direct—baby food and housing starts move together; –1 means there is a negative relationship—the more housing starts there are, the less baby food is sold; a coefficient of zero means there is no relationship between the two factors.

Regression analysis is also used in securities' markets analysis and in the risk-return analyses basic to PORTFOLIO THEORY.

REGRESSIVE TAX
1. system of taxation in which tax rates decline as the tax base rises. For example, a system that taxed values of $1000 to $5000 at 5%, $5000 to $10,000 at 4% and so on would be regressive. A regressive tax is the opposite of a PROGRESSIVE TAX.
2. tax system that results in a higher tax for the poor than for the rich, in terms of percentage of income. In this sense, a sales tax is regressive even though the same rate is applied to all sales, because people with lower incomes tend to spend most of their incomes on goods and services. Similarly, payroll taxes are regressive because they are borne largely by wage earners and not by higher income groups. Local property taxes also tend to be regressive because poorer people spend more of their incomes on housing costs, which are directly affected by property taxes. *See also* FLAT TAX.

REGULAR BOND bond that pays interest, usually twice a year, at a fixed interest rate.

Brokers sell regular bonds with a minimum purchase limit as low as $5000 but more typically $50,000 or more. Small investors are better off buying bond funds because, for amounts as small as $100, they can obtain units of a portfolio rather than investing in one specific bond. Holding bonds directly is safer, however, because full repayment of principal at maturity is usually guaranteed, whereas a bond fund manager will buy and sell bonds as he or she sees fit, rarely holding them to full maturity.

REGULAR DELIVERY stipulation that, unless otherwise stipulated, sellers of stock must deliver it on or before the third business day after the sale.

REGULATED COMMODITIES all commodity futures and options contracts traded on organized futures exchanges.

REHYPOTHECATION pledging by brokers of securities in customers' MARGIN ACCOUNTS to banks as collateral for broker loans under a GENERAL LOAN AND COLLATERAL AGREEMENT. Broker loans cover the positions of brokers who have made margin loans to customers for margin purchases and SELLING SHORT. Margin loans are collateralized by the HYPOTHECATION of customers securities to the broker. Their rehypothecation is authorized when the customer originally signs a GENERAL ACCOUNT agreement.

REIMBURSEMENT paying someone back for out-of-pocket expenses. For example, a company reimburses employees for their out-of-pocket business-related expenses when employees file expense reports. Insurance companies reimburse policyholders for out-of-pocket expenses incurred paying medical bills (for health insurance) or for home repairs (homeowner's insurance).

REINSTATEMENT in INSURANCE, the restoration of coverage after a policy has lapsed because premium payments have not been made. Typically, life insurance can be reinstated within a three-year period if premiums are paid and subject to evidence of continued insurability.

REINSURANCE sharing of RISK among insurance companies. Part of the insurer's risk is assumed by other companies in return for a part of the premium fee paid by the insured. By spreading the risk, reinsurance allows an individual company to take on clients whose coverage would be too great a burden for one insurer to carry alone.

REINVESTMENT act of reinvesting investment earnings, usually associated with mutual funds.

REINVESTMENT PRIVILEGE right of a shareholder to reinvest dividends in order to buy more shares in the company or MUTUAL FUND, usually at no additional sales charge.

REINVESTMENT RATE rate of return resulting from the reinvestment of the interest from a bond or other fixed-income security. The reinvestment rate on a ZERO-COUPON BOND is predictable and locked in, since no interest payments are ever made, and therefore all imputed interest is reinvested at the same rate. The reinvestment rate on coupon bonds is less predictable because it rises and falls with market interest rates.

REINVESTMENT RISK risk that rates will fall causing cash flows from an investment (dividends or interest), assuming reinvestment, to earn less than the original investment.

REIT *see* REAL ESTATE INVESTMENT TRUST.

REJECTION
Banking: refusal to grant credit to an applicant because of inadequate financial strength, a poor credit history, or some other reason.
Insurance: refusal to underwrite a risk, that is, to issue a policy.

Securities: refusal of a broker or a broker's customer to accept the security presented to complete a trade. This usually occurs because the security lacks the necessary endorsements. or because of other exceptions to the rules for GOOD DELIVERY.

RELATIVE STRENGTH rate at which a stock falls relative to other stocks in a falling market or rises relative to other stocks in a rising market. Analysts reason that a stock that holds value on the downside will be a strong performer on the upside and vice versa.

RELEASE CLAUSE provision in a MORTGAGE agreement allowing the freeing of pledged property after a proportionate amount of payment has been made.

RELEVANT CASH INFLOWS incremental after-tax net operating cash inflows (i.e., the combined incremental after-tax cash operating and the tax savings for each period) and the salvage value expected to result from the investment.

REMAINDER remaining interest in a TRUST or ESTATE after expenses and after prior beneficiaries have been satisfied. *See also* CHARITABLE REMAINDER TRUST.

REMAINING MONTHLY BALANCE amount of debt remaining unpaid on a monthly statement. For example, a credit card customer may charge $300 worth of merchandise during a month, and pay $100, leaving a remaining monthly balance of $200, on which interest charges would accrue.

REMARGINING putting up additional cash or eligible securities to correct a deficiency in EQUITY deposited in a brokerage MARGIN ACCOUNT to meet MINIMUM MAINTENANCE REQUIREMENTS. Remargining usually is prompted by a MARGIN CALL.

REMIT pay for purchased goods or services by cash, cheque, or electronic payment.

RENEWABLE TERM LIFE INSURANCE term life insurance policy offering the policyholder the option to renew for a specific period of time—frequently one year—for a particular length of time. Some term life policies stipulate a maximum age benefit. Some policies offer fixed premium rates for a certain number of years, usually ten, after which they are renewable at a higher premium rate. Other term policies are renewable every year, and charge escalating premium rates as the policyholder ages.

RENT payment from a tenant to a building owner for use of the specified property. For example, an apartment dweller must pay monthly rent to a landlord for the right to inhabit the apartment. A commercial tenant in an office or store must pay monthly rent to the building owner for the use of the commercial space.

RENT CONTROL state and local government regulation restricting the amount of rent landlords can charge their tenants. Rent control is used to regulate the quality of rental dwellings, with controls implemented only against those units that do not conform to building codes, or used across the board to deal with high rents resulting from a gross imbalance between housing supply and demand. If a landlord violates rent control laws, the tenant may protest at the local housing authority charged with enforcing the law. While tenants may like rent control, landlords argue that it reduces their ability to earn a profit on their property, thereby discouraging them from investing any further to maintain or upgrade the property. In some cases, landlords argue that rent control encourages owners to abandon their property altogether since it will never be profitable to retain it.

REORGANIZATION financial restructuring of a firm in BANKRUPTCY. *See also* TRUSTEE IN BANKRUPTCY; VOTING TRUST CERTIFICATE.

REORGANIZATION BOND debt security issued by a company in REORGANIZATION proceedings. The bonds are generally issued to the company's creditors on a basis whereby interest is paid only if and when it is earned. *See also* ADJUSTMENT BOND; INCOME BOND.

REPATRIATION return of the financial assets of an organization or individual from a foreign country to the home country.

REPLACEMENT COST cost to replace an asset with another of similar utility at today's prices. Also called *current cost* and *replacement value*. *See also* BOOK VALUE, REPLACEMENT COST INSURANCE.

REPLACEMENT COST ACCOUNTING accounting method allowing additional DEPRECIATION on part of the difference between the original cost and current replacement cost of a depreciable asset.

REPLACEMENT COST INSURANCE property and casualty insurance that replaces damaged property. Replacement cost contents insurance pays the dollar amount needed to replace damaged personal property with items of like kind and quality, without deducting for depreciation. Replacement cost dwelling insurance pays the policyholder the cost of replacing the damaged property without deduction for depreciation, but limited by the maximum dollar amount indicated on the declarations page of the policy. *See also* REPLACEMENT COST.

REPORTING ISSUER corporation that has issued or has outstanding securities that are held by the public and is subject to continuous disclosure requirements of securities administrators.

REQUIRED RATE OF RETURN return required by investors before they will commit money to an investment at a given level of risk. Unless the expected return exceeds the required return, an investment is unacceptable. *See also* HURDLE RATE; INTERNAL RATE OF RETURN; MEAN RETURN.

REQUIRED RESERVE RATE factor used to determine the amount of reserves a bank must maintain on its deposits.

RESCHEDULED LOANS bank loans that, as an alternative to DEFAULT, were restructured, usually by lengthening the maturity to make it easier for the borrower to meet repayment terms.

RESCIND cancel a contract agreement. Contracts may also be rescinded in cases of fraud, failure to comply with legal procedures, or misrepresentation. For example, a contract signed by a child under legal age may be rescinded, since children do not have the right to take on contractual obligations. Depending on the province, a consumer is allowed from 3 to 7 business days as a cooling-off period on most conditional sales contracts.

RESCISSION *see* RIGHT OF RESCISSION.

RESEARCH AND DEVELOPMENT (R&D) scientific and marketing evolution of a new product or service. Once such a product has been created in a laboratory or other research setting, marketing specialists attempt to define the market for the product. Then, steps are taken to manufacture the product to meet the needs of the market. Research and development spending is often listed as a separate item in a company's financial statements. In industries such as high-technology and pharmaceuticals, R&D spending is quite high, since products are outdated or attract competition quickly. Investors looking for companies in such fast-changing fields check on R&D spending as a percentage of sales because they consider this an important indicator of the company's prospects.

RESEARCH AND DEVELOPMENT LIMITED PARTNERSHIP plan whose investors put up money to finance new product RESEARCH AND DEVELOPMENT. In return, the investors get a percentage of the product's profits, if any, together with such benefits as tax credits and loss write-offs. R&D partnerships may be offered publicly or privately, usually through brokerage firms.

RESEARCH DEPARTMENT division within a brokerage firm, investment company, bank trust department, insurance company, or other institutional investing organization that analyzes markets and securities. Research departments include analysts who focus on particular securities, commodities, and whole industries as well as generalists who forecast movements of the markets as a whole, using both FUNDAMENTAL ANALYSIS and TECHNICAL ANALYSIS. An analyst whose advice is followed by many investors can have a major impact on the prices of individual securities.

RESERVE
  1. segregation of RETAINED EARNINGS to provide for such payouts as dividends, contingencies, improvements, or retirement of preferred stock.

2. VALUATION RESERVE, also called ALLOWANCE, for DEPRECIATION, BAD DEBT losses, shrinkage of receivables because of discounts taken, and other provisions created by charges to the PROFIT AND LOSS STATEMENT.
3. hidden reserves, represented by understatements of BALANCE SHEET values.
4. deposit maintained by a commercial bank in a FEDERAL RESERVE BANK to meet the Fed's RESERVE REQUIREMENT.

RESERVE REQUIREMENT rule mandating the financial assets that member banks must keep in the form of cash and other liquid assets as a percentage of DEMAND DEPOSITS and TIME DEPOSITS.

RESET BONDS bonds issued with a provision that on specified dates the initial interest rate must be adjusted so that the bonds trade at their original value. Although reset provisions can work in an issuer's favour by lowering rates should market rates fall or credit quality improve, they were designed as a protective feature for investors to enhance the marketability of JUNK BOND issues. Should market rates rise or credit quality decline (causing prices to decline), the interest rate would be increased to bring the bond price to PAR or above. The burden of increased interest payments on a weak issuer could prompt DEFAULT.

RESIDENTIAL MORTGAGE mortgage on a residential property.

RESIDENTIAL PROPERTY property zoned for single-family homes, townhouses, multifamily apartments, condominiums, and co-ops. Residential property falls under different zoning and taxation regulations than commercial property.

RESIDUAL DIVIDEND THEORY theory suggesting that a business pays cash dividends if and only when acceptable investment opportunities for these funds are currently unavailable, i.e., cash dividends are viewed as residual funds that cannot be used in some acceptable investment opportunity.

RESIDUAL SECURITY SECURITY that has a potentially dilutive effect on earnings per common share. Warrants, rights, convertible bonds, and preferred stock are potentially dilutive because exercising or converting them into common stock would increase the number of common shares competing for the same earnings, and earnings per share would be reduced. *See also* DILUTION: FULLY DILUTED EARNINGS PER (COMMON) SHARE.

RESIDUAL VALUE
1. realizable value of a FIXED ASSET after costs associated with the sale.
2. amount remaining after all allowable DEPRECIATION charges have been subtracted from the original cost of a depreciable asset.
3. scrap value, which is the value to a junk dealer. Also called *salvage value.*

RESISTANCE LEVEL price ceiling at which technical analysts note persistent selling of a commodity or security. If XYZ's stock generally trades between a low of $50 and a high of $60 a share, $50 is called the SUPPORT LEVEL and $60 is called the resistance level. Technical analysts think it significant when the stock breaks through the resistance level because that means it usually will go on to new high prices. *See also* BREAKOUT; TECHNICAL ANALYSIS.

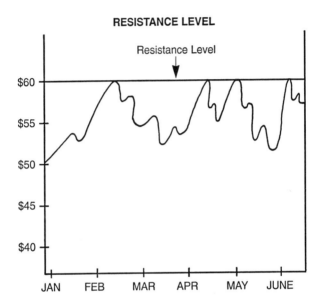

RESISTANCE LEVEL

RESOLUTION
1. in general, expression of desire or intent.
2. formal document representing an action of a corporation's BOARD OF DIRECTORS—perhaps a directive to management, such as in the declaration of a dividend, or a corporate expression of sentiment, such as acknowledging the services of a retiring officer. A *corporate resolution,* which defines the authority and powers of individual officers, is a document given to a bank.
3. legal order or contract by a government entity—called a *bond resolution*—authorizing a bond issue and spelling out the rights of bondholders and the obligations of the issuer.

RESOLUTION TRUST CORPORATION (RTC) U.S. government agency created by the 1989 bailout bill to merge or close savings and loan institutions becoming insolvent between 1989 and August 1992. RTC was scheduled to terminate after 1996 and shift its responsibilities to the SAVINGS ASSOCIATION INSURANCE FUND (SAIF), a unit of the FEDERAL DEPOSIT INSURANCE CORPORATION. The *Resolution Trust Corporation Oversight Board,* an arm of the executive branch, was charged with overseeing broad policy and the dispensing of funds to sick thrifts by RTC.

RESTRICTED SHARES shares that participate in a company's earnings and assets (in liquidation), as common shares do, but generally has either voting rights with restrictions or no voting rights.

RESTRICTED SURPLUS portion of RETAINED EARNINGS not legally available for the payment of dividends. Among the circumstances giving rise to such restriction: dividend arrearages in CUMULATIVE PREFERRED stock, a shortfall in the minimum WORKING CAPITAL ratio specified in an INDENTURE, or simply a vote by the BOARD OF DIRECTORS. Also called *restricted retained earnings.*

RESTRICTIVE COVENANT *see* COVENANT.

RESTRICTIVE ENDORSEMENT signature on the back of a cheque specifying the transfer of the amount of that cheque, under specific conditions. The most common type of restrictive endorsement is "for deposit only," meaning the cheque must be deposited in the payee's bank account and cannot be cashed.

RESTRICTIVE LOAN PROVISIONS *see* COVENANT.

RETAIL HOUSE brokerage firm that caters to retail investors instead of institutions. Such a firm may be a large national broker called a WIRE HOUSE, with a large RESEARCH DEPARTMENT and a wide variety of products and services for individuals, or it may be a small BOUTIQUE serving an exclusive clientele with specialized research or investment services.

RETAIL INVESTOR investor who buys securities and commodities futures on his own behalf, not for an organization. Retail investors typically buy shares of stock or commodity positions in much smaller quantities than institutions such as mutual funds, bank trust departments, and pension funds and therefore are usually charged commissions higher than those paid by the institutions. In recent years, market activity has increasingly been dominated by INSTITUTIONAL INVESTORS.

RETAIL PRICE price charged to retail customers for goods and services. Retailers buy goods from wholesalers, and increase the price to cover their costs, plus a profit. Manufacturers list suggested retail prices for their products; retailers may adhere to these prices or offer discounts from them.

RETAIL SALES sale of goods to the consumer by a merchant who buys them at wholesale prices. Since retail sales make up more than half the total level of demand in the economy, an increase in retail sales is likely to mean increased industrial production and investment.

RETAINED EARNINGS net profits kept to accumulate in a business after dividends are paid. Also called *undistributed profits* or *earned surplus.* Retained earnings are distinguished from *contributed capital*—capital received in exchange for stock, which is reflected in CAPITAL STOCK or CAPITAL SURPLUS and DONATED STOCK or DONATED SURPLUS. STOCK DIVIDENDS—the distribution of additional shares of capital stock with no cash payment—reduce retained earnings and increase capital stock. Retained earnings plus the total of all the capital accounts represent the NET WORTH of a firm. Retained earnings can also mean the accumulated earnings after taxes and can be negative if a company has net accumulated losses. *See also* ACCUMULATED PROFITS TAX; PAID-IN CAPITAL.

RETAINED EARNINGS STATEMENT reconciliation of the beginning and ending balances in the RETAINED EARNINGS account on a company's BALANCE SHEET. It breaks down changes affecting the account, such as profits or losses from operations, dividends declared, and any other items charged or credited to retained earnings. A retained earnings statement is required by GENERALLY ACCEPTED ACCOUNTING PRINCIPLES whenever comparative balance sheets and income statements are presented. It may appear in the balance sheet, in a combined PROFIT AND LOSS STATEMENT and retained earnings statement, or as a separate schedule. It may also be called *statement of changes in earned surplus* (or *retained income).*

RETENTION in securities underwriting, the number of units allocated to a participating investment banker (SYNDICATE member) minus the units held back by the syndicate manager for facilitating institutional sales and for allocation to firms in the selling group that are not also members of the syndicate. *See also* UNDERWRITE.

RETENTION RATE percentage of net earnings available for reinvestment into the company after dividends are paid to stockholders. The retention rate is also the inverse of the dividend payout ratio. If the payout ratio is 25%, the retention rate is 75%.

RETIREMENT
1. cancellation of stock or bonds that have been reacquired or redeemed. *See also* CALLABLE; REDEMPTION.
2. removal from service after a fixed asset has reached the end of its useful life or has been sold and appropriate adjustments have been made to the asset and depreciation accounts.
3. repayment of a debt obligation.
4. permanent withdrawal of an employee from gainful employment in accordance with an employer's policies concerning length of service, age, or disability. A retired employee may have rights to a pension or other retirement provisions offered by the employer. Such benefits may in some circumstances supplement payments from a Registered Retirement Savings Plan.

RETIREMENT AGE age at which employees no longer work. Though there is no longer any mandatory retirement age, many institutions do impose a retirement age. Many corporations have a retirement age of 65, although this has become more flexible and is no longer standard. Employees reaching age 60 may start to receive Canada Pension.

RETIREMENT PLAN *see* PENSION PLAN.

RETRACTABLE a feature that can be included in a new debt or preferred issue, granting the holder the option under specified conditions to redeem the security on a stated date, prior to maturity in the case of a bond.

RETRACTABLE PREFERRED SHARE share that may be cashed in by the owner at the company on a specified date for a specified price.

RETURN
Finance and investment: profit on a securities or capital investment, usually expressed as an annual percentage rate. For comparison purposes, it is important to know whether returns are before or after tax. *See also* RATE OF RETURN; RETURN ON EQUITY; RETURN ON INVESTED CAPITAL; RETURN ON SALES; TOTAL RETURN.
Retailing: exchange of previously sold merchandise for REFUND or CREDIT against future sales.
Taxes: form on which taxpayers submit information required by the government when they file with the Revenue Canada.
Trade: physical return of merchandise for credit against an invoice.

RETURN ITEM negotiable instrument sent to another bank for collection and payment and returned unpaid, e.g., NSF cheque. Return items are sent back via the same route according to the various bank endorsements on the back of the item.

RETURN OF CAPITAL distribution of cash resulting from DEPRECIATION tax savings, the sale of a CAPITAL ASSET or of securities in a portfolio, or any other transaction unrelated to RETAINED EARNINGS. Returns of capital are not directly taxable but may result in higher CAPITAL GAINS taxes later on if they reduce the acquisition cost base of the property involved. Also called *return of basis.*

RETURN ON COMMON EQUITY *see* RETURN ON EQUITY; RETURN ON INVESTED CAPITAL.

RETURN ON EQUITY (ROE) amount, expressed as a percentage, earned on a company's common stock investment for a given period. It is calculated by dividing common stock equity (NET WORTH) at the beginning of the accounting period into NET INCOME for the period after preferred stock dividends but before common stock dividends. Return on equity tells common shareholders how effectually their money is being employed. Comparing percentages for current and prior periods reveals trends, and comparison with industry composites reveals how well a company is holding its own against its competitors.

RETURN ON INVESTED CAPITAL amount, expressed as a percentage, earned on a company's total capital—its common and preferred stock EQUITY plus its long-term FUNDED DEBT—calculated by dividing total capital into earnings after interest, taxes, and dividends. (In the United States, the division is usually made before taxes.) Return on invested capital, usually termed *return on investment,* or *ROI,* is a useful means of comparing companies, or corporate divisions, in terms of efficiency of management and viability of product lines.

RETURN ON INVESTMENT (ROI) sometimes called the return on total assets. It can be calculated by dividing the firm's net profit after taxes by its total assets or by multiplying its net profit margin by the total asset turnover. In the United States, the division is usually made before taxes.

RETURN ON SALES net pretax profits as a percentage of NET SALES— a useful measure of overall operational efficiency when compared with prior periods or with other companies in the same line of business. It is important to recognize, however, that return on sales varies widely from industry to industry. A supermarket chain with a 2% return on sales might be operating efficiently, for example, because it depends on high volume to generate an acceptable RETURN ON INVESTED CAPITAL. In contrast, a manufacturing enterprise is expected to average 4% to 5%, so a return on sales of 2% is likely to be considered highly inefficient.

REVALUATION change in the value of a country's currency relative to others that is based on the decision of authorities rather than on fluctuations in the market. Revaluation generally refers to an increase in the currency's value; DEVALUATION refers to a decrease. *See also* FLOATING EXCHANGE RATE; PAR VALUE OF CURRENCY.

REVENUE NEUTRAL a change in tax legislation that results in no net tax increase to taxpayers or no net increase in government revenue.

REVENUE SHARING
Limited partnerships: percentage split between the general partner and limited partners of profits, losses, cash distributions, and other income or losses which result from the operation of a real estate, oil and gas, film and R&D, or other partnership. *See also* LIMITED PARTNERSHIP.
Taxes: return of tax revenue to a unit of government by a larger unit, such as from a province to one of its municipalities.

REVERSAL change in direction in the stock or commodity futures markets, as charted by technical analysts. If the Toronto Stock Exchange 300 Index has been climbing steadily from 4000 to 4900, for instance, chartists would speak of a reversal if the average started a sustained fall back toward 4000. *See* chart on next page*See* chart on next page

REVERSAL

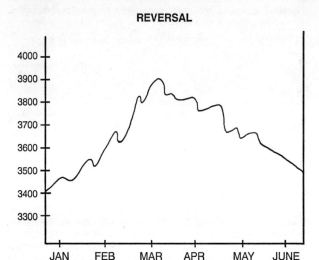

REVERSE ANNUITY MORTGAGE (RAM) MORTGAGE instrument that allows an elderly person to live off the equity in a fully paid-for house. Such a homeowner would enter into a reverse annuity mortgage agreement with a financial institution which would guarantee a life-long fixed monthly income in return for gradually giving up ownership of the house. The longer the payments continue, the less equity the elderly owner would retain. At the owner's death the lender gains title to the real estate, which it can sell at a profit.

Only a few institutions, including some credit unions, offer reverse mortgages, and people need expert advice before embarking on them because there are pitfalls for the unwary. In a Term Reverse Mortgage, the amount owing seems to grow quite quickly because it is accumulating without any repayment. In a Reverse Annuity Mortgage (RAM), if the annuitant (mortgagor) dies early, the heirs often feel cheated, since the annuity provides no value to the estate and the value of the house is much less after retiring the mortgage. Neither of these problems seems too serious when real estate prices are rising, but if they fall, the effect is severe.

Reverse mortgages are indeed mortgages, because the security is the home. The homeowner buys an annuity with the cash received through an installment loan that is contingent on the value of the house and, in the case of a RAM, on the life of the annuitant. Conceptually, the mortgagor has a put option to make the issuer of the reverse mortgage take either the house or the value of the mortgage, whichever is less. The value of the put option rises with the length of time to expiry. In a RAM, that time is uncertain.

If property values are increasing and the RAM payments are finished, a lender may enter into an extended RAM if the owner's equity in the home justifies a further loan. If the RAM cannot be extended, the homeowner must continue making mortgage payments until the debt is paid. If the homeowner has no other income, the home may have to be sold, and, if house prices have decreased, the homeowner could be in considerable financial difficulty.

See also ARM'S LENGTH TRANSACTION.

REVERSE A SWAP restore a bond portfolio to its former position following a swap of one bond for another to gain the advantage of a YIELD SPREAD or a tax loss. The reversal may mean that the yield differential has disappeared or that the investor, content with a short-term profit, wishes to stay with the original bond for the advantages that may be gained in the future. *See also* BOND SWAP.

REVERSE CONVERSION technique whereby brokerage firms earn interest on their customers' stock holdings. A typical reverse conversion would work like this: A brokerage firm sells short the stocks it holds in customers' margin accounts, then invests this money in short-term money market instruments. To protect against a sharp rise in the markets, the firm hedges its short position by buying CALL options and selling PUT options. To unwind the reverse conversion, the firms buys back the stocks, sells the call, and buys the put. *See also* MARGIN ACCOUNT; OPTION.

REVERSE LEVERAGE situation, the opposite of FINANCIAL LEVERAGE, where the interest on money borrowed exceeds the return on investment of the borrowed funds.

REVERSE LEVERAGED BUYOUT process of bringing back into publicly traded status a company—or a division of a company—that had been publicly traded and taken private. In the 1980s, many public companies were taken private in LEVERAGED BUYOUTS by corporate raiders who borrowed against the companies' assets to finance the deal. When some or all of the debt incurred in the leveraged buyout was repaid, many of these companies were in sufficiently strong financial condition to go public again, enriching the private stockholders as well as the investment bankers who earned fees implementing these deals.

REVERSE MORTGAGE arrangement whereby a homeowner borrows against home equity and receives regular payments (tax-free) from the lender until the accumulated principal and interest reach the credit limit of equity; at that time, the lender either gets repayment in a lump sum or takes the house. They are appropriate for cash-poor but house-rich older borrowers who want to stay in their homes and expect to live long enough to amortize high up-front fees but not so long that the lender winds up with the house.

REVERSE REPURCHASE AGREEMENT *see* REPURCHASE AGREEMENT.

REVERSE SPLIT like CONSOLIDATION, a procedure whereby a corporation reduces the number of shares outstanding. The total number of shares will have the same market value immediately after the reverse split as before it, but each share will be worth more. For example, if a firm with 10 million outstanding shares selling at $10 a share executes a reverse 1 for 10 split, the firm will end up with 1 million shares selling for $100 each. Such splits are usually initiated by companies wanting to raise the price of their outstanding shares because they think the price is too low to attract investors. Also called *split down. See also* SPLIT.

REVISIONARY TRUST IRREVOCABLE TRUST that becomes a REVOCABLE TRUST after a specified period, usually over 10 years or upon the death of the GRANTOR.

REVOCABLE TRUST agreement whereby income-producing property is deeded to heirs. The provisions of such a TRUST may be altered as many times as the GRANTOR pleases, or the entire trust agreement can be canceled, unlike irrevocable trusts. The grantor receives income from the assets, but the property passes directly to the beneficiaries at the grantor's death, without having to go through PROBATE court proceedings. Since the assets are still part of the grantor's estate, however, this kind of trust differs from an IRREVOCABLE TRUST, which permanently transfers assets from the estate during the grantor's lifetime.

REVOLVING CREDIT
Commercial banking: contractual agreement between a bank and its customer, usually a company, whereby the bank agrees to make loans up to a specified maximum for a specified period, usually a year or more. As the borrower repays a portion of the loan, an amount equal to the repayment can be borrowed again under the terms of the agreement. In addition to interest borne by notes, the bank charges a fee for the commitment to hold the funds available. A COMPENSATING BALANCE may be required in addition.
Consumer banking: loan account requiring monthly payments of less than the full amount due, and the balance carried forward is subject to a financial charge. Also, an arrangement whereby borrowings are permitted up to a specified limit and for a specified period, usually a year, with a fee charged for the commitment. Also called *open-end credit* or *revolving line of credit.*

REVOLVING LINE OF CREDIT *see* REVOLVING CREDIT.

RICH
1. term for a security whose price seems too high in light of its price history. For bonds, the term may also imply that the yield is too low.

2. term for rate of interest that seems too high in relation to the borrower's risk.

3. synonym for *wealthy.*

RIDER written form attached to an insurance policy that alters the policy's coverage, terms, or conditions. For example, after buying a diamond bracelet, a policyholder may want to add a rider to his or her homeowner's insurance policy to cover the jewellery. *See also* FLOATER.

RIGGED MARKET situation in which the prices for a security are manipulated so as to lure unsuspecting buyers or sellers. *See also* MANIPULATION.

RIGHT *see* SUBSCRIPTION RIGHT.

RIGHT OF FIRST REFUSAL right of someone to be offered a right before it is offered to others. For example, a baseball team may have the right of first refusal on a ballplayer's contract, meaning that the club can make the first offer, or even match other offers, before the player works for another team. A company may have the right of refusal to distribute or manufacture another company's product. A publishing company may have the right of refusal to publish a book proposed by one of their authors.

RIGHT OF REDEMPTION right to recover property transferred by a MORTGAGE or other LIEN by paying off the debt either before or after foreclosure. Also called *equity of redemption.*

RIGHT OF RESCISSION right of a purchaser of a new issue to rescind the purchase contract within the applicable time limits.

RIGHT OF SURVIVORSHIP right entitling one owner of property held jointly to take title to it when the other owner dies. *See also* JOINT TENANTS WITH RIGHT OF SURVIVORSHIP; TENANTS IN COMMON.

RIGHTS OFFERING offering of COMMON STOCK to existing shareholders who hold rights that entitle them to buy newly issued shares at a discount from the price at which shares will later be offered to the public. Rights offerings are usually handled by INVESTMENT BANKERS under what is called a STANDBY COMMITMENT, whereby the investment bankers agree to purchase any shares not subscribed to by the holders of rights. *See also* PREEMPTIVE RIGHT; SUBSCRIPTION RIGHT.

RIGHT OF WITHDRAWAL right of a purchaser of a new issue to withdraw from the purchase agreement within two business days after being deemed to have received the prospectus.

RING location on the floor of an exchange where trades are executed. The circular arrangement where traders can make bid and offer prices is also called a *pit,* particularly when commodities are traded.

RISING BOTTOMS technical chart pattern showing a rising trend in the low prices of a security or commodity. As the range of prices is charted daily, the lows reveal an upward trend. Rising bottoms signify higher and higher basic SUPPORT LEVELS for a security or commodity. When combined with a series of ASCENDING TOPS, the pattern is one a follower of TECHNICAL ANALYSIS would call bullish.

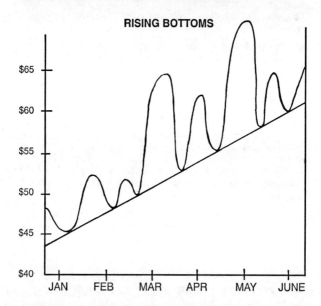

RISING BOTTOMS

RISK measurable possibility of losing or not gaining value. Risk is differentiated from uncertainty, which is not measurable. Term that refers to the variability of returns associated with a project or the forecast values of the firm. In a statistical sense, risk exists when a decision maker can estimate the probabilities associated with various outcomes. Risk is not the same as uncertainty which is not measurable. Among the commonly encountered types of risk are these:

Actuarial risk: risk an insurance underwriter covers in exchange for premiums, such as the risk of premature death.

Business risk: an economic or operating risk reflected in the variability of a firm's earnings.

Exchange risk: chance of loss on foreign currency exchange.

Inflation risk: chance that the value of assets or of income will be eroded as inflation shrinks the value of a country's currency.

Interest rate risk: possibility that a fixed-rate debt instrument will decline in value as a result of a rise in interest rates.

Inventory risk: possibility that price changes, obsolescence, or other factors will shrink the value of INVENTORY.

Liquidity risk: possibility that an investor will not be able to buy or sell a commodity or security quickly enough or in sufficient quantities because buying or selling opportunities are limited.

Political risk: possibility of NATIONALIZATION or other unfavourable government action.

Repayment (credit) risk: chance that a borrower or trade debtor will not repay an obligation as promised.

Risk of principal: chance that invested capital will drop in value.

Underwriting risk: risk taken by an INVESTMENT BANKER that a new issue of securities purchased outright will not be bought by the public and/or that the market price will drop during the offering period.

RISK-ADJUSTED DISCOUNT RATE in PORTFOLIO THEORY and CAPITAL BUDGET analysis, the rate necessary to determine the PRESENT VALUE of an uncertain or risky stream of income; it is the risk-free rate plus a risk premium that is based on an analysis of the risk characteristics of the particular investment or project.

RISK ARBITRAGE ARBITRAGE involving risk, as in the simultaneous purchase of stock in a company being acquired and sale of stock in its proposed acquirer. Also called *takeover arbitrage.* Traders called *arbitrageurs* attempt to profit from TAKEOVERS by cashing in on the expected rise in the price of the target company's shares and drop in the price of the acquirer's shares. If the takeover plans fall through, the traders may be left with enormous losses. Risk arbitrage differs from riskless arbitrage, which entails locking in or profiting from the differences in the prices of two securities or commodities trading on different exchanges. *See also* RISKLESS TRANSACTION.

RISK AVERSE term referring to the assumption that, given the same return and different risk alternatives, a rational investor will seek the security offering the least risk—or, put another way, the higher the degree of risk, the greater the return that a rational investor will demand. *See also* CAPITAL ASSET PRICING MODEL; EFFICIENT PORTFOLIO; MEAN RETURN; PORTFOLIO THEORY.

RISK-BASED CAPITAL RATIO FIRREAH-imposed requirement that banks maintain a minimum ratio of estimated total capital to estimated risk-weighted assets.

RISK CAPITAL *see* VENTURE CAPITAL.

RISK CATEGORY classification of risk elements used in analyzing MORTGAGES.

RISK-FREE RETURN YIELD on a risk-free investment. The 90-day Treasury bill is considered a riskless investment because it is a direct obligation of the Canadian government and its term is short enough to minimize the risks of inflation and market interest rate changes. The

CAPITAL ASSET PRICING MODEL (CAPM) used in modern PORTFOLIO THEORY has the premise that the return on a security is equal to the risk-free return plus a RISK PREMIUM.

RISK PREMIUM in PORTFOLIO THEORY, the difference between the RISK-FREE RETURN and the TOTAL RETURN from a risky investment. In the CAPITAL ASSET PRICING MODEL (CAPM), the risk premium reflects market-related risk (SYSTEMATIC RISK) as measured by BETA. Other models also reflect specific risk as measured by ALPHA.

RISK-RETURN TRADE-OFF concept, basic in investment management, that RISK equals (varies with) RETURN; in other words, the higher the return the greater the risk and vice versa. In practice, it means that a speculative investment, such as stock in a newly formed company, can be expected to provide a higher potential return than a more conservative investment, such as BLUE CHIP or a BOND. Conversely, if you don't want the risk, don't expect the return. *See also* PORTFOLIO THEORY.

RISKS indicates or measures any threat to the value of original invested capital; for example, market risk, liquidity risk, and share-price volatility.

RISK TRANSFER shifting of risk, as with INSURANCE or the SECURITIZATION of debt.

ROAD SHOW presentation by an issuer of securities to potential buyers about the merits of the issue. Management of the company issuing stocks or bonds doing a road show travel around the country presenting financial information and an outlook for the company and answering the questions of analysts, fund managers, and other potential investors. Also known as a *dog and pony show.*

ROCKET SCIENTIST investment firm creator of innovative securities.

ROLL DOWN move from one OPTION position to another one having a lower EXERCISE PRICE. The term assumes that the position with the higher exercise price is closed out.

ROLL FORWARD move from one OPTION position to another with a later expiration date. The term assumes that the earlier position is closed out before the later one is established. If the new position involves a higher EXERCISE PRICE, it is called a *roll-up and forward;* if a lower exercise price, it is called a *roll-down and forward.* Also called *rolling over.*

ROLLING STOCK equipment that moves on wheels, used in the transportation industry. Examples include railroad cars and locomotives, tractor-trailers, and trucks.

ROLLOVER
1. movement of funds from one investment to another. For instance, an INDIVIDUAL RETIREMENT ACCOUNT may be rolled over when a person retires into an ANNUITY or other form of pension plan payout system.

When a BOND or CERTIFICATE OF DEPOSIT matures, the funds may be rolled over into another bond or certificate of deposit. The proceeds from the sale of a house may be rolled over into the purchase of another house within two years without tax penalty. A stock may be sold and the proceeds rolled over into the same stock, establishing a different cost basis for the shareholder. *See also* THIRTY DAY WASH RULE.

2. term often used by banks when they allow a borrower to delay making a PRINCIPAL payment on a loan. Also, a country that has difficulty in meeting its debt payments may be granted a rollover by its creditors. With governments themselves, rollovers in the form of REFUNDINGS or REFINANCINGS are routine.

See also CERTIFICATE OF DEPOSIT ROLLOVER.

ROLL UP move from one OPTION position to another having a higher EXERCISE PRICE. The term assumes that the earlier position is closed out before the new position is established. *See also* MASTER LIMITED PARTNERSHIP.

ROUND LOT generally accepted unit of trading on a securities exchange. On most exchanges, for example, a round lot is 100 shares for stock and $1000 or $5000 par value for bonds. In inactive stocks, the round lot is 10 shares. Increasingly, there seems to be recognition of a 500-share round lot for trading by institutions.

ROUND TRIP TRADE purchase and sale of a security or commodity within a short time. For example, a trader who continually is making short-term trades in a particular commodity is making round trip or *round turn* trades. Commissions for such a trader are likely to be quoted in terms of the total for a purchase and sale—$100 for the round trip, for instance. Excessive round trip trading is called CHURNING.

ROYALTY payment to the holder for the right to use property such as a patent, copyrighted material, or natural resources. For instance, inventors may be paid royalties when their inventions are produced and marketed. Authors may get royalties when books they have written are sold. Land owners leasing their property to an oil or mining company may receive royalties based on the amount of oil or minerals extracted from their land. Royalties are set in advance as a percentage of income arising from the commercialization of the owner's rights or property.

RRSP ELIGIBLE FUND fund that has enough Canadian investments to avoid contravening the RRSP and RRIF foreign investment restrictions. As of 1995, funds were allowed 20% foreign investment.

RUBBER CHEQUE cheque for which insufficient funds are available. It is called a rubber cheque because it bounces. *See also* OVERDRAFT.

RULE OF 72 formula for approximating the time it will take for a given amount of money to double at a given COMPOUND INTEREST rate. The formula is simply 72 divided by the interest rate. In six years $100 will double at a compound annual rate of 12%, thus: 72 divided by 12 equals 6.

RULE OF THE 78s method of computing REBATES of interest on installment loans. It uses the SUM-OF-THE-YEAR'S-DIGITS basis in determining
the interest earned by the FINANCE COMPANY for each month of a year,
assuming equal monthly payments, and gets its name from the fact
that the sum of the digits 1 through 12 is 78. Thus interest is equal to
$^{12}/_{78}$ of the total annual interest in the first month, $^{11}/_{78}$ in the second
month, and so on.

RUMOURTRAGE stock traders' term, combining rumour and ARBI-
TRAGE, for buying and selling based on rumour of a TAKEOVER. *See
also* DEAL STOCK; GARBATRAGE.

RUN
Banking: demand for their money by many depositors all at once. If
large enough, a run on a bank can cause it to fail, as hundreds of banks
did in the Great Depression of the 1930s. Such a run is caused by a
breach of confidence in the bank, perhaps as a result of large loan
losses or fraud.
Securities:
1. list of available securities, along with current bid and asked prices,
   which a market maker is currently trading. For bonds the run may
   include the par value as well as current quotes.
2. when a security's price rises quickly, analysts say it had a quick run
   up, possibly because of a positive earnings report.

RUNDOWN
In general: status report or summary.
Municipal bonds: summary of the amounts available and the prices
on units in a SERIAL BOND that has not yet been completely sold to the
public.

RUNNING AHEAD illegal practice of buying or selling a security for a
broker's personal account before placing a similar order for a customer. For example, when a firm's analyst issues a positive report on
a company, the firm's brokers may not buy the stock for their own
accounts before they have told their clients the news. Some firms pro-
hibit brokers from making such trades for a specific period, such as
two full days from the time of the recommendation.

RUNOFF printing of an exchange's closing prices on a TICKER tape after
the market has closed. The runoff may take a long time when trading
has been very heavy and the tape has fallen far behind the action.

RUSSELL INDEXES market capitalization weighted indexes published
by Frank Russell Company of Tacoma, Washington. The *Russell 3000
Index* consists of the 3000 largest U.S. stocks in terms of market capitalization. The stocks in the index have a market capitalization range
of approximately $91 million to $85 billion, with an average of $1.5
billion. The highest-ranking 1000 stocks comprise the *Russell 1000
Index*, which is highly correlated to the S&P 500 Index and has an

average market capitalization of $4 billion; the smallest company in the index has an average market capitalization of $672 million. The *Russell 2000 Index* consists of the other 2000 stocks and represent approximately 11% of the Russell 3000 Index's total market capitalization, with an average capitalization of $255 million. The largest company in the index has an approximate market capitalization of $672 million. The Russell 2000 is a popular measure of the stock price performance of small companies.

The *Russell 2500 Index* consists of the bottom 800 securities in the Russell 1000, with the market capitalization of the largest company approximately $4.6 billion. The *Russell Top 200 Index* consists of the 200 largest securities in the Russell 1000, the "blue chip" index, with average market capitalization of $13 billion. The smallest stock in the index has an average capitalization of $4.5 billion. Four indexes, based on the Russell 1000 Index and Russell 2000 Index, reflect specialized growth orientation. The *Russell 1000 Value Index* and *Russell 2,000 Value Index* contain those securities in the underlying indexes with a less-than-average growth orientation. Companies generally have low price-to-book and price-earnings ratios, higher dividend yields, and lower forecasted growth values. Average market capitalization is $3.9 billion and $126 million, respectively. The *Russell 1000 Growth Index* and *Russell 2000 Growth Index* contain those securities in the underlying indexes with a greater than average growth orientation, and generally higher price-to-book and price-earnings ratios. Average market capitalization is $4.1 billion and $129 million, respectively. *See also* STOCK INDEXES AND AVERAGES.

RUST BELT geographical area of the United States, mainly in Pennsylvania, West Virginia, and the industrial Midwest, where iron and steel is produced and where there is a concentration of industries that manufacture products using iron and steel. Term is used broadly to mean traditional American manufacturing with its largely unmodernized plants and facilities.

S

SAFE HARBOUR form of SHARK REPELLENT whereby a TARGET COMPANY acquires a business so onerously regulated it makes the target less attractive, giving it, in effect, a safe harbour.

SAFEKEEPING storage and protection of a customer's financial assets, valuables, or documents, provided as a service by an institution serving as AGENT and, where control is delegated by the customer, also as custodian. An individual, corporate, or institutional investor might rely on a bank or a brokerage firm to hold stock certificates or bonds, keep track of trades, and provide periodic statements of changes in position. Investors who provide for their own safekeeping usually use a *safe deposit box,* provided by financial institutions for a fee. *See also* SELLING SHORT AGAINST THE BOX; STREET NAME.

SAFETY concept of preservation and stability of original invested capital.

SALARY regular wages received by an employee from an employer on a weekly, biweekly, or monthly basis. Many salaries also include such employee benefits as health and life insurance and savings plans. Salary income is taxable by the federal, and provincial government through payroll withholding.

SALARY FREEZE cessation of increases in salary throughout a company for a period of time. Companies going through a business downturn will freeze salaries in order to reduce expenses. When business improves, salary increases are frequently reinstated.

SALE
In general: any exchange of goods or services for money. *Contrast with* BARTER.
Finance: income received in exchange for goods and services recorded for a given accounting period, either on a cash basis (as received) or on an accrual basis (as earned). *See also* GROSS SALES.
Securities: in securities trading, a sale is executed when a buyer and a seller have agreed on a price for the security.

SALE AND LEASEBACK form of LEASE arrangement in which a company sells an asset to another party—usually an insurance or finance company, a leasing company, a limited partnership, or an institutional investor—in exchange for cash, then contracts to lease the asset for a specified term. Typically, the asset is sold for its MARKET VALUE, so the lessee has really acquired capital that would otherwise have been tied up in a long-term asset. Such arrangements frequently have tax benefits for the lessee, although there is normally little difference in the effect on income between the lease payments and the interest payments that would have existed had the asset been purchased with borrowed money. A company generally opts for the sale and leaseback arrangement as an alternative to straight financing when the rate it would have to pay a lender is higher than the cost of rental or when it wishes to show less debt on its BALANCE SHEET (called *off-balance-sheet financing*). *See also* CAPITAL LEASE.

SALES CHARGE fee paid to a brokerage house by a buyer of shares in a load MUTUAL FUND or a LIMITED PARTNERSHIP. Normally, the sales charge for a mutual fund starts at 4.5% to 5% of the capital invested and decreases as the size of the investment increases. The sales charge for a limited partnership can be even higher—as much as 10%. In return for the sales charge, investors are entitled to investment advice from the broker on which fund or partnership is best for them. A fund that carries no sales charge is called a NO-LOAD FUND. *See also* BACK-END LOAD; FRONT-END LOAD; LETTER OF INTENT; LOAD FUND; REDEMPTION FEES; 12B-1 MUTUAL FUND.

SALES LITERATURE

In general: written material designed to help sell a product or a service.

Investments: written material issued by a securities brokerage firm, mutual fund, underwriter, or other institution selling a product that explains the advantages of the investment product. Such literature must be truthful and must comply with disclosure regulations issued by securities commissions.

SALES LOAD *see* SALES CHARGE.

SALES TAX a regressive, consumption tax based on a percentage of the selling price of goods and services. The retail buyer pays the sales tax to the retailer, who passes it on to the sales tax collection agency of the government. For an item costing $1000 in a province with an 8% sales tax, the buyer pays $80 in sales tax, for a total of $1080. Sales taxes are not deductible.

SALE TRANSACTION transaction in which an investor who has bought or holds an option terminates his or her position by selling an option with the same terms.

SALOMON BROTHERS WORLD EQUITY INDEX (SBWEI) a comprehensive top-down, float capitalization-weighted index that includes shares of approximately 6000 companies in 22 countries. It is one member of a family of Salomon Brothers performance indexes that measure domestic and international fixed income and equity markets. The index includes all companies with available market capitalization greater than $100 million. Each issue is weighted by the proportion of its available equity capital, its float, rather than by its total equity capital. The index is the successor to the Salomon-Russell Global Equity Index. Other SBWEI equity products include GDP and weighted indexes, and emerging market indexes.

SALVAGE VALUE *see* RESIDUAL VALUE.

SAME-DAY SUBSTITUTION offsetting changes in a MARGIN ACCOUNT in the course of one day, resulting in neither a MARGIN CALL nor a credit to the SPECIAL MISCELLANEOUS ACCOUNT. Examples: a purchase and a sale of equal value; a decline in the MARKET VALUE of some margin securities offset by an equal rise in the market value of others.

SAMURAI BONDS bonds denominated in yen issued by non-Japanese companies for sale mostly in Japan. The bonds are not subject to Japanese withholding taxes, and therefore offer advantages to Japanese buyers.

SANDWICH GENERATION middle-aged working people who feel squeezed by the financial pressures of supporting their aging parents, the costs of raising and educating their children, and the need to save for their own retirement.

SANTA CLAUS RALLY rise in stock prices in the week between Christmas and New Year's Day. Also called the *year-end rally*. Some analysts attribute this rally to the anticipation of the JANUARY EFFECT, when stock prices rise in the first few days of the year as pension funds add new money to their accounts.

SAO PAULO STOCK EXCHANGE *see* BOLSA DE VALORES DE SAO PAULO (BOVESPA).

S&P PHENOMENON tendency of stocks newly added to the STANDARD & POOR'S INDEX to rise temporarily in price as S&P-related INDEX FUNDS adjust their portfolios, creating heavy buying activity.

SATURDAY NIGHT SPECIAL sudden attempt by one company to take over another by making a public TENDER OFFER. The term was coined in the 1960s after a rash of such surprise maneuvers, which were often announced over weekends.

SAUCER technical chart pattern (see next page) signaling that the price of a security or a commodity has formed a bottom and is moving up. An inverse saucer shows a top in the security's price and signals a downturn. *See also* TECHNICAL ANALYSIS.

SAVE HARMLESS clause in a contract whereby one party to a transaction tries to protect itself from a past or subsequent liability caused, usually unwittingly, by the other party. For example, in the sale of a company the vendor might be required to save the purchaser harmless from a third party suit trying to set aside the deal from undisclosed tax liabilities. Also called *indemnity clause.*

SAVING RATE ratio of personal saving to disposable personal income. Disposable personal income is personal income less personal tax and nontax payments. Personal saving is disposable personal income less personal outlays.

SAUCER

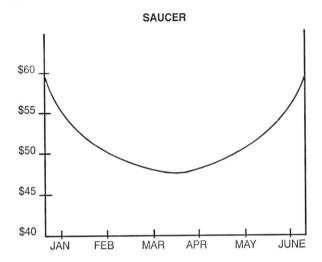

SAVINGS ACCOUNT deposit account at a bank or trust company that pays interest, usually from a day-of-deposit to day-of-withdrawal basis. Savings accounts are insured for $60,000 by the Canada Deposit Insurance Corporation.

SAVINGS BOND Canadian government bond issued in FACE VALUE denominations ranging from $50 to $10,000. These are really savings certificates and rates may fall according to market conditions. Interest is payable annually on the regular bonds or compound until the term of the bond and are payable on cashing. They are taxable when the interest is earned, not when the interest is received.

Provincial savings bonds are now available. They carry variable interest rates and can be purchased only twice a year. They have a slightly higher rate than federal savings bonds.

SAVINGS DEPOSITS interest-earning cash balances that can be withdrawn on demand, kept for the purpose of savings, trusts, banks and credit unions. Passbook savings and statement savings are examples of savings deposits.

SAVINGS ELEMENT cash value accumulated inside a life insurance policy. A cash value policy has two components: a death benefit paid to beneficiaries if the insured dies, and a savings element, which is the amount of premium paid in excess of the cost of protection. This excess is invested by the insurance company in stocks, bonds, real estate, and other ventures and the returns build up tax-deferred inside the policy. A policyholder can borrow against this cash value or take it out of the policy, at which point it becomes taxable income. Once a policyholder reaches retirement age, he or she can ANNUITIZE the accumulated cash value and receive a regular payment from the insurance company for life. Insurance companies encourage people to buy policies with a savings element because it provides a disciplined way to save.

SCALE
Labour: wage rate for specific types of employees. For example: "Union scale for carpenters is $15.60 per hour."
Production economics: amount of production, as in "economy or diseconomy of scale." *See also* MARGINAL COST.
  See also SCALE ORDER.

SCALE ORDER order for a specified number of shares that is to be executed in stages in order to average the price. Such an order might provide for the purchase of a total of 5000 shares to be executed in lots of 500 shares at each quarter-point interval as the market declines. Since scale orders are clerically cumbersome, not all brokers will accept them.

SCALPER
In general: speculator who enters into quasi-legal or illegal transactions to turn a quick and sometimes unreasonable profit. For example, a scalper buys tickets at regular prices for a major event and when the event becomes a sellout, resells the tickets at the highest price possible.
Securities:
1. investment adviser who takes a position in a security before recommending it, then sells out after the price has risen as a result of the recommendation. .
2. market maker who adds an excessive markup or takes an excessive MARKDOWN on a transaction.
3. commodity trader who trades for small gains, usually establishing and liquidating a position within one day.

SCALPING in securities, trading for small gains by buying and selling many times during a trading day. This is a very difficult way of making money because of the brokerage fees that have to be paid for all transactions.

SCORCHED-EARTH POLICY technique used by a company that has become the target of a TAKEOVER attempt to make itself unattractive to the acquirer. For example, it may agree to sell off the most attractive parts of its business, called the CROWN JEWELS, or it may schedule all debt to become due immediately after a MERGER. *See also* JONESTOWN DEFENSE; POISON PILL; SHARK REPELLENT.

SCREEN (STOCKS) to look for stocks that meet certain predetermined investment and financial criteria. Often, stocks are screened using a computer and a data base containing financial statistics on thousands of companies. For instance, an investor may want to screen for all those companies that have a PRICE/EARNINGS RATIO of less than 10, an earnings growth rate of more than 15%, and a dividend yield of more than 4%.

SCRIP

In general: receipt, certificate, or other representation of value recognized by both payer and payee. Scrip is not currency, but may be convertible into currency up to a specified date, after which it may have no value.

Securities: temporary document that is issued by a corporation and that represents a fractional share of stock resulting from a SPLIT, exchange of stock, or SPIN-OFF. Scrip certificates may be aggregated or applied toward the purchase of full shares. Scrip dividends have historically been paid in lieu of cash dividends by companies short of cash.

SCRIPOPHILY practice of collecting stock and bond certificates for their scarcity value, rather than for their worth as securities. The certificate's price rises with the beauty of the illustration on it and the importance of the issuer in world finance and economic development. Many old certificates, such as those issued by railroads in the 19th century or by Standard Oil before it was broken up in the early 20th century, have risen greatly in value since their issue, even though the issuing companies no longer exist.

SEASONALITY variations in business or economic activity that recur with regularity as the result of changes in climate, holidays, and vacations. The retail toy business, with its steep sales buildup between Thanksgiving and Christmas and pronounced dropoff thereafter, is an example of seasonality in a dramatic form, though nearly all businesses have some degree of seasonal variation. It is often necessary to make allowances for seasonality when interpreting or projecting financial or economic data, a process economists call *seasonal adjustment.*

SEASONED securities that have been trading in the secondary market for a lengthy period of time, and have established a track record of significant trading volume and price stability. Many investors prefer buying only seasoned issues instead of new securities that have not stood the test of time.

SEASONED ISSUE securities (usually from established companies) that have gained a reputation for quality with the investing public and enjoy LIQUIDITY in the SECONDARY MARKET.

SEAT figurative term for a membership on a securities or commodities exchange. Seats are bought and sold at prices set by supply and demand. Seats on the Toronto Stock Exchange have traded in a range from $100,000 to $300,000. A seat on the New York Stock Exchange, for example, traded for over $1 million U.S. prior to BLACK MONDAY in 1987 and just over $400,000 U.S. in late 1989.

SEC *see* SECURITIES AND EXCHANGE COMMISSION.

SECONDARY DISTRIBUTION public sale of previously issued securities held by large investors, usually corporations, institutions, or other AFFILIATED PERSONS, as distinguished from a NEW ISSUE or PRIMARY DISTRIBUTION, where the seller is the issuing corporation. As with a primary offering, secondaries are usually handled by INVESTMENT BANKERS, acting alone or as a syndicate, who purchase the shares from the seller at an agreed price, then resell them, sometimes with the help of a SELLING GROUP, at a higher PUBLIC OFFERING PRICE, making their profit on the difference, called the SPREAD. Since the offering is registered with the appropriate securities commission, the syndicate manager can legally stabilize—or peg—the market price by bidding for shares in the open market. Buyers of securities offered this way pay no commissions, since all costs are borne by the selling investor. If the securities involved are listed, the CONSOLIDATED TAPE will announce the offering during the trading day, although the offering is not made until after the market's close.

SECONDARY MARKET
1. exchanges and over-the-counter markets where securities are bought and sold subsequent to original issuance, which took place in the PRIMARY MARKET. Proceeds of secondary market sales accrue to the selling dealers and investors, not to the companies that originally issued the securities.
2. market in which money-market instruments are traded among investors.

SECONDARY MORTGAGE MARKET buying, selling, and trading of existing mortgage loans and mortgage-backed securities. Original lenders are thus able to sell loans in their portfolios in order to build LIQUIDITY to support additional lending.

SECONDARY OFFERING *see* SECONDARY DISTRIBUTION.

SECONDARY STOCKS used in a general way to mean stocks having smaller MARKET CAPITALIZATION, less quality, and more risk than BLUE CHIP issues represented by the Toronto Stock Exchange 300 Index or Dow Jones Industrial Average.

SECOND MORTGAGE LENDING advancing funds to a borrower that are secured by real estate previously pledged in a FIRST MORTGAGE loan. In the case of DEFAULT, the first mortgage has priority of claim over the second.

A variation on the second mortgage is the *home equity loan,* in which the loan is secured by independent appraisal of the property value. A home equity loan may also be in the form of a line of credit, which may be drawn down on by using a cheque or even a credit card. *See also* HOMEOWNER'S EQUITY ACCOUNT; RIGHT OF RESCISSION.

SECOND-PREFERRED STOCK preferred stock issue that ranks below another preferred issue in terms of priority of claim on dividends and on assets in liquidation. Second-preferred shares are often issued with a CONVERTIBLE feature or with a warrant to make them more attractive to investors. *See also* JUNIOR SECURITY; PREFERRED STOCK; PRIOR-PREFERRED STOCK; SUBSCRIPTION WARRANT.

SECOND ROUND intermediate stage of VENTURE CAPITAL financing, coming after the SEED MONEY (or START-UP) and *first round* stages and before the MEZZANINE LEVEL, when the company has matured to the point where it might consider a LEVERAGED BUYOUT by management or an INITIAL PUBLIC OFFERING (IPO).

SECOND-TO-DIE INSURANCE insurance policy that pays a death benefit upon the death of the spouse who dies last. Such insurance typically is purchased by a couple wanting to pass a large estate on to their heirs. When the first spouse dies, the couple's assets are passed tax-free to the second spouse under the MARITAL DEDUCTION. When the second spouse dies, the remaining estate could be subject to large estate taxes. The proceeds from the second-to-die insurance are designed to pay the estate taxes, leaving the remaining estate for the heirs. Such insurance is appropriate only for those facing large estate tax liabilities. Because the policy is based on the joint life expectancy of both husband and wife, premiums typically cost less than those on traditional cash value policies on both lives insured separately. Also called *survivorship life insurance.*

SECTOR particular group of stocks, usually found in one industry. SECURITIES ANALYSTS often follow a particular sector of the stock market, such as airline or chemical stocks.

SECTOR FUND *see* SPECIALIZED MUTUAL FUND.

SECULAR long-term (10–50 years or more) as distinguished from seasonal or cyclical time frames.

SECURED BOND bond backed by the pledge of COLLATERAL, a MORTGAGE, or other LIEN. The exact nature of the security is spelled out in the INDENTURE. Secured bonds are distinguished from unsecured bonds, called DEBENTURES.

SECURED DEBT debt guaranteed by the pledge of assets or other COLLATERAL. *See also* ASSIGN; HYPOTHECATION.

SECURITIES ACT name for provincial acts administered by the Securities Commission in each province that set down the rules under which securities may be issued and traded.

SECURITIES ADMINISTRATOR general term referring to the provincial regulatory authority (e.g., Securities Commission or Provincial Registrar) responsible for administering a provincial Securities Act.

SECURITIES ADVISOR person or company registered with applicable securities commissions to advise the public generally about specific securities, often through publications.

SECURITIES ANALYST individual, usually employed by a stock brokerage house, bank, or investment institution, who performs investment research and examines the financial condition of a company or group of companies in an industry and in the context of the securities markets. Many analysts specialize in a single industry or SECTOR and make investment recommendations to buy, sell, or hold in that area. Among a corporation's financial indicators most closely followed by ANALYSTS are sales and earnings growth, CAPITAL STRUCTURE, stock price trend and PRICE/EARNINGS RATIO, DIVIDEND PAYOUTS, and RETURN ON INVESTED CAPITAL. Securities analysts promote corporate financial disclosure by sponsoring forums through local associations. *See also* FORECASTING; FUNDAMENTAL ANALYSIS; QUALITATIVE ANALYSIS; QUANTITATIVE ANALYSIS; TECHNICAL ANALYSIS.

SECURITIES AND COMMODITIES EXCHANGES organized exchanges where securities, options, and futures contracts are traded by members for their own accounts and for the accounts of customers. The stock exchanges are registered with and regulated by the Ontario Securities Commission and the B.C. Securities Commission in Canada and by the SECURITIES AND EXCHANGE COMMISSION (SEC) in the United States; the commodities exchanges are registered with and regulated by the Commodity Futures Trading Commission (*see* REGULATED COMMODITIES); where options are traded on an exchange, such activity is regulated by the SEC.

STOCKS, BONDS, SUBSCRIPTION RIGHTS, SUBSCRIPTION WARRANTS and in some cases OPTIONS are traded on 4 STOCK EXCHANGES in Canada and 9 STOCK EXCHANGES in the United States. The FUTURES MARKET is represented by 13 leading commodities exchanges.

Exchanges listing basic securities—stocks, bonds, rights, warrants, and options on individual stocks—are described under the entries for the TORONTO STOCK EXCHANGE, VANCOUVER STOCK EXCHANGE, NEW YORK STOCK EXCHANGE, AMERICAN STOCK EXCHANGE, and REGIONAL STOCK EXCHANGES.

The exchanges listing commodity and other futures contracts and options in addition to those on individual stocks are:

American Stock Exchange (New York) *index options:* Biotechnology Index, Computer Technology Index, Eurotop 100 Index, Hong Kong 30 Index, Institutional Index, Japan Index, Major Market Index, Mexico Index, Morgan Stanley Cyclical Index, Morgan Stanley Consumer Index, Natural Gas Index, North American Telecommunications Index, Oil Index, Oscar Gruss Israel Index, Pharmaceutical Index, Security Broker/Dealer Index, S&P MidCap 400 Index. *interest rate options:* Treasury bills, Treasury notes; LEAPS; FLEX options on underlying indices.

Chicago Board of Trade (Chicago) *futures:* wheat, corn, oats, soybeans, soybean oil, soybean meal, rice, diammonium phosphate, anhydrous ammonia, edible oil index, barge freight index, structural panel index, Eastern catastrophic insurance, Midwest catastrophic insurance, national catastrophic insurance, silver (1,000 ounces, 5,000 ounces), gold (kilo, 100 ounces) U.S. Treasury bonds, Treasury notes (10-year, 5-year, 2-year), Municipal Bond Index, Canadian government bonds, 30-day Fed funds, U.S. dollar index, Major Market Index, Wilshire Small Cap Index. *options:* wheat, corn, oats, soybeans, soybean oil, soybean meal, rice, Eastern catastrophic insurance, Midwest catastrophic insurance, national catastrophic insurance, Western insurance—annual, silver (1,000 ounces), U.S. Treasury bonds, Treasury notes (10-year, 5-year, 2-year), Municipal Bond Index, Canadian government bond, Flexible U.S. Treasury bonds, Flexible Treasury notes (10-year, 5-year, 2-year), Major Market Index, Wilshire Small Cap Index.

Chicago Board Options Exchange (Chicago) *equity options; equity LEAPS; index options:* Standard & Poor's 100 Index, Standard & Poor's 500 Index, OEX CAPS, OEX LEAPS, S&P 500 long-dated options, S&P 500 end-of-quarter options, SPX LEAPS, SPX CAPS, FLEX options, NASDAQ-100 Index, Russell 2000 Index, Russell 2000 Index LEAPS, FT-SE 100 Index, CBOE Mexico Index, CBOE Mexico Index LEAPS, Nikkei 300 Index, Nikkei 300 Index LEAPS, S&P Banks Index, CBOE BioTech Index, CBOE BioTech Index LEAPS, S&P Chemical Index, CBOE Computer Software Index, CBOE Environmental Index, CBOE Gaming Index, S&P Health Care Index, S&P Insurance Index, S&P Retail Index, CBOE US Telecommunications Index, S&P Transportation Index. *interest rate options:* 13-week Treasury bill, 5-year Treasury note, 10-year Treasury note, 30-year Treasury bond.

Chicago Mercantile Exchange (Chicago) *foreign currency futures:* Australian dollar, British pound, British pound Rolling Spot, Canadian dollar, Deutsche mark, Deutsche mark Rolling Spot, Deutsche mark/Japanese yen cross rate, DM currency forward, 3-month Eurodollar, 3-month Euromark, French franc, Japanese yen, Swiss franc. *commodity futures:* live hogs, pork bellies, live cattle, feeder cattle, lumber. *financial futures:* 1-month LIBOR (London Interbank Offer Rate), 90-day Treasury bills, 1-year Treasury bills, S&P 500 Index, S&P 400 Index, FT-SE 100, Major Market Index, Russell 2000 Index, Goldman Sachs Commodity Index. *options on futures:* Australian dollar, British pound, British pound Rolling Spot, Canadian dollar, Deutsche mark, Deutsche mark Rolling Spot, 3-month Eurodollar, 3-month Euromark, French franc, Japanese yen, Swiss franc, Deutsche mark/yen cross, 1-month LIBOR, 90-day Treasury bill; live hogs, pork bellies, live cattle, feeder cattle, lumber; Nikkei 225, S&P 500 Index, S&P 400 Index, Major Market Index, Russell 2000 Index, Goldman Sachs Commodity Index.

Coffee, Sugar and Cocoa Exchange* (New York) *futures:* cocoa, coffee, sugar No. 11, sugar No. 14, white sugar, cheddar cheese, nonfat dry milk. *options on futures:* cocoa, coffee, sugar No. 11, cheddar cheese, nonfat dry milk.

Kansas City Board of Trade (Kansas City) *futures:* wheat, Value Line Index, Mini Value Line. *options on futures:* wheat, Mini Value Line.

Mid-America Commodity Exchange (Chicago) *futures:* wheat, corn, oats, soybeans, soybean meal new, live cattle, live hogs, rough rice, NY silver, NY gold, platinum, U.S. Treasury bonds, U.S. Treasury bills, Treasury notes (10-year, 5-year), Eurodollars, U.S. dollar index, British pound, Swiss franc, Canadian dollar, Deutsche mark, Japanese yen. *options on futures:* wheat, corn, soybeans, rough rice, NY gold, U.S. Treasury bonds.

Minneapolis Grain Exchange (Minneapolis) *futures:* wheat, white wheat, oats, shrimp. *options on futures:* American spring wheat, European spring wheat, white wheat, oats, shrimp.

New York Cotton Exchange* (New York) *futures:* cotton, frozen concentrated orange juice. *options on futures:* cotton, frozen concentrated orange juice. *FINEX (division of NYCE) futures:* U.S. dollar index (USDX), U.S. dollar-based currency, cross-rate currency, Treasury auction U.S. Treasury notes (5-year, 2-year). *options on futures:* USDX, U.S. dollar based currency, Treasury auction U.S. Treasury notes (5-year, 2-year).

New York Futures Exchange (division of the NYCE) (New York) *futures:* Knight-Ridder Commodity Research Bureau Index, New York Stock Exchange Composite Index, Treasury bonds. *options on futures:* NYSE Composite Index, KR-CRB Index.

New York Mercantile Exchange* (New York) *NYMEX division: futures:* light, sweet crude oil, sour crude, New York Harbor unleaded gasoline, Gulf Coast unleaded gasoline, heating oil, natural gas, propane, electricity, platinum, palladium. *options on futures:* light, sweet crude, heating oil, New York Harbor unleaded gasoline, natural gas, platinum. *COMEX division: futures:* copper, gold, silver, Eurotop 100 Index. *options on futures:* copper, gold, silver, Eurotop 100 Index.

New York Stock Exchange (New York) *index options:* NYSE Composite Index options, NYSE Utility Index options.

Pacific Stock Exchange (San Francisco) *index options:* Wilshire Small Cap Index, Telegraph Ltd. Israel Index.

Philadelphia Board of Trade (Philadelphia): *futures:* Australian dollar, British pound, Canadian dollar, Deutsche mark, European Currency Unit (ECU), French franc, Japanese yen, Swiss franc.

Philadelphia Stock Exchange (Philadelphia) *foreign currency options:* Australian dollar, British pound, Canadian dollar, Deutsche mark,

---

*These exchanges though independent, share space and other facilities at 4 World Trade Center, in New York City, and are collectively called the Commodity Exchange Center.

European Currency Unit (ECU), French franc, Japanese yen, Swiss franc, cash settled Deutsche mark, DM/yen, British pound/DM. *index options:* Utility Index, Value Line Index, Phone Index, Semiconductor Index, Gold/Silver Index, Bank Index, Big Cap Index, OTC Index.

SECURITIES AND EXCHANGE COMMISSION (SEC) U.S. federal agency created by the SECURITIES EXCHANGE ACT OF 1934 to administer that act and the SECURITIES ACT OF 1933, formerly carried out by the FEDERAL TRADE COMMISSION. The SEC is made up of five commissioners, appointed by the President of the United States on a rotating basis for five-year terms. The chairman is designated by the President and, to insure its independence, no more than three members of the commission may be of the same political party. The statutes administered by the SEC are designed to promote full public DISCLOSURE and protect the investing public against malpractice in the securities markets. All issues of securities offered in interstate commerce or through the mails must be registered with the SEC; all national securities exchanges and associations are under its supervision, as are INVESTMENT COMPANIES, investment counselors and advisers, OVER THE COUNTER brokers and dealers, and virtually all other individuals and firms operating in the investment field. In addition to the 1933 and 1934 securities acts, responsibilities of the SEC include the PUBLIC UTILITY HOLDING COMPANY ACT of 1935, the TRUST INDENTURE ACT of 1939, the INVESTMENT COMPANY ACT of 1940 and the INVESTMENT ADVISERS ACT of 1940. It also administers the SECURITIES ACTS AMENDMENTS OF 1975, which directed the SEC to facilitate the establishment of a NATIONAL MARKET SYSTEM and a nationwide system for clearance and settlement of transactions and established the Municipal Securities Rulemaking Board, a self-regulatory organization whose rules are subject to SEC approval. In Canada, there is no national regulatory authority, and securities legislation is provincially administered.

SECURITIES EXCHANGE OF THAILAND (SET) only stock market in Thailand, based in Bangkok. The *SET Index,* calculated by the exchange, and the *Bangkok Book Club Price Index,* compiled by the Book Club Finance and Securities Co. Ltd., include all corporate stocks and mutual funds and are the most widely watched. Trading is conducted through the ASSET automated electronic trading system Monday through Friday from 10 A.M. to 12:30 P.M., and 2 P.M. to 4 P.M. Trades are settled on the third business day after the trade date.

SECURITIES LOAN
1. loan of securities by one broker to another, usually to cover a customer's short sale. The lending broker is secured by the cash proceeds of the sale.
2. in a more general sense, loan collateralized by MARKETABLE SECURITIES. *See also* HYPOTHECATION; LENDING AT A PREMIUM; LENDING AT A RATE; LENDING SECURITIES; REHYPOTHECATION; SELLING SHORT.

SECURITIES MARKETS general term for markets in which securities are traded, including both ORGANIZED SECURITIES EXCHANGES and OVER-THE-COUNTER (OTC) markets.

SECURITIZATION process of converting loans of various sorts into marketable securities by packaging the loans into pools. In a broader sense, it refers to the development of markets for a variety of debt instruments that permit the ultimate borrower to bypass the banks and other deposit-taking institutions and to borrow directly from lenders.

SECURITY
Finance: collateral offered by a debtor to a lender to secure a loan called *collateral security.* For instance, the security behind a mortgage loan is the real estate being purchased with the proceeds of the loan. If the debt is not repaid, the lender may seize the security and resell it.

Personal security refers to one person or firm's GUARANTEE of another's primary obligation.

Investment: instrument that signifies an ownership position in a corporation (a stock), a creditor relationship with a corporation or governmental body (a bond), or rights to ownership such as those represented by an OPTION, SUBSCRIPTION RIGHT, and SUBSCRIPTION WARRANT.

SECURITY DEPOSIT money paid in advance to protect the provider of a product or service against damage or nonpayment by the buyer. For example, landlords require a security deposit of one month's rent when a tenant signs a lease, to cover the possibility that the tenant will move out without paying the last month's rent, or that the tenant will inflict substantial damage on the property while living there. In such a case, the money from the security deposit is used to cover repairs. Similarly, car leasing companies typically demand security deposits for the last month's lease payment to protect the leasing company against damage to the car or nonpayment of the lease. If all payments are made on time and there is no damage, security deposits must be returned to those who paid them.

SECURITY MARKET LINE relationship between the REQUIRED RATE OF RETURN on an investment and its SYSTEMATIC RISK.

SECURITY RATINGS evaluations of the credit and investment risk of securities issues by commercial RATING agencies.

SECURITY STREET NAME securities registered in the name of a broker rather than the name of the real or beneficial owner.

SEED MONEY venture capitalist's first contribution toward the financing or capital requirements of a START-UP business. It frequently takes the form of a loan, often SUBORDINATED, or an investment in convertible bonds or preferred stock. Seed money provides the basis for additional capitalization to accommodate growth. *See also* MEZZANINE LEVEL; SECOND ROUND; VENTURE CAPITAL.

SEEK A MARKET to look for a buyer (if a seller) or a seller (if a buyer) of securities.

SEGMENT REPORTING *see* BUSINESS SEGMENT REPORTING.

SELECTED DEALER AGREEMENT agreement governing the SELLING GROUP in a securities underwriting and distribution. *See also* UNDERWRITE.

SELECT TEN PORTFOLIO in the United States, UNIT INVESTMENT TRUST offered on a quarterly basis by a group of brokers including Merrill Lynch, Paine Webber, Dean Witter, and Prudential Securities that buys and holds for one year the ten stocks in the Dow Jones Industrial Average (DJIA) with the highest dividend yields. Stocks thus selected have usually outperformed the DJIA. The strategy was first popularized by Michael B. O'Higgins in *Beating the Dow*.

SELF-INSURED PLAN plan that a business decides to fund using money set aside from its operating budget to cover items such as public liability and general insurance, instead of going to an insurance company.

SELF-REGULATORY ORGANIZATION (SRO) principal means contemplated by provincial and U.S. federal securities laws for the enforcement of fair, ethical, and efficient practices in the securities and commodities futures industries. It is these organizations (such as the Investment Dealers Association of Canada) that are being referred to when "industry rules" are mentioned, as distinguished from the regulatory agencies.

SELF-TENDER *see* SHARE REPURCHASE PLAN.

SELLER FINANCING financing provided by the owner/seller of real estate, who takes back a secured note. The buyer may be unable to qualify for a mortgage from a lending institution, or interest rates may have risen so high that the buyer is unwilling to take on a market-rate loan. In order to sell their property, sellers offer to lend the buyer the money needed, often at a below-market interest rate. The buyer takes full title to the property when the loan is fully repaid. If the buyer defaults on the loan, the seller can repossess the property. Also called *creative financing*.

SELLER'S MARKET situation in which there is more demand for a security or product than there is available supply. As a result, the prices tend to be rising, and the sellers can set both the prices and the terms of sale. It contrasts with a buyer's market, characterized by excess supply, low prices, and terms suited to the buyer's desires.

SELLER'S OPTION securities transaction in which the seller, instead of making REGULAR WAY DELIVERY, is given the right to deliver the security to the purchaser on the date the seller's option expires or before, provided written notification of the seller's intention to deliver is given to the buyer one full business day prior to delivery. Seller's option deliveries are normally not made before 6 business days following the transaction or after 60 days.

SELLING CLIMAX sudden plunge in security prices as those who hold stocks or bonds panic and decide to dump their holdings all at once. Technical analysts see a climax as both a dramatic increase in volume and a sharp drop in prices on a chart. To these analysts, such a pattern usually means that a short-term rally will soon follow since there are few sellers left after the climax. Sometimes, a selling climax can signal the bottom of a BEAR MARKET, meaning that after the climax the market will start to rise.

SELLING CLIMAX

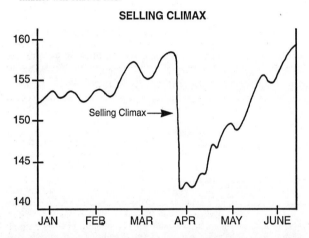

SELLING CONCESSION discount at which securities in a NEW ISSUE offering (or a SECONDARY DISTRIBUTION) are allocated to the members of a SELLING GROUP by the underwriters. Since the selling group cannot sell to the public at a price higher than the PUBLIC OFFERING PRICE, its compensation comes out of the difference between the price paid to the issuer by the underwriters and the public offering price, called the SPREAD. The selling group's portion, called the CONCESSION, is normally one half or more of the gross spread, expressed as a discount off the public offering price. *See also* FLOTATION COST; UNDERWRITE; UNDERWRITING SPREAD.

SELLING DIVIDENDS questionable practice by sales personnel dealing in MUTUAL FUNDS whereby a customer is induced to buy shares in a fund in order to get the benefit of a dividend scheduled in the near future. Since the dividend is already part of the NET ASSET VALUE of the fund and therefore part of the share price, the customer derives no real benefit.

SELLING, GENERAL, AND ADMINISTRATIVE (SG&A) EXPENSES grouping of expenses reported on a company's PROFIT AND LOSS STATEMENT between COST OF GOODS SOLD and INCOME DEDUCTIONS. Included are such items as salespersons' salaries and commissions, advertising and promotion, travel and entertainment, office payroll and expenses, and executives' salaries. SG&A expenses do not include such items as interest or amortization of INTANGIBLE ASSETS, which would be listed as income deductions. *See also* OPERATING PROFIT (OR LOSS).

SELLING GROUP group of dealers appointed by the syndicate manager of an UNDERWRITING GROUP, as AGENT for the other underwriters, to market a new or secondary issue to the public; also called *selling syndicate.* The selling group typically includes members of the underwriting group but varies in size with the size of the issue, sometimes running into several hundred dealers. The selling group is governed by the selling group agreement, also called the SELECTED DEALER AGREEMENT. It sets forth the terms of the relationship, establishes the commission (or SELLING CONCESSION, as it is called), and provides for the termination of the group, usually in 30 days. The selling group may or may not be obligated to purchase unsold shares. *See also* UNDERWRITE.

SELLING OFF selling securities or commodities under pressure to avoid further declines in prices. Technical analysts call such action a *sell-off. See also* DUMPING.

SELLING ON THE GOOD NEWS practice of selling a stock soon after a positive news development is announced. Most investors, cheered by the news of a successful new product or higher earnings, buy a stock because they think it will go higher: this pushes up the price. Someone selling on this good news believes that the stock will have reached its top price once all those encouraged by the development have bought the stock. Therefore, it is better to sell at this point than to wait for more good news or to be holding the stock if the next announcement is disappointing. *Compare with* BUYING ON THE BAD NEWS.

SELLING SHORT sale of a security or commodity futures contract not owned by the seller; a technique used (1) to take advantage of an anticipated decline in the price or (2) to protect a profit in a LONG POSITION *(see* SELLING SHORT AGAINST THE BOX).

An investor borrows stock certificates for delivery at the time of short sale. If the seller can buy that stock later at a lower price, a profit results; if the price rises, however, a loss results.

A commodity sold short represents a promise to deliver the commodity at a set price on a future date. Most commodity short sales are COVERED before the DELIVERY DATE.

Example of a short sale involving stock: An investor, anticipating a decline in the price of XYZ shares, instructs his or her broker to sell short 100 XYZ when XYZ is trading at $50. The broker then lends the investor 100 shares of XYZ, using either its own inventory, shares in the MARGIN ACCOUNT of another customer, or shares borrowed from another broker. These shares are used to make settlement with the buying broker within five days of the short sale transaction, and the proceeds are used to secure the loan. The investor now has what is known as a SHORT POSITION—that is, he or she still does not own the 100 XYZ and, at some point, must buy the shares to repay the lending broker. If the market price of XYZ drops to $40, the investor can buy the shares for $4000, repay the lending broker, thus covering the short sale, and claim a profit of $1000, or $10 a share.

It is illegal for a seller not to declare a short sale when placing the order.

SELLING SHORT AGAINST THE BOX SELLING SHORT stock actually owned by the seller but held in SAFEKEEPING, called the BOX. The motive for the practice, which assumes that the securities needed to COVER are borrowed as with any short sale, may be simply inaccessibility of the box or that the seller does not wish to disclose ownership. The main motive is to protect a CAPITAL GAIN in the shares that are owned, while deferring a LONG-TERM GAIN into another tax year.

SELLING THE SPREAD spread where the sold option is trading at a higher premium than the purchased option. For example, purchasing a shorter term option and selling a longer term option (assuming both options have the same EXERCISE PRICE) would usually result in a net credit. *See* CALENDAR SPREAD. Another example would be purchasing a call with a higher exercise price and selling a call with a lower exercise price, assuming both options have the same expiration date. *See also* CREDIT SPREAD.

SELL-OFF massive selling of stocks or bonds after a steep decline in prices. Traders sell quickly in order to avoid further losses.

SELL ORDER order by an investor to a broker to sell a particular stock, bond, option, future, mutual fund, or other holding. There are several kinds of sell orders, including DAY ORDERS, GOOD-TILL-CANCELED ORDERS (GTC), LIMIT ORDERS, MARKET-ON-CLOSE ORDERS, MARKET ORDERS, ON THE CLOSE ORDERS, ON THE OPENING ORDERS, STOP-LIMIT ORDERS, STOP LOSS ORDERS, and STOP ORDERS.

SELL OUT
1. liquidation of a MARGIN ACCOUNT by a broker after a MARGIN CALL has failed to produce additional equity to bring the margin to the required level. *See also* CLOSE A POSITION; MARGIN REQUIREMENT; MINIMUM MAINTENANCE.
2. action by a broker when a customer fails to pay for securities purchased and the securities received from the selling broker are sold to cover the transaction. Term also applies to commodities futures transactions.

3. expression used when all the securities in a NEW ISSUE underwriting have been distributed.

SELL PLUS sell order with instructions to execute only if the trading price in a security is higher than the last different preceding price. *See also* SHORT-SALE RULE.

SELL-STOP ORDER *see* STOP ORDER.

SELL THE BOOK order to a broker by the holder of a large quantity of shares of a security to sell all that can be ABSORBED at the current bid price. The term derives from the SPECIALIST'S BOOK—the record of all the buy and sell orders members have placed in the stock he or she handles. In this scenario, the buyers potentially include those in the specialist's book, the specialist for his or her own account, and the broker-dealer CROWD.

SENIOR BOND ISSUE corporate bond issue that has priority over other bonds as to its claim on the company's assets and earnings. Example: first mortgage bond. *See also* SENIOR MORTGAGE BOND.

SENIOR DEBT loans or DEBT SECURITIES that have claim prior to junior obligations and EQUITY on a corporation's assets in the event of LIQUIDATION. Senior debt commonly includes funds borrowed from banks, insurance companies, or other financial institutions, as well as notes, bonds, or debentures not expressly defined as junior or subordinated.

SENIOR MORTGAGE BOND bond with the highest claim on the assets of the issuer in case of bankruptcy or liquidation. Senior mortgage bondholders are paid off in full before any payments are made to junior bondholders. *See also* SENIOR BOND.

SENIOR REFUNDING replacement of securities maturing in 5 to 12 years with issues having original maturities of 15 years or longer. The objectives may be to reduce the bond issuer's interest costs, to consolidate several issues into one, or to extend the maturity date.

SENIOR SECURITY security that has claim prior to a junior obligation and EQUITY on a corporation's assets and earnings. Senior securities are repaid before JUNIOR SECURITIES in the event of LIQUIDATION. Debt, including notes, bonds, and debentures, is senior to stock; first mortgage bonds are senior to second mortgage bonds; and all mortgage bonds are senior to debentures, which are unsecured.

SENSITIVE MARKET market easily swayed by good or bad news.

SENSITIVITY ANALYSIS study measuring the effect of a change in a variable (such as sales) on the risk or profitability of an investment.

SENTIMENT INDICATORS measures of the bullish or bearish mood of investors. Many technical analysts look at these indicators as contrary indicators—that is, when most investors are bullish, the market is about to drop, and when most are bearish, the market is about to rise. Some financial newsletters measure swings in investor sentiment by tabulating the number of INVESTMENT ADVISORY SERVICES that are bullish or bearish.

SEPARATE ACCOUNT account or group of similar accounts (of a customer of a member firm of any one of the five Sponsoring Self-Regulatory Organizations) that are treated as if each belongs to a separate customer. Each is therefore entitled to the maximum coverage offered by the Canadian Investor Protection Fund, currently $500,000 per account. Separate accounts include various tax-deferral plans and trusts (e.g., Self-Directed Retirement Savings Plans). *See also* CANADIAN INVESTOR PROTECTION FUND.

SEPARATELY REPORTABLE SEGMENT *see* BUSINESS SEGMENT REPORTING.

SERIAL BOND bond issue, with various MATURITY DATES scheduled at regular intervals until the entire issue is retired. Each bond certificate in the series has an indicated REDEMPTION DATE.

SERIAL DEBENTURE *see* SERIAL BOND.

SERIAL REDEMPTION redemption of a SERIAL BOND.

SERIES options of the same class having the same exercise price and expiry date. Each class can have several option series trading at any given time.

SERIES MONTH calendar month during which a commodity futures contract is deliverable or is settled.

SERIES OF OPTION class of OPTION, either all CALL OPTIONS or all PUT OPTIONS, on the same underlying security, all of which have the same EXERCISE PRICE (strike price) and maturity date. For example, all XYZ May 50 calls would form a series of options.

SET-ASIDE percentage of a job set aside for bidding to minority contractors. In the securities business, many municipal and some corporate bond underwritings require that a certain percentage of the offering be handled by a minority-owned broker/dealer underwriting firm. Other government and corporate contracts for products and services also stipulate that a certain percentage of the business must be handled by minority firms. Set-aside programs are designed to help minority firms become established more quickly than they might if they had to compete on an equal footing with entrenched competitors.

SETTLE
In general: to pay an obligation.
Estates: distribution of an estate's assets by an executor to beneficiaries after all legal procedures have been completed.
Law: (1) to resolve a legal dispute short of adjudication; (2) to arrange for disposition of property, such as between spouses or between parents and children, if there has been a dispute such as a divorce.

Securities: to complete a securities trade between brokers acting as AGENTS or between a broker and his or her customer. A trade is settled when the customer has paid the broker for securities bought or when the customer delivers securities that have been sold and the customer receives the proceeds from the sale. *See also* CONTINUOUS NET SETTLEMENT.

SETTLEMENT in general, a resolution of differences among various parties. For example, a labour dispute resulting in a strike may finally be settled by a new contract, or a conflict between a landlord and tenant may be settled in a housing court.

Securities: conclusion of a securities transaction in which a broker/dealer pays for securities bought for a customer or delivers securities sold and receives payment from the buyer's broker. REGULAR WAY DELIVERY AND SETTLEMENT is completed on the third full business day following the date of the transaction for stocks, called the SETTLEMENT DATE. Government bonds and options trades are settled the next business day. *See also* CONTINUOUS NET SETTLEMENT.

Futures/Options: the final price, established by exchange rule, for the prices prevailing during the closing period and upon which futures contracts are marked to market.

SETTLEMENT CHANGE difference between the previous day's and today's settlement price.

SETTLEMENT DATE date by which an executed order must be settled, either by a buyer paying for the securities with cash or by a seller delivering the securities and receiving the proceeds of the sale for them. In a REGULAR-WAY DELIVERY of stocks and bonds, the settlement date is three business days after the trade was executed. For listed options and government securities, settlement is required by the next business day. *See also* SELLER'S OPTION.

SETTLEMENT OPTIONS options available to beneficiaries when a person insured by a life insurance policy dies. The DEATH BENEFIT may be paid in one lump sum, in several installments over a fixed period of time, or in the form of an ANNUITY for the rest of the beneficiary's life, among other options.

SETTLOR person who creates an INTER VIVOS TRUST as distinguished from a TESTAMENTARY TRUST. Also called *donor, grantor,* or *trustor.*

SEVERALLY BUT NOT JOINTLY form of agreement used to establish the responsibility for selling a portion of the securities in an underwriting. UNDERWRITING GROUP members agree to buy a certain portion of an issue (severally) but do not agree to joint liability for shares not sold by other members of the syndicate. In a less common form of underwriting arrangement, called a *several and joint agreement,* syndicate members agree to sell not only the shares allocated to them, but also any shares not sold by the rest of the group. *See also* UNDERWRITE.

SEVERANCE PAY money paid to an employee who has been laid off by an employer. The money may be paid in the form of a LUMP SUM, as an ANNUITY, or in the form of paycheques for a specified period of time. The size of the termination benefit is based on the length of service and job level of the employee, union contracts, and other factors. Also called *termination benefit*.

SG&A EXPENSES *see* SELLING, GENERAL, AND ADMINISTRATIVE EXPENSES.

SHAKEOUT change in market conditions that results in the elimination of marginally financed participants in an industry. For example, if the market for microcomputers suddenly becomes glutted because there is more supply than demand, a shakeout will result, meaning that companies will fall by the wayside. In the securities markets, a shakeout occurs when speculators are forced by market events to sell their positions, usually at a loss.

SHAM transaction conducted for the purpose of avoiding taxation. Once discovered by tax authorities, it will be considered null and void, and the parties to the transaction will have to pay the taxes due.

SHARE
1. unit of equity ownership in a corporation. This ownership is represented by a stock certificate, which names the company and the shareowner. The number of shares a corporation is authorized to issue is detailed in its corporate charter. Corporations usually do not issue the full number of AUTHORIZED SHARES.
2. unit of ownership in a mutual fund. *See also* INVESTMENT COMPANY.
3. interest, normally represented by a certificate, in a general or LIMITED PARTNERSHIP.

SHARE BROKER DISCOUNT BROKER whose charges are based on the number of shares traded. The more shares in a trade, the lower the per-share cost will be. Trading with a share broker is usually advantageous for those trading at least 500 shares, or for those trading in high-priced shares, who would otherwise pay a percentage of the dollar amount. Those trading in small numbers of shares, or lower-priced ones, may pay lower commissions with a VALUE BROKER, the other kind of discount brokerage firm.

SHARED APPRECIATION MORTGAGE (SAM) mortgage in which the borrower receives a below-market rate of interest in return for agreeing to share part of the appreciation in the value of the underlying property with the lender in a specified number of years. If the borrower does not want to sell at that time, he or she must pay the lender its share of the appreciation in cash. If the borrower does not have that amount of cash on hand, the lender may force the borrower to sell the property to satisfy their claim.

SHARE CLASS designation given when a company issues or sells more than one kind of common or preferred share to show that there is a distinction between them, e.g., Class A Common, and Class B Common shares.

SHARE DRAFT instrument similar to a bank cheque that is used by credit unions to withdraw from interest-bearing share draft accounts.

SHAREHOLDER
1. owner of one or more shares of STOCK in a corporation. A common shareholder is normally entitled to four basic rights of ownership: (1) claim on a share of the company's undivided assets in proportion to number of shares held; (2) proportionate voting power in the election of DIRECTORS and other business conducted at shareholder meetings or by PROXY; (3) DIVIDENDS when earned and declared by the BOARD OF DIRECTORS; and (4) PREEMPTIVE RIGHT to subscribe to additional stock offerings before they are available to the general public except when overruled by the ARTICLES OF INCORPORATION or in special circumstances, such as where stock is issued to effect a merger.
2. owner of one or more shares or units in a MUTUAL FUND. Mutual fund investors have voting rights similar to those of stock owners.
   Shareholders' rights can vary according to the articles of incorporation or BYLAWS of the particular company.
   See also PREFERRED STOCK.

SHAREHOLDER REPORT *see* STOCKHOLDER'S REPORT.

SHAREHOLDER'S EQUITY total ASSETS minus total LIABILITIES of a corporation. Equity divided by number of shares outstanding gives equity per share. Also called *stockholder's equity,* EQUITY, and NET WORTH.

SHARE PROFIT calculated by dividing the profit after dividend rights of preferred shares by the average number of common shares outstanding. This calculation may be done either before or after taking any extraordinary items into account. If the company had a loss instead of a profit, the same calculations would result in a share loss before or after extraordinary items.

SHARE PURCHASE PLAN fringe benefits occasionally offered to employees that allow them to purchase their company's shares at a discount or on a matching basis, with the company absorbing part of the cost.

SHARE REPURCHASE PLAN program by which a corporation buys back its own shares in the open market. It is usually done when shares are UNDERVALUED. Since it reduces the number of shares outstanding and thus increases EARNINGS PER SHARE, it tends to elevate the market value of the remaining shares held by stockholders. *See also* GOING PRIVATE; TREASURY STOCK.

SHARES AUTHORIZED number of shares of stock provided for in the ARTICLES OF INCORPORATION of a company. This figure is ordinarily indicated in the capital accounts section of a company's BALANCE SHEET and is usually well in excess of the shares ISSUED AND OUTSTANDING. A corporation cannot legally issue more shares than authorized. The number of authorized shares can be changed only by amendment to the corporate charter, with the approval of the shareholders. The most common reason for increasing authorized shares in a public company is to accommodate a stock SPLIT.

SHARES OUTSTANDING *see* ISSUED AND OUTSTANDING.

SHARK REPELLENT measure undertaken by a corporation to discourage unwanted TAKEOVER attempts. Also called *porcupine provision*. For example:
(1) fair price provision requiring a bidder to pay the same price to all shareholders. This raises the stakes and discourages TENDER OFFERS designed to attract only those shareholders most eager to replace management.
(2) GOLDEN PARACHUTE contract with top executives that makes it prohibitively expensive to get rid of existing management.
(3) defensive merger, in which a TARGET COMPANY combines with another organization that would create antitrust or other regulatory problems if the original, unwanted takeover proposal was consummated. *See also* SAFE HARBOR.
(4) STAGGERED BOARD OF DIRECTORS, a way to make it more difficult for a corporate RAIDER to install a majority of directors sympathetic to his or her views.
(5) supermajority provision, which might increase from a simple majority to two-thirds or three-fourths the shareholder vote required to ratify a takeover by an outsider.
See also POISON PILL; SCORCHED-EARTH POLICY.

SHARK WATCHER firm specializing in the early detection of TAKEOVER activity. Such a firm, whose primary business is usually the solicitation of proxies for client corporations, monitors trading patterns in a client's stock and attempts to determine the identity of parties accumulating shares.

SHELF REGISTRATION term which allows a corporation to comply with REGISTRATION requirements up to two years prior to a PUBLIC OFFERING of securities. With the registration on the shelf, the corporation, by simply updating regularly filed annual, quarterly, and related reports, can go to the market as conditions become favourable with a minimum of administrative preparation. The flexibility corporate issuers enjoy as the result of shelf registration translates into substantial savings of time and expense. This is most commonly used in the United States.

SHELL CORPORATION company that is incorporated but has no significant assets or operations. Such corporations may be formed to obtain financing prior to starting operations, in which case an investment in them is highly risky. The term is also used of corporations set up by fraudulent operators as fronts to conceal tax evasion schemes.

SHOCK ABSORBERS *see* CIRCUIT BREAKERS.

SHOGUN SECURITY security issued and distributed exclusively in Japan by a non-Japanese company and denominated in a currency other than yen.

SHOP
1. area of a business location where production takes place, as distinguished from the office or warehouse areas.
2. factory work force of an employer, as in a "union shop."
3. office of a broker-dealer in securities.
4. the act of canvassing dealers for the most favourable price, as in shopping securities dealers for the best bid or offer.
5. a small retail establishment.

SHORT selling a security that the seller does not own in the hope of buying it back later at a lower price. *See also* SELLING SHORT.

SHORT AGAINST THE BOX *see* SELLING SHORT AGAINST THE BOX.

SHORT BOND
1. bond with a short maturity; a somewhat subjective concept, but generally meaning two years or less. *See also* SHORT TERM.
2. bond repayable in one year or less and thus classified as a CURRENT LIABILITY in accordance with the accounting definition of SHORT-TERM DEBT.
3. SHORT COUPON bond.

SHORT COUPON
1. bond interest payment covering less than the conventional six-month period. A short coupon payment occurs when the original issue date is less than a half year from the first scheduled interest payment date. Depending on how short the coupon is, the ACCRUED INTEREST makes a difference in the value of the bond at the time of issue, which is reflected in the offering price.
2. bond with a relatively short maturity, usually two years or less. *See also* LONG COUPON.

SHORT COVERING actual purchase of securities by a short seller to replace those borrowed at the time of a short sale. *See also* LENDING SECURITIES; SELLING SHORT.

SHORTFALL amount by which a financial objective has not been met. For example, a municipality expecting $100 million in tax revenue will say there is a $10 million shortfall if it collects only $90 million. For individual investors, a shortfall is the amount by which investment objectives have not been reached. For instance, investors execting to earn 15% a year will have a 5% shortfall if they earn 10% a year.

SHORT HEDGE transaction that limits or eliminates the risk of declining value in a security or commodity without entailing ownership. Examples:

(1) SELLING SHORT AGAINST THE BOX leaves the owned securities untouched, possibly to gain in value, while protecting against a decline in value, since that would be offset by a profit on the short sale.

(2) purchasing a PUT OPTION to protect the value of a security that is owned limits loss to the cost of the option.

(3) buying a futures contract on raw materials at a specific price protects a manufacturer committed to sell a product at a certain price at a specified future time but who cannot buy the raw materials at the time of the commitment. Thus, if the price of the materials goes up, the manufacturer makes a profit on the contract; if the price goes down, he or she makes a profit on the product.

Compare with LONG HEDGE.

SHORT INTEREST total amount of shares of stock that have been sold short and have not yet been repurchased to close out SHORT POSITIONS. The short interest figure for the New York Stock Exchange, which is published monthly in newspapers, indicates how many investors think stock prices are about to fall. The Exchange repor. l issues in which there are at least 5000 shares sold short, and in which the short interest position had changed by at least 2000 shares in the preceding month. The higher the short interest, the more people are expecting a downturn. Such short interest also represents potential buying pressure, however, since all short sales must eventually be covered by the purchase of shares. For this reason, a high short interest position is viewed as a bullish sign by many sophisticated market watchers. *See also* SELLING SHORT; SHORT INTEREST THEORY.

SHORT INTEREST THEORY theory that a large SHORT INTEREST in a stock presages a rise in the market price. It is based on the reasoning that even though short selling reflects a belief that prices will decline, the fact that short positions must eventually be covered is a source of upward price pressure. It is also called the CUSHION THEORY, since short sales can be viewed as a cushion of imminent buy orders. *See also* MEMBERS SHORT-SALE RATIO; ODD-LOT SHORT-SALE RATIO; SELLING SHORT; SPECIALIST'S SHORT-SALE RATIO.

SHORT MARKET market in which a trader has sold commodities futures before actually buying any.

SHORT POSITION
Commodities: contract in which a trader has agreed to sell a commodity at a future date for a specific price.
Stocks: stock shares that an individual has sold short (by delivery of borrowed certificates) and has not covered as of a particular date. *See also* COVER; SELLING SHORT.

SHORT SALE *see* SELLING SHORT.

SHORT-SALE RULE rule requiring that short sales be made only in a rising market; also called PLUS TICK rule. A short sale can be transacted only under these conditions: (1) if the last sale was at a higher price than the sale preceding it (called an UPTICK or PLUS TICK); (2) if the last sale price is unchanged but higher than the last preceding different sale (called a ZERO-PLUS TICK). The short sale rule was designed to prevent abuses perpetuated by so-called pool operators, who would drive down the price of a stock by heavy short selling, then pick up the shares for a large profit.

SHORT SQUEEZE situation when prices of a stock or commodity futures contract start to move up sharply and many traders with short positions are forced to buy stocks or commodities in order to COVER their positions and prevent losses. This sudden surge of buying leads to even higher prices, further aggravating the losses of short sellers who have not covered their positions. *See also* SELLING SHORT.

SHORT TERM
   Accounting: assets expected to be converted into cash within the normal operating cycle (usually one year), or liabilities coming due in one year or less. *See also* CURRENT ASSETS; CURRENT LIABILITY.
   Investment: investment with a maturity of one year or less. This includes bonds, although in differentiating between short-, medium-, and long-term bonds short term often is stretched to mean two years or less. *See also* SHORT BOND; SHORT-TERM DEBT; SHORT-TERM GAIN OR LOSS.
   Taxes: HOLDING PERIOD of less than one year, used to differentiate SHORT-TERM GAIN OR LOSS from LONG-TERM GAIN and LONG-TERM LOSS. *See also* CAPITAL GAINS TAX.

SHORT-TERM BOND bond or debenture maturing within 3 to 5 years.

SHORT-TERM BOND FUND bond mutual fund investing in short-to-intermediate term bonds. Such bonds, maturing in 3 to 5 years, typically pay higher yields than the shortest maturity bonds of 1 year or less, which are held by ULTRA-SHORT-TERM BOND FUNDS. Short-term bond funds also usually pay higher yields than money market mutual funds, which buy short-term commercial paper maturing in 90 days or less. However, short-term bond funds usually yield less than long-term bond funds holding bonds maturing in 10 to 30 years. Short-term bond funds, while yielding less than long-term bond funds, are also considerably less volatile, meaning that their value falls less when interest rates rise and rises less when interest rates fall.

SHORT-TERM DEBT all debt obligations coming due within one year; shown on a balance sheet as current liabilities. *See also* CURRENT LIABILITY.

SHORT-TERM INVESTMENT *see* SHORT-TERM.

SHOTGUN clause in a buy-sell agreement whereby, if one party offers to buy out the other at a certain price, the other party has, within a limited period, either to accept the price or buy the offerer out at the same price.

SHOW STOPPER legal barrier erected to prevent a takeover attempt from becoming successful. For example, a target company may appeal to the state legislature to pass laws preventing the takeover. Or the company may embark on a SCORCHED-EARTH POLICY, making the company unappealing to the suitor. *See also* SHARK REPELLENT.

SHRINKAGE difference between the amount of inventory recorded in a firm's books and the actual amount of inventory on hand. Shrinkage may occur because of theft, deterioration, loss, clerical error, and other factors.

SIDE-BY-SIDE TRADING trading of a security and an OPTION on that security on the same exchange.

SIDEWAYS MARKET period in which prices trade within a narrow range, showing only small changes up or down. Also called HORIZONTAL PRICE MOVEMENT. *See also* FLAT MARKET.

SIGNATURE GUARANTEE written confirmation by a financial institution such as a bank or brokerage firm that a customer's signature is valid. The institution will compare a new signature from a customer with the signature on file. Transfer agents require signature guarantees when transferring stocks, bonds, mutual funds, or other securities from one party to another to ensure that the transactions are legitimate.

SIGNATURE LOAN unsecured loan requiring only the borrower's signature on a loan application. The lender agrees to make the loan because the borrower has good credit standing. Collateral is not required. Also known as a *good-faith loan* or *character loan.*

SIGNIFICANT INFLUENCE holding of a large enough equity stake in a corporation to require accounting for it in financial statements. Usually, a company that holds at least 20% of the voting stock in another company is considered a holder of significant influence. A company with such a large holding is likely represented on the board of directors of the other firm. The company owning such a stake has to declare its equity holdings, and all dividends received from the position, in its financial reports.

SIGNIFICANT ORDER order to buy or sell securities that is significant enough to affect the price of the security. Many institutional investors, such as mutual funds, will try to spread out their significant buying or selling of a particular security over several days or weeks so they do not adversely affect the price at which they buy or sell.

SIGNIFICANT ORDER IMBALANCE large number of buy or sell orders for a stock, causing an unusually wide spread between bid and offer prices. Stock exchanges frequently halt trading of a stock with a significant order imbalance until more buyers or sellers appear and an orderly market can be reestablished. A significant order imbalance on the buying side can occur when there is an announcement of an impending takeover of the company, better-than-expected earnings, or other unexpected positive news. A significant order imbalance on the selling side can occur when a takeover offer has fallen through, a key executive has left the company, earnings came in far worse than expected, or there is other unexpected negative news.

SILENT PARTNER
1. limited partner, such as real estate and oil and gas limited partnerships, in which CASH FLOW and tax benefits are passed directly through to shareholders. Such partners are called silent because, unlike general partners, they have no direct role in management and no liability beyond their individual investment.
2. general partner in a business who has no role in management but represents a sharing of the investment and liability. Silent partners of this type are often found in family businesses, where the intent is to distribute tax liability.
   See also LIMITED PARTNERSHIP.

SILVER *see* GOLD.

SILVER FIX price setting that occurs in London twice each trading day right after the gold fix.

SILVER FUTURES *see* GOLD FUTURES.

SILVER THURSDAY the day—March 27, 1980—when the extremely wealthy Hunt brothers of Texas failed to meet a MARGIN CALL by the brokerage firm of Bache Halsey Stuart Shields (which later became Prudential-Bache Securities) for $100 million in silver futures contracts. Their position was later covered and Bache survived, but the effects on the commodities markets and the financial markets in general were traumatic.

SIMPLE INTEREST interest calculation based only on the original principal amount. Simple interest contrasts with COMPOUND INTEREST, which is applied to principal plus accumulated interest. For example, $100 on deposit at 12% simple interest would yield $12 per year (12% of $100). The same $100 at 12% interest compounded annually would yield $12 interest only in the first year. The second year's interest would be 12% of the first year's accumulated interest and principal of $112, or $13.44. The third year's payment would be 12% of $125.44— the second year's principal plus interest—or $15.05. For computing interest on loans, simple interest is distinguished from various methods of calculating interest on a precomputed basis. *See also* PRECOMPUTE.

SIMPLE RATE OF RETURN rate of return that results from dividing the income and capital gains from an investment by the amount of capital invested. For example, if a $1000 investment produced $50 in income and $50 in capital appreciation in one year, the investment would have a 10% simple rate of return. This method of calculation does not factor in the effects of compounding.

SINGLE-COUNTRY MUTUAL FUNDS mutual funds investing in the securities of just one country. Such funds may be open-end, meaning they continue to create new shares as more money comes into the fund, or closed-end, meaning they issue a limited number of shares which then trade on the stock exchange at a premium or discount to net asset value. Single-country funds offer investors a PURE PLAY on the fortunes of securities in that country. This means that these funds typically are far more volatile than REGIONAL MUTUAL FUNDS holding securities in a wider region, or GLOBAL MUTUAL FUNDS investing in markets around the world. There are many single-country funds, including funds for Argentina, Australia, Canada, China, France, Germany, Israel, Japan, Korea, Mexico, Spain, Switzerland, the United Kingdom, and the United States.

SINGLE OPTION term used to distinguish a PUT OPTION or a CALL OPTION from a SPREAD or a STRADDLE, each of which involves two or more put or call options. *See also* OPTION.

SINGLE-PREMIUM LIFE INSURANCE WHOLE LIFE INSURANCE policy requiring one premium payment. Since this large, up-front payment begins accumulating cash value immediately, the policy holder will earn more than holders of policies paid up in installments.

SINGLE TAX SYSTEM *see* FLAT TAX.

SINKER bond on which interest and principal payments are made from the proceeds of a SINKING FUND.

SINKING FUND money accumulated on a regular basis in a separate custodial account that is used to redeem debt securities or preferred stock issues. A bond indenture or preferred stock charter may specify that payments be made to a sinking fund, thus assuring investors that the issues are safer than bonds (or preferred stocks) for which the issuer must make payment all at once, without the benefit of a sinking fund. *See also* PURCHASE FUND.

SITUATIONAL AUDIT study done to identify external factors (competitors, economic conditions, new technology, new rules and regulations) that influence the formulation and implementation of business strategies.

SIZE
1. number of shares or bonds available for sale. A market maker will say, when asked for a quote, that a particular number of shares (the size) is available at a particular price.
2. term used when a large number of shares are for sale—a trader will say that "shares are available in size," for instance.

SKIP-PAYMENT PRIVILEGE
1. clause in some MORTGAGE contracts and installment loan agreements allowing borrowers to miss payments if ahead of schedule.

2. option offered some bank credit-card holders whereby they may defer the December payment on balances due.

SLD LAST SALE indication, meaning "sold last sale," that appears on the CONSOLIDATED TAPE when a greater than normal change occurs between transactions in a security. The designation, which appears after the STOCK SYMBOL, is normally used when the change is a point or more on lower-priced issues (below $20) or two points or more on higher-priced issues.

SLEEPER stock in which there is little investor interest but which has significant potential to gain in price once its attractions are recognized. Sleepers are most easily recognized in retrospect, after they have already moved up in price.

SLEEPING BEAUTY potential TAKEOVER target that has not yet been approached by an acquirer. Such a company usually has particularly attractive features, such as a large amount of cash, or undervalued real estate or other assets.

SLUMP short-term drop in performance. The economy may enter a slump when it goes into a RECESSION. An individual stock or mutual fund may be in a slump if its price falls over several weeks or months. A normally productive employee may go into a slump and be less productive if he or she is having financial or emotional difficulties. A slump is considered to be a temporary phenomenon, from which the economy, investment or employee will soon recover.

SMALL BUSINESS ADMINISTRATION (SBA) U.S. federal agency created in 1953 to provide financial assistance (through direct loans and loan guarantees) as well as management assistance to businesses that lack the access to CAPITAL MARKETS enjoyed by larger more creditworthy corporations. Further legislation authorized the SBA to contribute to the VENTURE CAPITAL requirements of START-UP companies by licensing and funding small business investment companies (SBICs), to maintain a loan fund for rehabilitation of property damaged by natural disasters (floods, hurricanes, etc.), and to provide loans, counseling and training for small businesses owned by minorities, the economically disadvantaged, and the disabled.

The SBA finances its activities through direct grants approved by the U.S. Congress.

SMALL BUSINESS DEDUCTION federal tax credit available to relatively small Canadian-controlled private corporations. It serves to reduce the basic federal corporate tax rate of 46% to 25% on the first $200,000 of active business income of eligible corporations. It can be as low as 18% if the province in which the business operates has a tax holiday in the first 3 years after startup. A tax holiday means that no taxes are payable for up to 3 years as an incentive to start a business.

SMALL CAP shorthand for *small capitalization stocks* or mutual funds holding such stocks. Small cap stocks usually have a market capitalization (number of shares outstanding multiplied by the stock price) of $500 million or less. Those under $50 million in market cap are known as *microcap issues*. Small capitalization stocks represent companies that are less well established, but in many cases faster-growing than *mid-cap stocks* (from $500 million to $3 billion–$5 billion) or *large cap stocks* ($1 billion or more). Since they are less established, small cap stocks are usually more volatile than BLUE CHIPS.

SMALL FIRM EFFECT tendency of stocks of smaller firms, defined by MARKET CAPITALIZATION, to outperform larger firms. Theories to explain this phenomenon vary, but include the following: (1) smaller companies tend to have more growth potential; (2) small capitalization groupings include more companies in financial difficulty; when fortunes recover, price gains are dramatic and lift the return of the group as a whole; (3) small firms are generally neglected by analysts and hence by institutions; once discovered, they become appropriately valued, registering dramatic gains in the process. *See also* ANKLE BITER.

SMALL INVESTOR individual investor who buys small amounts of stock or bonds, often in ODD LOT quantities; also called the RETAIL INVESTOR. Although there are millions of small investors, their total holdings are dwarfed by the share ownership of large institutions such as mutual funds and insurance companies. Together with the proliferation of mutual funds, recent developments in the brokerage industry and its diversification along full-service lines have brought new programs specifically designed to make investing more convenient for small investors. Thus, much cash traditionally kept in savings banks has found its way into the stock and bond markets.

SMART MONEY investors who make profitable investment moves at the right time, no matter what the investing environment. In a bull market, such investors buy the stocks that go up the most. In bear markets, they sell stocks short that fall the most. Smart money investors also have access to information about companies, either positive or negative, in advance of when the typical small investor learns of it. The term is also used in a more general sense to convey what sophisticated investors are doing now. Analysts will say "the smart money is buying cyclical stocks now because the economy is improving," for example.

SMOKESTACK INDUSTRIES basic manufacturing industries, such as autos, chemicals, steel, paper, and rubber, which typically have smokestacks on their plants. The fate of these industries, when viewed by analysts, is closely tied to the ups and downs of the economy—they are therefore called CYCLICAL stocks.

SNAKE SYSTEM agreement between European countries linking their currencies in an exchange-rate system in order to minimize fluctuations.

Participating countries include Denmark, Germany, the Netherlands, Norway, and Sweden.

SNOWBALLING process by which the activation of STOP ORDERS in a declining or advancing market causes further downward or upward pressure on prices, thus triggering more stop orders and more price pressure, and so on.

SOCIAL CONSCIOUSNESS MUTUAL FUND mutual fund that is managed for capital appreciation while at the same time investing in securities of companies that do not conflict with certain social priorities. As a product of the social consciousness movements of the 1960s and 1970s, this type of mutual fund might not invest in companies that derive significant profits from weapons or whose activities cause environmental pollution, nor in companies with significant interests in countries with repressive or racist governments. *See also* ETHICAL FUND.

SOCIAL SECURITY in the United States, benefits provided under the Social Security Act (1935), financed by the SOCIAL SECURITY TAX authorized by the FEDERAL INSURANCE CONTRIBUTORS ACT (FICA), and administered by the Social Security Administration. Term usually refers to retirement income benefits, but other benefits include SOCIAL SECURITY DISABILITY INCOME INSURANCE; Aid to Families with Dependent Children (AFDC); the Food Stamp program; Unemployment Insurance; Medicare; Medicaid; Public Assistance for the Aged, Blind and Disabled; Veterans' Compensation and Pensions; Housing Subsidies and Public Housing; Nutritional Programs for Children; and Student Aid.

SOCIAL RESPONSIBILITY principle that businesses should actively contribute to the welfare of society and not only maximize profits. Most corporate annual reports will highlight what the company has done to further education, help minorities, give to the arts and social welfare agencies, and in general improve social conditions. The concept is also used by investors in picking companies that are fair to their employees, do not pollute or build weapons, and make beneficial products. *See also* SOCIAL CONSCIOUSNESS MUTUAL FUND; ETHICAL FUND.

SOES acronym for the computerized *Small Order Entry (or Execution) System* used by NASDAQ, in which orders for under 1000 shares bypass brokers and are aggregated and executed against available firm quotes by market makers on the NASDAQ system. *See also* ORDER SPLITTING.

SOCIALISM political-economic doctrine that, unlike CAPITALISM, which is based on competition, seeks a co-operative society in which the means of production and distribution are owned by the government or collectively by the people.

SOFT CURRENCY funds of a country that are not acceptable in exchange for the hard currencies of other countries. Soft currencies, such as Russia's ruble, are fixed at unrealistic exchange rates and are not backed by gold, so that countries with hard currencies, like Canadian dollars or British pounds, are reluctant to convert assets into them. *See also* HARD MONEY (HARD CURRENCY).

SOFT DOLLARS means of paying brokerage firms for their services through commission revenue, rather than through direct payments, known as *hard-dollar fees.* For example, a mutual fund may offer to pay for the research of a brokerage firm by executing trades generated by that research through that brokerage firm. The broker might agree to this arrangement if the fund manager promises to spend at least $100,000 in commissions with the broker that year. Otherwise, the fund would have to pay a hard-dollar fee of $50,000 for the research. *Compare with* HARD DOLLARS.

SOFT LANDING term used to describe a rate of growth sufficient to avoid recession but slow enough to prevent high inflation and interest rates. When the economy is growing very strongly, the Bank of Canada typically tries to engineer a soft landing by raising interest rates to head off inflation. If the economy threatens to fall into a recession, the Bank may lower rates to stimulate growth.

SOFT MARKET market characterized by an excess of supply over demand. A soft market in securities is marked by inactive trading, wide bid-offer spreads, and pronounced price drops in response to minimal selling pressure. Also called *buyer's market.*

SOFTS term used to refer to tropical commodities—coffee, sugar, and cocoa—but in a broader sense could include grains, oilseeds, cotton, and orange juice. Metals, financial futures, and livestock generally are excluded from this category.

SOFT SPOT weakness in selected stocks or stock groups in the face of a generally strong and advancing market.

SOLD-OUT MARKET commodities market term meaning that futures contracts in a particular commodity or maturity range are largely unavailable because of contract liquidations and limited offerings.

SOLVENCY state of being able to meet maturing obligations as they come due. See *also* INSOLVENCY.

SOUR BOND bond in DEFAULT on its interest or principal payments. The issue will typically trade at a deep discount and have a low credit rating. Traders say that the bond has "gone sour" when it defaults.

SOURCES AND APPLICATIONS (or USES) OF FUNDS STATE-MENT financial statement section that analyzed changes affecting WORKING CAPITAL (or, optionally, cash) and that appeared as part of the annual reports of the publicly held companies prior to 1988. It is now called a STATEMENT OF CHANGES IN FINANCIAL POSITION.

SOVEREIGN RISK risk that a foreign government will default on its loan or fail to honour other business commitments because of a change in national policy. A country asserting its prerogatives as an independent nation might prevent the REPATRIATION of a company or country's funds through limits on the flow of capital, tax impediments, or the nationalization of property. Sovereign risk became a factor in the growth of international debt that followed the oil price increases of the 1970s. Several developing countries that borrowed heavily from Western banks to finance trade deficits had difficulty later keeping to repayment schedules. Banks had to reschedule loans to such countries as Mexico and Argentina to keep them from defaulting. These loans ran the further risk of renunciation by political leaders, which also would have affected loans to private companies that had been guaranteed by previous governments. Beginning in the 1970s, banks and other multinational corporations developed sophisticated analytical tools to measure sovereign risk before committing to lend, invest, or begin operations in a given foreign country. Also called *country risk* or *political risk.*

SPDR acronym for *Standard & Poor's Depositary Receipt,* traded on the American Stock Exchange under the ticker symbol "SPY." Called *spiders,* they are securities that represent ownership in a long-term unit investment trust that holds a portfolio of common stocks designed to track the performance of the S&P 500 INDEX. A SPDR entitles a holder to receive proportionate quarterly cash distributions corresponding to the dividends that accrue to the S&P 500 stocks in the underlying portfolio, less trust expenses.

SPECIAL ARBITRAGE ACCOUNT special MARGIN ACCOUNT with a broker reserved for transactions in which the customer's risk is hedged by an offsetting security transaction or position. The MARGIN REQUIREMENT on such a transaction is substantially less than in the case of stocks bought on credit and subject to price declines. *See also* HEDGE/HEDGING.

SPECIAL BID infrequently used U.S. method of purchasing a large block of stock whereby a MEMBER FIRM, acting as a broker, matches the buy order of one client, usually an institution, with sell orders solicited from a number of other customers.

SPECIAL DISTRICT BOND *see* SPECIAL ASSESSMENT BOND.

SPECIAL DRAWING RIGHTS (SDR) measure of a nation's reserve assets in the international monetary system; known informally as "paper gold." First issued by the INTERNATIONAL MONETARY FUND (IMF) in 1970, SDRs are designed to supplement the reserves of gold and convertible currencies (or hard currencies) used to maintain stability in the foreign exchange market. For example, if the Bank of Canada sees that the British pound's value has fallen precipitously in relation to the dollar, it can use its store of SDRs to buy excess pounds on the foreign exchange market, thereby raising the value of the remaining supply of pounds.

This neutral unit of account was made necessary by the rapid growth in world trade during the 1960s. International monetary officials feared that the supply of the two principal reserve assets—gold and U.S. dollars—would fall short of demand, causing the value of the U.S. currency to rise disproportionately in relation to other reserve assets. (At the time SDRs were introduced, the price of gold was fixed at about $35 per ounce.)

The IMF allocates to each of its more than 140 member countries an amount of SDRs proportional to its predetermined quota in the fund, which in turn is based on its GROSS NATIONAL PRODUCT (GNP). Each member agrees to back its SDRs with the full faith and credit of its government, and to accept them in exchange for gold or convertible currencies.

Originally, the value of one SDR was fixed at one dollar and at the dollar equivalent of other key currencies on January 1, 1970. As world governments adopted the current system of FLOATING EXCHANGE RATES, the SDR's value fluctuated relative to the "basket" of major currencies. Increasing reliance on SDRs in settling international accounts coincided with a decline in the importance of gold as a reserve asset.

Because of its inherent equilibrium relative to any one currency, the SDR has been used to denominate or calculate the value of private contracts, international treaties, and securities on the EUROBOND market. *See also* EUROPEAN CURRENCY UNIT (ECU).

SPECIALIST member of a stock exchange who maintains a fair and orderly market in one or more securities. A specialist or SPECIALIST UNIT performs two main functions: executing LIMIT ORDERS on behalf of other exchange members for a portion of the FLOOR BROKER'S commission, and buying or selling—sometimes SELLING SHORT—for the specialist's own account to counteract temporary imbalances in supply and demand and thus prevent wide swings in stock prices. The specialist is prohibited by exchange rules from buying for his or her own account when there is an unexecuted order for the same security at the same price in the SPECIALIST'S BOOK, the record kept of limit orders in each price category in the sequence in which they are received. Specialists must meet strict minimum capital requirements before receiving formal approval by a stock exchange. *See also* SPECIALIST BLOCK PURCHASE AND SALE; SPECIALIST'S SHORT SALE RATIO.

SPECIALIST BLOCK PURCHASE AND SALE transaction whereby a SPECIALIST on a stock exchange buys a large block of securities either to sell for his or her own account or to try and place with another block buyer and seller, such as a FLOOR TRADER. Exchange rules require that such transactions be executed only when the securities cannot be ABSORBED in the regular market. *See also* NOT HELD.

SPECIALIST'S BOOK record maintained by a SPECIALIST that includes the specialist's own inventory of securities, market orders to sell short, and LIMIT ORDERS and STOP ORDERS that other stock exchange members have placed with the specialist. The orders are listed in chronological sequence. For example, for a stock trading at 57 a broker might ask for 500 shares when the price falls to 55. If successful at placing this limit order, the specialist notifies the member broker who entered the request, and collects a commission. The specialist is prohibited from buying the stock for his or her own account at a price for which he or she has previously agreed to execute a limit order.

SPECIALIZED MUTUAL FUND mutual fund concentrating on one industry. By so doing, shareholders have a PURE PLAY on the fortunes of that industry, for better or worse. Some of the many industries with specialized mutual funds include banking, biotechnology, chemicals, energy, environmental services, natural resources, precious metals, technology, telecommunications, and utilities. These funds tend to be more volatile than funds holding a diversified portfolio of stocks in many industries. Also called *sector funds* or *specialty funds.*

SPECIAL OFFERING method of selling a large block of stock that is similar to a SECONDARY DISTRIBUTION but is limited to stock exchange members and takes place during normal trading hours. The selling member announces the impending sale on the CONSOLIDATED TAPE, indicating a fixed price, which is usually based on the last transaction price in the regular market. All costs and commissions are borne by the seller. The buyers are member firms that may be buying for customer accounts or for their own inventory.

SPECIAL SITUATION
1. undervalued stock that should soon rise in value because of an imminent favourable turn of events. A special situation stock may be about to introduce a revolutionary new product or be undergoing a needed management change. Many securities analysts concentrate on looking for and analyzing special situation stocks.
2. stock that fluctuates widely in daily trading, often influencing market averages, because of a particular news development, such as the announcement of a TAKEOVER bid.

SPECIALTY FUND fund that concentrates on purchasing shares of a group of companies in one industry (e.g., oil and gas), in one geographic location (e.g., Japan), or in one segment of the capital market (e.g., natural resources). Although there is diversification in their portfolios, these funds tend to be more risky and speculative than most types of common stock funds.

SPECTAIL term for broker-dealer who is part retail broker but preponderantly dealer/speculator.

SPECULATION assumption of risk in anticipation of gain but recognizing a higher than average possibility of loss. Speculation is a necessary and productive activity. It can be profitable over the long term when engaged in by professionals, who often limit their losses through the use of various HEDGING techniques and devices, including OPTIONS trading, SELLING SHORT, STOP LOSS ORDERS, and transactions in FUTURES CONTRACTS. The term speculation implies that a business or investment risk can be analyzed and measured, and its distinction from the term INVESTMENT is one of degree of risk. It differs from gambling, which is based on random outcomes.

    See also VENTURE CAPITAL.

SPECULATOR market participant who tries to profit from buying and selling futures and options contracts by anticipating future price movements. Speculators assume market price risk and add liquidity and capital to the futures markets. Speculators may purchase volatile stocks or mutual funds, and hold them for a short time in order to reap a profit. They may also sell stocks short and hope to cash in when the stock price drops quickly.

SPIDERS *see* SPDR.

SPIN-OFF form of corporate DIVESTITURE that results in a subsidiary or division becoming an independent company. In a traditional spin-off, shares in the new entity are distributed to the parent corporation's shareholders of record on a PRO RATA basis. Spin-offs can also be accomplished through a LEVERAGED BUYOUT by the subsidiary or division's management.

SPINS acronym for *Standard & Poor's 500 Index Subordinated Notes,* as Salomon Brothers' product combining features of debt, equity, and options.

SPLIT increase in a corporation's number of outstanding shares of stock without any change in the shareholders' EQUITY or the aggregate MARKET VALUE at the time of the split. In a split, also called a *split up,* the share price declines. If a stock at $100 par value splits 2-for-1, the number of authorized shares doubles (for example, from 10 million to 20 million) and the price per share drops by half, to $50. A holder of 50 shares before the split now has 100 shares at the lower price. If the same stock splits 4-for-1, the number of shares quadruples to 40 million and the share price falls to $25. Dividends per share also fall proportionately. Directors of a corporation will authorize a split to make ownership more affordable to a broader base of investors. Where stock splits require an increase in AUTHORIZED SHARES and/or a change in PAR VALUE of the stock, shareholders must approve an amendment of the corporate charter.

    See also REVERSE SPLIT.

SPLIT COMMISSION commission divided between the securities broker who executes a trade and another person who brought the trade to the broker, such as an investment counselor or financial planner. Split commissions between brokers are also common in real estate transactions.

SPLIT COUPON BOND debt instrument that begins as a zero-coupon bond and converts to an interest-paying bond at a specified date in the future. These bonds, issued by corporations and governments, are advantageous to issuers because they do not have to pay out cash interest for several years. They are attractive to investors, particularly in tax-sheltered accounts like RRSPs, because they have locked in a reinvestment rate for several years, and then can receive cash interest.

SPLIT DOWN *see* REVERSE SPLIT.

SPLIT FINANCING *see* SPLIT.

SPLIT OFFERING new municipal bond issue, part of which is represented by SERIAL BONDS and part by term maturity bonds.

SPLIT ORDER large transaction in securities that, to avoid unsettling the market and causing fluctuations in the market price, is broken down into smaller portions to be executed over a period of time.

SPLIT RATING in the United States, situation in which two major rating agencies, such as Standard & Poor's and Moody's Investors Service, assign a different rating to the same security.

SPLIT UP *see* SPLIT.

SPONSOR
Limited partnerships: GENERAL PARTNER who organizes and sells a LIMITED PARTNERSHIP. Sponsors (also called *promoters)* rely on their reputation in past real estate, oil and gas, or other deals to attract limited partners to their new deals.
Mutual funds: investment company that offers shares in its funds. Also called the *underwriter.*
Stocks: important investor—typically, an institution, mutual fund, or other big trader—whose favourable opinion of a particular security influences other investors and creates additional demand for the security. Institutional investors often want to make sure a stock has wide sponsorship before they invest in it, since this should ensure that the stock will not fall dramatically.

SPONSORING SELF REGULATORY ORGANIZATION *see* CANADIAN INVESTOR PROTECTION FUND.

SPOT COMMODITY COMMODITY traded with the expectation that it will actually be delivered to the buyer, as contrasted to a FUTURES CONTRACT that will usually expire without any physical delivery taking place. Spot commodities are traded in the SPOT MARKET.

SPOT DELIVERY MONTH nearest month of those currently being traded in which a commodity could be delivered. In late January, therefore, the spot delivery month would be February for commodities with a February contract trade.

SPOT GOLD selling price for gold in the spot (i.e., current) market for immediate delivery as opposed to delivery sometime in the future.

SPOT MARKET commodities market in which goods are sold for cash and delivered immediately. Trades that take place in FUTURES CONTRACTS expiring in the current month are also called *spot market trades.* The spot market tends to be conducted OVER-THE-COUNTER— that is, through telephone trading—rather than on the floor of an organized commodity exchange. Also called *actual market, cash market* or *physical market. See* also FUTURES MARKET.

SPOT PRICE current delivery price of a commodity traded in the cash market. Also called *cash price.*

SPOUSAL RRSP Registered Retirement Savings Plan that may be opened in the name of a nonworking spouse. The maximum annual contribution is that of the qualifying income times 18% of the working spouse, which can be allocated in whole or part. The contribution is deductible by the working spouse but it produces a retirement income for the nonworking spouse taxed at a lower rate. If contributions are withdrawn in less than 3 years, they are taxed in the hands of the working spouse.

SPREAD

Commodities: in futures trading, the difference in price between delivery months in the same market, or between different or related contracts. *See also* MOB SPREAD; NOB SPREAD; TED SPREAD.

Fixed-income securities: (1) difference between yields on securities of the same quality but different maturities. For example, the spread between 6% short-term Treasury bills and 10% long-term Treasury bonds is 4 percentage points. (2) difference between yields on securities of the same maturity but different quality. For instance, the spread between a 10% long-term government bond and a 14% long-term bond of a B-rated corporation is 4 percentage points, since an investor's risk of default is so much less with the government bond. *See also* YIELD SPREAD.

Foreign exchange: spreading one currency versus another, or multiple spreads within various currencies. An example would be a long position in Deutsche marks versus a short position in the British pound, or a long position in Deutsche marks versus a short position in the British pound or Japanese yen. An example of an intermonth spread would be a long March spot position in Swiss francs versus a short March position in the same currency. Spreads are frequently done in cash and futures markets. Interest rate differentials often have significant impact.

Options: position usually consisting of one long call and one short call option, or one long put and one short put option, with each option representing one "leg" of the spread. The two legs, if taken independently, would profit from opposite directional price movements.

Spreads usually have lower cost and lower profit potential than an outright long option. They are entered into to reduce risk, or to profit from the change in the relative prices of the options. *See also* BEAR SPREAD; BULL SPREAD; BUTTERFLY SPREAD; CALENDAR SPREAD; CREDIT SPREAD; DEBIT SPREAD; DIAGONAL SPREAD; OPTION; PRICE SPREAD; SELLING THE SPREAD; VERTICAL SPREAD.

Stocks and bonds: (1) difference between the bid and offer price. If a stock is bid at $45 and offered at $46, the spread is $1. This spread narrows or widens according to supply and demand for the security being traded. *See also* BID-ASKED SPREAD; DEALER SPREAD. (2) difference between the high and low price of a particular security over a given period.

Underwriting: difference between the proceeds an issuer of a new security receives and the price paid by the public for the issue. This spread is taken by the underwriting syndicate as payment for its services. A security issued at $100 may entail a spread of $2 for the underwriter, so the issuer receives $98 from the offering. *See also* UNDERWRITING SPREAD.

SPREADING practice of buying and selling OPTION contracts of the same CLASS on the same underlying security in order to profit from moves in the price of that security. *See also* SPREAD.

SPREAD OPTION SPREAD position involving the purchase of an OPTION at one EXERCISE PRICE and the simultaneous sale of another option on the same underlying security at a different exercise price and/or expiration date. *See also* DIAGONAL SPREAD; HORIZONTAL SPREAD; VERTICAL SPREAD.

SPREAD ORDER OPTIONS market term for an order designating the SERIES of LISTED OPTIONS the customer wishes to buy and sell, together with the desired SPREAD—or difference in option premiums (prices)—shown as a net debit or net credit. The transaction is completed if the FLOOR BROKER can execute the order at the requested spread.

SPREAD POSITION status of an account in which a SPREAD has been executed.

SPREADSHEET ledger sheet on which a company's financial statements, such as BALANCE SHEETS, INCOME STATEMENTS, and sales reports, are laid out in columns and rows. Spreadsheets are used by securities and credit analysts in researching companies and industries. Since the advent of personal computers, spreadsheets have come into wide use, because software makes them easy to use. In an electronic spreadsheet on a computer, any time one number is changed, all the other numbers are automatically adjusted according to the relationships the computer operator sets up. For instance, in a spreadsheet of a sales report of a company's many divisions, the updating of a single division's sales figure will automatically change the total sales for the company, as well as the percentage of total sales that division produced.

SPRINKLING TRUST trust under which no beneficiary has a right to receive any trust income. Instead, the trustee is given discretion to divide, or "sprinkle," the trust's income as the trustee sees fit among a designated group of persons. Sprinkling trusts can be created both by LIVING TRUST agreements and by WILLS.

SPX ticker symbol for the Standard & Poor's 500 stock index options traded on the Chicago Board Options Exchange. The European-style index options contract is settled in cash, and can be exercised only on the last business day before expiration. The SPX is one of the most heavily traded of all index options contracts.

SQUEEZE

Finance: (1) tight money period, when loan money is scarce and interest rates are high, making borrowing difficult and expensive—also called a *credit crunch;* (2) any situation where increased costs cannot be passed on to customers in the form of higher prices.

Investments: situation when stocks or commodities futures start to move up in price, and investors who have sold short are forced to COVER their short positions in order to avoid large losses. When done by many short sellers, this action is called a SHORT SQUEEZE. *See also* SELLING SHORT; SHORT POSITION.

SRO *see* SELF-REGULATORY ORGANIZATION.

STABILIZATION

Currency: buying and selling of a country's own currency to protect its exchange value, also called PEGGING.

Economics: leveling out of the business cycle, unemployment, and prices through fiscal and monetary policies.

Market trading: action taken by REGISTERED COMPETITIVE TRADERS on the New York Stock Exchange in accordance with an exchange requirement that 75% of their trades be stabilizing—in other words, that their sell orders follow a PLUS TICK and their buy orders a MINUS TICK.

New issues underwriting: intervention in the market by a managing underwriter in order to keep the market price from falling below the PUBLIC OFFERING PRICE during the offering period. The underwriter places orders to buy at a specific price, an action called PEGGING that, in any other circumstance, is a violation of laws prohibiting MANIPULATION in the securities and commodities markets.

STAG speculator who makes it a practice to get in and out of stocks for a fast profit, rather than to hold securities for investment.

STAGFLATION term coined by economists in the 1970s to describe the previously unprecedented combination of slow economic growth and high unemployment (stagnation) with rising prices (inflation). The principal factor was the fourfold increase in oil prices imposed by the Organization of Petroleum Exporting Countries (OPEC) cartel in 1973–74, which raised price levels throughout the economy while further slowing economic growth. As is characteristic of stagflation, fiscal and monetary policies aimed at stimulating the economy and reducing unemployment only exacerbated the inflationary effects.

STAGGERED BOARD OF DIRECTORS board of directors of a company in which a portion of the directors are elected each year, instead of all at once. A board is often staggered in order to thwart unfriendly TAKEOVER attempts, since potential acquirers would have to wait a longer time before they could take control of a company's board through the normal voting procedure. Normally, all directors are elected at the annual meeting.

STAGGERING MATURITIES technique used to lower risk by a bond investor. Since long-term bonds are more volatile than short-term ones, an investor can HEDGE against interest rate movements by buying short-, medium- and long-term bonds. If interest rates decline, the long-term bonds will rise faster in value than the shorter-term bonds. If rates rise, however, the shorter-term bonds will hold their value better than the long-term debt obligations, which could fall precipitously.

STAGNATION
Economics: period of no or slow economic growth or of economic decline, in real (inflation-adjusted) terms. Economic growth of 3% or less per year—as was the case in the late 1970s, measured according to increases in the gross national product—generally is taken to constitute stagnation.
Securities: period of low volume and inactive trading.

STAGS acronym for *Sterling Transferable Accruing Government Securities.* A British version of U.S. government STRIPS, STAGS are deep discount zero-coupon bonds backed by British Treasury securities. *See also* ZERO-COUPON SECURITY.

STANDARD & POOR'S CORPORATION subsidiary of McGraw-Hill, Inc. that provides a broad range of investment services, including RATING corporate and municipal bonds, common stocks, preferred stocks, and COMMERCIAL PAPER; compiling the Standard & Poor's Composite Index of 500 Stocks, the Standard & Poor's 400 Industrial Index, and the Standard & Poor's 100 Index among other indexes; publishing a wide variety of statistical materials, investment advisory reports, and other financial information, including: *Bond Guide,* a summary of data on corporate and municipal bonds; *Earnings Forecaster,* earnings-per-share estimates on more than 1600 companies; *New Issue Investor,* information and analysis on the new issue market; *Stock Guide,* investment data on listed and unlisted common and preferred stocks and mutual funds; *Analyst's Handbook,* per-share data on the stocks and industry groups making up the 400 index, plus 15 transportation, financial and utility groups; *Corporation Records,* six volumes of information on more than 10,000 publicly held companies; *Stock Reports,* 2-page analytical reports on listed and unlisted companies. A subsidiary publishes the daily BLUE LIST of municipal and corporate bonds. Standard & Poor's also publishes

Poor's Register, a national directory of companies and their officers, and *Securities Dealers of North America,* a directory of investment banking and brokerage firms in North America. *See also* STANDARD & POOR'S RATING; STOCK INDEXES AND AVERAGES.

STANDARD & POOR'S INDEX broad-based measurement of changes in stock market conditions based on the average performance of 500 widely held common stocks; commonly known as the *Standard & Poor's 500* (or *S&P 500*). The selection of stocks, their relative weightings to reflect differences in the number of outstanding shares, and publication of the index itself are services of STANDARD & POOR'S CORPORATION, a financial advisory, securities rating, and publishing firm. The index tracks industrial, transportation, financial, and utility stocks; it is a large cap index. The composition of the 500 stocks is flexible and the number of issues in each sector varies over time. Standard & Poor's also publishes several other important indexes including the *S&P MidCap 400,* the *S&P 600 SmallCap Index,* and the *S&P 1500 Super Composite Index,* which totals the S&P 500, 400, and 600 indices. These three indices represent approximately 82% of the total market capitalization of stocks traded in the U.S. equity market. S&P also maintains over 90 individual industry indexes.

> *See also* S&P PHENOMENON; STANDARD & POOR'S CORPORATION; STOCK INDEXES AND AVERAGES.

STANDARD & POOR'S RATING classification of stocks and bonds according to risk issued by STANDARD & POOR'S CORPORATION. S&P's top four debt grades—called INVESTMENT GRADE AAA, AA, A, and BBB—indicate a minimal risk that a corporate or municipal bond issue will DEFAULT in its timely payment of interest and principal. Common stocks are ranked A+ through C on the basis of growth and stability, with a ranking of D signifying REORGANIZATION. *See also* EVENT RISK; LEGAL LIST; RATING.

STANDARD BAR GOLD standard sizes of gold bullion bars, e.g., 100, 400, and 1000 ounces of 99.9% pure gold.

STANDARD BAR SILVER silver bar or ingot that comes in a standard size of 1000 ounces of 99.9% pure silver.

STANDARD COST estimate, based on engineering and accounting studies, of what costs of production should be, assuming normal operating conditions. Standard costs differ from budgeted costs, which are forecasts based on expectations. Variances between standard costs and actual costs measure productive efficiency and are used in cost control.

STANDARD DEVIATION statistical measure of the degree to which an individual value in a probability distribution tends to vary from the mean of the distribution. It is widely applied in modern PORTFOLIO THEORY, for example, where the past performance of securities is used to determine the range of possible future performances and a probability is attached to each performance. The standard deviation of performance can then be calculated for each security and for the portfolio as a whole. The greater the degree of dispersion, the greater the risk. *See also* PORTFOLIO THEORY; REGRESSION ANALYSIS.

STANDARD INDUSTRIAL CLASSIFICATION (SIC) SYSTEM federally designed standard numbering system identifying companies by industry and providing other information. It is widely used by market researchers, securities analysts, and others. Computerized data bases frequently make use of this classification system.

STANDARD OF LIVING degree of prosperity in a nation, as measured by income levels, quality of housing and food, medical care, educational opportunities, transportation, communications, and other measures. The standard of living in different countries is frequently compared based on annual per capita income. On an individual level, the standard of living is a measure of the quality of life in such areas as housing, food, education, clothing, transportation, and employment opportunities.

STANDBY COMMITMENT

Securities: agreement between a corporation and an investment banking firm or group (the *standby underwriter)* whereby the latter contracts to purchase for resale, for a fee, any portion of a stock issue offered to current shareholders in a RIGHTS OFFERING that is not subscribed to during the two- to four-week standby period. A right, often issued to comply with laws guaranteeing the shareholder's PREEMPTIVE RIGHT, entitles its holder, either an existing shareholder or a person who has bought the right from a shareholder, to purchase a specified amount of shares before a PUBLIC OFFERING and usually at a price lower than the PUBLIC OFFERING PRICE.

The risk to the investment banker in a standby commitment is that the market price of shares will fall during the standby period. *See also* LAY OFF for a discussion of how standby underwriters protect themselves. *See also* FLOTATION COST; SUBSCRIPTION RIGHT; UNDERWRITE.

Lending: a bank commitment to loan money up to a specified amount for a specific period, to be used only in a certain contingency. The most common example would be a commitment to repay a construction lender in the event a permanent mortgage lender cannot be found. A COMMITMENT FEE is normally charged.

STANDBY FEE fee charged on the unused portion of credit under a revolving credit or line-of-credit arrangement.

STANDBY UNDERWRITER *see* STANDBY COMMITMENT.

STANDSTILL AGREEMENT accord by a RAIDER to abstain from buying shares of a company for a specified period. *See also* GREENMAIL.

START-UP new business venture. In VENTURE CAPITAL parlance, start-up is the earliest stage at which a venture capital investor or investment pool will provide funds to an enterprise, usually on the basis of a business plan detailing the background of the management group along with market and financial PROJECTIONS. Investments or loans made at this stage are also called SEED MONEY.

STATED INTEREST RATE
Banking: rate paid on savings instruments, such as savings accounts. The stated interest rate does not take into account any compounding of interest.

Bonds: interest rate stated on a bond coupon. A bond with a 7% coupon has a 7% stated interest rate. This rate is applied to the face value of the bond, normally $1000, so that bondholders will receive 7% annually for every $1000 in face value of bonds they own.

STATED VALUE assigned value given to a corporation's stock for accounting purposes in lieu of par value. For example, the stated value may be set at $1 a share, so that if a company issued 10 million shares, the stated value of its stock would be $10 million. The stated value of the stock has no relation to its market price. It is, however, the amount per share that is credited to the CAPITAL STOCK account for each share outstanding and is therefore the legal capital of the corporation.

STATEMENT
1. summary for customers of the transactions that occurred over the preceding month. A bank statement lists all deposits and withdrawals, as well as the running account balances. A brokerage statement shows all stock, bond, commodity futures, or options trades, interest and dividends received, margin debt outstanding, and other transactions, as well as a summary of the worth of the accounts at month end. A trade supplier provides a summary of open account transactions.
2. statement drawn up by businesses to show the status of their ASSETS and LIABILITIES and the results of their operations as of a certain date. *See also* FINANCIAL STATEMENT.

STATEMENT OF CASH FLOWS analysis of CASH FLOW included as part of the financial statements in annual reports of publicly held companies. The statement shows how changes in balance sheet and income accounts affected cash and cash equivalents and breaks the analysis down according to operating, investing, and financing activities. As an analytical tool, the statement of cash flows reveals healthy or unhealthy trends and makes it possible to predict future cash requirements. It also shows how actual cash flow measured up to estimates and permits comparisons with other companies.

STATEMENT OF CHANGES IN FINANCIAL POSITION financial statement that provides information as to how a company generated and spent its cash during the year. It assists users in evaluating the company's ability to generate cash internally, repay debts, reinvest, and pay dividends to shareholders.

STATEMENT OF CONDITION
    Banking: sworn accounting of a bank's resources, liabilities, and capital accounts as of a certain date, submitted in response to periodic "calls" by bank regulatory authorities.
    Finance: summary of the status of assets, liabilities, and equity of a person or a business organization as of a certain date. *See also* BALANCE SHEET.

STATEMENT OF INCOME *see* PROFIT AND LOSS STATEMENT.

STATEMENT OF MATERIAL FACTS document presenting the relevant facts about a company and compiled in connection with an underwriting or secondary distribution of its shares. It is used only when the shares underwritten or distributed are listed on a recognized stock exchange and takes the place of a prospectus in such cases.

STATEMENT OF OPERATIONS *see* PROFIT AND LOSS STATEMENT.

STATUTE OF LIMITATIONS statute describing the limitations on how many years can pass before the right to sue for a wrongful action is given up. For example, Revenue Canada has up to 6 years to assess back taxes from the time the return is filed, unless tax fraud is charged.

STATUTORY HOLIDAYS federally, provincially, or municipally declared holidays, for example, Christmas and Thanksgiving. In some communities, special statutory holidays are allowed to accommodate individuals whose religious beliefs are other than Christian.

STATUTORY INVESTMENT investment specifically authorized by state law for use by a trustee administering a trust under that state's jurisdiction.

STATUTORY MERGER legal combination of two or more corporations in which only one survives as a LEGAL ENTITY. It differs from *statutory consolidation,* in which all the companies in a combination cease to exist as legal entities and a new corporate entity is created. *See also* MERGER.

STATUTORY PROSPECTUS *see* PROSPECTUS.

STATUTORY VOTING one-share, one-vote rule that governs voting procedures in most corporations. Shareholders may cast one vote per share either for or against each nominee for the board of directors, but may not give more than one vote to one nominee. The result of statutory voting is that, in effect, those who control over 50% of the shares control the company by ensuring that the majority of the board will represent their interests. *Compare with* CUMULATIVE VOTING. *See also* PROPORTIONAL REPRESENTATION.

STAYING POWER ability of an investor to stay with (not sell) an investment that has fallen in value. For example, a commodity trader with staying power is able to meet margin calls as the commodities FUTURES CONTRACTS he or she has bought fall in price. The commodity trader can afford to wait until the trade ultimately becomes profitable. In real estate, an investor with staying power is able to meet mortgage and maintenance payments on his or her properties and is therefore not harmed as interest rates rise or fall, or as the properties become temporarily difficult to sell.

STEP DOWN NOTE type of FLOATING RATE whose interest rate declines at specified times in the course of the loan.

STICKY DEAL new securities issue that the underwriter fears will be difficult to sell. Adverse market conditions, bad news about the issuing entity, or other factors may lead underwriters to say, "This will be a sticky deal at the price we have set." As a result, the price may be lowered or the offering withdrawn from the market.

STOCK

1. ownership of a CORPORATION represented by shares that are a claim on the corporation's earnings and assets. COMMON STOCK usually entitles the shareholder to vote in the election of directors and other matters taken up at shareholder meetings or by proxy. PREFERRED STOCK generally does not confer voting rights but it has a prior claim on assets and earnings—dividends must be paid on preferred stock before any can be paid on common stock. A corporation can authorize additional classes of stock, each with its own set of contractual rights. *See also* ARTICLES OF INCORPORATION; AUTHORIZED SHARES; BLUE CHIP; BOOK VALUE; CAPITAL STOCK; CERTIFICATE; CLASS; CLASSIFIED STOCK; CLOSELY HELD; COMMON STOCK; COMMON STOCK EQUIVALENT; CONVERTIBLES; CONTROL STOCK; CORPORATION; CUMULATIVE PREFERRED; DIVIDEND; EARNINGS PER SHARE; EQUITY; FLOAT; FRACTIONAL SHARES; GOING PUBLIC; GROWTH STOCK; INACTIVE STOCK; INITIAL PUBLIC OFFERING; ISSUED AND OUTSTANDING; JOINT STOCK COMPANY; LETTER SECURITY; LISTED SECURITY; MARKET VALUE; NONVOTING STOCK; NO-PAR VALUE STOCK; OVER THE COUNTER; PAR VALUE; PARTICIPATING PREFERRED; PENNY STOCK; PREEMPTIVE RIGHT; PREFERENCE SHARES; PREFERRED STOCK; PRIOR PREFERRED STOCK; QUARTER STOCK; REGISTERED SECURITY; REGISTRAR; REVERSE SPLIT; SCRIP; SECURITY; SHARE; SHAREHOLDER; SPLIT; STATED VALUE; STOCK CERTIFICATE; STOCK DIVIDEND; STOCK EXCHANGE; STOCKHOLDER; STOCKHOLDER OF RECORD; STOCK MARKET; STOCK POWER; STOCK PURCHASE PLAN; STOCK SYMBOL; STOCK WATCHER; TRANSFER AGENT; TREASURY STOCK; VOTING STOCK; VOTING TRUST CERTIFICATE; WATERED STOCK.

2. inventories of accumulated goods in manufacturing and retailing businesses.

3. *see* ROLLING STOCK.

STOCK AHEAD situation in which two or more orders for a stock at a certain price arrive about the same time, and the exchange's PRIORITY rules take effect. Most exchange rules stipulate that the bid made first should be executed first or, if two bids came in at once, the bid for the larger number of shares receives priority. The bid that was not executed is then reported back to the broker, who informs the customer that the trade was not completed because there was stock ahead. *See also* MATCHED AND LOST.

STOCK BONUS PLAN plan established and maintained by an employer to provide benefits similar to those of a profit-sharing plan. Contributions by the employer, however, are not necessarily dependent on profits, and the benefits are distributed in shares of stock in the employer company. Stock bonus plans reward employee performance, and by giving employees a stake in the company they are used to help motivate them to perform at maximum efficiency.

STOCKBROKER *see* REGISTERED REPRESENTATIVE; BROKER.

STOCK BUYBACK corporation's purchase of its own outstanding stock. A buyback may be financed by borrowings, sale of assets, or operating CASH FLOW. Its purpose is commonly to increase EARNINGS PER SHARE and thus the market price, often to discourage a TAKEOVER. When a buyback involves a PREMIUM paid to an acquirer in exchange for a promise to desist from takeover activity, the payment is called GREENMAIL. A buyback having a formula and schedule may also be called a SHARE REPURCHASE PLAN or SELF-TENDER. *See also* TREASURY STOCK.

STOCK CERTIFICATE documentation of a shareholder's ownership in a corporation. Stock certificates are engraved intricately on heavy paper to deter forgery. They indicate the number of shares owned by an individual, their PAR VALUE (if any), the CLASS of stock (for example, common or preferred), and attendant voting rights. To prevent theft, shareholders often store certificates in safe deposit boxes or take advantage of a broker's SAFEKEEPING service. Stock certificates become negotiable when endorsed.

STOCK CLOSE closing price of a stock underlying an option, based on the day's last call. This may not be the closing price of the stock for that day, especially if the last call was sold early in the day.

STOCK DIVIDEND payment of a corporate dividend in the form of stock rather than cash. The stock dividend may be additional shares in the company, or it may be shares in a SUBSIDIARY being spun off to shareholders. The dividend is usually expressed as a percentage of the shares held by a shareholder. For instance, a shareholder with 100 shares would receive 5 shares as the result of a 5% stock dividend. From the corporate point of view, stock dividends conserve cash needed to operate the business. From the stockholder point of view, the advantage is that additional stock is not taxed until sold, unlike a cash dividend, which is declarable as income in the year it is received.

STOCK EXCHANGE organized marketplace in which stocks, COMMON STOCK EQUIVALENTS, and bonds are traded by members of the exchange, acting both as agents (brokers) and as principals (dealers or traders). Such exchanges have a physical location where brokers and dealers meet to execute orders from institutional and individual investors to buy and sell securities. Each exchange sets its own requirements for membership; the Toronto and New York Stock Exchanges have the most stringent requirements. *See also* MONTREAL STOCK EXCHANGE; VANCOUVER EXCHANGE; CALGARY EXCHANGE; AMERICAN STOCK EXCHANGE; LISTING REQUIREMENTS; NEW YORK STOCK EXCHANGE; REGIONAL STOCK EXCHANGES; SECURITIES AND COMMODITIES EXCHANGES.

STOCK EXCHANGE INDEX indices of stock prices for a variety of industry classifications, compiled and published by the Toronto Stock Exchange (TSE) and the Montreal Exchange (ME). These indices, and dividend yields and price earnings ratios based on the TSE 300 Composite Index are included in the *Bank of Canada Review* and also appear in financial weekly and daily newspapers in Canada and elsewhere. Indices based on securities traded on the Vancouver and Alberta Exchanges are also published regularly by each of these exchanges in the press. In addition, certain securities firms prepare indicators for different market sectors. These are covered in the press and are widely followed.

STOCK EXCHANGE OF SINGAPORE (SES) only stock exchange in Singapore, trading through a fully computerized system called CLOB. A direct link between the SES and the NASDAQ Stock Market was established in 1988, with all prices quoted in U.S. currency. The *Straits Times Industrial Index* and the *SES Share Indices* are the most widely followed indicators of share performance. Trades are settled on a five-day settlement. Trading hours are 9:30 A.M. to 12:30 P.M. and 2 P.M. to 5 P.M., Monday through Friday. Trades are settled five business days after the trade date.

STOCK FUND *see* EQUITY FUND.

STOCKHOLDER individual or organization with an ownership position in a corporation; also called a SHAREHOLDER or *shareowner.* Stockholders must own at least one share, and their ownership is confirmed by either a stock certificate or a record by their broker, if shares are in the broker's custody.

STOCKHOLDER OF RECORD common or preferred stockholder whose name is registered on the books of a corporation as owning shares as of a particular date. Dividends and other distributions are made only to shareholders of record. Common stockholders are usually the only ones entitled to vote for candidates for the board of directors or on other matters requiring shareholder approval.

STOCKHOLDER'S EQUITY *see* OWNER'S EQUITY.

STOCKHOLDER'S REPORT company's ANNUAL REPORT and supplementary quarterly reports giving financial results and usually containing an ACCOUNTANT'S OPINION. Special stockholder's reports are sometimes issued covering major corporate developments. Also called *shareholder's report. See also* DISCLOSURE.

STOCKHOLM STOCK EXCHANGE only market in Sweden for official equity trading. The Stockholm Automatic Exchange (SAX) electronic trading system, introduced in 1989, includes all traded shares. A parallel system, called SOX, operates for fixed-interest securities. Clearing and settlement occur on the third business day following the trade. Trading is conducted Monday through Friday from 10 A.M. to 4 P.M.

STOCK INDICES AND AVERAGES indicators used to measure and report value changes in representative stock groupings. Strictly speaking, an AVERAGE is simply the ARITHMETIC MEAN of a group of prices, whereas an INDEX is an average expressed in relation to an earlier established BASE MARKET VALUE. (In practice, the distinction between indices and averages is not always clear; the AMEX Major Market Index is an average, for example.) Indices and averages may be broad based—that is, comprising of many stocks and designed to be representative of the overall market—or narrowly based, meaning they are made up of a smaller number of stocks and designed to reflect a particular industry or market SECTOR. Selected indices and averages are also used as the underlying value of STOCK INDEX FUTURES, INDEX OPTIONS, or options on index futures, which enable investors to HEDGE A POSITION against general market movement at relatively little cost. An extensive number and variety of indices and averages exist. Among the best known and most widely used are the following U.S. ones:

AMEX Major Market Index (XMI): price-weighted (high-priced issues have more influence than low-priced issues) average of 20 BLUE CHIP industrial stocks. It is designed to closely track the Dow Jones Industrial Average (DJIA) in measuring representative performance in the stocks of major industrial corporations. It is produced by the American Stock Exchange (AMEX) but is composed of 20 stocks listed on the New York Stock Exchange (NYSE), 15 of which are also components of the DJIA. Futures on the Major Market Index are traded on the Chicago Mercantile Exchange. Options on the XMI are listed on the AMEX.

AMEX Market Value Index (XAM): on September 4, 1973, the XAM replaced the ASE Index, which tracked the performance of American Stock Exchange issues. It is not a trading index. The Market Value Index is a capitalization-weighted index (i.e., the impact of a component's market change is proportionate to the overall market value of the issue) introduced at a base level of 100.00 in September 1973 and adjusted to half that level in July 1983. It measures the collective performance of more than 800 issues, representing all major industry groups traded on the AMEX, including AMERICAN DEPOSITARY RECEIPTS and warrants as well as common stocks. Uniquely, cash dividends paid by component stocks are assumed to be reinvested and are thus reflected in the index.

Dow Jones Industrial Average (DJIA): price-weighted average of 30 actively traded BLUE CHIP stocks, primarily industrials but including American Express Co., Walt Disney Co., J.P. Morgan, and other service-oriented firms. Prepared and published in the United States by Dow Jones & Co., it is the oldest and most widely quoted of all the market indicators. The components, which change from time to time, represent between 15% and 20% of the market value of NYSE stocks. The DJIA is calculated by adding the trading prices of the component stocks and using a divisor that is adjusted for STOCK DIVIDENDS and SPLITS, and cash equivalent distributions equal to 10% or more of the closing prices of an issue, as well as for substitutions and mergers. The average is quoted in points, not dollars. Dow Jones & Co. has refused to allow the DJIA to be used as a basis for speculation with futures or options. Other averages similarly prepared by Dow Jones & Co. are the *Dow Jones Transportation Average*—20 stocks representative of the airline, trucking, railroad, and shipping businesses (*see also* DOW THEORY); and the *Dow Jones Utility Average* (DJUA)—15 geographically representative gas and electric utilities. The combination of the Dow Industrials, Transportation and Utility Averages, encompassing 65 stocks, is known as the *Dow Jones Composite Average,* also known as the *65 Stock Average.*

Dow Jones Equity Market Index: a broad-based, capitalization-weighted (price times the shares outstanding for each company) index (June 30, 1982 = 100) of about 700 stocks traded on the NYSE, the AMEX, and NASDAQ, representing approximately 80% of the U.S. equity market. It is the U.S. portion of the Dow Jones World Stock Index.

Dow Jones World Stock Index: a broad-based, capitalization-weighted index (December 31, 1991 = 100) tracking more than 2600 companies in a growing list of countries and representing about 80% of the equity capital on stock markets around the globe. Currently, the index includes 25 countries in North America, Europe and Asia/Pacific regions.

Dow Jones Industry Group and Economic Sector Indices are: comprised of companies in the Dow Jones World Stock Index, classified on the basis of their type of business, which then are sorted into more than 100 industry groups and nine broad economic sectors. The indices are computed to measure the movement of stock prices by industry groups and broad economic sectors on a global, regional, and national basis. These indices are tracked in real time.

Country indices are calculated in each country's own currency, plus the U.S. dollar, British pound, German mark, and Japanese yen. The regional and world indices are calculated in these four global currencies. All indices can be converted to any currency.

NASDAQ Composite Index: market value-weighted index that measures all U.S.-based securities as well as those based in other countries, more than 4700 companies, listed on the NASDAQ Stock Market. The index was introduced on February 5, 1971, with a base value of 100. The market value—the last-sale price multiplied by total shares outstanding—is calculated through the trading day, and is related to the total value of the index. Each security in the index is assigned to a NASDAQ sub-index: Bank, Biotechnology, Computer, Industrial, Insurance, Other Finance, Transportation, Telecommunications. Values for the sub-indices began in February 1971, except for Biotechnology, Computer, and Telecommunications, which started November 1993.

NASDAQ-100 Index: begun in January 1985, it includes 100 of the largest nonfinancial companies listed on the NASDAQ Stock Market's National Market. Each security is proportionally represented by its market capitalization in relation to the total market value of the index. In October 1993, all index components had a market value of at least $400 million and were selected on the basis of trading volume, the company's visibility, the continuity of the components in the index and a good mix of industries represented in the NASDAQ Stock Market. In February 1994, the index value was reduced by half when options on the index began trading on the Chicago Board Options Exchange. The NASDAQ-100 option is a European-style option, and can be exercised only on its expiration date.

New York Stock Exchange Composite Index: market value-weighted index which relates all NYSE stocks to an aggregate market value as of December 31, 1965, adjusted for capitalization changes. The base value of the index is $50 and point changes are expressed in U.S. dollars and cents. NYSE sub-indices include the *NYSE Industrial, NYSE Transportation, NYSE Utility,* and *NYSE Financial Composite Indexes.*

Russell Indexes: market capitalization-weighted indexes published by Frank Russell Company of Tacoma, Washington. The *Russell 3000 Index* consists of the largest U.S. stocks in terms of market capitalization. The highest-ranking 1000 comprise the *Russell 1000 Index,* and the other 2000, which have market value ranging from $91 million to $672 million, make up the *Russell 2000 Small Stock Index,* a popular measure of the stock price performance of small companies. Seven other indices are built from these three. They are the *Russell 2500 Index, Russell Midcap Index, Russell Top 200 Index, Russell 1000 Value Index, Russell 1000 Growth Index, Russell 2000 Value Index and Russell 2000 Growth Index. See also* RUSSELL INDEXES.

Standard & Poor's Composite Index of 500 Stocks: market value-weighted index showing the change in the aggregate market value of 500 stocks relative to the base period 1941–43. Mostly NYSE-listed companies with some AMEX and NASDAQ Stock Market stocks, it comprises 381 industrial stocks, 47 utilities, 56 financials, and 16 transportation issues representing about 74% of the market value of all issues traded on the NYSE. Index options are traded on the Chicago Board of Trade and futures and futures options are traded on the Chicago Mercantile Exchange. The *Standard & Poor's 100 Index*

(OEX), calculated on the same basis as the 500 Stock Index, is made up of stocks for which options are listed on the Chicago Board Options Exchange. Its components are mainly NYSE industrials, with some transportation, utility, and financial stocks. Options on the 100 Index are listed on the Chicago Board of Trade and futures are traded on the Chicago Mercantile Exchange. Futures options are not traded.

Value Line Composite Average: equally weighted geometric average of approximately 1700 NYSE, AMEX, and over the counter stocks tracked by the VALUE LINE INVESTMENT SURVEY. The index uses a base value of 100.00 established June 30, 1961, and changes are expressed in index numbers rather than dollars and cents. This index is designed to reflect price changes of typical stocks (industrials, transportation, and utilities) and being neither price- nor market value-weighted, it largely succeeds. Futures on the index are traded on the Kansas City Board of Trade and futures options are traded on the Philadelphia Stock Exchange.

Wilshire 5000 Equity Index: broadest of all the averages and indexes, the Wilshire Index is market value-weighted and represents the value of all U.S. headquartered equities on the NYSE, AMEX, and NASDAQ National Market system for which quotes are available, more than 6000 stocks in all. Changes are measured against a base value established December 31, 1980. Options and futures are not traded on the Wilshire Index, which is prepared by Wilshire Associates Inc. of Santa Monica, California.

Many indices and averages track the performance of stock markets around the world. The major indices include the: ALL ORDINARIES INDEX; CAC 40 INDEX; MORGAN STANLEY CAPITAL INTERNATIONAL INDICES; EAFE INDEX; EMERGING MARKET FREE (EMF) INDEX; HANG SENG INDEX; INTERNATIONAL MARKET INDEX; SALOMON BROTHERS WORLD EQUITY INDEX.

See also BARRON'S CONFIDENCE INDEX; BOND BUYER'S INDEX; COMMODITY INDICES; ELVES; LIPPER MUTUAL FUND INDUSTRY AVERAGE; MONEY MAGAZINE SMALL INVESTOR INDEX; SECURITIES AND COMMODITIES EXCHANGES.

STOCK INDEX FUTURE security that combines features of traditional commodity futures trading with securities trading using composite stock indexes. Investors can speculate on general market performance or can buy an index future contract to hedge a LONG POSITION or SHORT POSITION against a decline in value. Settlement is in cash, since it is obviously impossible to deliver an index of stocks to a futures buyer. Among the most popular stock index futures traded are the Toronto Futures Exchange, the New York Stock Exchange Composite Index on the New York Futures Exchange (NYFE), the Standard & Poor's 500 Index on the Chicago Mercantile Exchange (CME), and the Value Line Composite Index on the Kansas City Board of Trade (KCBT).

It is also possible to buy options on stock index futures; the Standard & Poor's 500 Stock Index futures options are traded on the

Chicago Mercantile Exchange and the New York Stock Exchange Composite Index futures options are traded on the New York Futures Exchange, for example. Unlike stock index futures or INDEX OPTIONS, however, futures options are not settled in cash; they are settled by delivery of the underlying stock index futures contracts.

See also FUTURES CONTRACT; HEDGE/HEDGING; SECURITIES AND COMMODITIES EXCHANGES.

STOCK INSURANCE COMPANY insurance company that is owned by stockholders, as distinguished from a MUTUAL COMPANY that is owned by POLICYHOLDERS. Even in a stock company, however, policyholders interests are ahead of shareholder's dividends.

STOCK JOCKEY stockbroker who actively follows individual stocks and frequently buys and sells shares in his or her client's portfolios. If the broker does too much short-term trading in accounts over which he or she has discretion, the broker may be accused of CHURNING.

STOCK LIST function of the organized stock exchanges that is concerned with LISTING REQUIREMENTS and related investigations, the eligibility of unlisted companies for trading privileges, and the delisting of companies that have not complied with exchange regulations and listing requirements. The New York Stock Exchange department dealing with listing of securities is called the Department of Stock List.

STOCK MARKET general term referring to the organized trading of securities through the various exchanges and the OVER THE COUNTER market. The securities involved include COMMON STOCK, PREFERRED STOCK, BONDS, CONVERTIBLES, OPTIONS, rights, and warrants. The term may also encompass commodities when used in its most general sense, but more often than not the stock market and the commodities (or futures) market are distinguished. *See also* SECURITIES AND COMMODITIES EXCHANGES.

STOCK OPTION

1. right to purchase or sell a stock at a specified price within a stated period. OPTIONS are a popular investment medium, offering an opportunity to hedge positions in other securities, to speculate in stocks with relatively little investment, and to capitalize on changes in the MARKET VALUE of options contracts themselves through a variety of options strategies.

   See also CALL OPTION; PUT OPTION.

2. widely used form of employee incentive and compensation, usually for the executives of a corporation. The employee is given an OPTION to purchase its shares at a certain price (at or below the market price at the time the option is granted) for a specified period of years.

   See also INCENTIVE STOCK OPTION; QUALIFIED STOCK OPTION.

STOCK POWER power of attorney form transferring ownership of a REGISTERED SECURITY from the owner to another party. A separate piece of paper from the CERTIFICATE, it is attached to the latter when the security is sold or pledged to a brokerage firm, bank, or other lender as loan COLLATERAL. Technically, the stock power gives the owner's permission to another party (the TRANSFER AGENT) to transfer ownership of the certificate to a third party. Also called *stock/bond power.*

STOCK PURCHASE PLAN organized program for employees of a company to buy shares of its stock. The plan could take the form of compensation if the employer matches employee stock purchases. In some companies, employees are offered the chance to buy stock in the company at a discount. Also, a corporation can offer to reinvest dividends in additional shares as a service to shareholders, or it can set up a program of regular additional share purchases for participating shareholders who authorize periodic, automatic payments from their wages for this purpose. *See also* AUTOMATIC INVESTMENT PROGRAM.

Another form of stock purchase plan is the EMPLOYEE SHARE PURCHASE PLAN (ESPP), whereby employees regularly accumulate shares and may ultimately assume control of the company.

STOCK RATING evaluation by rating agencies of common stocks, usually in terms of expected price performance or safety. Standard & Poor's and Value Line's respective quality and timeliness ratings are among the most widely consulted.

STOCK RECORD control, usually in the form of a ledger card or computer report, used by brokerage films to keep track of securities held in inventory and their precise location within the firm. Securities are recorded by name and owner.

STOCK RIGHT *see* SUBSCRIPTION RIGHT.

STOCK SPLIT *see* SPLIT.

STOCK SYMBOL letters used to identify listed companies on the securities exchanges on which they trade. These symbols, also called *trading symbols,* identify trades on the CONSOLIDATED TAPE and are used in other reports and documents whenever such shorthand is convenient. Some examples: TD (Toronto Dominion Bank), BNS (Bank of Nova Scotia), ABT (Abbott Laboratories), AA (Aluminum Company of America), XON (Exxon), KO (Coca Cola). Stock symbols are not necessarily the same as abbreviations used to identify the same companies in the stock tables of newspapers. *See also* COMMITTEE ON UNIFORM SECURITIES IDENTIFICATION PROCEDURES (CUSIP).

STOCK-TRANSFER AGENT *see* TRANSFER AGENT.

STOCK WARRANT *see* SUBSCRIPTION WARRANT.

STOCK WATCHER (NYSE) computerized service that monitors all trading activity and movement in stocks listed on the Toronto and New York Stock Exchange. The system is set up to identify any unusual activity due to rumours or MANIPULATION or other illegal practices. The stock watch departments of the TSE and NYSE are prepared to conduct investigations and to take appropriate action, such as issuing clarifying information or turning questions of legality over to the Ontario Securities Commission or, in the United States, to the Securities and Exchange Commission. *See also* SURVEILLANCE DEPARTMENT OF EXCHANGES.

STOCK YIELD yield that is calculated by expressing the annual dividend as a percentage of the current market price of the stock.

STOP BUY/LOSS ORDER orders to buy or sell, placed above or below the market price, which become market orders as soon as the price of a BOARD LOT of the stock rises or falls to the specified price. A stop buy order is used to protect against losses in a short sale, whereas a STOP LOSS ORDER may be used to protect a paper profit or to limit a possible loss when shares are already owned. Since such orders become market orders when the stop price is reached, there is no certainty they will be executed at that price.

STOP-LIMIT ORDER order to a securities broker with instructions to buy or sell at a specified price or better (called the *stop-limit price)* but only after a given *stop price* has been reached or passed. It is a combination of a STOP ORDER and a LIMIT ORDER. For example, the instruction to the broker might be "buy 100 XYZ 55 STOP 56 LIMIT" meaning that if the MARKET PRICE reaches $55, the broker enters a limit order to be executed at $56 or a better (lower) price. A stop-limit order avoids some of the risks of a stop order, which becomes a MARKET ORDER when the stop price is reached; like all price-limit orders, however, it carries the risk of missing the market altogether, since the specified limit price or better may never occur.

STOP LOSS

Insurance: promise by a reinsurance company that it will cover losses incurred by the company it reinsures over and above an agreed-upon amount.

Stocks: customer order to a broker that sets the sell price of a stock below the current MARKET PRICE. A stop-loss order therefore will protect profits that have already been made or prevent further losses if the stock drops.

STOP ORDER order to a securities broker to buy or sell at the MARKET PRICE once the security has traded at a specified price called the *stop price.* A stop order may be a DAY ORDER, a GOOD-TILL-CANCELED ORDER, or any other form of time-limit order. A stop order to buy, always at a stop price above the current market price, is usually designed to protect a profit or to limit a loss on a short sale *(see* SELLING SHORT). A stop order to sell, always at a price below the current market price, is usually designed to protect a profit or to limit a loss on a security already purchased at a higher price. The risk of stop orders is that they may be triggered by temporary market movements or that they may be executed at prices several points higher or lower than the stop price because of market orders placed ahead of them. Also called *stop-loss order. See also* GATHER IN THE STOPS; STOP LIMIT ORDER; STOPBUY/LOSS ORDER; STOP LOSS (stocks).

STOP-OUT PRICE lowest dollar price at which Treasury bills are sold at a particular auction. This price and the beginning auction price are averaged to establish the price at which smaller purchasers may purchase bills under the NONCOMPETITIVE BID system. *See also* BILL; DUTCH AUCTION.

STOP PAYMENT revocation of payment on a cheque after the cheque has been sent or delivered to the payee. So long as the cheque has not been cashed, the writer has up to six months in which to request a stop payment. The stop payment right does not carry over to electronic funds transfers.

STOPPED OUT term used when a customer's order is executed under a STOP ORDER at the price predetermined by the customer, called the *stop price.* For instance, if a customer has entered a stop-loss order to sell XYZ at $30 when the stock is selling at $33, and the stock then falls to $30, his or her position will be stopped out. A customer may also be stopped out if the order is executed at a guaranteed price offered by a SPECIALIST. *See also* GATHER IN THE STOPS; STOPPED STOCK.

STOPPED STOCK guarantee by a SPECIALIST that an order placed by a FLOOR BROKER will be executed at the best bid or offer price then in the SPECIALIST'S BOOK unless it can be executed at a better price within a specified period of time.

STOP PRICE *see* STOP ORDER.

STORY STOCK/BOND security with values or features so complex that a "story" is required to persuade investors of its merits. Story stocks are frequently from companies with some unique product or service that is difficult for competitors to copy. In a less formal sense, term is used by news organizations to mean stocks most actively traded.

STRADDLE strategy consisting of an equal number of PUT OPTIONS and CALL OPTIONS on the same underlying stock, stock index, or commodity future at the same STRIKE PRICE and maturity date. Each OPTION may be exercised separately, although the combination of options is usually bought and sold as a unit. *See* SPREAD.

STRADDLE WRITING *see* STRADDLE.

STRAIGHT LIFE ANNUITY annuity that provides an agreed-upon payment until death, with nothing to the estate. The rate paid by a straight life annuity is the highest of all annuities per dollar of principal.

STRAIGHT-LINE DEPRECIATION method of depreciating a fixed asset whereby the asset's useful life is divided into the total cost less the estimated salvage value. The procedure is used to arrive at a uniform

annual DEPRECIATION expense to be charged against income before fig
uring income taxes. Thus, if a new machine purchased for $1200 was
estimated to have a useful life of ten years and a salvage value of $200,
annual depreciation under the straight-line method would be $100,
charged at $100 a year.

STRAIGHT TERM INSURANCE POLICY term life insurance policy
for a specific number of years in which the death benefit remains
unchanged. A level premium policy will charge the same premium for
a number of years, usually ten, and then increase. An annual renewable term policy will charge slightly higher premiums each year.

STRANGLE sale or purchase of a put option and a call option on the
same underlying instrument, with the same expiration, but at strike
prices equally OUT OF THE MONEY. A strangle costs less than a STRAD-
DLE because both options are out of the money, but profits are made
only if the underlying instrument moves dramatically.

STRAP OPTION contract combining one PUT OPTION and two CALL
OPTIONS of the same SERIES, which can be bought at a lower total premium than that of the three options bought individually. The put has
the same features as the calls—same underlying security, exercise
price, and maturity. Also called *triple option. Compare with* STRIP.

STRATEGIC BUYOUT ACQUISITION based on analysis of the operational benefits of consolidation. Implicitly contrasts with the type of
TAKEOVER based on "paper values" that characterized the "merger
mania" of the 1980s—undervalued stock bought using JUNK BONDS
ultimately repayable from the liquidation of acquired assets and activities. A strategic buyout focuses on how companies fit together and
anticipates enhanced long-term earning power. *See also* SYNERGY.

STREET short for Wall Street, referring to the financial community in
New York City and elsewhere. It is common to hear "The Street likes
XYZ." This means there is a national consensus among securities ana-
lysts that XYZ's prospects are favourable. *See also* STREET NAME.

STREET CERTIFICATE stock certificate registered in the name of an
investment dealer or stock broker whose name makes it more attractive to buyers and thus increases its negotiability, but beneficially
(actually) owned by someone else. When fully paid, they are segre-
gated from the securities of the dealer.

STREET NAME phrase describing securities held in the name of a broker or another nominee instead of a customer. Since the securities are
in the broker's custody, transfer of the shares at the time of sale is easier than if the stock were registered in the customer's name and physical certificates had to be transferred.

STRIKE PRICE *see* EXERCISE PRICE.

STRIP BOND   relatively new on the bond market, strip bonds can be purchased through a stockbroker for self directed RRSPs, with a minimum of $5,000. Like Treasury bills, they are priced at a deep discount and they mature at face value. The guaranteed yield protects against inflation. (The name "strip" is an acronym for Separately Traded Residual and Interest Payment bonds.)

A 20-year Ontario government bond, for example, carries an annual yield to maturity of 9.72%. Based on current prices of 7.625%, $10,000 invested in mid-1995 would yield $43,000 by the January, 2015 maturity date.

Market values of strip bonds can be volatile. If the interest rates shoot up, the long wait until maturity will cause your investment to plunge sharply in value. Therefore, you should buy and hold for the long term. If interest rates fall sharply, as they did between 1989 and 1992 and March, 1995 to July, 1995, substantial capital gain can be realized, especially in the body of an RRSP, making it largely tax-deferred capital gain.

A broker will buy a high-quality federal or provincial government bond. After the bond has been stripped of remaining coupons, the bond principal, called the residual, then trades separately from the strip of detached coupons, both at substantial discounts from par.

Generally, those who invest in zero-coupon or strip bonds, want (1) no reinvestment risk, (2) a guaranteed yield to maturity or, (3) a specific amount of money at a specified future date, and to achieve this goal with certainty.

Options: OPTION contract consisting of two PUT OPTIONS and one CALL OPTION on the same underlying stock or stock index with the same strike and expiration date. *Compare with* STRAP.

Stocks: to buy stocks with the intention of collecting their dividends. Also called *dividend stripping*. *See also* DIVIDEND ROLLOVER PLAN.

STRIPPED BOND   bond separated into its two components: periodic interest payments and principal repayment. Each of the interest payments and the principal repayment are stripped apart by a brokerage firm and sold individually as ZERO-COUPON SECURITIES. Investors therefore have a wide choice of maturities to pick from when shopping for a zero-coupon bond.

STRIPPED DEBENTURE   debentures that have been separated from other securities such as warrants with which they were originally issued. They may be separated in order to make them more saleable, cheaper, or strippable for use as a fee by the seller.

STRONG DOLLAR   dollar that can be exchanged for a large amount of a foreign currency. In the past, this has been true of the Canadian dollar, but can now only be said of the U.S. dollar. The U.S. dollar can gain strength in currency markets because the United States is considered a haven of political and economic stability, or because yields on American securities are attractive. A strong dollar is a blessing for

American travelers going abroad, because they get more Canadian dollars, pounds, francs, marks, and yen and other currencies for their greenbacks. However, a strong dollar makes it difficult for American firms to export their goods to foreign countries because it raises the cost to foreigners of purchasing American products. *See also* EXCHANGE RATE; WEAK DOLLAR.

STRUCTURED NOTE

1. derivative instrument based on the movement of an underlying index. For example, a structured note issued by a corporation may pay interest to noteholders based on the rise and fall of oil prices. This gives investors the opportunity to earn interest and profit from the change in price of a commodity at the same time.

2. complex debt instrument, usually a medium-term note, in which the issuer enters into one or more SWAP arrangements to change the cash flows it is required to make. A simple form utilizing interest-rate swaps might be, for example, a three-year FLOATING RATE NOTE paying the London Interbank Offered Rate (LIBOR) plus a premium semiannually. The issuer arranges a swap transaction whereby it agrees to pay a fixed semiannual rate for three years in exchange for the LIBOR. Since the floating rate payments (cash flows) offset each other, the issuer has synthetically created a fixed-rate note.

STUB STOCK common stocks or instruments convertible to equity in a company that is overleveraged as the result of a BUYOUT or RECAPITALIZATION and may have DEFICIT NET WORTH. Stub stock is highly speculative and highly volatile but, unlike JUNK BONDS, has unlimited potential for gain if the company succeeds in restoring financial balance.

SUBCHAPTER S section of the Internal Revenue Code in the United States, giving a corporation that has 35 or fewer shareholders and meets certain other requirements the option of being taxed as if it were a PARTNERSHIP. Thus a small corporation candistribute its income directly to shareholders and avoid the corporate income tax while enjoying the other advantages of the corporate form. These companies are known as *Subchapter S corporations, tax-option corporations,* or *small business corporations.*

SUBJECT investment term referring to a bid and/or offer that is negotiable—that is, a QUOTATION that is not firm. For example, a broker looking to place a sizable order might call several dealers with the question, "Can you give me a *subject quote* on 20,000 shares of XYZ?"

SUBJECT BID bid that indicates the buyer's interest in a security, but does not commit the bidder to purchase of the security at that price or time.

SUBJECT OFFER offer made for a security that indicates the seller's interest but does not commit the offeror to the sale of the security at that price or time.

SUBJECT QUOTE *see* SUBJECT.

SUBORDINATED junior in claim on assets to other debt, that is, repayable only after other debts with a higher claim have been satisfied. Some subordinated debt may have less claim on assets than other subordinated debt; a *junior subordinated debenture* ranks below a subordinated DEBENTURE, for example.

It is also possible for unsubordinated (senior) debt to become subordinated at the request of a lender by means of a subordination agreement. For example, if an officer of a small company has made loans to the company instead of making a permanent investment in it, a bank might request the officer's loan be subordinated to its own loan as long as the latter is outstanding. This is accomplished by the company officer's signing a subordination agreement. *See also* EFFECTIVE NET WORTH; JUNIOR SECURITY.

SUBORDINATION CLAUSE clause in a MORTGAGE loan agreement that permits a mortgage recorded at a subsequent date to have preference over the original mortgage.

SUBSCRIPTION agreement of intent to buy newly issued securities. *See also* NEW ISSUE; SUBSCRIPTION RIGHT; SUBSCRIPTION WARRANT.

SUBSCRIPTION AGREEMENT application submitted by an investor seeking to join a limited partnership. All prospective limited partners must be approved by the general partner before they are allowed to become limited partners.

SUBSCRIPTION PRICE price at which existing shareholders of a corporation are entitled to purchase common shares in a RIGHTS OFFERING or at which subscription warrants are exercisable. *See also* SUBSCRIPTION RIGHT; SUBSCRIPTION WARRANT.

SUBSCRIPTION PRIVILEGE right of existing shareholders of a corporation, or their transferees, to buy shares of a new issue of common stock before it is offered to the public. *See also* PREEMPTIVE RIGHT; SUBSCRIPTION RIGHT.

SUBSCRIPTION RATIO *see* SUBSCRIPTION RIGHT.

SUBSCRIPTION RIGHT privilege granted to existing shareholders of a corporation to subscribe to shares of a new issue of common stock before it is offered to the public; better known simply as a *right*. Such a right, which normally has a life of two to four weeks, is freely transferable and entitles the holder to buy the new common stock below the PUBLIC OFFERING PRICE. While in most cases one existing share entitles the stockholder to one right, the number of rights needed to buy a share of a new issue (called the *subscription ratio*) varies and is determined by a company in advance of an offering. To subscribe, the holder sends or delivers to the company or its agent the required number of rights plus the dollar price of the new shares.

Rights are sometimes granted to comply with state laws that guarantee the shareholders' PREEMPTIVE RIGHT—their right to maintain a proportionate share of ownership. It is common practice, however, for corporations to grant rights even when not required by law; protecting shareholders from the effects of DILUTION is seen simply as good business.

The actual certificate representing the subscription is technically called a SUBSCRIPTION WARRANT, giving rise to some confusion. The term *subscription warrant,* or simply *warrant,* is commonly understood in a related but different sense—as a separate entity with a longer life than a right—maybe 5, 10, or 20 years or even perpetual—and with a SUBSCRIPTION PRICE higher at the time of issue than the MARKET VALUE of the common stock.

Subscription rights are offered to shareholders in what is called a RIGHTS OFFERING, usually handled by underwriters under a STANDBY COMMITMENT.

SUBSCRIPTION WARRANT type of security, usually issued together with a BOND or PREFERRED STOCK, that entitles the holder to buy a proportionate amount of common stock at a specified price, usually higher than the market price at the time of issuance, for a period of years or to perpetuity; better known simply as a *warrant.* In contrast, rights, which also represent the right to buy common shares, normally have a subscription price lower than the current market value of the common stock and a life of two to four weeks. A warrant is usually issued as a SWEETENER, to enhance the marketability of the accompanying fixed income securities. Warrants are freely transferable and are traded on the major exchanges. They are also called *stock-purchase warrants. See also* PERPETUAL WARRANT; SUBSCRIPTION RIGHT.

SUBSIDIARY company of which more than 50% of the voting shares are owned by another corporation, called the PARENT COMPANY. *See also* AFFILIATE.

SUBSIDY amount created when revenues do not meet opportunity costs, requiring that the loan be justified on higher order economic or social needs.

SUBSTANDARD HEALTH ANNUITY annuity that provides a higher payment than a straight life annuity to a qualifying person who can demonstrate a sufficiently serious health problem, such as heart disease or cancer, that lowers life expectancy significantly.

SUBSTITUTION

Banking: replacement of COLLATERAL by other collateral.

Contracts: replacement of one party to a contract by another. *See also* NOVATION.

Economics: concept that, if one product or service can be replaced by another, their prices should be similar.

Law: replacement of one attorney by another in the exercise of stock powers relating to the purchase and sale of securities. *See also* STOCK POWER.

Securities:

1. exchange or SWAP of one security for another in a client's PORTFOLIO. Securities analysts often advise substituting a stock they currently favour for a stock in the same industry that they believe has less favourable prospects.

2. substitution of another security of equal value for a security a cting as COLLATERAL for a MARGIN ACCOUNT. *See also* SAME-DAY-SUBSTITUTION.

SUICIDE PILL POISON PILL with potentially catastrophic implications for the company it is designed to protect. An example might be a poison pill providing for an exchange of stock for debt in the event of a *hostile takeover;* that would discourage an acquirer by making the TAKEOVER prohibitively expensive, but its implementation could put the TARGET COMPANY in danger of bankruptcy.

SUITABILITY RULES guidelines that those selling sophisticated and potentially risky financial products, such as limited partnerships or commodities futures contracts, must follow to ensure that investors have the financial means to assume the risks involved. Such rules are enforced through self-regulation administered by such organizations as the NATIONAL ASSOCIATION OF SECURITIES DEALERS, the SECURITIES AND COMMODITIES EXCHANGES, and other groups operating in the securities industry. Individual brokerage firms selling the products have their own guidelines and policies. They typically require the investor to have a certain level of NET WORTH and LIQUID ASSETS, so that he or she will not be irreparably harmed if the investment sours. A brokerage firm may be sued if it has allowed an unsuitable investor to buy an investment that goes sour. *See also* KNOW YOUR CUSTOMER.

SUM-OF-THE-YEARS'-DIGITS METHOD (SOYD) method of ACCELERATED DEPRECIATION that results in higher DEPRECIATION charges and greater tax savings in the earlier years of a FIXED ASSET'S useful life than the STRAIGHT-LINE DEPRECIATION method, where charges are uniform throughout. Sometimes called just *sum-of-digits method,* it allows depreciation based on an inverted scale of the total of digits for the years of useful life. Thus, for four years of life, the digits 4, 3, 2, and 1 are added to produce 10. The first year's rate becomes $\frac{4}{10}$ of the depreciable cost of the asset (cost less salvage value), the second year's rate $\frac{3}{10}$, and so on. The effects of this method of accelerated depreciation are compared with the straight-line method in the following illustration, which assumes an asset with a total cost of $1000, a useful life of four years, and no salvage value:

YEAR	STRAIGHT LINE		SUM-OF-YEARS' DIGITS	
	Expense	Cumulative	Expense	Cumulative
1	$250	$250	$400	$400
2	$250	$500	$300	$700
3	$250	$750	$200	$900
4	$250	$1000	$100	$1000
	$1000		$1000	

See also MODIFIED ACCELERATED COST RECOVERY SYSTEM (MACRS).

SUNK COSTS costs already incurred in a project that cannot be changed by present or future actions. For example, if a company bought a piece of machinery five years ago, that amount of money has already been spent and cannot be recovered. It should also not affect the company's decision on whether or not to buy a new piece of machinery if the five-year old machinery has worn out.

SUNRISE INDUSTRIES figurative term for the emerging growth sectors that some believe will be the mainstays of the future economy, taking the place of declining *sunset industries.* Although the latter, including such mature industries as the automobile, steel, and other heavy manufacturing industries, will continue to be important, their lead role as employers of massive numbers of workers is expected to be superseded by the electronics and other computer-related high-technology, biotechnology, and genetic engineering sectors and by service industries.

SUNSET PROVISION condition in a law or regulation that specifies an expiration date unless reinstated by legislation.

SUPER BOWL INDICATOR in the United States, technical indicator that holds that if a team from the old American Football League pre-1970 wins the Super Bowl, the stock market will decline during the coming year. If a team from the old pre-1970 National Football League wins the Super Bowl, the stock market will end the coming year higher. The indicator has been a remarkably accurate predictor of stock market performance for many years.

SUPER DOT *see* DESIGNATED ORDER TURNAROUND (DOT).

SUPERMAJORITY AMENDMENT corporate AMENDMENT requiring that a substantial majority (usually 67% to 90%) of stockholders approve important transactions, such as mergers.

SUPER SINKER BOND bond with long-term coupons (which might equal a 20-year-bond's yield) but with short maturity. Typically, super sinkers are HOUSING BONDS, which provide home financing. If home-owners move from their homes and prepay their mortgages, bond-holders receive their principal back right away. Super sinkers may therefore have an actual life of as little as three to five years, even though their yield is about the same as bonds of much longer maturities. *See also* COUPON BOND.

SUPERVISORY ANALYST member firm research analyst who has passed a special examination and is deemed qualified to approve publicly distributed research reports.

SUPPLEMENTAL AGREEMENT agreement that amends a previous agreement and contains additional conditions.

SUPPLY-SIDE ECONOMICS theory of economics, popular in the U.S. and the U.K., contending that drastic reductions in tax rates will stimulate productive investment by corporations and wealthy individuals to the benefit of the entire society. Championed in the late 1970s by Professor Arthur Laffer *(see* LAFFER CURVE) and others, the theory held that MARGINAL TAX RATES had become so high (primarily as a result of big government) that major new private spending on plant, equipment, and other "engines of growth" was discouraged. Therefore, reducing the size of government, and hence its claim on earned income, would fuel economic expansion.

Supporters of the supply-side theory claimed they were vindicated in the first years of the administration of President Ronald W. Reagan, when marginal tax rates were cut just prior to a sustained economic recovery. However, members of the opposing KEYNESIAN ECONOMICS school maintained that the recovery was a classic example of "demand-side" economics—growth was stimulated not by increasing the supply of goods, but by increasing consumer demand as disposable incomes rose. Also clashing with the supply-side theory were MONETARIST economists, who contended that the most effective way of regulating aggregate demand is for the Federal Reserve to control growth in the money supply. *See also* AGGREGATE SUPPLY.

SUPPORT LEVEL price level at which a security tends to stop falling because there is more demand than supply. Technical analysts identify support levels as prices at which a particular security or market has bottomed in the past. When a stock is falling towards its support level, these analysts say it is "testing its support," meaning that the stock should rebound as soon as it hits the support price. If the stock continues to drop through the support level, its outlook is considered very bearish. The opposite of a support level is a RESISTANCE LEVEL. *See* chart on next page.

SURCHARGE charge added to a charge, cost added to a cost, or tax added to a tax. *See also* SURTAX.

SURETY individual or corporation, usually an insurance company, that guarantees the performance or faith of another. Term is also used to mean *surety bond,* which is a bond that backs the performance of the person bonded, such as a contractor, or that pays an employer if a bonded employee commits theft.

SUPPORT LEVEL

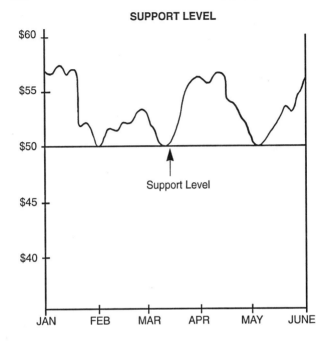

Support Level

SURRENDER VALUE *see* CASH SURRENDER VALUE.

SURPLUS connotes either CAPITAL SURPLUS or EARNED SURPLUS. *See also* PAID-IN CAPITAL; RETAINED EARNINGS.

SURTAX tax applied to corporations or individuals who have earned a certain level of income. For example, many provinces have a 5% to 10% or 20% surtax on provincial income tax.

SURVEILLANCE DEPARTMENT OF EXCHANGES division of a stock exchange that is constantly watching to detect unusual trading activity in stocks, which may be a tipoff to an illegal practice. These departments cooperate with the provincial securities commissions in investigating misconduct. *See also* STOCK WATCHER.

SURVIVING SPOUSE spouse remaining alive when his or her spouse dies (in other words, the spouse who lives longer). In most provinces, the surviving spouse cannot be totally disinherited, but has a right to receive a share of the deceased spouse's estate, with the size of that share determined by provincial law usual ⅓ to ½ of the estate.

SURVIVORSHIP ACCOUNT *see* JOINT TENANTS WITH RIGHT OF SURVIVORSHIP.

SURVIVORSHIP LIFE INSURANCE *see* SECOND-TO-DIE INSURANCE.

SUSPENDED TRADING temporary halt in trading in a particular security, in advance of a major news announcement or to correct an imbalance of orders to buy and sell. Using telephone alert procedures, listed companies with material developments to announce can give advance notice to the Toronto Stock Exchange. The exchanges can then determine if trading in the securities affected should be suspended temporarily to allow for orderly dissemination of the news to the public. Where advance notice is not possible, a *floor governor* may halt trading to stabilize the price of a security affected by a rumour or news development. Destabilizing developments might include a MERGER announcement, an unfavourable earnings report, or a major resource discovery. *See also* CIRCUIT BREAKER; DISCLOSURE; INVESTOR RELATIONS DEPARTMENT.

SUSPENSE ACCOUNT in accounting, an account used temporarily to carry receipts, disbursements, or discrepancies, pending their analysis and permanent classification.

SWAP traditionally, an exchange of one security for another to change the maturities of a bond PORTFOLIO or the quality of the issues in a stock or bond portfolio, or because investment objectives have shifted. Investors with bond portfolio losses often swap for other higher-yielding bonds to be able to increase the return on their portfolio and realize tax losses. Recent years have seen explosive growth in more complex *currency swaps,* used to link increasingly global capital markets, and in *interest-rate swaps,* used to reduce risk by synthetically matching the DURATION of assets and liabilities of financial institutions as interest rates got higher and more volatile. In a simple currency swap (swaps can be done with varying degrees of complexity), two parties sell each other a currency with a commitment to re-exchange the principal amount at the maturity of the deal. Originally done to get around the problems of exchange controls, currency swaps are widely used to tap new capital markets, in effect to borrow funds irrespective of whether the borrower requires funds within that market. The INTERNATIONAL BANK FOR RECONSTRUCTION AND DEVELOPMENT (WORLD BANK) has been an active participant in currency swaps with Canadian corporations.

An interest-rate swap is an arrangement whereby two parties (called counterparties) enter into an agreement to exchange periodic interest payments. The dollar amount the counterparties pay each other is an agreed-upon periodic interest rate multiplied by some predetermined dollar principal, called the *notational principal amount.* No principal (no notational amount) is exchanged between parties to the transaction; only interest is exchanged. In its most common and simplest variation, one party agrees to pay the other a fixed rate of interest in exchange for a floating rate. The benefit of interest-rate swaps, which can be used to synthetically extend or shorten the duration characteristics of an asset or liability, is that direct changes in the contractual characteristics of the assets or the liabilities become matters affecting only administrative, legal, and investment banking costs. *See also* BOND SWAP; SUBSTITUTION.

SWAP ORDER *see* CONTINGENT ORDER.

SWAPTION option to enter an interest rate swap. A *payer swaption* gives its purchaser the right, but not the obligation, to enter into an interest-rate swap at a preset rate within a specific period of time. The swaption buyer pays a premium to the seller for this right. A *receiver swaption* gives the purchaser the right to receive fixed payments. The seller agrees to provide the specified swap if called upon, though it is possible for him or her to hedge that risk with other offsetting transactions.

SWEAT EQUITY equity created in a property by the hard work of the owner. For example, a small business may be built up more on the efforts of its founders than on the capital raised to finance it. Homeowners who renovate a house with their own labour create rising value with the sweat of their own brows, not the general increase in housing prices from inflation.

SWEETENER feature added to a securities offering to make it more attractive to purchasers. A bond may have the sweetener of convertibility into common stock added, for instance. *See also* KICKER.

SWISS OPTIONS AND FINANCIAL FUTURES EXCHANGE (SOFFEX) first fully electronic trading system in the world, with a completely integrated and automated clearing system. Contracts include traded options on equities; low exercise price options; futures and options on the Swiss government bond; and futures and long-term options (LTO) on the Swiss Market Index, the index that includes the largest capitalization stocks traded on Switzerland's three stock exchanges.

SWITCHING
Mutual funds: moving assets from one mutual fund to another, either within a FUND FAMILY or between different fund families. There is no charge for switching within a no-load family of mutual funds, which offer a variety of stock, bond, and money market funds. A sales charge might have to be paid when switching from one LOAD FUND to another. Customers of many discount brokerage firms can switch among fund families, sometimes at no fee and sometimes by paying a brokerage commission. Switching usually occurs at the shareholder's initiative, as a result of changes in market conditions or investment objectives. Some investment advisers and investment advisory newsletters recommend when to switch into or out of different mutual funds. *See also* NO-LOAD FUND.

Securities: selling stocks or bonds to replace them with other stocks and bonds with better prospects for gain or higher yields. *See also* SWAP.

SWITCH ORDER *see* CONTINGENT ORDER.

SYNDICATE *see* PURCHASE GROUP.

SYNDICATE MANAGER *see* MANAGING UNDERWRITER.

SYNERGY ideal sought in corporate mergers and acquisitions that the performance of a combined enterprise will exceed that of its previously separate parts. For example, a MERGER of two oil companies, one with a superior distribution network and the other with more reserves, would have synergy and would be expected to result in higher earnings per share than previously. *See also* STRATEGIC BUYOUT.

SYNTHETIC ASSET value that is artificially created by using other assets, such as securities, in combination. For example, the simultaneous purchase of a CALL OPTION and sale of a PUT OPTION on the same stock creates *synthetic stock* having the same value, in terms of CAPITAL GAIN potential, as the underlying stock itself.

SYNTHETIC SECURITIES *see* STRUCTURED NOTE; SYNTHETIC ASSET.

SYSTEMATIC INVESTMENT PLAN plan in which investors make regular payments into a stock, bond, mutual fund, or other investment. This may be accomplished through an AUTOMATIC INVESTMENT PROGRAM, such as a salary reduction plan with an employer, a dividend reinvestment plan with a company or mutual fund, or an automatic investment plan in which a mutual fund withdraws a set amount from a bank chequing or savings account on a regular basis. By investing systematically, investors are benefiting from the advantages of DOLLAR-COST AVERAGING.

SYSTEMATIC WITHDRAWAL PLAN MUTUAL FUND option whereby the shareholder receives specified amounts at specified intervals.

SYSTEMATIC RISK that part of a security's risk that is common to all securities of the same general class (stocks and bonds) and thus cannot be eliminated by DIVERSIFICATION; also known as *market risk.* The measure of systematic risk in stocks is the BETA COEFFICIENT. *See also* PORTFOLIO BETA SCORE, PORTFOLIO THEORY.

T

TACTICAL ASSET ALLOCATION shifting percentages of portfolios among stocks, bonds, or cash, depending on the relative attractiveness of the respective markets. *See also* ASSET ALLOCATION.

TAFT-HARTLEY ACT U.S. federal law (in full, Labor Management Relations Act) enacted in 1947, which restored to management in unionized industries some of the bargaining power it had lost in prounion legislation prior to World War II. Taft-Hartley prohibited a union from
- refusing to bargain in good faith
- coercing employees to join a union
- imposing excessive or discriminatory dues and initiation fees
- forcing employers to hire union workers to perform unneeded or non-existent tasks (a practice known as *featherbedding)*
- striking to influence a bargaining unit's choice between two contesting unions (called a *jurisdictional strike)*
- engaging in secondary boycotts against businesses selling or handling nonunion goods
- engaging in sympathy strikes in support of other unions

Taft-Hartley also
- imposed disclosure requirements to regulate union business dealings and uncover fraud and racketeering
- prohibited unions from directly making contributions to candidates running for federal offices
- authorized the President of the United States to postpone strikes in industries deemed essential to national economic health or national security by declaring an 80-day "cooling-off period"
- permitted states to enact right-to-work laws, which outlaw compulsory unionization.

TAIL
Insurance: interval between receipt of premium income and payment of claims. For example, REINSURANCE companies have a long tail as compared to CASUALTY INSURANCE companies.
U.S. Treasury auctions: spread in price between the lowest COMPETITIVE BID accepted by the U.S. Treasury for bills, bonds, and notes and the average bid by all those offering to buy such Treasury securities. *See also* TREASURIES.
Underwriting: decimal places following the round-dollar amount of a bid by a potential UNDERWRITER in a COMPETITIVE BID underwriting. For instance, in a bid of $97.3347 for a particular bond issue, the tail is .3347.

TAILGATING unethical practice of a broker who, after a customer has placed an order to buy or sell a certain security, places an order for the same security for his or her own account. The broker hopes to profit either because of information the customer is known or presumed to have or because the customer's purchase is of sufficient size to put pressure on the security price.

TAIWAN STOCK EXCHANGE exchange of the Republic of China, located in Taipei. The *Taiwan Stock Exchange Capitalization Weighted Stock Index* is the oldest and most widely quoted of three leading indices, and is comparable to the STANDARD & POOR'S 500 INDEX in terms of its construction. Trading hours are Monday through Friday from 9 A.M. to noon, and Saturday from 9 A.M. to 11 A.M. Settlement by delivery of stock or cash payment must be made to the commissioning broker by the next business day.

TAKE
In general:
1. profit realized from a transaction.
2. gross receipts of a lottery or gambling enterprise.
3. open to bribery, as in *being on the take.*
Law: to seize possession of property. When a debtor defaults on a debt backed by COLLATERAL, that property is taken back by the creditor.
Securities: act of accepting an OFFER price in a transaction between brokers or dealers.

TAKE A BATH to suffer a large loss on a SPECULATION or investment, as in "I took a bath on my XYZ stock when the market dropped last week."

TAKE A FLIER to speculate, that is, to buy securities with the knowledge that the investment is highly risky.

TAKE A POSITION
1. to buy stock in a company with the intent of holding for the long term or, possibly, of taking control of the company. An acquirer who takes a position of 5% or more of a company's outstanding stock must file information with the Securities and Exchange Commission, the exchange the TARGET COMPANY is listed on, and the target company itself.
2. phrase used when a broker/dealer holds stocks or bonds in inventory. A position may be either long or short. *See also* LONG POSITION; SHORT POSITION.

TAKEDOWN
1. each participating INVESTMENT BANKER'S proportionate share of the securities to be distributed in a new or a secondary offering.
2. price at which the securities are allocated to members of the UNDERWRITING GROUP, particularly in municipal offerings.
    See also UNDERWRITE.

TAKE-HOME PAY amount of salary remaining after all deductions have been taken out. Some of the most common deductions are for federal and provincial income tax withholding; CPP; UI; medical and dental care; union dues; and contributions to pensions and other retirement savings plans.

TAKE OFF to rise sharply. For example, when positive news about a company's earnings is released, traders say that the stock takes off. The term is also used referring to the overall movement of stock prices, as in "When the Bank of Canada lowered interest rates, the stock market took off."

TAKEOUT

Real estate finance: long-term mortgage loan made to refinance a short-term construction loan (INTERIM LOAN). *See also* STANDBY COMMITMENT.

Securities: withdrawal of cash from a brokerage account, usually after a sale and purchase has resulted in a net CREDIT BALANCE.

TAKEOVER change in the controlling interest of a corporation. A takeover may be a friendly acquisition or an unfriendly bid that the TARGET COMPANY may fight with SHARK REPELLENT techniques. A hostile takeover (aiming to replace existing management) is usually attempted through a public TENDER OFFER. Other approaches might be unsolicited merger proposals to directors, accumulations of shares in the open market, or PROXY FIGHTS that seek to install new directors. *See also* ANY-AND-ALL BID; ARBITRAGEUR; ASSET STRIPPER; BEAR HUG; BLITZKREIG TENDER OFFER; BUST-UP TAKEOVER; CRAM-DOWN DEAL; CROWN JEWELS; DAWN RAID; DEAL STOCK; FAIR-PRICE AMENDMENT; GAP OPENING; GARBATRAGE; GODFATHER OFFER; GOLDEN PARACHUTE; GOODBYE KISS; GREENMAIL; GREY KNIGHT; HIGHLY CONFIDENT LETTER; HIGHJACKING; HOSTILE TAKEOVER; IN PLAY; INSIDER TRADING; KILLER BEES; LADY MACBETH STRATEGY; LEVERAGED BUYOUT; LEVERAGED RECAPITALIZATION; LOCK-UP OPTION; MACARONI DEFENSE; MANAGEMENT BUYOUT; MATERIALITY; MERGER; PAC-MAN STRATEGY; PEOPLE PILL; POISON PILL; POISON PUT; RADAR ALERT; RAIDER; RISK ARBITRAGE; REVERSE LEVERAGED BUYOUT; RUMORTRAGE; SAFE HARBOR; SATURDAY NIGHT SPECIAL; SCORCHED EARTH POLICY; SHARK WATCHER; SHOW STOPPER; SLEEPING BEAUTY; STAGGERED BOARD OF DIRECTORS; STANDSTILL AGREEMENT; STOCK BUYBACK; STRATEGIC BUYOUT; SUICIDE PILL; SUPERMAJORITY AMENDMENT; TAKEOVER TARGET; TWO-TIER BID; WAR CHEST; WHITE KNIGHT; WHITEMAIL; WHITE SQUIRE.

TAKEOVER ARBITRAGE *see* RISK ARBITRAGE.

TAKEOVER BID offer made to security holders of a company to purchase voting securities of the company that, with the offeror's already owned securities, will in total exceed 20% of the outstanding voting securities of the company. For federally incorporated companies, the equivalent requirement is more than 10% of the outstanding voting shares of the target company. These percentages are statutory requirements set by federal and provincial securities regulations.

TAKEOVER TARGET company that is the object of a takeover offer, whether the offer is friendly or unfriendly. In a HOSTILE TAKEOVER attempt, management tries to use various defensive strategies to repel the acquirer. In a friendly takeover situation, management cooperates with the acquirer, negotiating the best possible price, and recommends that shareholders vote to accept the final offer. *See also* TAKEOVER.

TAKING DELIVERY

In general: accepting receipt of goods from a common carrier or other shipper, usually documented by signing a bill of lading or other form of receipt.

Commodities: accepting physical delivery of a commodity under a FUTURES CONTRACT or SPOT MARKET contract. Delivery requirements, such as the size of the contract and the necessary quality of the commodity, are established by the exchange on which the commodity is traded.

Securities: accepting receipt of stock or bond certificates that have recently been purchased or transferred from another account.

TALON coupon or certificate similar to a warrant attached to another security and carrying some right or privilege. *See also* WARRANT.

TANGIBLE ASSET any asset not meeting the definition of an INTANGIBLE ASSET, which is a nonphysical right to something presumed to represent an advantage in the marketplace, such as a trademark or patent. Thus tangible assets are clearly those having physical existence, like cash, real estate, or machinery. Yet in accounting, assets such as ACCOUNTS RECEIVABLE are considered tangible, even though they are no more physical than a licence or a lease, both of which are considered intangible. In summary: if an asset has physical form it is tangible; if it doesn't, consult a list of what accountants have decided are intangible assets.

TANGIBLE COST oil and gas drilling term meaning the cost of items that can be used over a period of time, such as casings, well fittings, land, and tankage, as distinguished from intangible costs such as drilling, testing, and geologist's expenses. In the most widely used LIMITED PARTNERSHIP sharing arrangements, tangible costs are borne by the GENERAL PARTNER (manager) while intangible costs are borne by the limited partners (investors), usually to be taken as tax deductions. In the event of a dry hole, however, all costs become intangibles. *See also* INTANGIBLE COST.

TANGIBLE NET WORTH total ASSETS less INTANGIBLE ASSETS and total LIABILITIES; also called *net tangible assets*. Intangible assets include nonmaterial benefits such as goodwill, patents, copyrights, and trademarks.

TAPE

1. service that reports prices and size of transactions on major exchanges. Also called *composite tape* and *ticker tape* (because of the sound made by the machine that printed the tape before the process was computerized).

2. tape of Dow Jones and other news wires, usually called the BROAD TAPE.

    See also CONSOLIDATED TAPE.

TAPE IS LATE situation in which trading volume is so heavy that the consolidated tape is running more than a minute behind when the actual trades are taking place on the floor of the exchange. The tape will not run faster than 900 characters a minute because the human eye cannot take in information any faster. When trading volume is heavy and the tape is running late, some price digits will first be deleted, and then volume digits will be deleted.

TARGET COMPANY firm that has been chosen as attractive for TAKEOVER by a potential acquirer. The acquirer may buy up to 5% of the target's stock without public disclosure, but it must report all transactions and supply other information to the Securities and Exchange Commission, the exchange the target company is listed on, and the target company itself once 5% or more of the stock is acquired. *See also* TOEHOLD PURCHASE; SLEEPING BEAUTY; TENDER OFFER.

TARGET PRICE

Finance: price at which an acquirer aims to buy a company in a TAKEOVER.

Options: price of the underlying security after which a certain OPTION will become profitable to its buyer. For example, someone buying an XYZ 50 call for a PREMIUM of $200 could have a target price of 52, after which point the premium will be recouped and the CALL OPTION will result in a profit when exercised.

Stocks: price that an investor is hoping a stock he or she has just bought will rise to within a specified period of time. An investor may buy XYZ at $20, with a target price of $40 in one year's time, for instance.

TARIFF

1. federal tax on imports or exports usually imposed either to raise revenue (called a *revenue tariff*) or to protect domestic firms from import competition (called a *protective tariff*). A tariff may also be designed to correct an imbalance of payments. The money collected under tariffs is called DUTY or *customs duty.*

2. schedule of rates or charges, usually for freight.

TAXABLE EVENT occurrence with tax consequences. For example, if a stock or mutual fund is sold at a profit, capital gains taxes may be due. Withdrawal of assets from a registered retirement savings plan is a taxable event because some or all of the proceeds may be considered taxable income in the year withdrawn. Proper TAX PLANNING can help taxpayers time taxable events to maximum advantage.

TAXABLE INCOME amount of income (after all allowable deductions and tax credits) subject to tax. On an individual's federal income tax return, taxable income is the sum of wages, salaries, dividends, interest, capital gains, business income, etc., less allowable expenses and personal tax credits. Once taxable income is known, the individual taxpayer finds the total income tax obligation for his or her TAX BRACKET by checking the Revenue Canada tax tables or by calculating the tax according to a rate schedule. TAX CREDITS reduce the tax liability dollar-for-dollar.

Taxable income of an incorporated business, also called *net income before taxes,* consists of total revenues less cost of goods sold, selling and administrative expenses, interest, and extraordinary items.

TAX AUDIT audit by Revenue Canada, or provincial ministry of revenue to determine if a taxpayer paid the correct amount of tax. Returns will be chosen for audits if they have suspiciously high claims for deductions or credits, or if reported income is suspiciously low, or if computer matching of income uncovers discrepancies. Audits may be done on a relatively superficial level, or in great depth. If the auditor finds a tax deficiency, the taxpayer may have to pay back-taxes, as well as interest and penalties. The taxpayer does have the right of appeal through the appeals process and, if warranted, to the Federal Court. There is a taxpayers' bill of rights.

TAX AVOIDANCE strategy to pay the least amount of tax possible through legal means. For example, taxpayers may buy tax sheltered investments; shelter gains inside tax-deferred RRSP accounts; shift capital gains to children who need not pay taxes on part of their income; make legitimate charitable contributions to generate tax credits; and establish trusts to avoid estate taxes. Illegal strategies to avoid paying taxes are called TAX EVASION.

TAX BASE total amount of taxable property, assets, and income that can be taxed within a specific jurisdiction. A town's tax base is the assessed value of the homes and apartments (minus exempted property), income from businesses, business taxes, and other sources of taxable activity. If a business moves out of the town, the tax base shrinks, shifting the tax burden onto remaining homeowners and businesses.

TAX BASIS
Finance: original cost of an ASSET, less accumulated DEPRECIATION, that goes into the calculation of a gain or loss for tax purposes. Thus, a property acquired for $100,000 that has been depreciated by $40,000 has a tax basis of $60,000 assuming no other adjustments; sale of that property for $120,000 results in a taxable CAPITAL GAIN of $60,000.
Investments: price at which a stock or bond was purchased, plus brokerage commission. The law requires that a PREMIUM paid on the purchase of an investment be amortized.

TAX BRACKET point on the income-tax rate schedules where TAXABLE INCOME falls; also called *marginal tax bracket.* It is expressed as a percentage to be applied to each additional dollar earned over the base amount for that bracket. Under a PROGRESSIVE TAX system, increases in taxable income lead to higher marginal rates in the form of higher brackets. There are 3 (17%, 26%, and 29%) tax brackets for individuals in Canada. Then provinces apply their taxes, usually as a percentage of federal taxes payable.

For corporations the corporate rate varies from as low as 18% for a small business with net income below $200,000 to 44%.

TAX CREDIT direct, dollar-for-dollar reduction in tax liability, as distinguished from a tax deduction, which reduces taxes only by the percentage of a taxpayer's TAX BRACKET. (A taxpayer in the 37% tax bracket would get a 37 cent benefit from each $1.00 deduction, for example.) In the case of a tax credit, a taxpayer owing $10,000 in tax would owe $9000 if he or she took advantage of a $1000 tax credit. Under certain conditions, tax credits are allowed for a pensioner above age 65, charitable and political donations, child care expenses, and conducting research and development.

TAX DEDUCTIBLE expense that generates a tax deduction. For individuals, some items that are tax deductible include charitable contributions, mortgage interest, and unreimbursed business expenses. In some cases, taxpayers must meet a minimum threshold before an expense is deductible. For example, unreimbursed medical expenses are deductible if they exceed 3% of net income in a tax year.

TAX DEDUCTION deductible expense that reduces taxable income for individuals or businesses. *See* TAX DEDUCTIBLE for examples of legal tax deductions.

TAX DEFERRED term describing an investment whose accumulated earnings are free from taxation until the investor takes possession of them. For example, the holder of an RRSP postpones paying taxes on interest, dividends, or capital appreciation if he or she waits until after age 71 and rolls the proceeds into an annuity or REGISTERED RETIREMENT INCOME FUND. Other examples of tax-deferred investment vehicles include INSURANCE, and UNIVERSAL LIFE INSURANCE policies and Employee Profit and Stock Purchase plans.

TAX EVASION illegal practice of intentionally evading taxes. Taxpayers who evade their true tax liability may underreport income, overstate deductions and exemptions, or participate in fraudulent tax shelters. If the taxpayer is caught, tax evasion is subject to criminal penalties, as well as payment of back taxes with interest, and civil penalties. Tax evasion is different from TAX AVOIDANCE, which is the legal use of the Tax Act to reduce tax liability.

TAX LIABILITY income, property, sales, or other taxes owed to a government entity. *See also* PROVISION FOR INCOME TAXES.

TAX HAVEN country offering outside businesses and individuals an environment with little or no taxation. Several Caribbean islands, such as the Cayman Islands, have attracted billions of dollars in bank deposits by creating a tax haven. Depositors and businesses not only lower the tax burdens in their home countries, but also are subject to less regulation and increased privacy for their financial affairs.

TAX LIEN statutory right obtained by a government to enforce a claim against the property of a person owing taxes until the debt is paid.

TAX LOSS CARRYBACK, CARRYFORWARD tax benefit that allows a company or individual to apply losses to reduce tax liability. A company may OFFSET the current year's capital or NET OPERATING LOSSES against profits in the three immediately preceding years, with the earliest year first. After the carryback, it may carry forward (also called a *carryover)* capital losses 7 years and net operating losses indefinitely. By then it will presumably have regained financial health.

Individuals may carry over capital losses until they are used up for 7 years to offset capital gains, and can carry back losses for 3 years to apply to prior years' tax returns.

TAX PLANNING strategy of minimizing tax liability for an individual or company by analyzing the tax implications of various options throughout a tax year. Tax planning involves choosing a FILING STATUS, figuring out the most advantageous time to realize capital gains and losses, knowing when to accelerate deductions and postpone income or vice versa, setting up a proper estate plan to reduce deemed disposition on death taxes, and other legitimate tax-saving moves.

TAX PREPARATION SERVICES businesses that specialize in preparing tax returns. Such services may range from national tax preparation chains such as H&R Block to local tax preparers, accountants, and tax lawyers. Services normally charge based on the complexity of the tax return and the amount of time needed to fill it out correctly. Many services can arrange to file a tax return with Revenue Canada electronically, which can result in a faster TAX REFUND.

TAX RATE percentage of tax to be paid on a certain level of income. Canada uses a system of marginal tax rates, meaning that the rates rise with taxable income. The top rate is paid only on the portion of income over the threshold. Currently, the federal government has 3 rates—17%, 26% and 29%. There is also a series of surtaxes based on income. Each province has its own tax rates and surtaxes.

TAX REFUND refund of overpaid taxes from the government to the taxpayer. Refunds are due when the taxpayer has been OVERWITHHOLDING, or has overestimated income or underestimated deductions, exemptions, and credits. Though taxpayers may like the fact that they are getting a tax refund, in fact they are granting the government an interest-free loan for most of the year, which is not astute TAX PLANNING.

TAX SCHEDULES tax forms used in addition to the basic form to report itemized deductions; dividend and interest income; investment income; profit or loss from business; capital gains and losses; property and child tax credits, transfer of tax credits, medical expenses, and charitable donations.

TAX SHELTER method used by investors to legally avoid or reduce tax liabilities. Legal shelters include those using DEPRECIATION of assets and operating losses like DEPLETION allowances for oil and gas exploration. LIMITED PARTNERSHIPS have traditionally offered investors limited liability and tax benefits including "flow through" operating losses usable to offset income from other sources. New at risk rules require full recourse financing to be in place for the invesment to be considered legal.

TAX SOFTWARE software that helps taxpayers plan for and prepare their tax returns. Software such as HomeTax and KwikTax helps taxpayers analyze their tax situation and take actions to minimize tax liability. Different versions of tax software are appropriate for large and small businesses, partnerships, individuals, and estates. When integrated with a personal finance software package, a taxpayer does not have to reenter data, which can easily be exchanged from the personal finance side into the tax preparation side of the package.

TAX UMBRELLA tax loss carryforwards stemming from losses of a firm in past years, which shield profits earned in current and future years from taxes. *See also* TAX LOSS CARRYBACK, CARRYFORWARD.

TEAR SHEET sheet from one of a dozen loose-leaf books comprising Standard & Poor's Stock Reports, which provide essential background and financial data on several thousand companies. Brokers often tear and mail these sheets to customers (hence the name).

TECHNICAL ANALYSIS research into the demand and supply for securities, options, mutual funds, and commodities based on trading volume and price studies. Technical analysts use charts or computer programs to identify and project price trends in a market, security, fund, or futures contract. Most analysis is done for the short- or intermediate-term, but some technicians also predict long-term cycles based on charts and other data. Unlike FUNDAMENTAL ANALYSIS, technical analysis is not concerned with the financial position of a company. *See also* ADVANCE/DECLINE (A/D); ASCENDING TOPS; BREAKOUT; CORRECTION; DEAD CAT BOUNCE; DESCENDING TOPS; DIP; DOUBLE BOTTOM; ELVES; FALL OUT OF BED; FLAG; FLURRY; GAP; GAP OPENING; HEAD AND SHOULDERS; HORIZONTAL PRICE MOVEMENT; MOVING AVERAGE; NEW HIGH/NEW LOW; PENNANT; POINT AND FIGURE CHART; PUT-CALL RATIO; RESISTANCE LEVEL; REVERSAL; RISING BOTTOMS; SAUCER; SELLING CLIMAX; SUPPORT LEVEL; TRADING PATTERN; TRIANGLE; V FORMATION; VERTICAL LINE CHARTING; W FORMATION.

TECHNICAL INSOLVENCY situation that occurs when a business is unable to pay bills as they fall due. Technical insolvency normally precedes bankruptcy, although business can overcome technical insolvency through borrowing.

TECHNICAL RALLY short rise in securities or commodities futures prices within a general declining trend. Such a rally may result because investors are bargain-hunting or because analysts have noticed a particular SUPPORT LEVEL at which securities usually bounce up. Technical rallies do not last long, however, and soon after prices resume their declining pattern.

TECHNICAL SIGN short-term trend that technical analysts can identify as significant in the price movement of a security or a commodity. *See also* TECHNICAL ANALYSIS.

TECHNICIAN *or* TECHNICAL ANALYST one who studies all factors related to the actual supply and demand of stocks, bonds, or commodities. The primary tools of the technician are stock charts and various technical indicators.

TED SPREAD difference between interest rates on U.S. Treasury bills and Eurodollars. The term *Ted* refers to *Treasuries over Eurodollars.* Many traders in the futures markets actively trade the Ted spread, speculating that the difference between U.S. Treasuries and Eurodollars will widen or narrow. The Ted spread also is used in the United States as an indicator of confidence in the government and the general level of fear or confidence in the markets for private financing. A narrow spread indicates confidence in financial markets in general and the U.S. Government in particular. When the spread is wide, confidence is diminished. *See also* FLIGHT TO QUALITY.

TEL AVIV STOCK EXCHANGE only stock exchange in Israel. Trading hours for stocks, warrants, and convertible bonds are 10:30 A.M. to 3:30 P.M., Sunday through Thursday. Options are traded on the 25 companies with highest market value that are part of the *Maof Index.* All other derivatives and all shares are reflected in the *General Share Index.* Trades are settled on the day following the trade.

TEMPORARY INVESTMENT investment designed to be held for a short period of time, typically a year or less. Some examples of temporary investments are money market mutual funds and T-bill accounts.

TEMPORARY LINE OF CREDIT temporary (e.g., 2 or 3 months) additional line of credit from a bank to cover a special or seasonal requirement. Also called a BULGE.

TENANCY AT WILL tenancy where a person holds or occupies real estate with the permission of the owner, for an unspecified term. A tenancy at will could occur when a lease is being negotiated, or under a valid oral lease or contract of sale. All the duties and obligations of a landlord-tenant relationship exist. Notice of termination is required by either party. The tenancy is not assignable.

TENANCY BY THE ENTIRETY (TBE) form of individual (versus corporate or partnership) co-ownership in which ownership passes automatically at the death of one co-owner to the surviving co-owner. The person with a TBE co-ownership interest lacks the power to freely dispose of that interest by WILL. In this respect, it is similar to JOINT TENANCY WITH RIGHT OF SURVIVORSHIP (JTWROS). Unlike JTWROS, however, the TBE ownership interests are limited to ownership by two persons who are husband and wife at the time the property is acquired. If the married couple then divorces, the form of ownership automatically changes to TENANCY IN COMMON (TIC). Generally, TBE ownership is limited to real estate, although about a dozen states permit TBE ownership of personal property.

TENANCY IN COMMON (TIC) ownership of real or personal property by two or more persons in which ownership at the death of one co-owner is part of the owner's disposable ESTATE, and does not pass to the co-owner(s). There is no limit to the number of persons who can acquire property as TIC, and those persons could be, but need not be married to each other.

TENANT
Real Estate: (1) holder or possessor of real property; (2) lessee.
Securities: part owner of a security.
  See also JOINT TENANTS WITH RIGHT OF SURVIVORSHIP; TENANCY IN COMMON.

TENANTS-IN-COMMON *see* TENANCY IN COMMON (TIC).

TENBAGGER stock that grows in value by ten times. The term comes from baseball lingo, since a double is called a two-bagger because it earns the hitter the right to two bases, or bags. Similarly, a triple is a three-bagger and a home run a four-bagger. The term, as applied to investing, is also used in larger multiples, such as a twenty-bagger, for a stock that grows twenty-fold.

TENDER
1. act of surrendering one's shares in a corporation in response to an offer to buy them at a set price. *See also* TENDER OFFER.
2. to submit a formal bid to buy a security, as in a Treasury bill auction. *See also* DUTCH AUCTION.
3. offer of money or goods in settlement of a prior debt or claim, as in the delivery of goods on the due date of a FUTURES CONTRACT.
4. agreed-upon medium for the settlement of financial transactions, such as a valid currency, which is labeled "legal tender for all debts, public and private."

TENDER CREDIT line of credit relating to certified cheques that accompany tenders submitted by a contractor. If the bid is unsuccessful, the cheques are returned and the line of credit paid down. If the bid is successful, the amount is secured by the tender.

TENDER OFFER offer to buy shares of a corporation, usually at a PRE-MIUM above the shares' market price, for cash, securities, or both, often with the objective of taking control of the TARGET COMPANY. A tender offer may arise from friendly negotiations between the company and a corporate suitor or may be unsolicited and possibly unfriendly, resulting in countermeasures being taken by the target firm.

TERM

1. period of time during which the conditions of a contract will be carried out. This may refer to the time in which loan payments must be made, or the time when interest payments will be made on a certificate of deposit or a bond or the time remaining until a bond reaches its maturity date. It also may refer to the length of time a life insurance policy is in force. *See also* TERM LIFE INSURANCE.

2. provision specifying the nature of an agreement or contract, as in *terms and conditions.*

3. period of time an official or board member is elected or appointed to serve. For example, Federal Reserve governors are appointed for 14-year terms.

TERM DEBT technically, any debt for which repayment is scheduled beyond one year.

TERM DEPOSIT DEPOSIT with a longer-term maturity date. Such deposits can range in length from 1 year to 7 years, though the most popular term deposits are those for one or two years. Deposit holders usually receive a fixed rate of interest, payable semiannually or quarterly during the term, and are subject to costly EARLY WITHDRAWAL PENALTIES if cashed in before the scheduled maturity.

TERM DEPOSIT RECEIPT deposit instrument most commonly available from chartered banks, requiring a minimum investment at a predetermined rate of interest for a stated term. The interest rate varies according to the amount invested and the term to maturity, but is competitive with comparable alternative investments. A reduced interest rate usually applies if funds are withdrawn prior to maturity.

TERMINATION BENEFIT *see* SEVERANCE PAY.

TERM LIFE INSURANCE form of life insurance, written for a specified period, that requires the policyholder to pay only for the cost of protection against death; that is, no cash value is built up as in WHOLE LIFE INSURANCE. Every time the policy is renewed, the premium is higher, since the insured is older and therefore statistically more likely to die. Term insurance is far cheaper than whole life, giving policyholders the alternative of using the savings to invest on their own.

TERM LOAN intermediate- to long-term (typically, two to ten years) secured credit granted to a company by a commercial bank, insurance company, or commercial finance company usually to finance capital equipment or provide working capital. The loan is amortized over a fixed period, sometimes ending with a BALLOON payment. Borrowers under term loan agreements are normally required to meet minimum WORKING CAPITAL and debt to net worth tests, to limit dividends, and to maintain continuity of management.

TERM LOAN INTEREST RATES two types of interest rates that are charged on term loans. On a variable-rate loan, the interest rate charged floats at a predetermined fixed percentage (spread) above the prime rate for the loan (or duration of the loan). On a fixed-rate loan, the interest rate charged by the lender is fixed for the term of the loan.

TERM TO 100 PERMATERM provision that the amount paid for a policy may remain the same every year or there may be some variation in the pattern of payments, but there is usually no cash value available if the policy is terminated.

TEST

In general: examination to determine knowledge, competence, or qualifications.

Finance: criterion used to measure compliance with financial ratio requirements of indentures and other loan agreements (e.g., a current asset to current liability test or a debt to net worth test). *See also* QUICK RATIO.

Securities: term used in reference to a price movement that approaches a SUPPORT LEVEL or a RESISTANCE LEVEL established earlier by a commodity future, security, or market. A test is passed if the levels are not penetrated and is failed if prices go on to new lows or highs. Technical analysts say, for instance, that if the Toronto Stock Exchange last formed a solid base at 4000, and prices have been falling from 4200, a period of testing is approaching. If prices rebound once the TSE hits 4000 and go up further, the test is passed. If prices continue to drop below 4000, however, the test is failed. *See also* TECHNICAL ANALYSIS.

TESTAMENT synonym for a WILL, a document that will dispose of property a person owns at his or her death. The testament is created by the TESTATOR or TESTATRIX, usually with the aid of an estate planning lawyer or will-writing software.

TESTAMENTARY TRUST trust created by a will, as distinguished from an INTER VIVOS TRUST created during the lifetime of the GRANTOR.

TESTATE having made and left a valid WILL; a person who dies with a will is said to die testate. A person who dies without a will is said to die INTESTATE.

TESTATOR/TESTATRIX a man/woman who has made and left a valid WILL at his/her death.

TFE Toronto Futures Exchange. *See also* TORONTO STOCK EXCHANGE.

THEORETICAL VALUE (OF A RIGHT) mathematically determined MARKET VALUE of a SUBSCRIPTION RIGHT after the offering is announced but before the stock goes EX-RIGHTS. The formula includes the current market value of the common stock, the subscription price, and the number of rights required to purchase a share of stock:

theoretical value of a right

$$= \frac{\text{market value of common stock} - \text{subscription price per share}}{\text{number of rights needed to buy 1 share} + 1}$$

Thus, if the common stock market price is $50 per share, the subscription price is $45 per share, and the subscription ratio is 4 to 1, the value of one right would be $1:

$$\frac{50 - 45}{4 + 1} \quad = \quad \frac{5}{5} \quad = 1$$

THIN MARKET market in which there are few bids to buy and few offers to sell. A thin market may apply to an entire class of securities or commodities futures such as small OVER THE COUNTER stocks or the platinum market—or it may refer to a particular stock, whether exchange-listed or over-the-counter. Prices in thin markets are more volatile than in markets with great LIQUIDITY, since the few trades that take place can affect prices significantly. Institutional investors who buy and sell large blocks of stock tend to avoid thin markets, because it is difficult for them to get in or out of a POSITION without materially affecting the stock's price.

THIRD MARKET nonexchange-member broker/dealers and institutional investors trading OVER THE COUNTER in exchange-listed securities. The third market rose to importance in the 1950s when institutional investors began buying common stocks as an inflation hedge and fixed commission rates still prevailed on the exchanges. By trading large blocks with nonmember firms, they both saved commissions and avoided the unsettling effects on prices that large trades on the exchanges produced. After commission rates were deregulated in the United States in May 1975, a number of the firms active in the third market became member firms so they could deal with members as well as nonmembers. At the same time, member firms began increasingly to move large blocks of stock off the floor of the exchanges, in effect becoming participants in the third market. Before selling securities off the exchange to a nonmember, however, a member firm must satisfy all LIMIT ORDERS on the SPECIALIST'S BOOK at the same price or higher. *See also* OFF-FLOOR ORDER.

THIRD-PARTY CHEQUE
1. cheque negotiated through a bank, except one payable to the writer of the cheque (that is, a cheque written for cash). The *primary party*

to a transaction is the bank on which a cheque is drawn. The *secondary party* is the drawer of the cheque against funds on deposit in the bank. The *third party* is the payee who endorses the cheque.

2. double-endorsed cheque. In this instance, the payee endorses the cheque by signing the back, then passes the cheque to a subsequent holder, who endorses it prior to cashing it. Recipients of cheques with multiple endorsers are reluctant to accept them unless they can verify each endorser's signature.

3. payable-through drafts and other negotiable orders not directly serviced by the providing company. Money orders and cheques drawn against a brokerage account are other examples of payable-through or third-party items.

THIRD WORLD name for the less developed countries of Africa, Asia, and Latin America.

THREE STEPS AND A STUMBLE RULE rule holding that stock and bond prices will fall if the U.S. Federal Reserve raises the DISCOUNT RATE three times in a row. By raising interest rates, the Federal Reserve both raises the cost of borrowing for companies and makes alternative investments such as money market funds relatively more attractive than stocks and bonds. Many market historians have tracked this rule, and found it to be a good predictor of drops in stock and bond prices.

THRIFT INSTITUTION in the United States, an organization formed primarily as a depository for consumer savings, the most common varieties of which are the SAVINGS AND LOAN ASSOCIATION and the SAVINGS BANK. Traditionally, savings institutions have lent most of their deposit funds in the residential mortgage market. Deregulation in the early 1980s expanded their range of depository services and allowed them to make commercial and consumer loans. Deregulation led to widespread abuse by savings and loans that used insured deposits to engage in speculative real estate lending.

TICK upward or downward price movement in a security's trades. Technical analysts watch the tick of a stock's successive up or down moves to get a feel of the stock's trend. The term also applies to the overall market. In futures and options trading, a minimum change in price up or down. *See also* CLOSING TICK; DOWNTICK; MINUS TICK; PLUS TICK; SHORT SALE RULE; TECHNICAL ANALYSIS; TRIN; UPTICK; ZERO-MINUS TICK; ZERO-PLUS TICK.

TICKER system that produces a running report of trading activity on the stock exchanges, called the TICKER TAPE. The name derives from machines that, in times past, printed information by punching holes in a paper tape, making an audible ticking sound as the tape was fed forth. Today's ticker tape is a computer screen and the term is used to refer both to the CONSOLIDATED TAPE, which shows the STOCK SYMBOL, latest price, and volume of trades on the exchanges, and to news ticker services. *See also* QUOTATION BOARD; TICKER TAPE.

TICKER SYMBOL letters that identify a security for trading purposes on the CONSOLIDATED TAPE, such as XON for Exxon Corporation. *See also* STOCK SYMBOL; TICKER TAPE.

TICKER TAPE device that relays the STOCK SYMBOL and the latest price and volume on securities as they are traded to investors around the world. Prior to the advent of computers, this machine had a loud printing device that made a ticking sound. Since 1975, the New York Stock Exchange and the American Stock Exchange have used a CONSOLIDATED TAPE that indicates the New York or REGIONAL STOCK EXCHANGE on which a trade originated. Other systems, known as news tickers, pass along the latest economic, financial and market news developments. See also TAPE. *See* illustration of consolidated tape, below.

TUX	INC	TD
5S27½	62⅝	3S49½

Sample section of the consolidated tape.

Trades in TuxGold, Inco, and the Toronto Dominion Bank are shown. In the lower line, where a number precedes the letter S, a multiple of 100 shares is indicated. Thus, 500 shares of TuxGold were transacted at a price of 27½ on the Toronto Stock Exchange; no shares of Inco were sold, and 300 shares of Toronto Dominion Bank shares were sold at 49½.

TICKET short for ORDER TICKET.

TIGER acronym for Treasury Investors Growth Receipt, a form of ZERO-COUPON SECURITY first created by the brokerage firm of Merrill Lynch, Pierce, Fenner & Smith. TIGERS are U.S. government-backed bonds that have been stripped of their COUPONS. Both the CORPUS (principal) of the bonds and the individual coupons are sold separately at a deep discount from their face value. Investors receive FACE VALUE for the TIGERS when the bonds mature but do not receive periodic interest payments. Under Internal Revenue Service rules, however, TIGER holders owe income taxes on the imputed interest they would have earned had the bond been a FULL COUPON BOND. To avoid having to pay taxes without having the benefit of the income to pay them from, most investors put TIGERS in Individual Retirement accounts or in other TAX DEFERRED plans. Also called *TIGR*.

TIGHT MARKET market in general or market for a particular security marked by active trading and narrow bid-offer price spreads. In contrast, inactive trading and wide spreads characterize a *slack market*. *See also* SPREAD.

TIGHT MONEY economic condition in which credit is difficult to secure, usually as the result of Federal Reserve action to restrict the MONEY SUPPLY. The opposite is *easy money. See also* MONETARY POLICY.

TIME DRAFT DRAFT payable at a specified or determinable time in the future, as distinguished from a *sight draft,* which is payable on presentation and delivery.

TIMELY DISCLOSURE obligation imposed by securities administrators or companies and their officers and directors, to release promptly to the news media any favourable or unfavourable corporate information of a material nature. Board dissemination of this news allows non-insiders to trade the company's securities with the same knowledge about the company as insiders. *See also* CONTINUOUS DISCLOSURE.

TIMES FIXED CHARGES *see* FIXED-CHARGE COVERAGE.

TIME SHARING
Computers: practice of renting time on a central computer through a smaller computer, frequently through modems and phone lines. The user can upload or download files, access electronic mail, use computer programs on the central computer, and perform other tasks, for a fee based on usage.
Real estate: practice of sharing a piece of real estate, such as a condominium, apartment, or house, with other owners. Typically, a buyer will purchase a particular block of time for a vacation, such as the second week of February, during which the buyer will have exclusive use of the property. In return, the buyer must pay his or her share of annual maintenance charges, whether he or she uses the property or not. One condominium may therefore be sold to 52 different parties, each for one week per year. Time share owners have the benefit of changing their weeks with other owners around the world through one of the worldwide exchange companies. Time shares should be viewed as a purchase of one's vacation, and not as a real estate investment.

TIMES INTEREST EARNED *see* FIXED-CHARGE COVERAGE.

TIME SPREAD OPTION strategy in which an investor buys and sells PUT OPTION and CALL OPTION contracts with the same EXERCISE PRICE but with different expiration dates. The purpose of this and other option strategies is to profit from the difference in OPTION PREMIUMS—the prices paid to buy the options. *See also* CALENDAR SPREAD; HORIZONTAL SPREAD; SPREAD.

TIME VALUE
In general: price put on the time an investor has to wait until an investment matures, as determined by calculating the PRESENT VALUE of the investment at maturity. *See also* YIELD TO MATURITY.
Options: that part of a stock option PREMIUM that reflects the time remaining on an option contract before expiration. The premium is composed of this time value and the INTRINSIC VALUE of the option.

Stocks: difference between the price at which a company is taken over and the price before the TAKEOVER occurs. For example, if XYZ Company is to be taken over at $30 a share in two months, XYZ shares might presently sell for $28.50. The $1.50 per share difference is the cost of the time value those owning XYZ must bear if they want to wait two months to get $30 a share. As the two months pass, the time value will shrink, until it disappears on the day of the takeover. The time that investors hold XYZ has a price because it could be used to invest in something else providing a higher return. *See also* OPPORTUNITY COST.

TIME-WEIGHTED RETURN portfolio accounting method that measures investment performance (income and price changes) as a percentage of capital "at work," effectively eliminating the effects of additions and withdrawals of capital and their timing that distort DOLLAR-WEIGHTED RETURN accounting. Since exact timing-weighting is impractical, the industry accepts an approximation that assumes all additions and withdrawals occur simultaneously at the midpoint of a reporting period. Performance thus equals the return on the value of assets at the beginning of the measuring period plus the return on the net amount of additions and withdrawals during the period divided in half. The periods, usually quarters, are then linked to produce a compound average TOTAL RETURN.

TIMING trying to pick the best time to make a decision. For example, MARKET TIMING involves the analysis of fundamental and technical data to decide when to buy or sell stocks, bonds, mutual funds or futures contracts. Timing is also important in making consumer decisions, such as when to make a major purchase. Consumers might want to time their purchase of real estate when prices and mortgage rates are especially attractive, or their purchase of a car when dealers are offering particularly good prices.

TIP
   In general: payment over and above a formal cost or charge, ostensibly given in appreciation for extra service, to a waiter, bellhop, cabdriver, or other person engaged in service. Also called a *gratuity*.
   Investments: information passed by one person to another as a basis for buy or sell action in a security. Such information is presumed to be of material value and not available to the general public. The provincial securities commissions regulate the use of such information by so-called insiders, and court cases have established the liability of persons receiving and using or passing on such information (called tippees) in certain circumstances. *See also* INSIDER; INSIDE INFORMATION.

TOEHOLD PURCHASE accumulation by an acquirer of less than 10% of the shares of a TARGET COMPANY. Once 10% is acquired, the acquirer is required to file with the Securities Commission, the appropriate stock exchange, and the target company, explaining what is happening and what can be expected.

TOKYO COMMODITY EXCHANGE (TOCOM) trades futures on gold, silver, platinum, palladium, rubber, cotton yarn, and woolen yarn. Metal contracts are traded from 9 A.M. to 11 A.M. and 1 p.m. to 3:30 P.M.; rubber is traded from 9:45 A.M. to 3:30 P.M.; and yarns are traded from 8:50 A.M. to 3:10 P.M.

TOKYO STOCK EXCHANGE largest stock exchange in Japan. The Tokyo Stock Exchange is one of the largest, most important, and most active stock markets in the world. The *Nikkei Stock Average*, known as the Nikkei 225, and Nikkei 500 are the principal indices and are calculated by a formula similar to the DOW JONES INDUSTRIAL AVERAGE. The TOPIX, the *Tokyo Stock Price Index*, is a composite of all stocks on the first section of the exchange. Trading takes place in two daily sessions, from 9 A.M. to 11 A.M., and from 1 P.M. to 3 P.M. The principal form of settlement is delivery on the third business day following the day of the contract.

TOKYO STOCK PRICE INDEX (TOPIX) *see* NIKKEI STOCK AVERAGE.

TOMBSTONE advertisement placed in newspapers by investment bankers in a PUBLIC OFFERING of securities. It gives basic details about the issue and lists the UNDERWRITING GROUP members involved in the offering in alphabetically organized groupings according to the size of their participations. It is not "an offer to sell or a solicitation of an offer to buy," but rather it calls attention to the PROSPECTUS, sometimes called the *offering circular.* A tombstone may also be placed by an investment banking firm to announce its role in a PRIVATE PLACEMENT, corporate MERGER, or ACQUISITION; by a corporation to announce a major business or real estate deal; or by a firm in the financial community to announce a personnel development or a principal's death. *See also* MEZZANINE BRACKET.

TON bond traders' jargon for $100 million.

TOP-DOWN APPROACH TO INVESTING method in which an investor first looks at trends in the general economy, and next selects industries and then companies that should benefit from those trends. For example, an investor who thinks inflation will stay low might be attracted to the retailing industry, since consumers' spending power will be enhanced by low inflation. The investor then might look at Sears, Wal-Mart, The GAP, The Limited, and other retailers to see which company has the best earnings prospects in the near term. Or, an investor who thinks there will be rapid inflation may identify the mining industry as attractive, and then look at particular gold, copper, and other mining companies to see which would benefit most from a trend of rising prices. The opposite method is called the BOTTOM-UP APPROACH TO INVESTING.

TOP-HAT PLAN benefit plan that provides business partners with additional or increased levels of life insurance protection.

TOPIX *see* NIKKEI STOCK AVERAGE.

TOPPING OUT term denoting a market or a security that is at the end of a period of rising prices and can now be expected to stay on a plateau or even to decline.

TORONTO FUTURES EXCHANGE wholly owned subsidiary of the TORONTO STOCK EXCHANGE (TSE), trading TSE 35 Index futures and TSE 100 Index futures. TSE index options, TIPs (Toronto 35 Index Participation units), and TIPs options trade on the TSE.

TORONTO STOCK EXCHANGE (TSE) largest stock exchange in Canada, listing some 1200 company stocks and 33 options. The TSE was founded as an association in 1852 by a small group of Toronto businessmen who met to trade securities for half an hour each morning. These founders operated as a partnership until, by an act of the Province of Ontario, the TSE was incorporated in 1878.

In 1899, a second stock exchange, the Toronto Stock and Mining Exchange (TSME), was organized to trade speculative mining equities. This exchange was succeeded by the Standard Stock and Mining Exchange in 1908, which carried on as a separate exchange until 1934. At that time, a merger was completed with the TSE so that mining and industrial stocks could be traded on one floor. From 1937 to 1983, the TSE was located on Bay Street. In May, 1983, the Exchange moved to the Exchange Tower and Trading Pavilion (behind the Exchange Tower) at York and Adelaide Streets.

On the TSE's 30,000 square-foot trading floor, 5½ trading posts are used for equity trading and 2 trading posts are used for trading equity and non-equity options. In 1984, the TSE established the Toronto Futures Exchange (TFE) as a separate exchange using 2 trading pits on the TSE's trading floor. Currently, the TFE uses only 1 trading pit. The TFE trades silver options and Toronto 35 index options and futures.

The TSE is home to many resource-based companies in the mining, paper, timber, and other natural resource industries, but also trades manufacturing, biotechnology, and telecommunications equities. The *TSE 300 Composite Index,* also known as the TSE 300, is the most widely quoted index tracking this marketplace. The *Toronto 35 Index,* comprising a cross-section of major Canadian stocks, is the base for derivative products such as the Toronto 35 Index option (TXO) and future (TXF). The *TSE 100 Index* is a performance benchmark for institutional investors, and is the base for the TSE 100 Index option and TSE 100 Index future contract. The *TSE 200 Index* is a small to mid-cap index comprising 200 stocks in the TSE 300 that are not represented in the TSE 100. Toronto 35 Index Participation Units, or TIPs, and TIPs options, are proprietary products. Each TIPs unit represents an interest in a trust that holds baskets of stocks in the Toronto 35 Index. TIPs options are American exercise and physically settled, while TXO options are European exercise and cash settled. TSE Index

35 options, TSE Index 100 options, and TIPs products trade on the TSE. The CANADIAN DEALING NETWORK (CDN) is a subsidiary of the exchange. The TSE's (and TFE's) mailing address is the Exchange Tower, 2 First Canadian Place, Toronto, Ontario M5X 1J2. TSE's trading hours are 9:30 A.M. to 4 P.M., Monday through Friday, with an after-hours crossing section until 5 P.M. Settlement is the third day following the trade. The exchange uses both open outcry and the Computer Assisted Trading System (CATS).

TOTAL CAPITALIZATION CAPITAL STRUCTURE of a company, including LONG-TERM DEBT and all forms of EQUITY.

TOTAL COST
Accounting: (usually pl.) sum of FIXED COSTS, semivariable costs, and VARIABLE COSTS.
Investments: contract price paid for a security plus the brokerage commission plus any ACCRUED INTEREST due the seller (if the security is a bond). The figure is not to be confused with the COST BASIS for the purpose of figuring the CAPITAL GAINS TAX, which may involve other factors such as amortization of bond premiums.

TOTAL DISABILITY injury or illness that is so serious that it prevents a worker from performing any functions for which he or she is educated and trained. Workers with total disability may qualify for DISABILITY INCOME INSURANCE, either though a private employer's plan or through Social Security's disability insurance program. There is normally a waiting period before disability insurance payments begin, to determine if the disability is long-term. Waiting periods vary, from a month to several months, and are determined by the plan and premium structure of the employer.

TOTAL RETURN annual return on an investment including appreciation and dividends or interest. For bonds held to maturity, total return is YIELD TO MATURITY. For stocks, future appreciation is projected using the current PRICE/EARNINGS RATIO. In options trading, total return means dividends plus capital gains plus premium income.

TOTAL VOLUME total number of shares or contracts traded in a stock, bond, commodity future, or option on a particular day. For stocks and bonds, this is the aggregate of trades on national exchanges like the Toronto, New York, and American stock exchanges and on regional exchanges. For commodities futures and options, it represents the volume of trades executed around the world in one day. For over-the-counter securities, total volume is measured by the NASDAQ index.

TOUT to promote a particular security aggressively, usually done by a corporate spokesman, public relations firm, broker, or analyst with a vested interest in promoting the stock. Touting a stock is unethical if it misleads investors.

T-PLUS-THREE *see* DELIVERY DATE.

TRADE
In general:
1. buying or selling of goods and services among companies, states, or countries, called *commerce.* The amount of goods and services imported minus the amount exported makes up a country's BALANCE OF TRADE. *See also* TARIFF; TRADE DEFICIT.
2. those in the business of selling products are called *members of the trade.* As such, they receive DISCOUNTS from the price the public has to pay.
3. group of manufacturers who compete in the same market. These companies form trade associations and publish trade journals.
4. commercial companies that do business with each other. For example, ACCOUNTS PAYABLE to suppliers are called *trade accounts payable;* the term TRADE CREDIT is used to describe accounts payable as a source of WORKING CAPITAL financing. Companies paying their bills promptly receive *trade discounts* when available.
5. synonymous with BARTER, the exchange of goods and services without the use of money.

Securities: to carry out a transaction of buying or selling a stock, a bond, or a commodity future contract. A trade is consummated when a buyer and seller agree on a price at which the trade will be executed. A TRADER frequently buys and sells for his or her own account securities for short-term profits, as contrasted with an investor who holds his or her positions in hopes of long-term gains.

TRADE BALANCE *see* BALANCE OF TRADE.

TRADE CREDIT open account arrangements with suppliers of goods and services, and a firm's record of payment with the suppliers. Trade liabilities comprise a company's ACCOUNTS PAYABLE. DUN & BRADSTREET is the largest compiler of trade credit information, rating commercial firms and supplying published reports. Trade credit data is also processed by MERCANTILE AGENCIES specializing in different industries.

Trade credit is an important external source of WORKING CAPITAL for a company, although such credit can be highly expensive. Terms of 2% 10 days, net 30 days (2% discount if paid in 10 days, the net [full] amount due in 30 days) translate into a 36% annual interest rate if not taken advantage of. On the other hand, the same terms translate into a borrowing rate of slightly over 15% if payment is made in 60 days instead of 30. *See also* TRADE DEFICIT OR SURPLUS.

TRADE DATE day on which a security or a commodity future trade actually takes place. The SETTLEMENT DATE usually follows the trade date by 5 business days for futures and 3 days for securities, but varies depending on the transaction and method of delivery used. *See also* DELAYED DELIVERY; DELIVERY DATE; REGULAR-WAY DELIVERY (AND SETTLEMENT); SELLER'S OPTION.

TRADE DEFICIT OR SURPLUS excess of imports over exports *(trade deficit)* or of exports over imports *(trade surplus),* resulting in a negative or positive BALANCE OF TRADE. The balance of trade is made up of transactions in merchandise and other movable goods and is only one factor comprising the larger *current account* (which includes services and tourism, transportation, and other *invisible items,* such as interest and profits earned abroad) in the overall BALANCE OF PAYMENTS. Factors influencing a country's balance of trade include the strength or weakness of its currency in relation to those of the countries with which it trades (a weak Canadian dollar, for example, makes goods produced in other countries relatively expensive for Canadians), production advantages in key manufacturing areas (Japanese automobiles, for instance), or the domestic economy of a trading country where production may or may not be meeting demand.

TRADEMARK distinctive name, symbol, motto, or emblem that identifies a product, service, or firm. In Canada, trademark rights—the right to prevent competitors from using similar marks in selling or advertising—arise out of use; that is, registration is not essential to establish the legal existence of a mark. A trademark registered with the Industry Canada is good for 17 years, renewable as long as used. Products may be both patented and protected by trademark, the advantage being that when the patent runs out, exclusivity can be continued indefinitely with the trademark. A trademark is classified on a BALANCE SHEET as an INTANGIBLE ASSET.

   Although, like land, trademarks have an indefinite life and cannot technically be amortized, in practice accountants do amortize trademarks over their estimated life, not to exceed 17 years.

TRADER
In general: anyone who buys and sells goods or services for profit; a DEALER or *merchant. See also* BARTER; TRADE.
Investments:
1. individual who buys and sells securities, such as STOCKS, BONDS, OPTIONS, or commodities, such as wheat, gold, or FOREIGN EXCHANGE, for his or her own account—that is, as a dealer or PRINCIPAL—rather than as a BROKER or AGENT.
2. individual who buys and sells securities or commodities for his or her own account on a short-term basis in anticipation of quick profits; a *speculator. See also* DAY TRADE; COMPETITIVE TRADER; FLOOR TRADER; REGISTERED COMPETITIVE MARKET MAKER; REGISTERED COMPETITIVE TRADER; SPECULATION.

TRADE SURPLUS *see* TRADE DEFICIT OR SURPLUS.

TRADING AUTHORIZATION document giving a brokerage firm employee acting as AGENT (BROKER) the POWER OF ATTORNEY in buy-sell transactions for a customer.

TRADING HALT *see* SUSPENDED TRADING.

TRADING LIMIT *see* DAILY TRADING LIMIT; LIMIT UP, LIMIT DOWN.

TRADING PATTERN long-range direction of a security or commodity future price. This pattern is charted by drawing a line connecting the highest prices the security has reached and another line connecting the lowest prices the security has traded at over the same time frame. These two lines will be pointing either up or down, indicating the security's long-term trading pattern. *See also* TECHNICAL ANALYSIS, TRENDLINE.

TRADING PATTERN

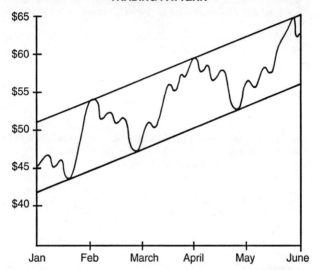

TRADING POST physical location on a stock exchange floor where particular securities are bought and sold. It is here that the SPECIALIST in a particular security performs his or her market-making functions and that the CROWD (floor brokers with orders in that security) congregates. The Toronto Stock Exchange, for example, has 7½ trading posts, most handling around 100 stocks. *See also* FLOOR BROKER; FLOOR TRADER; MAKE A MARKET.

TRADING PROFIT profit earned based on short-term trades. For assets such as stocks, bonds, futures contracts, and mutual funds held under a year, such trading profits are taxed at regular income tax rates. In general commerce, *trading profit* refers to the difference between what a product is sold for by a retailer and what it costs to buy or produce at the wholesale or producer level.

TRADING RANGE
  Commodities: trading limit set by a COMMODITIES futures exchange

for a particular commodity. The price of a commodity future contract may not go higher or lower than that limit during one day's trading. *See also* LIMIT UP, LIMIT DOWN.

Securities: range between the highest and lowest prices at which a security or a market has traded. The trading range for XYZ Corporation might be $40 to $60 over the last two years, for example. If a security or a market seems to be stuck in a narrow price range, analysts say that it is a trading range market, which will eventually be followed by a significant up or down move. *See also* FLAG; PENNANT; TRIANGLE; WEDGE.

TRADING UNIT number of SHARES, BONDS, or other securities that is generally accepted for ordinary trading purposes on the exchanges, *See also* ODD LOT; ROUND LOT; UNIT OF TRADING.

TRADING VARIATION fractions to which securities transaction prices are rounded. For example, stocks are rounded up or down to the nearest eighth of a point. Options over $3 are also rounded to an eighth, but options under $3 are rounded to $\frac{1}{16}$. Corporate bonds are rounded to $\frac{1}{8}$, medium- and long-term government bonds to $\frac{1}{32}$, and shorter-term government bonds to $\frac{1}{64}$. *See also* PLUS.

TRANCH CD *see* TRANCHES.

TRANCHES
1. in the United Kingdom, fixed-rate security issues are often prearranged by governments, local authorities, or corporations, then brought out in successive rounds, termed tranches. One thus speaks of new tranches of existing securities. A variation of the term, *tranchettes,* refers to small tranches of gilt-edged securities (government bonds) sold by the government to the Bank of England, which then sells them into the market at times it deems appropriate.
2. subunits of a large ($10–$30 million) Eurodollar certificate of deposit that are marketed to smaller investors in $10,000 denominations. Tranches are represented by separate certificates and have the same interest rate, issue date, interest payment date, and maturity of the original instrument, which is called a *tranch CD.*

TRANCHETTES *see* TRANCHES.

TRANSACTION
Accounting: event or condition recognized by an entry in the books of account.
Securities: execution of an order to buy or sell a security or commodity futures contract. After the buyer and seller have agreed on a price, the seller is obligated to deliver the security or commodity involved, and the buyer is obligated to accept it. *See also* TRADE.

TRANSACTION COSTS cost of buying or selling a security, which consists mainly of the *brokerage commission,* and the dealer MARKDOWN or markup or fee.

TRANSACTION DATE date on which the purchase or sale of a security takes place.

TRANSFER exchange of ownership of property from one party to another. For example, a piece of real estate may be transferred from seller to buyer through the execution of a sales contract. Securities and mutual funds are typically transferred through a transfer agent, who electronically switches ownership of the securities. In banking, *transfer* refers to the movement of funds from one account to another, such as from a savings account to a chequing account.

TRANSFER AGENT agent, usually a trust company, appointed by a corporation, to maintain records of stock and bond owners, to cancel and issue certificates, to resolve problems arising from lost, destroyed, or stolen certificates, and to send out dividend cheques.

TRANSFER PAYMENTS money transferred to people and the provinces from the government. Many payments under government benefit programs are considered transfer payments, including health care Canada pensions, disability payments, unemployment compensation, welfare, and veterans' benefits. A large portion of the federal government's yearly budget goes to make transfer payments.

TRANSFER PRICE price charged by individual entities in a multi-entity corporation on transactions among themselves; also termed *transfer cost*. This concept is used where each entity is managed as a PROFIT CENTRE—that is, held responsible for its own RETURN ON INVESTED CAPITAL—and must therefore deal with the other internal parts of the corporation on an arm's-length (or market) basis. *See also* ARM'S LENGTH TRANSACTION.

TRANSFER TAX
1. combined federal tax on gifts and estates. *See* ESTATE TAX; GIFT TAX.
2. federal tax on the sale of all bonds (except obligations of the United States, foreign governments, states, and municipalities) and all stocks. The tax is paid by the seller at the time ownership is transferred and involves a few pennies per $100 of value.
3. tax levied by some provinces on the transfer of such documents as deeds to property, securities, or licenses. Such taxes are paid, usually with stamps, by the seller or donor and are determined by the location of the transfer agent. Land transfer tax is most common on the sale of a property and the registration of the deed.

TRANSMITTAL LETTER letter sent with a document, security, or shipment describing the contents and the purpose of the transaction.

TRAVEL, ACCIDENT INSURANCE insurance that covers the policyholder while, he or she is traveling on company business. It can be purchased by an individual to benefit his or her family or by the company for which he or she works.

TRAVEL AND ENTERTAINMENT ACCOUNT separate account set up by an employer to track and reimburse employees' travel and entertainment expenses. Many employers give special credit cards to employees so that all travel and entertainment expenses can be tracked separately from personal expenses. Employers need to track travel and entertainment expenses carefully if they are to claim the appropriate tax deductions for these business expenses.

TRAVEL AND ENTERTAINMENT EXPENSE expense for travel and entertainment that may qualify for a tax deduction. Under current tax law, employers may deduct 50% of legitimate travel and entertainment expenses. Expenses are deductible if they are directly related to business. For example, a business meal must include a discussion that produces a direct business benefit.

TRAVELER'S CHEQUE cheque issued by a financial institution such as American Express, Visa, or Mastercard that allows travelers to carry travel funds in a more convenient way than cash. The traveler buys the cheques, often for a nominal fee, with cash, a credit card, or a regular cheque at a bank or travel service office and then signs each traveler's cheque. The cheque can then be used virtually anywhere in the world once it has been countersigned with the same signature. The advantage to the traveler is that the traveler's cheque cannot be used by someone else if it is lost or stolen, and can be replaced usually anywhere in the world. Traveler's cheques are also issued in many foreign currencies, allowing a traveler to lock in at a particular exchange rate before the trip begins. Many issuers of traveler's cheques offer a type of cheque that enables two travelers to share the same travel funds. American Express was the first issuer to introduce this form of cheque. Institutions issuing traveler's cheques profit from the FLOAT, earning interest on the money from the time the customer buys the cheque to the time they use the check.

TREASURER company officer responsible for the receipt, custody, investment, and disbursement of funds, for borrowings, and, if it is a public company, for the maintenance of a market for its securities. Depending on the size of the organization, the treasurer may also function as the CONTROLLER, with accounting and audit responsibilities. Provincial laws require only one officer for most corporations, functioning in several roles, but federal corporations have a secretary-treasurer. *See also* CHIEF FINANCIAL OFFICER (CFO).

TREASURY BILL commonly called a T-bill by money market people, a Treasury bill is a short-term government security issued for a term of 19 or 182 days and bought mainly by large institutional investors through stockbrokers and fully licenced investment dealers. They are issued in denominations of 1, 5, 10, 25, or 100 thousand dollars, or even 1 million dollars. They do not pay interest but are sold below their face value and then mature at their par value (i.e., discounted).

The difference between the issue price and the par value is in effect the interest payment.

TREASURY BILL FUND very specific type of money market mutual fund that invests very conservatively and exclusively in Treasury bills issued by the Government of Canada.

TREASURY BILL RATE interest payable on one-year government securities that are bought mainly by large institutional investors.

TREASURY SHARE authorized but unissued stock of a company or previously issued share that has been reacquired by the corporation.

TREASURY STOCK stock reacquired by the issuing company and available for RETIREMENT or resale. It is issued but not outstanding. It cannot be voted and it pays or accrues no dividends. It is not included in any of the ratios measuring values per common share. Among the reasons treasury stock is created are (1) to provide an alternative to paying taxable dividends, since the decreased amount of outstanding shares increases the per share value and often the market price; (2) to provide for the exercise of stock options and warrants and the conversion of convertible securities; (3) in countering a TENDER OFFER by a potential acquirer; (4) to alter the DEBT-TO-EQUITY RATIO by issuing bonds to finance the reacquisition of shares; (5) as a result of the STABILIZATION of the market price during a NEW ISSUE. Also called *reacquired stock* and *treasury shares. See also* ISSUED AND OUTSTANDING; UNISSUED STOCK.

TREND
In general: any general direction of movement. For example: "There is an upward (downward, level) trend in XYZ sales," or "There is a trend toward increased computerization of trading on Bay Street."
Securities: long-term price or trading volume movements either up, down, or sideways, which characterize a particular market, commodity or security. Also applies to interest rates and yields.

TRENDLINE line used by technical analysts to chart the past direction of a security or commodity future in order to help predict future price movements. The trendline is made by connecting the highest or lowest prices to which a security or commodity has risen or fallen within a particular time period. The angle of the resulting line will indicate if the security or commodity is in a downtrend or uptrend. If the price rises above a downward sloping trendline or drops below a rising uptrend line, technical analysts say that a new direction may be emerging. *See* chart on next page. *See also* TECHNICAL ANALYSIS; TRADING PATTERN.

TRIANGLE technical chart pattern that has two base points and a top point, formed by connecting a stock's price movements with a line. In a typical triangle pattern, the apex points to the right, although in reverse triangles the apex points to the left. In a typical triangle, there are a series of two or more rallies and price drops where each succeeding peak is lower than the preceding peak, and each bottom is higher than the preceding bottom. In a right-angled triangle, the sloping part of the formation often points in the direction of the breakout. Technical analysts find it significant when a security's price breaks out of the triangle formation, either up or down, because that usually means the security's price will continue in that direction. *See* chart on next page. *See also* PENNANT; TECHNICAL ANALYSIS; WEDGE.

TRENDLINE

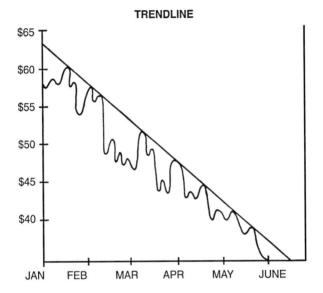

TRICKLE DOWN theory that economic growth can best be achieved by letting businesses flourish, since their prosperity will ultimately trickle down to middle- and lower-income people, who will benefit by increased economic activity. Proponents say that it produces more long-term growth than direct welfare grants to the middle- and lower-income sectors. *See also* SUPPLY-SIDE ECONOMICS.

TRIN measure of stock market strength that relates the ADVANCE-DECLINE ratio (the number of issues that advanced in price divided by the number of issues that declined in price) to the advance volume-decline volume ratio (the total number of shares that advanced divided by the total number of shares that declined). For example, if 800 stocks advanced and 750 issues declined while a total of 68 million shares advanced and 56 million shares declined, the trin would be calculated as follows:

$$\frac{\text{Advances } 800 \div \text{Declines } 750}{\text{Advance volume } 68{,}000{,}000 \div \text{Decline volume } 56{,}000{,}000} = \frac{1.067}{1.214}$$

$$= 0.88$$

A trin of under 1.00 is considered bullish while a trin over 1.00 is considered bearish. The above trin of 0.88 is thus a bullish sign. A trin based on closing figures is called a *closing trin. See also* CLOSING TICK.

TRIANGLE

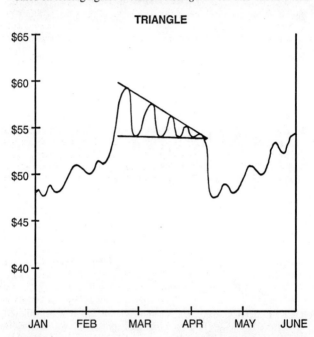

TRIPLE NET LEASE lease requiring tenants to pay all ongoing maintenance expenses such as utilities, taxes, insurance, and upkeep of the property. There are many LIMITED PARTNERSHIPS investing in triple net lease real estate deals. In such a deal, the limited partnership owns the property and collects rent, but the tenants pay most of the operating expenses. This results in higher returns for limited partners with lower risks, because tenants bear any increased costs for utilities, insurance, or taxes.

TRIPLE NINE highest purity of gold bullion or silver, .999 fineness or 99.9% pure.

TRIPLE WITCHING DAY in the United States, third Friday in March, June, September, and December when OPTIONS, INDEX OPTIONS, AND FUTURES CONTRACTS all expire simultaneously. At times there may be massive trades in index futures, options, and the underlying stocks by hedge strategists, arbitrageurs, and other investors, resulting in volatile markets on those days. In the past, all contracts expired in the same hour, but steps were taken so that contracts now expire at the open as well as the close of the day instead of all at once. Smaller-scale witching days occur in the other eight months, usually on the third Friday, when other options, index options, and futures contracts expire concurrently. *See also* DOUBLE WITCHING DAY.

TRUNCATION shortening of processing steps, in an effort to reduce paperwork and operating costs. For example, cheque truncation, or cheque SAFEKEEPING, where the bank holds the cheques or microfilm records of them in a central file.

TRUST
Business: type of corporate combination that engaged in monopolies and restraint of trade and that operated freely until the Competition Act of the late 19th century and early 20th century. The name derived from the use of the voting trust, in which a small number of trustees vote a majority of the shares of a corporation. The voting trust survives as a means of facilitating the reorganization of firms in difficulty. *See also* INVESTMENT COMPANY; VOTING TRUST CERTIFICATE.
Law: FIDUCIARY relationship in which a person, called a *trustee,* holds title to property for the benefit of another person, called a BENEFICIARY. The agreement that establishes the trust, contains its provisions, and sets forth the powers of the trustee is called the *trust indenture.* The person creating the trust is the *creator, settlor,* GRANTOR, or *donor;* the property itself is called the CORPUS, *trust res, trust fund,* or *trust estate,* which is distinguished from any income earned by it. If the trust is created while the donor is living, it is called a *living trust* or INTER VIVOS TRUST. A trust created by a will is called a TESTAMENTARY TRUST. The trustee is usually charged with investing trust property productively and, unless specifically limited, can sell, mortgage, or lease the property as he or she deems warranted. *See also* CHARITABLE REMAINDER TRUST; INVESTMENT TRUST; REVISIONARY TRUST; TRUST COMPANY; TRUSTEE IN BANKRUPTCY; TRUST INDENTURE ACT OF 1939.

TRUST COMPANY organization, usually combined with a bank, which is engaged as a trustee, FIDUCIARY, or AGENT for individuals or businesses in the administration of TRUST funds, estates, custodial arrangements, stock transfer and registration, and other related services. Trust companies also engage in fiduciary investment management functions and estate planning. They are regulated by provincial law.

TRUSTEE *see* TRUST.

TRUSTEE IN BANKRUPTCY trustee appointed by a court or by creditors to administer the affairs of a bankrupt company or individual. Under the Bankruptcy Act and Company's Creditors Arrangement Act, the trustee has the responsibility for liquidating the property of the company and making distributions of liquidating dividends to creditors. Under the bankruptcy provision, which provides for REORGANIZATION, a trustee may or may not be appointed. If one is, the trustee is responsible for seeing that a reorganization plan is filed and often assumes responsibility for the company.

TRUST FUND *see* TRUST.

TSE INDEX index of stock prices compiled and published by the Toronto Stock Exchange (TSE) initiated in 1934. In January, 1977 the present TSE 300 Composite Index Systems was introduced with historical series dating back to January, 1956.

This Composite Index measures changes in the market value of a portfolio of 300 stocks resulting from changes in the prices of the individual stocks. Each stock is weighted by the total number of shares outstanding (less known control blocks of 20% or more).

The 300 stocks have also been classified by the industry so that 14 major group indices and 43 sub-group indices are also computed. The base year for all stock price indices is 1975 when the base value was set equal to an index level of 1000.

In 1980, the TSE introduced a set of Total Return Indices, computed once a day, which complement the basic market value indices. They measure changes in the portfolio due only to stock price fluctuations but also to the reinvestment of dividends from the stocks. Thus, these indices show the compound return available from investing in stocks on a continuing basis. The base for all Total Return Indices was set equal to 1000 as of December 31, 1976.

Complete historical data on both sets of indices as well as related earnings, price-earnings ratio, dividends, and other data are available from the TSE. Generally, composite PE ratios are low and dividend yields are high when the market is at or near the bottom of a cycle. At market peaks, the opposite is true. However, factors such as new accounting procedures, or structural changes to the asset evaluation can affect PC valuations, making it necessary to proceed cautiously with any comparative analysis of PE levels.

The TSE introduced a 35-stock index on May 27, 1987. The index consists of 35 of the most widely traded stocks on the TSE.

Industry Grouping TSE 300 Composite Index

Metals and Minerals	15
Gold and Silver	25
Oil and Gas	39
Paper and Forest Products	18
Consumer Products	35
Industrial Products	42

Real Estate and Construction	10
Transportation	7
Pipelines	4
Utilities	17
Communications and Media	19
Merchandising	25
Financial Services	32
Conglomerates	11
TSE 300 Composite	300

Proportions TSE 300 Composite Index

Metals and Minerals	8.11
Gold and Silver	6.56
Oil and Gas	7.09
Paper and Forest Products	2.63
Consumer Products	11.23
Industrial Products	11.99
Real Estate and Construction	0.71
Transportation	2.33
Pipelines	2.26
Utilities	12.91
Communications and Media	5.49
Merchandising	4.11
Financial Services	18.99
Conglomerates	5.51
TSE 300 Composite	100.00

TSE 35 INDEX a 35-stock index composed of 35 of the largest Canadian companies drawn from a variety of industrial groups. The companies represented include: Air Canada, Alcan Aluminum, Bank of Montreal, Bank of Nova Scotia, BCE Inc., Bombardier Inc., Class B, Canadian Imperial Bank of Commerce, Canadian Pacific Ltd., Canadian Tire Corporation Limited, Echo Bay Mines Ltd., Gulf Canada Resources Limited, Imasco Limited, Imperial Oil Limited, Inco Limited, LAC Minerals Ltd., Laidlaw Inc., Class B, Maclean Hunter Limited, MacMillan Bloedel Incorporated, Moore Corporation Limited, National Bank of Canada, Noranda Inc., Nortel Limited, Nova Corporation of Alberta, Placer Dome Inc., Power Corporation of Canada, The Seagram Company Ltd., Stelco Inc., Series A.

TURKEY disappointing investment. The term may be used with reference to a business deal that went awry, or to the purchase of a stock or bond that dropped in value sharply, or to a new securities issue that did not sell well or had to be sold at a loss.

TURNAROUND favourable reversal in the fortunes of a company, a market, or the economy at large. Stock market investors speculating that a poorly performing company is about to show a marked improvement in earnings might profit handsomely from its turnaround.

TURNKEY any project constructed or manufactured by a company that ultimately turns it over in finished form to the company that will use it, so that all the user has to do is turn the key, so to speak, and the project is underway. The term is used of housing projects that, after construction, are turned over to property managers. There are also turnkey computer systems, for which the user needs no special computer knowledge and which can therefore be put right to work once they are installed.

TURNOVER
Finance:
1. number of times a given asset is replaced during an accounting period, usually a year. *See also* ACCOUNTS RECEIVABLE TURNOVER; INVENTORY TAKEOVER.
2. ratio of annual sales of a company to its NET WORTH, measuring the extent to which a company can grow without additional capital investment when compared over a period. *See also* CAPITAL TURNOVER.

Great Britain: annual sales volume.
Industrial relations: total employment divided by the number of employees replaced during a given period.
Securities: volume of shares traded as a percentage of total shares listed on an exchange during a period, usually either a day or a year. The same ratio is applied to individual securities and the portfolios of individual or institutional investors.

TWISTING unethical practice of convincing a customer to trade unnecessarily, thereby generating a commission for the broker or salesperson. Examples: A broker may induce a customer to sell one mutual fund with a sales charge in order to buy another fund, also with a sales charge, thereby generating a commission. A life insurance salesperson may persuade a policyholder to cancel his or her policy or allow it to lapse, in order to sell the insured a new policy, which would be more costly but which would produce sizable commissions for the salesperson. Also called CHURNING.

TWO-DOLLAR BROKER in the United States, FLOOR BROKER who executes orders for other brokers too busy to do it themselves; a "broker's broker." Such brokers once were paid two dollars for a ROUND LOT trade, hence the name. Today they receive a negotiated commission rate varying with the dollar value of the transaction. *See also* INDEPENDENT BROKER.

TWO-SIDED MARKET market in which both the BID AND ASKED sides are firm, such as that which a SPECIALIST and others who MAKE A MARKET are required to maintain. Both buyers and sellers are thus assured of their ability to complete transactions. Also called *two-way market.*

TWO-TIER BID TAKEOVER bid where the acquirer offers to pay more for the shares needed to gain control than for the remaining shares; contrasts with ANY-AND-ALL BID.

TWO-WAY SECURITY   security, usually a debenture or preferred share, which is convertible into, or exchangeable for, another security (usually common shares) of the same company. Also indirectly refers to the possibility of profiting in the future from upward movements in the underlying common shares as well as receiving in the interim interest or dividend payments.

U

ULTRA VIRES ACTIVITIES actions of a corporation that are not authorized by its charter and that may therefore lead to shareholder or third-party suits. *See also* ARTICLES OF INCORPORATION.

UNAMORTIZED BOND DISCOUNT difference between the FACE VALUE (par value) of a bond and the proceeds received from the sale of the bond by the issuing company, less whatever portion has been amortized, that is, written off to expense as recorded periodically on the PROFIT AND LOSS STATEMENT. At the time of issue, a company has two alternatives: (1) it can immediately absorb as an expense the amount of discount plus costs related to the issue, such as legal, printing, REGISTRATION, and other similar expenses, or (2) it can decide to treat the total discount and expenses as a DEFERRED CHARGE, recorded as an ASSET to be written off over the life of the bonds or by any other schedule the company finds desirable. The amount still to be expensed at any point is the unamortized bond discount.

UNAMORTIZED PREMIUMS ON INVESTMENTS unexpensed portion of the amount by which the price paid for a security exceeded its PAR value (if a BOND or PREFERRED STOCK) or MARKET VALUE (if common stock). A PREMIUM paid in acquiring an investment is in the nature of an INTANGIBLE ASSET, and conservative accounting practice dictates it be written off to expense over an appropriate period. *See also* GOING-CONCERN VALUE.

UNBUNDLING trend in banking toward costing and pricing separately for services provided.

UNCERTAINTY term that refers to the variability of outcomes associated with a specific project or event. In a statistical sense, uncertainty is used when a decision maker has no historical data from which to develop a probability distribution.

UNCOLLECTED FUNDS portion of bank deposit made up of cheques that have not yet been collected by the depository bank—that is, payment has not yet been acknowledged by the bank on which a cheque was drawn. A bank will usually not let a depositor draw on uncollected funds. *See also* FLOAT.

UNCOLLECTIBLE ACCOUNT customer account that cannot be collected because of the customer's unwillingness or inability to pay. A business normally writes off such a receivable as worthless after several attempts at collecting the funds.

UNCOVERED OPTION short option that is not fully collateralized. A short call position is uncovered if the writer does not have long stock to deliver or does not own another call on the same security with a lower or same strike price, and with a longer or same time of expiration. Also called NAKED OPTION. *See also* NAKED POSITION; COVERED OPTION; COVERED WRITER.

UNCOVERED WRITER   writer (seller) who has sold stock or an option contract for stock that he or she does not own.

UNDERBANKED said of a NEW ISSUE underwriting when the originating INVESTMENT BANKER is having difficulty getting other firms to become members of the UNDERWRITING GROUP, or syndicate. *See also* UNDERWRITE.

UNDERBOOKED said of a NEW ISSUE of securities during the preoffering REGISTRATION period when brokers canvassing lists of prospective buyers report limited INDICATIONS OF INTEREST. The opposite of underbooked would be *fully circled. See also* CIRCLE.

UNDERCAPITALIZATION situation in which a business does not have enough capital to carry out its normal business functions. *See also* CAPITALIZATION; WORKING CAPITAL.

UNDERLYING INTEREST   interest that, in the case of an index option, is the index that is the subject of the option. *See* UNDERLYING SECURITY.

UNDERLYING INTEREST OPTION   interest that, for equity options, is covered by one option contract. It is generally 100 shares of a specific common stock.

UNDERLYING SECURITY
Options: security that must be delivered if a PUT OPTION or CALL OPTION contract is exercised. Stock INDEX OPTIONS and STOCK INDEX FUTURES, however, are settled in cash, since it is not possible to deliver an index of stocks.
Securities: common stock that underlies certain types of securities issued by corporations. This stock must be delivered if a SUBSCRIPTION WARRANT or SUBSCRIPTION RIGHT is exercised, if a CONVERTIBLE bond or PREFERRED STOCK is converted into common shares, or if an INCENTIVE STOCK OPTION is exercised.

UNDERMARGINED ACCOUNT MARGIN ACCOUNT that has fallen below MARGIN REQUIREMENTS or MINIMUM MAINTENANCE requirements. As a result, the broker must make a MARGIN CALL to the customer.

UNDERSUBSCRIBED   new issue of shares or bonds that is not sold out.

UNDERVALUED security selling below its LIQUIDATION value or the MARKET VALUE analysts believe it deserves. A company's stock may be undervalued because the industry is out of favour, because the company is not well known or has an erratic history of earnings, or for many other reasons. Fundamental analysts try to spot companies that are undervalued so their clients can buy before the stocks become

FULLY VALUED. Undervalued companies are also frequently targets of TAKEOVER attempts, since acquirers can buy assets cheaply this way. *See also* FUNDAMENTAL ANALYSIS.

UNDERWATER OPTION OUT-OF-THE MONEY option. Being out of the money indicates the option has no intrinsic value; all of its value consists of time value. A call option is out of the money if its exercise price is higher than the current price of the underlying contract. A put option is out of the money if its exercise price is lower than the current price of the underlying contract.

UNDERWITHHOLDING situation in which taxpayers have too little federal, or provincial income tax withheld from their salaries. Because they have underwithheld, these taxpayers may owe income taxes when they file their tax returns. If the underwithholding is large enough, penalties and interest also may be due.

UNDERWRITE
Insurance: to assume risk in exchange for a PREMIUM.
Investments: to assume the risk of buying a NEW ISSUE of securities from the issuing corporation or government entity and reselling them to the public, either directly or through dealers. The UNDERWRITER makes a profit on the difference between the price paid to the issuer and the PUBLIC OFFERING PRICE, called the UNDERWRITING SPREAD.

Underwriting is the business of investment bankers, who usually form an UNDERWRITING GROUP (also called a PURCHASE GROUP or syndicate) to pool the risk and assure successful distribution of the issue. The syndicate operates under an AGREEMENT AMONG UNDERWRITERS, also termed a *syndicate contract* or PURCHASE GROUP contract.

The underwriting group appoints a MANAGING UNDERWRITER, also known as *lead underwriter, syndicate manager,* or simply *manager,* that is usually the *originating investment banker*—the firm that began working with the issuer months before to plan details of the issue and prepare the REGISTRATION materials to be filed with the SECURITIES COMMISSION. The manager, acting as agent for the group, signs the UNDERWRITING AGREEMENT (or *purchase contract*) with the issuer. This agreement sets forth the terms and conditions of the arrangement and the responsibilities of both issuer and underwriter. During the offering period, it is the manager's responsibility to stabilize the MARKET PRICE of the issuer's shares by bidding in the open market, a process called PEGGING. The manager may also appoint a SELLING GROUP, comprising dealers and the underwriters themselves, to assist in DISTRIBUTION of the issue.

Strictly speaking, *underwrite* is properly used only in a FIRM COMMITMENT underwriting, also known as a BOUGHT DEAL, where the securities are purchased outright from the issuer.

Other investment banking arrangements to which the term is sometimes loosely applied are BEST EFFORT, ALL OR NONE, and STANDBY COMMITMENTS; in each of these, the risk is shared between the issuer and the INVESTMENT BANKER.

The term is also sometimes used in connection with a REGISTERED SECONDARY OFFERING, which involves essentially the same process as a new issue, except that the proceeds go to the selling investor, not to the issuer. For these arrangements, the term *secondary offering* or SECONDARY DISTRIBUTION is preferable to *underwriting,* which is usually reserved for new, or primary, distributions.

There are two basic methods by which underwriters are chosen by issuers and underwriting spreads are determined: NEGOTIATED UNDERWRITINGS and COMPETITIVE BID underwritings. Generally, the negotiated method is used in corporate equity (stock) issues and most corporate debt (bond) issues, whereas the competitive bidding method is used by municipalities and public utilities.

See also ALLOTMENT; BLOWOUT; FLOATING AN ISSUE; FLOTATION COST; HOT ISSUE; INITIAL PUBLIC OFFERING; PRESOLD ISSUE; PRIMARY MARKET; PUBLIC OFFERING; STANDBY UNDERWRITER.

UNDERWRITER
Insurance: company that assumes the cost risk of death, fire, theft, illness, etc., in exchange for payments, called *premiums.*
Securities: INVESTMENT BANKER who, singly or as a member of an UNDERWRITING GROUP or syndicate, agrees to purchase a NEW ISSUE of securities from an issuer and distribute it to investors, making a profit on the UNDERWRITING SPREAD. *See also* UNDERWRITE.

UNDERWRITING AGREEMENT agreement between a corporation issuing new securities to be offered to the public and the MANAGING UNDERWRITER as agent for the UNDERWRITING GROUP. Also termed the *purchase agreement* or *purchase contract,* it represents the underwriters' commitment to purchase the securities, and it details the PUBLIC OFFERING PRICE, the UNDERWRITING SPREAD (including all discounts and commissions), the net proceeds to the issuer, and the SETTLEMENT DATE.

The issuer agrees to pay all expenses incurred in preparing the issue for resale, including the costs of REGISTRATION with the SECURITIES COMMISSION and of the PROSPECTUS, and agrees to supply the managing underwriter with sufficient copies of both the PRELIMINARY PROSPECTUS (red herring) and the final, statutory prospectus. The issuer guarantees (1) to make all required securities filings; (2) to assume responsibility for the completeness, accuracy, and proper certification of all information in the registration statement and prospectus; (3) to disclose all pending litigation; (4) to use the proceeds for the purposes stated; (5) to comply with provincial securities laws; (6) to work to get listed on the exchange agreed upon; and (7) to indemnify the underwriters for liability arising out of omissions or misrepresentations for which the issuer had responsibility.

The underwriters agree to proceed with the offering as soon as the registration is cleared by the Securities Commission or at a specified date thereafter. The underwriters are authorized to make sales to members of a SELLING GROUP.

The underwriting agreement is not to be confused with the AGREEMENT AMONG UNDERWRITERS. *See also* BEST EFFORT; FIRM COMMITMENT; STANDBY COMMITMENT; UNDERWRITE.

UNDERWRITING GROUP temporary association of investment bankers, organized by the originating INVESTMENT BANKER in a NEW ISSUE of securities. Operating under an AGREEMENT AMONG UNDERWRITERS, it agrees to purchase securities from the issuing corporation at an agreed-upon price and to resell them at a PUBLIC OFFERING PRICE, the difference representing the UNDERWRITING SPREAD. The purpose of the underwriting group is to spread the risk and assure successful distribution of the offering. Most underwriting groups operate under a *divided syndicate contract,* meaning that the liability of members is limited to their individual participations. Also called DISTRIBUTING SYNDICATE, PURCHASE GROUP, *investment banking group,* or *syndicate. See also* FIRM COMMITMENT; UNDERWRITE; UNDERWRITING AGREEMENT.

UNDERWRITING SPREAD difference between the amount paid to an issuer of securities in a PRIMARY DISTRIBUTION and the PUBLIC OFFERING PRICE. The amount of SPREAD varies widely, depending on the size of the issue, the financial strength of the issuer, the type of security involved (stock, bonds, rights), the status of the security (senior, junior, secured, unsecured), and the type of commitment made by the investment bankers. The range may be from a fraction of 1% for a bond issue of a big company to 25% for the INITIAL PUBLIC OFFERING of a small company. The division of the spread between the MANAGING UNDERWRITER, the SELLING GROUP, and the participating underwriters also varies, but in a two-point spread the manager might typically get 0.25%, the selling group 1%, and the underwriters 0.75%. It is usual, though, for the underwriters also to be members of the selling group, thus picking up 1.75% of the spread, and for the manager to be in all three categories, thus picking up the full 2%. *See also* COMPETITIVE BID; FLOTATION COST; GROSS SPREAD; NEGOTIATED UNDERWRITING; SELLING CONCESSION; UNDERWRITE.

UNDIGESTED SECURITIES newly issued stocks and bonds that remain undistributed because there is insufficient public demand at the OFFERING PRICE. *See also* UNDERWRITE.

UNDISTRIBUTED PROFITS (EARNINGS, NET INCOME) *see* RETAINED EARNINGS.

UNDIVIDED PROFITS account shown on a bank's BALANCE SHEET representing profits that have neither been paid out as DIVIDENDS nor transferred to the bank's SURPLUS account. Current earnings are credited to the undivided profits account and are then either paid out in dividends or retained to build up total EQUITY. As the account grows, round amounts may be periodically transferred to the surplus account.

UNEARNED DISCOUNT account on the books of a lending institution recognizing interest deducted in advance and which will be taken into income as earned over the life of the loan. In accordance with accounting principles, such interest is initially recorded as a LIABILITY. Then, as months pass and it is gradually "earned," it is recognized as income, thus increasing the lender's profit and decreasing the corresponding liability. *See also* UNEARNED INCOME.

UNEARNED INCOME (REVENUE)

Accounting: income received but not yet earned, such as rent received in advance or other advances from customers. Unearned income is usually classified as a CURRENT LIABILITY on a company's BALANCE SHEET, assuming that it will be credited to income within the normal accounting cycle. *See also* DEFERRED CHARGE.

Income taxes: income from sources other than wages, salaries, tips, and other employee compensation—for example, DIVIDENDS, INTEREST, rent.

UNEARNED INTEREST interest that has already been collected on a loan by a financial institution, but that cannot yet be counted as part of earnings because the principal of the loan has not been outstanding long enough. Also called DISCOUNT and UNEARNED DISCOUNT.

UNEMPLOYED OR UNEMPLOYMENT condition of being out of work involuntarily. The federal unemployment insurance commission makes cash payments directly to laid-off workers. There are up to 52 weeks of payments for those who have worked at least 12 weeks a year or more. In general, to collect unemployment benefits a person must have previously held a job and must be actively seeking employment. Unemployed people apply for and collect unemployment compensation from the federal government. The system is financed both by worker and employee contributions.

UNEMPLOYMENT INSURANCE COMMISSION federal commission that oversees unemployment insurance for short-term out-of-work employees.

UNEMPLOYMENT RATE percentage of the labour force actively looking for work but unable to find jobs. The rate is compiled by Statistics Canada, and released to the public on the first Friday of every month. The unemployment rate is affected by the number of people entering the workforce as well as the number of unemployed people and it is adjusted for seasonal occurrences such as the influx of students in the summer months and the loss of jobs in fishing, forest, and construction industries in the winter months which covers data on hours, earnings, and employment. The unemployment report is one of the most closely watched of all government reports, because it gives the clearest indication of the direction of the economy. A rising unemployment rate will be seen by analysts and the Bank of Canada as a sign of a weakening economy, which might call for an easing of monetary policy by the Bank. On the other hand, a drop in the unemployment rate shows that the economy is growing, which may spark fears of higher inflation on the part of the Bank, which may raise interest rates as a result.

UNENCUMBERED property free and clear of all liens (creditors' claims). When a homeowner pays off his or her mortgage, for example, the house becomes unencumbered property. Securities bought with cash instead of on MARGIN are unencumbered.

UNFUNDED PENSION PLAN pension plan that is funded by the employer out of current income as funds are required by retirees or beneficiaries. Also known as a *pay-as-you-go* pension plan, or a plan using the *current disbursement funding approach.* This contrasts with an ADVANCE FUNDED PENSION PLAN, under which the employer puts aside money on a regular basis into a separate fund that is invested in stocks, bonds, real estate, and other assets.

UNIFORM COMMERCIAL CODE (UCC) in the United States, legal code adopted by most states that codifies various laws dealing with commercial transactions, primarily those involving the sale of goods, both tangible and intangible, and secured transactions. It was drafted by the National Conference of Commissioners of Uniform State Laws and covers bank deposits, bankruptcy, commercial letters of credit, commercial paper, warranties, and other commercial activities. Article 8 of the UCC applies to transactions in investment securities.

UNIFORM PRACTICE CODE rules of the NATIONAL ASSOCIATION OF SECURITIES DEALERS (NASD) concerned with standards and procedures for the operational handling of OVER THE COUNTER securities transactions, such as delivery, SETTLEMENT DATE, EX-DIVIDEND DATE, and other ex-dates (such as EX-RIGHTS and EX-WARRANTS), and providing for the arbitration of disputes through Uniform Practice committees.

UNISSUED STOCK shares of a corporation's stock authorized in its charter but not issued. They are shown on the BALANCE SHEET along with shares ISSUED AND OUTSTANDING. Unissued stock may be issued by action of the board of directors, although shares needed for unexercised employee STOCK OPTIONS, rights, warrants, or convertible securities must not be issued while such obligations are outstanding. Unissued shares cannot pay dividends and cannot be voted. They are not to be confused with TREASURY STOCK, which is issued but not outstanding.

UNIT

In general: any division of quantity accepted as a standard of measurement or of exchange. For example, in the commodities markets, a unit of wheat is a bushel, a unit of coffee a pound, and a unit of shell eggs a dozen. The unit of the Canadian currency is the dollar.

Banking: bank operating out of only one office, and with no branches, as required by states having unit banking laws.

Finance:

1. segment or subdivision (division or subsidiary, product line, or plant) of a company.

2. in sales or production, quantity rather than dollars. One might say, for example, "Unit volume declined but dollar volume increased after prices were raised."

Securities:

1. minimum amount of stocks, bonds, commodities, or other securities accepted for trading on an exchange. *See also* ODD LOT; ROUND LOT; UNIT OF TRADING.
2. group of specialists on a stock exchange, who maintain fair and orderly markets in particular securities. *See also* SPECIALIST; SPECIALIST UNIT.
3. more than one class of securities traded together; one common share and one SUBSCRIPTION WARRANT might sell as a unit, for example.
4. in primary and secondary distributions of securities, one share of stock or one bond.

UNITED STATES GOVERNMENT SECURITIES direct GOVERNMENT OBLIGATIONS—that is, debt issues of the U.S. government, such as Treasury bills, notes, and bonds and Series EE and Series HH SAVINGS BONDS as distinguished from government-sponsored AGENCY issues. *See also* GOVERNMENT SECURITIES; TREASURIES.

UNITIZATION combining of producing leases in oil and gas wells to be managed by an operator in which each working interest has a predetermined fixed equity. This makes for economies in futures costs.

UNIT OF TRADING normal number of shares, bonds, or commodities comprising the minimum unit of trading on an exchange. For stocks, this is usually 100 shares, although inactive shares trade in 10-share units. For corporate bonds on the TSE, the unit for exchange trading is $1000 or $5000 par value. Commodities futures units vary widely, according to the COMMODITY involved. *See also* FUTURES CONTRACT; ODD LOT; ROUND LOT.

UNIVERSAL LIFE INSURANCE form of life insurance that combines the low-cost protection of TERM LIFE INSURANCE with a savings portion, which is invested in a tax-deferred account earning money-market rates of interest, although these rates are not guaranteed. The policy is flexible; that is, as age and income change, a policyholder can increase or decrease premium payments and coverage, or shift a certain portion of premiums into the savings account, without additional sales charges or complications. A new form of the policy; called *universal variable life insurance,* combines the flexibility of universal life with the growth potential of variable life. *See also* VARIABLE LIFE INSURANCE; WHOLE LIFE INSURANCE.

UNIVERSE OF SECURITIES group of stocks sharing a common characteristic. For example, one analyst may define a universe of securities as those with $100 to $500 million in outstanding market capitalization. Another may define it as stocks in a particular industry, such as communications, paper, or airlines. A mutual fund will often define itself to investors as limiting itself to a particular universe of securities, allowing investors to know in advance which kinds of securities that fund will buy and hold.

UNLISTED SECURITY security that is not listed on an organized exchange, such as the TORONTO, MONTREAL, VANCOUVER, NEW YORK, or the AMERICAN STOCK EXCHANGE, and is traded in the OVER THE COUNTER market.

UNLISTED TRADING trading of securities not listed on an organized exchange but traded on that exchange as an accommodation to its members. An exchange wishing to trade unlisted securities must file an application with the SECURITIES COMMISSION and make the necessary information available to the investing public.

UNLOADING
Finance: selling off large quantities of merchandise inventory at below-market prices either to raise cash quickly or to depress the market in a particular product.
Investments: selling securities or commodities when prices are declining to preclude further loss.
See also PUMP; PROFIT TAKING; SELLING OFF.

UNMARGINED ACCOUNT brokerage CASH ACCOUNT.

UNPAID DIVIDEND dividend that has been declared by a corporation but has still not been paid. A company may declare a dividend on July 1, for example, payable on August 1. During July, the declared dividend is called an unpaid dividend. *See also* EX-DIVIDEND.

UNQUALIFIED OPINION independent auditor's opinion that a company's financial statements are fairly presented, in all material respects, in conformity with generally accepted accounting principles. The justification for the expression of the auditor's opinion rests on the conformity of his or her audit with generally accepted auditing standards and on his or her feelings. Materiality and audit risk underly the application of auditing standards. *See also* ACCOUNTANT'S OPINION; ADVERSE OPINION; QUALIFIED OPINION.

UNREALIZED PROFIT (OR LOSS) profit or loss that has not become actual. It becomes a REALIZED PROFIT (OR LOSS) when the security or commodity future contract in which there is a gain or loss is actually sold. Also called a *paper profit or loss.*

UNREGISTERED STOCK *see* LETTER SECURITY.

UNSECURED DEBT obligation not backed by the pledge of specific COLLATERAL.

UNSECURED LOAN loan without COLLATERAL.

UNSYSTEMATIC RISK firm, specific risk caused by events peculiar to one company only and not to the entire market.

UNWIND A TRADE to reverse a securities transaction through an offsetting transaction. *See also* OFFSET.

UPGRADING increase in the quality rating of a security. An analyst may upgrade a company's bond or stock rating if its finances improve, profitability is enhanced, and its debt level is reduced. For municipal bond issues, upgrading will occur if tax revenues increase and expenses are reduced. The upgrading of a stock or bond issue may in itself raise the price of the security because investors will feel more confident in the financial soundness of the issuer. The credit rating of issuers is constantly being evaluated, which may lead to further upgradings, or, if conditions deteriorate, downgradings. The term *upgrading* is also applied to an entire portfolio of securities. For example, a mutual fund manager who wants to improve the quality of his or her bond holdings will say that he or she is in the process of upgrading his portfolio.

UPSET PRICE term used in auctions that represents the minimum price at which a seller of property will entertain bids.

UPSIDE POTENTIAL amount of upward price movement an investor or an analyst expects of a particular stock, bond, or commodity. This opinion may result from either FUNDAMENTAL ANALYSIS or TECHNICAL ANALYSIS.

UPSTAIRS MARKET transaction completed within the broker-dealer's firm and without using the stock exchange. Securities and Exchange Commission and stock exchange rules exist to ensure that such trades do not occur at prices less favourable to the customer than those prevailing in the general market. *See also* OFF BOARD.

UPSWING upward movement in the price of a security or commodity after a period of falling prices. Analysts will say "that stock has bottomed out and now has started an upswing which should carry it to new highs." The term is also used to refer to the general condition of the economy. An economy that is recovering from a prolonged downturn or recession is said to be in an upswing.

UPTICK transaction executed at a price higher than the preceding transaction in that security; also called PLUS TICK. A plus sign is displayed throughout the day next to the last price of each stock that showed a higher price than the preceding transaction in that stock at the TRADING POST of the SPECIALIST on the floor of the Toronto Stock Exchange. Short sales may only be executed on upticks or ZERO-PLUS TICKS. *See* also MINUS TICK; SELLING SHORT; TICK.

UPTICK RULE Securities and Exchange Commission rule that selling short may only be done on an UPTICK. In 1990, interpretation of the rule was extended to cover PROGRAM TRADING.

UPTREND upward direction in the price of a stock, bond, or commodity future contract or overall market. *See also* TRENDLINE.

USEFUL LIFE estimated period of time during which an asset subject to DEPRECIATION is judged to be productive in a business. Also called *depreciable life.*

USES OF FUNDS *see* SOURCES AND APPLICATIONS (OR USES) OF FUNDS STATEMENT.

USURY LAWS federal laws limiting excessive interest rates on loans.

UTILITY power company that owns or operates facilities used for the generation, transmission, or distribution of electric energy. Utilities provide electric, gas, and water to their customers. Many are controlled by municipalities. In the United States, utilities are regulated at the state and federal level. Public utility commissions regulate retail rates.

V

VALUABLE PAPERS   *see* OFFICE CONTENT INSURANCE/VALUABLE PAPERS.

VALUATION placing a value or worth on an asset. Stock analysts determine the value of a company's stock based on the outlook for earnings and the market value of assets on the balance sheet. Stock valuation is normally expressed in terms of price/earnings (P/E) ratios. A company with a high P/E is said to have a high valuation, and a low P/E stock has a low valuation. Other assets, such as real estate and bonds, are given valuations by analysts who recommend whether the asset is worth buying or selling at the current price. Estates also go through the valuation process after someone has died.

VALUATION RESERVE reserve or allowance, created by a charge to expenses (and therefore, in effect, taken out of profits) in order to provide for changes in the value of a company's assets. Accumulated DEPRECIATION, allowance for BAD DEBTS, and UNAMORTIZED BOND DISCOUNT are three familiar examples of valuation reserves. Also called *valuation account.*

VALUE-ADDED TAX (VAT) consumption tax levied on the value added to a product at each stage of its manufacturing cycle as well as at the time of purchase by the ultimate consumer. The value-added tax is a fixture in European countries and a major source of revenue for the European Community. Advocates of retaining Canada's value-added tax (the GSI) contend that it is the most efficient method of raising revenue and that the size of its receipts would eventually permit a reduction in income tax rates. Opponents argue that in its pure form it is the equivalent of a national sales tax and therefore unfair and regressive, putting the greatest burden on those who can least afford it. As an example, for each part that goes into the assembling of an automobile, the auto manufacturer pays a value-added tax to the supplier. When the finished car is sold, the consumer pays a value-added tax on the cost of the finished product less the material and supply costs that were taxed at earlier stages. This avoids double taxation and thus differs from a flat sales tax based on the total cost of purchase.

VALUE CHANGE change in a stock price adjusted for the number of outstanding shares of that stock, so that a group of stocks adjusted this way are equally weighted. A unit of movement of the group—called an INDEX—is thus representative of the average performance.

VALUE DATE
  Banking: official date when money is transferred, that is, becomes good funds to the depositor. The value date differs from the *entry date* when items are received from the depositor, since the items must then

be forwarded to the paying bank or otherwise collected. The term is used mainly with reference to foreign accounts, either maintained in a domestic bank or maintained by a domestic bank in foreign banks. *See also* FLOAT.

Eurodollar and foreign currency transactions: synonymous with SETTLEMENT DATE or DELIVERY DATE, which on spot transactions involving North American currencies (Canadian dollar, U.S. dollar, and Mexican peso) is one business day and on spot transactions involving other currencies, two business days. In the forward exchange market, value date is the maturity date of the contract plus one business day for North American currencies, two business days for other currencies. *See also* FORWARD EXCHANGE TRANSACTION; SETTLEMENT DATE; SPOT MARKET.

VALUE LINE INVESTMENT SURVEY in the United States, investment advisory service that ranks about 1700 stocks for "timeliness" and safety. Using a computerized model based on earnings momentum, Value Line projects which stocks will have the best or worst relative price performance over the next 6 to 12 months. In addition, each stock is assigned a risk rating, which identifies the VOLATILITY of a stock's price behaviour relative to the market average. The service also ranks all major industry groups for timeliness. Value Line's ranking system for both timeliness and safety of an individual stock is as follows:

       1—highest rank
       2—above average rank
       3—average rank
       4—below average rank
       5—lowest rank

The weekly writeups of companies that Value Line subscribers receive include detailed financial information about a company, as well as such data as corporate INSIDER buying and selling decisions and the percentage of a company's shares held by institutions.

Value Line offers several specialized financial surveys. The *Value Line Convertibles Survey* is a subscription service that evaluates convertible securities. The *Value Line Mutual Fund Survey* offers details on fund holdings and performance and ranks funds on expected returns. Value Line also sponsors its own family of mutual funds. Value Line also produces several stock indices and averages, the most important of which is the *Value Line Composite Average,* which tracks the stocks followed by the *Value Line Investment Survey.*

VALUE OF SHARES value of the shares to be issued as stock in place of the dividend; when such is to be paid. The Board of Directors, makes the decision, and the value is usually the market value of the shares on the record date.

VALUE OF STOCK DIVIDEND number of shares owned × dividend value per share × market value per share on the record date or that set by the board of directors.

VANCOUVER STOCK EXCHANGE securities and options exchange in Vancouver, British Columbia, incorporated by Special Act of the B.C. Legislature in 1907. The VSE specializes in venture capital companies. Its securities market trades stocks, rights, warrants, and units, while its options market focuses on equity and gold options. Mining stocks account for most of the trading, with junior mining companies making up the largest single group. Billions of dollars have been raised by natural resource companies on the exchange. The number of technology, entertainment, real estate, and financial services companies listed on the exchange is increasing. Traditionally between 10% and 20% of the financings originate in the United States, with 20% to 25% from Europe and Asia. The *VSE Index* (100.00—January 1982), is capital-weighted and comprises three sub-indices: Commercial/Industrial, Resource, and Venture. In 1990, with the introduction of Vancouver Computerized Trading (VCT), the VSE became the first North American exchange to convert from open outcry to a completely automated trading system with over 150 trading terminals now located in member firms offices. Computerized clearing is conducted through the West Canada Clearing Corp. Settlement is on the third business day following a trade. The VSE's address is Stock Exchange Tower, P.O. Box 10333, 609 Granville Street, Vancouver, BC V7Y 1H1, and trading hours are 9 A.M. to 5 P.M., Monday through Friday.

VARIABLE ANNUITY life insurance ANNUITY contract whose value fluctuates with that of an underlying securities PORTFOLIO or other INDEX of performance. The variable annuity contrasts with a conventional or FIXED ANNUITY, whose rate of return is constant and therefore vulnerable to the effects of inflation. Income on a variable annuity may be taken periodically, beginning immediately or at any future time. The annuity may be a single-premium or multiple-premium contract. The return to investors may be in the form of a periodic payment that varies with the MARKET VALUE of the portfolio or a fixed minimum payment with add-ons based on the rate of portfolio appreciation. *See also* SINGLE PREMIUM DEFERRED ANNUITY.

VARIABLE CAPITAL form of equity investment. Applies to businesses on which there is a possibility of unusually high returns along with generally high risks for the investor.

VARIABLE COST cost that changes directly with the amount of production—for example, direct material or direct labour needed to complete a product. As sales fluctuate, so do variable costs. *See also* FIXED COST.

VARIABLE INTEREST RATE interest rate on a loan that rises and falls based on the movement of an underlying index of interest rates. For example, many credit cards charge variable interest rates, based on a specific spread over the prime rate. Most home equity loans charge variable rates tied to the prime rate. Also called *adjustable interest rate.*

VARIABLE LIFE INSURANCE innovation in WHOLE LIFE INSURANCE that allows the cash value of the policy to be invested in stock, bond, or money market portfolios. Investors can elect to move from one portfolio to another or can rely on the company's professional money managers to make such decisions for them. As in whole life insurance, the annual premium is fixed, but part of it is earmarked for the investment PORTFOLIO. The policyholder bears the risk of securities investments, while the insurance company guarantees a minimum death benefit unaffected by any portfolio losses. When portfolio investments rise substantially, a portion of the increased cash value is put into additional insurance coverage. As in usual whole life policies, borrowings can be made against the accumulated cash value, or the policy can be cashed in.

Variable life insurance is different from UNIVERSAL LIFE INSURANCE. Universal life allows policyholders to increase or decrease premiums and change the death benefit. It also accrues interest at market-related rates on premiums over and above insurance charges and expenses.

VARIABLE RATE *see* FLOATING RATE.

VARIABLE-RATE DEMAND NOTE note representing borrowings (usually from a commercial bank) that is payable on demand and that bears interest tied to the bank PRIME RATE. The rate on the note is adjusted upward or downward each time the base rate changes.

VARIABLE RATE MORTGAGE (VRM) *see* ADJUSTABLE RATE MORTGAGE (ARM).

VARIABLE RATE PREFERRED STOCK *see* ADJUSTABLE RATE PREFERRED STOCK (ARP).

VARIANCE
Accounting: difference between actual cost and STANDARD COST in the categories of direct material, direct labour, and DIRECT OVERHEAD. A positive variation (when the actual cost is lower than the standard or anticipated cost) would translate into a higher profit unless offset by negative variances elsewhere.
Finance: (1) difference between corresponding items on a comparative BALANCE SHEET and PROFIT AND LOSS STATEMENT. (2) difference between actual experience and budgeted or projected experience in any financial category. For example, if sales were projected to be $2 million for a period and were actually $2.5 million, there would be a positive variance of $500,000, or 25%.
Real estate: allowed exception to zoning rules. If a particular neighbourhood were zoned for residential use only, a person wanting to open a store would need to be granted a variance from the zoning board in order to proceed.
Statistics: measure of the dispersion of a distribution. It is the sum of the squares of the deviation from the mean. *See also* STANDARD DEVIATION.

VELOCITY rate of spending, or turnover of money—in other words, how many times a dollar is spent in a given period of time. The more money turns over, the faster velocity is said to be. The concept of "income velocity of money" was first explained by the economist Irving Fisher in the 1920s as bearing a direct relationship to GROSS DOMESTIC PRODUCT (GDP). Velocity usually is measured as the ratio of GDP to the money supply. Velocity affects the amount of economic activity generated by a given money supply, which includes bank deposits and cash in circulation. Velocity is a factor in the Bank of Canada's management of MONETARY POLICY, because an increase in velocity may obviate the need for a stimulative increase in the money supply. Conversely, a decline in velocity might reflect dampened economic growth, even if the money supply holds steady. *See also* FISCAL POLICY.

VENDOR
1. supplier of goods or services of a commercial nature; may be a manufacturer, importer, or wholesale distributor. For example, one component of the Index of LEADING INDICATORS is vendor performance, meaning the rate at which suppliers of goods are making delivery to their commercial customers.
2. retailer of merchandise, especially one without an established place of business, as in *sidewalk vendor.*

VENTURE CAPITAL important source of financing for START-UP companies or others embarking on new or TURNAROUND ventures that entail some investment risk but offer the potential for above average future profits; also called *risk capital.* Sources of venture capital include wealthy individual investors; groups of investment banks and other financing sources who pool investments in venture capital funds or small business labour-sponsored VENTURE CAPITAL CORPORATIONS. Venture capital financing supplements other personal or external funds that an ENTREPRENEUR is able to tap, or takes the place of loans of other funds that conventional financial institutions are unable or unwilling to risk. Some venture capital sources invest only at a certain stage of entrepreneurship, such as the start-up or SEED MONEY stage, the *first round* or SECOND ROUND phases that follow, or at the MEZZANINE LEVEL immediately preceding an INITIAL PUBLIC OFFERING. In return for taking an investment risk, venture capitalists are usually rewarded with some combination of PROFITS, PREFERRED STOCK, ROYALTIES on sales, and capital appreciation of common shares.

VENTURE CAPITAL CORPORATION labour-sponsored mutual fund of small business shares usually held for at least 5 years. Investors are eligible for a 20% federal + 20% provincial tax credit, and units qualify for the RRSP. Very popular in Ontario, Québec, and BC.

VERTICAL LINE CHARTING form of technical charting on which the high, low, and closing prices of a stock or a market are shown on one vertical line with the closing price indicated by a short horizontal mark. Each vertical line represents another day, and the chart shows the trend of a stock or a market over a period of days, weeks, months, or years. Technical analysts discern from these charts whether a stock or a market is continually closing at the high or low end of its trading range during a day. This is useful in understanding whether the market's action is strong or weak, and therefore whether prices will advance or decline in the near future. *See also* TECHNICAL ANALYSIS.

VERTICAL LINE CHARTING

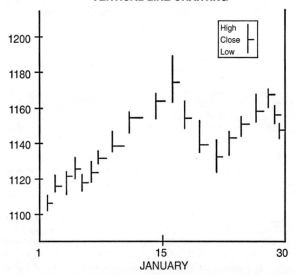

VERTICAL MERGER merger between a company that supplies goods and services and a company that buys those goods and services. For example, if a publishing company buys a paper producer, it is considered a vertical merger because the publisher buys large amounts of paper. In some cases, vertical mergers may be challenged by the government if they are found to violate ANTITRUST LAWS. *See also* MERGER.

VERTICAL SPREAD OPTION strategy that involves purchasing an option at one STRIKE PRICE while simultaneously selling another option of the same class at the next higher or lower strike price. Both options have the same expiration date. For example, a vertical spread is created by buying an XYZ May 30 call and selling an XYZ May 40 call. The investor who buys a vertical spread hopes to profit as the difference between the option premium on the two option positions widens or narrows. Also called a PRICE SPREAD. *See also* OPTION PREMIUM.

VESTED INTEREST in law, an interest in something that is certain to occur as opposed to being dependent on an event that might not happen. In general usage, an involvement having the element of personal gain. *See also* VESTING.

VESTING right an employee gradually acquires by length of service at a company to receive employer-contributed benefits, such as payments from a PENSION FUND, PROFIT-SHARING PLAN

V FORMATION technical chart pattern that forms a V. The V pattern indicates that the stock, bond, or commodity being charted has bottomed out and is now in a bullish (rising) trend. An upside-down (inverse) V is considered bearish (indicative of a falling market). *See also* BOTTOM; TECHNICAL ANALYSIS.

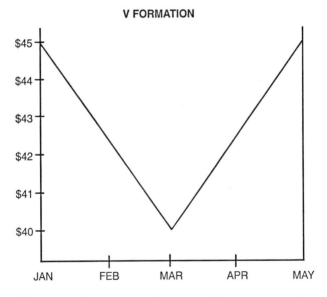

V FORMATION

VIENNA STOCK EXCHANGE founded in 1771 as a state institution to provide a market for state-issued bonds, it is one of the world's oldest exchanges. The VSE represents some two-thirds of Austrian stock transactions, with the balance over-the-counter. The *VSE Share Index* is made up of all domestic shares listed on the official market, while the *Austrian Traded Index* (ATX) includes the 19 most actively traded shares. Trades are settled on the second Monday following order execution. Trading is conducted from 9:30 A.M. to 1:30 P.M., Monday through Friday. Futures and options are traded on the Osterreichische Termin-und Optionenborse, or OTOB. Products include ATX futures, Austrian government bond futures, American-style stock options, and European-style ATX options.

VOID deprived of legal force or effect, as a CONTRACT.

VOIDABLE contract that can be annulled by either party after it is signed because fraud, incompetence, or another illegality exists or because a RIGHT OF RESCISSION applies.

VOLATILE tending to rapid and extreme fluctuations. The term is used to describe the size and frequency of the fluctuations in the price of a particular stock, bond, or commodity. A stock may be volatile because the outlook for the company is particularly uncertain, because there are only a few shares outstanding (*see also* THIN MARKET), or because of various other reasons. Where the reasons for the variation have to do with the particular security as distinguished from market conditions, return is measured by a concept called ALPHA. A stock with an alpha factor of 1.25 is projected to rise in price by 25% in a year on the strength of its inherent values such as growth in earnings per share and regardless of the performance of the market as a whole. Market-related volatility, also called SYSTEMATIC RISK, is measured by BETA. *See also* DURATION.

VOLATILITY characteristic of a security, commodity, or market to rise or fall sharply in price within a short-term period. A measure of the relative volatility of a stock to the overall market is its BETA. *See also* VOLATILE.

VOLUME total number of stock shares, bonds, or commodities futures contracts traded in a particular period. Volume figures are reported daily by exchanges, both for individual issues trading and for the total amount of trading executed on the exchange. Technical analysts place great emphasis on the amount of volume that occurs in the trading of a security or a commodity futures contract. A sharp rise in volume is believed to signify future sharp rises or falls in price, because it reflects increased investor interest in a security, commodity, or market. *See also* TECHNICAL ANALYSIS; TURNOVER.

VOLUME DELETED note appearing on the TICKER TAPE, usually when the tape is running behind by two minutes or more because of heavy trading, that only the STOCK SYMBOL and the trading price will be displayed for transactions of less than 5000 shares.

VOLUME DISCOUNT any reduction in price based on the purchase of a large quantity.

VOLUNTARY BANKRUPTCY legal proceeding that follows a petition of BANKRUPTCY filed by a debtor in the appropriate court under the Bankruptcy and Insolvency Act. Petitions for voluntary bankruptcy can be filed by any insolvent business or individual.

VOLUNTARY SETTLEMENT "out-of-court" settlement or discharge with a company's creditors that leaves a technically insolvent or bankrupt company in a position to continue operations or to be liquidated. A voluntary settlement enables the company to bypass many of the costs involved in formal legal proceedings.

VOTING RIGHT stockholder's right to vote in the affairs of his or her company. Most common shares have one vote each. Preferred stocks usually have the right to vote when their dividends are in arrears. The right to vote may be delegated by the shareholder to another person (PROXY).

VOTING RIGHTS rights afforded by the possession of common shares allowing the shareholder to vote at annual and special meetings. Owners of preferred shares have no voting rights unless dividends or interest are in arrears.

VOTING STOCK shares in a corporation that entitle the shareholder to voting and PROXY rights. When a shareholder deposits such stock with a CUSTODIAN that acts as a voting TRUST, the shareholder retains rights to earnings and dividends but delegates voting rights to the trustee. *See also* COMMON STOCK; PROPORTIONAL REPRESENTATION; VOTING TRUST CERTIFICATE.

VOTING TRUST arrangement by which shareholders surrender their voting rights, placing the control of a company in the hands of certain managers for a given period of time, or until certain results have been achieved.

VSE INDEX four indices published by the Vancouver Stock Exchange (VSE): the VSE Composite Index, and 3 sub-indices: the Resource Index and the Commercial/Industrial Index, both of which track price changes by the "Senior Board" companies; and the Venture Index, which tracks junior companies. The current VSE Index is a composite of the 3 sub-indices that were introduced on June 1, 1990. The indices are all capital-weighted—the largest or most widely capitalized companies have the greatest impact on Index movement. The VSE Composite Index was first introduced on a capital-weighted basis in January, 1986.

VULTURE FUND type of LIMITED PARTNERSHIP that invests in depressed property, usually real estate, aiming to profit when prices rebound, usually a REAL ESTATE INVESTMENT TRUST.

W

WAGE GARNISHMENT *see* GARNISHMENT.

WAGE-LOSS REPLACEMENT *see* DISABILITY INSURANCE.

WAGE-PUSH INFLATION inflationary spiral caused by rapid increases in wages. *See also* COST-PUSH INFLATION; DEMAND-PULL INFLATION; INFLATION.

WAITING PERIOD period of time before something goes into effect. In securities, there is a waiting period between the filing of registration statements and the time when securities may be offered for sale to the public. This waiting period may be extended if the Securities Commission requires revisions to the registration statement. In DISABILITY INCOME INSURANCE, there is a waiting period of several months from the time the disability occurs to the time when disability benefits are paid. For insurance claims, the waiting period is also known as the *elimination period.*

WAIVER OF PREMIUM clause in an insurance policy providing that all policy premiums will be waived if the policyholder becomes seriously ill or disabled, either permanently or temporarily, and therefore is unable to pay the premiums. Some policies include a waiver-of-premium clause automatically, while in other cases it is an optional feature that must be paid with additional premiums. During the waiver period, all policy benefits remain in force.

WALLFLOWER *see* ORPHAN STOCK.

WALLPAPER worthless securities. The implication of the term is that certificates of stocks and bonds that have gone bankrupt or defaulted have no other use than as wallpaper. However, there may be value in the worthless certificates themselves by collectors of such certificates, who prize rare or historically significant certificates. The practice of collecting such certificates is known as SCRIPOPHILY.

WALL STREET
1. common name for the financial district at the lower end of Manhattan in New York City, where the New York and American Stock Exchanges and numerous brokerage firms are headquartered. The New York Stock Exchange is actually located at the corner of Wall and Broad Streets.
2. investment community, such as in "Wall Street really likes the prospects for that company" or "Wall Street law firm," meaning a firm specializing in securities law and mergers. Also referred to as "the Street."

WANTED FOR CASH TICKER tape announcement that a bidder will pay cash the same day for a specified block of securities. Cash trades are executed for delivery and settlement at the time the transaction is made.

WAR CHEST fund of liquid assets (cash) set aside by a corporation to pay for a takeover or to defend against a takeover. Traders will say that a company has a war chest that it plans to use to take over another company. Or traders might say that a particular company will be difficult to take over because it has a large war chest that it can use to defend itself by buying back its stock, making an acquisition of its own, paying for legal fees to mount defenses, or taking other defensive measures. *See also* TAKEOVER.

WAREHOUSE RECEIPT document listing goods or commodities kept for SAFEKEEPING in a warehouse. The receipt can be used to transfer ownership of that commodity, instead of having to deliver the physical commodity. Warehouse receipts are used with many commodities, particularly precious metals like gold, silver, and platinum, which must be safeguarded against theft.

WARRANT *see* SUBSCRIPTION WARRANT.

WARRANTY contract between the seller and the buyer of a product specifying the conditions under which the seller will make repairs or remedy other problems that may arise, at no additional cost to the buyer. The warranty document describes how long the warranty remains in effect, and which specific repairs will be performed at no extra charge. Warranties usually cover workmanship or the failure of the product if used normally, but not negligence on the part of the user if the product is used in ways for which it was not designed. Warranties are commonly issued for automobiles, appliances, electronic gear, and most other products. In some cases, manufacturers will offer extended warranties for several years beyond the original warranty period, at an extra charge. Consumers should consult federal and provincial laws for more extensive applications or interpretations of warranties.

WASH SALE purchase and sale of a security either simultaneously or within a short period of time. It may be done by a single investor or (where MANIPULATION is involved) by two or more parties conspiring to create artificial market activity in order to profit from a rise in the security's price. Also known as *wash trade.*

WASTING ASSET
1. fixed asset, other than land, that has a limited useful life and is therefore subject to DEPRECIATION.
2. natural resource that diminishes in value because of extractions of oil, ores, or gas, or the removal of timber, or similar depletion and that is therefore subject to AMORTIZATION.
3. security with a value that expires at a particular time in the future. An OPTION contract, for instance, is a wasting asset, because the chances of a favourable move in the underlying stock diminish as the contract approaches expiration, thus reducing the value of the option.

WATCH LIST list of securities singled out for special surveillance by a brokerage firm or an exchange or other self-regulatory organization to spot irregularities. Firms on the watch list may be TAKEOVER candidates, companies about to issue new securities, or others that seem to have attracted an unusually heavy volume of trading activity. *See also* STOCK WATCHER; SURVEILLANCE DEPARTMENT OF EXCHANGES.

WATERED STOCK stock representing ownership of OVERVALUED assets, a condition of overcapitalized corporations, whose total worth is less than their invested capital. The condition may result from inflated accounting values, gifts of stock, operating losses, or excessive stock dividends. Among the negative features of watered stock from the shareholder's standpoint are inability to recoup full investment in LIQUIDATION, inadequate return on investment, possible liability exceeding the PAR value of shares, low MARKET VALUE because of poor dividends and possible adverse publicity, reduced ability of the firm to issue new stock or debt securities to capitalize on growth opportunity, and loss of competitive position because of the need to raise prices to provide a return acceptable to investors. To remedy the situation, a company must either increase its assets without increasing its OUTSTANDING shares or reduce outstanding shares without reducing assets. The alternatives are to increase RETAINED EARNINGS or to adjust the accounting values of assets or of stock.

WEAK DOLLAR dollar that has fallen in value against foreign currencies. This means that those holding dollars will get fewer pounds, yen, marks, francs, U.S. dollars or other currencies in exchange for their dollars. A weak Canadian dollar makes it easier for companies to export their goods to other countries because foreigners' buying power is enhanced. The dollar may weaken because of loose Canadian monetary policy (creating too many dollars) and lack of confidence in the Canadian government, large trade and budget deficits, unattractive interest rates on dollar-denominated investments compared to investments denominated in other currencies, or other reasons.

WEAK HANDS term that refers to people who believe that declining markets will decline further since the traders with long positions are not bona fide HEDGERS and will not accept delivery but will sell before maturity to reduce their risk.

WEAK MARKET market characterized by a preponderance of sellers over buyers and a general declining trend in prices.

WEALTH MAXIMIZATION strategy of maximizing the value of the owner's or shareholder's investment in a company, generally measured by the market value of the company's shares. This strategy is not necessarily consistent with a strategy of profit maximization.

WEDGE technical chart pattern similar to but varying slightly from a TRIANGLE. Two converging lines connect a series of peaks and troughs to form a wedge. These converging lines move in the same direction, unlike a triangle, in which one rises while the other falls or one rises or falls while the other line stays horizontal. Falling wedges usually occur as temporary interruptions of upward price rallies, rising wedges as interruptions of a falling price trend. *See also* TECHNICAL ANALYSIS.

WEDGE

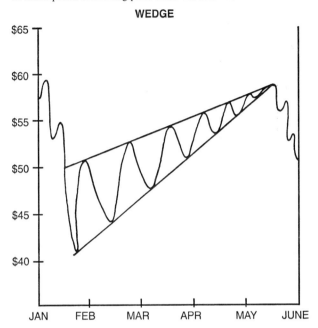

WEIGHTED AVERAGE COST OF CAPITAL measure of the cost of capital calculated by weighting the marginal cost of each type of capital (i.e., debt, preferred shares, common equity, etc.) by the proportion of that type of capital in the firm's capital structure.

WEIGHTED AVERAGE MATURITY also called *average life* or *weighted average life* and used in mortgage-backed PASS-THROUGH SECURITIES meaning the weighted-average time to the return of a dollar of principal. It is arrived at by multiplying each portion of principal received by the time at which it is received, and then summing and dividing by the total amount of principal. Fabozzi's *Handbook of Fixed Income Securities* uses this example: Consider a simple annual-pay, four-year bond with a face value of $100 and principal payments of $40 the first year, $30 the second year, $20 the third year, and $10 the fourth year. The average life would be calculated as: Average life = .4 × 1 year + .3 × 2 years + .2 × 3 years + .1 × 4 years = 2 years. An alternative measure of investment life is DURATION.

W FORMATION technical chart pattern of the price of a stock, bond, or commodity that shows the price has hit a SUPPORT LEVEL two times and is moving up; also called a *double bottom.*

A reverse W is just the opposite; the price has hit a resistance level and is headed down. This is called a DOUBLE TOP.

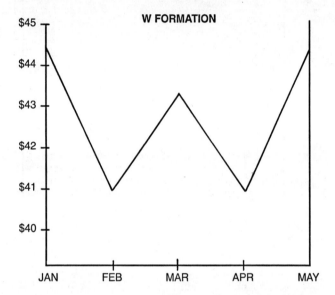

WHEN DISTRIBUTED transactions conditional on the SECONDARY DISTRIBUTION of shares ISSUED AND OUTSTANDING but CLOSELY HELD, as those of a wholly owned subsidiary, for example. *See also* WHEN ISSUED.

WHEN ISSUED short form of "when, as, and if issued." Term refers to a transaction made conditionally because a security, although authorized, has not yet been issued. NEW ISSUES of stocks and bonds, stocks that have SPLIT, and Treasury securities are all traded on a when issued basis. In a newspaper listing, a "WI" is placed next to the price of such a security. *See also* WHEN DISTRIBUTED.

WHIPSAWED to be caught in VOLATILE price movements and make losing trades as prices rise and fall. A trader is whipsawed if he or she buys just before prices fall and sells just before prices rise.

Term is also used in TECHNICAL ANALYSIS referring to misleading signals in the chart trends of markets or particular securities.

WHISPER STOCK stock that is rumoured to be a takeover target. Speculators, arbitrageurs, and other investors may buy shares in the company hoping that the "whispers" they have heard are true, allowing them to reap huge profits when the takeover is officially announced. Whisper stocks may trade in heavier-than-usual volume once the rumours about the takeover spread widely. Investing in whisper stocks is risky, however, because the takeover rumours may prove to be inaccurate.

WHISTLE BLOWER employee or other person with inside knowledge of wrongdoing inside a company or government agency. The employee is supposed to be protected from retribution by the employer by several federal laws protecting whistle blowers, though whistle blowers frequently are punished for revealing wrongdoing by their employer. Whistle blowers who provide Revenue Canada with information about illegal insider trading or other illegal activity that leads to a conviction may qualify for a bounty, a percentage bonus based on what is collected.

WHITE COLLAR WORKER office worker in professional, managerial, or administrative position. Such workers typically wear shirts with white collars. Those working in factories or doing manual labour typically wear blue collars, and are therefore called *blue-collar workers.*

WHITE KNIGHT friendly acquirer sought by the target of an unfriendly TAKEOVER.

WHITEMAIL anti-TAKEOVER device whereby a vulnerable company sells a large amount of stock to a friendly party at below-market prices. This puts a potential raider in a position where it must buy a sizable amount of stock at inflated prices to get control and thus helps perpetuate existing management.

WHITE SHEETS list of prices published by the NATIONAL QUOTATION BUREAU for market makers in OVER-THE-COUNTER stocks traded in Chicago, Los Angeles, and San Francisco.

WHITE-SHOE FIRM anachronistic characterization of certain broker-dealers as venerable, "upper-crust" and "above" such practices as participating in hostile takeovers. Derives from the '50s culture of Ivy League colleges, where white buck shoes were *de rigueur* in elite fraternities and clubs.

WHITE SQUIRE WHITE KNIGHT who buys less than a majority interest.

WHOLE LIFE INSURANCE form of life insurance policy that offers protection in case the insured dies and also builds up cash value. The policy stays in force for the lifetime of the insured, unless the policy is canceled or lapses. The policyholder usually pays a level PREMIUM for whole life, which does not rise as the person grows older (as in the case of TERM INSURANCE). The earnings on the cash value in the policy accumulate tax-deferred, and can be borrowed against in the form of a POLICY LOAN. The death benefit is reduced by the amount of the loan, plus interest, if the loan is not repaid.

Traditionally, life insurance companies invest insurance premiums conservatively in bonds, stocks, and real estate in order to generate increases in cash value for policyholders. Policyholders have no input into the investment decision-making process in a whole life insurance policy. Other forms of cash value policies, such as UNIVERSAL LIFE INSURANCE and VARIABLE LIFE INSURANCE give policyholders more options, such as stocks, and bonds, to choose from in investing their premiums. Whole life insurance is also known as *ordinary life, permanent life, or straight life insurance. See also* ADEQUACY OF COVERAGE; ANNUAL EXCLUSION; CASH VALUE INSURANCE; CONTINGENT BENEFICIARY; CONVERTIBILITY; DEATH BENEFIT; EXPERIENCE RATING; FINANCIAL NEEDS APPROACH; FIXED PREMIUM; FULLY PAID POLICY; GUARANTEED INSURABILITY; HIDDEN LOAD; INCOME EXCLUSION RULE; INSURABILITY; INSURABLE INTEREST; INSURANCE AGENT; INSURANCE CLAIM; INSURANCE DIVIDEND; INSURANCE POLICY; INSURANCE PREMIUM; INSURANCE SETTLEMENT; INSURED; LAPSE; LIFE INSURANCE; LIFE INSURANCE POLICY; LIVING BENEFITS; LUMP SUM; MORTALITY RISK; NONCONTESTABILITY CLAUSE; NONPARTICIPATING LIFE INSURANCE POLICY; PAID UP; PAID UP POLICY; PARTICIPATING DIVIDENDS; PARTICIPATING INSURANCE; SAVINGS ELEMENT; SECOND-TO-DIE INSURANCE; SETTLEMENT OPTIONS; SINGLE-PREMIUM LIFE INSURANCE; SURRENDER VALUE.

WHOLESALE PRICE INDEX *see* PRODUCER PRICE INDEX.

WHOLESALER
In general: middleman or DISTRIBUTOR who sells mainly to retailers, JOBBERS, other merchants, and industrial, commercial, and institutional users as distinguished from consumers. *See also* VENDOR.
Securities:
1. INVESTMENT BANKER acting as an UNDERWRITER in a NEW ISSUE or as a distributor in a secondary offering of securities. *See also* SECONDARY DISTRIBUTION.
2. broker-dealer who trades with other broker-dealers, rather than with the retail investor, and receives discounts and selling commissions.
3. SPONSOR of a MUTUAL FUND.

WHOLLY OWNED SUBSIDIARY SUBSIDIARY whose common stock is virtually 100%-owned by the PARENT COMPANY.

WIDE OPENING abnormally large SPREAD between the BID AND ASKED prices of a security at the OPENING of a trading session.

WIDGET symbolic American gadget, used wherever a hypothetical product is needed to illustrate a manufacturing or selling concept.

WIDOW-AND-ORPHAN STOCK stock that pays high dividends and is very safe. It usually has a low BETA COEFFICIENT and is involved in a noncyclical business. For years Bell Canada was considered a widow-and-orphan stock. Canadian Pacific, Imperial Oil, and TransCanada Pipelines are still considered widow-and-orphan stocks by and large.

WILDCAT DRILLING exploring for oil or gas in an unproven area. A wildcat OIL AND GAS LIMITED PARTNERSHIP is structured so that investors take high risks but can reap substantial rewards if oil or gas is found in commercial quantities.

WILL document, also called a *testament,* that, when signed and witnessed, gives legal effect to the wishes of a person, called a *testator,* with respect to disposal of property upon death.

WILSHIRE 5000 EQUITY INDEX market value-weighted index of approximately 6500 U.S.-based equities traded on the New York Stock Exchange, American Stock Exchange, and NASDAQ Stock Market. The index is prepared by Wilshire Associates, Inc., of Santa Monica, California. Changes are measured against its base value, equal to its market value in billions of dollars, on December 31, 1980. The Wilshire 5000 is widely followed as an indicator of the broad trend in stock prices. Some index mutual funds are designed to replicate the Wilshire 5000. *See also* STOCK INDICES AND AVERAGES.

WINDFALL PROFIT profit that occurs suddenly as a result of an event not controlled by the person or company profiting from the event. For example, oil companies profited in the 1970s from an explosion in the price of oil brought about by the Arab oil embargo and the price increases demanded by the Organization of Petroleum Exporting Countries.

WINDFALL PROFITS TAX tax on profits that result from a sudden windfall to a particular company or industry.

WINDOW
1. limited time during which an opportunity should be seized, or it will be lost. For example, a period when new stock issues are welcomed by the public only lasts for a few months, or maybe as long as a year—that time is called the *window of opportunity.*
2. cashier department of a brokerage firm, where delivery and settlement of securities transactions takes place.

WINDOW DRESSING
1. trading activity near the end of a quarter or fiscal year that is designed to dress up a PORTFOLIO to be presented to clients or shareholders. For example, a fund manager may sell losing positions in his or her portfolio in order to display only positions that have gained in value.
2. accounting gimmickry designed to make a FINANCIAL STATEMENT show a more favourable condition than actually exists—for example by omitting certain expenses, by concealing liabilities, by delaying WRITE-OFFS, by anticipating sales, or by other such actions, which may or may not be fraudulent.

WINN Winnipeg Commodity Exchange.

WINNIPEG COMMODITY EXCHANGE (WSE) incorporated by an Act of the Province of Manitoba in March, 1903, it is Canada's only agricultural futures and options exchange. It conducts the world's only futures market for canola, flaxseed, and rye, and also trades oats, feed grades of wheat, and barley. The WSE is located at 2901 One Lombard Place, Winnipeg, Manitoba R3B 0Y2, and trading is conducted Monday through Friday, from 9:30 A.M.–1:15 P.M. for futures, and 9:30 A.M.–1:20 P.M. for options.

WIRE HOUSE national or international brokerage firm whose branch offices are linked by a communications system that permits the rapid dissemination of prices, information, and research relating to financial markets and individual securities. Although smaller retail and regional brokers currently have access to similar data, the designation of a firm as a wire house dates back to the time when only the largest organizations had access to high-speed communications. Therefore, *wire house* still is used to refer to the biggest brokerage houses.

WIRE ROOM operating department of a brokerage firm that receives customers' orders from the REGISTERED REPRESENTATIVE and transmits the vital data to the exchange floor, where a FLOOR TICKET is prepared, or to the firm's trading department for execution. The wire room also receives notices of executed trades and relays them to the appropriate registered representatives. Also called *order department, order room,* or *wire and order.*

WITCHING HOUR *see* TRIPLE WITCHING HOUR.

WITHDRAWAL PLAN program available through most open-end MUTUAL FUND companies in which shareholders can receive fixed payments of income or CAPITAL GAINS (or both) on a regular basis, usually monthly or quarterly. Also called *systematic withdrawal.*

WITHHOLDING deduction from salary payments and other compensation to provide for an individual's tax liability. Federal income taxes and Canada Pension Plan and unemployment insurance contributions are remitted by the employer biweekly. Contributions are withheld from paycheques. The yearly amount of withholding is reported on a reporting slip, the T-4, which must be submitted with the federal and provincial tax returns.

WITHOUT DIVIDEND *see* EX-DIVIDEND.

WORKERS' COMPENSATION BOARD body in each province that oversees compensation for employees injured in work-related accidents and for beneficiaries if an accident results in death.

WORKERS' COMPENSATION INSURANCE managed by the provincial workers' compensation board, INSURANCE that pays benefits on behalf of an insured employer to employees or their families in the case of injury, disability, or death resulting from occupational hazards.

WORKING CAPITAL funds invested in a company's cash, ACCOUNTS RECEIVABLE, INVENTORY, and other CURRENT ASSETS *(gross working capital);* usually refers to *net working capital*—that is, current assets minus CURRENT LIABILITIES. Working capital finances the CASH CONVERSION CYCLE of a business—the time required to convert raw materials into finished goods, finished goods into sales, and accounts receivable into cash. These factors vary with the type of industry and the scale of production, which varies in turn with seasonality and with sales expansion and contraction. Internal sources of working capital include RETAINED EARNINGS, savings achieved through operating efficiencies and the allocation of CASH FLOW from sources like DEPRECIATION or deferred taxes to working capital. External sources include bank and other short-term borrowings, TRADE CREDIT, and term debt and EQUITY FINANCING not channeled into long-term assets. *See also* CURRENT RATIO; NET CURRENT ASSETS.

WORKING CAPITAL MANAGEMENT area of finance concerned with the management of a company's current accounts that include its current assets and current liabilities. If a firm cannot maintain a satisfactory working capital position, it may become technically insolvent and may be forced into bankruptcy.

WORKING CONTROL control of a company by a shareholder or shareholders. Theoretically, ownership of 51% of a company's voting stock is necessary to exercise control. In practice, and this is particularly true in the case of a large corporation, effective control can be exerted through ownership, individually, or by a group acting in consort, of less than 50%.

WORKING INTEREST property ownership agreement whereby each owner pays exploration and development costs for a property in proportion to ownership.

WORK-IN-PROCESS *see* INVENTORY.

WORKOUT situation, such as a bad loan or troubled firm, where remedial measures are being taken.

WORKSHEET computerized page allowing the user to manipulate many columns and rows of numbers. The worksheet can contain formulas so that if one number is changed, the entire worksheet is automatically updated, based on those formulas. Analysts, investors, and accountants track a company's financial statements, balance sheets, and other data on worksheets.

WORLD BANK *see* INTERNATIONAL BANK FOR RECONSTRUCTION AND DEVELOPMENT.

WRAP ACCOUNT investment consulting relationship in which a client's funds are placed with one or more money managers, and all administrative and management fees, along with commissions, are wrapped into one comprehensive fee, which is paid quarterly. The wrap fee varies, but usually ranges from 1% to 3% of the value of the assets in the account. Wrap accounts usually require a minimum initial investment of anywhere from $25,000 to $10 million for individual accounts. The term *wrap* has been expanded to involve mutual fund asset allocation programs. Technically, these are not wrap programs because they are not "all inclusive." Transaction commissions in these programs on mutual funds are still a variable and they are pooled accounts as distinguished from individual accounts. From the customer's point of view, a wrap account provides access to top investment managers. The broker overseeing the account is paid an ongoing fee to monitor the performance of the money managers. Although brokers may switch assets to other managers within the program if one manager consistently starts to underperform, most sponsors of wrap programs suggest a three- to five-year time horizon to reach investment goals.

WRINKLE novel feature that may attract a buyer for a new product or a security. For example, ZERO COUPON SECURITIES were a new wrinkle when they were introduced but soon thereafter became quite commonplace.

WRITEDOWNS downward reevaluation of an asset that was previously recognized at a larger value by the company.

WRITE-OFF charging an ASSET amount to expense or loss. The effect of a write-off is to reduce or eliminate the value of the asset and reduce profits. Write-offs are systematically taken in accordance with allowable tax DEPRECIATION of a FIXED ASSET, and with the AMORTIZATION of certain other assets, such as an INTANGIBLE ASSET and a capitalized cost (like premiums paid on investments). Write-offs are also taken when assets are, for whatever reason, deemed worthless, the most common example being uncollectible ACCOUNTS RECEIVABLE. Where such write-offs can be anticipated and therefore estimated, the usual practice has been to charge income regularly in amounts needed to maintain a RESERVE, the actual losses then being charged to the reserve.

WRITE OUT procedure followed when a SPECIALIST on an exchange makes a trade involving his or her own inventory, on one hand, and an order he or she is holding for a FLOOR BROKER, on the other. Exchange rules require a two-part transaction: the broker first completes a trade with the specialist, who then completes the transaction by a separate trade with the customer. The write out involves no charge other than the normal broker's commission.

WRITER
1. person who sells PUT OPTION and CALL OPTION contracts, and therefore collects PREMIUM INCOME. The writer of a put option is obligated

to buy (and the writer of a call option is obligated to sell) the UNDERLYING SECURITY at a predetermined price by a particular date if the OPTION is exercised. *See also* COVERED CALL; NAKED OPTION; WRITING NAKED.

2. insurance UNDERWRITER.

WRITE UP/WRITE DOWN upward or downward adjustment of the accounting value of an asset according to GENERALLY ACCEPTED ACCOUNTING PRINCIPLES GAAP. *See also* WRITE-OFF.

WRITING CASH-SECURED PUTS OPTION strategy that a trader who wants to sell PUT OPTIONS uses to avoid having to use a MARGIN ACCOUNT. Rather than depositing MARGIN with a broker, a put WRITER can deposit cash equal to the option EXERCISE PRICE. With this strategy, the put option writer is not subject to additional margin requirements in the event of changes in the underlying stock's price. The put writer can also be earning money by investing the PREMIUM he or she receives in MONEY MARKET instruments.

WRITING NAKED strategy used by an OPTION seller in which the trader does not own the UNDERLYING SECURITY. This strategy can lead to large profits if the stock moves in the hoped-for direction, but it can lead to large losses if the stock moves in the other direction, since the trader will have to go into the marketplace to buy the stock in order to deliver it to the option buyer. *See also* NAKED OPTION.

WRITING PUTS TO ACQUIRE STOCK strategy used by an OPTION writer (seller) who believes a stock is going to decline and that its purchase at a given price would represent a good investment. By writing a PUT OPTION exercisable at that price, the writer cannot lose. If the stock, contrary to his expectation, goes up, the option will not be exercised and he is at least ahead the amount of the PREMIUM he received. If, as expected, the stock goes down and the option is exercised, he has bought the stock at what he had earlier decided was a good buy, and he has the premium income in addition.

WRITTEN-DOWN VALUE BOOK VALUE of an asset after DEPRECIATION or other AMORTIZATION; also called *net book value.* For example, if the original cost of a piece of equipment was $1000 and accumulated depreciation charges totaled $400, the written-down value would be $600. *See also* INTANGIBLE ASSET.

WT abbreviation for *warrant. See also* SUBSCRIPTION WARRANT.

X Y Z

X or XD symbol used in newspapers to signify that a stock is trading EX-DIVIDEND, that is, without dividend. The symbol X is also used in bond tables to signify without interest.

XR symbol used in newspapers to signify that a stock is trading EX-RIGHTS, that is, without rights attached. *See also* SUBSCRIPTION RIGHT.

XW symbol used in newspapers to signify that a stock is trading EX-WAR-RANTS, that is, without warrants attached. *See also* SUBSCRIPTION WARRANT.

YANKEE BOND MARKET dollar-denominated bonds issued in the U.S. by foreign banks and corporations. The bonds are issued in the U.S. when market conditions there are more favourable than on the EUROBOND market or in domestic markets overseas. Similarly, Yankee CERTIFICATES OF DEPOSIT are negotiable CDs issued in the U.S. by branches and agencies of foreign banks.

YEAR-END BONUS bonus payment given to employees at the end of a year, based on the employee's performance and the performance of the company. Most securities firms operate on a bonus system, providing employees with huge bonuses in highly profitable years and little or no bonuses in lean years. Many salespeople also operate on a year-end bonus system, in which they receive bonuses if they met or exceeded certain sales goals during the year.

YEAR-END DIVIDEND an additional or special DIVIDEND declared based on a company's profits during the fiscal year.

YEAR-TO-DATE (YTD) period from the beginning of the calendar year (or FISCAL YEAR (FY) if so indicated) to the reporting date. For example third-quarterly results of a company would be reported for the quarter alone and for the year-to-date, which would be nine months.

YELLOW SHEETS daily publication of the NATIONAL QUOTATION BUREAU in the United States that details the BID AND ASKED prices and firms that MAKE A MARKET in CORPORATE BONDS traded in the OVER THE COUNTER (OTC) market. Much of this information is not available in the daily OTC newspaper listings. The sheets are named for their colour. OTC equity issues are covered separately on PINK SHEETS and regional OTC issues of both classes are listed on white sheets.

YEN BOND in general terms, any bond issue denominated in Japanese yen. International bankers using the term are usually referring to yen-denominated bonds issued or held outside Japan.

YIELD

In general: RETURN on an investor's CAPITAL INVESTMENT. A piece of real estate may yield a certain return, or a business deal may offer a particular yield. *See also* RETURN ON INVESTED CAPITAL.

Agriculture: agricultural output in terms of quantity of a crop.

Bonds:

1. COUPON rate of interest divided by the purchase price, called CURRENT YIELD. For example, a bond selling for $1000 with a 10% coupon offers a 10% current yield. If that same bond were selling for $500, however, it would offer a 20% yield to an investor who bought it for $500. (As a bond's price falls, its yield rises and vice versa.)

2. rate of return on a bond, taking into account the total of annual interest payments, the purchase price, the redemption value, and the amount of time remaining until maturity; called *maturity yield* or YIELD TO MATURITY. *See also* DURATION; YIELD TO AVERAGE LIFE; YIELD TO CALL.

Lending: total money earned on a loan—that is, the ANNUAL PERCENTAGE RATE of interest multiplied by the term of the loan.

Stocks: percentage rate of return paid on a common or preferred stock in dividends. For example, a stock that sells for $20 and pays an annual dividend of $2 per share has a yield, also called a *dividend yield,* of 10%.

Taxes: amount of revenue received by a governmental entity as a result of a tax.

YIELD ADVANTAGE extra amount of return an investor will earn if he or she purchases a CONVERTIBLE security instead of the common stock of the same issuing corporation. If an XYZ Corporation convertible yields 10% and an XYZ common share yields 5%, the yield advantage is 5%. *See also* YIELD SPREAD.

YIELD CURVE graph showing the term structure of interest rates by plotting the yields of all bonds of the same quality with maturities ranging from the shortest to the longest available. The resulting curve shows if short-term interest rates are higher or lower than long-term rates. If short-term rates are lower, it is called a POSITIVE YIELD CURVE. If short-term rates are higher, it is called a NEGATIVE (or INVERTED) YIELD CURVE. If there is little difference between short-term and long-term rates, it is called a *flat yield* curve. For the most part, the yield curve is positive, since investors who are willing to tie up their money for a longer period of time usually are compensated for the extra risk they are taking by receiving a higher yield. The most common version of the yield curve graph plots T-bills with 90-day maturities against 10- to 30-year government bonds.

Fixed-income analysts study the yield curve carefully in order to make judgments about the direction of interest rates. *See also* DURATION.

YIELD SPREAD difference in YIELD between various issues of securities. In comparing bonds, it usually refers to issues of different credit quality since issues of the same maturity and quality would normally have the same yields, as with government securities, for example.

Yield spread also refers to the differential between dividend yield on stocks and the CURRENT YIELD on bonds. The comparison might be made, for example, between the TSE 300 Index dividend yield and the current yield of an index of corporate bonds. A significant difference in bond and stock yields, assuming similar quality, is known as a *yield gap.*

YIELD TO AVERAGE LIFE yield calculation used, in lieu of YIELD TO MATURITY or YIELD TO CALL, where bonds are retired systematically during the life of the issue, as in the case of a SINKING FUND with contractual requirements. Because the issuer will buy its own bonds on the open market to satisfy its sinking fund requirements if the bonds are trading below PAR, there is to that extent automatic price support for such bonds; they therefore tend to trade on a yield-to-average-life basis.

YIELD TO CALL yield on a bond assuming the bond will be redeemed by the issuer at the first CALL date specified in the INDENTURE agreement. The same calculations are used to calculate yield to call as YIELD TO MATURITY except that the principal value at maturity is replaced by the first CALL PRICE and the maturity date is replaced by the first call date. Assuming the issuer will put the interest of the company before the interest of the investor and will call the bonds if it is favourable to do so, the lower of the yield to call and the yield to maturity can be viewed as the more realistic rate of return to the investor. *See also* DURATION.

YIELD TO MATURITY yield on a bond, other than a Canada Savings Bond, that changes as interest rates rise or fall. An investor who purchases a bond on any day other than its issue date or at a price other than its par value must refer to the bond's yield to maturity for its earning power. The yield to maturity is calculated to incorporate the purchase price of the bond, the coupon, and the assumed rate of interest at which the coupon will be reinvested.

YO-YO STOCK stock that fluctuates in a VOLATILE manner, rising and falling quickly like a yo-yo.

ZACKS ESTIMATE SYSTEM service offer by Zacks Investment Research of Chicago compiling earnings estimates and brokerage buy/hold/sell recommendations from more than 200 Wall Street research firms, covering more than 4500 stocks. Zacks tracks the number of analysts following each stock, how many analysts have raised or lowered their estimates, and the high, low and average earnings estimate for each quarter and fiscal year. Zacks offers a multiple selection of data bases, of print reports, and software for institutional and individual investors. *See also* I/B/E/S INTERNATIONAL INC.

ZERO BALANCE ACCOUNT DISBURSING (ZBA) unique type of corporate chequing account used for disbursement control. The maintenance of a zero balance at all times is its differentiating characteristic. As cheques drawn against a ZBA clear, the total dollar amount accumulates and results in a debit total. At the close of the business day, a transfer of funds is made from a master account of the corporation to cover this debit total and to return the account to a zero balance. ZBAs are typically used by corporations that wish central cash control while allowing decentralized disbursing operations.

ZERO-BASE BUDGETING (ZBB) method of setting budgets for corporations and government agencies that requires a justification of all expenditures, not only those that exceed the prior year's allocations. Thus all budget lines are said to begin at a zero base and are funded according to merit rather than according to the level approved for the preceding year, when circumstances probably differed.

ZERO COUPON BOND *see* ZERO-COUPON SECURITY.

ZERO-COUPON SECURITY security that makes no periodic interest payments but instead is sold at a deep discount from its face value. The buyer of such a bond receives the rate of return by the gradual APPRECIATION of the security, which is redeemed at FACE VALUE on a specified maturity date. For tax purposes, Revenue Canada maintains that the holder of a zero-coupon bond owes income tax on the interest that has accrued each year, even though the bondholder does not actually receive the cash until maturity. Revenue Canada calls this interest *imputed interest.* Because of this interpretation, many financial advisers recommend that zero-coupon securities be used in RRSP accounts, where they remain tax-sheltered.

There are many kinds of zero-coupon securities. The most commonly known is the zero-coupon bond, which either may be issued at a deep discount by a government entity or may be created by a brokerage firm when it strips the coupons off a bond and sells the CORPUS and the coupons separately. .

Because zero-coupon securities bear no interest, they are the most VOLATILE of all fixed-income securities. Since zero-coupon bondholders do not receive interest payments, zeros fall more dramatically than bonds paying out interest on a current basis when interest rates rise. However, when interest rates fall, zero-coupon securities rise more rapidly in value than full-coupon bonds, because the bonds have locked in a particular rate of reinvestment that becomes more attractive the further rates fall. The greater the number of years that a zero-coupon security has until maturity, the less an investor has to pay for it, and the more LEVERAGE is at work for him or her. For instance, a bond maturing in 5 years may double, but one maturing in 25 years may increase in value 10 times, depending on the interest rate of the bond.

See also ACCRUAL BONDS; COUPON BOND; DEEP DISCOUNT BOND, SPLIT-COUPON BONDS; STAGS; STRIPPED BOND; ZERO-COUPON CONVERTIBLE SECURITY.

ZERO-MINUS TICK sale that takes place at the same price as the previous sale, but at a lower price than the last different price; also called a *zero downtick.* For instance, stock trades may be executed consecutively at prices of $52, $51, and $51. The final trade at $51 was made at a zero-minus tick, because it was made at the same price as the previous trade, but at a lower price than the last different price.

ZERO-PLUS TICK securities trade that takes place at the same price as the previous transaction but at a higher price than the last different price; also called *zero uptick.* For instance, with trades executed consecutively at $51, $52, and $52, the last trade at $52 was made at a zero-plus tick—the same price as the previous trade but a higher price than the last different price. Short sales must be executed only on zero-plus ticks or on PLUS TICKS. *See also* SHORT SALE RULE.

ZERO-SUM GAME situation in which the gains of the winners are matched by the losses of the losers. For example, futures and options trading are zero-sum games because for every investor holding a profitable contract, there is another investor on the other side of the trade who is losing money. The total amount of wealth held by all the traders in a zero-sum game remains the same, but the wealth is shifted from some traders to others.

ZOMBIES companies that continue to operate even though they are insolvent and bankrupt. Such companies, in addition to being called zombies, are called *brain dead* or *living dead.*

ZONING LAWS municipal ordinances that authorize the establishment of zoning boards to administer regulations concerning the use of property and buildings in designated areas.

ZURICH STOCK EXCHANGE largest of three Swiss exchanges, followed by Geneva and Basel. The three exchanges operate simultaneously and are linked by computers, enabling orders to be executed on any of the three exchanges, regardless of origin. Trading is by open outcry, although an electronic system has been under lengthy development. The *Swiss Performance Index,* the official and most widely used index, is computed on three-minute intervals using real-time prices at all three exchanges. There are three different market segments: the official market, official parallel market, and unofficial market. The official market is open from 10 A.M. to 1 P.M. and 2 P.M. to 4 P.M., while the official parallel market is open from 9:15 A.M. to 10 A.M., all Monday through Friday. Trades are settled on the third business day after the trade date.

ABBREVIATIONS AND ACRONYMS

A

A Includes Extra (or Extras) (in stock listings of newspapers)

AB Aktiebolag (Swedish stock company)

ABA American Bankers Association

ABA American Bar Association

ABS Automated Bond System

ACE AMEX Commodities Exchange

ACRS Accelerated Cost Recovery System

A-D Advance-Decline Line

ADB Adjusted Debit Balance

ADR American Depositary Receipt

ADR Automatic Dividend Reinvestment

ADRS Asset Depreciation Range System

ADS American Depositary Shares

AE Account Executive

AFL-CIO American Federation of Labor-Congress of Industrial Organizations

AICPA American Institute of Certified Public Accountants

AG Aktiengesellschaft (West German stock company)

AMA American Management Association

AMA Asset Management Account

AMEX American Stock Exchange

AMPS Auction Market Preferred Stock

AON All or None

APB Accounting Principles Board

APR Annual Percentage Rate

APS Auction Preferred Stock

Arb Arbitrageur

ARM Adjustable Rate Mortgage

ARPS Adjustable Rate Preferred Stock

ASAP As Soon as Possible

ASE American Stock Exchange

ATM Automatic Teller Machine

ATP Arbitrage Trading Program

B

B Annual Rate Plus Stock Dividend (in stock listings of newspapers)

BAC Business Advisory Council

BAN Bond Anticipation Note

BBB Better Business Bureau

BD Bank Draft

BD Bills Discontinued

B/D Broker-Dealer

BE Bill of Exchange

BEACON Boston Exchange Automated Communication Order-routing Network

BF Brought Forward

BIC Bank Investment Contract

BIF Bank Insurance Fund

BL Bill of Lading

BO Branch Office

BO Buyer's Option

BOM Beginning of the Month

BOP Balance of Payments

BOT Balance of Trade

BOT Bought

BOT Board of Trustees

BR Bills Receivable

BS Balance Sheet

BS Bill of Sale

BW Bid Wanted

C

C Liquidating Dividend (in stock listings of newspapers)

CA Capital Account
CA Chartered Accountant
CA Commercial Agent
CA Credit Account
CA Current Account
CACM Central American Common Market
CAD Cash against Documents
CAF Cost Assurance and Freight
C&F Cost and Freight
CAMPS Cumulative Auction Market Preferred Stocks
CAPM Capital Asset Pricing Model
CAPS Convertible Adjustable Preferred Stock
CARs Certificate for Automobile Receivables
CARDS Certificates for Amortizing Revolving Debts
CATV Community Antenna Television
CAW Canadian Auto Workers' Union
CBA Cost Benefit Analysis
CBA Capital Cost Allowance
CBD Cash Before Delivery
CBO Collateralized Bond Obligation
CBT Chicago Board of Trade
CC Chamber of Commerce
CCA Capital Cost Allowance
CCH Commerce Clearing House
CD Certificate of Deposit
CD Commercial Dock
CDIC Canada Deposit Insurance Corporation
CEA Council of Economic Advisors
CEO Chief Executive Officer
CF Certificates (in bond listings of newspapers)
CF Carried Forward
CFA Chartered Financial Analyst
CFC Consolidated Freight Classification

CFI Cost, Freight, and Insurance
CFIB Canadian Federation of Independent Business
CFO Chief Financial Officer
CFP Certified or Chartered Financial Planner
CFTC Commodities Futures Trading Commission
CH Clearing House
CH Custom House
ChFC Chartered Financial Consultant
Cía Compañía (Spanish company)
Cie Compagnie (French company)
CIF Corporate Income Fund
CIF Cost, Insurance, and Freight
CIPs Cash Index Participations
CLD Called (in stock listings of newspapers)
CLU Chartered Life Underwriter
CMA Canadian Manufacturers Association
CME Chicago Mercantile Exchange
CMHC Central Mortgage Housing Corporation
CMO Collateralized Mortgage Obligation
CMV Current Market Value
CN Consignment Note
CN Credit Note
CNS Continuous Net Settlement
CO Cash Order
CO Certificate of Origin
Co. Company
COB Close of Business (with date)
COD Cash on Delivery
COD Collect on Delivery
CODA Cash or Deferred Arrangement
COLA Cost-of-Living Adjustment
COLTS Continuously Offered Longer-Term Securities

COMEX Commodity Exchange (New York)

COMSAT Communications Satellite Corporation

CPA Certified Public Accountant

CPPF Cost Plus Fixed Fee

CPI Consumer Price Index

CPM Cost per Thousand

CPP Canada Pension Plan

CPPC Cost plus a Percentage of Cost

CR Carrier's Risk

CR Class Rate

CR Company's Risk

CR Current Rate

CSA Canadian Standards Association

CSB Canada Savings Bond

CSE Cincinnati Stock Exchange

CSVLI Cash Surrender Value of Life Insurance

CUNA Credit Union National Association

CUSIP Committee on Uniform Securities Identification Procedures

CV Convertible Security (in bond and stock listings of newspapers)

CWO Cash with Order

D

DA Deposit Account

DA Documents against Acceptance

DAC Delivery against Cost

D&B Dun and Bradstreet

DBA Doing Business As

DC Deep Discount Issue (in bond listings of newspapers)

DCFM Discounted Cash Flow Method

DDB Double-Declining-Balance Depreciation Method

DENKS Dual-Employed, No Kids

DEWKS Dual Employed, With Kids

DF Damage Free

DINKS Dual-Income, No Kids

DJIA Dow Jones Industrial Average

DJTA Dow Jones Transportation Average

DJUA Dow Jones Utility Average

DK Don't Know

DN Debit Note

DNR Do Not Reduce

D/O Delivery Order

DOT Designated Order Turnaround

DP Documents against Payment

DPI Disposable Personal Income

DS Days After Sight

DUNS Data Universal Numbering System (Dun's Number)

DVP Delivery Versus Payment

E

E Declared or Paid in the Preceding 12 Months (in stock listings of newspapers)

E&OE Errors and Omissions Excepted

EBIT Earnings Before Interest and Taxes

EBITA Earnings Before Interest, Taxes, Depreciation, and Amortization

ECM Emerging Company Marketplace

ECM European Common Market

ECT Estimated Completion Time

EDD Estimated Delivery Date

ECU European Currency Unit

EEC European Economic Community

EEOC Equal Employment Opportunity Commission

EMP   End-of-Month Payment

EOA   Effective On or About

EOD   Every Other Day (advertising)

EOM   End of Month

EPR   Earnings Price Ratio

EPS   Earnings Per Share

ERM   Exchange Rate Mechanism

ESOP   Employee Stock Ownership Plan

ESP   Exchange Stock Portfolio

ETA   Estimated Time of Arrival

ETD   Estimated Time of Departure

ETLT   Equal To or Less Than

F

F   Dealt in Flat (in bond listings in newspapers)

FA   Free Alongside

FACT   Factor Analysis Chart Technique

FAS   Free Alongside

FASB   Financial Accounting Standards Board

FAT   Fixed Asset Transfer

FAX   Facsimile

FB   Freight Bill

FBOB   Federal Business Development Bank

FCA   Fellow of the Institute of Chartered Accountants

FCC   Federal Communications Commission

FDIC   Federal Deposit Insurance Corporation

Fed   Federal Reserve System

F&F   Furniture and Fixtures

FHA   Federal Housing Administration

FICO   Financing Corporation

FIFO   First In, First Out

FIT   Federal Income Tax

FNMA   Federal National Mortgage Association (Fannie Mae)

FOB   Free on Board

FOC   Free of Charge

FOCUS   Financial and Operations Combined Uniform Single Report

FOI   Freedom of Information Act

FOK   Fill or Kill

FOR   Free on Rail (or Road)

FOT   Free on Truck

FP   Floating Policy

FP   Fully Paid

FPM   Fixed-Payment Mortgage

FRA   Federal Reserve Act

FRB   Federal Reserve Bank

FRB   Federal Reserve Board

FRS   Federal Reserve System

FS   Final Settlement

FTC   Federal Trade Commission

FVO   For Valuation Only

FX   Foreign Exchange

FY   Fiscal Year

FYA   For Your Attention

FYI   For Your Information

G

G   Dividends and Earnings In Canadian Dollars (in stock listings of newspapers)

GAAP   Generally Accepted Accounting Principles

GAAS   Generally Accepted Auditing Standards

GAI   Guaranteed Annual Income

GAO   General Accounting Office

GATT   General Agreement on Tariffs and Trade

GDP   Gross Domestic Product

GIC   Guaranteed Investment Certificate

GIS   Guaranteed Income Supplement

GINNIE MAE   Government National Mortgage Association

GIT   Guaranteed Income (or Investment) Contract

GM   General Manager

GmbH Gesellschaft mit beschränkter Haftung (West German limited liability company)

GNP Gross National Product

GO General Obligation Bond

GPM Graduated Payment Mortgage

GST Goods and Services Tax

GTC Good Till Canceled

GTM Good This Month

GTW Good This Week

GULP Group Universal Life Policy

H

H Declared or Paid After Stock Dividend or Split-Up (in stock listings of newspapers)

HEL Home Equity Loan

H/F Held For

HFR Hold For Release

HIBOR Hong Kong Interbank Offered Rate

HLT Highly Leveraged Transaction

HQ Headquarters

HR U.S. House of Representatives

HR U.S. House of Representatives Bill (with number)

HUD Department of Housing and Urban Development

I

I Paid This Year, Dividend Omitted, Deferred, or No Action Taken at Last Dividend Meeting (in stock listings of newspapers)

IAFP International Association for Financial Planning

IARFP International Association of Registered Financial Planners

IBES Institutional Broker's Estimate System

IBRD International Bank for Reconstruction and Development (World Bank)

ICC Interstate Commerce Commission

ICFP Institute of Certified Financial Planners

ICFTU International Confederation of Free Trade Unions

ICMA Institute of Cost and Management Accountants

IDA Investment Dealers Association

IFC International Finance Corporation

IFIC Investment Funds Institute of Canada

ILA International Longshoremen's Association

ILGWU International Ladies' Garment Workers' Union

ILO International Labor Organization

IMF International Monetary Fund

IMM International Monetary Market of the Chicago Mercantile Exchange

Inc. Incorporated

INSTINET Institutional Networks Corporation

IO Interest Only

IOC Immediate-Or-Cancel Order

IOU I Owe You

IPO Initial Public Offering

IR Investor Relations

IRA Individual Retirement Account

IRR Internal Rate of Return

IRS Internal Revenue Service

ISBN International Standard Book Number

ISE International Stock Exchange of the U.K. and the Republic of Ireland

ISIS Intermarket Surveillance Information System

ISSN International Standard Serial Number

ITS Intermarket Trading System

J

JA Joint Account

K

K Declared or Paid This Year on a Cumulative Issue with Dividends in Arrears (in stock listings of newspapers)

K Kilo- (prefix meaning multiplied by one thousand)

KCBT Kansas City Board Of Trade

KD Knocked Down (disassembled)

KK Kabushiki-Kaisha (Japanese stock company)

KW Kilowatt

KWH Kilowatt-hour

KYC Know Your Customer Rule

L

L Listed (securities)

LBO Leveraged Buyout

L/C Letter Of Credit

LCL Less-Than-Carload Lot

LCM Least Common Multiple (mathematics)

LDC Less Developed Country

LEAPS Long-Term Equity AnticiPation Securities

L/I Letter of Intent

LIBOR London Interbank Offered Rate

LIFO Last In, First Out

LP Limited Partnership

Ltd Limited (British, Canadian Corporation)

LTV Loan To Value

M

M Matured Bonds (in bond listings in newspapers)

M Milli- (prefix meaning divided by one thousand)

M Mega- (prefix meaning multiplied by one million)

M One Thousand (Roman Numeral)

MACRS Modified Accelerated Cost Recovery System

Max Maximum

MBA Master of Business Administration

MBO Management By Objective

MBS Mortgage-Backed Security

MC Marginal Credit

MD Months After Date

MFN Most Favored Nation (tariff regulations)

MGM Milligram

MIG-1 Moody's Investment Grade

MIMC Member of the Institute of Management Consultants

Min Minimum

MIS Management Information System

Misc Miscellaneous

MIT Market if Touched

M&L Matched And Lost

MLP Master Limited Partnership

MLR Minimum Lending Rate

MM Millimeter (metric unit)

MMDA Money Market Deposit Account

MO Money Order

MP Member of Parliament

MSE Midwest Stock Exchange

MSE Montreal Stock Exchange

MTN Medium-term Note

MTU Metric Units

N

N New Issue (in stock listings of newspapers)

NAFTA North American Free Trade Agreement

NAIC National Association of Investors Corporation

NAPA National Association of Purchasing Agents

NAPM National Association of Purchasing Managers

NASD National Association of Securities Dealers

NASDAQ National Association of Securities Dealers Automated Quotation

NATO North Atlantic Treaty Organization

NAV Net Asset Value

NBS National Bureau of Standards

NC No Charge

NCV No Commercial Value

ND Next Day Delivery (in stock listings of newspapers)

NEMS National Exchange Market System

NH Not Held

NIC Net Interest Cost

NICS Newly Industrialized Countries

NIP Normal Investment Practice

NIT Negative Income Tax

NL No Load

NMS National Market System

NNP Net National Product

NOW Negotiable Order of Withdrawal

NP No Protest (banking)

NP Notary Public

N/P Notes Payable

NPV Net Present Value

NPV No Par Value

NQB National Quotation Bureau

NQB No Qualified Bidders

NR Not Rated

NSCC National Securities Clearing Corporation

NSF Not Sufficient Funds (banking)

NSTS National Securities Trading System

NTU Normal Trading Unit

NV Naamloze Vennootschap (Dutch corporation)

NYCSCE New York Coffee, Sugar and Cocoa Exchange

NYCTN, CA New York Cotton Exchange, Citrus Associates

NYFE New York Futures Exchange

NYM New York Mercantile Exchange

NYSE New York Stock Exchange

O

O Old (in options listing of newspapers)

OAPEC Organization of Arab Petroleum Exporting Countries

OB Or Better

OBV On-Balance Volume

OCC Option Clearing Corporation

OD Overdraft, overdrawn

OECD Organization for Economic Cooperation and Development

OEX Standard & Poor's 100 Stock Index

OID Original Issue Discount

OPD Delayed Opening

OPEC Organization of Petroleum Exporting Countries

OPM Options Pricing Model

OPM Other People's Money

OSC Ontario Securities Commission

O/T Overtime

OTC Over The Counter

OTS Office of Thrift Supervision

OW Offer Wanted

P

P Paid this Year (in stock listings of newspapers)

P Put (in options listings of news-papers)

PA Power of Attorney
PA Purchasing Agent
PAC Put and Call (options market)
PAL Passive Activity Loss
PAYE Pay as You Earn
PBR Price-to-Book Value Ratio
PC Participation Certificates
PE Price Earnings Ratio (in stock listings of newspapers)
PER Price Earnings Ratio
PERCS Preferred Equity Redemption Cumulative Stock
PERLS Principal Exchange-Rate-Linked Securities
PFD Preferred Stock
PHLX Philadelphia Stock Exchange
P&I Principal and Interest
PIG Passive Income Generator
PIK Securities Payment-In-Kind Securities
PIN Personal Identification Number
PITI Principal, Interest, Taxes, and Insurance
P&L Profit and Loss Statement
PL Price List
PLC Public Liability Company
PLC (British) Public Limited Company
PMV Private Market Value
PN Project Note
PN Promissory Note
PO Principal Only
POA Power of Attorney
POD Pay on Delivery
POE Port of Embarkation
POE Port of Entry
POR Pay on Return
PPP Penultimate Profit Prospect
PPS Prior Preferred Stock
PR Public Relations
PRIME Prescribed Right to Income and Maximum Equity
Prop Proprietor
PST Provincial Sales Tax

PSE Pacific Stock Exchange
PVR Profit/Volume Ratio

Q

QB Qualified Buyers
QC Quality Control
QI Quarterly Index
QT Questioned Trade

R

R Declared or Paid in the Preceding 12 Months plus Stock Dividend (in stock listings of newspapers)
R Option Not Traded (in option listings in newspapers)
RAM Reverse Annuity Mortgage
RAN Revenue Anticipation Note
R&D Research and Development
RCMM Registered Competitive Market Maker
REDs Refunding Escrow Deposits
REFCORP Resolution Funding Corporation
REIT Real Estate Investment Trust
Repo Repurchase Agreement
RFP Registered Financial Planner
ROB Report on Business (Globe & Mail)
ROC Return on Capital
ROE Return on Equity
ROI Return on Investment (Return on Invested Capital)
ROP Registered Options Principal
ROS Return on Sales
RP Repurchase Agreement
RRP Reverse Repurchase Agreement
RRSP Registered Retirement Savings Plan
RT Royalty Trust

RTC   Resolution Trust Corporation

RTW   Right to Work

S

S   No Option Offered (in option listings of newspapers)

S   Signed (before signature on typed copy of a document, original of which was signed)

S   Split or Stock Dividend (in stock listings of newspapers)

SA   Sociedad Anónima (Spanish corporation)

SA   Société Anonyme (French corporation)

SAA   Special Arbitrage Account

SAB   Special Assessment Bond

S&L   Savings and Loan

S&L   Sale and Leaseback

S&P   Standard & Poor's

SB   Savings Bond

SB   U.S. Senate Bill (with number)

SB   Short Bill

SBA   Small Business Administration

SBIC   Small Business Investment Corporation

SD   Standard Deduction

SDBL   Sight Draft, Bill of Lading Attached

SDRs   Special Drawing Rights

SE   Shareholders' Equity

SEAQ   Stock Exchange Automated Quotations

SEC   Securities and Exchange Commission

Sen   Senator

SEP   Simplified Employee Pension Plan

SET   Securities Exchange of Thailand

SF   Sinking Fund

SG&A   Selling, General and Administrative Expenses

SIC   Standard Industrial Classification

SL   Sold

SLO   Stop-Limit Order, Stop-Loss Order

SMA   Society of Management Accountants

SMA   Special Miscellaneous Account

SN   Stock Number

SOES   Small Order Entry (or Execution) System

SOP   Standard Operating Procedure

SOYD   Sum of the Years' Digits Method

SpA   Società per Azioni (Italian corporation)

SPDA   Single Premium Deferred Annuity

SPDR   Standard & Poor's Depository Receipt

SPQR   Small Profits, Quick Returns

SPRI   Société de Personnes a Responsabilité Limitée (Belgian corporation)

Sr   Senior

SRO   Self-Regulatory Organization

SRP   Salary Reduction Plan

SRT   Spousal Remainder Trust

SS   Social Security

STB   Special Tax Bond

SU   Set Up (freight)

T

T-   Treasury (as in T-bill)

TA   Trade Acceptance

TA   Transfer Agent

TAN   Tax Anticipation Note

TBA   To Be Announced

TD   Time Deposit

TIP   To Insure Promptness

TL   Trade-Last

TM   Trademark

TSE   Toronto Stock Exchange

TT   Testamentary Trust

TVA   Tennessee Valley Authority

U

UAW   United Automobile Workers
UCC   Uniform Commercial Code
UIC   Unemployment Insurance Commission
UL   Underwriters' Laboratories
ULC   Underwriter's Laboratories of Canada
ULI   Underwriter's Laboratories, Inc.
UMW   United Mine Workers
UN   United Nations
UPC   Uniform Practice Code
US   United States (of America)
USA   United States of America
USBS   United States Bureau of Standards
USC   United States Code
UW   Underwriter

V

VAT   Value Added Tax
VD   Volume Deleted
Veep   Vice President
VIP   Very Important Person
VL   Value Line Investment Survey
VOL   Volume
VP   Vice President
VRM   Variable Rate Mortgage
VSE   Vancouver Stock Exchange

W

WAM   Weighted Average Maturity
WB   Waybill
WCB   Workers' Compensation Act

WD   When Distributed (in stock listings of newspapers)
WI   When Issued (in stock listings of newspapers)
WR   Warehouse Receipt
WSJ   Wall Street Journal
WT   Warrant (in stock listings of newspapers)
W/Tax   Withholding Tax
WW   With Warrants (in bond and stock listings of newspapers)

X

X   Ex-Interest (in bond listings of newspapers)
XD   Ex-Dividend (in stock listings of newspapers)
X-Dis   Ex-Distribution (in stock listings of newspapers)
XR   Ex-Rights (in stock listings of newspapers)
XW   Ex-Warrants (in bond and stock listings of newspapers)

Y

Y   Ex-Dividend and Sales in Full (in stock listings of newspapers)
YLD   Yield (in stock listings of newspapers)
YTB   Yield to Broker
YTC   Yield to Call
YTM   Yield to Maturity

Z

Z   Zero
ZBA   Zero Bracket Amount
ZBB   Zero-Based Budgeting
ZR   Zero Coupon Issue (Security) (in bond listings of newspapers)